Semantic Mining Technologies for Multimedia Databases

Dacheng Tao
Nanyang Technological University, Singapore

Dong Xu
Nanyang Technological University, Singapore

Xuelong Li
University of London, UK

INFORMATION SCIENCE REFERENCE

Hershey · New York

Director of Editorial Content:	Kristin Klinger
Senior Managing Editor:	Jamie Snavely
Managing Editor:	Jeff Ash
Assistant Managing Editor:	Carole Coulson
Typesetter:	Amanda Appicello
Cover Design:	Lisa Tosheff
Printed at:	Yurchak Printing Inc.

Published in the United States of America by
Information Science Reference (an imprint of IGI Global)
701 E. Chocolate Avenue, Suite 200
Hershey PA 17033
Tel: 717-533-8845
Fax: 717-533-8661
E-mail: cust@igi-global.com
Web site: http://www.igi-global.com/reference

and in the United Kingdom by
Information Science Reference (an imprint of IGI Global)
3 Henrietta Street
Covent Garden
London WC2E 8LU
Tel: 44 20 7240 0856
Fax: 44 20 7379 0609
Web site: http://www.eurospanbookstore.com

Library of Congress Cataloging-in-Publication Data

Semantic mining technologies for multimedia databases / Dacheng Tao, Dong Xu, and Xuelong Li, editors.
    p. cm.
 Includes bibliographical references and index.
 Summary: "This book provides an introduction to the most recent techniques in multimedia semantic mining necessary to researchers new to the field"--Provided by publisher.
 ISBN 978-1-60566-188-9 (hardcover) -- ISBN 978-1-60566-189-6 (ebook) 1. Multimedia systems. 2. Semantic Web. 3. Data mining. 4. Database management. I. Tao, Dacheng, 1978- II. Xu, Dong, 1979- III.Li, Xuelong, 1976-
 QA76.575.S4495 2009 006.7--dc22
                    2008052436

-

British Cataloguing in Publication Data
A Cataloguing in Publication record for this book is available from the British Library.

All work contributed to this book is new, previously-unpublished material. The views expressed in this book are those of the authors, but not necessarily of the publisher.

Table of Contents

Section III
Semantic Analysis

Detailed Table of Contents

Section I
Multimedia Information Representation

Video processing and segmentation are important stages for multimedia data mining, especially with the advance and diversity of video data available. The aim of this chapter is to introduce researchers, especially new ones, to the "video representation, processing, and segmentation techniques". This includes an easy and smooth introduction, followed by principles of video structure and representation, and then a state-of-the-art of the segmentation techniques focusing on the shot-detection. Performance evaluation and common issues are also discussed before concluding the chapter.

Multimedia data mining is a critical problem due to the huge amount of data available. Efficient and reliable data mining solutions requires both appropriate features to be extracted from the data and relevant techniques to cluster and index the data. In this chapter, the authors deal with the first problem which is feature extraction for image representation. A wide range of features has been introduced in the literature, and some attempts have been made to build standards (e.g. MPEG-7). These features are extracted with image processing techniques, and the authors focus here on a particular image processing toolbox, namely the mathematical morphology, which stays rather unknown from the multimedia mining community, even if it offers some very interesting feature extraction methods. They review here these morphological features, from the basic ones (granulometry or pattern spectrum, differential morphological profile) to more complex ones which manage to gather complementary information.

The authors present a face recognition scheme based on semantic features' extraction from faces and tensor subspace analysis. These semantic features consist of eyes and mouth, plus the region outlined by three weight centres of the edges of these features. The extracted features are compared over images in tensor subspace domain. Singular value decomposition is used to solve the eigenvalue problem and to project the geometrical properties to the face manifold. They also compare the performance of the proposed scheme with that of other established techniques, where the results demonstrate the superiority of the proposed method.

Section II
Learning in Multimedia Information Organization

Computer-aided foliage image retrieval systems have the potential to dramatically speed up the process of plant species identification. Despite previous research, this problem remains challenging due to the large intra-class variability and inter-class similarity of leaves. This is particularly true when a large number of species are involved. In this chapter, the authors present a shape-based approach, the inner-distance shape context, as a robust and reliable solution. They show that this approach naturally captures part structures and is appropriate to the shape of leaves. Furthermore, they show that this approach can be easily extended to include texture information arising from the veins of leaves. They also describe a real electronic field guide system that uses our approach. The effectiveness of the proposed method is demonstrated in experiments on two leaf databases involving more than 100 species and 1000 leaves.

Motion estimation necessitates an appropriate choice of similarity function. Because generic similarity functions derived from simple assumptions are insufficient to model complex yet structured appearance variations in motion estimation, the authors propose to learn a discriminative similarity function to match images under varying appearances by casting image matching into a binary classification problem. They use the LogitBoost algorithm to learn the classifier based on an annotated database that exemplifies the structured appearance variations: An image pair in correspondence is positive and an image pair out of correspondence is negative. To leverage the additional distance structure of negatives, they present a location-sensitive cascade training procedure that bootstraps negatives for later stages of the cascade from the regions closer to the positives, which enables viewing a large number of negatives and steering the training process to yield lower training and test errors. They also apply the learned similarity function to estimating the motion for the endocardial wall of left ventricle in echocardiography and to performing visual tracking. They obtain improved performances when comparing the learned similarity function with conventional ones.

Chapter VI

Jian Cheng, National Laboratory of Pattern Recognition, Institute of Automation, Chinese Academy of Sciences, China
Kongqiao Wang, Nokia Research Center, Beijing, China
Hanqing Lu, National Laboratory of Pattern Recognition, Institute of Automation, Chinese Academy of Sciences, China

Relevance feedback is an effective approach to boost the performance of image retrieval. Labeling data is indispensable for relevance feedback, but it is also very tedious and time-consuming. How to alleviate users' burden of labeling has been a crucial problem in relevance feedback. In recent years, active learning approaches have attracted more and more attention, such as query learning, selective sampling, multi-view learning, etc. The well-known examples include Co-training, Co-testing, SVMactive, etc. In this literature, the authors will introduce some representative active learning methods in relevance feedback. Especially they will present a new active learning algorithm based on multi-view learning, named Co-SVM. In Co-SVM algorithm, color and texture are naturally considered as sufficient and uncorrelated views of an image. SVM classifier is learned in color and texture feature subspaces, respectively. Then the two classifiers are used to classify the unlabeled data. These unlabeled samples that disagree in the two classifiers are chose to label. The extensive experiments show that the proposed algorithm is beneficial to image retrieval.

Chapter VII

Juliusz L. Kulikowski, Polish Academy of Sciences, Poland

Visual data mining is a procedure aimed at a selection from a document's repository subsets of documents presenting certain classes of objects; the last may be characterized as classes of objects' similarity or, more generally, as classes of objects satisfying certain relationships. In this chapter attention will be focused on selection of visual documents representing objects belonging to similarity classes.

The insufficiency of labeled training samples is a major obstacle in automatic semantic analysis of large scale image/video database. Semi-supervised learning, which attempts to learn from both labeled and unlabeled data, is a promising approach to tackle this problem. As a major family of semi-supervised learning, graph-based methods have attracted more and more recent research. In this chapter, a brief introduction is given on popular semi-supervised learning methods, especially the graph-based methods, as well as their applications in the area of image annotation, video annotation, and image retrieval. It is well known that the pair-wise similarity is an essential factor in graph propagation based semi-supervised learning methods. A novel graph-based semi-supervised learning method, named Structure-Sensitive Anisotropic Manifold Ranking (SSAniMR), is derived from a PDE based anisotropic diffusion framework. Instead of using Euclidean distance only, SSAniMR further takes local structural difference into account to more accurately measure pair-wise similarity. Finally some future directions of using semi-supervised learning to analyze the multimedia content are discussed.

With the explosive growth in the amount of video data and rapid advance in computing power, extensive research efforts have been devoted to content-based video analysis. In this chapter, they authors will give a broad discussion on this research area by covering different topics such as video structure analysis, object detection and tracking, event detection, visual attention analysis, etc. In the meantime, different video representation and indexing models are also presented.

Semantic mining is an essential part in knowledgebase and decision support systems where it enables the extraction of useful knowledge form available databases with the ultimate goal of supporting the decision making process. In process systems engineering, decisions are made throughout plant / process / product life cycles. The provision of smart semantic mining techniques will improve the decision making process for all life cycle activities. In particular, safety and environmental related decisions are highly dependent on process internal and external conditions and dynamics with respect to equipment geometry and plant layout. This chapter discusses practical methods for semantic mining using systematic knowledge representation as integrated with process modeling and domain knowledge. POOM or plant/process object oriented modeling methodology is explained and used as a basis to implement semantic mining as applied on process systems engineering. Case studies are illustrated for biological process engineering, in particular MoFlo systems focusing on process safety and operation design support.

Chapter XI

Efficient and effective techniques for managing and browsing large image databases are increasingly sought after. This chapter presents a simple yet efficient and effective approach to navigating image datasets. Based on the concept of a globe as visualisation and navigation medium, thumbnails are projected onto the surface of a sphere based on their colour. Navigation is performed by rotating and tilting the globe as well as zooming into an area of interest. Experiments based on a medium size image database demonstrate the usefulness of the presented approach.

Section IV
Multimedia Resource Annotation

Although important in practice, manual image annotation and retrieval has rarely been studied by means of formal modeling methods. In this paper, we propose a set of formal models to characterize the annotation times for two commonly-used manual annotation approaches, i.e., tagging and browsing. Based on the complementary properties of these models, we design new hybrid approaches, called frequency-based annotation and learning-based annotation, to improve the efficiency of manual image annotation as well as retrieval. Both our simulation and experimental results show that the proposed algorithms can achieve up to a 50% reduction in annotation time over baseline methods for manual image annotation, and produce significantly better annotation and retrieval results in the same amount of time.

Chapter XIII

This chapter introduces the application of active learning in video annotation. The insufficiency of training data is a major obstacle in learning-based video annotation. Active learning is a promising approach to dealing with this difficulty. It iteratively annotates a selected set of most informative samples, such that the obtained training set is more effective than that gathered randomly. We present a brief review of the typical active learning approaches. We categorize the sample selection strategies in these methods into five criteria, i.e., *risk reduction*, *uncertainty*, *positivity*, *density*, and *diversity*. In particular, we introduce the Support Vector Machine (SVM)-based active learning scheme which has been widely applied. Afterwards, we analyze the deficiency of the existing active learning methods for video annotation, i.e., in most of these methods the to-be-annotated concepts are treated equally without preference and only one modality is applied. To address these two issues, we introduce a multi-concept multi-modality active learning scheme. This scheme is able to better explore human labeling effort by considering both the learnabilities of different concepts and the potential of different modalities.

Xin-Jing Wang, Microsoft Research Asia, China
Lei Zhang, Microsoft Research Asia, China
Xirong Li, Microsoft Research Asia, China
Wei-Ying Ma, Microsoft Research Asia, China

Although it has been studied for years by computer vision and machine learning communities, image annotation is still far from practical. In this paper, we propose a novel attempt of modeless image annotation, which investigates how effective a data-driven approach can be, and suggest annotating an uncaptioned image by mining its search results. We collected 2.4 million images with their surrounding texts from a few photo forum websites as our database to support this data-driven approach. The entire process contains three steps: 1) the search process to discover visually and semantically similar search results; 2) the mining process to discover salient terms from textual descriptions of the search results; and 3) the annotation rejection process to filter noisy terms yielded by step 2). To ensure real time annotation, two key techniques are leveraged – one is to map the high dimensional image visual features into hash codes, the other is to implement it as a distributed system, of which the search and mining processes are provided as Web services. As a typical result, the entire process finishes in less than 1 second. Since no training dataset is required, our proposed approach enables annotating with unlimited vocabulary, and is highly scalable and robust to outliers. Experimental results on real web images show the effectiveness and efficiency of the proposed algorithm.

Yonghong Tian, Peking University, China
Shuqiang Jiang, Chinese Academy of Sciences, China
Tiejun Huang, Peking University, China
Wen Gao, Peking University, China

With the rapid growth of image collections, content-based image retrieval (CBIR) has been an active area of research with notable recent progress. However, automatic image retrieval by semantics still remains a challenging problem. In this chapter, we will describe two promising techniques towards semantic image retrieval — semantic image classification and automatic image annotation. For each technique, four aspects are presented: task definition, image representation, computational models, and evaluation. Finally, we will give a brief discussion of their application in image retrieval.

Section V
Other Topics Related to Semantic Mining

Chapter XVI

  Arun Kulkarni, The University of Texas at Tyler, USA
  Leonard Brown, The University of Texas at Tyler, USA

With advances in computer technology and the World Wide Web there has been an explosion in the amount and complexity of multimedia data that are generated, stored, transmitted, analyzed, and accessed. In order to extract useful information from this huge amount of data, many content-based image retrieval (CBIR) systems have been developed in the last decade. A Typical CBIR system captures image features that represent image properties such as color, texture, or shape of objects in the query image and try to retrieve images from the database with similar features. Recent advances in CBIR systems include relevance feedback based interactive systems. The main advantage of CBIR systems with relevance feedback is that these systems take into account the gap between the high-level concepts and low-level features and subjectivity of human perception of visual content. CBIR systems with relevance feedback are more efficient than conventional CBIR systems; however, these systems depend on human interaction. In this chapter, we describe a new approach for image storage and retrieval called association-based image retrieval (ABIR). We try to mimic human memory. The human brain stores and retrieves images by association. We use a generalized bi-directional associative memory (GBAM) to store associations between feature vectors that represent images stored in the database. Section I introduces the reader to the CBIR system. In Section II, we present architecture for the ABIR system, Section III deals with preprocessing and feature extraction techniques, and Section IV presents various models of GBAM. In Section V, we present case studies.

Chapter XVII

  Gerald Schaefer, Aston University, UK

Image retrieval and image compression have been typically pursued separately. Only little research has been done on a synthesis of the two by allowing image retrieval to be performed directly in the compressed domain of images without the need to uncompress them first. In this chapter we show that such compressed domain image retrieval can indeed be done and lead to effective and efficient retrieval performance. We introduce a novel compression algorithm – colour visual pattern image coding (CVPIC) – and present several retrieval algorithms that operate directly on compressed CVPIC data. Our experiments demonstrate that it is not only possible to realise such midstream content access, but also that the presented techniques outperform standard retrieval techniques such as colour histograms and colour correlograms.

Chapter XVIII

M. Singh, Middlesex University, UK
X. Cheng, Middlesex University, UK & Beijing Normal University, China
X. He, Reading University, UK

Discovery of the multimedia resources on network is the focus of the many researches in post semantic web. The task of resources discovery can be automated by using agent. This chapter reviews the current most used technologies that facilitate the resource discovery process. The chapter also the presents the case study to present a fully functioning resource discovery system using mobile agents.

Chapter XIX

Zhu Li, Hong Kong Polytechnic University, Hong Kong
Yun Fu, BBN Technologies, USA
Junsong Yuan, Northwestern University, USA
Ying Wu, Northwestern University, USA
Aggelos Katsaggelos, Northwestern University, USA
Thomas S. Huang, University of Illinois at Urbana-Champaign, USA

The rapid advances in multimedia capture, storage and communication technologies and capabilities have ushered an era of unprecedented growth of digital media content, in audio, visual, and synthetic forms, and both personal and commercially produced. How to manage these data to make them more accessible and searchable to users is a key challenge in current multimedia computing research. In this chapter, we discuss the problems and challenges in multimedia data management, and review the state of the art in data structures and algorithms for multimedia indexing, media feature space management and organization, and applications of these techniques in multimedia data management.

Preface

With the explosive growth of multimedia databases in terms of both size and variety, effective and efficient indexing and searching techniques for large-scale multimedia databases have become an urgent research topic in recent years.

For data organization, the conventional approach is based on keywords or text description of a multimedia datum. However, it is tedious to give all data text annotation and it is almost impossible for people to capture as well. Moreover, the text description is also not enough to precisely describe a multimedia datum. For example, it is unrealistic to utilize words to describe a music clip; an image says more than a thousand words; and keywords-based video shot description cannot characterize the contents for a specific user. Therefore, it is important to utilize the content based approaches (CbA) to mine the semantic information of a multimedia datum.

In the last ten years, we have witnessed very significant contributions of CbA in semantics targeting for multimedia data organization. CbA means that the data organization, including retrieval and indexing, utilizes the contents of the data themselves, rather than keywords provided by human. Therefore, the contents of a datum could be obtained from techniques in statistics, computer vision, and signal processing. For example, Markov random fields could be applied for image modeling; spatial-temporal analysis is important for video representation; and the Mel frequency cepstral coefficient has been shown to be the most effective method for audio signal classification.

Apart from the conventional approaches mentioned above, machine learning also plays an indispensable role in current semantic mining tasks, for example, random sampling techniques and support vector machine for human computer interaction, manifold learning and subspace methods for data visualization, discriminant analysis for feature selection, and classification trees for data indexing.

The goal of this IGI Global book is to provide an introduction about the most recent research and techniques in multimedia semantic mining for new researchers, so that they can go step by step into this field. As a result, they can follow the right way according to their specific applications. The book is also an important reference for researchers in multimedia, a handbook for research students, and a repository for multimedia technologists.

The major contributions of this book are in three aspects: (1) collecting and seeking the recent and most important research results in semantic mining for multimedia data organization, (2) guiding new researchers a comprehensive review on the state-of-the-art techniques for different tasks for multimedia database management, and (3) providing technologists and programmers important algorithms for multimedia system construction.

This edited book attracted submissions from eight countries including Canada, China, France, Japan, Poland, Singapore, United Kingdom, and United States. Among these submissions, 19 have been accepted. We strongly believe that it is now an ideal time to publish this edited book with the 19 selected chapters. The contents of this edited book will provide readers with cutting-edge and topical information for their related research.

Accepted chapters are solicited to address a wide range of topics in semantic mining from multimedia databases and an overview of the included chapters is given below.

This book starts from new multimedia information representations (Video Representation and Processing for Multimedia Data Mining) (Image Features from Morphological Scale-spaces) (Face Recognition and Semantic Features), after which learning in multimedia information organization, an important topic in semantic mining, is studied by four chapters (Shape Matching for Foliage Database Retrieval) (Similarity Learning For Motion Estimation) (Active Learning for Relevance Feedback in Image Retrieval) (Visual Data Mining Based on Partial Similarity Concepts). Thereafter, four schemes are presented for semantic analysis in four chapters (Image/Video Semantic Analysis by Semi-Supervised Learning) (Content-Based Video Semantic Analysis) (Semantic Mining for Green Production Systems) (Intuitive Image Database Navigation by Hue-sphere Browsing). The multimedia resource annotation is also essential for a retrieval system and four chapters provide interesting ideas (Hybrid Tagging and Browsing Approaches for Efficient Manual Image Annotation) (Active Video Annotation: To Minimize Human Effort) (Image Auto-Annotation by Search) (Semantic Classification and Annotation of Images). The last part of this book presents other related topics for semantic mining (Association-Based Image Retrieval) (Compressed-domain Image Retrieval based on Colour Visual Patterns) (Multimedia Resource Discovery using Mobile Agent) (Multimedia Data Indexing).

Dacheng Tao
Email: dctao@ntu.edu.sg
Nanyang Technological University, Singapore

Dong Xu
Email: dongxu@ntu.edu.sg
Nanyang Technological University, Singapore

Xuelong Li
Email: xuelong@dcs.bbk.ac.uk
University of London, UK

Section I
Multimedia Information Representation

Chapter I
Video Representation and Processing for Multimedia Data Mining

Amr Ahmed
University of Lincoln, UK

ABSTRACT

Video processing and segmentation are important stages for multimedia data mining, especially with the advance and diversity of video data available. The aim of this chapter is to introduce researchers, especially new ones, to the "video representation, processing, and segmentation techniques". This includes an easy and smooth introduction, followed by principles of video structure and representation, and then a state-of-the-art of the segmentation techniques focusing on the shot-detection. Performance evaluation and common issues are also discussed before concluding the chapter.

I. INTRODUCTION

With the advances, which are progressing very fast, in the digital video technologies and the wide availability of more efficient computing resources, we seem to be living in an era of explosion in digital video. Video data are now widely available, and being easily generated, in large volumes. This is not only on the professional level. It can be found everywhere, on the internet, especially with the video uploading and sharing sites, with the personal digital cameras and camcorders, and with the camera mobile phones that became almost the norm.

People use the existing easy facilities to generate video data. But at some point, sooner or later, they realize that managing these data can be a bottleneck. This is because the available techniques and tools for accessing, searching, and retrieving video data are not on the same level as for other traditional data, such as text. The advances in the video access, search, and retrieval techniques have not been progressing with the same pace as the digital video technologies and its generated data volume. This could be attributed, at least partly, to the nature of the video data and its richness, compared to text data. But it can also be attributed to the increase of our demands. In text, we are no longer just satisfied by searching for exact match of sequence of characters or strings, but need to find similar meanings and other higher level matches. We are also looking forward to do the same on video data. But the nature of the video data is different.

Video data is more complex and naturally larger in volume than the traditional text data. They usually combine visual and audio data, as well as textual data. These data need to be appropriately annotated and indexed in an accessible form for search and retrieval techniques to deal with it. This can be achieved based on either textual information, visual and/or audio features, and more importantly on semantic information. The textual-based approach is theoretically the simplest. Video data need to be annotated by textual descriptions, such as keywords or short sentences describing the contents. This converts the search task into the known area of searching in the text data, where the existing relatively advanced tools and techniques can be utilized. The main bottleneck here is the huge time and effort that are needed to accomplish this annotation task, let alone any accuracy issues. The feature-based approach, whether visual and/or audio, depends on annotating the video data by combinations of their extracted low-level features such as intensity, color, texture, shape, motion, and other audio features. This is very useful in doing a query-by-example task. But still not very useful in searching for specific event or more semantic attributes. The semantic-based approach is, in one sense, similar to the text-based approach. Video data need to be annotated, but in this case, with high-level information that represents the semantic meaning of the contents, rather than just describing the contents. The difficulty of this annotation is the high variability of the semantic meaning, of the same video data, among different people, cultures, and ages, to name just a few. It will depend on so many factors, including the purpose of the annotation, the domain and application, cultural and personal views, and could even be subject to the mood and personality of the annotator. Hence, generally automating this task is highly challenging. For specific domains, carefully selected combinations of the visual and/or audio features correlate to useful semantic information. Hence, the efficient extraction of those features is crucial to the high-level analysis and mining of the video data.

In this chapter, we focus on the core techniques that facilitate the high-level analysis and mining of the video data. One of the important initial steps in segmentation and analysis of video data is the shot-boundary detection. This is the first step in decomposing the video sequence to its logical structure and components, in preparation for analysis of each component. It is worth mentioning that the subject is enormous and this chapter is meant to be more of an introduction, especially for new researchers. Also, in this chapter, we only focus on the visual modality of the video. Hence, the audio and textual modalities are not covered.

After this introductory section, section II provides the principles of video data, so that we know the data that we are dealing with and what does it represent. This includes video structure and representation, both for compressed and uncompressed data. The various types of shot transitions are defined in section III, as well as the various approaches of classifying them. Then, in section IV, the key categories of the shot-boundary detection techniques are discussed. First, the various approaches of categorizing the shot-detection techniques are discussed, along with the various factors contributing to that. Then, a selected hierarchical approach is used to represent the most common techniques. This is followed by discussion of the performance evaluation measures and some common issues. Finally the chapter is summarized and concluded in section V.

II. VIDEO STRUCTURE AND REPRESENTATION

In this section, it is aimed to introduce, mainly new, researchers to the principles of video data structure and representation. This is an important introduction to understand the data that will be dealt with and what does it represent. This introduction is essential to be able to follow the subsequent sections, especially the shot-transition detection.

This section starts by an explanation of the common structure of a video sequence, and a discussion of the various levels in that structure. The logical structure of the video sequence is particularly important for segmentation and data mining.

A. Video Structure

The video consists of a number of frames. These frames are usually, and preferably, adjacent to each other on the storage media, but should definitely be played back in the correct order and speed to convey the recorded sequences of actions and/or motion. In fact, each single frame is a still image that consists of pixels, which are the smallest units from the physical point of view. These pixels are dealt with when analyzing the individual frames, and the processing usually utilizes a lot of image processing techniques. However, the aim of most applications of analyzing the video is to identify the basic elements and contents of the video. Hence, logical structure and elements are of more importance than the individual pixels.

Video is usually played back with frequencies of 25 or 30 frames per second, as described in more details in section 'B' below. These speeds are chosen so that the human eye do not detect the separation between the frames and to make sure that motion will be smooth and seems to be continuous. Hence, as far as we, the human beings, are concerned, we usually perceive and process the video on a higher level structure. We can easily detect and identify objects, people, and locations within the video. Some objects may change position on the screen from one frame to another, and recording locations could be changing between frames as well. These changes allow us to perceive the motion of objects and people. But more importantly, it allows us to detect higher level aspects such as behaviors and sequences, which we can put together to detect and understand a story or an event that is recorded in the video.

According to the above, the video sequence can be logically represented as a hierarchical structure, as depicted in fig. 1 and illustrated in fig. 2. It is worth mentioning that as we go up in the hierarchy, more detailed sub-levels may be added or slightly variations of interpretations may exist. This is mainly depend on the domain in hand. But at least the *shot* level, as in the definition below, seems to be commonly understood and agreed upon.

The definition of each level in the hierarchy is given below, in the reverse order, i.e. bottom-up:

- **Frame:** The frame is simply a single still image. It is considered as the smallest logical unit in this hierarchy. It is important in the analysis of the other logical levels.
- **Shot:** The shot is a sequence of consecutive frames, temporally adjacent, that has been recorded continuously, within the same session and location, by the same single camera, and without substantial change in the contents of the picture. So, a shot is highly expected to contain a continuous action in both space and time. A shot could be a result of what you continuously record, may be with a camcorder or even a mobile video camera, since you press the record button, until you stop the recording. But off course, if you drop the camera or the mobile, or someone has quickly passed

Figure 1. Hierarchy of the video logical structure

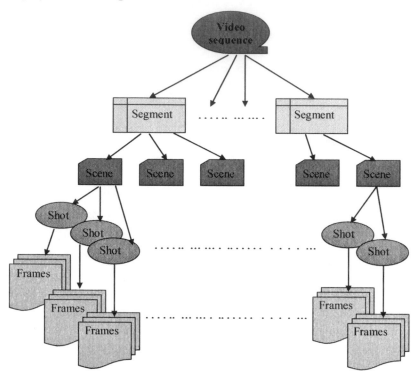

in front of your camera, this would probably cause a sudden change in the picture contents. If such change is significant, it may results in breaking the continuity and may then not be considered as a single shot.

- **Scene:** The scene is a collection of related shots. Normally, those shots are recorded within the same session, at the same location, but can be recorded from different cameras. An example could be a conversation scene between few people. One camera may be recording the wide location and have all people in the picture, while another camera focuses on the person who is currently talking, and may be another camera is focusing on the audience. Each camera is continuously recording its designated view, but the final output to the viewer is what the director selects from those different views. So, the director can switch between cameras at various times within the conversation based on the flow of the conversation, change of the talking person, reaction from the audience, and so on. Although the finally generated views are usually substantially different, for the viewer, the scene still seems to be logically related, in terms of the location, timing, people and/or objects involved. In fact, we are cleverer than that. In some cases, the conversation can elaborate from one point to another, and the director may inject some images or sub-videos related to the discussion. This introduces huge changes in the pictures shown to the viewer, but still the viewer can follow it up, identify that they are related. This leads to the next level in the logical structure of the video.

- **Segment:** The video segment is a group of scenes related to a specific context. It does not have to have been recorded in the same location or in the same time. And off course, it can be recorded with various cameras. However, they are logically related to each other within a specific semantic

Figure 2. Illustration of the video logical structure

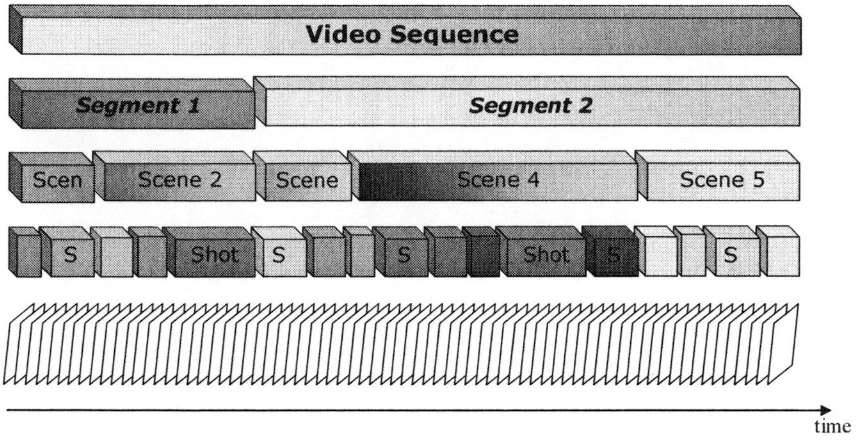

context. The various scenes of the same event, or related events, within the news broadcast are an example of a video segment.

- **Sequence:** A video sequence consists of a number of video segments. They are usually expected to be related or share some context or semantic aspects. But in reality it may not always be the case.

Depending on the application and its domain, the analysis of the video to extract its logical components can fall into any of the above levels. However, it is worth mentioning that the definitions may slightly differ with the domain, as they tend to be based on the semantic, especially towards the top levels (i.e. Scenes and segments in particular). However, a more common and highly potential starting point is the video shot. Although classified as a part of the logical structure, it also has a tight link with the physical recording action. As it is a result of a continuous recording from a single camera within the same location and time, the shot usually has the same definition in almost all applications and domains. Hence, the shot is a high candidate starting point for extracting the structure and components of the video data.

In order to correctly extract shots, we will need to detect their boundaries, lengths, and types. To do so, we need to be aware of how shots are usually joined together in the first place. This is discussed in details in section III and the various techniques of shot detection are reviewed in section IV.

B. Video Representation

In this sub-section we discuss the video representation for both compressed and uncompressed data. We first explore the additional dimensionality of video data and frame-rates with their associated redundancy in uncompressed data. Then, we discuss the compressed data representation and the techniques of reducing the various types of redundancies, and how that can be utilized for shot-detection.

1) Uncompressed Video Data

The video sequence contains groups of successive frames. They are designed so that when they are played back, the human eye perceives continuous motion of objects within the video and no flickers are recognized due to the change from one frame to another. The film industry uses a frame-rate of 24 frames/sec for films. But the most two common TV standard formats are PAL and NTSC. The frame-rate in those two standards is either 25 frames/sec, for PAL TV standard, or 30 frames/sec for the NTSC TV standard. In case of the videos that are converted from films, some care need to be taken, especially due to the different frame-rates involved in the different standards. A machine, called *telecine*, is usually used in that conversion that involves the 2:2 pulldown or 3:2 pulldown process for PAL or NTSC respectively.

Like the still image, each pixel within the frame has a value or more, such as intensity or colors. But video data has an extra dimension, in addition to the spatial dimensions of the still images, which is the temporal dimension. The changes between various frames in the video can be exhibited in any of the above attributes, pixel values, spatial and/or temporal. And the segmentation of video, as discussed in later sections, is based on detecting the changes in one or more of the above attributes, or their statistical properties and/or evolution.

The video data also carry motion information. Motion information are among the useful information that can be used for segmenting video, as it give an indication of the level of activities and its dynamics within the video. Activity levels can change between the different parts of the video and in fact can characterize its parts. Unlike the individual image properties and pixel values, the motion information are embedded within the video data. Techniques that are based on motion information, as discussed in section V, have to extract them first. This is usually a computationally expensive task.

From the discussion above, it can be noticed that in many cases, the video data will usually contain redundancy. For example, some scenes can be almost stationary where there are almost no movements or changes happening. In such cases, the 25 frames produced every second, assuming using the PAL standard, will be very similar, which is a redundancy. This example represents a redundancy in the temporal information, which is between the frames. Similarly, if large regions of the image have the same attributes, this represents a redundancy in the spatial information, which is within the same image. Both types of redundancy can be dealt with or reduced as described in the next subsections, with the compressed video data.

2) Compressed Video Data

Video compression aims to reduce the redundancy exist in video data, with minimum visual effect on the video. This is useful in multimedia storage and transmission, among others. The compression can be applied on one or more of the video dimensions; spatial and/or temporal. Each of them is described, with focus on the MPEG standards, as follows:

Spatial-Coding (Intra-Coding)
The compression in the spatial dimension deals with reducing the redundancy within the same image or frame. There is no need to refer to any other frame. Hence, it is also called *intra*-coding, and the term "*intra*" here means "within the same image or frame". The Discrete Cosine Transform (DCT)

is widely used for intra-coding in the most common standards such as JPEG, MPEG-1, MPEG-2, and MPEG-4, although the wavelet transform is also incorporated in MPEG-4.

One benefit of the intra-coding is that, as each individual frame is compressed independently, any editing of individual frames or re-ordering of the frames on the time axis can be done without affecting any other frames in the compressed video sequence.

Temporal-Coding (Inter-Coding)

The compression in the temporal dimension aims at reducing the redundancy between successive frames. This type of compression is also known as the *inter*-coding, and the term "*inter*" here means "across or between frames". Hence, the coding of each frame is related to its neighboring ones, on the time axis. In fact, it is mainly based on the differences from neighboring frames. This makes editing, inserting, or deleting individual frames not a straight-forward task, as the neighboring frames will be affected, if not also affecting the process.

As it deals with changes between frames, motion plays a dominant factor. A simple translation of an object between two frames, without any other changes such as deformation, would result in unnecessarily large differences. This is because of the noticeable differences in pixel values in the corresponding positions. These differences will require more bits to be coded, which increases the bit-rate. To achieve better compression rates, one of the factors is to reduce the bit-rate. This is done through *motion compensation* techniques. The motion compensation estimates the motion of an object, between successive frames, and takes that into account when calculating the differences. So, the differences are mainly representing the changes in the objects properties such as shape, color, and deformation, but not usually the motion. This reduces the differences and hence the bit-rate.

The motion compensation process results in important parts of the motion information. That are the *motion vectors*, which indicate the motion of various parts of the image between the successive frames, and the *residual*, which are the errors resulting from the motion compensation process. In fact, one big advantage of the temporal-coding is the extraction of the motion information that are highly important in video segmentation, and shot detection, as discussed in section IV.

As the MPEG standards became one of the most commonly used in industry, a brief explanation of the MPEG structure and information, mainly those that are related to the techniques discussed in section IV, is below.

MPEG

MPEG stands for *Moving Pictures Experts Group*. In the MPEG standards, the frame is usually divided into blocks, 8x8 pixels each. The spatial-coding, or intra-coding, is achieved by using the Discrete Cosine Transform (DCT) on each block. The DCT is also used in encoding the differences between frames and the residual errors from the motion compensation. On the other hand, the temporal-coding, or inter-coding, is achieved by block-based motion compensation techniques. In MPEG, the unit area that is used for motion compensation is usually a block of 16x16 pixels, called macro-blocks (MB). However, in MPEG-4, moving objects can be coded through arbitrary shapes rather than the fixed-size macro-blocks.

There are various types of frames in the MPEG standards. The *I*-frames, which are the intra-coded frames, the *P*-frames and B-frames, which are the frames that are predicted through motion compensation and the calculated differences between original frames. Each two successive *I*-frames will usually have

Figure 3. The sequence of the MPEG's I-, P-, and B-frames

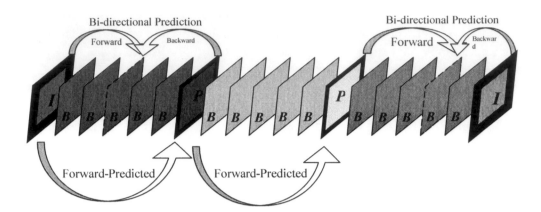

a number of *P*-frames and *B*-frames in between them, as depicted in fig. 3. The sequence of one *I*-frame followed by a number of *P*- and *B*-frames, till the next *I*-frame, is called a group of pictures (GOP)

The MPEG provides various useful information about the changes between frames, including motion vectors, residual errors, macro-blocks types, and group of pictures. These information are usually utilized by shot-detection techniques that works on the MPEG compressed video data, as discussed in section IV.

III. VIDEO SHOT TRANSITIONS

In order to be able to extract the shots, it is important that we understand how they were joined together when scenes were created in the first place. Shots can be joined together using various types of transition effects. The simplest of these transition effects is the straight-forward cut and paste of individual shots adjacent to each other, without any kind of overlapping. However, with digital video and the advance in editing tools and software, more complex transition types are commonly used nowadays.

Shot transitions can be classified in many ways, based on their behavior, the properties or features that they modify, the length and amount of overlapping, to name just a few. In this section, the most common shot transition types are introduced and defined. We start by presenting various classification approaches and their criteria. Then, a classification approach is chosen and its commonly used transition types are identified and explained. The chosen classification and its identified transition types will be referred to in the rest of the chapter.

The first classification approach is based on the applied spatial and/or color modifications to achieve the transition. In this approach, shot transitions can be classified to one of the following four types:

- *Identity* **transition:** In an analogy with the identity matrix, this transition type does not involve any modification, neither in the color nor in the spatial information. That is none of the two shots that are involved in this transition will be subject to any modification. They will just be joined together as they are.

- ***Spatial* transition:** As the name suggests, the main modification in this type is in the spatial details. The involved shots are subject to spatial transformations only.
- ***Chromatic* transition:** Again, as the name implies, the chromatic details will be the main target for modification. So, the involved shots are subject to modifications in their chromatic details, such as color and/or intensity.
- ***Spatio-Chromatic* transition:** This is the most general type of transition. This is because it can involve combinations of both chromatic and spatial modifications.

The second classification approach is based on the length of the transition period and the amount of overlapping between the two involved shots. This seems to be more common and its terminology can be identified in most video editing tools and software. In this approach, shot transitions can be classified to one of the following two main types:

- ***Hard-Cut* transition:** This type of transition happens suddenly between two consecutive frames. The last frame of the first shot is directly followed by the first frame of the second shot, with no gaps or modifications in between. Hence, there is no overlapping at all. This is illustrated in fig. 4.a.
- ***Gradual* transition:** In the gradual transitions, the switch from the first shot to the second shot happens over a period of time, not suddenly as in the hard-cut. The transition occupies multiple frames, where the two involved shots are usually overlapping. The length of the transition period varies widely, and in most cases it is one of the parameters that can be set within the editing tool, by the ordinary user. There are almost unlimited combinations of the length of transition period and the modifications that can be done on the overlapping frames from both shots. This results in enormous forms of the gradual transitions. However, the most commonly known ones are:
  - ° **Fade-out:** This is a transition from the last frame of the first shot, to a monochrome frame, gradually over a period of time, as illustrated in the left half of fig. 4.c.
  - ° **Fade-in:** This is almost the opposite of the fade-out. The fade in is a transition from a monochrome frame to the first frame of the following shot, gradually over a period of time, as illustrated in the right half of fig. 4.c.

Figures 4. Illustrations of the various types of shot-transition a) hard-cut b) gradual transition c) fade-in and fade-out

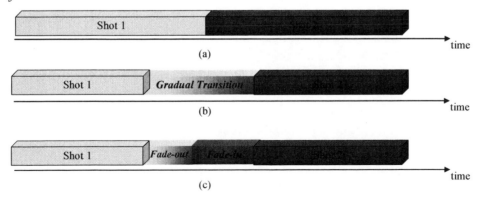

○ **Dissolve:** The dissolve involves the end and start frames of the first and second shots, respectively. The pixels' values of the transitional frames, between the original two shots, are determined by the linear combination of the spatially corresponding pixel values from those end and start frames. This is illustrated in fig. 4.b.

○ **Wipe:** The wipe transition is achieved by gradually replacing the final frames of the first shot, by the initial frames of the second shot, on spatial basis. This could be horizontally, vertically, or diagonally.

With the above overview of the most common shot-transition types, and their definitions, we are almost ready to explore the shot-boundary detection techniques, which is the focus of the next section.

IV. SHOT-BOUNDARY DETECTION TECHNIQUES

After the above introduction to the most common shot-transitions, in this section we introduce the key approaches for the shot-transition detection. As you may imagine, the work in this area became numerous, and is still growing, and an exhaustive survey of the field is beyond the scope of just one chapter, if not beyond a full book. However, the aim in this chapter is to introduce the researchers to the main categories and key work in this field.

Shot-boundary detection techniques can be categorized in a number of ways, depending on various factors, such as the type of the input video data, change measures, processing complexity and domain, as well as the type of shots tackled. The following is a brief overview of the various possible categorizations, based on each of those factors:

1. **The type of the input video data:** Some techniques work directly on the ***compressed data*** and others work on the original ***uncompressed data***. As we will see, most compression formats are designed in a way that provide some useful information and allow the detection techniques to work directly without need for decompression. This may improve the detection performance.

2. **The change measures** are another important factor. As discussed before, segmenting the video into shots is based on detecting the changes between the different shots, which are significantly higher than changes within the same shot. The question is "what changes are we looking for?, and equally important, how to measure them?" There are various elements of the image that can exhibit changes and various techniques may consider various elements and/or combination of elements to look for changes in order to detect the shot boundaries. The image, and subsequently its features, is affected by the changes of its contents. Hence, measuring the changes in the image features will help in detecting the changes and deciding on the shot-boundary.

   Changes can be within the ***local features*** of each frame, such as the intensity or color values of each ***pixel*** and existing ***edges*** within the image. Changes can also be detected in a more gross fashion by comparing the ***global features***, such as the ***histogram*** of intensity levels or color values. As we will see, the latter (i.e. global features) does not account for the spatial details, as it is usually calculated over the entire image, although some special cases of local histograms were developed. More ***complex features*** could be also be utilized, such as ***corners, moments, and phase correlation*** (Gao, Li, & Shi, 2006), (Camara-Chavez et al., 2007).

Other sources of changes within the video include ***motion*** of the objects and/or camera movements and operations, such as pan, tilt, and zoom. However, for the purpose of shot detection, the changes due to camera movements and operations need to be ignored, or more precisely compensated for, as long as the recording is still continuous with the same camera as in the definition of the shot in section II. This is another issue, referred to as the *camera ego motion*, where the camera movements and operations need to be detected from the given video and those motions are compensated for, to reduce false detections.

Also, on a higher level, the ***objects*** included within the images as well as the simulation of the human ***attention*** models (Ma, Lu, Zhang, & Li, 2002) can be utilized to detect the changes and identify the various shots.

3. **Processing time and complexity:** Various applications have different requirements in terms of the processing time and computational complexity. The majority, so far, can accommodate the ***off-line processing*** of the video data. So, video can be captured and recorded, then later be processed and analyzed, for example for indexing and summarization. Other applications can not afford for that and need immediate and ***real-time*** fast and efficient processing of the video stream. An example of that is the processing of the incoming TV/video broadcast. In such a case, fast processing is needed to adjust the playback frame rate to match the modern advanced displaying devices that have high refresh frame rates. This is to provide smoother motions and better viewing options.

4. **Processing domain:** This is a classical classification in image processing. Some techniques apply the ***time-domain*** analysis, while others apply the ***frequency-domain*** analysis. Also, various transforms can be utilized, such as Discrete Cosine Transform (DCT) and wavelets transforms. This is especially when compressed data are involved.

5. **Type of shot-transition:** As we discussed in section II, there are various types of shot-transitions, each has its own properties. Although the ultimate aim is to have techniques that can detect almost all transitions, this is always have a drawback somehow, such as the complexity and/or accuracy. Hence, for more accurate and computationally efficient performance, some techniques are more specialized in one or more related type of transitions, with the main overview categorizations is between the **Hard-cut** and **Gradual** transitions. Even the gradual transitions are usually broken down to various sub-types, due to the high variations and possibilities provided by the current digital video editing and effects software. In fact, some efforts are trying to model specific effects and use these models in detecting those transitions, whether from scratch or from the result of a more general shot-boundary detection techniques (Nam & Tewfik, 2005).

It can be noticed that many shot-boundary detection techniques can fall into more than one category of the above classifications. And depending on the specific domain and application, or even the interest of the reader, one or more classification could be more useful than others. But, if we try to present the detection techniques following each and every classification of the above, we will end up repeating a large portion of the discussion. For this reason, we prefer to pick the most common classifications that serve the wide majority of the domains and applications.

We prefer to present the key detection techniques in a hierarchical approach. If you are thinking of dealing with video data for whatever application, and need to do shot-boundary detection, you would usually try to select techniques that are suitable to the type of your input data with the application constraints in mind. Hence, the type of the input video data would be one of the initial factors in such a selection. This will help you to focus on those techniques that are applicable to either compressed or uncompressed data, depending on the type of your input data. Then, the focus is on detecting changes, quantitatively measuring those changes, and making the decision of detecting a boundary or not. To that extent, the classification that is based on the change measures would be useful. We can also distinguish between the main two types of transitions; hard-cut and gradual transitions. The summary of this hierarchical classification approach is depicted in fig. 5.

In the following sub-sections, we present the key shot-boundary detection techniques according to the classification depicted in fig. 5. They are organized into three main sub-sections; (a) shot-cut detection from uncompressed data, (b) gradual-transitions from uncompressed data, (c) shot-boundary detection from compressed data. In addition, the performance evaluation is also discussed in sub-section "*D*" and some common issues are discussed in sub-section "*E*". But first, let us agree on the following notations that will be used later:

F_i: represents the ith frame in the video sequence.

$I_{F_i}(x,y)$: represents the intensity I of a pixel that is located at the (x,y) coordinates, in the ith frame.

$C_{F_i}^k(x,y)$: represents the kth color component of a pixel that is located at the (x,y) coordinates, in the ith frame.

$H_{F_i}(v)$: represents the intensity histogram value for the vth bin of the ith frame.

$H_{F_i}^{C^k}(v)$: represents the color histogram value for the vth bin within the histogram of the kth color component, of the ith frame.

Figure 5. Hierarchical classification of shot-boundary detection techniques

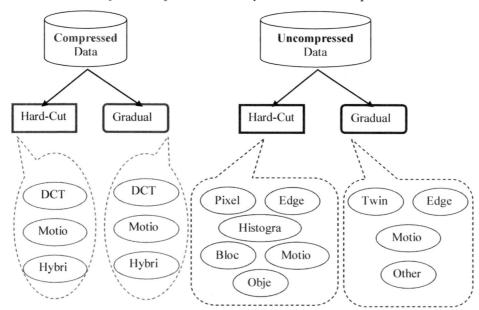

A. Shot-Cut Detection from "Uncompressed Data"

The uncompressed video data is the original video data, which are mainly the frames that are represented by their pixel contents. So, detection techniques need to utilize features from the original data contents, rather than from coding cues as in the compressed data. In the rest of this sub-section, the key shot-cut detection techniques that deal with the uncompressed data, are presented. They are grouped according to the main change measures as follows:

1) Local Features

The local feature is calculated for specific location, or a region, within the image. It takes the spatial information into account. Examples of local features include the individual pixel's intensity and color as well as edges, to name just a few. The following are the key shot-cut detection techniques that rely on the most common local features:

a) Pixel-Based Differences

This category is considered as the very basic approach for detecting changes between frames. It is based simply on comparing the spatially corresponding pixel values, intensity or color. For each consecutive pair of frames, the difference is calculated between each pair of pixels that are in the same spatial location within their corresponding frames. The sum of those differences is calculated and a shot is detected if the sum is greater than a pre-defined threshold (Nagasaka & Tanaka, 1991) as follows:

$$\left(\sum_{x=1}^{X} \sum_{y=1}^{Y} \left| I_{F_i}(x,y) - I_{F_{i-1}}(x,y) \right| \right) > T \tag{1}$$

And for the color images, this is extended as follows:

$$\left(\sum_{x=1}^{X} \sum_{y=1}^{Y} \sum_{k=1}^{3} \left| C_{F_i}^k(x,y) - C_{F_{i-1}}^k(x,y) \right| \right) > T \tag{2}$$

The above technique is known as the pair-wise pixel comparison, as it based on comparing the spatially corresponding pair of pixels in consecutive frames.

A slight variation of this technique is introduced in (H. J. Zhang, Kankanhalli, & Smoliar, 1993). Instead of calculating and accumulating the differences in the pixel values, it only counts the number of pixels that are considered to be changed between consecutive frames and compare that with a threshold, as follows:

$$\left(\sum_{x=1}^{X} \sum_{y=1}^{Y} D_{F_i, F_{i-1}}(x,y) \right) > T \tag{3}$$

Where

$$D_{F_i, F_{i-1}}(x,y) = \begin{cases} 1 & if \left| I_{F_i}(x,y) - I_{F_{i-1}}(x,y) \right| > T_D \\ 0 & otherwise \end{cases}$$

Then the detection decision is based on comparing the number of changed pixels against a pre-defined threshold. In its strict form, when $T_D = 0$ in (3), it could be more computationally efficient, which is an important factor for the real-time applications. But it is clear that it will be very sensitive to any variations in the pixel values between frames.

A common drawback in this category of techniques is that they are very sensitive to object and camera motions and operations. With even the simplest object movement, its position in the image will change, and hence its associated pixels. Hence, the spatially corresponding pixel-pairs, from consecutive frames, may not be corresponding to the same object anymore. This will simply indicate a change, according to the above formulas, that can exceed the defined threshold. Once the change is above the defined threshold, a decision will be made that a shot boundary has been detected, which is a false detection in such a case.

As the measure is usually calculated between pairs of consecutive frames, this category is usually more suitable for detecting hard-cut transitions, as it happens abruptly. However, it is worth mentioning that some research has introduced the use of evolution of pixels' values, over multiple frames, to detect gradual transitions (Taniguchi, Akutsu, & Tonomura, 1997), (Lawrence, Ziou, Auclair-Fortier, & Wang, 2001).

b) Edge-Based Differences

Edges are important image feature that are commonly used, especially in image segmentation. Edges are detected from the discontinuity in the pixel intensity and/or color. This is with the assumption that pixels belonging to the same object are expected to exhibit continuity in their intensity or color values. So, edges could indicate a silhouette of a person or object, or separation between different objects as well as the background. This gives an idea of the contents of the image, which is considered a relatively higher level cue than the individual pixels. Hence, the change in those edges is expected to indicate the changes in the image contents, and when significant enough, indicates a shot change.

The straight forward test, especially for detecting hard-cut shot transitions, is to compare the number of edge pixels between consecutive frames. If the difference is above a certain threshold, then there have been enough changes to consider a shot change. However, as discussed in the following sub-section (global features), this simple approach does not take the spatial information into account. As a result, we may have more missed shot boundaries. This happens when frames from different shots contain similar number of edge pixels, but in significantly different spatial locations.

For the above reason, motion compensation techniques are utilized to compensate for motion between consecutive frames first (Zabih, Miller, & Mai, 1999). Then, the edges are compared, with indication of their spatial information. The number of edge pixels from the previous frame, which are within a certain distance from edges in the current frame, is called the exiting edge pixels, P_{ex}. Similarly, the number of edge pixels from the current frame, which are within a certain distance from edges in the previous frame, is called the entering edge pixels P_{en}. Those are usually normalized by the total number of pixels in the frame. The two quantities are calculated for every pair of consecutive frames and the maximum value among them is selected to represent the difference measure. The decision of detecting a shot-boundary is based on locating the maxima points of the curve representing the above difference measure. Sharp peaks, on the curve of the difference measure, are usually an indication of hard-cut transitions. But low and wide peaks, which occupy longer time periods than the hard-cuts, are usually an indication of gradual transitions.

In fact, for detecting the gradual transitions, the process needs to be extended to cover multiple frames (Smeaton et al., 1999), instead of only two consecutive frames. More details may be identified for detecting specific types of gradual transitions. For example, for detecting dissolve transitions, edges can be classified into weak and strong edges, using extra two thresholds, as introduced in (Lienhart, 1999).

As we can see, the edge-based differences approach can be used for both hard-cut and gradual transitions detection. However, its main limitation is its relatively high computational costs that makes it slow.

2) Global Features

Unlike the local features, the global feature is calculated over the entire image. It is expected to give an indication of an aspect of the image contents or its statistics. For example, the mean and/or variance of pixel intensities or colors, over the entire image, can be used as a global representation of the frame's contents. This measure can be compared between frames and a boundary can be detected if the difference is above a pre-determined threshold. Other statistical measures, such as the likelihood-ratio, can also be utilized. However, the histogram is the most popular and widely used global feature as discussed below.

a) Histogram-Based Differences
For the intensity level histogram, the intensity range is divided into quantized levels, called bins, and each pixel is classified into the nearest bin. Then the histogram represents the number of pixels associated with each bin. The same applies for the color histograms. The histogram of the intensity levels is usually used for grey-level images, and the color histograms are utilized for color images.

Once the histogram is constructed for each frame, the change measure is calculated by comparing the histograms of the pair of consecutive frames. The change measure can be as simple as the differences between the histograms. Then the sum of those differences is again compared with a pre-defined threshold to decide about the detection. For intensity histogram, this can be as follows:

$$\left(\sum_{v=0}^{V} \left| H_{F_i}(v) - H_{F_{i-1}}(v) \right| \right) > T \tag{4}$$

But for the color histogram, the following is an extended form that takes the various color components into account:

$$\left(\sum_{k=1}^{K} \sum_{v=0}^{V} \left| H_{F_i}^{C^k}(v) - H_{F_{i-1}}^{C^k}(v) \right| \right) > T \tag{5}$$

The color components could be the RGB components, with $K=3$ in (5), or any other components of other color spaces. Although normally only two components are used, i.e. $K=2$. In fact, one of the issues related with the color histogram is the selection of the appropriate color space (Gargi, Kasturi, & Strayer, 2000), as in the discussion sub-section below.

As can be seen above, the histogram is relatively easy to calculate. More importantly, it is less sensitive to object and camera motion than the pixel comparison techniques. This is because it is a global feature that does not involve spatial details within the frame. But, for the same reason, the technique may miss shot-cuts when different shots have similar range of total intensity or color values. A simple example is two frames, one contains a checker board, and the other contains a rectangle with half black and half white. Using the histogram, with the same number of bins, the histogram values will be the same. On the other hand, false detections can also be encountered, due to intensity and/or color changes within the frames contents, although within the same shot. An improved color histogram-based technique was introduced in (Ionescu, Lambert, Coquin, & Buzuloiu, 2007), for animated movies, where the frame is divided into quadrants to localize the measures.

3) Intermediate Level

As we saw in the above sub-sections, local and global features based techniques, each has its own advantages and limitations. The ultimate aim is to achieve more accurate shot-boundary detection, but also with less computation complexities. The block-based techniques are trying to address this balance between the advantages and limitations of using the local- and global feature-based techniques, to achieve those aims.

a) Block-Based Differences

In this approach, each frame is divided into equal-size areas, called blocks (Katsuri & Fain, 1991). These blocks are not spatially overlapping. The more blocks, the more the spatial details will be involved, with the extreme is having number of blocks equal to the number of pixels. Once the frame is divided into blocks, the rest of the work deals with the block as the smallest unit within the frame, instead of pixels.

Although each block consists of a number of pixels, an individual block can be dealt with either as a single value, as we dealt with pixels, or as a sub-image. In the case of dealing with the block as a sub-image, histogram-based techniques can be applied (AhmedM, 1999), (Bertini, Del Bimbo, & Pala, 2001). In such a case, a histogram is calculated for each individual block. Then, the histograms of the spatially corresponding blocks, from consecutive frames, are compared and the difference measure is tested against a pre-defined threshold. The same difference measures of histogram-based techniques can be utilized here, as discussed in the above sub-section (Histogram-based differences). This approach is also known as the local histograms, as it involves spatial details to some extent.

The block can also be dealt with as a single value, in an analogy to pixels. This can be seen as a reduced dimension of the original image, as every group of pixels will be replaced by the single value of the individual block that contains them. But first, we need to select the criteria for determining the block value that appropriately represents its contained pixels.

Variety of measures can be used to determine the block value. For example, the mean and/or variance of pixel intensities or colors can be used (M. S. Lee, Yang, & Lee, 2001). Other statistical measures, such as the likelihood-ratio, can also be utilized (Ren, Sharma, & Singh, 2001).

The above two ways of dealing with the block, as a single value or as a sub-image, can also be combined together (Dugad, Ratakonda, & Ahuja, 1998). Given the relatively cheaper computations of the histogram, it is used as a initial pass to detect hard-cut transitions and indicate potential gradual transitions. Then, the candidates are further checked using mean, variance, or likelihood-ratio tests between spatially corresponding blocks as usual.

Involving multiple frames, and especially for off-line processing, the evolution over time of the above difference measures can also be tracked, processed, and compared with a threshold to detect shot-boundaries (Demarty & Beucher, 1999), (Lefevre, Holler, & Vincent, 2000). In (Lefevre et al.,

2000), the evolution of the difference values were used to indicate the potential start of gradual transitions, while the derivative of the difference measures, over time, has been utilized to detect the hard-cut transitions.

As we mentioned above, the block-based techniques are considered as intermediate between local and global feature-based techniques. Hence, they are relatively less sensitive to the object and camera motions, than the pixel-based techniques, as the spatial resolution is reduced by using blocks instead of individual pixels. On the other hand, it can be relatively more computationally expensive than the global histogram-based techniques.

4) Motion-Based

In the previously discussed techniques, the main principle was finding the changes in some features of the contents of consecutive frames. This is, at least implicitly, based on the concept that the video can abstractly be considered as a sequence of individual frames or still images. However, the video sequence has more than just playing back a group of still images, otherwise, it can be considered as a uniform slide-presentation.

The video sequence carries other extra information, than a slide-show of still images. One of the extra important information in the video data is the motion information. The motion is conveyed by the temporal changes of object and/or camera positions and orientations over consecutive frames. We should recall that the video frame rates, especially the playback frame rates, are designed to convey smooth motion to the human eye. That is the rate of change of the displayed images is more than what the human eye can recognize, hence, no flickers can be noticed.

Given the above, and recalling the shot definition from section II, it is expected that the motion encountered among the frames of the same shot will have continuity. However, the motion among frames from different shots will exhibit discontinuity. So, this continuity criterion can be utilized in detection of the shot-boundary.

We should also differentiate between the motion originated from the movements of the contained objects and the motion originated from the camera movements and operations, such as pan, tilt, or zoom. The camera movements will usually result in a similar motion of the contents, assuming no moving objects. That is all the frame's pixels or blocks will shift, translate, or rotate consistently, almost in the same direction. This is except for zooming, although it can be seen in a similar fashion as motion will be radially consistent from/to the centre of the image. The motion originated from the camera movements or operations is known as the *global motion*, as it is usually exhibited over the entire image. The objects motion can be a bit more complicated. First of all, we would usually have more than one object in the video, each may be moving in different direction. With occlusion, things become even more complicated. This is all with the assumption that objects are simply rigid. In fact, deformable objects, like our skin, could also add to this complexity. Within the normal video sequence, many combinations of the above motions can be found. These are all challenges faced by motion estimation and compensation techniques.

Based on the above discussion, various techniques were developed that utilize one or more of the above motion properties. When utilizing the global motion, it is assumed that it will be coherent within the same shot. If the coherence of the global motion is broken, a shot-boundary is flagged (Cherfaoui & Bertin, 1995). A template could also be designed where each pixel is represented by a coefficient that indicates how coherent it is with the estimated dominant motion. The evolution of the number of pixels that are coherent with the dominant motion, with a pre-determined threshold, are used to decide on shot-boundary detection (Bouthemy, Gelgon, Ganansia, & IRISA, 1999).

In utilizing the objects motion, techniques from the motion estimation are utilized to calculate motion vectors and correlation coefficients, of corresponding blocks, between frames. The similarity measure is calculated from those correlation coefficients, and critical points on its evolution curve correspond to shot-boundaries (Akutsu, Tonomura, Hashimoto, & Ohba, 1992), (Shahraray, 1995). Other techniques were developed that are based on the optical flow (Fatemi, Zhang, & Panchanathan, 1996) or correlation in the frequency domain (Porter, Mirmehdi, & Thomas, 2000).

The computational cost of the motion estimation techniques are relatively high (Lefèvre, Holler, & Vincent, 2003), which can affect the performance of the techniques discussed above, in terms of the processing time. However, motion estimation are already incorporated in the current compression standards such as MPEG (see "video compression" in section II). Hence, more work has been done in this category but for the compressed data, as discussed in their corresponding section later in this chapter.

5) Object-Based

Instead of applying the difference measures on individual pixels or fixed size blocks changes, in this category, efforts are made to obtain differences based on object-level changes. Based on color, size, and position of recognized objects, differences between frames can be computed (Vadivel, Mohan, Sural, & Majumdar, 2005). Objects are constructed by pixel grouping, through *k-means* clustering, followed by post-processing that includes *connected component analysis* to merge tiny size regions. Although it was presented on *I*-frames, an MPEG frame type, the techniques seems to be applicable for uncompressed data.

Also, a semantic objects tracking approach was introduced in (Cheng & Wu, 2006) for the detection of both shot-cut and gradual transitions. Foreground objects are recognized and tracked based on a combined color and motion segmentation process. The numbers of entering and exiting objects or regions help in detecting shot changes, while the motion vectors help in detecting the camera motion.

Although it is easy for humans to recognize and identify objects from images and videos, achieving this automatically is still an ongoing research challenge. Hence, the object-based approaches will always benefit from the advances in the image analysis and understanding field.

B. Gradual-Transition Detection from "Uncompressed Data"

As explained in section III, the gradual transitions exhibit much less changes between consecutive frames, than in the case of hard-cut transitions. Consequently, the pre-determined threshold that is used to detect hard-cuts will always miss the gradual transitions. On the other hand, using a lower threshold will increase the false detection, due to motion and camera operations that introduce changes in a relative order to the changes from the gradual transitions.

As the gradual transition occurs over longer period of time, the difference measure between two consecutive frames, which is used in most of the techniques described earlier, is not always useful to accurately detect such transitions. We need to track the changes over longer periods, i.e. multiple frames. One way, especially for off-line detection, is to track the evolution of the difference measure over the time of the given sequence. In a pixel-based approach introduced in (Taniguchi et al., 1997), the variation of pixel intensities is tracked and pixels are labeled according to the behavior of their variation over time; sudden, gradual, random, or constant. The gradual transition can be detected by analyzing the percentage of the gradually changing pixels.

In the rest of this sub-section, the most common techniques, for detecting gradual transitions, are discussed.

1) Twin-Threshold Approach

This approach, introduced in (H. J. Zhang et al., 1993), is based on two observations. Firstly, although the differences between consecutive frames are not high, during the gradual transition, the difference between the two frames, just before and after the transition, is significant. It is usually in the order of the changes that occur in hard-cut, as those two frames are from different shots. Secondly, the changes during the gradual transition are slightly higher than the usual changes within the same shot. They also occupy longer period of time, as depicted in fig. 6.

The twin-threshold algorithm, as the name suggests, has two thresholds, instead of one. The first threshold, T_H, is similar to thresholds discussed before, and is usually high enough to identify the hard-cut transitions. The second threshold, T_L, is the new introduced threshold. This threshold is adjusted so that the start of a potential gradual transition period can be detected. In other words, this threshold is set to identify the changes due to the gradual transition, from changes between frames within the same shot. Once the difference between two consecutive frames exceeds the T_L, but still less than T_H, this will mark the start of a potential gradual transition. From this frame onwards, an extra accumulated difference will be calculated, in addition to the difference between consecutive frames. This will continue until the difference between consecutive frames fall again below the threshold T_L. This is potentially the end of gradual transition, if any. To confirm, whether a gradual transition was detected or not, the accumulated difference is compared to the threshold T_H. If the accumulated difference exceeds the threshold T_H, a gradual transition is considered. Otherwise, the marked potential start, of gradual transition, will be ignored and the procedure starts again. The procedure, from one of our experiments, is illustrated in fig. 7, with the addition that the value of T_L is computed adaptively based on the average of the difference

Figure 6. Example of the difference measure for hard-cut and gradual transition

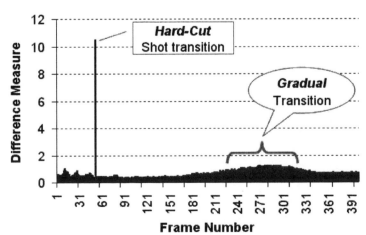

measure from previous frames, to adapt to the video contents. Choosing the threshold value is one of the important issues and discussed in a later sub-section with other common issues.

One limitation of this algorithm is that it could produce false detection if significant object and/or camera motion and operations occurred. This is because those significant motions are expected to produce frame differences of almost the same order as the differences exhibited during the gradual transition. One suggested solution to reduce this false detection is to analyze detected transitions to distinguish real gradual transitions from global motion of camera and camera operations (H. J. Zhang et al., 1993).

2) Edge-Based Detection of Gradual Transitions

The edge-based comparison has already been discussed earlier. In this subsection, we emphasize on its use for detecting gradual transitions. As edges are related to the objects within the images, its changes and strength can also help identifying the various types of gradual transitions.

Based on the properties of each type of the gradual transition, as discussed in section III, the number and ratios of the entering and exiting edge pixels can indicate a potential shot change. In fade-out, the transition is usually end up with a constant color frame, which means that it has almost no entering edges. Hence, the exiting edges will be expected to be much higher. In the fade-in, the opposite will happen. In fade-in, the transition usually starts from a constant color frame that has almost no edges. Hence, the entering edges, from the new shot, will be expected to be much higher. So, by analyzing the ratios of the entering and exiting edges, fade-in and fade-out can potentially be detected. Dissolve transitions can also be detected as they are usually a combination of the fade-in and fade-out. Wipe transition needs a bit more attention due to the special changes in the spatial distribution. Based on the hypothesis that the gradual curve can mostly be characterized by the variance distribution of edge information, a localized edge blocks techniques was presented in (Yoo, Ryoo, & Jang, 2006). However, as mentioned earlier, the edge-based comparison is computationally expensive and relatively slower than others.

3) Motion-Based Detection of Gradual Transitions

As discussed earlier, for the uncompressed data, most of the motion-based techniques use the evolution of the motion measure, whether global motion, motion vectors, correlation, or others, to decide on the shot-boundaries.

A histogram-based approach is utilized in (H. J. Zhang et al., 1993) for detecting two directions of wipe transitions, specifically horizontal and vertical wipes. As in (Bouthemy et al., 1999), pixels that are not coherent with the estimated motion are flagged first. Then, vertical and horizontal histograms, of those flagged non-coherent pixels, are constructed for each frame. The histogram differences, of corresponding histograms of consecutive frame, are calculated and thresholds are used to detect a horizontal or a vertical wipe transition.

In (Hu, Han, Wang, & Lin, 2007), motion vectors were filtered first to obtain the *reliable motion vectors*. Then, those reliable motion vectors are used to support a color-based technique and enhance the detection accuracy, for soccer video analysis. Also, the analysis of discontinuity in the optical flow between frames can be utilized in shot detection (Bruno & Pellerin, 2002).

Other Combined Techniques for Detection of Gradual Transitions

Some other techniques, that may not fit exactly within the above categories, are discussed here. The Hidden Markov Models (HMM) were employed in (W. Zhang, Lin, Chen, Huang, & Liu, 2006) for detection of various types of shot transitions. An HHM is constructed and trained for each type of the shot transitions, which model its temporal characteristics. One of the advantages is that the issue of selecting threshold values is avoided.

More advanced features can be employed such as corners, moments, and phase correlation. In (Gao et al., 2006), corners are extracted at the initial frame and then tracked, using Kalman filter, through the rest of the sequence. The detection is based on the characteristics of the changing measure. In another system, a two-pass hierarchical supervised approach was introduced (Camara-Chavez et al., 2007) that is based on a kernel-based Support Vector Machine (SVM) classifier. A feature vector, combining color histograms and few moment measures as well as the phase correlation, is extracted for each frame. In the first pass, shot-cuts are detected and used as guides for the second pass, where the gradual transitions are to be detected in-between shot-cuts.

Figure 7. The difference measure (top) and the accumulated difference measure (bottom) of the twin-threshold technique, for detection gradual transitions

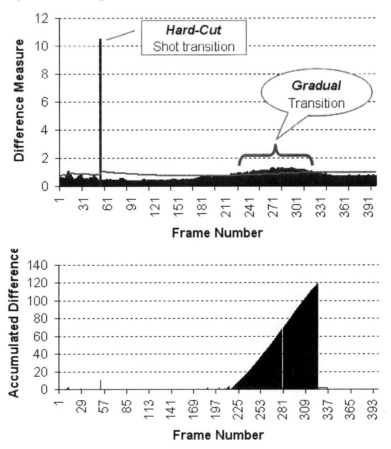

Finally, some efforts are made to model the various editing effects and detect the transitions by fitting the corresponding edit model as in (Nam & Tewfik, 2005). While it could achieve promising results, the main concern is the almost unlimited, and ever increasing, number and variations of editing effects that are even customizable by video editing software users.

C. Shot-Boundary Detection from "Compressed Data"

Compressed video data result from processing the original video data by coding the data, inter- or intra-coding as explained in section II, in such a way to reduce redundancy. This coding also provides useful information that helps the detection techniques. Examples include the motion vectors, and various types of frames and macro-blocks in the MPEG compression. The coding usually facilitates the shot-boundary detection without decompression. Hence, it could also improve the detection performance, in terms of the computational costs.

In MPEG compression, the frame is divided into 8x8 blocks. Blocks within the I-frames are intra-coded using the Discrete Cosine Transform (DCT). For P-frames and B-frames, motion vectors, correlations and residual errors are calculated. Hence, different types of frames contain some different types of information.

The rest of this subsection presents the detection techniques that deal with the compressed data. They are based on the most common features that can be extracted, usually directly without need for decompression, from the compressed data.

1) DCT-Based

The *I*-frames of the MPEG compressed data, see section II, which are intra-coded frames, contains all the DCT coefficients. On the other hand, the *P*-frames and *B*-frames do not usually include the DCT coefficients as most of their blocks are inter-coded rather than intra-coded. Most blocks within those *P*- and *B*-frames include the DCT coefficients of the residual error resulting from the motion compensation.

The DCT coefficients are representatives of the frame contents. In fact, the DC coefficients alone represent a low-resolution, or iconic, version of the image and are considered as an iconic version of the image. Hence, most of the pixel-based and histogram-based techniques could be applied for shot-boundary detection. Also, the difference in feature vectors, extracted from the DC components, is used to detect shot-cuts (Taskiran et al., 2004). The feature vector contains standard deviation and color histogram intersection of the YUV color space components, as well as other information about the various types of macro-blocks and the type of the frame.

For gradual transitions, and for off-line processing, both the absolute difference and the variance of the DC coefficients are utilized to detect gradual transitions (Yeo & Liu, 1995), (Meng, Juan, & Chang, 1995). Gradual transition is represented by a plateau in the curve depicting the absolute difference between two frames separated by *n* frames, where n is longer than the known length of gradual transitions (Yeo & Liu, 1995). On the other hand, a dissolve will produce a downward parabolic curve when the variance of the DC coefficients is plotted (Meng et al., 1995).

As mentioned above, the DCT coefficients, of frame contents, are mainly available within the *I*-frames. However, *I*-frames are only a percentage of the total frames in MPEG, as there are several *P*-frames and *B*-frames in-between *I*-frames. This introduces some temporal gaps, if only *I*-frames are used with DCT-based techniques, which increases the false detection. The straight forward solution is to use the *P*-frames and *B*-frames as well, by obtaining the best possible estimation of their DCT coefficients. Alternatively, the technique can be combined with other techniques as discussed in the hybrid techniques section below.

2) Motion-Based

As discussed in the motion-based detection techniques, from uncompressed data, the motion is an important property in video. And based on the shot definition, it is expected that the motion measure will have continuity over time, within the same shot. But will exhibit discontinuity across different shots.

The computational cost of obtaining the motion vectors are relatively high (Lefèvre et al., 2003). But fortunately, motion information can be extracted from compressed data that have been coded through the currently available compression standards such as MPEG (see "video compression" in section II). This dramatically reduces the computational cost of the motion-based shot-boundary detection.

From the MPEG coding, the blocks contained in the *I*-frames are all intra-coded. But the blocks in the *P*-frames and *B*-frames are of various types. *P*-frames contain both intra-coded as well as forward-predicted blocks. *B*-frames are more complicated as they can contain any combination of forward-predicted, backward-predicted, bi-directional predicted, intra-coded, and/or skipped blocks. The number and the ratios between the various types of blocks can give some indication of changes and motion continuity (Yi, Rajan, & Chia, 2006), hence, helps in detecting shot-boundaries. For example, the more continuous and coherent the motion is, the less intra-coded blocks to be found. In other words, blocks that have high residual errors as a result of motion compensation, indicates a discontinuity of motion. Those blocks are intra-coded by the MPEG encoder. So, when the ratio of the intra-coded blocks is higher than a pre-defined threshold, a potential shot-boundary is flagged (Meng et al., 1995).

The bit-rate for encoding the blocks, in MPEG compression, also exhibit variations, especially with the changes associated with shot-cuts. By monitoring and analysing the variations in the number of bits required to encode each block, shot-cuts can be detected when the differences in bit-rate exceed certain threshold (FENG, Kwok-Tung, & MEHRPOUR, 1996).

Exhaustive survey of the compressed video data, and more features that can be utilized in shot detection, can be found in (Wang, Divakaran, Vetro, Chang, & Sun, 2003), (Vadivel et al., 2005).

3) Hybrid Techniques

One or more techniques can be combined together to achieve better detection performance, whether the accuracy and/or the processing speed. A hierarchical multi-pass approach was introduced in (H. Zhang, Low, & Smoliar, 1995). This combines the DCT coefficients technique and the motion-based techniques. The DCT coefficients, which are already available in the *I*-frames, are utilized to locate potential shot-transitions. Then, motion information, from the in-between P-frames and B-frames, are utilized to confirm and refine the identified shot-boundary. As we can see, the motion information is only utilized from the frames lying in-between the two *I*-frames around the identified potential transition. This improves the computational costs. Also, by using the appropriate thresholds, it was reported that both shot-cuts and gradual-transitions can be detected.

A similar two-pass hybrid approach was presented in (Koprinska & Carrato, 2002), although only use motion vectors and macro-blocks information. Potential shot-boundaries are identified by a rule-based module, then a refined pass using a neural structure detect and classify the various types, especially gradual transitions. In (Zhao & Cai, 2006), a technique utilizing Adaboost and fuzzy theory was introduced. It utilizes various features and information, such as DCT coefficients, macro-block types, and color histograms. The important reported advantage is the robustness of the technique's performance against camera motion and large objects fast movements.

The bit-rate variation technique from (FENG, Kwok-Tung, & MEHRPOUR, 1996) can also be combined with other techniques, such as those that use the DCT coefficients, to improve the detection (Divakaran, Ito, Sun, & Poon, 2003), (Boccignone, De Santo, & Percannella, 2000).

D. Performance Evaluation

There are two main performance aspects that need to be assessed when evaluating or comparing shot-detection techniques, as well as many other techniques. These two aspects are the *accuracy* and the *computational complexity*. As we can expect, these aspects could be seen as being on opposite sides of a coin, or as two ends of one string. Usually improving one aspect would be on the cost of the other one. So, usually to improve the accuracy, more complicated techniques are developed, which will usually require more computational requirements. On the other hand, if we are after a real-time system, we might have to compromise and accept some less accuracy. Also, for the evaluation to be truly representative and trustable for comparing various techniques, it needs to be done in similar conditions and with very similar, if not the same, datasets. Hence, there is a need for benchmarks to be used. TRECVID (Over, Ianeva, Kraaij, & Smeaton, 2005) is one of the initiatives within the video retrieval task. Other efforts also facilitate reproducing the research results so that people can test it themselves. Some even allow the user to upload their own data and apply the techniques on it (Vadivel et al., 2005) , which provide a fair comparison. Otherwise, researchers will have to re-implement previous techniques to compare with, which waste time and effort, and can still be not accurate due to various interpretations and implementation decisions.

In this section, we discuss the above two aspects of performance evaluation, the accuracy and the computational complexity, and the common metrics of measuring them for the shot-boundary detection.

1) Accuracy

Ideally, we would hope that the detection technique can detect all the *correct* shot-boundaries, without missing any of them. However, the reality is that for some reasons, some shots can be *missed*, and also some non-existing boundaries may seem to be detected, which is called the *false detection* or *false positive*.

One way of quantitatively evaluating the accuracy is by calculating the *detection-rate* and the *error-rate* (Tian & Zhang, 1999). The detection-rate is the percentage of the correctly detected shots, relative to the total number of shots. The total number of shots should be identified, somehow but usually manually, as a ground-truth. Similarly, the error-rate is the percentage of the falsely detected shots, relative to the total number of shots.

The most commonly measures that are used to evaluate the accuracy of the detection techniques are the *recall* and the *precision*. The recall measure is similar to the detection rate, described above. The precision measure gives an indication on how precise the detection is, correct or false. We can denote the number of correctly detected shots by N_c, the number of falsely detected shots by N_f, and the missed shots by N_m. Hence, the $N_c + N_m$ represents the total number of shots, while the $N_c + N_f$ represents the total number of detections by the detection technique. And the recall and precision can be obtained as follows:

$$\mathrm{Re}call = \frac{N_c}{N_c + N_m} \tag{6}$$

$$\mathrm{Pr}ecision = \frac{N_c}{N_c + N_f} \tag{7}$$

From the above definitions, the good detection techniques are expected to have high recall and high precision at the same time.

It can be noticed that the above measures are mainly evaluating the performance in terms of the number of shots, whether correct, missed, or false. However, the accuracy in determining the length of the transition periods also needs to be evaluated. Additional measures, brought from the field of image segmentation, have been employed, namely over-segmentation and under-segmentation (Y. J. Zhang & Beijing, 2006). The lengths of the detected shots are compared with the lengths of the corresponding shots in the ground-truth. It is preferred to have low over- and under-segmentation values.

So, overall, the good detection technique is expected to have high recall, high precision, low over-segmentation, and low under-segmentation values.

2) Computational Complexity

Most of the evaluation is usually focused on the accuracy aspect of the performance. That could be acceptable for off-line applications. But once the processing time becomes a factor in the application, such as real-time applications, the computation costs have to be incorporated in the performance evaluation.

In fact, most research of the literature provides quantitative figures of the accuracy of the presented detection techniques. But it is rare to find quantitative figures for the computational complexity. However, an exhaustive survey, where the evaluation is focused on the computational complexity, was presented in (Lefèvre et al., 2003). This was crucial as the survey was reviewing the real-time shot detection techniques, from uncompressed data.

Their computational complexity measure considers the arithmetic and logical operations only. It represents the number of operations per frame where each arithmetic or logical operation, including the absolute operation, increments the computational complexity measure by one. Other operations, such as loops and conditional branching were not considered in that complexity measure.

For the pixel-based techniques, the complexity measure will be a function of the number of pixels in each frame, which is denoted by P. So, for the intensity-based computations, the complexity is $O(3P)$, while for the color version, the complexity is $O(9P)$. Another estimated complexity, for edge-based techniques, is $O(26P)$. However, for the block-based techniques, the number of blocks per frame is also incorporated, which is denoted by B. The complexity measure is estimated to be between $O(2P+10B)$ and $O(3P+15B)$, depending on the specific technique used.

Similarly, for the histogram-based techniques, the measure will be a function of the number of bins, denoted by L. It was reported that, for intensity histogram difference, the complexity is $O(3L)$. The complexity of the color version is $O(6L)$, based on using only two color components, for the reasons mentioned in the discussion section next.

E. Common Issues

From the above review, and the preceded discussion about the various classifications, it is clear that the topic is large and interrelated in various ways. There are also some issues that are considered to be common to various groups of techniques. To avoid repeating them in various places, which is a redundancy that we tried to avoid, we preferred to discuss them in this sub-section.

It can be noticed from the above review, that in almost all the techniques, the detection decision involves a pre-defined thresholds. Determining the values of those thresholds is one of the common issues. It is expected and understood that the value of many of those thresholds will depend on the domain and application as well as the particular video data. Fixed threshold values are usually chosen based on heuristics or through statistics of the existing data. Fixed pre-defined values would be acceptable for specific domains, given that they have been carefully chosen. However, adaptive and automatically chosen threshold values (Volkmer, Tahaghoghi, & Williams, 2004), (Bescos, Cisneros, Martinez, Menendez, & Cabrera, 2005), (Ionescu et al., 2007) would be much desirable to reduce the need for human intervention and to adapt to the varying data ranges. In fact, avoiding the thresholds would be even better as in (Yu, Tian, & Tang, 2007), where the Self-Organizing Map (SOM) network was used, which avoided the need for thresholds.

Another issue, especially with the color histogram techniques, is selecting the appropriate color space. Usually, the images are converted from the RGB color space to other color spaces such as YUV, HSV, or YCbCr (Gargi et al., 2000). This is because those color spaces are closer to the color perception model of humans. Also, the intensity value component is usually not included in the color histogram to reduce false detections. The YCbCr color space is used in the MPEG video.

For the gradual transitions in particular, large and sudden object motion and fast camera operations in dynamic scenes increases the false detection. This is because they produce relatively large differences that are in the order of the changes of the gradual transitions.

From the detected and classified shots, higher logical components in the logical video structure can be constructed, such as video scenes and segments. Those higher level components are usually more dependent on the application domain and more semantic information. However, it is worth mentioning that some recent efforts of scene detection have been reported in(M. H. Lee, Yoo, & Jang, 2006), (Rasheed & Shah, 2005), (Adjeroh & Lee, 2004).

V. SUMMARY AND CONCLUSION

Video data are now available, and being easily generated, in large volumes. This puts a high demand for efficient access, search, and retrieval of these data, which have not been progressed in the same rate. To facilitate that, the data need to be annotated and indexed, by text, features, or semantic descriptions. This can be done manually, but given the huge volumes of data, it became impractical to do so. Hence, automatic or even semi-automatic video content analysis techniques need to be able to efficiently extract the video structure and components. Most of these techniques require processing and segmentation of the given video data.

In this chapter, we presented the principles of the video representation and processing in preparation for video data mining, with focus on the shot-boundary detection as an important initial step. Firstly, the video structure and representation were explained, followed by definition and classification of the common shot transitions. Then, the stat-of-the-art, of the key techniques for the shot-boundary detection, was presented. We have only focused on the visual modality of the video. Hence, audio and text modalities were not covered. Research in multi-modal detection can be found in the literature, but it was beyond the scope of this chapter.

As can be seen from the review, a lot of research has been going on for the shot boundary detection, both on the compressed and uncompressed data. In uncompressed data, most techniques trying to detect changes based on comparing differences in *pixel values, histograms, edges,* and *motion information.* In compressed data, techniques are relying on the representation of the compressed data and the information provided in it. Compressed-domain techniques are based on DCT coefficients, motion information, or a hybrid. Other higher-level techniques, such as object-based techniques have also been presented. It was reported, through comparisons between various methods, that the histogram-based techniques are usually more reliable and efficient. But it has its limitations, in terms of sensitivity to changing illumination conditions within the shot and missing shot boundaries especially in the global histograms. Localized histograms address these problems to some extent. The edge-based techniques, although useful in detecting both shot-cut and gradual transitions, are computationally expensive. Motion-based techniques are useful in utilizing the temporal information, but expensive to compute on the uncompressed data. On the other hand, compressed-based techniques utilize the spatial and temporal coded information, mainly the motion and block types, to detect changes. As these information are already available within the compression coding, motion-based techniques are more efficient on the compressed data. However, may not be on the same level of accuracy. It is obvious that there is no individual technique that solves the problem completely. Hence, hybrid methods that combine two or more techniques were employed to improve the performance.

The performance evaluation of the shot detection techniques includes both the accuracy and computational complexity. Accuracy evaluation is always the dominant and has been the focus of most papers in the literature. However, the computational complexity is also important, especially with real-time applications, and the rapid increase of the data volumes. Accuracy is evaluated through the precision and recall measures. They are calculated based on the number of correctly and falsely detected shots, as well as the missed one. Another important issue with the evaluation is that it needs to be done using a common data sets, and standards to be truly representative. Some initiatives have been made and more improvements are still needed.

Common issues in almost all the detection algorithms include the selection of the threshold values and the appropriate color space to work with. Adaptive threshold were suggested, based on some statistical properties of the video data. For the color space, most techniques convert the images from the RGB color space to other color spaces such as YUV, HSV, or YCbCr, as they are closer to the color perception model of humans. It has also been noticed that, especially with the gradual transitions, large and sudden object motion and fast camera operations in dynamic scenes increases the false detection. This is because they produce relatively large differences that are in the order of the changes of the gradual transitions. Some specific models are designed to fit specific gradual transitions, which improves the accuracy and reduce the false detection. However, the increasing number, variability, and options of the possible digital effects these days makes it difficult to include models for all possible effects.

Finally, the detected shots are expected to be classified and grouped to construct the higher components in the logical video structure; that are the scenes and segments. This can be done based on temporal, contents similarity, and/or semantic inputs. But they are usually more dependent on the specific application domain among other factors. Hence, most probably they involve some level of user interaction, especially for the semantics. We also mentioned some efforts in scene detection that have been reported in the last couple of years.

ACKNOWLEDGMENT

I would like to thank my lovely wife (Mrs G. Mohamed) very much for her kind help, support, and encouragement all the way through. Thanks also to my lovely children (Noran, Yusof, and AbdulRahman) for their patient and understanding during the time I have been working on this chapter. I also would like to thank my parents (Mr Adel Hassan, and Mrs Afaf Zaky) for their continuous support and encouragement.

REFERENCES

Adjeroh, D., & Lee, M. (2004). Scene-adaptive transform domain video partitioning. *IEEE Transactions on Multimedia, 6*(1), 58-69.

Ahmed M, K. A. (1999). Video segmentation using an opportunistic approach. *Multimedia Modeling,* 389–405.

Akutsu, A., Tonomura, Y., Hashimoto, H., & Ohba, Y. (1992). Video indexing using motion vectors. *SPIE,* (1992) 1522-1530.

Bertini, M., Del Bimbo, A., & Pala, P. (2001). Content-based indexing and retrieval of TV news. *Pattern Recognition Letters, 22*(5), 503-516.

Bescos, J., Cisneros, G., Martinez, J., Menendez, J., & Cabrera, J. (2005). A unified model for techniques on video-shot transition detection. *IEEE Transactions On Multimedia, 7*(2), 293-307.

Boccignone, G., De Santo, M., & Percannella, G. (2000). An algorithm for video cut detection in MPEG sequences. *SPIE Conference on Storage and Retrieval of Media Databases,* 523–530.

Bouthemy, P., Gelgon, M., Ganansia, F., & IRISA, R. (1999). A unified approach to shot change detection and camera motion characterization. *IEEE Transactions On Circuits And Systems For Video Technology, 9*(7), 1030-1044.

Bruno, E., & Pellerin, D. (2002). Video shot detection based on linear prediction of motion. *IEEE International Conference on Multimedia and Expo,*

Camara-Chavez, G., Precioso, F., Cord, M., Philipp-Foliguet, S., De, A., & Araujo, A. (2007). Shot boundary detection by a hierarchical supervised approach. *14th International Workshop on Systems, Signals and Image Processing, 2007 and 6th EURASIP Conference Focused on Speech and Image Processing, Multimedia Communications and Services.* 197-200.

Cheng, S. C., & Wu, T. L. (2006). Scene-adaptive video partitioning by semantic object tracking. *Journal of Visual Communication and Image Representation, 17*(1), 72-97.

Cherfaoui, M., & Bertin, C. (1995). Temporal segmentation of videos: A new approach. *SPIE,* 38.

Demarty, C. H., & Beucher, S. (1999). Morphological tools for indexing video documents. *IEEE International Conference on Multimedia Computing and Systems, , 2* 991-1002.

Divakaran, A., Ito, H., Sun, H., & Poon, T. (2003). Scene change detection and feature extraction for MPEG-4 sequences. *SPIE, 545.*

Dugad, R., Ratakonda, K., & Ahuja, N. (1998). Robust video shot change detection. *IEEE Second Workshop on Multimedia Signal Processing, 376-381.*

Fatemi, O., Zhang, S., & Panchanathan, S. (1996). Optical flow based model for scene cut detection. *Canadian Conference on Electrical and Computer Engineering, 470-473.*

FENG, J., Kwok-Tung, L., & MEHRPOUR, H. (1996). Scene change detection algorithm for MPEG video sequence. *IEEE International Conference on Image Processing, 821-824.*

Gao, X., Li, J., & Shi, Y. (2006). A video shot boundary detection algorithm based on feature tracking. *Lecture Notes In Computer Science, 4062,* 651.

Gargi, U., Kasturi, R., & Strayer, S. (2000). Performance characterization of video-shot-change detection methods. *IEEE Transactions On Circuits And Systems For Video Technology, 10*(1), 1-13.

Hu, Y., Han, B., Wang, G., & Lin, X. (2007). Enhanced shot change detection using motion features for soccer video analysis. *2007 IEEE International Conference on Multimedia and Expo, 1555-1558.*

Ionescu, B., Lambert, P., Coquin, D., & Buzuloiu, V. (2007). The cut detection issue in the animation movie domain. *Journal Of Multimedia, 2*(4)

Katsuri, R., & Fain, R. (1991). Dynamic vision. In R. Katsuri, & R. Fain (Eds.), *Computer vision: Advances and applications* (pp. 469-480) IEEE Computer Society Press, Los Alamitos, California.

Koprinska, I., & Carrato, S. (2002). Hybrid rule-Based/Neural approach for segmentation of MPEG compressed video. *Multimedia Tools and Applications, 18*(3), 187-212.

Lawrence, S., Ziou, D., Auclair-Fortier, M. F., & Wang, S. (2001). Motion insensitive detection of cuts and gradual transitions in digital videos. *International Conference on Multimedia Modeling, , 266*

Lee, M. H., Yoo, H. W., & Jang, D. S. (2006). Video scene change detection using neural network: Improved ART2. *Expert Systems with Applications, 31*(1), 13-25.

Lee, M. S., Yang, Y. M., & Lee, S. W. (2001). Automatic video parsing using shot boundary detection and camera operation analysis. *Pattern Recognition, 34*(3), 711-719.

Lefevre, S., Holler, J., & Vincent, N. (2000). Real time temporal segmentation of compressed and uncompressed dynamic colour image sequences. *International Workshop on Real Time Image Sequence Analysis, 56-62.*

Lefèvre, S., Holler, J., & Vincent, N. (2003). A review of real-time segmentation of uncompressed video sequences for content-based search and retrieval. *Real-Time Imaging, 9*(1), 73-98.

Lienhart, R. (1999). Comparison of automatic shot boundary detection algorithms. *SPIE,* 290–301.

Ma, Y. F., Lu, L., Zhang, H. J., & Li, M. (2002). A user attention model for video summarization. *Proceedings of the Tenth ACM International Conference on Multimedia*, 533-542.

Meng, J., Juan, Y., & Chang, S. F. (1995). Scene change detection in an MPEG compressed video sequence. *IS&T/SPIE Symposium*,

Nagasaka, A., & Tanaka, Y. (1991). Automatic video indexing and full-video search for object appearance. *Second Working Conference on Visual Database Systems*, 113-127.

Nam, J., & Tewfik, A. (2005). Detection of gradual transitions in video sequences using B-spline interpolation. *IEEE Transactions On Multimedia, 7*(4), 667-679.

Over, P., Ianeva, T., Kraaij, W., & Smeaton, A. F. (2005). TRECVID 2005-an overview. *TRECVID, , 2005*

Porter, S., Mirmehdi, M., & Thomas, B. (2000). Video cut detection using frequency domain correlation. *15th International Conference on Pattern Recognition*, 413-416.

Rasheed, Z., & Shah, M. (2005). Detection and representation of scenes in videos. *IEEE Transactions On Multimedia, 7*(6), 1097-1105.

Ren, W., Sharma, M., & Singh, S. (2001). Automated video segmentation. *International Conference on Information, Communication, and Signal Processing*,

Shahraray, B. (1995). Scene change detection and content-based sampling of video sequences. *SPIE*, 2-13.

Smeaton, A., Gilvarry, J., Gormley, G., Tobin, B., Marlow, S., & Murphy, M. (1999). An evaluation of alternative techniques for automatic detection of shot boundaries in digital video. *Irish Machine Vision and Image Processing Conference (IMVIP'99)*, 45-60.

Taniguchi, Y., Akutsu, A., & Tonomura, Y. (1997). PanoramaExcerpts: Extracting and packing panoramas for video browsing. *Fifth ACM International Conference on Multimedia*, 427-436.

Taskiran, C., Chen, J. Y., Albiol, A., Torres, L., Bouman, C., & Delp, E. (2004). *IEEE Transactions On Multimedia, 6*(1), 103-118.

Tian, Q., & Zhang, H. J. (1999). Video shot detection and analysis: Content-based approaches. In C. Chen, & Y. Zhang (Eds.), *Visual information representation, communication, and image processing* () Marcel Dekker, Inc.

Vadivel, A., Mohan, M., Sural, S., & Majumdar, A. (2005). Object level frame comparison for video shot detection. *IEEE Workshop on Motion and Video Computing*,

Volkmer, T., Tahaghoghi, S., & Williams, H. (2004). Gradual transition detection using average frame similarity. *Computer Vision and Pattern Recognition Workshop*, 139.

Wang, H., Divakaran, A., Vetro, A., Chang, S. F., & Sun, H. (2003). Survey of compressed-domain features used in audio-visual indexing and analysis. *Journal of Visual Communication and Image Representation, 14*(2), 150-183.

Yeo, B. L., & Liu, B. (1995). Unified approach to temporal segmentation of motion JPEG and MPEG video. *International Conference on Multimedia Computing and Systems,* 2-13.

Yi, H., Rajan, D., & Chia, L. T. (2006). A motion-based scene tree for browsing and retrieval of compressed videos. *Information Systems, 31*(7), 638-658.

Yoo, H. W., Ryoo, H. J., & Jang, D. S. (2006). Gradual shot boundary detection using localized edge blocks. *Multimedia Tools and Applications, 28*(3), 283-300.

Yu, J., Tian, B., & Tang, Y. (2007). Video segmentation based on shot boundary coefficient. *2nd International Conference on Pervasive Computing and Applications,* 630-635.

Zabih, R., Miller, J., & Mai, K. (1999). A feature-based algorithm for detecting and classifying production effects. *Multimedia Systems, 7*(2), 119-128.

Zhang, H., Low, C. Y., & Smoliar, S. W. (1995). Video parsing and browsing using compressed data. *Multimedia Tools and Applications, 1*(1), 89-111.

Zhang, H. J., Kankanhalli, A., & Smoliar, S. (1993). Automatic partitioning of full-motion video. *Multimedia Systems, 1,* 10-28.

Zhang, W., Lin, J., Chen, X., Huang, Q., & Liu, Y. (2006). Video shot detection using hidden markov models with complementary features. 593-596.

Zhang, Y. J., & Beijing, C. (2006). In Zhang Y. J., Beijing C. (Eds.), *Advances in image and video segmentation* IRM Press.

Zhao, Z., & Cai, A. (2006). Shot boundary detection algorithm in compressed domain based on adaboost and fuzzy theory. *Lecture Notes In Computer Science, 4222,* 617.

Chapter II
Image Features from Morphological Scale–Spaces

Sébastien Lefèvre
University of Strasbourg — CNRS, France

ABSTRACT

Multimedia data mining is a critical problem due to the huge amount of data available. Efficient and reliable data mining solutions require both appropriate features to be extracted from the data and relevant techniques to cluster and index the data. In this chapter, we deal with the first problem which is feature extraction for image representation. A wide range of features have been introduced in the literature, and some attempts have been made to build standards (e.g. MPEG-7). These features are extracted using image processing techniques, and we focus here on a particular image processing toolbox, namely the mathematical morphology, which stays rather unknown from the multimedia mining community, even if it offers some very interesting feature extraction methods. We review here these morphological features; from the basic ones (granulometry or pattern spectrum, differential morphological profile) to more complex ones which manage to gather complementary information.

INTRODUCTION

With the growth of multimedia data available on personal storage or on the Internet, the need for robust and reliable data mining techniques becomes more necessary than ever. In order these techniques to be really useful with multimedia data, the features used for data representation should be chosen attentively and accurately depending on the data considered: images, video sequences, audio files, 3-D models, web pages, etc.

As features are of primary importance in the process of multimedia mining, a wide range of features have been introduced in particular since the last decade. Some attempts have been made to gather the most relevant and robust features into commonly adopted standards, such as MPEG-7 (Manjunath,

Salembier, & Sikora, 2002). For the description of still images, MPEG-7 contains an heterogeneous but complementary set of descriptors which are related to various properties (e.g. colour, texture, 2-D shape, etc).

In addition to well-known standards such as MPEG-7, local or global descriptions of digital images can be achieved through the use of various toolboxes from the image analysis and processing field. Among these toolboxes, Mathematical Morphology offers a robust theoretical framework and a set of efficient tools to describe and analyse images. We believe it can be a very relevant solution for image representation in the context of multimedia mining. Indeed, its nonlinear behaviour comes with several attractive properties, such as translation invariance (both in spatial and intensity domains) and other properties (e.g. idempotence, extensivity or anti-extensivity, increasingness, connectedness, duality and complementariness, etc), depending on the morphological operator under consideration. Moreover, it allows very easily the construction of image scale-spaces from which can be extracted some robust features.

The goal of this chapter is not to present once again a well-known standard such as MPEG-7 but rather to focus on a specific theory, namely the Mathematical Morphology, and to review how the tools it offers can be used to generate global or local features for image representation. This chapter is organized as follows. First we recall the foundations of Mathematical Morphology and give the necessary definitions and notations. Then we present the morphological one-dimensional features which can be computed from the images either at a local or a global scale but always from a scale-space analysis of the images. In a third section we review several extensions which have been proposed to gather more information than these standard features through multidimensional morphological features. Next we focus on the implementation aspects, and give indications on the available methods for efficient processing, which is needed as soon as these features are used with multimedia indexing. We underline the potential of these features in a following section by giving a brief survey of their use in various application fields. Finally we give some concluding remarks and suggest further readings related to the topic addressed in this chapter.

BASICS OF MATHEMATICAL MORPHOLOGY

Mathematical Morphology is a theory introduced about 50 years ago by Georges Matheron and Jean Serra. Since then, it has been a growing and very active field of research, with its regular International Symposium on Mathematical Morphology (ISMM) taking place every two years and a half, and several recent special issues of journals (Ronse, 2005; Ronse, Najman, & Decencière, 2007).

Theoretical Foundations

Basically, Mathematical Morphology relies on the spatial analysis of images through a pattern called structuring element (SE) and consists in a set of nonlinear operators which are applied on the images considering this SE. Thus it can be seen as a relevant alternative to other image processing techniques such as purely statistical approaches or linear approaches. First works in Mathematical Morphology were related to binary image processing. The theoretical framework involved initially was very logically the set theory. Within this framework, the morphological operators were defined by means of set operators such as inclusion, union, intersection, difference, etc. However, despite initial efforts leading to stack approaches, this theory has been shown insufficient as soon as more complex images such as greyscale images were considered. So another theoretical framework, namely the (complete) lattice theory, is now widely considered as appropriate to define morphological operators (Ronse, 1990).

In order to define the main morphological operators from the lattice theory viewpoint, let us note $f : E \rightarrow T$ a digital image, where E is the discrete coordinate grid (usually $\mathbb{N}^2$ for a 2-D image, or $\mathbb{N}^3$ for a 3-D image or a 2-D+t image sequence) and T is the set of possible image values. In the case of a binary image, $T = \{0, 1\}$ where the objects and the background are respectively represented by values equal to 1 and 0. In the case of a greyscale image, T can be defined on $\mathbb{R}$, but it is often defined rather on a subset of $\mathbb{Z}$, most commonly [0, 255]. In case of multidimensional images such as colour images, multispectral or multimodal images, T is defined on $\mathbb{R}^n$ or $\mathbb{Z}^n$, with n the number of image channels.

A complete lattice is defined from three elements:

- a partially ordered set $(T, \geq)$, which could be the set inclusion order for binary images, the natural order of scalars for greyscale images, etc,
- an infimum or greatest lower bound $\wedge$, which is most often computed as the minimum operator (this choice will also be made here for the sake of simplicity),
- a supremum or least upper bound $\vee$, which is similarly most often computed as the maximum operator.

Once a complete lattice structure has been imposed on the image data, it is possible to apply morphological operators using a structuring pattern. It is called structuring function (SF) or functional structuring element and noted g when defined as a function on a subset of T, and called structuring element (SE) and noted b when defined as a set on E. In this chapter and for the sake of simplicity, we will assume the latter case unless otherwise mentioned, and use the so-called flat structuring elements. Let us notice however that the features reviewed in this chapter can be easily computed with structuring functions without important modification (if any).

Erosion and Dilation

From these theoretical requirements, one can define the two basic morphological operators. The first one called erosion is defined as:

$$\varepsilon_b(f)(p) = \wedge_{q \in b} f(p + q), p \in E$$

where p is the pixel coordinates, e.g. $p = (x, y)$ in 2-D images or $p = (x, y, z)$ in 3-D images. The coordinates within the SE are denoted by q and most commonly defined in the same space as p. In binary images, erosion will reduce white areas (or enlarge black areas). In greyscale or more complex images, it will spread the lowest pixel values (i.e. the darkest pixels in case of greyscale images) while removing the highest ones (i.e. the brightest pixels in case of greyscale images). In other words, the erosion results in an image where each pixel p is associated with the local minimum of f computed in the neighbourhood defined by the SE b.

The main other morphological operator is called dilation and is defined in a dual way as:

$$\delta_b(f)(p) = \vee_{q \in \bar{b}} f(p + q), p \in E$$

Here the result is an image where each pixel p is associated to the local maximum of f in the neighbourhood defined by the SE b. Thus it will enlarge areas with highest values (i.e. brightest pixels) while reducing areas with lowest values (i.e. darkest pixels). Another main difference is related to the SE: contrary to the erosion where b is considered, here the dilation is applied using the reflected SE $\breve{b} = \{-q \mid q \in b\}$. In other words, the dilation can be defined as:

$$\delta_b(f)(p) = \vee_{q \in b} f(p - q), p \in E$$

Mathematical morphology is of particular interest due to the numerous properties verified by its operators. Indeed, morphological operators such as erosion and dilation (but also the more complex ones) are invariant to (spatial and greyscale) translations, and are commutative, associative, increasing, distributive, dual with respect to the complementation, and can most often be broken down into simple operators.

Erosion and dilation, as many other morphological operators, require the definition of a structuring element b. This parameter has a strong impact on the results returned by an operator. Main SE shapes are diamond ♦, square ■, cross +, disc •, and line ⁻ or |. A pixel and its 4- or 8-neighbourhood correspond respectively to a 3×3 pixel diamond- or square-shaped SE, also called elementary isotropic (or symmetric) SE. The shape of the SE can also be defined from a basic shape and an homothetic parameter (or SE size), so we will use the notation $b_\lambda = \lambda b$ to represent a SE of shape b and size λ. For most of the SE shapes, b_λ can be generated from $\lambda - 1$ successive dilations, i.e. $b_\lambda = \delta^{(\lambda - 1)}(b)$. This is obviously not true with disc-shaped SE, where $\bullet_\lambda = \{p : d(p,o) \leq \lambda\}$ with o the origin or centre of the disc, and d the exact or approximated Euclidean distance. Moreover, we can also consider a growing factor κ between successive λ sizes, i.e. $b_\lambda = \kappa \lambda b$. For the sake of simplicity, the b parameter may be omitted in formulas, e.g. $\varepsilon_\lambda = \varepsilon_{b_\lambda}$ and $\delta_\lambda = \delta_{b_\lambda}$. For elementary structuring elements (e.g. ■₁ or ♦₁), we may also omit the $\lambda = 1$ parameter, i.e. $\varepsilon = \varepsilon_1$ and $\delta = \delta_1$, thus resulting in elementary erosion and dilation. We also state that $\varepsilon_0(f) = \delta_0(f) = f$. Figure 1 illustrates the basic structuring elements used in mathematical morphology.

Since morphological operators are often applied several times successively, we will use the notation $\varepsilon^{(n)}(f)$ and $\delta^{(n)}(f)$ to denote respectively the n successive applications of ε and δ on f. In other words, $\varepsilon^{(n)}(f) = \varepsilon^{(1)}(\varepsilon^{(n-1)}(f))$ and $\delta^{(n)}(f) = \delta^{(1)}(\delta^{(n-1)}(f))$, with $\varepsilon^{(1)} = \varepsilon$ and $\delta^{(1)} = \delta$.

Figure 1. Illustrative examples of basic SE with increasing size λ

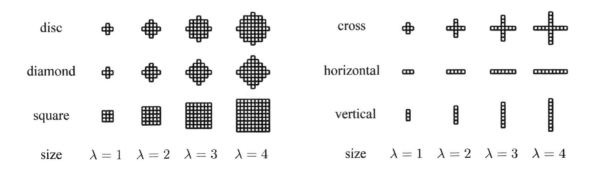

Figure 2. Binary erosion and dilation with square-shaped SE 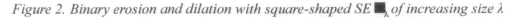 *of increasing size λ*

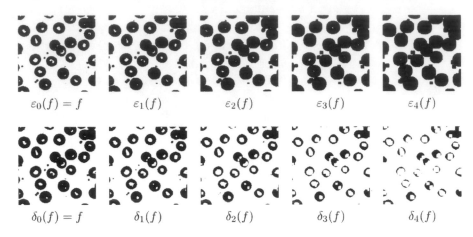

$\varepsilon_0(f) = f$ $\varepsilon_1(f)$ $\varepsilon_2(f)$ $\varepsilon_3(f)$ $\varepsilon_4(f)$

$\delta_0(f) = f$ $\delta_1(f)$ $\delta_2(f)$ $\delta_3(f)$ $\delta_4(f)$

Figure 3. Greyscale erosion and dilation with square-shaped SE  *of increasing size λ*

$\varepsilon_0(f) = f$ $\varepsilon_2(f)$ $\varepsilon_4(f)$ $\varepsilon_6(f)$ $\varepsilon_8(f)$

$\delta_0(f) = f$ $\delta_2(f)$ $\delta_4(f)$ $\delta_6(f)$ $\delta_8(f)$

Even if most of the features presented in this chapter will be defined with flat SE b (i.e. sets), they can be easily defined also with structuring functions (SF) g. In this case, the basic operations are defined as:

$$\varepsilon_g(f)(p) = \bigwedge_{q \,\in\, \text{supp}(g)} f(p+q) - g(q), \quad p \in E$$

and

$$\delta_g(f)(p) = \bigvee_{q \,\in\, \text{supp}(g)} f(p-q) + g(q), \quad p \in E$$

with supp(g) representing the support of g, i.e. the points for which the SF is defined.

Figure 2 and 3 illustrate the effects of morphological erosions and dilations applied respectively on binary and greyscale images with 8-connected elementary SE ■$_\lambda$ of increasing size λ.

Opening and Closing

Erosion and dilation are used to build most of the other morphological operators. Among these operators, we can mention the well-known opening and closing filters where erosion and dilation are applied successively to filter the input image, starting with erosion for the opening and with dilation for the closing. Opening is defined by

$$\gamma_b(f) = \delta_{\bar{b}}(\varepsilon_b(f))$$

while closing is defined by

$$\varphi_b(f) = \varepsilon_{\bar{b}}(\delta_b(f))$$

These two operators respectively result in a removal of local maxima or minima and return filtered images which are respectively lower and higher than the input image. This is called the anti-extensivity property of the opening with $\gamma(f) \leq f$ and the extensivity property of the closing with $f \leq \varphi(f)$ (with the $\leq$ relation being replaced by the $\subseteq$ relation if set theory is considered). Moreover, both opening and closing share some very nice properties (in addition to those of erosion and dilation). First they have the idempotence property since $\gamma_b(\gamma_b(f)) = \gamma_b(f)$ and $\varphi_b(\varphi_b(f)) = \varphi_b(f)$. Second they also ensure the increasingness property, i.e. if $f \leq g$, $\gamma_b(f) \leq \gamma_b(g)$ and $\varphi_b(f) \leq \varphi_b(g)$. Since they verify these two properties, they are called morphological filters.

Figure 4 and 5 illustrate the effects of morphological openings and closings applied respectively on binary and greyscale images with 8-connected elementary SE ■$_\lambda$ of increasing size λ.

The main concern with these two morphological filters is their very strong sensitivity to the SE shape, which will have a straight influence on the shapes visible in the filtered image. In order to avoid this problem, it is possible to involve the so-called algebraic filters which are a generalization of the morphological opening and closing defined above. For the sake of conciseness, we will use in this chapter the operator ψ to represent any morphological filter (e.g. γ or φ).

Algebraic Filters

The term algebraic opening (respectively closing) is related to any transformation which is increasing, anti-extensive (respectively extensive) and idempotent. Thus morphological (also called structural) opening and closing are a particular case of algebraic filters. The two main ways of creating algebraic opening and closing are recalled here.

The first option relies on opening and closing by reconstruction, which are useful to preserve original object edges. More precisely, let us note $\varepsilon_g^{(1)}(f)$ the geodesic erosion of size 1 of the marker image f with respect to the mask image g:

$$\varepsilon_g^{(1)}(f)(p) = \varepsilon^{(1)}(f)(p) \vee g(p)$$

where the elementary erosion is limited (through a lower bound) within the mask, i.e. $\varepsilon_g \geq \varepsilon$.

Figure 4. Binary opening and closing with square-shaped SE ■$_\lambda$ of increasing size λ

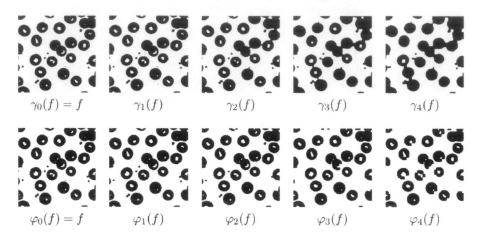

$\gamma_0(f) = f$ $\gamma_1(f)$ $\gamma_2(f)$ $\gamma_3(f)$ $\gamma_4(f)$

$\varphi_0(f) = f$ $\varphi_1(f)$ $\varphi_2(f)$ $\varphi_3(f)$ $\varphi_4(f)$

Figure 5. Greyscale opening and closing with square-shaped SE ■$_\lambda$ of increasing size λ

$\gamma_0(f) = f$ $\gamma_2(f)$ $\gamma_4(f)$ $\gamma_6(f)$ $\gamma_8(f)$

$\varphi_0(f) = f$ $\varphi_2(f)$ $\varphi_4(f)$ $\varphi_6(f)$ $\varphi_8(f)$

Similarly, the geodesic dilation of size 1 is defined by:

$$\delta_g^{(1)}(f)(p) = \delta^{(1)}(f)(p) \wedge g(p)$$

where the elementary dilation is limited (through an upper bound) within the mask, i.e. $\delta_g \leq \delta$.

These two operators are usually applied several times iteratively, thus we will use the following notations:

$$\varepsilon_g^{(n)}(f) = \varepsilon_g^{(1)}(\varepsilon_g^{(n-1)}(f))$$

and

$$\delta_g^{(n)}(f) = \delta_g^{(1)}(\delta_g^{(n-1)}(f))$$

From these two geodesic operators, it is possible to build reconstruction filters ρ which consist in successive applications of these operators until convergence. More precisely, the morphological reconstruction by erosion and by dilation are respectively defined by:

$$\rho_g^\varepsilon(f) = \varepsilon_g^{(j)}(f) \text{ with } j \text{ such as } \varepsilon_g^{(j)}(f) = \varepsilon_g^{(j-1)}(f)$$

and

$$\rho_g^\delta(f) = \delta_g^{(j)}(f) \text{ with } j \text{ such as } \delta_g^{(j)}(f) = \delta_g^{(j-1)}(f)$$

Based on these reconstruction filters, new morphological filters which preserve object edges can be defined. Indeed, the opening by reconstruction $\gamma_b^\rho(f)$ of the image f using the SE b is defined as:

$$\gamma_b^\rho(f) = \rho_f^\delta(\varepsilon_b(f))$$

while the closing by reconstruction $\varphi_b^\rho(f)$ is defined by:

$$\varphi_b^\rho(f) = \rho_f^\varepsilon(\delta_b(f))$$

In other words, for the opening (resp. closing) by reconstruction, the image f is used both as input for the first erosion (resp. dilation) and as mask for the following iterative geodesic dilations (resp. erosions). Contrary to their standard counterparts, these morphological filters by reconstruction remove details without modifying the structure of remaining objects.

The second option consists in computing various openings (respectively closings) and select their supremum (respectively infimum). Here each opening is related to a different condition or SE. Let us consider a set $B = (b)_i$ of SE, we can then define respectively the algebraic openings and closings by:

$$\gamma_B^\alpha(f) = \bigvee_{b \in B} \gamma_b(f)$$

and

$$\varphi_B^\alpha(f) = \bigwedge_{b \in B} \varphi_b(f)$$

and we will use the shortcuts $\gamma_\lambda^\alpha = \gamma_{\lambda B}^\alpha$ and $\varphi_\lambda^\alpha = \varphi_{\lambda B}^\alpha$ with $\lambda B = (\lambda b)_i$.

Among the main algebraic filters, we can mention the area-based operators, which have the very interesting property to be invariant to the shape of the SE b under consideration. To do so, they consider the whole set of all SE of a given size λ, thus resulting in the following operators:

$$\gamma_\lambda^a(f) = \bigvee_b \{\gamma_b(f) \mid b \text{ is connected and } \operatorname{card}(b) = \lambda\}$$

and

$$\varphi_\lambda^a(f) = \bigwedge_b \{\varphi_b(f) \mid b \text{ is connected and } \operatorname{card}(b) = \lambda\}$$

Area filters ψ^a are a special case of more general attribute filters ψ^χ, with the attribute or criterion χ to be satisfied being related to the area, i.e. the Boolean function $\chi(b, \lambda) = \{\text{card}(b) = \lambda\}$. Other attribute filters can be elaborated, in particular shape-related ones, involving for instance the perimeter $\chi(b, \lambda) = \{\text{card}(b - \varepsilon(b)) = \lambda\}$ or the moment of inertia

$$\chi(b, \lambda) = \{\sum_{q \in b} d(q,o) = \lambda\}$$

(with d the Euclidean distance and o the origin of the SE b). More generally, attribute filters can be defined as:

Figure 6. Comparison between binary standard (structural) filters, filters by reconstruction, and area filters with increasing λ parameter

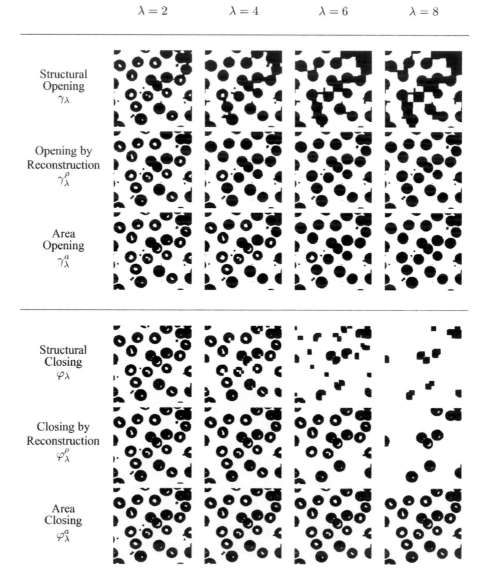

Figure 7. Comparison between greyscale standard (structural) filters, filters by reconstruction, and area filters with increasing λ parameter

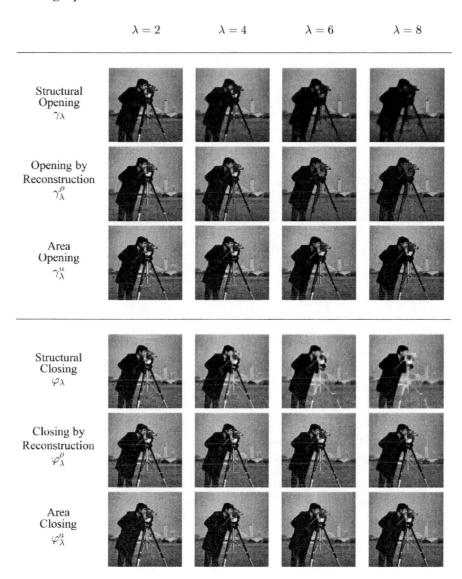

$$\gamma_\lambda^\chi(f) = \bigvee_b \{\gamma_b(f) \mid b \text{ is connected and } (\chi b, \lambda)\}$$

and

$$\varphi_\lambda^\chi(f) = \bigwedge_b \{\varphi_b(f) \mid b \text{ is connected and } \chi(b, \lambda)\}$$

In Figure 6 and 7 are given some visual comparisons between structural filters, filters by reconstruction, and area filters, respectively on binary and greyscale images. We can observe the interest of filters by reconstruction and area filters to limit the sensitivity to the SE shape.

Apart from these basic operators, mathematical morphology offers a wide range of operators or methods to process images. We can cite the morphological gradient, the hit-or-miss transform to perform template matching or object skeletonisation, the watershed or levelling approaches for segmentation, the alternating sequential filters (ASF) for image simplification, etc. In this chapter, we will focus on morphological features extracted from the previously presented operators and we will not deal with some other morphological operators. The interested reader will find in the book from Soille (2003) a good overview of the morphological toolbox for image processing and analysis.

STANDARD MORPHOLOGICAL IMAGE FEATURES

Image features are most often dedicated to a single type of information (e.g. colour, texture, spatial distribution, shape, etc). The most famous example is undoubtedly the image histogram which measures the probability density function of the intensity values in the image and which can be analysed through various measures (e.g. moments, entropy, uniformity, etc). However it is limited to intensity distribution and does not take into account the spatial relationships between pixels.

On the opposite, approaches known under the terms of pattern spectra, granulometries, or morphological profiles are built from series of morphological filtering operations and thus involve a spatial information. We review here these different (either global or local) features in an unified presentation.

Multiscale Representation Using Morphological Filters

We have introduced in section 1 the main morphological filters (i.e. opening and closing filters) which aim at removing details in the image, either bright details (with the opening) or dark details (with the closing), by preserving or not object edges. Thus they can be used to build multiscale representations of digital images by means of mathematical morphology.

Most of these multiscale representations can be seen as nonlinear scale-spaces, if some of the original constraints are relaxed. The concept of scale space introduced by Witkin (1983) is defined as a family of filtered images $\{\Upsilon_t(f)\}_{t\geq 0}$, with $\Upsilon_0(f) = f$ and various axioms (Duits, Florack, Graaf, & Haar Romeny, 2004), the multiscale representation being computed most often by means of a convolution by a Gaussian kernel:

$$\Upsilon_t(f)(x,y) = f(x,y) * g(x,y,t) = \int_{-\infty}^{+\infty} f(u,v)\frac{1}{2\pi t^2}e^{-\frac{(x-u)^2+(y-v)^2}{2t^2}}\, du\, dv$$

The main properties of a scale-space are relatively compatible with some of the morphological operators as pointed out by the work of Jackway (1992):

- causality, i.e. no additional structures are created in the image when t increases (indeed both height and position of extrema are preserved);
- recursivity
  $$\Upsilon_t(\Upsilon_s(f)) = \Upsilon_s(\Upsilon_t(f)) = \Upsilon_{t+s}(f), \quad \forall t, s \geq 0$$
- increasingness
  $$f \leq g, \quad \Upsilon_t(f) < \Upsilon_t(g), \quad \forall t > 0$$

- either extensivity

$$\Upsilon_t(f) \geq f, \quad \forall t \geq 0$$

or anti-extensivity

$$\Upsilon_t(f) \leq f, \quad \forall t \geq 0$$

which leads respectively to

$$t_1 \leq t_2, \Upsilon_{t_1}(f) \leq \Upsilon_{t_2}(f), \forall t > 0$$
$$t_1 \leq t_2, \Upsilon_{t_1}(f) \geq \Upsilon_{t_2}(f), \forall t > 0$$

Thus some scale-spaces can be built straightforward from successive applications of morphological operators (such as erosion and dilations (Jackway & Deriche, 1996), or ASF (Matsopoulos & Marshall, 1992; K. Park & Lee, 1996; Bangham, Ling, & Harvey, 1996)), or using advanced morphological representations such as max-tree (Salembier, Oliveras, & Garrido, 1998). Here we will use the term (morphological) scale-space even for scale-spaces where the recursivity property is replaced by the absorption law defined by Matheron (1975) which is relevant for morphological filters:

$$\forall t, s \geq 0, \quad \Upsilon_t(\Upsilon_s(f)) = \Upsilon_s(\Upsilon_t(f)) = \Upsilon_{\max(t,s)}(f)$$

In addition to this property, the idempotence property also holds:

$$\Upsilon_t(\Upsilon_t(f)) = \Upsilon_t(f)$$

A wide range of morphological operators can lead to scale spaces, such as openings and closings (Chen & Yan, 1989).

Figure 8 illustrates the difference between a scale-space built with Gaussian and morphological (bottom) closing filters. One can clearly see the interest of morphological scale-spaces to retain object edges even with basic (i.e. structural) morphological filters.

So morphological scale-spaces can be built by applying some morphological operators Υ_t on the input image f, with increasing parameter t. In the morphological framework, t is directly related to the size λ of the structuring element b, and we will use the notation $\Upsilon_\lambda = \Upsilon_{b_\lambda}$. Indeed, for a given morphological filter ψ_λ, λ denotes the size of the SE, i.e. the size of neighbourhood used to compute minima or maxima (or the filter window). Then when λ increases, the morphological filter ψ_λ will remove more and more details from the input image (as shown by Figure 9), thus respecting the main property of scale-spaces (i.e. causality). Moreover, to satisfy the absorption property, the SE b under consideration has to be a compact convex set (Matheron, 1975).

Let us note $\Pi^\psi(f) = \{\Pi_\lambda^\psi(f)\}_{\lambda \geq 0}$ the morphological scale-space, i.e. the series of successive filtered images using ψ with growing SE size λ:

$$\Pi^\psi(f) = \left\{\Pi_\lambda^\psi(f) \mid \Pi_\lambda^\psi(f) = \psi_\lambda(f)\right\}_{0 \leq \lambda \leq n}$$

where $\psi_0(f) = f$ and $n + 1$ is the length of the series (including the original image). This Π series is a nonlinear scale-space, with less and less details as λ is increasing from 0 to n. Instead of using a single SE, a SE set or generator $B = (b)_i$ can be used (Matheron, 1975), thus resulting in series made from algebraic filters:

Figure 8. Comparison between Gaussian (top) and morphological (bottom) scale-spaces

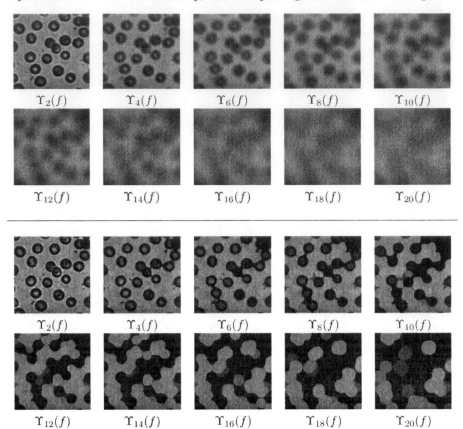

$$\Pi^{\psi^{\alpha}}(f) = \left\{ \Pi_{\lambda}^{\psi^{\alpha}}(f) \mid \Pi_{\lambda}^{\psi^{\alpha}}(f) = \psi_{\lambda}^{\alpha}(f) \right\}_{0 \le \lambda \le n}$$

with $\Psi_{\lambda}^{\alpha} = \Psi_{\lambda B}^{\alpha}$. The initial definition leading to Euclidean granulometries was considering the same growing factor κ for all SE b_i in B, i.e. $(b_i)_{\lambda} = \lambda \kappa_i b_i$. It is also possible to make the κ factor depends on b, thus either $B = (b, \kappa)_i$ (where $(b_i)_{\lambda} = \lambda \kappa_i b_i$) for homogeneous multivariate series (Batman & Dougherty, 1997) or $B = (b, t, k)_i$ (with t_i being a strictly increasing function of κ_i, thus $(b_i)_{\lambda} = \lambda t_i(\kappa_i) b_i$ for heterogeneous multivariate series (Batman, Dougherty, & Sand, 2000).

Moreover, these series Π^{ψ} can be made using any ψ filter (see (Soille, 2003) for a deeper review of morphological filters). Thus, Π is also anti-extensive for any opening filter and extensive for any closing filter, resulting respectively in lower and lower images or higher and higher images as λ increases. Indeed, if we have $\lambda_1 \le \lambda_2$, then $\Pi_{\lambda_2}^{\gamma}(f) \le \Pi_{\lambda_1}^{\gamma}(f)$ and $\Pi_{\lambda_2}^{\varphi}(f) \ge \Pi_{\lambda_1}^{\varphi}(f)$.

In order to avoid their highly asymmetric behaviour (Π^{ψ} is either anti-extensive or extensive), it is possible to gather opening and closing series to generate a single Π series of length $2n + 1$:

Figure 9. Details removal by means of successive openings (top) and closings (bottom) by reconstruction

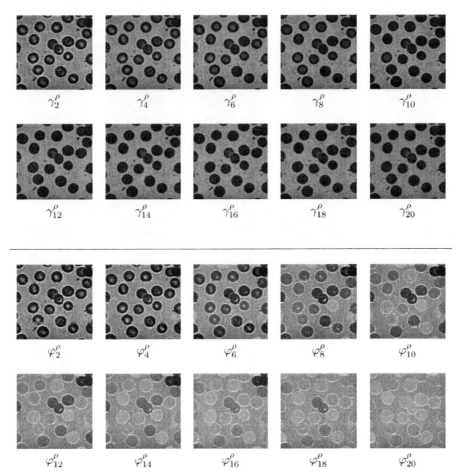

$$\Pi(f) = \left\{ \Pi_\lambda(f) \mid \Pi_\lambda(f) = \begin{cases} \Pi^\gamma_{-\lambda}(f), & \lambda < 0 \\ \Pi^\varphi_\lambda(f), & \lambda > 0 \\ f, & \lambda = 0 \end{cases} \right\}_{-n \le \lambda \le n}$$

We can also build these symmetric series using any of the pair of opening/closing filters, and we will denote by Π^ρ, Π^α, Π^a, Π^χ the series created respectively with ψ^ρ, ψ^α, ψ^a, ψ^χ. An illustration of this kind of dual series is given in Figure 10.

Let us note that the merging of openings and closings can also be made by means of alternate sequential filters (ASF), which consists in successive openings and closing with SE of increasing size λ. Using ASF to compute the Π series results in the following definition:

Figure 10. From top left to bottom right, Π series of length $2n + 1$ with $n = 7$ using structural filters γ and φ and 4-connected elementary SE ◆

$$\Pi^{ASF}(f) = \left\{ \Pi_\lambda^{ASF}(f) \mid \Pi_\lambda^{ASF}(f) = \begin{cases} \gamma_{\lceil \lambda/2 \rceil}(\Pi_{\lambda-1}^{ASF}(f)) & \text{if } \lambda \text{ is odd} \\ \varphi_{\lceil (\lambda-1)/2 \rceil}(\Pi_{\lambda 1}^{ASF}(f)) & \text{if } \lambda \text{ is even} \\ f, & \text{if } \lambda = 0 \end{cases} \right\}_{0 \leq \lambda \leq n}$$

Of course the morphological filters γ and φ can again be replaced by any of their variants, e.g. their reconstruction-based counterparts γ^ρ and φ^ρ, thus resulting in the Π^{ASF^ρ} series. ASF have been proven to be a specific case of more general concepts, M- and N- sieves (Bangham et al., 1996). Another related feature is the lomo filter (Bosworth & Acton, 2003), which consists in the mean of two ASF applied until convergence, one starting with an opening (i.e. being defined as $\varphi_n \gamma_n ... \varphi_1 \gamma_1$) and the other starting with a closing operation (i.e. being defined as $\gamma_n \varphi_n ... \gamma_1 \varphi_1$). It is also possible to associate to each scale λ the difference between the union and the intersection of the ASF with successive λ size (Xiaoqi & Baozong, 1995), i.e. $(\Pi_\lambda^{ASF} \vee \Pi_{\lambda-1}^{ASF}) - (\Pi_\lambda^{ASF} \wedge \Pi_{\lambda-1}^{ASF})$.

Features can be extracted directly from the series Π^ψ (or from their symmetrical version Π), but most often it is more relevant to compute the differential version Δ^ψ of this series where removed details are emphasized for each λ size. For anti-extensive filters such as openings, we have:

$$\Delta^\gamma(f) = \left\{ \Delta_\lambda^\gamma(f) \mid \Delta_\lambda^\gamma(f) = \Pi_{\lambda-1}^\gamma(f) - \Pi_\lambda^\gamma(f) \right\}_{0 \leq \lambda \leq n}$$

while for extensive filters such as closings, we have:

$$\Delta^\varphi(f) = \left\{ \Delta_\lambda^\varphi(f) \mid \Delta_\lambda^\varphi(f) = \Pi_\lambda^\varphi(f) - \Pi_{\lambda-1}^\varphi(f) \right\}_{0 \leq \lambda \leq n}$$

thus resulting in a single definition

$$\Delta^{\psi}(f) = \left\{\Delta_{\lambda}^{\psi}(f) \mid \Delta_{\lambda}^{\psi}(f) = \left|\Pi_{\lambda}^{\psi}(f) - \Pi_{\lambda-1}^{\psi}(f)\right|\right\}_{0 \leq \lambda \leq n}$$

with the assumption $\Delta_{0}^{\psi} = 0$. In this series, a pixel p will appear (i.e. have a non null value) in $\Delta_{\lambda}^{\psi}(f)$ if it is removed by ψ_{λ}, the morphological filter ψ of size λ (or in other words, if it was present in $\psi_{\lambda-1}(f)$ but not anymore in $\psi_{\lambda}(f)$).

Similarly for the Π^{ψ} series, it is possible to compute a symmetric version of Δ^{ψ} by taking into account both opening and closing filters:

$$\Delta(f) = \left\{\Delta_{\lambda}(f) \mid \Delta_{\lambda}(f) = \begin{cases} \Delta_{-\lambda}^{\gamma}(f), & \lambda < 0 \\ \Delta_{\lambda}^{\varphi}(f), & \lambda > 0 \\ 0, & \lambda = 0 \end{cases} \right\}_{-n \leq \lambda \leq n}$$

As an illustration, Figure 11 is the Δ counterpart of the Π series presented in Figure 10 using structural filters with diamond shaped-SE, while Figure 12 is the differential series built from the one presented in Figure 9 using filters by reconstruction.

We also have to notice that even basic operators (not necessarily filters) can be used to build morphological series. Indeed, one can apply successive erosions ε or dilations δ to build a Π or Δ series:

$$\Pi^{\nu}(f) = \left\{\Pi_{\lambda}^{\nu}(f) \mid \Pi_{\lambda}^{\nu}(f) = \nu_{\lambda}(f)\right\}_{0 \leq \lambda \leq n}$$

Figure 11. From top left to bottom right, Δ series of length $2n + 1$ with $n = 7$ using structural filters γ and φ and 4-connected elementary SE Grey levels have been inverted and normalised for the sake of readability.

where ν denotes the basic morphological operator under consideration (e.g. ε or δ). The properties of these series will be however weaker than the previous series built from morphological filters. Depending on the desired properties of the series, one can even relax the constraint on the shape (compactness and convexity) of the SE in use.

Among these operators which do not belong to morphological filters, we can even use difference operators. For instance, by considering the morphological gradient $G_\lambda(f) = \delta_\lambda(f) - \varepsilon_\lambda(f)$ with increasing scale λ, we can build some morphological fractal measures (Soille, 2003). Another example is related to top-hats and the so called hat scale-spaces (Jalba, Wilkinson, & Roerdink, 2004). More precisely, the top-hat by opening is defined by $\tau^\gamma(f) = f - \gamma(f)$ while the top-hat by closing (or bottom-hat) is defined by $\tau^\varphi(f) = \varphi(f) - f$. From these hat scale-spaces can be extracted the so called fingerprints introduced by Jackway and Deriche (1996) as local maxima or minima in the images filtered at different scales. Fingerprints can also be obtained by the filters by reconstruction (Rivas-Araiza, Mendiola-Santibanez, & Herrera-Ruiz, 2008). Various robust features can also be extracted from the analysis of scale-spaces made with top- and bottom-hat by reconstruction (W. Li, Haese-Coat, & Ronsin, 1997). Of course we

Figure 12. Details emphasized by means of differences between successive openings and closing by reconstruction. Grey levels have been inverted and normalised for the sake of readability.

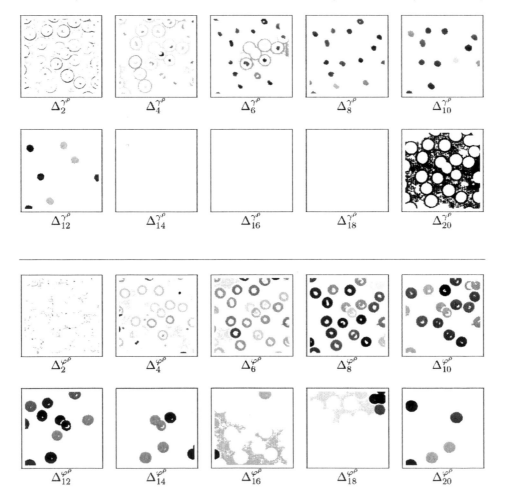

can also build other versions of these operators, e.g. using filters by reconstruction γ^{ρ} and φ^{ρ}. Any of the resulting series $\Pi^{\tau^{\psi}}$ can then be analyzed in a similar manner as the standard Π series.

These different series are the basis of the standard morphological features widely used in image analysis and visual pattern recognition. These features are computed either at a local scale or a global scale.

Local Morphological Features

The simplest way to extract morphological features from a digital image f using one of the Π^{ψ} or Δ^{ψ} series consists in associating to each pixel p the vector $\Pi^{\psi}(f)(p) = (\Pi^{\psi}_{\lambda}(f)(p))_{0 \leq \lambda \leq n}$ of size $n + 1$.

In the remote sensing field, this principle led to the so called differential morphological profile (DMP) proposed by Pesaresi and Benediktsson in (Pesaresi & Benediktsson, 2001; Benediktsson, Pesaresi, & Arnason, 2003) which is computed using the reconstruction-based differential series:

$$DMP(f)(p) = \Delta^{\rho}(f)(p)$$

Figure 13 illustrates the behaviour of the DMP feature for pixels belonging to different areas of an image.

This feature is a kind of structural feature, and an interesting alternative to spectral or textural features. Its size (initially equal to $2n + 1$) can be strongly reduced by considering only the few most important maxima. It has been shown in (Benediktsson et al., 2003) that using only the first and second maximum values of $\Delta^{\rho}(f)(p)$ for each pixel p ensures satisfactory recognition rates in supervised classification of remotely sensed images.

Moreover, an attempt has been made in (Chanussot, Benediktsson,&Pesaresi, 2003) to use reconstruction-based alternate sequential filters through the $\Delta^{ASF^{\rho}}$ series as an alternative to the original DMP, thus defining $DMP_{ASF}(f)(p) = \Delta^{ASF^{\rho}}(f)(p)$. Alternatively, ASF-based scale-space representations can also be computed from the area-filters (Acton & Mukherjee, 2000b).

Figure 13. Input image with 4 sample points (left) and corresponding DMP values (right) using 20 openings (negative indices) and 20 closings (positive indices).

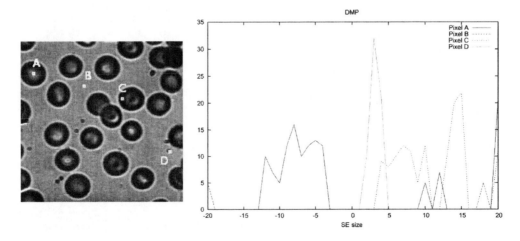

In case of binary images, pixelwise feature extraction from morphological scale-space may consist in assigning to each pixel p of f the scale, or size λ, for which the filter (e.g. opening) manages to remove the pixel, thus resulting in the so called opening transform when considering successive applications of the opening filter (similarly, the closing transform is related to the scale-space obtained from successive closings). The definition is given by:

$$\Xi^{\psi}(f)(p) = \max\{\lambda \geq 0 \mid \psi_{\lambda}(f)(p) > 0\}$$

with the convention $\Xi^{\psi}(f)(p) = 0$ if $f(p) = 0$.

Figure 14. Illustration of various opening and closing transforms obtained with different filters and SE shapes

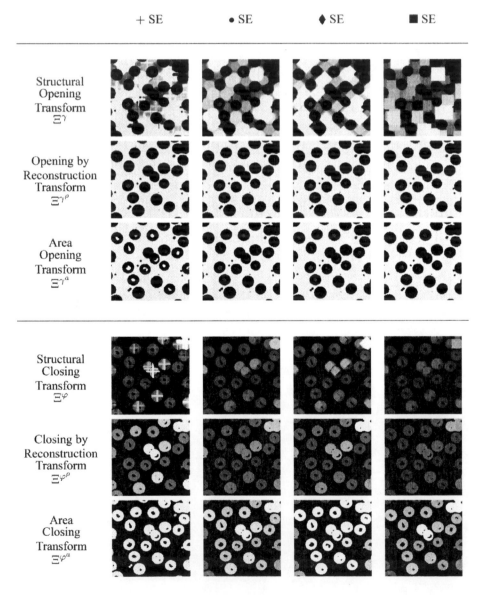

In other words, it can be easily computed by analysing the series Π and looking at each pixel p for the first image (with filter size $\lambda + 1$) such as $\Pi_{\lambda+1}^{\psi}(f)(p) = 0$.

Figure 14 illustrates the opening and closing transforms considering various morphological filters and SE. The extension of this principle to greyscale images can lead to the definition of opening trees (Vincent, 2000). However, if one wants to keep a single value for each pixel, it is recommended to select the λ value resulting in the biggest drop in greyscale intensity when applying $\psi_{\lambda}(f)(p)$, thus following the recommendation of Pesaresi and Benediktsson with DMP.

Global Morphological Features

Besides the use of morphological series directly on a per-pixel basis, it is possible to involve them in global image features. In this case, pattern spectra and granulometries are certainly the most famous morphological features in the image analysis community (Soille, 2003).

Granulometries and antigranulometries (also called size and anti-size distributions) are built by gathering the values of the series over all pixels p of the filtered image $\psi(f)$ through a Lebesgue measure, for instance a volume or sum operation. In the particular case of binary images, the image volume can either be computed as the sum of pixel values or as the amount of white pixels (or 1-pixels). The granulometry uses openings:

$$\Omega^{\gamma}(f) = \left\{ \Omega_{\lambda}^{\gamma}(f) \mid \Omega_{\lambda}^{\gamma}(f) = \sum_{p \in E} \Pi^{\gamma}_{\lambda}(f)(p) \right\}_{0 \leq \lambda \leq n}$$

while the antigranulometry relies on closings:

$$\Omega^{\varphi}(f) = \left\{ \Omega_{\lambda}^{\varphi}(f) \mid \Omega_{\lambda}^{\varphi}(f) = \sum_{p \in E} \Pi^{\varphi}_{\lambda}(f)(p) \right\}_{0 \leq \lambda \leq n}$$

From the properties of morphological filters, we can observe that Ω^{γ} is monotonically decreasing while Ω^{φ} is monotonically increasing. In order these measures to be invariant to image size and to represent cumulative distribution functions, they are worth being normalized, thus resulting in the new definition:

$$\Gamma^{\psi}(f) = \left\{ \Gamma_{\lambda}^{\psi}(f) \mid \Gamma_{\lambda}^{\psi}(f) = 1 - \frac{\Omega_{\lambda}^{\psi}(f)}{\Omega_{0}^{\psi}(f)} \right\}_{0 \leq \lambda \leq n}$$

with ψ denoting either γ or ψ. In Figure 15 are given the granulometric curves Γ for both opening and closing filters, considering the main standard SE.

Another very interesting morphological global feature is the pattern spectrum Φ introduced by Maragos (1989), also called pecstrum (Anastassopoulos & Venetsanopoulos, 1991). It can be seen as the morphological counterpart of the well-known image histogram. Instead of measuring the distribution of intensities within an image, it aims at measuring the distribution of sizes (and to a lesser extent, of shapes). To do so, it gathers values of the differential series Δ over all pixels:

$$\Phi(f) = \left\{ \Phi_{\lambda}(f) \mid \Phi_{\lambda}(f) = \sum_{p \in E} \Delta_{\lambda}(f)(p) \right\}_{-n \leq \lambda \leq n}$$

Figure 15. Input image (left) and corresponding granulometric curve Γ (right) using 20 openings (negative indices) and 20 closings (positive indices).

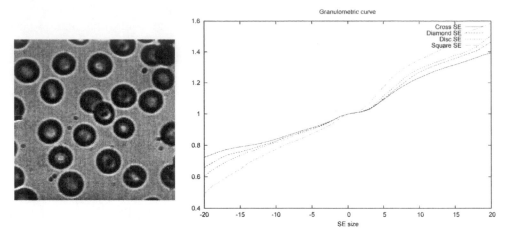

Figure 16. Input image (left) and corresponding pattern spectrum Δ (right) using structural filters, filters by reconstruction and area filters

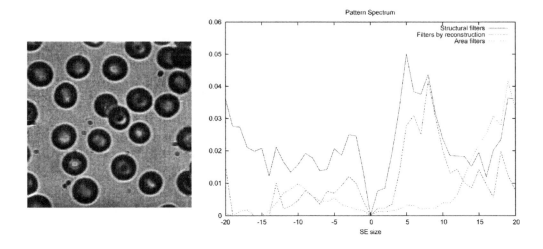

and the normalization ensures measures independent of the image size:

$$\Lambda(f) = \left\{ \Lambda_\lambda(f) \mid \Lambda_\lambda(f) = \frac{\Phi_\lambda(f)}{\Omega_0(f)} \right\}_{-n \le \lambda \le n}$$

Moreover, let us notice that the pattern spectrum can be easily computed as the histogram of the opening (or/and closing) transform.

In Figure 16 are given the pattern spectra Λ for both opening and closing filters, using respectively structural filters, filters by reconstruction and area filters. Moreover, Figure 17 illustrates the relevance of the pattern spectrum in case of image with similar greylevel distribution.

When dealing with greyscale images, it is also possible to involve greyscale (or volume) SE, thus dealing with spatial but also to a lesser extent with intensity information.

Moreover, some scalar attributes can be extracted from the previous 1-D morphological series. As representative examples, we can cite the average size and roughness (Maragos, 1989) computed respectively as the mean and the entropy of the signal, or the statistical moments computed on the granulometric 1-D curve and called granulometric moments (Dougherty, Newell, & Pelz, 1992; Sand & Dougherty, 1999).

Besides the use of morphological filters to build global morphological filters, it is also possible to involve any operator v and to exploit the morphological series (e.g. Π_v) of images processed with this operator. In this case, the obtained series Ω_v are called pseudo-granulometries since they do not respect the fundamental requirements of granulometries (Soille, 2003). As another representative example of using Π_v series, we can cite the covariance feature K, a morphological counterpart of the autocorrelation operator. To compute this feature, the SE b under consideration consists in a set of two points p_1 and p_2 and is defined by both a size $2\lambda = \| \overrightarrow{p_1 p_2} \|$ and an orientation: $\vec{v} = \overrightarrow{p_1 p_2} / \| \overrightarrow{p_1 p_2} \|$

$$K^{\vec{v}}(f) = \left\{ K^{\vec{v}}_\lambda(f) \mid K^{\vec{v}}_\lambda(f) = \sum_{p \subset E} \Pi^{\varepsilon}_{\lambda, \vec{v}}(f)(p) \right\}_{0 \le \lambda \le n}$$

Figure 17. Two input images (left) with similar histograms (top right) but different pattern spectra Λ (bottom right)

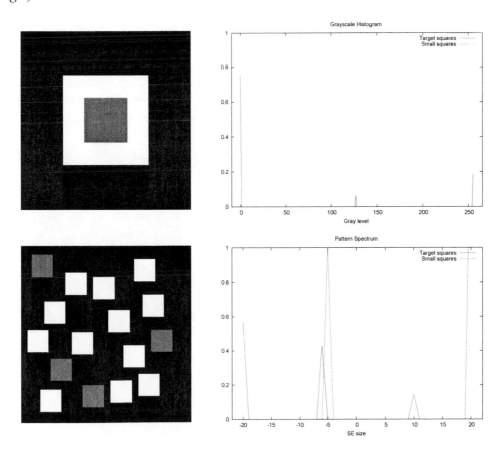

where

$$\varepsilon_{\lambda,\vec{v}}(f)(p) = f(p-\lambda\vec{v}) \wedge f(p+\lambda\vec{v})$$

This feature is illustrated by Figure 18.

Another definition of the covariance has been given by Serra (1982) where the autocorrelation function is used, thus resulting in the operator ε' defined by

$$\varepsilon'_{\lambda,\vec{v}}(f)(p) = f(p-\lambda\vec{v})\cdot f(p+\lambda\vec{v})$$

where the intersection $\wedge$ is replaced by a product ˙ operation.

We have not dealt yet with the case of semi-local features, i.e. features computed on an intermediate scale. The processing units at this scale are neither the single pixels nor the whole image, but rather parts of it, e.g. blocks or image regions. In this case, the global features can be computed similarly but within a limited area of the image, thus resulting in one morphological feature per block or region. An illustrative example of this approach is the work from Dougherty where each pixel is characterized by the granulometry computed from its neighbouring window (Dougherty, Pelz, Sand, & Lent, 1992).

Even if these features (either local or global) appear as particularly relevant alternatives to usual image features such as image histograms, wavelets, or other textural features (just to mention a few), they still are limited to a single evolution curve and so cannot consider simultaneously several dimensions. More precisely, they deal only with the structural information extracted from morphological filters applied with growing SE sizes.

MULTIDIMENSIONAL EXTENSIONS OF MORPHOLOGICAL FEATURES

Despite their broad interest in image representation, the well-known morphological features reviewed so far are limited by their one-dimensional nature (i.e. they are computed as single evolution curves and thus cannot consider simultaneously several dimensions).

Figure 18. Input image (left) and corresponding covariance curves $K^{\vec{v}}$ (right) using 25 vector sizes λ and 4 different orientations θ for $\vec{v}$.

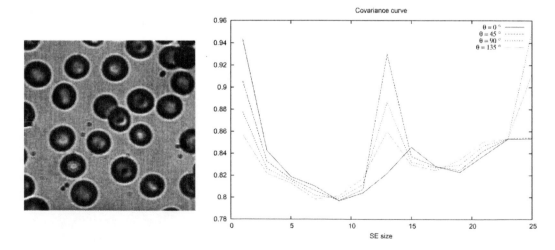

We review here some recent multidimensional extensions which allow to build *n*-D (mostly 2-D) series of morphological measures. These extensions help to gather complementary information (e.g. spatial, intensity, spectral, shape, etc) in a single local or global morphological representation.

Size-Shape

In the morphological series defined in the previous section, a unique parameter λ was considered for measuring the size evolution, through the SE b_λ. We have indicated various ways to build the series of SE b_λ based on the increasing λ parameter. Here we consider the SE κ as a growing factor of the initial shape b, i.e. $b_\lambda = \delta_\kappa^{(\lambda-1)}(b)$ with various shapes for κ (e.g. one of the basic shapes introduced in section 1.2). Let us notice that the size of κ has to be rather small to build measurements at a precise scale (or conversely large for coarse measurements) since it represents the growing factor of the SE series. Moreover, one has also to set the initial condition b, i.e. the initial SE, which can be of arbitrary shape, even equal to κ (thus resulting in the definition given in section 1.2).

This definition assuming a single size varying parameter λ prevents us from performing accurate measurements. Indeed, it is not adequate to elliptical or rectangular shapes for instance, where the two independent axes should be taken into account. So several attempts have been made to build bivariate morphological series, thus allowing to obtain size-shape measurements.

Figure 19. Three input images (top) and their respective 2-D Δ feature (middle). As a comparison, standard pattern spectra using square SE (bottom left), horizontal line SE (bottom centre) and vertical line SE (bottom right) are also given.

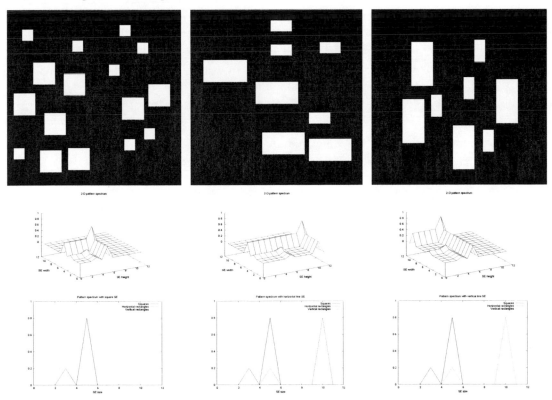

Lefèvre, Weber, & Sheeren (2007) consider structuring elements with two different size parameters α and β that vary independently. More precisely, a way to define the 2-D series of SE $b_{\alpha,\beta}$ is given by $b_{\alpha,\beta} = \delta_{\kappa_1}^{(\alpha-1)}(\delta_{\kappa_2}^{(\beta-1)}(b)) = \delta_{\kappa_2}^{(\beta-1)}(\delta_{\kappa_1}^{(\alpha-1)}(b))$ with κ_1 and κ_2 denoting the structuring elements used as growing factors in the two dimensions, and b the initial SE. In the case of rectangular SE series, a relevant choice for κ_1 and κ_2 consists in 1-D SE such as horizontal and vertical lines respectively (with a length proportional to the degree of coarseness desired) and an initial rectangular SE b.

The new Π series built using the 2-D set of SE $b_{\alpha,\beta}$ is then computed as:

$$\Pi^{\psi}(f) = \left\{ \Pi_{\alpha,\beta}^{\psi}(f) \mid \Pi_{\alpha,\beta}^{\psi}(f) = \psi_{\alpha,\beta}(f) \right\}_{\substack{0 \leq \alpha \leq m \\ 0 \leq \beta \leq n}}$$

where the application of ψ on f with a SE $b_{\alpha,\beta}$ is noted $\psi_{\alpha,\beta}(f)$ and with the convention $\psi_{0,0}(f) = f$. Similarly, the Δ series measures the differential in both size dimensions:

$$\Delta^{\psi}(f) = \left\{ \Delta_{\alpha,\beta}^{\psi}(f) \mid \Delta_{\alpha,\beta}^{\psi}(f) = \frac{1}{2} \left| 2\Pi_{\alpha-1,\beta-1}^{\psi}(f) - \Pi_{\alpha-1,\beta}^{\psi} - \Pi_{\alpha,\beta-1}^{\psi}(f) \right| \right\}_{\substack{0 \leq \alpha \leq m \\ 0 \leq \beta \leq n}}$$

where $\Delta_{\alpha,0}^{\psi} = \Delta_{\alpha}^{\psi} \Delta_{0,\beta}^{\psi} = \Delta_{\beta}^{\psi} \Delta_{0,0}^{\psi} = 0$.

Figure 19 illustrates the potential interest of such 2-D features for sample images where standard granulometries are irrelevant.

A similar approach has been proposed by Ghosh and Chanda (1998) who introduce conditional parametric morphological operators, and who build a 2D set of SE with increasing size, both on the horizontal and vertical dimensions. From this set of SE they finally compute the bivariate pattern spectrum for binary images. Bagdanov and Worring (2002) introduce the same feature under the term rectangular granulometry, while a slightly different definition has been given by Barnich, Jodogne, & Droogenbroeck (2006) to limit the SE to the largest non-redundant rectangles within the analysed object (in binary images). Moreover, a more general expression of m-parametric SE has been used in (Gadre & Patney, 1992) to define multiparametric granulometries.

Batman et al. in (Batman & Dougherty, 1997; Batman et al., 2000) propose an alternative definition of this series using Euclidean series $\Pi^{\psi^{\alpha}}(f)$ with the set of SE $B = \{-_1, |_1\}$ where $-$ and $|$ denote respectively elementary horizontal and vertical SE. Moreover, they also introduce a univariate series by combining through the sum operations two series of SE b_{α} and c_{β} built from initial SE b and c:

$$\Pi^{\psi}(f) = \left\{ \Pi_{\alpha,\beta}^{\psi}(f) \mid \Pi_{\alpha,\beta}^{\psi}(f) = \psi_{b_{\alpha}}(f) + \psi_{c_{\beta}}(f) \right\}_{\substack{0 \leq \alpha \leq m \\ 0 \leq \beta \leq n}}$$

Urbach, Roerdink, & Wilkinson (2007) also propose to combine size and shape information in a single 2-D granulometry. They rely on attribute filters (Breen & Jones, 1996) ψ^{χ} and use a max-tree representation (Salembier et al., 1998) of the image for computational reasons. Their 2-D series can be defined as:

$$\Pi^{\psi^{\chi_1 \cdot \chi_2}}(f) = \left\{ \Pi_{\alpha,\beta}^{\psi}(f) \mid \Pi_{\alpha,\beta}^{\psi}(f) = \psi_{\alpha}^{\chi_1}(f) \wedge \psi_{\beta}^{\chi_2}(f) \right\}_{\substack{0 \leq \alpha \leq m \\ 0 \leq \beta \leq n}}$$

where the two criteria χ_1 and χ_2 are respectively related to the area (i.e. defining size) and the ratio of the moment of inertia to the square of the area (i.e. defining shape). While the first dimension (indexed by α and related to the criterion χ_1) is related to size and respect the axioms of morphological scale-spaces, the second dimension (indexed by β and related to the criterion χ_2) is related to shape and should be scale-invariant, thus the increasingness property is replaced by the scale-invariance property, i.e. $S_\lambda(Y_t(f)) = Y_t(S_\lambda(f))$, $\forall t > 0$ with the transform $S_\lambda(f)$ being the scaling of the image f by a scalar factor λ.

Size-Orientation

Besides the size of the SE, one can also vary its orientation (Werman & Peleg, 1985). Naturally this is relevant only with anistropic structuring elements and not for disc-shaped SE, nor with area-based filters. Let us note $b_{\lambda,\theta}$ a SE of size λ and orientation θ. This SE is built from a rotation of the initial SE b_λ with an angle θ, i.e. $\angle(b_\lambda, b_{\lambda,\theta}) = \theta$ with $\angle(b_1, b_2)$ the measured angle between orientations of b_1 and b_2.

Based on this principle, the morphological series is then defined as:

$$\Pi^\psi (f) = \left\{ \Pi^\psi_{\lambda,\theta}(f) \mid \Pi^\psi_{\lambda,\theta}(f) = \psi_{\lambda,\theta}(f) \right\}_{\substack{0 \leq \lambda \leq n \\ \theta_0 \leq \theta \leq \theta_m}}$$

where $\{\theta_0,...,\theta_m\}$ represents the set (of cardinality $|\theta|$) of orientations considered, and $\psi_{\lambda,\theta}$ is a shortcut for $\psi_{b_{\lambda,\theta}}$. Figure 20 illustrates the interest of such size-orientation features when the standard granulometry is useless.

Apart from the most simple angles (i.e. $\theta = k\pi/4$), one has to tackle very carefully the problem of discretisation for rotated SE. Accurate approximations can be obtained by periodic lines (see the work from Jones and Soille (1996)) and require the use of several SE to get an accurate discrete representation of a continuous segment (Soille & Talbot, 2001). It is also possible to retain for each pixel at a given size, only the maximum or minimum value from the results returned by the morphological filter with the various orientations (Maragos, 1989). In this case however, the result is a 1-D series similar to the one which could be obtained by means of radial filters (Soille, 2003). Finally, from these size-orientation measures, other features can be extracted such as orientation maps proposed by Soille & Talbot (2001).

Size-Spectral or Size-Colour

Since digital images contain very often spectral or colour information, it is worth involving the spectral signature or colour of each pixel in the computation of the morphological representation.

To do so, it is possible to first compute a morphological signature for each of the k spectral components (or bands) and then to combine these k signatures into a single one. With this two-step approach, the morphological series Π can be expressed as:

$$\Pi^\psi (f) = \left\{ \Pi^\psi_{\lambda,\omega}(f) \mid \Pi^\psi_{\lambda,\omega}(f) = \psi_\lambda(f_\omega) \right\}_{\substack{1 \leq \omega \leq k \\ 0 \leq \lambda \leq n}}$$

where f_Ω is a greyscale image representing the Ωth spectral component of the multispectral or colour image $f = \{f_w\}_{1 \leq \Omega \leq k}$. In this definition, morphological filters are applied independently on each image band, thus the marginal strategy is used and the correlation among the different spectral channels is completely ignored. Moreover it can result in new spectral signatures or colours in the filtered images.

To avoid these limitations, it is possible to rather consider a vectorial ordering when applying the morphological operators on the multispectral input image f (Aptoula & Lefèvre, 2007a). The purpose of a vectorial ordering is to give a way to order vectors and thus to compute vectorial extrema by means of the two operators sup^v and inf^v. Assuming a given vectorial ordering, the fundamental dilation and erosion operators are written:

$$\varepsilon_b^v(f)(p) = \inf_{q \in b}^v f(p+q), \quad p \in E$$

$$\delta_b^v(f)(p) = \sup_{q \in b}^v f(p-q), \quad p \in E$$

and from these operators it is possible to write all vectorial versions of the morphological operators described previously in this chapter.

The new size-spectral morphological series is finally computed as:

$$\Pi^\psi(f) = \left\{ \Pi_{\lambda,\omega}^\psi(f) \mid \Pi_{\lambda,\omega}^\psi(f) = \left(\psi_\lambda^v(f) \right)_\omega \right\}_{\substack{1 \le \omega \le k \\ 0 \le \lambda \le n}}$$

where $\left(\psi_\lambda^v(f) \right)_\omega = \psi_\lambda(f_\omega)$ in the specific case of a marginal ordering. A comparison of marginal and vectorial strategies is given in Figure 21, considering a similar size distribution but a different spatial distribution in each colour band.

For a comprehensive review of vectorial orderings and multivariate mathematical morphology, the reader can refer to the survey from Aptoula & Lefèvre (2007a). An example of colour pattern spectrum can be found in (Ledda & Philips, 2005) while a comparison between several vectorial orderings has also been proposed recently by Gimenez and Evans(2008) using the series $\Pi^{\mathrm{ASF^a}}(f)$. Nes and d'Ornellas (1999) consider colour pattern spectra with linear SE of variable directions (at each scale λ, the maximum pattern spectrum among the various orientations is selected). Rivest (2006) deals with radar signals and propose adequate granulometry and power spectrum by introducing a vector ordering dedicated to complex data.

Size-Intensity

In greyscale images, the pixel intensity values are used either directly (at local scale) or gathered with the sum operator (at global scale). So the distribution of intensity values in the image is not taken into account with standard morphological features, which can be a real issue since intensity distribution (usually measured by an histogram) is a key feature to represent image content.

Computing the histogram on morphological scale-spaces has been proposed by Lefèvre (2007) to take into account both size and intensity distributions. To do so, let us use the Kronecker delta function:

$$\delta_{i,j} = \begin{cases} 1 & \text{if } i = j \\ 0 & \text{if } i \ne j \end{cases}$$

and the histogram function $h_f : T \to \mathbb{Z}$:

$$h_f(\eta) = \sum_{p \in E} \delta_{\eta, f(p)}$$

which measures the number of occurrences of each greylevel η in the image f. Alternatively, we can also use the normalised histogram function $h_f' : T \to [0,1]$ where

$$h_f'(\eta) = \frac{h_f(\eta)}{|\operatorname{supp}(f)|}$$

with $|\text{supp}(f)|$ the cardinality of the support of f, i.e. the number of pixels in f.

The formulation of the 2-D size-intensity morphological feature is then given by the following Π series:

$$\Pi^{\Psi}(f) = \left\{ \Pi^{\Psi}_{\lambda,\eta}(f) \mid \Pi^{\Psi}_{\lambda,\eta}(f) = h_{\Psi(f)}(\eta) \right\}_{\substack{\eta_0 \leq \eta \leq \eta_m \\ 0 \leq \lambda \leq n}}$$

where $\{\eta_0,\ldots,\eta_m\}$ represents the different greylevels or bins in the histogram.

Figure 22 shows the relevance of size-intensity morphological features when both granulometry and histogram are irrelevant. For the sake of clarity, greylevel 0 (i.e. black pixels) has been omitted in the plots.

Its derivative counterpart can be given by the following Δ series:

$$\Delta^{\Psi}(f) = \left\{ \Delta^{\Psi}_{\lambda,\eta}(f) \mid \Delta^{\Psi}_{\lambda,\eta}(f) = h_{\Psi_{\lambda}(f) - \Psi_{\lambda-1}(f)}(\eta) \right\}_{\substack{\eta_0 \leq \eta \leq \eta_m \\ 0 \leq \lambda \leq n}}$$

This feature can be seen as a morphological alternative to the very effective multiresolution histograms computed from Gaussian linear scale-spaces (Hadjidemetriou, Grossberg, & Nayar, 2004).

Spatial and intensity information can also be gathered by the use of structuring functions (SF) as proposed by Lotufo and Trettel (1996). More precisely, let us define the SF $g_{\lambda,\eta}$ as a non-planar cylinder of radius λ and amplitude η. A size-intensity feature is then built using various λ and η values:

$$\Pi^{\Psi}(f) = \left\{ \Pi^{\Psi}_{\lambda,\eta}(f) \mid \Pi^{\Psi}_{\lambda,\eta}(f) = \Psi_{\lambda,\eta}(f) \right\}_{\substack{\eta_0 \leq \eta \leq \eta_m \\ 0 \leq \lambda \leq n}}$$

where $\Psi_{\lambda,\eta}$ is here a shortcut for $\Psi_{g_{\lambda,\eta}}$. It has been noticed in (Lotufo & Trettel, 1996) that both the classic histogram and the pattern spectrum can be derived from this measure by considering respectively $\lambda = 0$ (i.e. a single pixel) and $\eta = 0$ (i.e. a flat disc-shaped SE).

A similar feature called granold has been proposed by D. Jones and Jackway (2000) by first decomposing the greyscale image into a stack of binary images and then computing the granulometry for each binary image (i.e. at each greyscale threshold), thus resulting in the following series:

$$\Pi^{\Psi}(f) = \left\{ \Pi^{\Psi}_{\lambda,\eta}(f) \mid \Pi^{\Psi}_{\lambda,\eta}(f) = \Psi_{\lambda}(T_{\eta}(f)) \right\}_{\substack{\eta_0 \leq \eta \leq \eta_m \\ 0 \leq \lambda \leq n}}$$

where T_{η} denotes the thresholding function:

$$T_{\eta}(f)(p) = \begin{cases} 1 & \text{if } (f\ p) \geq \eta \\ 0 & \text{if } (f\ p) < \eta \end{cases}$$

Despite their different definitions, both (Lotufo & Trettel, 1996) and (D. Jones & Jackway, 2000) lead to similar measures.

Size-Spatial

All the previous features were considering the spatial information through the successive applications of morphological operators which rely on a spatial neighbourhood. But they did not retain any information about the spatial distribution of the pixels at a given scale λ. A first attempt to deal with this problem was made by Wilkinson (2002) who proposed to compute spatial moments on the filtered binary images, thus resulting in spatial pattern spectra:

Figure 20. Two input images (left), their respective (similar) granulometric curve with vertical SE (centre) and their 2-D size-orientation granulometric curve (right) considering four angles.

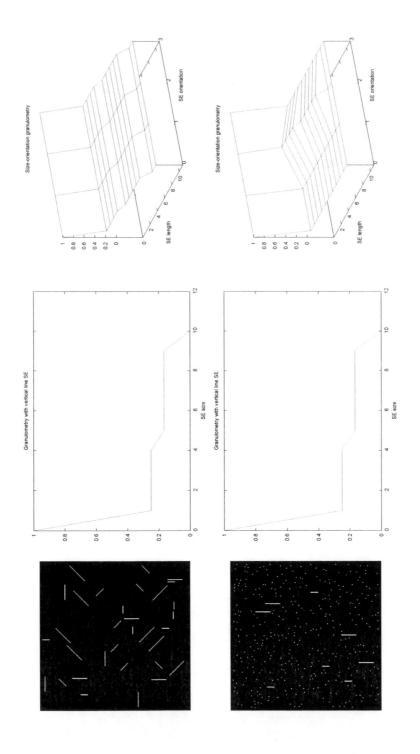

$$\Phi(f) = \left\{ \Phi_\lambda(f) \mid \Phi_\lambda(f) = m_{ij}\left(\Delta_\lambda(f)\right) \right\}_{\substack{m_{ij} \\ -n \le \lambda \le n}}$$

where m_{ij} denotes the moment of order (i, j), computed on an image f as:

$$m_{ij}(f) = \sum_{(x,y)\in E} x^i y^j f(x,y)$$

This idea was later followed by Aptoula and Lefèvre (2006) where a normalised spatial covariance involving normalised unscaled central moments μ_{ij} is proposed to ensure scale and translation invariance:

$$K^{\vec{v}}(f) = \left\{ K_\lambda^{\vec{v}} \mid K_\lambda^{\vec{v}} = \mu_{ij}\left(\Pi^\varepsilon_{\lambda\vec{v}}(f)(p)\right)/\mu_{ij}(f) \right\}_{\substack{\mu_{ij} \\ 0 \le \lambda \le n}}$$

with μ_{ij} defined by:

$$\mu_{ij}(f) = \frac{\sum\limits_{(x,y)\in E}(x-\overline{x})^i(y-\overline{y})^j f(x,y)}{(m_{00}(f))^\alpha} \quad \text{with } 1\alpha = \frac{i+j}{2} \, | \, , \quad \forall i+j \ge 2$$

and $\overline{x} = m_{10}(f)/m_{00}(f)$, $\overline{y} = m_{01}(f)/m_{00}(f)$.

Alternatively, Ayala and Domingo (2001) proposed spatial size distributions where filtered images of the morphological series are replaced by their intersection with filtered translated images, intersection being computed on a linear way with a product rather than on a nonlinear way with a minimum. Thus their feature can be obtained by comparing the linear covariances applied on both initial and filtered images, for all possible vectors in a set defined by κb, with increasing κ values:

$$\Omega(f) = \left\{ \Omega_{\lambda,\kappa} \mid \Omega_{\lambda,\kappa} = \frac{1}{\left(\sum\limits_{p\in E} f(p)\right)^2} \sum_{q\in\kappa b} K_1'^{\vec{q}}(f) - K_1'^{\vec{q}}(\Pi_\lambda(f)) \right\}_{\substack{0\le\kappa\le k \\ 0\le\lambda\le n}}$$

where $\vec{q}$ is a shortcut for the vector $\overrightarrow{oq}$ with o the centre or origin of the SE b, and q any neighbour belonging to the SE. Here we have used the notation K' to denote the autocorrelation function (cf. section 2.3). The spatial-size distribution can finally be computed as a 2-D differential measure, in a way similar to the computation of the Δ measure from the associated Π one. Zingman, Meir, & El-Yaniv (2007) propose the pattern density spectrum with a rather similar definition but relying on some concepts of fuzzy sets (actually their density opening operator is similar to a rank-max opening (Soille, 2003)). Combined with the standard pattern spectrum, they obtain the 2D size-density spectrum.

Finally, Aptoula and Lefèvre (2007b) consider a composite SE built from two different SE, and introduce two parameters λ and κ to deal with both the size of the two SE and the shift between them. Their new operator combines the filtering properties of the granulometry and the covariance, thus resulting in a series:

Figure 21. Two input images (left), their respective granulometric curves computed with a marginal strategy (center) and with a vectorial strategy (right).

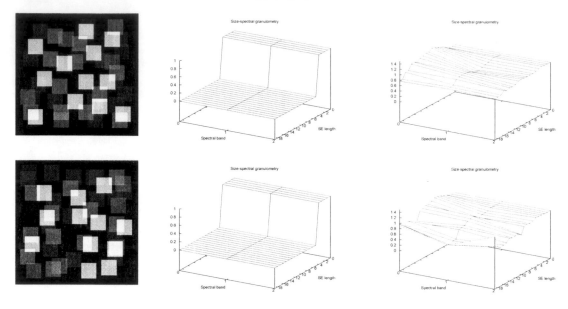

$$\Pi^{\psi,\vec{v}}(f) = \left\{ \Pi^{\psi,\vec{v}}_{\lambda,\kappa}(f) \mid \Pi^{\psi\vec{v}}_{\lambda\kappa}(f) = \Psi_{\lambda,\vec{v}\kappa}(f) \right\}_{\substack{0 \le \kappa k \\ 0 \le \lambda \le n}}$$

with $\Psi_{\lambda,\kappa\vec{v}}$ a shortcut for $\Psi_{b_{\lambda,\kappa\vec{v}}}$, and the composite SE being defined as $b_{\lambda,\kappa\vec{v}} = b_{\lambda} \cup (b_{\lambda} + \kappa\vec{v})$, i.e. a pair of SE b of size λ separated by a vector $\kappa\vec{v}$. The following normalized measure can then be computed from the previous series:

$$\Gamma^{\psi,\vec{v}}(f) \left\{ \Gamma^{\psi,\vec{v}}_{\lambda,\kappa}(f) \mid \Gamma^{\psi\vec{v}}_{\lambda\kappa}(f) = \frac{\sum\limits_{p \in E} \Pi^{\psi,\vec{v}}_{\lambda,\kappa}(f)(p)}{\sum\limits_{p \in E} f(p)} \right\}_{\substack{0 \le \kappa k \\ 0 \le \lambda \le n}}$$

Figure 23 illustrates the interest of size-spatial features, considering the spatial covariance defined in Eq. (3.20) with vertical information taken into account.

We have presented various features which can be extracted from morphological scale-spaces. We will now discuss the issues related to their practical implementation.

PRACTICAL IMPLEMENTATION ISSUES

In support to the theoretical presentation introduced above, we discuss here the issues related to the practical implementation of morphological features. Naturally, straight coding of the features described previously will lead to prohibitive computation time, thus making morphological features irrelevant for

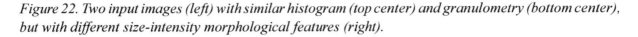

Figure 22. Two input images (left) with similar histogram (top center) and granulometry (bottom center), but with different size-intensity morphological features (right).

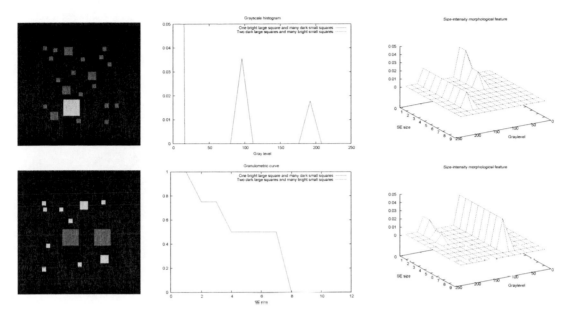

most of the real-life problems. However a lot of work has been done on efficient algorithms and operators in the field of mathematical morphology. So all the features presented in the previous sections can be computed very efficiently and thus be involved actually in any real (even real-time) system. Moreover, other issues have often to be taken into account, for instance noise robustness, definition of optimal parameters, etc.

Efficient Algorithms

Features presented previously need the application of a given morphological filter many times to build the scale-space from which they can be extracted.

In case of features based on standard filters (e.g. structural openings and closings), the reader will find in the paper of Vincent (2000) a comprehensive set of fast algorithms. We recall here the main ideas of this paper. When dealing with binary images, two different cases have to be considered. The most simple case is related to linear SE for which a run-length technique can be involved. The principle for horizontal SE is to scan each line of the image from left to right, and add the length of each discovered run (i.e. series of successive white pixels) to the associated Φ_λ bin of the pattern spectrum Φ. With more complex SE, creating an opening transform is most of the time a prerequisite for fast algorithms, and can be performed using a distance transform. Once the opening transform has been computed, extracting the granulometry or pattern spectrum is very straightforward. In (Vincent, 2000) are given very efficient algorithms compatible with SE which can be decomposed into most simple ones (horizontal, vertical or diagonal SE). The distance transform computed with city-block distance metric may also be an appropriate basis for disc-shaped SE (P. Ghosh, Chanda, & Mali, 2000). In his paper, Vincent has extended the opening transform for binary images to the opening tree for greyscale images. Linear SE

Figure 23. Three input images (left), their respective covariance curve with vertical SE (centre) and 2-D size-spatial granulometric curve (right) considering vertical spatial moments.

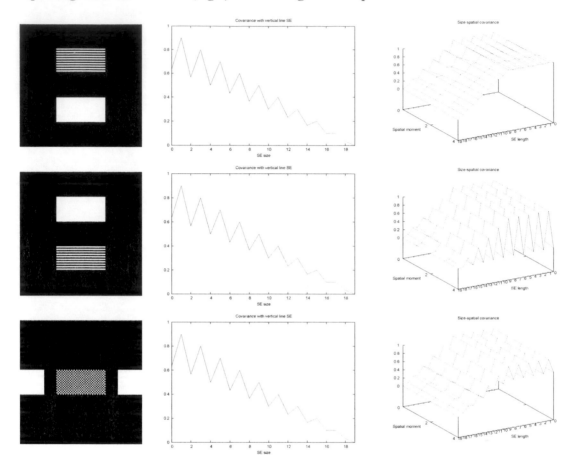

are tackled with a run-length technique rather similar to the binary case, with an additional step which consists in opening the segments found in the input image iteratively to fill all the related bins in the pattern spectrum. For the other kinds of SE (from which a decomposition into simple SE is possible), it is necessary to compute an opening tree. In such a structure, each node represents a plateau in the image (i.e. a series of successive pixels having a value higher or equal to a level l). The tree root is related to the lowest level $l = 0$ while the leaves correspond to local maxima. The pattern spectrum can then be obtained by analysing the successive nodes of the opening tree for each pixel. Vincent also introduces some techniques to deal with semi-local computation of granulometries.

As far as attribute-based operators are concerned, several efficient algorithms have also been proposed. Vincent (1993) introduces an algorithm for area-based filters which starts from all image maxima and iteratively analyse their neighbourhoods by increasing the greyscale range until the area parameter is reached. His work was extended to general attribute-based filters by Breen and Jones (1996), while Salembier et al. (1998) introduced another solution for attribute-based filters using new data structures, the max and min tree. More recently, Meijster and Wilkinson (2002) give an alternative solution to the use of queues based on the very efficient union-find structure and compare their approach with previously cited works.

In order to reduce the computation time, it is necessary to limit the number of comparisons needed when applying a morphological operator. This can be achieved either by decomposing a 2-D SE into smaller 1-D or 2-D SE, or by optimising a given morphological operator through analysis of its behaviour (in particular with linear SE), and a recent review has been made by Van Droogenbroeck and Buckley (2005) (the case of filters using a rectangular SE is considered in a previous paper from Van Droogenbroeck (2002)). To illustrate the first case, let us assume a SE b can be written as a combination of smaller SE b_1 and b_2 such as $b = \delta_{b_1} b_2$. Then the morphological filtering simplifies, e.g. $\varepsilon_b(f) = \varepsilon_{b_1} \varepsilon_{b_2}(f)$. Similarly, the SE b with size λ can be defined as $b_\lambda = \lambda b = \delta_b^{(\lambda-1)}(b)$. Thus various solutions have been introduced in the literature for SE decomposition, mainly dealing with convex flat SE. Among the earliest works, Zhuang and Haralick (1986) proposed an efficient tree search technique and later on Park and Chin(1995) consider the decomposition of a SE into its prime factors. More recently, Hashimoto and Barrera (2003) introduced a greedy algorithm which minimizes the number of SE used in the decomposition. But all the deterministic approaches are related to convex SE, some are even dedicated to a particular shape (e.g. a disc in (Vanrell & Vitria, 1997)). When dealing with nonconvex SE, solutions can be obtained through the use of genetic algorithms (Shih & Wu, 2005) or linear programming (H. Yang & Lee, 2005) for instance. In case of structuring functions, one can refer for instance to the work of Engbers, Boomgaard, & Smeulders (2001). Moreover, it is also possible to perform a 1.5-D scan of the 2-D SE as proposed by Fredembach and Finlayson (2008). To the best knowledge of the author, the most up-to-date technique is from Urbach and Wilkinson (2008) who do not decompose a SE into smaller SE but into chords, and for which the C source code is freely available from the authors.

Besides efficient algorithms to ensure low computation time, one can also rely on hardware implementation of the morphological operators (Mertzios & Tsirikolias, 1998; Sivakumar, Patel, Kehtarnavaz, Balagurunathan, & Dougherty, 2000). In case of hyperspectral data, Plaza, Plaza, & Valencia (2007) consider a parallel architecture built from a cluster of workstations.

Robustness and Adaptation

In addition to computational efficiency, several other issues have to be considered when using features from morphological scale-spaces in real-life applications.

Robustness to various artefacts, and mainly noise, should be achieved. Asano and Yokozeki (1996) propose the multiresolution pattern spectrum (MPS) to measure size distributions accurately even in the presence of noise in binary images. They suggest to precede each opening by a closing of the same size, so their MPS is nothing more than the Φ^{ASF} feature. Dougherty and Cheng (1995) introduce exterior granulometries to perform recognition of noisy shapes. If the size of the feature set is large (which could be easily observed with 2-D or n-D features), it is necessary to proceed to data or dimension reduction to ensure robustness of the method to the size of the feature set. Naturally statistical approaches such as PCA or MNF may be involved, but one can also rely on genetic algorithms (Ramos & Pina, 2005). Moreover, data discretisation may also bring some problems, and robustness against it has to be solved if features with low λ values are analysed. To do so, it is possible to build a new larger and oversampled image from f and to compute morphological features on this image, thus avoiding the problems related to data discretisation (Hendriks, Kempen, & Vliet, 2007).

Morphological scale-spaces may require the definition of the underlying SE shape, or the window size and shape when used at a semi-local scale, thus allowing the adaptation of the morphological feature to the data under consideration. Since these parameters have a very strong influence on the resulting features, this is a critical issue. Jan and Hsueh propose to define the window size used with semi-local granulometries using analysis of the global covariance measure (Jan & Hsueh, 1998). Asano, Miyagawa, & Fujio (2000) propose to define the structuring function which best models a given texture through the use of a pattern spectrum, by first defining the optimal size of the SE and then determining the appropriate SE values. Balagurunathan and Dougherty (2003) deal with the same problem and propose a solution based on a Bayesian framework and dedicated to the binary case.

APPLICATIONS

The different features reviewed in this chapter have been used in the literature to solve various problems. We present here the main areas where they have been applied, as illustrative examples to help the reader to understand the benefit of morphological features over conventional features when dealing with real-life problems.

Texture Segmentation and Classification

Since granulometries and pattern spectrum were first proposed to determine the distribution of grains in binary images, the main usage of such morphological features is related to texture analysis, i.e. image segmentation and classification based on textural properties. Indeed, morphological features can achieve to describe the shape, size, orientation, and periodicity of ordered textures, and are also relevant to extract some properties of disordered textures (Soille, 2002).

When computed at a local or semi-local scale, morphological features have been used to perform segmentation of textured images. Early work in this field is due to Dougherty, Pelz, et al. (1992) who proposed to consider several features (mean and variance of the pattern spectrum, or more generally the granulometric moments) leading to various studies since then. Among them we can cite (Fletcher & Evans, 2005) where area-based filters are considered. A supervised segmentation scheme is proposed in (Racky & Pandit, 1999) which requires to learn the different textures before applying the segmentation algorithm. For each image in the morphological scale-space, mean and standard deviation are computed with 3 different SE (square, horizontal and vertical line segments) and lead to the identification of the scales which are relevant for texture recognition.

When applied at a global scale, morphological features can allow texture classification. The Brodatz dataset has been extensively used to deal with this problem, e.g. considering hat scale-spaces (Jalba et al., 2004) or comparing between various dimensionality reduction techniques (Velloso, Carneiro, & Souza, 2007).

Micrographs were studied in (D. Ghosh & Wei, 2006) where a k nearest neighbours (k-NN) classifier is involved to distinguish between various texture classes. The morphological feature here is a 3-D pattern spectrum with various height, width, and greylevel of the structuring function. Similarly, size-intensity morphological measures have been used to qualify granite textures (Ramos & Pina, 2005), involving also a k-NN classifier and a genetic algorithm to reduce the feature space.

Comparison of different morphological features for texture analysis has also been investigated, for instance in the context of nondestructive and quantitative assessment of stone decay (Mauricio & Figueirdo, 2000), for Brodatz (Ayala, Diaz, Demingo, & Epifanio, 2003) and for Outex (Southam & Harvey, 2005) texture databases. This last database has also been used in the comparative evaluations made by Aptoula and Lefèvre (2006,2007a,2007b).

Biomedical Imaging

In the field of biomedical imaging, features built from morphological scale-spaces have been successfully involved in the resolution of various problems due to the high importance of the shape information within visible structures. We give here some examples related to medical imaging and biological imaging.

In the field of Ophthalmology, binary images obtained from specular microscopy are analysed by means of granulometric moments either at a global scale (Ayala, Diaz, & Martinez-Costa, 2001) or at a semi-local scale (Zapater, Martinez-Costa, Ayala, & Domingo, 2002) to determine the corneal endothelium status. Segmentation of X-ray mammographies is performed in (Baeg et al., 1999) by relying on a clustering algorithm. Each pixel is characterised by some features which consist of the 3 first moments computed on several semi-local granulometric curves obtained using 10 different SE (both flat and nonflat). In (Korn, Sidiropoulos, Faloutsos, Siegel, & Protopapas, 1998), shape matching in the context of tumour recognition in medical images is considered. The difference between two shapes is computed at every scale between aligned shapes (i.e. after a spatial registration of the two shapes) and is finally integrated over all scales to give a global difference measure. The problem of atherosclerotic carotid plaque classification from ultrasound images is tackled in (Kyriacou et al., 2008). The greyscale input image is thresholded to generate three binary images isolating the different tissues. The pattern spectrum is then computed both on these binary images and on the initial greylevel image and used as an image feature for a subsequent SVM classifier. Skin lesion images acquired with diffuse reflectance spectroscopic imaging are analysed in (Mehrubeoglu, Kehtarnavaz, Marquez, & Wang, 2000) through several pattern spectra computed with various SE and SF. Granulometric features are used in (Summers et al., 2001) to quantify the size of renal lesions from binarised CT scans.

As biology is concerned, Diatom shells are classified using some features computed on scale-spaces built using top-hat operators by reconstruction (i.e. Π^{r^ρ} series) (Jalba et al., 2004) and using size-shape features (Urbach et al., 2007). In (Ruberto, Dempster, Khan, & Jarra, 2002), granulometry is used to define accurate parameters in a global image analysis procedure of infected blood cell images. Based on this work, a technique was proposed more recently (Ross, Pritchard, Rubin, & Duse, 2006) to segment and classify malaria parasites. Malaria-infected blood slide images are also analysed in (Mohana-Rao & Dempster, 2001) with area-based granulometries. In the field of quantitative cytology, scale-spaces computed with openings by reconstruction are used to perform shape description (Metzler, Lehmann, Bienert, Mottahy, & Spitzer, 2000). Histological images of breast tissue are classified using an SVM with size-density features in (Zingman et al., 2007). In (Wada, Yoshizaki, Kondoh, & Furutani-Seiki, 2003), classification of medaka embryo is performed using a neural network fed with pattern spectrum values computed on binary images. Granulometric moments help to count and classify white blood cells in (Theera-Umpon & Dhompongsa, 2007). Granulometry is involved in (You & Yu, 2004) to determine accurate parameters to separate overlapping cells. Greyscale granulometries and Fourier boundary descriptors are combined in (Tang, 1998) to perform classification of underwater plankton images with a neural network.

Remote Sensing

Morphological features have also been applied to remote sensing, or satellite image analysis.

Interpretation of multispectral images has been elaborated by Aptoula and Lefèvre (2007a) with the comparison of various vector ordering schemes for computing the DMP used in a subsequent supervised pixelwise classification. Lefèvre et al. (2007) consider a size-shape pattern spectrum with rectangular SE to determine automatically the optimal parameters for a noise removal step based on an opening, in the context of a morphological approach to building detection in panchromatic remotely-sensed images. The analysis of DEM (Digital Elevation Map) images was performed by Jackway & Deriche (1996) using scale-space fingerprints computed in a semi-local way considering circular regions in order to recognise these areas using a predefined set of fingerprint models. Remotely-sensed textures have also been analysed by means of pattern spectrum in (Velloso et al., 2007). Finally, some works have been done in pixelwise classification of hyperspectral images, e.g. Benediktsson, Pesaresi, & Arnason (2005) and Plaza, Martinez, Perez, & Plaza (2004). The problem of dimensionality reduction has also been tackled (Plaza et al., 2007). Post-conflict reconstruction assessment has been addressed in (Pesaresi & Pagot, 2007), and building detection studied in (Shackelford, Davis, & Wang, 2004). In (Bellens, Martinez-Fonte, Gautama, Chan, & Canters, 2007), operators by partial reconstruction are used as intermediate filters between standard filters and filters by reconstruction.

Document Analysis

Document images also exhibit strong shape properties, that make them a good support for applying morphological features.

A block-based analysis of binary images is performed in (Sabourin, Genest, & Prêteux, 1997) where the authors use the 3 first granulometric moments computed with SE of various orientations to build an off-line signature recognition system. A 2-D granulometry with rectangular SE as features (reduced by means of a PCA transform) for classifying several types of documents (images of PDF files) is proposed in (Bagdanov & Worring, 2002). In (Hiary & Ng, 2007), a pattern spectrum helps to determine an optimal opening filter for background subtraction in a problem related to watermark analysis in document images.

Content-Based Image Retrieval and Categorization

With new morphological scale-spaces being defined for greyscale and colour images, CBIR starts to be a possible application field of morphological features.

In (Nes & d'Ornellas, 1999), each colour image is associated to its colour pattern spectrum. Several SE with various orientations are combined by keeping at each scale the maximum value of the pattern spectra. The resulting feature is included in the Monet CBIR system. The COIL-20 dataset has been used for object recognition with several morphological features, such as shape features extracted from hat scale-spaces (Jalba, Wilkinson, & Roerdink, 2006), quantised size-shape 2-D pattern spectra using attribute scale-spaces (Urbach et al., 2007), or the morphological size-intensity feature (Lefèvre, 2007). In (Tushabe & Wilkinson, 2007), the size-shape pattern spectra (Urbach et al., 2007) is computed on each colour band independently to solve the problem of colour image retrieval.

As far as the image categorisation problem is concerned, we can mention (Ianeva, Vries, & Rohrig, 2003) where the problem of automatic video-genre classification (cartoons vs. photographs) is tackled. Several features are involved, among which a pattern spectrum computed with isotropic structuring functions with a 2-D parabolic profile. In (Bangham, Gibson, & Harvey, 2003), the problem of non-photorealistic rendering of colour images is considered and the proposed solution relies on ASF scale-space filters to extract edge maps similar to sketch-like pictures. With new morphological scale-spaces being defined for greyscale and colour images, CBIR starts to be a possible application field of morphological features.

Biometrics and Shape Recognition

Biometrics is a very topical issue, and mathematical morphology is a possible tool to compute reliable features as long as image data are available.

In (Barnich et al., 2006), some measures are computed from rectangular size distributions to perform silhouette classification in real-time. Silhouettes are also classified with hat scale-spaces in (Jalba et al., 2006). 2D shape smoothing is performed in (Jang & Chin, 1998) based on the scale-space proposed by Chen & Yan (1989), by keeping at each scale λ only pixels which appear in both differential series of openings and closing, i.e. Δ^γ and Δ^φ. Binary shapes are also compared at several scales to perform silhouette matching in (Y. Li, Ma, & Lu, 1998). The gender of walking people can be determined by analysing the binary silhouette with entropy of the pattern spectrum (Sudo, Yamato, & Tomono, 1996).

Xiaoqi & Baozong (1995) propose the high-order pattern spectrum (computed from difference between union and intersection of successive ASF) as a measure for shape recognition. In (Anastassopoulos & Venetsanopoulos, 1991), the authors explore how the pattern spectrum can be effectively used to perform shape recognition, and they consider binary images representing planes.

In (Omata, Hamamoto, & Hangai, 2001), pattern spectrum is used as an appropriate feature to distinguish between lips. For each individual, several colour images are acquired considering the pronunciation of different vowels, and then binarised to highlight the lip which will be further analysed by means of pattern spectrum with square, horizontal and vertical SE. The fingerprints computed from scale-spaces by reconstruction are evaluated as appropriate features for face description in (Rivas-Araiza et al., 2008). Soille and Talbot (2001) introduce orientation fields by analysing the $\{\Pi^\psi_{\lambda\theta}(f)(p)\}$ series in each pixel p and scale λ. More precisely, they compute for each pair (p, λ) the main orientation and its strength by looking for maximal and minimal values of the series with various θ angles. These features are finally used to extract fingerprints. An effective smoothing method for footprint images is proposed in (S. Yang, Wang, & Wang, 2007), which relies on the analysis of the morphological scale-space by reconstruction. Su, Crookes, & Bouridane (2007) introduce the topologic spectrum to deal with shoeprint recognition in binary images. They replace the sum of pixels (or object area) by the Euler number as the Lebesgue measure, thus measuring at each scale the number of components versus holes, and similarly to the pattern spectrum consider the differential series instead of the original one.

Other Applications

Beyond the main applications presented above, morphological features have also been used in other domains.

Acton and Mukherjee explore area scale-space to solve various problems in image processing. In (Acton & Mukherjee, 2000b) they introduce a new fuzzy clustering algorithm based on area scale-space which performs better than standard ones for pixel classification considering various object identification tasks (coins, cells, connecting rod). In (Acton & Mukherjee, 2000a) they propose a new edge detector relying on the area scale-space and which does not require any threshold. Gimenez & Evans (2008) consider the problems of noise reduction and segmentation of colour images using area-based scale-spaces. Noise reduction has been already addressed by Haralick, Katz, & Dougherty (1995) with the opening spectrum, a morphological alternative to the Wiener filter. Warning traffic signs are recognised by means of oriented pattern spectrum in (Yi, Gangyi, & Yong, 1996). Soilsection images have been analysed in (Doulamis, Doulamis, & Maragos, 2001; Tzafestas & Maragos, 2002) by means of pattern spectra computed either with area-based or more complex connected filters. The process of preparation of electronic ink is considered in (Wang, Li, & Shang, 2006) where the size distribution of microcapsules is of primary importance to evaluate the ink quality. Thus the proposed method relies on the analysis of granulometric curve obtained with openings by reconstruction. Pattern recognition based on pattern spectrum and neural network is applied to partial discharges in order to evaluate insulation condition of high voltage apparatuses (Yunpeng, Fangcheng, & Yanqing, 2005).

CONCLUSION

Mathematical morphology is a very powerful framework for nonlinear image processing. When dealing with image description, it has been shown that scale-space representations are of major importance. So in this chapter, we have presented a review of image features computed from morphological scale-spaces, i.e. scale-spaces generated with operators from Mathematical Morphology. In our study, we consider both local (or semi-local) and global features, from the earliest and probably most famous 1-D features such as granulometries, pattern spectra and morphological profiles, to some recent multidimensional features which gather many complementary information in a single feature.

Due to space constraints, we have limited our study to morphological features which are extracted from scale-spaces built using mainly structural morphological operators (i.e. operators relying on a structuring element or function). To be complete, we have to mention several other works which could have been included in this chapter. Wilkinson (2007) focuses on attribute filters to build attribute-spaces, which offer several advantages over structural operators (e.g. no need to define a SE, more invariant, more efficient). Ghadiali, Poon, & Siu (1996) brings the fuzzy logic framework to the morphological features by introducing a fuzzy pattern spectrum. Soille (2003) proposes the self-dual filters which are particularly effective when dealing with objects which are neither the brightest nor the darkest in the image.

Among the works related to morphological scale-spaces which have not been detailed here, we can mention the use of PDE (Boomgaard & Smeulders, 1994; Maragos, 2003), the multiscale connectivities (Braga-Neto & Goutsias, 2005; Tzafestas & Maragos, 2002), the generalisations with pseudolinear scale spaces (Florack, 2001; Welk, 2003), adjunction pyramids (Goutsias & Heijmans, 2000) or an algebraic framework (Heijmans & Boomgaard, 2002), and finally the use of morphological levellings (Meyer & Maragos, 2000).

To conclude, morphological scale-spaces are a particularly relevant option to build robust image features, due to the numerous desired properties of mathematical morphology. Despite their theoretical interest and the very active community in mathematical morphology, their practical use stays however limited, in particular for more recent multidimensional features. With the comprehensive review presented here and the various usage examples which have been given, we hope the readers will understand their benefits in mining of multimedia data.

REFERENCES

Acton, S., & Mukherjee, D. (2000a). Image edges from area morphology. In *International Conference on Acoustics, Speech, and Signal Processing (ICASSP)* (pp. 2239–2242). Istanbul, Turkey.

Acton, S., & Mukherjee, D. (2000b, April). Scale space classification using area morphology. *IEEE Transactions on Image Processing, 9*(4), 623–635.

Anastassopoulos, V., & Venetsanopoulos, A. (1991). The classification properties of the pecstrum and its use for pattern identification. *Circuits, Systems and Signal Processing, 10*(3), 293–326.

Aptoula, E., & Lefèvre, S. (2006, September). Spatial morphological covariance applied to texture classification. In *International Workshop on Multimedia Content Representation, Classification and Security (IWMRCS), 4105*, 522–529. Istanbul, Turkey: Springer-Verlag.

Aptoula, E., & Lefèvre, S. (2007a, November). A comparative study on multivariate mathematical morphology. *Pattern Recognition, 40*(11), 2914–2929.

Aptoula, E., & Lefèvre, S. (2007b, October). On morphological color texture characterization. In *International Symposium on Mathematical Morphology (ISMM)* (pp. 153–164). Rio de Janeiro, Brazil.

Asano, A., Miyagawa, M., & Fujio, M. (2000). Texture modelling by optimal grey scale structuring elements using morphological pattern spectrum. In *IAPR International Conference on Pattern Recognition (ICPR)* (pp. 475–478).

Asano, A., & Yokozeki, S. (1996). Multiresolution pattern spectrum and its application to optimization of nonlinear filter. In *IEEE International Conference on Image Processing (ICIP)* (pp. 387–390). Lausanne, Switzerland.

Ayala, G., Diaz, E., Demingo, J., & Epifanio, I. (2003). Moments of size distributions applied to texture classification. In *International Symposium on Image and Signal Processing and Analysis (ISPA)* (pp. 96–100).

Ayala, G., Diaz, M., & Martinez-Costa, L. (2001). Granulometric moments and corneal endothelium status. *Pattern Recognition, 34*, 1219–1227.

Ayala, G., & Domingo, J. (2001, December). Spatial size distribution: applications to shape and texture analysis. *IEEE Transactions on Pattern Analysis and Machine Intelligence, 23*(12), 1430–1442.

Baeg, S., Batman, S., Dougherty, E., Kamat, V., Kehtarnavaz, N., Kim, S., et al. (1999). Unsupervised morphological granulometric texture segmentation of digital mammograms. *Journal of Electronic Imaging, 8*(1), 65–73.

Bagdanov, A., & Worring, M. (2002). Granulometric analysis of document images. In *IAPR International Conference on Pattern Recognition (ICPR)* (pp. 468–471). Quebec City, Canada.

Balagurunathan, Y., & Dougherty, E. (2003). Granulometric parametric estimation for the random boolean model using optimal linear filters and optimal structuring elements. *Pattern Recognition Letters, 24*, 283–293.

Bangham, J., Gibson, S., & Harvey, R. (2003). The art of scale-space. In *British Machine Vision Conference (BMVC)*.

Bangham, J., Ling, P., & Harvey, R. (1996, May). Scale-space from nonlinear filters. *IEEE Transactions on Pattern Analysis and Machine Intelligence, 18*(5), 520–528.

Barnich, O., Jodogne, S., & Droogenbroeck, M. van. (2006). Robust analysis of silhouettes by morphological size distributions. In *International Workshop on Advanced Concepts for Intelligent Vision Systems (ACIVS), 4179*, 734–745. Springer-Verlag.

Batman, S., & Dougherty, E. (1997). Size distribution for multivariate morphological granulometries: texture classification and statistical properties. *Optical Engineering, 36*(5), 1518–1529.

Batman, S., Dougherty, E., & Sand, F. (2000). Heterogeneous morphological granulometries. *Pattern Recognition, 33*, 1047–1057.

Bellens, R., Martinez-Fonte, L., Gautama, S., Chan, J., & Canters, F. (2007). Potential problems with using reconstruction in morphological profiles for classification of remote sensing images from urban areas. In *IEEE International Geosciences and Remote Sensing Symposium (IGARSS)* (pp. 2698–2701).

Benediktsson, J., Pesaresi, M., & Arnason, K. (2003, September). Classification and feature extraction for remote sensing images from urban areas based on morphological transformations. *IEEE Transactions on Geoscience and Remote Sensing, 41*(9), 1940–1949.

Benediktsson, J., Pesaresi, M., & Arnason, K. (2005, March). Classification of hyperspectral data from urban areas based on extended morphological profiles. *IEEE Transactions on Geoscience and Remote Sensing, 43*(3), 480–491.

Boomgaard, R. van den, & Smeulders, A. (1994, November). The morphological structure of images: the differential equations of morphological scale-space. *IEEE Transactions on Pattern Analysis and Machine Intelligence, 16*(11), 1101–1113.

Bosworth, J., & Acton, S. (2003). Morphological scale-space in image processing. *Digital Signal Processing, 13*, 338–367.

Braga-Neto, U., & Goutsias, J. (2005). Constructing multiscale connectivities. *Computer Vision and Image Understanding, 99*, 126–150.

Breen, E., & Jones, R. (1996, November). Attribute openings, thinnings, and granulometries. *Computer Vision and Image Understanding, 64*(3), 377–389.

Chanussot, J., Benediktsson, J., & Pesaresi, M. (2003). On the use of morphological alternated sequential filters for the classification of remote sensing images from urban areas. In *IEEE International Geosciences and Remote Sensing Symposium (IGARSS)*. Toulouse, France.

Chen, M., & Yan, P. (1989, July). A multiscale approach based on morphological filtering. *IEEE Transactions on Pattern Analysis and Machine Intelligence, 11*(7), 694–700.

Dougherty, E., & Cheng, Y. (1995). Morphological pattern-spectrum classification of noisy shapes: exterior granulometries. *Pattern Recognition, 28*(1), 81–98.

Dougherty, E., Newell, J., & Pelz, J. (1992, October). Morphological texture-based maximum-likelihood pixel classification based on local granulometric moments. *Pattern Recognition, 25*(10), 1181–1198.

Dougherty, E., Pelz, J., Sand, F., & Lent, A. (1992). Morphological image segmentation by local granulometric size distributions. *Journal of Electronic Imaging, 1*, 46–60.

Doulamis, A., Doulamis, N., & Maragos, P. (2001). Generalized multiscale connected operators with applications to granulometric image analysis. In *IEEE International Conference on Image Processing (ICIP)* (pp. 684–687).

Droogenbroeck, M. van. (2002). Algorithms for openings of binary and label images with rectangular structuring elements. In *International Symposium on Mathematical Morphology (ISMM)* (pp. 197–207).

Droogenbroeck, M. van, & Buckley, M. (2005). Morphological erosions and openings: fast algorithms based on anchors. *Journal of Mathematical Imaging and Vision, 22*, 121–142.

Duits, R., Florack, L., Graaf, J. D., & Haar Romeny, B. ter. (2004). On the axioms of scale space theory. *Journal of Mathematical Imaging and Vision, 20*, 267–298.

Engbers, E., Boomgaard, R. van den, & Smeulders, A. (2001). Decomposition of separable concave structuring functions. *Journal of Mathematical Imaging and Vision, 15*, 181–195.

Fletcher, N., & Evans, A. (2005). Texture segmentation using area morphology local granulometries. In *International Symposium on Mathematical Morphology (ISMM)* (p. 367-376).

Florack, L. (2001). Non-linear scale-spaces isomorphic to the linear case with applications to scalar, vector, and multispectral images. *International Journal of Computer Vision, 42*(1/2), 39–53.

Fredembach, C., & Finlayson, G. (2008). The 1.5d sieve algorithm. *Pattern Recognition Letters, 29*, 629–636.

Gadre, V., & Patney, R. (1992). Multiparametric multiscale filtering, multiparametric granulometries and the associated pattern spectra. In *IEEE International Symposium on Circuits and Systems* (pp. 1513–1516).

Ghadiali, M., Poon, J., & Siu, W. (1996, September). Fuzzy pattern spectrum as texture descriptor. *IEE Electronic Letters, 32*(19), 1772–1773.

Ghosh, D., & Wei, D. T. (2006). Material classification using morphological pattern spectrum for extracting textural features from material micrographs. In *Asian Conference on Computer Vision (ACCV)* (Vol. 3852, pp. 623–632). Springer-Verlag.

Ghosh, P., & Chanda, B. (1998, October). Bi-variate pattern spectrum. In *International symposium on computer graphics, image processing and vision* (pp. 476–483). Rio de Janeiro.

Ghosh, P., Chanda, B., & Mali, P. (2000). Fast algorithm for sequential machine to compute pattern spectrum via city-block distance transform. *Information Sciences, 124*, 193–217.

Gimenez, D., & Evans, A. (2008). An evaluation of area morphology scale-space for colour images. *Computer Vision and Image Understanding, 110*, 32–42.

Goutsias, J., & Heijmans, H. (2000, November). Nonlinear multiresolution signal decomposition schemes. Part I: Morphological pyramids. *IEEE Transactions on Image Processing, 9*(11), 1862–1876.

Hadjidemetriou, E., Grossberg, M., & Nayar, S. (2004, July). Multiresolution histograms and their use in recognition. *IEEE Transactions on Pattern Analysis and Machine Intelligence, 26*(7), 831–847.

Haralick, R., Katz, P., & Dougherty, E. (1995, January). Model-based morphology: the opening spectrum. *Computer Vision, Graphics and Image Processing: Graphical Models and Image Processing, 57*(1), 1–12.

Hashimoto, R., & Barrera, J. (2003). A greedy algorithm for decomposing convex structuring elements. *Journal of Mathematical Imaging and Vision, 18*, 269–289.

Heijmans, H., & Boomgaard, R. van den. (2002). Algebraic framework for linear and morphological scale-spaces. *Journal of Visual Communication and Image Representation, 13*, 269–301.

Hendriks, C. L., Kempen, G. van, & Vliet, L. van. (2007). Improving the accuracy of isotropic granulometries. *Pattern Recognition Letters, 28*, 865–872.

Hiary, H., & Ng, K. (2007). A system for segmenting and extracting paper-based watermark designs. *International Journal of Document Libraries, 6*, 351–361.

Ianeva, T., Vries, A. de, & Rohrig, H. (2003). Detecting cartoons: a case study in automatic video-genre classification. In *IEEE International Conference on Multimedia and Expo (ICME)* (pp. 449–452).

Jackway, P. (1992). Morphological scale-space. In *IAPR International Conference on Pattern Recognition (ICPR)* (p. C:252-255).

Jackway, P., & Deriche, M. (1996, January). Scale-space properties of the multiscale morphological dilation-erosion. *IEEE Transactions on Pattern Analysis and Machine Intelligence, 18*(1), 38–51.

Jalba, A., Wilkinson, M., & Roerdink, J. (2004, May). Morphological hat-transform scale spaces and their use in pattern classification. *Pattern Recognition, 37*(5), 901–915.

Jalba, A., Wilkinson, M., & Roerdink, J. (2006). Shape representation and recognition through morphological curvature scale spaces. *IEEE Transactions on Image Processing, 15*(2), 331–341.

Jan, S., & Hsueh, Y. (1998). Window-size determination for granulometric structural texture classification. *Pattern Recognition Letters, 19*, 439–446.

Jang, B., & Chin, R. (1998, May). Morphological scale space for 2d shape smoothing. *Computer Vision and Image Understanding, 70*(2), 121–141.

Jones, D., & Jackway, P. (2000). Granolds: a novel texture representation. *Pattern Recognition, 33*, 1033–1045.

Jones, R., & Soille, P. (1996). Periodic lines: definitions, cascades, and application to granulometries. *Pattern Recognition Letters, 17*, 1057–1063.

Korn, P., Sidiropoulos, N., Faloutsos, C., Siegel, E., & Protopapas, Z. (1998). Fast and effective retrieval of medical tumor shapes. *IEEE Transactions on Knowledge and Data Engineering, 10*(6), 889–904.

Kyriacou, E., Pattichis, M., Pattichis, C., Mavrommatis, A., Christodoulou, C., Kakkos, S., et al. (2008). Classification of atherosclerotic carotid plaques using morphological analysis on ultrasound images. *Applied Intelligence*, online first.

Ledda, A., & Philips, W. (2005). Majority ordering and the morphological pattern spectrum. In *International Workshop on Advanced Concepts for Intelligent Vision Systems (ACIVS)* (Vol. 3708, pp. 356–363). Springer-Verlag.

Lefèvre, S. (2007, June). Extending morphological signatures for visual pattern recognition. In *IAPR International Workshop on Pattern Recognition in Information Systems (PRIS)* (pp. 79–88). Madeira, Portugal.

Lefèvre, S., Weber, J., & Sheeren, D. (2007, April). Automatic building extraction in VHR images using advanced morphological operators. In *IEEE/ISPRS Joint Workshop on Remote Sensing and Data Fusion over Urban Areas*. Paris, France.

Li, W., Haese-Coat, V., & Ronsin, J. (1997). Residues of morphological filtering by reconstruction for texture classification. *Pattern Recognition, 30*(7), 1081–1093.

Li, Y., Ma, S., & Lu, H. (1998). A multi-scale morphological method for human posture recognition. In *International Conference on Automatic Face and Gesture Recognition (FG)* (pp. 56–61).

Lotufo, R., & Trettel, E. (1996). Integrating size information into intensity histogram. In *International Symposium on Mathematical Morphology (ISMM)* (pp. 281–288). Atlanta, USA.

ManJunath, B., Salembier, P., & Sikora, T. (2002). *Introduction to mpeg-7: Multimedia content description interface*. Wiley.

Maragos, P. (1989, July). Pattern spectrum and multiscale shape representation. *IEEE Transactions on Pattern Analysis and Machine Intelligence, 11*(7), 701–716.

Maragos, P. (2003). Algebraic and pde approaches for lattice scale-spaces with global constraints. *International Journal of Computer Vision, 52*(2/3), 121–137.

Matheron, G. (1975). *Random sets and integral geometry*. New York: Wiley.

Matsopoulos, G., & Marshall, S. (1992). A new morphological scale space operator. In *IEE Conference on Image Processing and its Applications* (pp. 246–249).

Mauricio, A., & Figueirdo, C. (2000). Texture analysis of grey-tone images by mathematical morphology: a non-destructive tool for the quantitative assessment of stone decay. *Mathematical Geology, 32*(5), 619–642.

Mehrubeoglu, M., Kehtarnavaz, N., Marquez, G., & Wang, L. (2000). Characterization of skin lesion texture in diffuse reflectance spectroscopic images. In *IEEE Southwest Symposium on Image Analysis and Interpretation* (pp. 146–150).

Meijster, A., & Wilkinson, M. (2002, April). A comparison of algorithms for connected set openings and closings. *IEEE Transactions on Pattern Analysis and Machine Intelligence, 24*(4), 484–494.

Mertzios, B., & Tsirikolias, K. (1998). Coordinate logic filters and their applications in image recognition and pattern recognition. *Circuits, Systems and Signal Processing, 17*(4), 517–538.

Metzler, V., Lehmann, T., Bienert, H., Mottahy, K., & Spitzer, K. (2000). Scale-independent shape analysis for quantitative cytology using mathematical morphology. *Computers in Biology and Medicine, 30*, 135–151.

Meyer, F., & Maragos, P. (2000). Nonlinear scale-space representation with morphological levelings. *Journal of Visual Communication and Image Representation, 11*, 245–265.

Mohana-Rao, K., & Dempster, A. (2001). Area-granulometry: an improved estimator of size distribution of image objects. *Electronic Letters, 37*(15), 950–951.

Nes, N., & d'Ornellas, M. (1999, January). Color image texture indexing. In *International Conference on Visual Information and Information Systems,1614*, 467–474. Springer-Verlag.

Omata, M., Hamamoto, T., & Hangai, S. (2001). Lip recognition using morphological pattern spectrum. In *International conference on audio- and video-based biometric person authentication,2091*, 108–114. Springer-Verlag.

Park, H., & Chin, R. (1995, January). Decomposition of arbitrarily shaped morphological structuring elements. *IEEE Transactions on Pattern Analysis and Machine Intelligence, 17*(1), 2–15.

Park, K., & Lee, C. (1996, November). Scale-space using mathematical morphology. *IEEE Transactions on Pattern Analysis and Machine Intelligence, 18*(11), 1121–1126.

Pesaresi, M., & Benediktsson, J. (2001, February). A new approach for the morphological segmentation of high-resolution satellite imagery. *IEEE Transactions on Geoscience and Remote Sensing, 39*(2), 309–320.

Pesaresi, M., & Pagot, E. (2007). Post-conflict reconstruction assessment using image morphological profile and fuzzy multicriteria approach on 1-m-resolution satellite data. In *IEEE/ISPRS Joint Workshop on Remote Sensing and Data Fusion over Urban Areas*.

Plaza, A., Martinez, P., Perez, R., & Plaza, J. (2004). A new approach to mixed pixel classification of hyperspectral imagery based on extended morphological profiles. *Pattern Recognition, 37*, 1097–1116.

Plaza, A., Plaza, J., & Valencia, D. (2007). Impact of platform heterogeneity on the design of parallel algorithms for morphological processing of high-dimensional image data. *The Journal of Supercomputing, 40*(1), 81–107.

Racky, J., & Pandit, M. (1999). Automatic generation of morphological opening-closing sequences for texture segmentation. In *IEEE International Conference on Image Processing (ICIP)* (pp. 217–221).

Ramos, V., & Pina, P. (2005). Exploiting and evolving r^n mathematical morphology feature spaces. In *International Symposium on Mathematical Morphology (ISMM)* (pp. 465–474). Paris, France.

Rivas-Araiza, E., Mendiola-Santibanez, J., & Herrera-Ruiz, G. (2008). Morphological multiscale fingerprints from connected transformations. *Signal Processing, 88*, 1125–1133.

Rivest, J. (2006). Granulometries and pattern spectra for radar signals. *Signal Processing, 86*, 1094–1103.

Ronse, C. (1990, October). Why mathematical morphology needs complete lattices. *Signal Processing, 21*(2), 129–154.

Ronse, C. (2005). Special issue on mathematical morphology after 40 years. *Journal of Mathematical Imaging and Vision, 22*(2-3).

Ronse, C., Najman, L., & Decencière, E. (2007). Special issue on ISMM 2005. *Image and Vision Computing, 25*(4).

Ross, N., Pritchard, C., Rubin, D., & Duse, A. (2006, May). Automated image processing method for the diagnosis and classification of malaria on thin blood smears. *Medical and Biological Engineering and Computing, 44*(5), 427–436.

Ruberto, C. D., Dempster, A., Khan, S., & Jarra, B. (2002). Analysis of infected blood cells images using morphological operators. *Image and Vision Computing, 20*, 133–146.

Sabourin, R., Genest, G., & Prêteux, F. (1997, September). Off-line signature verification by local granulometric size distributions. *IEEE Transactions on Pattern Analysis and Machine Intelligence, 19*(9), 976–988.

Salembier, P., Oliveras, A., & Garrido, L. (1998, April). Antiextensive connected operators for image and sequence processing. *IEEE Transactions on Image Processing, 7*(4), 555–570.

Sand, F., & Dougherty, E. (1999). Robustness of granulometric moments. *Pattern Recognition, 32*, 1657–1665.

Serra, J. (1982). *Image analysis and mathematical morphology.* Academic Press.

Shackelford, A., Davis, C., & Wang, X. (2004). Automated 2-d building footprint extraction from high resolution satellite multispectral imagery. In *IEEE International Geosciences and Remote Sensing Symposium (IGARSS)* (pp. 1996–1999).

Shih, F., & Wu, Y. (2005). Decomposition of binary morphological structuring elements based on genetic algorithms. *Computer Vision and Image Understanding, 99*, 291–302.

Sivakumar, K., Patel, M., Kehtarnavaz, N., Balagurunathan, Y., & Dougherty, E. (2000). A constant-time algorithm for erosions/dilations with applications to morphological texture feature computation. *Journal of Real-Time Imaging, 6*, 223–239.

Soille, P. (2002). Morphological texture analysis: an introduction. In *Morphology of condensed matter, 600*, 215–237. Springer-Verlag.

Soille, P. (2003). *Morphological image analysis : Principles and applications.* Berlin: Springer-Verlag.

Soille, P., & Talbot, H. (2001, November). Directional morphological filtering. *IEEE Transactions on Pattern Analysis and Machine Intelligence, 23*(11), 1313–1329.

Southam, P., & Harvey, R. (2005). Texture granularities. In *IAPR International Conference on Image Analysis and Processing (ICIAP), 3617*, 304–311. Springer-Verlag.

Su, H., Crookes, D., & Bouridane, A. (2007). Shoeprint image retrieval by topological and pattern spectra. In *International Machine Vision and Image Processing Conference* (pp. 15–22).

Sudo, K., Yamato, J., & Tomono, A. (1996). Determining gender of walking people using multiple sensors. In *International Conference on Multisensor Fusion and Integration for Intelligent Systems* (pp. 641–646).

Summers, R., Agcaoili, C., McAuliffe, M., Dalal, S., Yim, P., Choyke, P., et al. (2001). Helical CT of von Hippel-Lindau: semi-automated segmentation of renal lesions. In *IEEE International Conference on Image Processing (ICIP)* (pp. 293–296).

Tang, X. (1998). Multiple competitive learning network fusion for object classification. *IEEE Transactions on Systems, Man, and Cybernetics, 28*(4), 532–543.

Theera-Umpon, N., & Dhompongsa, S. (2007, May). Morphological granulometric features of nucleus in automatic bone marrow white blood cell classification. *IEEE Transactions on Information Technology in Biomedicine, 11*(3), 353–359.

Tushabe, F., &Wilkinson, M. (2007). Content-based image retrieval using shape-size pattern spectra. In *Cross Language Evaluation Forum 2007 Workshop, Imageclef Track*. Budapest, Hungary.

Tzafestas, C., & Maragos, P. (2002). Shape connectivity: multiscale analysis and application to generalized granulometries. *Journal of Mathematical Imaging and Vision, 17*, 109–129.

Urbach, E., Roerdink, J., & Wilkinson, M. (2007, February). Connected shape-size pattern spectra for rotation and scale-invariant classification of gray-scale images. *IEEE Transactions on Pattern Analysis and Machine Intelligence, 29*(2), 272–285.

Urbach, E., & Wilkinson, M. (2008, January). Efficient 2-d grayscale morphological transformations with arbitrary flat structuring elements. *IEEE Transactions on Image Processing, 17*(1), 1–8.

Vanrell, M., & Vitria, J. (1997). Optimal 3 x 3 decomposable disks for morphological transformations. *Image and Vision Computing, 15*, 845–854.

Velloso, M., Carneiro, T., & Souza, F. D. (2007). Pattern sepctra for texture segmentation of gray-scale images. In *International Conference on Intelligent Systems Design and Applications* (pp. 347–352).

Vincent, L. (1993). Grayscale area openings and closings: their applications and efficient implementation. In *EURASIP Workshop on Mathematical Morphology and its Applications to Signal Processing* (pp. 22–27). Barcelona, Spain.

Vincent, L. (2000, January). Granulometries and opening trees. *Fundamenta Informaticae, 41*(1-2), 57–90.

Wada, S., Yoshizaki, S., Kondoh, H., & Furutani-Seiki, M. (2003). Efficient neural network classifier of medaka embryo using morphological pattern spectrum. In *International Conference on Neural Networks and Signal Processing* (pp. 220–223).

Wang, X., Li, Y., & Shang, Y. (2006). Measurement of microcapsules using morphological operators. In *IEEE International Conference on Signal Processing*.

Welk, M. (2003). Families of generalised morphological scale spaces. In *Scale Space Methods in Computer Vision,2695*, pp. 770–784. Springer-Verlag.

Werman, M., & Peleg, S. (1985, November). Min-max operators in texture analysis. *IEEE Transactions on Pattern Analysis and Machine Intelligence, 7*(6), 730–733.

Wilkinson, M. (2007). Attribute-space connectivity and connected filters. *Image and Vision Computing*, *25*, 426–435.

Wilkinson, M. H. F. (2002, August). Generalized pattern spectra sensitive to spatial information. In *IAPR International Conference on Pattern Recognition (ICPR)*, *1*, 21–24. Quebec City, Canada.

Witkin, A. (1983). Scale-space filtering. In *International Joint Conference on Artificial Intelligence* (pp. 1019–1022). Karlsruhe, Germany.

Xiaoqi, Z., & Baozong, Y. (1995). Shape description and recognition using the high order morphological pattern spectrum. *Pattern Recognition*, *28*(9), 1333-1340.

Yang, H., & Lee, S. (2005, April). Decomposition of morphological structuring elements with integer linear programming. *IEE Proceedings on Vision, Image and Signal Processing*, *152*(2), 148–154.

Yang, S., Wang, C., & Wang, X. (2007). Smoothing algorithm based on multi-scale morphological reconstruction for footprint image. In *International Conference on Innovative Computing, Information and Control*.

Yi, Z., Gangyi, J., & Yong, C. (1996). Research of oriented pattern spectrum. In *IEEE International Conference on Signal Processing*.

You, Y., & Yu, H. (2004). A separating algorithm based on granulometry for overlapping circular cell images. In *International Conference on Intelligent Mechatronics and Automation* (pp. 244–248).

Yunpeng, L., Fangcheng, L., & Yanqing, L. (2005). Pattern recognition of partial discharge based on its pattern spectrum. In *International Symposium on Electrical Insulating Materials* (pp. 763–766).

Zapater, V., Martinez-Costa, L., Ayala, G., & Domingo, J. (2002). Classifying human endothelial cells based on individual granulometric size distributions. *Image and Vision Computing*, *20*, 783–791.

Zhuang, X., & Haralick, R. (1986). Morphological structuring element decomposition. *Computer Vision, Graphics and Image Processing*, *35*, 370–382.

Zingman, I., Meir, R., & El-Yaniv, R. (2007). Size-density spectra and their application to image classification. *Pattern Recognition*, *40*, 3336–3348.

Chapter III
Face Recognition and Semantic Features

Huiyu Zhou
Brunel University, UK

Yuan Yuan
Aston University, UK

Chunmei Shi
People's Hospital of Guangxi, China

ABSTRACT

The authors present a face recognition scheme based on semantic features' extraction from faces and tensor subspace analysis. These semantic features consist of eyes and mouth, plus the region outlined by three weight centres of the edges of these features. The extracted features are compared over images in tensor subspace domain. Singular value decomposition is used to solve the eigenvalue problem and to project the geometrical properties to the face manifold. They compare the performance of the proposed scheme with that of other established techniques, where the results demonstrate the superiority of the proposed method.

INTRODUCTION

Face recognition and modeling is a vital problem of prime interest in computer vision. Its applications have been commonly discovered in surveillance, information retrieval and human-computer interface. For decades studies on face recognition have addressed the problem of interpreting faces by machine, their efforts over time leading to a considerable understanding of this research area and rich practical applications. However, in spite of their impressive performance, the established face recognition systems to some extent exhibit deficiency in the cases of partial occlusion, illumination changes, etc. This is due to the fact that these systems mainly rely on the low-level attributes (e.g. color, texture, shape, and motion), which may change significantly and then lose effectiveness in the presence of image occlusion or illumination variations.

Classical image-based face recognition algorithms can be categorised into appearance- and model-based. The former normally consists of linear (using basis vectors) and non-linear analysis. These approaches represent an object using raw intensity images, being considered as high-dimensional vectors. For example, Beymer (Beymer, 1993) described a pose estimation algoithm to align the probe images to candidate poses of the gallery subjects. Pentland *et al.* (Pentland et al, 1994) compared the performance of a parametric eigenspace with view-based eigenspaces. The latter includes 2-D or 3-D model based schemes, where the facial variations with prior knowledge are encoded in a model to be constructed. Examples can be found in (Cootes et al, 2002; Lanitis, et al, 1997; Romdhani et al, 1999).

As one of the linear appearance algorithms, the well-known Eigenface algorithm (Turk & Pentland, 1991) uses the principal component analysis (PCA) for dimensionality reduction in order to find the best vectorised components that represent the faces in the entire image space. The face vectors are projected to the basis vectors so that the projection coefficients are used as the feature representation of each face image (Turk & Pentland, 1991). Another example of the linear appearance approaches is the application of Independent component analysis (ICA). ICA is very similar to PCA except that the distribution of the components is assumed to be non-Gaussian. One of these ICA based algorithms is the FastICA scheme that utilised the InfoMax algorithm (Draper et al, 2003). The Fisherface algorithm (Belhumeur et al, 1996), derived from the Fisher Linear Discriminant (FLD), defines different classes with different statistics. Faces with similar statistics will be grouped together by FLD rules. Tensorface (Vasilescu & Terzopoulos, 2003) recruits a higher-order tensor to describe the set of face images and extend singular value decomposition (SVD) to the higher-order tensor data. Non-linear appearance algorithms, such as principal component analysis (KPCA) (Yang, 2002), ISOMAP (Tenebaum et al, 2000) and Local Linear Embedding (LLE) (Roweis & Saul, 2000), have much more complicated process than the linear ones. Unlike the classical PCA, KPCA uses more eigenvector projections than the input dimensionality. Meanwhile, ISOMAP and LLE have been well established with stable topologically rendering capability.

Model-based face recognition normally contains three steps: model construction, model fitting to the face images, and similarity check by evaluation of the model parameters. An Active Appearance Model (AAM) is a statistical model that integrates shape variations with the appearance in a shape-normalized frame (Edwards et al, 1998). Model parameters are rendered so that the difference between the synthesized model and the face image can be minimized. Face matches will be found after this minimisation has been reached. 3-D facial information can be used to better describe the faces in the existence of illumination and pose changes, where 2-D descriptors sometimes turn out to be less effective. One example is reported in (Blanz et al, 2002). In this work, a 3-D morphable face model fusing shape and texture was proposed, and an algorithm for extracting the model parameters was established as well.

Traditional approaches as shown above do not directly extract or use the semantic descriptors of the faces, e.g. positions and length of eyes, eyebrows, mouth or nose. These semantic features inherently encode facial geometric properties (e.g. scaling, rotation, translation, and shearing) (Hsu & Jain, 2002). If these semantic components were applied, then the similarity check between a face image and its counterpart in the database might become much easier. These semantic facial features can be detected using spectral or temporal analysis (Hsu & Jain, 2002)]. Although the concept of semantic face recognition

Figure 1. Examples of face images in ORL database

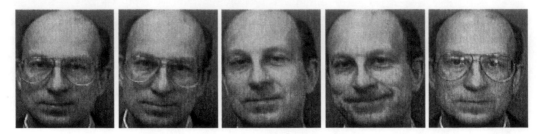

has been raised for years, a little work has been done so far. For example, Hsu and Jain (Hsu & Jain, 2003) introduced a semantic face graph for describing the properties of facial components. This is an extension work of (Hsu and Jain, 2002), and used interactive snakes to extract those facial features, e.g. eyes, mouth, etc. Martinez (Martinez, 2000) reported a new approach that considered facial expressions for the improvement of classification.

In this paper, we take advantage of the contribution of the semantic descriptors in the domain of tensor analysis for face recognition. The proposed algorithm deploys the established tensor subspace analysis (TSA) (Martinez, 2000), where an image of size n1×n2 is treated as a second order tensor in the tensor space of $R^{n_1} \oplus R^{n_2}$. TSA is used so as to find an optimal projection, representing the geometrical structure, that linearly approximates the face manifold in the domain of local isometry.

EIGENFACE BASED FACE RECOGNITION

Eigenface is a set of eigenvectors used for human face recognition. This approach was originally developed by Turk and Pentland (Turk & Pentland, 1991). The eigenvectors can be derived from the covariance matrix of the probability distribution of the high-dimensional vector space of possible faces of people. Let a face image $I(x,y)$ be a two dimensional N by N array of intensity values. An image can also be treated as a vector of dimension N^2. An image is then mapped to this huge vector space. Principal component analysis is then used to find the vectors that most fits the distribution of the face image within this space. Examples of face images are illustrated in Fig. 1.

Let the training set of the face images be T_1, T_2, T_3,....T_M The mean of this training data set is required in order to calculate the covariance matrix or eigenvectors. The average face is calculated as

$$\psi = (1/M)\sum_1^M T_i.$$

Each image in the data set has dissimilarity to the average face expressed by the vector $\Phi = Ti - \Psi$.

The covariance matrix is

$$C = (1/M)\sum_1^M \varphi_i \varphi_i^T = AA^T (1)$$

where $A = [\varphi_1, \varphi_2,...,\varphi_M]$. The matrix C is a N^2 by N^2 matrix and will generate N^2 eigenvectors and eigenvalues. It is very difficult to achieve calculation on an image of sizes 256 by 256 or even less due to the computational efforts.

A computationally feasible method is to compute the eigenvectors instead. If the number of images in the training set is less than the number of pixels in an image (i.e. $M < N^2$), then we can solve an M by M matrix instead of solving a N^2 by N^2 matrix. Consider the covariance matrix as $A^T A$ instead of AA^T. Now the eigenvector v_i can be calculated as follows,

$$AA^T v_i = \mu_i v_i, \tag{2}$$

where μ_i is the eigenvalue. Here the size of covariance matrix is M by M. We then have m eigenvectors instead of N^2. Multiplying Equation 2 by A, we have

$$AA^T A v_i = \mu_i A v_i. \tag{3}$$

The right hand side of the above equation brings us M eigenfaces of N^2 by 1. Such a process leads to an image space of dimensionality M.

Since an approximate reconstruction of the face is intended, we can reduce the dimensionality to M' instead of M. This is performed by selecting M' eigenfaces, which have the largest associated eigenvalues. These eigenfaces now span a M'-dimensional subspace instead of N^2.

A new image T is transformed into its eigenface components (projected into 'face space') by the following operation,

$$w_k = u_k^T (T - \psi), \tag{4}$$

where k = 1,2,....M'. The weights obtained as above constitute a vector $\Omega_T = [w_1, w_2, w_3, ..., w_M]$ that describes the contribution of each eigenface in representing the input face image. This vector can be used in a standard classification algorithm to explore the best shot in the database that describes the income face image. The face class in the database is formulated by averaging the weight vectors for the images of one individual. the face classes will depend on the overall images where subjects wear spectacles. With this face class, classification can be made if the subject has spectacles or not. The Euclidean distance of the weight vector of the new image from the face class weight vector can be calculated as follows,

$$\varepsilon_k = \| \Omega - \Omega_k \|, \tag{5}$$

where Ω_k is a vector representing the kth face class. Euclidean distance formula can be found in (Turk & Pentland, 1991). The face is classified as belonging to class k when the distance ε_k is below some

Figure 2. Eigenfaces of the examples shown in Figure 1

threshold value $\theta\varepsilon$. Otherwise the face is classified as unknown. Also it can be found whether an image is a face image or not by simply finding the squared distance between the mean adjusted input image and its projection onto the face space.

$$\varepsilon^2 = \|\varphi - \varphi_f\|, \tag{6}$$

where ϕ_f is the face space and $\Phi = Ti - \Psi$ is the mean adjusted input. Using this criterion, we can classify the image as known face image, unknown face image and not a face image. Fig. 2 denotes the eigenfaces of Fig. 1.

Recently, research attention is focused on dimensionality reduction. One of the examples is the work established by Gunturk et al. (Gunturk et al, 2003), where they proposed to transfer the super-resolution reconstruction from pixel domain to a lower dimensional face space. This dimensional reduction was based on the Karhunnen-Loeve Transformation (KLT). In the meantime, Yang *et al.* (Yang et al, 2004) proposed a new technique coined two-dimensional PCA. As opposed to traditional PCA techniques, this new approach was based on 2D image matrices rather than 1D vector so the image matrix does not have to be transformed into a vector prior to feature extraction. Alternatively, an image covariance matrix is constructed using the original image matrices and the eigenvectors were derived for image feature extraction. Zhao and Yang (Zhao & Yang, 1999) proposed a new method to compute the scatter matrix using three images each taken with different lighting conditions to account for arbitrary illumination effects. Pentland et al. (Pentland et al, 1994) extended their early work on eigenfaces to modular eigenfeatures corresponding to face components, such as the eyes, nose, and mouth (referred to as eigeneyes, eigennose, and eigenmouth).

FISHERFACE BASED FACE RECOGNITION

Fisherface works in a combinatorial scheme, where one performs dimensionality reduction using linear projection and then applies Fisher's Linear Discriminant (FLD) (Fisher, 1936) for classification in the reduced feature space. This approach intends to find an optimal projection where the ration of the between-class scatter and the within-class scatter is maximized (Belhumeur et al, 1996). Let the between-class scatter matrix be

$$S_B = \sum_{i=1}^{C} N_i (\mu_i - \mu)(\mu_i - \mu)^T, \tag{7}$$

and the within-class scatter matrix is defined as

$$S_W = \sum_{i=1}^{C} \sum_{X_K \in X_i} (X_k - \mu_i)(X_k - \mu_i)^T, \tag{8}$$

where μ_i is the mean image of class X_i, and N_i is the sample number in class X_i. If S_W is non-singular, the optimal projection W_o will be the one with orthonormal columns that satisfy the following equation,

$$W_o = \underset{W}{\operatorname{argmax}} \frac{|W^T S_B W|}{|W^T S_W W|} = [W_1, W_2, \ldots, W_m],$$ (9)

where W_i ($i = 1,2,\ldots,m$) is a set of generalised eigenvectors of S_B and S_W corresponding to the m largest eigenvalues λ_i, equivalently,

$$S_B W_i = \lambda_i S_W W_i, \, i = 1, 2, \ldots, m.$$ (10)

In real cases of face recognition, the within-class matrix SW is normally singular. This is due to the fact that rank of SW is at most $N - c$, and the number of images in the learning set N is smaller than that of image pixels. To tackle this problem, Fisherfaces uses PCA to reduce the dimension of the feature space to $N - c$, and then employs a standard FLD scheme to reduce the dimension to $c - 1$. Therefore, the optimal projection matrix is

$$W_0^T = W_{FLD}^T W_{PCA}^T,$$ (11)

Where

$$W_{PCA} = \underset{W}{\operatorname{arg\,max}} |W^T S_T W|$$

$$W_{FLD} = \underset{W}{\operatorname{arg\,max}} \frac{|W^T W_{PCA}^T S_B W_{PCA} W|}{|W^T W_{PCA}^T S_W W_{PCA} W|}.$$ (12)

$WPCA$ is optimised over $[n, (N - c)]$ matrices with orthonormal columns while $WFLD$ is optimised over $[(N - c), m]$ matrices with orthonormal columns. Such a procedure can be illustrated in Fig. 3. Fig. 4 illustrates the exemplar outcomes of Fisherface.

TENSOR SUBSPACE ANALYSIS

Let us start with the problem of linear dimensionality reduction. One of the common approaches is the use of Laplacian eigenmap with the objective function as follows:

$$\min_f \sum_{i,j} (f(x_i) - f(x_j))^2 S_{ij},$$ (13)

where S denotes the similarity matrix, and x is the functional variables, e.g. image vectors.

Let the face data set be $X_1, \ldots, X_m$ in the space $R^{n_1} \oplus R^{n_2}$. If a face image X matches its template Y in the database, then we can decompose Y into the multiplication of U, V and X, where U and V have size $n_1 \times l_1$ and $n_2 \times l_2$, respectively. In fact, we shall have $Y_i = U^T X_i V$.

Given m data points from the face sub-manifold $\mathbf{M} \in R^{n_1} \oplus R^{n_2}$, we intend to find a nearest graph $\mathbf{G}$ to simulate the geometry of $\mathbf{M}$. The similarity matrix S can be

Figure 3. Illustration of PCA and FLD in between-class and inter-class discrimination with orthonormal columns

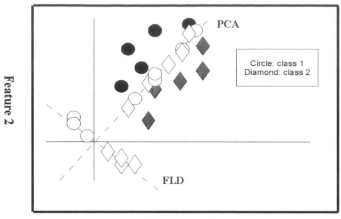

Figure 4. Fisherface examples of Figure 1

$$S_{ij} = \begin{cases} \exp^{-\frac{\|x_i - x_j\|^2}{e}}, & if \; \| x_i - x_j \| \leq \eta, \\ o & otherwise. \end{cases} \qquad (14)$$

where c is a constant and $\|.\|$ is the Frobenius form. Eq. (1) is equivalent to the following form:

$$\min_{U,V} \sum_{i,j} \| U^T X_i V - U^T X_j V \|^2 S_{ij}, \qquad (15)$$

Let **D** be a diagonal matrix with $D_{ii} = \Sigma_j S_{i,j}$. Then we can have the following representation:

$$(\sum_{i,j} \| U^T X_i V - U^T X_j V \|^2 S_{ij})/2 = tr(\sum_i D_{ii} Y_i Y_i^T - \sum_{i,j} S_{ij} Y_i Y_{ji}^T)$$

$$\cong tr(U^T (D_V - S_V)U), \qquad (16)$$

where

$$D_V = \sum_i D_u X_i^T V V^T X_i^T \tag{17}$$

and

$$S_V = \sum_i S_{ii} X_i^T V V^T X_j^T \tag{18}$$

Similarly, we have

$$(\sum_{i,j} \| U^T X_i V - U^T X_j V \|^2 S_{ij}) / 2 \cong tr(V^T (D_U - S_U) V), \tag{18}$$

where

$$D_U = \sum_i D_{ii} X_i^T U U^T X_i^T \tag{19}$$

and

$$S_U - \sum_i S_{ii} X_i^T U U^T X_j^T \tag{20}$$

To find an optimal face match, we have to minimise $tr(V^T(D_V - S_V)V)$ together with $tr(V^T(D_U - S_U)V)$.

Large global variance on the manifold may help the discrimination of different data sets. As a result, during the face recognition we amplify the similarity distance in the feature space. This leads to the following relationship:

$$var(Y) = \sum_i \| Y_i \|^2 D_i = tr(V^T D_U V), \tag{21}$$

assuming a zero mean distribution. We also have another similar form as follows:

$$var(Y) = \sum_i tr(Y_i Y_i^T) D_{ii} = tr(U^T D_V U). \tag{22}$$

Through the analysis above, a matched face in the database is subject to the following constraint

$$\begin{cases} \min_{U,V} (\dfrac{tr(U^T(D_V - S_V)U)}{tr(U^T D_V U)}) \\ \min_{U,V} (\dfrac{tr(V^T(D_U - S_U)V)}{tr(V^T D_U V)}). \end{cases} \tag{23}$$

Eq. 23 cannot be easily dealt with due to the computational cost. A simpler solution to this optimisation problem has been found as follows. Firstly, U is fixed; V can be computed by solving a generalized eigenvector problem:

$$(D_U - S_U)\hat{V} = \lambda D_U \hat{V}. \tag{24}$$

Once V is available, we then update U by this eigenvector process: d, V can be computed by solving a generalized eigenvector problem,

$$(D_V - S_V)\hat{U} = \lambda D_V \hat{U}. \tag{25}$$

Repeating this procedure, we eventually have an appropriate solution. Note that initially U is set to be identity matrix. Figs. 5-6 show exemplar Laplacianfaces and Tensorfaces of Fig. 1.

SEMANTIC FACE GRAPH

A semantic face graph consists of necessary components that denote a high-level description of a face and its bound contents. A semantic face graph is illustrated in Fig. 7. In this chapter, we only focus on the use of left and right eyes and mouth in 2-D, although generic semantic components contain eyes, eyebrow, mouth, nose, hair and face boundary/outline. The reason to extract these three aspects is that their extraction or detection has now become well developed so these components can play a reliable and stable role in the recognition stage.

Suppose that we have a semantic face graph G_0. Let H be the entire set of semantic facial components, and H_P is a subset of H including three components in the current work (i.e. left and right eyes and mouth). G is the 2-D projection of H_P. The detected edge/boundary coordinates of G are denoted by $(x_i(n), y_i(n))$, where $n = 0,1,..., N_i\text{-}1$ (vertices of the components) and $i = 1,2,3$.

To proceed the discussion, we assume that edges/boundaries of these three semantic components have been obtained. The absolute and relative positions of the three semantic components are so important

Figure 5. Laplacianface examples of Figure 1

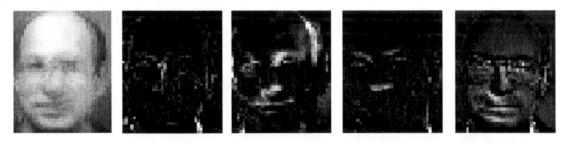

Figure 6. Tensorface examples of Figure 1

Figure 7. Illustration of a semantic face graph: (a) generic semantic descriptors depicted by edges, and (b) eyes and mouth detection (red ellipses).

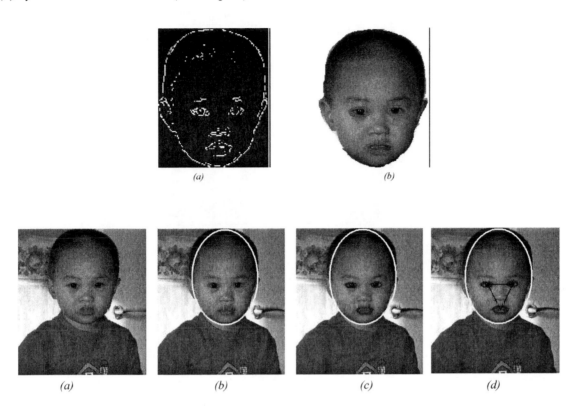

that they will be calculated and stored for later applications, e.g. (Huang & Chen, 1992). In addition, in order to enhance the face recognition, the region outlined by the weight centres of these three edges needs to be evaluated in terms of its intensity and colour histogram, e.g. (Tjahyadi et al, 2007). This histogram especially helps reduce mis-classification rates in the case of facial rotation.

First of all, a Canny edge detector (Canny, 1986) was applied to extract edges/contours from a face image. This is followed by the dilation and erosion operation for connected curves (Gonzlez & Woods, 1992). An eye/mouth detection algorithm, similar to the method reported in (Huang & Chen, 1992), will be used to extract these three features. Physiological evidence can be used in this eye/mouth extraction stage for the purpose of simplicity. For instance, the position of the left eyebrow is about one-fourth of the facial width. Localising the positions of two eyes will make the extraction of the mouth much easier. For example, the lip is of higher intensity than the surrounding areas. Finally, weight centre of individual curves are computed.

As an example, Fig. 8 demonstrates the working flow as described above. Corresponding to Fig. 8, Fig. 9 shows the intensity histogram of the triangle area outlined by the three semantic components. This histogram can be used as a feature for similarity check of face images. Similarly, Fig. 10 shows the intensity histograms of 1-4 images shown in Fig. 1.

Fig. 8 Illustration of determination of semantic features: (a) original face image, (b) face detection, (c) morphological results, and (d) weight centres of three semantic components.

INTEGRATION OF SEMANTIC WITH TSA

Let us denote appearance and semantic components of a face image by $X = [X_a, X_s]$. We also assume location and scale independence are available, given a relation model θ to match X and Y. Then we can have the joint probability of the image similarity

$$p(X,Y|\theta) = p(Y|\hat{\theta})\prod_k p(X^k|Y,\theta) = p(Y|\hat{\theta})\prod_k p(X_a^k|\theta^k)p(X_s^k|Y^k,\theta^k).$$

(26)

Gaussianity assumptions will lead to the following forms:

$$\begin{cases} p(X_a^k|\theta^k) = N(X_a^k|\mu_a^k,\sigma_a^k), \\ p(X_s^k|Y^k,\theta^k) = N((\log X_s^k)-\log(\theta)|\mu_s^k,\sigma_s^k), \end{cases}$$

(27)

where N denotes the Gaussian density with mean μ and covariance matrix θ. Finding a match between the two face images is equivalent to seeking the maximisation as follows:

$$\max(\log p(X|Y,\theta^k)).$$

(28)

The similarity matrix S, shown before, can possess the following form:

$$S = \sum_i w_i \exp(-\|X_i - X_j\|^2 / c).$$

(29)

That is to say, similarity distance now will be computed by weighting the most dominant features in the feature space. If the semantic features can better describe the relationship between two images,

Figure 9. Intensity histogram of the triangle area outlined in Figure 8(d)

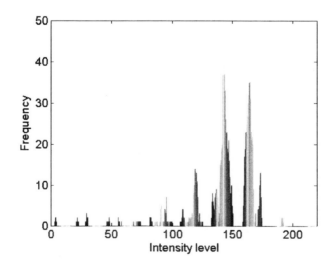

then these features will be kept for the similarity check. Otherwise, the appearance model parameters in the TSA model will be used instead.

In terms of the selection of weights, we here employ the Euclidean distance between two groups of image points/structures,

$$
w_i = \begin{cases} \exp^{-\frac{\|x_s^i - x_s^j\|^2}{c}} & if \; \| x_s^i - x_s^j \| \le d, \\ 0 & othrwise. \end{cases}
$$

(30)

Before starting, we tend to more trust the appearance components with larger weights. This assignment will be automatically updated once the dimensionality reduction is iterated.

EXPERIMENTAL WORK

In this section, we evaluate the proposed semantic based TSA scheme for face recognition. This proposed algorithm is compared with the Eigenface, Fisherface, Laplacianface and classical TSA algorithms. Two face databases were used, following the experimental configuration in (He et al, 2005; Zhou et al, 2008). The first database is the PIE from CMU, and the second one is the ORL database. In the experiments, pre-processing for obtaining good faces was performed. Faces were extracted by our method and these images were cropped in order to create a 32x32 size. The image is represented as a 1024-dimensional vector, and the classical TSA and semantic based algorithms used 32x32-dimensional matrix. The purpose of this evaluation is to (1) train the face recognition systems; (2) a new face image is projected to d-dimensional subspace (e.g. PCA, ICA, and LPP) or ($d \times d$ -dimensional tensor subspace; and (3) the nearest neighbour classifier was applied for face identification. The overall experiments were conducted on a PC with a 1.5 GHz Intel(R) Pentium(R) CPU and Matlab implementation.

Fig. 10 denotes some image frames of the ORL database. Figs. 12-15 show the outcomes using the Eigenface, Fisherface, Laplacianface and Tensorface approaches, respectively.

PIE Experiments

The CMU PIE database consists of 68 subjects with about 41,000 face images. In spite of its rich image background, we choose the five front poses (C05, C07, C09, C27, C29) with different illuminations and facial expressions. For individual persons, 5, 10, 20, 30 images are randomly selected for the training stage. The training process engaged is very similar to that reported in (He et al, 2005).

Fig. 7 illustrates the plots of error rate versus dimensionality reduction for the Eigenface, Fisherface, Laplacianface, TSA and semantic methods. It shows that as the number of dimensions varies, the performance of all the algorithms is changed. We also observe that the proposed semantic based approach performs better than any of the others with different numbers of training samples (5,10,20,30) per face. Table 1 tabulates the running time in seconds of each algorithm. It shows that the semantic and TSA based methods have more efficient computational capability.

Figure 10. Intensity histogram of 1-4 images shown in Fig. 1, given the triangulation areas outlined by eyes and noses

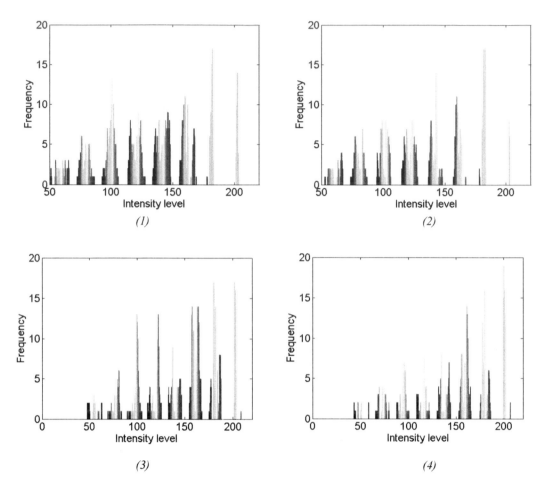

Table 1. Performance comparison of different algorithms on PIE database

Algorithm	5 Train			20 Train		
	Error	Dim	Time(s)	Error	Dim	Time(s)
Semantic	24.5%	136	0.64	10.7%	178	7.0
TSA	28.9%	121	0.61	11.2%	169	7.23
Eigenface	66.8%	242	0.83	47.0%	627	12.9
Fisherface	32.6%	61	1.62	14.8%	62	27.7
Laplacianface	31.5%	61	1.77	15.6%	148	29.9

Figure 11. Examples of ORL database

ORL Experiments

The ORL database contains 400 face images with 40 people (10 different views per person). The images were collected at different times and some people possess different expressions and facial details. For example, glasses were worn in some cases. The experimental setup is the same as shown in the last subsection. Fig. 8 plots the error rate versus dimensionality reduction for the individual methods. Again, the proposed semantic algorithm outperforms other methods due to faster convergence and less error rates.

The computational speeds have been tabulated in Table 2, where clearly the proposed algorithm becomes more efficient as more trains were applied, compared to other methods. Note that in this table the computational time is in millisecond.

CONCLUSIONS AND FUTURE WORK

We have presented a method for face recognition, based on the extraction of semantic features and a TSA method. This approach considers three semantic features, i.e. left and right eyes and mouth, which encode the geometrical properties of the faces inherently. A probabilistic strategy is recruited to fuse the extracted semantic features into the TSA scheme. In fact, TSA is applied to iterate the optimisation process so as to seek the best matches in the database. Furthermore, TSA solves the eigenvector problem via SVD so the entire system works very fast. In recognition tasks, our method compares favourably

Table 2. Performance comparison of different algorithms on ORL database

Algorithm	2 Train			5 Train		
	Error	Dim	Time(s)	Error	Dim	Time(s)
Semantic	22.7%	118	71.0	6.3%	118	353.4
TSA	23.8%	100	62.5	7.0%	100	407.2
Eigenface	31.2%	88	44.2	8.6%	146	301.3
Fisherface	24.8%	30	64.3	7.8%	36	344.5
Laplacianface	24.5%	40	54.7	8.2%	42	411.2

Figure 12. Eigenface of the exemplar images shown in Figure 10

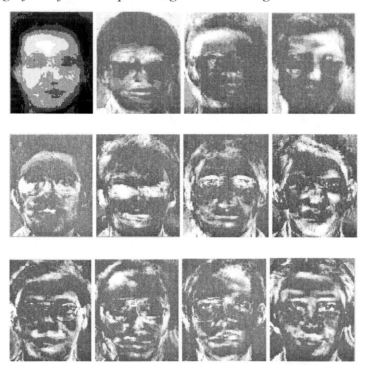

with several established dimensionality reduction methods. In efficiency task its performance has been verified to be competitive.

While our recognition results are optimistic, we recognise that the recognition performance of the proposed approach relies on better feature extraction and representation. Therefore, in some cases such as significantly large illumination changes the proposed method may not be so favourable due to unstable

Figure 13. Fisherface of the exemplar images shown in Figure 10

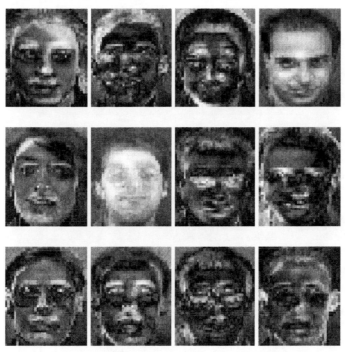

Figure 14. Laplacianface of the exemplar images shown in Figure 10

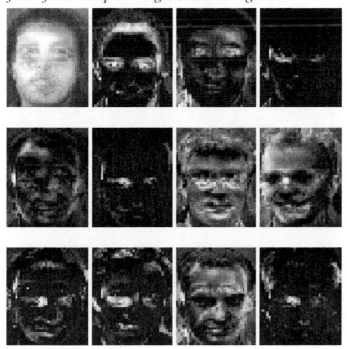

Figure 15. Tensorface of the exemplar images shown in Figure 10

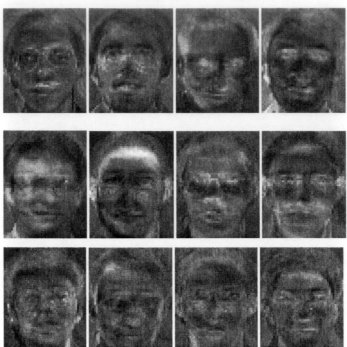

Figure 16. Error rates against dimensionality reduction on PIE database

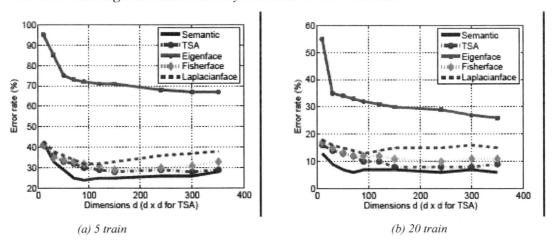

(a) 5 train   (b) 20 train

and inaccurate eye/mouth localisation. In these circumstances, 3-D model based face recognition may be of better performance due to its less sensitivity to the light changes or occlusions. However, 3-D modelling demands expensive computational efforts. Our future work shall be focused on the compromise between the efficiency and accuracy improvement using a 3-D model based scheme. Although this type of work has been started by other researchers, up to date a complete success has not been achieved yet. We intend to continue our research along this direction.

Figure 17. Error rates against dimensionality reduction on ORL database

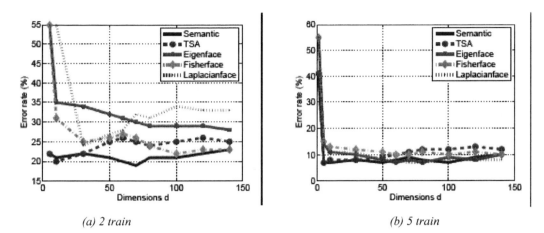

(a) 2 train   (b) 5 train

REFERENCES

Belhumeur, P., Hespanha, J., & Kriegman, D. (1996). Eigenfaces vs. Fisherfaces: recognition using class specific linear projection. In *Proc. Of European Conference on Computer Vision*, (pp. 45-58).

Beymer, D. (1993). *Face recognition under varying pose*. Technical Report AIM-1461. MIT AI Laboratory.

Blanz, V., Rornhani, S., & Vetter, T. (2002). Face identification across different poses and illuminations with a 3D morphable model. In *Proc. of IEEE International Conference on Automatic Face and Gesture Recognition*, (pp. 202-207).

Canny, J. (1986). *A computational approach to edge detection. IEEE Trans. Patt. Analysis and Mach. Intell.*, *8*(6), 679-698.

Cootes, T., Wheeler, G., Walker, K., & Taylor, C. (2002). View-based active appearance model. *Image and Vision Computing, 20*, 657-664.

Draper, B., Baek, K., Bartlett, M., & Beveridge, J. (2003). Recognising faces with PCA and ICA. *Comuter Vision and Image Understanding, 91*(1-2), 115-137.

Edwards, G., Cootes, T., & Taylor, C. (1998). Face recognition using active appearance models. In *Proc. of European Conference on Computer Vision*, (pp. 581-595).

Fisher, R.A. (1936). The Use of Multiple Measures in Taxonomic Problems. *Ann. Eugenics, 7*, 179-188.

Gonzalez, R. & Woods, R. (1992). *Digital image processing.*Reading, MA, USA: Addison Wesley.

Gunturk, B.K., Batur, A.U., Altunbasak, Y., Kayes, M.H., & Mersereau, R.M. (2003). Eigenface-domain super-resolution for face recognition. *IEEE Trans. On Image Proc., 12*(5), 597-606.

He, X., Cai, D., & Niyogi, P. (2005). Tensor subspace analysis. In *Proc. of Advances in Neural Information Processing*, (p. 18).

Hsu, R., & Jain, A. (2002). *Semantic face matching*. In *Proc. of IEEE International Conference on Multimedia and Expo*, (pp. 145-148).

Hsu, R., & Jain, A. (2003). Generating discriminating Carton faces using interacting snakes. *IEEE Trans. on Patter. Recogn. And Machine Intell.*, *25*(11), 1388-1398.

Huang, C., & Chen, C. (1992). Human facial feature extraction for face interpretation and recognition. *Pattern Recognition*, *25*(12), 1435-1444.

Lanitis, A., Taylor, C., & Cootes, T. (1997). Automatic interpretation and coding of face images using flexible models. *IEEE Trans. Patter. Analy. And Mach. Intell.*, *19*(7), 743-756.

Martinez, A. (2000). Semantic access of frontal face images: the expression-invariant problem. In *Proc. of IEEE Workshop on Content-based access of images and video libraries*.

Pentland, A., Moghaddam, B., & Starner, T. (1994). View-based and modular eigenspaces for face recognition. In Proc. Of the IEEE Conf. on Comput. Vis. and Patter. Recog., (pp. 84-91).

Romdhani, S., Gong, S., & Psarrou, A. (1999). A multi-view nonlinear active shape model using kernel PCA. In *Proc. of 10th British Machine Vision Conference*, (pp. 483-492).

Roweis, S., & Saul, L. (2000). Nonlinear dimensionality reduction by locally linear embeddings. *Science, 290*, 2323-2326.

Tenebaum, B., Silva, V., & Langford, J. (2000). A global geometric framework for nonlinear dimensionality. *Science, 290*, 23190-2323.

Tjahyadi, R., Liu, W., An, S., & Venkatesh, S. (2007). Face recognition via the overlapping energy histogram. In *Proc. of International Conf. on Arti. Intell.*, (pp. 2891-2896).

Turk, M., & Pentland, A. (1991). Eigenfaces for recognition. *Journal of Cognitive Neuroscience, 3*(1), 71-86.

Vasilescu, M., & Terzopoulos, D. (2003). Multilinear subspace analysis for image ensembles. In *Proc. Of Intl. Conf. On Compt. Vis. and Patter. Recog.*, (pp. 93-99).

Yang, M.-H. (2002). Kernel eigenfaces vs. kernel fisherfaces: Face recognition using kernel methods. *International Conf. on Auto. Face and Gest. Recog.*, (pp. 215-220).

Yang, J., Zhang, D., Frangi, A.F., & Yang, J. (2004). Two-*dimensional PCA: a new approach to appearance-based face representation and recognition. IEEE Trans. on Patt. Analy. And Mach. Intellig.*, *26*(1), 131-137.

Zhao, L., & Yang, Y.H. (1999). Theoretical analysis of illumination in PCA-based vision systems. *Pattern Recogn.*, *32*(4), 547-564.

Zhou, H., Yuan, Y., & Sadka, A.H. (2008). Application of semantic features in face recognition. *Pattern Recognition, 41*, 3251-3256.

Section II
Learning in Multimedia Information Organization

Chapter IV
Shape Matching for Foliage Database Retrieval

Haibin Ling
Temple University, USA

David W. Jacobs
University of Maryland, USA

ABSTRACT

Computer-aided foliage image retrieval systems have the potential to dramatically speed up the process of plant species identification. Despite previous research, this problem remains challenging due to the large intra-class variability and inter-class similarity of leaves. This is particularly true when a large number of species are involved. In this chapter, the authors present a shape-based approach, the inner-distance shape context, as a robust and reliable solution. The authors show that this approach naturally captures part structures and is appropriate to the shape of leaves. Furthermore, they show that this approach can be easily extended to include texture information arising from the veins of leaves. They also describe a real electronic field guide system that uses our approach. The effectiveness of the proposed method is demonstrated in experiments on two leaf databases involving more than 100 species and 1,000 leaves.

INTRODUCTION

Plant species identification is critical to the discovery of new plant species, as well as in monitoring changing patterns of species distribution due to development and climate change. However, biologists are currently hampered by the shortage of expert taxonomists, and the time consuming nature of species identification even for trained botanists. Computer-aided foliage identification has the potential to speed up expert identification and improve the accuracy with which non-experts can identify plants.

While recent advances in user interface hardware and software make such a system potentially afford-able and available for use in the field, a reliable and efficient computer vision recognition algorithm is needed to allow users to access such a system with a simple, general interface. In this chapter we will describe our recent work using computer vision techniques for this task.

Due to the reasons we have mentioned, foliage image retrieval has recently started attracting research efforts in computer vision and related areas (Agarwal, et al. (2006), Mokhtarian & Abbasi 2004, Weiss & Ray 2005, Im, Hishida, & Kunii 1998, Saitoh & Kaneko 2000, Soderkvist 2001, Yahiaoui, Herve, & Boujemaa 2005). Leaf images are very challenging for retrieval tasks due to their high inter-class similarity and large intra-class deformations. In addition, occlusion and self-folding often damage leaf shape. Furthermore, some species have very similar shape but different texture, which therefore makes the combination of shape and texture desirable. In summary, the challenges mainly come from several reasons:

- The between class similarity is great (see the first row in Fig. 1).
- Self occlusion happens for some species, especially for composite leaves (see the second row in Fig. 1).
- Some species have large intra class deformations. For example, composite leaves often have large articulations (see the second row in Fig. 1).

Figure 1. Example of challenging leaves. First row: Three leaves from three different species (from the Swedish leaf database). Second row: Self occlusions due to overlapping leaflets and deformation of composite leaves. The left two leaves come from the same species; so do the right two leaves. Third row: damaged leaves.

- In practice, leaves are often damaged due to folding, erosion, etc. (see the third row in Fig. 1).
- Usually the hundreds, if not thousands of species are present in a region. So that we can begin to address problems of this scale, one of the databases in our test contains leaves from about 100 species.

The shapes of leaves are one of the key features used in their identification, and are also relatively easy to determine automatically from images. This makes them especially useful in species identification. Variation in leaf shape also provides an interesting test domain for general work on shape comparison (Felzenszwalb 2005, Mokhtarian & Abbasi 2004, Sclaroff & Liu 2001).

Part structure plays a very important role in classifying complex shapes in both human vision and computer vision (Biederman 1987, Hoffman & Richards 1985, Kimia, Tannenbaum, & Zucker 1995, etc). However, capturing part structure is not a trivial task, especially considering articulations, which are nonlinear transformations between shapes. To make things worse, sometimes shapes can have ambiguous parts (e.g. [4]). Unlike many previous methods that deal with part structure explicitly, we propose an implicit approach to this task.

For this purpose we introduce the *inner-distance*, defined as the length of the shortest path within the shape boundary, to build shape descriptors. It is easy to see that the inner-distance is insensitive to shape articulations. For example, in Fig. 2, although the points on shape (a) and (c) have similar spatial distributions, they are quite different in their part structures. On the other hand, shapes (b) and (c) appear to be from the same category with different articulations. The inner-distance between the two marked points is quite different in (a) and (b), while almost the same in (b) and (c). Intuitively, this example shows that the inner-distance is insensitive to articulation and sensitive to part structures, a desirable property for complex shape comparison. Note that the Euclidean distance does not have these properties in this example. This is because, defined as the length of the line segment between landmark points, the Euclidean distance does not consider whether the line segment crosses shape boundaries. In this example, it is clear that the inner-distance reflects part structure and articulation without explicitly decomposing shapes into parts. We will study this problem in detail and give more examples in the following sections.

It is natural to use the inner-distance as a replacement for other distance measures to build new shape descriptors that are invariant or insensitive to articulation. Two approaches have been proposed and tested with this idea. In the first approach, by replacing the geodesic distance with the inner-distance,

*Figure 2. Three objects. The dashed lines denote shortest paths within the shape boundary that connect landmark points. Reprinted with permission from "Shape Classification Using the Inner-Distance", H. Ling and D.W. Jacobs, IEEE Trans on Pattern Anal. and Mach. Intell. (**PAMI**), 29(2):286-299, (2007). © 2007 IEEE.*

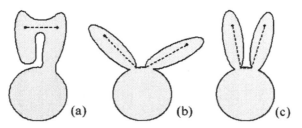

we extend the bending invariant signature for 3D surfaces (Elad & Kimmel 2003) to the articulation invariant signature for 2D articulated shapes. In the second method, the inner-distance replaces the Euclidean distance to extend the shape context (Belongie, Malik, & Puzicha 2002). We design a dynamic programming method for silhouette matching that is fast and accurate since it utilizes the ordering information between contour points. Both approaches are tested on a variety of shape databases and excellent performance is observed.

It is worth noting that articulation happens a lot for leaves. This is particularly true for leaves with petioles and compound leaves (see Fig. 1 and Fig. 5). Therefore, the inner-distance is a natural choice for leaf recognition tasks. In this chapter we will apply our methods to two leaf database. The first one is the Swedish leaf database containing 15 species. The second one is the Smithsonian leaf database containing 93 species. We will also describe the application of the proposed approach in a foliage retrieval system.

For some foliage retrieval tasks, it is often desirable to combine shape and texture information for object recognition. For example, leaves from different species often share similar shapes but have different vein structures (see Fig. 13 for examples). Using the gradient information along the shortest path, we propose a new shape descriptor, shortest path texture context, which naturally takes into account the texture information inside a given shape. The new descriptor is applied to a foliage image task and excellent performance is observed.

The rest of this chapter is organized as follows. Sec. II discusses related works. Sec. III describes the proposed inner-distance and shows how it can be used for shape matching tasks, including building articulation invariant signatures using multi-dimensional scaling (MDS) and the inner-distance shape context. Then Sec. IV extends the inner-distance based descriptor to include the texture information along shortest paths. After that, Sec. V gives a brief overview of an electronic field guide system that applies the proposed approaches in a foliage retrieval prototype system. Finally, Sec. VI presents and analyzes experiments on shape matching on an articulated shape database and two leaf shape databases. Much of the material described in this chapter has appeared previously in (Ling & Jacobs 2005, Hoffman & Richards 1985).

RELATED WORK

In this section, we first introduce some related work on foliage image retrieval. Then we discuss previous work on representing and matching shapes with part structures. After that, we discuss two works that we will extend using the inner-distance.

Foliage Image Retrieval

Biological shapes have been attracting scientists' attention for a long time. One of the earliest discussions, first published almost a hundred years ago, appeared in D'Arcy Thompson's famous book "On Growth and Form" (Thompson 1992). As a fundamental problem in computer vision and pattern recognition, biological shape analysis has motivated a lot of work in recent decades (Blum 1973). Among them, one of the most recent and comprehensive works is by Grenander, Srivastava, & Saini (2007).

Most of current foliage retrieval systems are based on shape analysis (Agarwal, et al. (2006), Mokhtarian & Abbasi 2004, Weiss & Ray 2005, Gandhi 2002, Im, Hishida, & Kunii 1998, Saitoh &

Kaneko 2000, Soderkvist 2001, Yahiaoui, Herve, & Boujemaa 2005). For example, in (Mokhtarian & Abbasi 2004) curvature scale space is proposed for shape analysis and applied to the classification of Chrysanthemum images. Soderkvist (2001) used a combination of several shape cues for retrieval with the Swedish leaf database involving 15 species. Gandhi (2002) applied dynamic warping on leaf shapes from six species.

In addition to the systems specific to foliage retrieval, leaf shapes are often used for the study of shape analysis due to the challenges they present. For example, it is used in (Felzenszwalb 2005, Felzenszwalb & Schwartz 2007, Ling & Jacobs 2005) to study shape deformation. It is also used in (Keogh et al. 2006) for demonstrating dynamic warping. Another interesting related work is [38], which uses a bag-of-words approach for a flower identification task.

Representation and Comparison of Shapes with Parts and Articulation

Biederman (1987) presented the recognition-by-components (RBC) model of human image understanding. He proposed that RBC is done with a set of geons, which are generalized-cone components. The geons are derived from edge properties in a two-dimensional image including curvature, co-linearity, symmetry, parallelism, and co-termination. In an overall introduction to human vision, Hoffman and Richards (1985) described the important role of part structure in human vision and showed how humans recognize objects through dividing and assembling parts. The important concept is part saliency, which is used by our visual system to identify parts. Concavity or negative curvature is used to determine saliency.

For general shape matching, a recent review is given in (Veltkamp & Hagedoorn 1999). Roughly speaking, works handling parts can be classified into three categories. The first category (Agarwal, Awan, & Roth 2004, Grimson 1990, Felzenszwalb & Hunttenlocher 2005, Schneiderman & Kanade 2004, Fergus, Perona, & Zisserman 2003, Weiss & Ray 2005) builds part models from a set of sample images, and usually with some prior knowledge such as the number of parts. After that, the models are used for retrieval tasks such as object recognition and detection. These works usually use statistical methods to describe the articulation between parts and often require a learning process to find the model parameters. For example, Grimson (1985) proposed some early work performing matching with precise models of articulation. Agarwal et al. (2004) proposed a framework for object detection via learning sparse, part-based representations. The method is targeted to objects that consist of distinguishable parts with relatively fixed spatial configurations. Felzenszwalb and Huttenlocher (2005) described a general method to statistically model objects with parts for recognition and detection. The method models appearance and articulation separately through parameter estimation. After that, the matching algorithm is treated as an energy minimization problem that can be solved efficiently by assuming that the pictorial representation has a tree structure. Schneiderman and Kanade (2004) used a general definition of parts that corresponds to a transform from a subset of wavelet coefficients to a discrete set of values, then built classifiers based on their statistics. Fergus et al. (2003) treated objects as flexible constellations of parts and probabilistically represented objects using their shape and appearance information. These methods have been successfully used in areas such as face and human motion analysis. However, for tasks where the learning process is prohibited, either due to the lack of training samples or due to the complexity of the shapes, they are hard to apply.

In contrast, the other two categories (Kimia et al. 1995, Basri et al. 1998, Sebastian, Klein, & Kimia 2004, Siddiqi et al. 1999, Gorelick et al. 2004, Liu & Geiger 1997) capture part structures from only one image. The second category (Basri et al. 1998, Liu & Geiger 1997) measures the similarity between shapes via a part-to-part (or segment-to-segment) matching and junction parameter distribution. These methods usually use only the boundary information such as the convex portions of silhouettes and curvatures of boundary points.

The third category, which our method belongs to, captures the part structure by considering the interior of shape boundaries. The most popular examples are the skeleton based approaches, particularly the *shock graph*-based techniques (Kimia et al. 1995, Sebastian et al. 2004, Siddiqi et al. 1999). Given a shape and its boundary, shocks are defined as the singularities of a curve evolution process that usually extracts the skeleton simultaneously. The shocks are then organized into a shock graph, which is a directed, acyclic tree. The shock graph forms a hierarchical representation of the shape and naturally captures its part structure. The shape matching problem is then reduced to a tree matching problem. Shock graphs are closely related to shape skeletons or the medial axis (Blum 1973, Kimia et al. 1995). Therefore, they benefit from the skeleton's ability to describe shape, including robustness to articulation and occlusion. However, they also suffer from the same difficulties as the skeleton, especially in dealing with boundary noise. Another related unsupervised approach is proposed by Gorelick et al. (2004). They used the average length of random walks of points inside a shape silhouette to build shape descriptors. The average length is computed as a solution to the Poisson equation. The solution can be used for shape analysis tasks such as skeleton and part extraction, local orientation detection, shape classification, etc.

The inner-distance is closely related to the skeleton based approaches in that it also considers the interior of the shape. Given two landmark points, the inner-distance can be "approximated" by first finding their closest points on the shape skeleton, then measuring the distance along the skeleton. In fact, the inner-distance can also be computed via the evolution equations starting from boundary points. The main difference between the inner-distance and the skeleton based approaches is that the inner-distance discards the structure of the path once their lengths are computed. By doing this, the inner-distance is more robust to disturbances along boundaries and becomes very flexible for building shape descriptors. For example, it can be easily used to extend existing descriptors by replacing Euclidean distances. In addition, the inner-distance based descriptors can be used for landmark point matching. This is very important for some applications such as motion analysis. The disadvantage is the loss of the ability to perform part analysis. It is an interesting topic for future work to see how to combine the inner-distance and skeleton based techniques.

Geodesic Distances for 3D Surfaces

The inner-distance is very similar to the geodesic distance on surfaces. The geodesic distances between any pair of points on a surface is defined as the length of the shortest path on the surface between them. Our work is partially motivated by Elad and Kimmel (2003) using geodesic distances for 3D surface comparison through multidimensional scaling (MDS). Given a surface and sample points on it, the surface is distorted using MDS, so that the Euclidean distances between the stretched sample points are as similar as possible to their corresponding geodesic distances on the original surface. Since the geodesic distance is invariant to bending, the stretched surface forms a bending invariant signature of the original surface.

Articulation invariance can be viewed as a special case of bending invariance. While bending invariance works well for surfaces by remapping the texture pattern (or intensity pattern) along the surface, articulation invariance cares about the shape itself. This sometimes makes the bending invariance a bit over-general, especially for 2D shape contours. In other words, the direct counterpart of the geodesic distance in 2D does not work for our purpose. Strictly speaking, the geodesic distance between two points on the "surface" of a 2D shape is the distance between them along the contour. If a simple (i.e. non self-intersecting), closed contour has length M, then for any point, p, and any d<M/2, there will be exactly two points that are a distance d away from p, along the contour. Therefore, a histogram of the geodesic distance to all points on the contour degenerates into something trivial, which does not capture shape. Unlike the geodesic distance, the inner-distance measures the length of the shortest path within the shape boundary instead of along the shape contour (surface). We will show that the inner distance is very informative and insensitive to articulation.

There are other works using geodesic distances in shape descriptions. For example, Hamza and Krim (2003) applied geodesic distance using *shape distributions* (Osada et al. 2002) for 3D shape classification. Zhao and Davis (2005) used the color information along the shortest path within a human silhouette. The articulation invariance of shortest paths is also utilized by them, but in the context of background subtraction. Ling and Jacobs (2005) proposed using the geodesic distance to achieve deformation invariance in intensity images.

Shape Contexts for 2D Shapes

The *shape context* was first introduced by Belongie et al. (2002). It uses the relative spatial distribution (distance and orientation) of landmark points to build shape descriptors. Given n sample points x_1, x_2, ..., x_n, on an object, its shape context at point x_i is defined as a histogram h_i of the relative coordinates of the remaining n-1 points

$$h_i(k) = \#\{x_j : j \neq i, x_j - x_i \in bin(k)\} \tag{1}$$

where the bins uniformly divide the log-polar space. The distance between two shape context histograms is defined using the χ^2 statistic.

For shape comparison, Belongie et al. used a framework combining shape context and thin-plate splines (Bookstein 1989) (SC+TPS). Given the points on two shapes A and B, first the point correspondences are found through a weighted bipartite matching. Then, TPS is used iteratively to estimate the transformation between them. After that, the similarity D between A and B is measured as a weighted combination of three parts

$$D = aD_{ac} + D_{sc} + bD_{bc} \tag{2}$$

where D_{ac} measures the appearance difference, and D_{be} measures the bending energy. The D_{sc} term, named the *shape context distance*, measures the average distance between a point on A and its most similar counterpart on B (in the sense of χ^2 distance). a and b are weights (a=1.6, b=0.3 in [6]).

The shape context uses the Euclidean distance to measure the spatial relation between landmark points. This means that the distance is the length of the straight line segment which connects the landmark points, regardless of whether the line crosses the shape boundary or not. This causes less discriminability for complex shapes with articulations (e.g., Figures 7 and 8). The inner-distance is a natural way to solve this problem since it captures the shape structure better than the Euclidean distance. We use the inner-distance to extend the shape context for shape matching. The advantages of the new descriptor are strongly supported by experiments.

The SC+TPS framework is shown to be very effective for shape matching tasks (Belongie et al. 2002). Due to its simplicity and discriminability, the shape context has become quite popular recently. Some examples can be found in (Mori & Malik 2003, Thayananthan et al. 2003, Tu & Yuille 2004, Leibe & Schiele 2003). Among these works, Thayananthan et al. (2003) is most related to our approach. Thayananthan et al. (2003) suggested including a figural continuity constraint for shape context matching via an efficient dynamic programming scheme. In our approach, we also include a similar constraint by assuming that contour points are ordered and use dynamic programming for matching the shape context at contour points along contours. Notice that usually dynamic programming encounters problems with shapes with multiple boundaries (e.g., scissors with holes). The inner-distance has no such problem since it only requires landmark points on the outermost silhouette, and the shortest path can be computed taking account of holes. This will be discussed in the following sections.

SHAPE MATCHING USING THE INNER-DISTANCE

The Inner-Distance

In this section, we will first give the definition of the inner-distance and discuss how to compute it. Then, the inner-distance's insensitivity to part articulations is proven. After that, we will discuss its ability to capture part structures.

The Inner-Distance and Its Computation

First, we define a shape O as a connected and closed subset of R^2. Given a shape O and two points $x, y \in O$ the inner-distance between x, y, denoted as $d(x, y; O)$, is defined as the length of the shortest path connecting x and y within O. One example is shown in Fig. 3.

Note: (1) There may exist multiple shortest paths between given points. However, in most cases, the path is unique. In rare cases where there are multiple shortest paths, we arbitrarily choose one. (2) We are interested in shapes defined by their boundaries, hence only boundary points are used as landmark points. In addition, we approximate a shape with a polygon formed by their landmark points.

A natural way to compute the inner-distance is using shortest path algorithms. This consists of two steps:

1. *Build a graph with the sample points.* First, each sample point is treated as a node in the graph. Then, for each pair of sample points p_1 and p_2, if the line segment connecting p_1 and p_2 falls entirely within the object, an edge between p_1 and p_2 is added to the graph with its weight equal to the Euclidean distance $|p_1 - p_2|$. An example is shown in Fig. 4. Note (1) Neighboring boundary points are always connected; (2) The inner-distance reflects the existence of holes without using sample points from hole boundaries, which allows dynamic programming algorithms to be applied to shapes with holes. Note that the points along hole boundaries may still be needed for computing the inner-distance, but not for building descriptors.

*Figure 3. Definition of the inner-distance. The dashed polyline shows the shortest path between point x and y. Reprinted with permission from "Shape Classification Using the Inner-Distance", H. Ling and D.W. Jacobs, IEEE Trans on Pattern Anal. and Mach. Intell. (**PAMI**), 29(2):286-299, (2007). © 2007 IEEE.*

2. *Apply an all pair's shortest path algorithm to the graph.* Many standard algorithms (Cormen et al. 2001) can be applied here, among them Johnson or Floyd-Warshall's algorithms have $O(n^3)$ complexity (n is the number of sample points).

In this chapter we are interested in the inner-distance between all pairs of points. Now we will show that this can be computed with $O(n^3)$ time complexity for n sample points. First, it takes time $O(n)$ to check whether a line segment between two points is inside the given shape (by checking the intersections between line $p_1 p_2$ and all other boundary line segments, with several extra tests). As a result, the complexity of graph construction is of $O(n^3)$. After the graph is ready, the all-pair shortest path algorithm has complexity of $O(n^3)$. Therefore, the whole computation takes $O(n^3)$.

Note that when O is convex, the inner-distance reduces to the Euclidean distance. However, this is not always true for non-convex shapes (e.g., Fig. 2). This suggests that the inner-distance is influenced by part structure to which the concavity of contours is closely related (Hoffman & Richards 1985, Feldman & Singh 2005). In the following subsections, we discuss this in detail.

Articulation Insensitivity of the Inner-Distance

As shown in Fig. 2, the inner-distance is insensitive to articulation. Intuitively, this is true because an articulated shape can be decomposed into rigid parts connected by junctions. Accordingly, the shortest path between landmark points can be divided into segments within each part. We will first give a very general model for part articulation and then formally prove articulation insensitivity of the inner-distance.

A Model of Articulated Objects

Before discussing the articulation insensitivity of the inner-distance, we need to provide a model of articulated objects. Note that our method does not involve any part models, the model here is only for the analysis of the properties of the inner-distance. Intuitively, when a shape O is said to have articulated parts, it means

* O can be decomposed into several *parts*, say, $O_1, O_2, ... , O_n$, where n is the number of parts. These parts are connected by *junctions*.

*Figure 4. Computation of the inner-distance. Left, the shape with the sampled silhouette landmark points. Middle, the graph built using the landmark points (it is easier to see the edges in the top part of the figure). Right, a detail of the right top of the graph. Note how the inner-distance captures the holes. Reprinted with permission from "Shape Classification Using the Inner-Distance", H. Ling and D.W. Jacobs, IEEE Trans on Pattern Anal. and Mach. Intell. (**PAMI**), 29(2):286-299, (2007). © 2007 IEEE.*

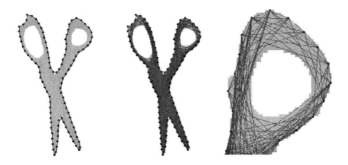

- The junctions between parts are very small compared to the parts they connect.
- The articulation of O as a transformation is rigid when limited to any part O_i, but can be non-rigid on the junctions.
- The new shape O' achieved from articulation of O is again an articulated object and can articulate *back* to O.

Based on these intuition, we define an articulated object $O \subset R^2$ of n parts together with an articulation f as:

$$O = \left\{ \bigcup_{i=1}^{n} O_i \right\} \cup \left\{ \bigcup_{i \neq j} J_{ij} \right\}$$

where

- $\forall i, 1 \leq i \leq n$, part $O_i \subset R^2$ is connected and closed and $O_i \bigcap O_j = null$, $\forall i \neq j, i, j = 1,...,n$.

*Figure 5. Examples of articulated objects. (a) An articulated shape with three parts, O_1, O_2, O_3 and two junctions J_{12}, J_{23}. (b) A compound leaf with three parts. (c) Ideal articulation. (a) and (c) are reprinted with permission from "Shape Classification Using the Inner-Distance", H. Ling and D.W. Jacobs, IEEE Trans on Pattern Anal. and Mach. Intell. (**PAMI**), 29(2):286-299, (2007). © 2007 IEEE.*

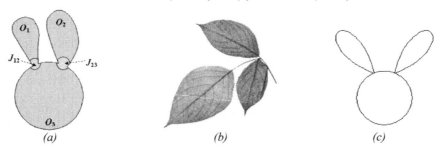

- $\forall i \neq j, 1 \leq i, j \leq n, J_{ij} \subset R^2$, connected and closed, is the junction between O_i and O_j. If there is no junction between O_i and O_j, then J_{ij}=*null*. Otherwise, $J_{ij} \cap O_i \neq null$, $J_{ij} \cap O_j \neq null$.
- $diam(J_{ij}) \leq \varepsilon$, where $diam(P) \equiv \max_{x,y \in P} d(x,y;P)$ is the *diameter* of a point set $P \subset R^2$ in the sense of the inner-distance. $\varepsilon \geq 0$ is constant and very small compared to the size of the articulated parts. A special case is when $\varepsilon=0$, which means that all junctions degenerate to single points and O is called an *ideal articulated object*.

Fig. 5 (a) shows an example articulated shape with three parts and two junctions.

The articulation from an articulated object O to another articulated object O' is a one-to-one continuous mapping f, such that:

- O' has the decomposition $O' = \left\{\bigcup_{i=1}^{n} O'_i\right\} \cup \left\{\bigcup_{i \neq j} J'_{ij}\right\}$. Furthermore, $O'_i = f(O_i)$, $\forall i, 1 \leq i \leq n$ are O' parts of and $J'_{ij} = f(J_{ij})$, $\forall i \neq j, 1 \leq i, j \leq n$ are junctions in O'. This preserves the topology between the articulated parts. In particular, the deformed junctions still have a diameter less than or equal to ε.
- f is rigid (rotation and translation only) when restricted to O_i, $\forall i, 1 \leq i \leq n$. This means inner-distances within each part will not change.

Notes: (1) In the above and following, we use the notation $f(P) \equiv \{f(x): x \in P\}$ for short. (2) It is obvious from the above definitions that f^{-1} is an articulation that maps O' to O.

The above model of articulation is very general and flexible. For example, there is no restriction on the shape of the junctions. Junctions are even allowed to overlap each other. Furthermore, the articulation f on the junctions are not required to be smooth. Fig. 5 (b) and (c) gives two more examples of articulated shapes.

Articulation Insensitivity

We are interested in how the inner-distance varies under articulation. From previous paragraphs we know that changes of the inner-distance are due to junction deformations. Intuitively, this means the change is very small compared to the size of parts. Since most pairs of points have inner-distances comparable to the sizes of parts, the relative change of the inner-distances during articulation are small. This roughly explains why the inner-distances are articulation insensitive.

We will use the following notations: (1) $\Gamma(x_1, x_2; P)$ denotes a shortest path $x_1 \in p$ from to $x_2 \in p$ for a closed and connected point set $P \subset R^2$ (so $d(x_1, x_2; P)$ is the length of $\Gamma(x_1, x_2; P)$). (2) We use prime "'" to indicate the image f of a point or a point set under an articulation e.g., $P' \equiv f(P)$ P for point set; $p' \equiv f(p)$ for a point P. 3) "[" and "]" denote the concatenation of paths.

Let us first point out two facts about the inner-distance within a part or crossing a junction. Both facts are direct results from our definitions of parts and junctions.

Fact 1:

$$d(x, y; O_i) = d(x', y'; O'_i) \qquad \forall x, y \in O_i, 1 \leq i \leq n$$

Fact 1 says that, for two points within the same part, the inner-distance between them is invariant to articulation. This is obvious because the transformation of a part is restricted to be rigid during articulation.

Fact 2:

$$|d(x, y; O) - d(x', y'; O')| \leq \varepsilon \qquad \forall x, y \in J_{i,j}, i \neq j, 1 \leq i, j \leq n, J_{i,j} \neq O$$

Fact 2 says that, for two points within the same junction, the change of the inner-distance between them is bounded by ε. This is because the size of a junction is limited by ε. Note that Fact 2 does not require the shortest path between x, y to lie within the junction J_{ij}.

The two facts describe the change of the inner-distances of restricted point pairs. For the general case, i.e. $x, y \in O$, we have the following theorem:

Theorem 1: *Let O be an articulated object and f be an articulation of O as defined above. $\forall x, y \in O$, suppose the shortest path $\Gamma(x, y; O)$ goes through m different junctions in O and $\Gamma(x', y'; O')$ goes through m' different junctions in O', then*

$$|d(x, y; O) - d(x', y'; O')| \leq \max\{m, m'\}\varepsilon$$

Proof: *The proof uses the intuition mentioned above. First we decompose $\Gamma(x, y; O)$ into segments. Each segment is either within a part or across a junction. Then, applying Fact 1 and Fact 2 to each segment leads to the theorem.*

First, $\Gamma(x, y; O)$ is decomposed into l segments:

$$\Gamma(x, y; O) = [\Gamma(p_0, p_1; R_1), \Gamma(p_1, p_2; R_2), ..., \Gamma(p_{l-1}, p_l; R_l)]$$

using point sequence $p_0, p_1, ..., p_l$ and regions $R_1, ..., R_l$ via the steps using Algorithm 1.

Algorithm 1: Decompose $\Gamma(x, y; O)$

$p_0 \leftarrow x$, $i \leftarrow 0$

while $p_i \neq y$

   /*find p_{i+1}*/

   $i \leftarrow I + 1$

   $R_i \leftarrow$ the region (a part or a junction) $\Gamma(x, y; O)$ enters after p_{i-1}

   if $R_i = O_k$ for some k

     /*enter a part (R_i is a part)*/

     Set p_i as a point in O_k such that

     1） $\Gamma(p_{i-1}, p_i; O_k) \subset \Gamma(x, y; O)$

       2) $\Gamma(x, y; O)$ enters a new region (a part or a junction) after p_i or $p_i = y$

   else

     /* $R_i = J_{rs}$ for some r, s (R_i is a junction), enter a junction*/]

     Set p_i as the point in $J_{rs} \bigcap \Gamma(x, y; O)$ such that $\Gamma(x, y; O)$ never re-enters J_{rs} after p_i

     $R_i \leftarrow$ the union of all the parts and junctions $\Gamma(p_{i-1}, p_i; O)$ passes through (note $J_{rs} \subset R_i$)

   endif

  endwhile

  $l \leftarrow i$

An example of this decomposition is shown in Fig. 6 (a). With this decomposition, $d(x, y; O)$ can be written as:

$$d(x, y; O) = \sum_{i=1}^{l} d(p_{i-1}, p_i; R_i)$$

Suppose m_1 of the segments cross junctions (i.e., segments not contained in any single part), then obviously $m_1 \le m$ ($m_1 < m$ when there are cross junction segments that are not contained within any single junction).

In O', we construct a path from x' to y' corresponding to $\Gamma(x, y; O)$ as follows (e.g. Fig. 6 (b)):

$$\tilde{C}(x', y'; O') = [\Gamma(p'_0, p'_1; R'_1), \Gamma(p'_1, p'_2; R'_2), ..., \Gamma(p'_{l-1}, p'_l; R'_l)]$$

Note that $\tilde{C}(x', y'; O')$ is not necessarily the shortest path in O'. Denote $\tilde{d}(x', y'; O')$ as the length of $\tilde{C}(x', y'; O')$, it has the following property due to Fact 1 and Fact 2:

$$| d(x, y; O) - \tilde{d}(x', y'; O') | \le m_1 \varepsilon \le m\varepsilon \tag{3}$$

*Figure 6. (a) Decomposition of $\Gamma(x, y; O)$ (the dashed line) with $x = p_0, p_3 = y$. Note that a segment can go through a junction more than once (e.g. $p_1 p_2$). (b) Construction of $\tilde{C}(x', y'; O')$ in o' (the dashed line). Note that $\tilde{C}(x', y'; O')$ is not the shortest path. Reprinted with permission from "Shape Classification Using the Inner-Distance", H. Ling and D.W. Jacobs, IEEE Trans on Pattern Anal. and Mach. Intell. (**PAMI**), 29(2):286-299, (2007). © 2007 IEEE.*

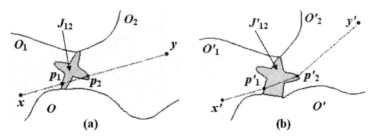

*Figure 7. With the same sample points, the distributions of Euclidean distances between all pair of points are indistinguishable for the four shapes, while the distributions of the inner-distances are quite different. Reprinted with permission from "Shape Classification Using the Inner-Distance", H. Ling and D.W. Jacobs, IEEE Trans on Pattern Anal. and Mach. Intell. (**PAMI**), 29(2):286-299, (2007). © 2007 IEEE.*

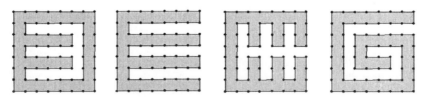

On the other hand, since O can be articulated from O' through f^{-1}, we can construct $\tilde{C}(x, y; O)$ from $\Gamma(x', y'; O')$ in the same way that we construct $\tilde{C}(x', y'; O')$ from $\Gamma(x, y; O)$. Then, similar to (3), we have

$$|d(x', y'; O') - \tilde{d}(x, y; O)| \leq m'\varepsilon \qquad (4)$$

Combining (3) and (4),

$$d(x, y; O) - m'\varepsilon \leq \tilde{d}(x, y; O) - m'\varepsilon \leq d(x', y'; O') \leq \tilde{d}(x', y'; O') \leq d(x, y; O) + m\varepsilon$$

This implies Theorem 1.   #

Regarding changes of inner-distances under articulation, two remarks can be made from Theorem 1:

- The inner-distance is strictly invariant for ideal articulated objects. This is obvious since $\varepsilon=0$ for ideal articulations.
- Since ε is very small by definition, for most pairs of x, y, the relative change of inner-distance is very small. This means the inner-distance is insensitive to articulations.

We further clarify several issues. First, the proof depends on the size limitation of junctions. The intuition is that a junction should have a relatively smaller size compared to parts, otherwise it is more like a part itself. A more precise part-junction definition may provide a tighter upper bound but sacrifice some generality. The definition also captures our intuition about what distinguishes articulation from deformation. Second, the part-junction model is not actually used at all when applying the inner-distance. In fact, one advantage of using the inner distance is that it *implicitly* captures part structure, whose definition is still not clear in general.

Inner-Distances and Part Structures

In addition to articulation insensitivity, we believe that the inner-distance captures part structures better than the Euclidean distance. This is hard to prove because the definition of part structure remains unclear. For example, Basri et al. (1998) gave a shape of shoe that has no clear part decomposition, although it feels like it has more than one part.

Instead of giving a rigorous proof, we show how the inner-distance captures part structure with examples and experiments. Figures 2, 7 and 12 show examples where the inner-distance distinguishes shapes with parts while the Euclidean distance runs into trouble because the sample points on the shape have the same spatial distributions. For example, the original shape context [6] may fail on these shapes. One may argue that the Euclidean distance will also work on these examples with an increased number of landmark points. This argument has several practical problems. First, the computational cost will be increased, usually in a quadratic order or higher. Second, no matter how many points are used, there can always be finer structures. Third, as shown in Fig. 8, for some shapes this strategy will not work.

During retrieval experiments using several shape databases, the inner-distance based descriptors all achieve excellent performance. Through observation we have found that some databases (e.g., MPEG7) are difficult for retrieval mainly due to the complex part structures in their shapes, though they have little articulation. These experiments show that the inner-distance is effective at capturing part structures (see Fig. 12 and (Ling & Jacobs 2007) for details).

Aside from part structures, examples in Fig. 8 show cases where the inner-distance can better capture some shapes without parts. We expect further studies on the relationship between inner-distances and shape in the future.

Articulation Invariant Signatures

To build shape descriptors with the inner-distance is straightforward. Theoretically, it can be used to replace other distance measures (e.g. the Euclidean distance) in any existing shape descriptors. In this section, the inner-distance is used to build articulation invariant signatures for 2D shapes using multi-dimensional scaling (MDS) similar to (Elad & Kimmel 2003). In the next section, we will show how to use the inner-distance to extend the shape context for shape matching.

Given sample points $P \equiv \{p_i\}_{i=1}^n$ on a shape O and the inner-distances $\{d_{ij}\}_{i,j=1}^n$ between them, MDS finds the transformed points $Q \equiv \{q_i\}_{i=1}^n$ such that the Euclidean distances $\{e_{ij}(Q) = \| q_i - q_j \|\}_{i,j=1}^n$ minimize the *stress* $S(Q)$ defined as:

$$S(Q) = \frac{\sum_{i<j} w_{ij}(d_{ij} - e_{ij})^2}{\sum_{i<j} d_{ij}^2} \tag{5}$$

where w_{ij} are weights. In our experiment, we use the least squares MDS with $w_{ij}=1$. The stress can be minimized using the SAMCOF (Scaling by Maximizing a Convex Function) algorithm (Borg & Groenen 1997). SAMCOF is an iterative algorithm that keeps decreasing the objective function, i.e., the stress (5). The details can be found in (Elad & Kimmel 2003).

Fig. 9 shows two examples of the articulation invariant signatures computed by the above approach. It can be seen that although the global shape of the two original objects are quite different due to articulation, their signatures are very similar to each other. More examples of articulation invariant signatures can be seen in Fig. 16.

It is attractive to use the articulation invariant signature for classifying articulated shapes. In our experiments we combine it with the shape context. The method contains three steps: (1) use the inner-distance and MDS to get the articulation invariant signatures; (2) build the shape context on the signa-

*Figure 8. With about the same number of sample points, the four shapes are virtually indistinguishable using distribution of Euclidean distances, as in Fig. 7. However, their distributions of the inner-distances are quite different except for the first two shapes. Note: (1) None of the shapes has (explicit) parts. (2) More sample points will not affect the above statement. Reprinted with permission from "Shape Classification Using the Inner-Distance", H. Ling and D.W. Jacobs, IEEE Trans on Pattern Anal. and Mach. Intell. (**PAMI**), 29(2):286-299, (2007). © 2007 IEEE.*

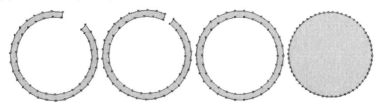

*Figure 9. (b) shows the articulation invariant signature of (a). (d) shows the articulation invariant signature of (c). Reprinted with permission from "Shape Classification Using the Inner-Distance", H. Ling and D.W. Jacobs, IEEE Trans on Pattern Anal. and Mach. Intell. (**PAMI**), 29(2):286-299, (2007). © 2007 IEEE.*

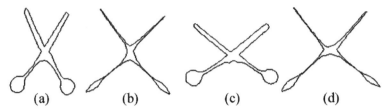

(a)　　　　(b)　　　　(c)　　　　(d)

tures; (3) use dynamic programming for shape context matching. The third step is described in detail in the next section. We call this approach MDS+SC+DP. The experimental results show significant improvement compared to the shape context on the original shapes.

Inner-Distance Shape Context: Matching and Retrieval

Inner-Distance Shape Context (IDSC)

To extend the shape context defined in (1), we redefine the bins with the inner-distance. The Euclidean distance is directly replaced by the inner-distance. The relative orientation between two points can be defined as the tangential direction at the starting point of the shortest path connecting them. However, this tangential direction *is* sensitive to articulation. Fortunately, for a boundary point p and its shortest path $\Gamma(p,q;O)$ to another point q, the angle between the contour tangent at p and the direction of $\Gamma(p,q;O)$ at p is insensitive to articulation (invariant to ideal articulation). We call this angle the *inner-angle* (e.g., see Fig. 11) and denote it as $\theta(p,q;O)$. The inner-angle is used for the orientation bins. A similar idea is used in [6], which uses the local coordinate system to achieve rotation invariance. In practice, the shape boundary may be distorted by noise that reduces the stability of the inner-angle. To deal with this problem, we smooth the contour using a small neighborhood before computing the inner-angle.

Note that the inner-angle may not be unique. However, the ambiguity only happens in very few situations so it does not significantly affect the shape descriptor we are going to build. The inner-angle is just a byproduct of the shortest path algorithms and does not affect the complexity. Once the inner-distances and orientations between all pair of points are ready, it takes $O(n^2)$ time to compute the histogram (1).

This extension can also be viewed as of first relocating the sample points according to the inner-distance, then counting to get the histogram. This is illustrated in Fig. 10 (d-f). Compared to (b), six points in (d) are moved to different bins, causing a change in of the numbers of points in some bins.

Fig. 12 shows examples of the shape context computed by the two different methods. It is clear that SC is similar for all three shapes, while IDSC is only similar for the beetles. From this figure we can see that the inner-distance is better at capturing parts than SC.

Shape Matching Through Dynamic Programming

The contour matching problem is formulated as follows: Given two shapes A and B, describe them by point sequences on their contour, say, $p_1,p_2...p_n$ for A with n points, and $q_1q_2...q_m$ for B with m points.

Without loss of generality, assume $n \geq m$. The matching ρ from A to B is a mapping from 1, 2, ... , n to 0, 1, 2, ... , m, where p_i is matched to $q_{\pi(i)}$ if $\pi(i) \neq 0$ and otherwise left unmatched. The matching ρ should minimize the match cost $H(\rho)$ defined as

$$H(\pi) = \sum_{i=1}^{n} c(i, \pi(i)) \tag{6}$$

where $c(i, 0) = \tau$ is the penalty for leaving p_i unmatched, and for $1 \leq j \leq m$, $c(i, j)$ is the cost of matching P_i to q_j. This is measured using the χ^2 statistic as in [6]

$$c(i, j) = \frac{1}{2} \sum_{k=1}^{K} \frac{(h_{A,i}(k) - h_{B,j}(k))^2}{h_{A,i}(k) + h_{B,j}(k)} \tag{7}$$

where $j_{A,i}$ and $h_{B,j}$ are the shape context histograms of p_i and q_j respectively, and K is the number of histogram bins.

Figure 10. Construction of the shape context (SC) and the inner-distance shape context (IDSC). (a) Sampled points along a shape. The SC and IDSC at point p will be built. Four log-distance bins and four orientation bins are used. (b) The bins and the number of points inside each bins. (c) SC at p. (d) When building IDSC, the inner-distance is used. It works as if moving some points to different bins according to the inner-distance and the inner-angle (θ in the graph). q is moved to q'. (e) The number of points inside each bin according to the inner-distance. (f) IDSC at p.

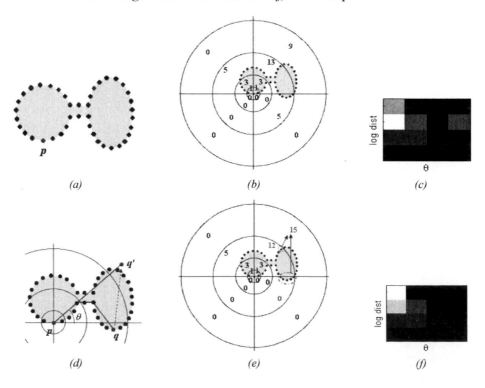

(a)   *(b)*   *(c)*

(d)   *(e)*   *(f)*

Since the contours provide orderings for the point sequences $p_1 p_2 \ldots p_n$ and $q_1 q_2 \ldots q_m$, it is natural to restrict the matching ρ with this order. To this end, we use dynamic programming (DP) to solve the matching problem. DP is widely used for contour matching. Detailed examples can be found in (Thayananthan et al. 2003, Petrakis et al. 2002, Basri et al. 1998). We use the standard DP method (Cormen et al. 2001) with the cost functions defined by (6) and (7).

In other words, we want to minimize (6) subject to the sequence ordering and starting points p_1, q_1. The key formula for the matching is

$$H(i,j) = \min \begin{cases} H(i-1, j-1) + c(i,j) \\ c(i-1, j) + \tau \\ c(i, j-1) + \tau \end{cases}$$

where $H(i,j)$ is the minimum matching cost of matching subsequence $p_1 p_2 \ldots p_i$ and $q_1 q_2 \ldots q_j$. And the cost of the whole matching is $H(\rho) = H(n, m)$.

*Figure 11. The inner-angle $\theta(p, q; O)$ between two boundary points. Reprinted with permission from "Shape Classification Using the Inner-Distance", H. Ling and D.W. Jacobs, IEEE Trans on Pattern Anal. and Mach. Intell. (**PAMI**), 29(2):286-299, (2007). © 2007 IEEE.*

*Figure 12. Shape context (SC) and inner-distance shape context (IDSC). The top row shows three objects from the MPEG7 shape database, with two marked points p, q on each shape. The next rows show (from top to bottom), the SC at p, the IDSC at p, the SC at q, the IDSC at q. Both the SC and the IDSC use local relative frames (i.e. aligned to the tangent). In the histograms, the x axis denotes the orientation bins and the y axis denotes log distance bins. Reprinted with permission from "Shape Classification Using the Inner-Distance", H. Ling and D.W. Jacobs, IEEE Trans on Pattern Anal. and Mach. Intell. (**PAMI**), 29(2):286-299, (2007). © 2007 IEEE.*

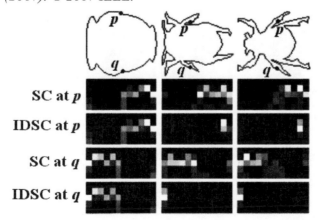

By default, the above method assumes the two contours are already aligned at their start and end points. Without this assumption, one simple solution is to try different alignments at all points on the first contour and choose the best one. The problem with this solution is that it raises the matching complexity from $O(n^2)$ to $O(n^3)$. Fortunately, for the comparison problem, it is often sufficient to try aligning a fixed number of points, say, k points. Usually k is much smaller than m and n, this is because shapes can be first rotated according to their moments. According to our experience, for n, m=100, k=4 or 8 is good enough and larger k does not demonstrate significant improvement. Therefore, the complexity remains $O(kn^2) = O(n^2)$.

Bipartite graph matching is used in (Belongie et al. 2002) to find the point correspondence ρ. Bipartite matching is more general since it minimizes the matching cost (6) without additional constraints. For example, it works when there is no ordering constraint on the sample points (while DP is not applicable). For sequenced points along silhouettes, however, DP is more efficient and accurate since it uses the ordering information provided by shape contours.

Shape Distances

Once the matching is found, we use the matching cost $H(\rho)$ as in (6) to measure the similarity between shapes. One thing to mention is that dynamic programming is also suitable for shape context. In the following, we use IDSC+DP to denote the method of using dynamic programming matching with the IDSC, and use SC+DP for the similar method with the SC.

In addition to the excellent performance demonstrated in the experiments, the IDSC+DP framework is simpler than the SC+TPS framework (2) (Belongie et al. 2002). First, besides the size of shape context bins, IDSC+DP has only two parameters to tune: (1) The penalty τ for a point with no matching, usually set to 0.3, and (2) The number of start points k for different alignments during the DP matching, usually set to 4 or 8. Second, IDSC+DP is easy to implement, since it does not require the appearance and transformation model as well as the iteration and outlier control. Furthermore, the DP matching is faster than bipartite matching, which is important for retrieval in large shape databases.

*Figure 13. Shapes of three leaves ((a), (b) and (c)) are not enough to distinguish them. Their texture ((d), (e) and (f) respectively) apparently helps. Reprinted with permission from "Shape Classification Using the Inner-Distance", H. Ling and D.W. Jacobs , IEEE Trans on Pattern Anal. and Mach. Intell. (**PAMI**), 29(2):286-299, (2007). © 2007 IEEE.*

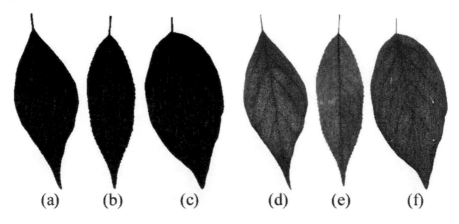

(a)　　(b)　　(c)　　(d)　　(e)　　(f)

The time complexity of the IDSC+DP consists of three parts. First, the computation of inner-distances can be achieved in $O(n^3)$ with Johnson or Floyd-Warshall's shortest path algorithms, where n is the number of sample points. Second, the construction of the IDSC histogram takes $O(n^2)$. Third, the DP matching costs $O(n^2)$, and only this part is required for all pairs of shapes, which is very important for retrieval tasks with large image databases. In our experiment using partly optimized Matlab code on a regular Pentium IV 2.8G PC, a single comparison of two shapes with $n=100$ takes about 0.31 second.

HANDLING TEXTURE

Shortest Path Texture Context

In real applications, shape information is often not enough for object recognition tasks. On the one hand, shapes from different classes sometimes are more similar than those from the same class (e.g., Fig. 13). On the other hand, shapes are often damaged due to occlusion and self-overlapping (some examples can be found in Fig. 1). A combination of texture and shape information is desirable for this problem. In (Belongie et al. 2002) appearance information is included in the SC+TPS framework by considering appearance around landmark points. In this section, we will introduce a new descriptor that considers the texture information inside the whole shape.

In previous sections, the inner-distance is shown to be articulation insensitive due to the fact that the shortest paths within shape boundaries are robust to articulation. Therefore, the texture information along these paths provides a natural articulation insensitive texture description. Note that this is true only when the paths are robust. In this section, we use local intensity gradient orientations to capture texture information because of their robustness and efficiency. To gain articulation invariance, the angles between intensity gradient directions and shortest path directions are used. In the following we call these angles *relative orientations*. Given shape O and two points p, v on it, we use $\alpha(p,v;O)$ to denote the relative orientation with respect to the shortest path $\Gamma(p,v;O)$. An example is shown in Fig. 14.

*Figure 14. (a) Relative orientation α(p, v; O) at point v. The arrow points to local intensity gradient direction. (b) The SPTC at a landmark point is a three-dimensional histogram. (a) is reprinted with permission from "Shape Classification Using the Inner-Distance", H. Ling and D.W. Jacobs, IEEE Trans on Pattern Anal. and Mach. Intell. (**PAMI**), 29(2):286-299, (2007). © 2007 IEEE.*

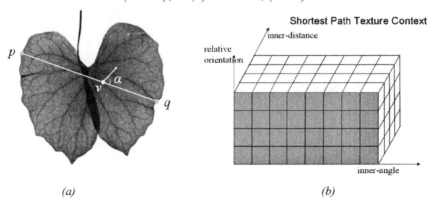

(a)   *(b)*

Based on the above idea, we propose the *shortest path texture context* (SPTC) as a combined shape and texture descriptor. SPTC is an extension of the IDSC in that it measures the distributions of (weighted) relative orientations along shortest paths instead of the joint distributions of inner-distance and inner-angle distributions of landmark points. In our application, the relative orientations are weighted by gradient magnitudes when building into SPTC. For texture undergoing large non-uniform illumination change, it might be better to use non-weighted relative orientations.

Given n landmark points $x_1, x_2, ..., x_n$ sampled from the boundary of shape O, the SPTC for each x_i is a three-dimensional histogram h_i (we abuse notation to use h_i again for the histograms). Similar to IDSC, SPTC uses the inner-distance and the inner-angle as the first two dimensions. The third dimension of SPTC is the (weighted) relative orientation that takes into account the texture information along shortest paths. To build h_i, for each x_j, $j \neq i$, a normalized histogram of relative orientation along the shortest path $\Gamma(x_i, x_j; O)$ is added into the relative orientation bin located at the inner-distance and inner-angle bin determined by x_j. The algorithm is described in Algorithm 2. Note that when the number of relative orientation bins $n_r=1$, SPTC reduces to IDSC.

A similar idea of using ``relative orientation'' is used by Lazebnik et al. (2005) for rotation invariant texture description. Shape context had also been extended for texture description by including intensity gradient orientation (Mikolajczyk & Schmid 2005). SPTC is different from these methods in three ways. First, SPTC combines texture information and global shape information while the above methods work for local image patches. Second, the above methods sample the orientations at a large number of pixels inside a patch, which is too expensive for our task without utilizing shortest paths. Third, none of the previous methods is articulation invariant. Another related work by Zhao and Davis (2005) used the color information along the shortest path for background subtraction. Instead of color information, we use gradient orientation, which is more robust to lighting change (Chen et al. 2000), which is very important for classification tasks. In the next section, SPTC is tested with two leaf image databases and excellent performance is observed.

FOLIAGE IMAGE RETRIEVAL IN AN ELECTRONIC FIELD GUIDE SYSTEM

In this section we briefly describe a prototype electronic field guide system. The prototype is the product of a collaboration between researchers from Columbia University, the Smithsonian Institution, and the University of Maryland [3]. The image retrieval system allows for online visual searching. In the field, a botanist can photograph an unknown leaf to the system and get the most visually similar leaves in the database. Another important target of an EFG system is to provide an easy-to-use browsing interface that helps not only botanists, but all users. For example, it would be very helpful to embed an EFG system in a web server, which further provides online access and browsing services.

Techniques from several research areas are necessary to fulfill this task:

1. *An image retrieval algorithm enables image-based browsing as well as query.* This is the main topic of this chapter. The inner-distance based approaches give a reliable solution to the problem. The shape matching algorithms not only play a key role in the visual search task, they also form the basis of visual clustering that has been shown to be very helpful in image browsing tasks (Agarwal 2005).

Figure 15. Modules of the electronic field guide prototype

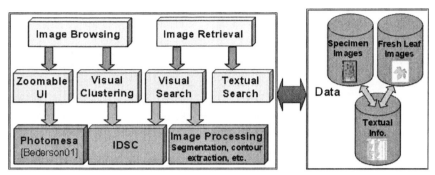

2. *Computing hardware.* A portable computing device is a must. This is much less of a problem nowadays than before, thanks to numerous popular mobile devices such as laptops, but more usable portable devices are still needed.

3. *A flexible interface.* The interface should provide an easy browsing environment as well as an easy interface to database systems that contain textual and image information.

4. *Interface hardware.* A traditional retrieval system is usually based on textual input. While this is easy and requires only a keyboard (or similar input device), it sacrifices convenience. In addition, it is often not easy to summarize an unknown species in a way that is appropriate for a text-based retrieval system. A natural extension is use image based searching. For this reason, an input device (usually a camera) is needed to provide a query image to the image-based retrieval system. Communication between a camera and a computing device can be easily and automatically done through wireless communication systems, such as Bluetooth, while systems with built in cameras will be even more convenient.

Figure 15 is a summary of the software part of our prototype system. On the top there are the two interfaces to users, image browsing and retrieval. In the middle are four modules that support the two interfaces, which are built on top of three modules, including Photomesa (Bederson 2001), which is a zoomable and reusable user interface toolkit, the inner-distance based shape matching (IDSC) techniques and an image processing module. Details of the system can be found in (Agarwal et al. 2006).

The system is tested in several real field test trips on the Plummers Island on the Potomac River near Washington DC. During these tests, the botanists picked leaves and took pictures of them. The pictures were then be automatically uploaded to our system and the searching results were provided by our system in real time. Both the reliability and usability of our system are confirmed in these real tests.

EXPERIMENTS AND REAL APPLICATIONS

Articulated Database

To show the articulation insensitivity of the inner-distance, we apply the proposed articulation invariant signature and the IDSC+DP approach to an articulated shape data set we collected. The dataset contains

Algorithm 2: Shortest path texture context h_i at landmark point x_i

$h_i \leftarrow$ 3-D matrix with zero entries everywhere

for $j=1$ to n, $j \neq i$

$\Gamma(x_i, x_j; O) \leftarrow$ shortest path from x_i to x_j

$\hat{h} \leftarrow$ 1-D weighted histogram of the relative orientations along $\Gamma(x_i, x_j; O)$

$\hat{h} \leftarrow \hat{h}/|\hat{h}|$ /   * Normalize $\hat{h}$ */

$d_{id} \leftarrow$ the inner-distance bin index computed from $d(x_i, x_j; O)$

$\theta_{id} \leftarrow$ the inner-angle bin index computed from $\theta(x_i, x_j; O)$

for $\alpha_{id} = 1$ to n_r /   * n_r is the number of relative orientation bins */

$h_i(d_{id}, \theta_{id}, \alpha_{id}) \leftarrow h_i(d_{id}, \theta_{id}, \alpha_{id}) + \hat{h}(\alpha_{id})$

endfor

endfor

$h_i \leftarrow h_i / |h_i|$ /   * Normalize h_i */

40 images from 8 different objects. Each object has 5 images articulated to different degrees (see Fig. 16). The dataset is very challenging because of the similarity between different objects (especially the scissors). The holes of the scissors make the problem even more difficult.

The parameters in the experiment are: $n=200$, $n_d=5$, $n_\theta=12$. Since all the objects are at the same orientation, we align the contours by forcing them to start from the bottom-left points and then set $k=1$ for DP matching. The articulation invariant signatures of the shapes are computed and shown in Fig. 16 (b).

To evaluate the recognition result, for each image, the four most similar matches are chosen from other images in the dataset. The retrieval result is summarized as the number of 1st, 2nd, 3rd and 4th most similar matches that come from the correct object. Table I shows the retrieval results. It demonstrates that both the articulation invariant signature and the IDSC help to improve recognition a lot. This verifies our claim that the inner-distance is very effective for objects with articulated parts. The experiment also shows that IDSC works better than MDS for the articulated shapes. One reason is that the MDS may cause loss of information since it uses the Euclidean distance to *approximate* the inner-distance.

Aside from the articulated dataset, the inner-distance based approaches have been applied to several other public datasets, including the MPEG7 shape dataset, Kimia datasets, ETH-80 datasets. Excellent performance is observed in all the experiments. Details of these experiments can be found in (Ling & Jacobs 2007).

Swedish Leaf Database

The Swedish leaf dataset comes from a leaf classification project at Linkoping University and the Swedish Museum of Natural History (Soderkvist 2001). The dataset contains isolated leaves from 15 different Swedish tree species, with 75 leaves per species. Fig. 17 shows some representative silhouette examples. Some preliminary classification work has been done in (Soderkvist 2001) by combining simple features like moments, area and curvature etc. We tested with Fourier descriptors, SC+DP, MDS+SC+DP,

Figure 16. (a) Articulated shape database. This dataset contains 40 images from 8 objects with articulation. Each column contains five images from the same object. (b) MDS of the articulated shape database using the inner-distances. Reprinted with permission from "Shape Classification Using the Inner-Distance", H. Ling and D.W. Jacobs, IEEE Trans on Pattern Anal. and Mach. Intell. (PAMI), 29(2):286-299, (2007). © 2007 IEEE.

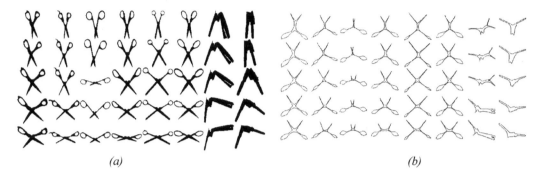

(a)   (b)

Table 1. Retrieval result on the articulate dataset

Distance Type	Top 1	Top 2	Top 3	Top 4
L_2	25/40	15/40	12/40	10/40
SC+DP	20/40	10/40	11/40	5/40
Art. Inv. Signature	36/40	26/40	17/40	15/40
IDSC+DP	40/40	34/40	35/40	27/40

Figure 17. Typical images from Swedish leaf data base, one image per species. Note that some species are quite similar, e.g. the 1st, 3rd and 9th species. Reprinted with permission from "Shape Classification Using the Inner-Distance", H. Ling and D.W. Jacobs, IEEE Trans on Pattern Anal. and Mach. Intell. (PAMI), 29(2):286-299, (2007). © 2007 IEEE.

IDSC+DP and SPTC+DP with parameters $n=128$, $n_d=8$, $n_\theta=12$, $n_r=8$ and $k=1$. Each species contains 25 training samples and 50 testing samples per species. The recognition results with 1-nearest-neighbor are summarized in Tab. II. Notice that unlike other experiments, the articulation invariant signature works a little better than IDSC on the leaf images. One possible explanation is that, as a real image dataset, the inner-angle for leaves are less robust due to boundary noise. Also notice that SPTC improves IDSC as we had expected.

Smithsonian Isolated Leaf Database

This data set comes from the Smithsonian project (Electronic Field Guide, 2008). We designed an Electronic Field Guide image retrieval system that allows online visual searching. The task is very challenging because it requires querying a database containing more than one hundred species and real time performance requires an efficient algorithm. In addition, the pictures taken in the field are vulnerable to lighting changes and the leaves may not be flattened well.

We evaluated the proposed approaches on a representative subset of the leaf image database in the system (http://www.ist.temple.edu/~hbling/data/SI-93.zip). The subset contains 343 leaves from 93 species (the number of leaves from different species varies). In the experiment, 187 of them are used as the training set and 156 as the testing set. Note that there are only two instances per class in the train-

Table 2. Recognition rates on the Swedish leaf dataset. Note that MDS+SC+DP and SPTC achieved the same rates

Method	[SODERKVIST 2001]	Fourier	SC+DP	MDS+SC+DP	IDSC+DP	SPTC+DP
Recognition Rate	82%	89.6%	8812.%	95.33%	94.13%	95.33%

Note that MDS+SC+DP and SPTC got same rates.

*Figure 18. The Smithsonian dataset. This dataset contains 343 leaf images from 93 species. Typical images from each species are shown. Reprinted with permission from "Shape Classification Using the Inner-Distance", H. Ling and D.W. Jacobs, IEEE Trans on Pattern Anal. and Mach. Intell. (**PAMI**), 29(2):286-299, (2007). © 2007 IEEE.*

ing set on average. The retrieval performance is evaluated using performance curves which show the recognition rate among the top N leaves, where N varies from 1 to 16.

For the efficiency reasons mentioned above, only 64 contour points are used (i.e. n=64). The similarity between leaves is measured by the shape context distance D_{sc} (see Sec. II or (Belongie et al. 2002). This distance is based on a greedy matching and should not be confused with the bipartite matching

*Figure 19. Recognition result on the Smithsonian leaf dataset. The ROC curves shows the recognition rate among the top N matched leaves. Reprinted with permission from "Shape Classification Using the Inner-Distance", H. Ling and D.W. Jacobs, IEEE Trans on Pattern Anal. and Mach. Intell. (**PAMI**), 29(2):286-299, (2007). © 2007 IEEE.*

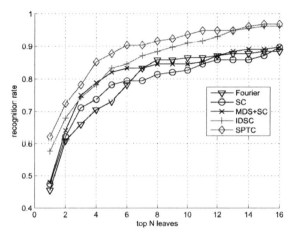

*Figure 20. Three retrieval examples for IDSC and SPTC. The left column shows the query images. For each query image, the top four retrieving results are shown to its right, using IDSC and SPTC respectively. The circled images come from the same species as the query image. Reprinted with permission from "Shape Classification Using the Inner-Distance", H. Ling and D.W. Jacobs, IEEE Trans on Pattern Anal. and Mach. Intell. (**PAMI**), 29(2):286-299, (2007). © 2007 IEEE.*

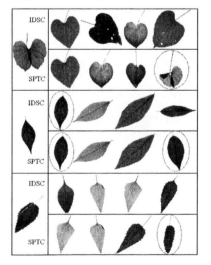

based approach. Therefore it is faster than DP-based matching. Other parameters used in the experiment are n_d=5, n_θ=12, and n_r=8. Note that k is not needed because DP is not used here. The performance is plotted in Fig. 19. It shows that SPTC works significantly better than other methods. Fig. 20 gives some detailed query results of SPTC and IDSC, from which we can see how SPTC improves retrieval result by also considering texture information.

CONCLUSION

In this chapter, we present an inner-distance based shape matching algorithm for the application of foliage image retrieval. With experiments on two leaf databases involving thousands of images, our method demonstrates excellent performance in comparison to several state-of-the-art approaches. The approach is adopted in an electronic field guide system that has been tested in several real field test trips.

There are two main issues that are worth future study. First, the algorithm requires segmentation for preprocessing. In our current system images are taken by putting leaves against a white paper background. This is apparently not an ideal solution especially for use in the field. Second, more efficient schemes are needed for fast retrieval and browsing, especially for a large database or an online system. One possibility is through smart indexing techniques instead of the currently used nearest neighbor algorithm. We look forward to future development in these directions.

ACKNOWLEDGMENT

We would like to thank J. W. Kress, R. Russell, N. Bourg, G. Agarwal, P. Belhumeur and N. Dixit for help with the Smithsonian leaf database, and O. Soderkvist for the Swedish leaf data. This work is supported in part by NSF (ITR-03258670325867) and by the US-Israel Binational Science Foundation grant number 2002/254.

REFERENCES

Agarwal, S., Awan, A., & Roth, D. (2004). Learning to Detect Objects in Images via a Sparse, Part-Based Representation. *IEEE Trans. on Pattern Analysis and Machine Intelligence, 26*(11), 1475-1490.

Agarwal, G. (2005). *Presenting Visual Information to the User: Combining Computer Vision and Interface Design.* Master Thesis, Univseristy of Maryland, 2005.

Agarwal, G., Belhumeur, P., Feiner, S., Jacobs, D., Kress, J.W., Ramamoorthi, R., Bourg, N., Dixit, N., Ling, H., Mahajan, D., Russell, R., Shirdhonkar, S., Sunkavalli, K., & White, S. (2006). First Steps Toward an Electronic Field Guide for Plants. *Taxon, 55*(3), 597-610.

Basri, R., Costa, L., Geiger, D., & Jacobs, D. (1998). Determining the Similarity of Deformable Shapes. *Vision Research, 38,* 2365-2385.

Bederson, B.B. (2001). PhotoMesa: A Zoomable Image Browser Using Quantum Treemaps and Bubblemaps. *ACM Symposium on User Interface Software and Technology, CHI Letters, 3*(2), 71-80.

Belongie, S., Malik, J., & Puzicha, J. (2002). Shape Matching and Object Recognition Using Shape Context. *IEEE Trans. on Pattern Analysis and Machine Intelligence, 24*(24), 509-522.

Biederman, I. (1987). Recognition--by--components: A theory of human image understanding. *Psychological Review, 94*(2), 115-147.

Blum, H. (1973). Biological Shape and Visual Science. *J. Theor. Biol., 38*, 205-287.

Bookstein, F. (1989). Principal Warps: Thin-Plate-Splines and Decomposition of Deformations. *IEEE Trans. on Pattern Analysis and Machine Intelligence, 11*(6), 567-585.

Borg, I., & Groenen, P. (1997). *Modern Multidimensional Scaling: Theory and Applications.* Springer.

Chen, H., Belhumeur, P., & Jacobs, D. (2000). In search of Illumination Invariants. *IEEE Conf. on Computer Vision and Pattern Recognition, I,* 254-261.

Cormen, T., Leiserson, T, Rivest, R., & Stein, C. (2001). *Introduction to Algorithms,* 2nd edition. The MIT Press.

Elad, A., & Kimmel, R. (2003). On Bending Invariant Signatures for Surfaces. *IEEE Trans. on Pattern Analysis and Machine Intelligence, 25*(10), 1285-1295

An Electronic Field Guide: Plant Exploration and Discovery in the 21st Century. (2008). Retrieved December 12, 2008, fromhttp://herbarium.cs.columbia.edu/.

Feldman, J., & Singh, M. (2005). Information along contours and object boundaries. *Psychological Review, 112*(1), 243-252.

Felzenszwalb, P. (2005). Representation and Detection of Deformable Shapes. *IEEE Trans. on Pattern Analysis and Machine Intelligence, 27*(2), 208-220.

Felzenszwalb, P., & Huttenlocher, D. (2005). Pictorial Structures for Object Recognition. *International Journal of Computer Vision, 61*(1), 55-79.

Felzenszwalb, P., & Schwartz, J. (2007). Hierarchical Matching of Deformable Shapes. *IEEE Conference on Computer Vision and Pattern Recognition.*

Fergus, R., Perona, P., & Zisserman, A. (2003). Object Class Recognition by Unsupervised Scale-Invariant Learning, *IEEE Conference on Computer Vision and Pattern Recognition, II,* 264-271.

Gandhi, A. (2002). *Content-based image retrieval: Plant species identification.* MS thesis. Oregon State University.

Gorelick, L., Galun, M., Sharon, A., Basri, R., & Brandt, A. (2004). Shape Representation and Classification Using the Poisson Equation. *IEEE Conference on Computer Vision and Pattern Recognition,* (pp. 61-67).

Grenander, U., Srivastava, A., & Saini, S. (2007). A Pattern-Theoretic Characterization of Biological Growth. *IEEE Transactions on Medical Imaging, 26*(5), 648-659.

Grimson, W.E.L. (1990). *Object Recognition by Computer: The Role of Geometric Constraints.* Cambridge, MA: MIT Press.

Hamza, A. B., & Krim, H. (2003). Geodesic Object Representation and Recognition. In I. Nystrom et al. (Eds.), *Discrete Geometry for Computer Imagery, LNCS, 2886,* 378-387.

Hoffman, D. D., & Richards, W. A. (1985). Parts of recognition. *Cognition, 18,* 65-96.

Im, C., Nishida, H., & Kunii, T. L. (1998). Recognizing plant species by leaf shapes-a case study of the Acer family. *International Conference on Pattern Recognition, 2,* 1171-1173.

Keogh, E., Wei, L., Xi, X., Lee, S-H., & Vlachos, M. (2006). LB_Keogh Supports Exact Indexing of Shapes under Rotation Invariance with Arbitrary Representations and Distance Measures. *VLDB.*

Kimia, B. B., Tannenbaum, A. R., & Zucker, S. W. (1995). Shapes, shocks, and deformations, I: The components of shape and the reaction-diffusion space. *International Journal of Computer Vision, 15*(3), 189-224.

Lazebnik, L., Schmid, C., & Ponce, J. (2005). A sparse texture representation using affine-invariant regions. *IEEE Trans. Pattern Anal. Mach. Intell., 27*(8), 1265-1278.

Leibe, B., & Schiele, B. (2003). Analyzing Appearance and Contour Based Methods for Object Categorization. *IEEE Conference on Computer Vision and Pattern Recognition, II,* 409-415.

Ling, H., & Jacobs, D. W. (2005). Using the Inner-Distance for Classification of Articulated Shapes. *IEEE Conference on Computer Vision and Pattern Recognition, II,* 719-726.

Ling, H., & Jacobs, D. W. (2005). Deformation Invariant Image Matching. *IEEE International Conference on Computer Vision, II,* 1466-1473.

Ling, H., & Jacobs, D. W. (2007). Shape Classification Using the Inner-Distance. *IEEE Trans on Pattern Anal. and Mach. Intell., 29*(2), 286-299.

Liu, T., & Geiger, D. (1997). Visual Deconstruction: Recognizing Articulated Objects. *Energy Minimization Methods in Computer Vision and Pattern Recognition,* (pp. 295-309).

Mikolajczyk, K., & Schmid, C. (2005). A Performance Evaluation of Local Descriptors. *IEEE Trans. Pattern Anal. Mach. Intell., 27*(10), 1615-1630.

Mokhtarian, F., & Abbasi, S. (2004). Matching shapes with self-intersections: application to leaf classification. *IEEE Trans. on Image Processing, 13*(5), 653-661.

Mori, G., & Malik, J. (2003). Recognizing Objects in Adversarial Clutter: Breaking a Visual CAPTCHA. *IEEE Conference on Computer Vision and Pattern Recognition, I,* 1063-6919.

Nilsback, M., & Zisserman, A. (2006). A Visual Vocabulary for Flower Classification. *IEEE Conf. on Computer Vision and Pattern Recognition, 2,* 1447-1454.

Osada, R., Funkhouser, T., Chazelle, B., & Dobkin, D. (2002). Shape Distributions. *ACM Trans. on Graphics, 21*(4), 807-832.

Petrakis, E.G.M., Diplaros, A., & Milios, E. (2002). Matching and Retrieval of Distorted and Occluded Shapes Using Dynamic Programming. *IEEE Trans. on Pattern Analysis and Machine Intelligence, 24*(11), 1501-1516.

Saitoh, T., & Kaneko, T. (2000). Automatic Recognition of Wild Flowers. *International Conference on Pattern Recognition, 2,* 2507-2510.

Sclaroff, S., & Liu, L. (2001). Deformable shape detection and description via model-based region grouping, *IEEE Trans. on Pattern Analysis and Machine Intelligence, 23*(5), 475-489.

Schneiderman, H., & Kanade, T. (2004). Object Detection Using the Statistics of Parts. *International Journal of Computer Vision, 56*(3), 151-177.

Sebastian, T.B., Klein, P.N., & Kimia, B.B. (2004). Recognition of Shapes by Editing Their Shock Graphs. *IEEE Trans. on Pattern Analysis and Machine Intelligence, 26*(5), 550-571.

Siddiqi, K, Shokoufandeh, A., Dickinson, S.J., & Zucker, S.W. (1999). Shock Graphs and Shape Matching. *International Journal of Computer Vision, 35*(1), 13-32.

Soderkvist, O. (2001). *Computer Vision Classification of Leaves from Swedish Trees.* Master Thesis. Linkoping University.

Thayananthan, A., Stenger, B., Torr, P.H.S., & Cipolla, R. (2003). Shape Context and Chamfer Matching in Cluttered Scenes. *IEEE Conference on Computer Vision and Pattern Recognition, I,* 127-133.

Thompson, D.W. (1992) *On Growth and Form.* (republished), Dover Publication.

Tu, Z., & Yuille, A.L. (2004). Shape Matching and Recognition-Using Generative Models and Informative Features. *European Conference on Computer Vision, 3,* 195-209.

Veltkamp, R.C., & Hagedoorn, M. (1999). State of the Art in Shape Matching, *Technical Report* UU-CS-1999-27, Utrecht.

Wang, Z., Chi, Z., & Feng, D. (2003). Shape based leaf image retrieval. *IEEI proc. Vision, Image and Signal Processing, 150*(1), 34-43.

Weiss, I., & Ray, M. (2005). Recognizing Articulated Objects Using a Region-Based Invariant Transform. *IEEE Trans. on Pattern Analysis and Machine Intelligence, 27*(10), 1660-1665.

Yahiaoui, I., Herve, N., & Boujemaa, N. (2005). *Shape-based image retrieval in botanical collections.*

Zhao, L., & Davis, L. S. (2005). Segmentation and Appearance Model Building from an Image Sequence. *IEEE International Conference on Image Processing, 1,* 321-324.

Chapter V
Similarity Learning for Motion Estimation

Shaohua Kevin Zhou
Siemens Corporate Research Inc., USA

Jie Shao
Google Inc., USA

Bogdan Georgescu
Siemens Corporate Research Inc., USA

Dorin Comaniciu
Siemens Corporate Research Inc., USA

ABSTRACT

Motion estimation necessitates an appropriate choice of similarity function. Because generic similarity functions derived from simple assumptions are insufficient to model complex yet structured appearance variations in motion estimation, the authors propose to learn a discriminative similarity function to match images under varying appearances by casting image matching into a binary classification problem. They use the LogitBoost algorithm to learn the classifier based on an annotated database that exemplifies the structured appearance variations: An image pair in correspondence is positive and an image pair out of correspondence is negative. To leverage the additional distance structure of negatives, they present a location-sensitive cascade training procedure that bootstraps negatives for later stages of the cascade from the regions closer to the positives, which enables viewing a large number of negatives and steering the training process to yield lower training and test errors. The authors apply the learned similarity function to estimating the motion for the endocardial wall of left ventricle in echocardiography and to performing visual tracking. They obtain improved performances when comparing the learned similarity function with conventional ones.

INTRODUCTION

Image Matching and Similarity Function

Image matching is fundamental to various computer vision tasks. In motion estimation, image matching happens along the temporal dimension, e.g., comparing consecutive frames to establish correspondences over time or tracking points of interest. In image registration, image matching happens along the spatial dimension, e.g., comparing two heterogeneous images for establishing spatial correspondences. Image matching is also vital to content-based retrieval, face recognition, and application of the same kind, where comparing testing and training image is needed.

Underlying an image matching process lays an indispensable component of similarity function. A similarity function is a two-input function $s(I, I')$ that measures how closely the test patch I' is visually similar to the template patch I. A typical use of similarity function in, say, motion estimation and image registration algorithms is as follows: given two images I and I' and a target point (u,v) whose motion vector or spatial correspondence to be estimated, one finds the shift that has the (local) maximum similarity. If the minimum is sought, one can simply negate the similarity function.

$$(\delta \hat{u}, \delta \hat{v}) = \arg \max_{(\delta u, \delta v) \in W} s(I(u,v), I'(u + \delta u, v + \delta v)), \tag{1}$$

where $I(u,v)$ is a local patch extracted from the image I, centered at (u,v), and W is the searching window. In motion estimation, the two images I and I' are successive frames, e.g., $I=I_{t-1}$ and $I'=I_t$; in image registration, the two images I and I' are the image pair to be registered. In retrieval and recognition applications, the use of similarity function is as follows:

$$\hat{n} = \arg \max_{n=1,..,N} s(I_n, I'), \tag{2}$$

where $\{I_n; n=1,2,...,N\}$ are gallery images stored in the database, and I' is a query image that is used to sort the database. The principal difference between (1) and (2) lies in the search space where the maximum is found: The search space for the first type of application (e.g., motion estimation and image registration) is a spatial window, and that for the second type of applications (e.g., retrieval and recognition) is on the index of the images in the gallery database.

In this chapter, we concentrate on the specific application of motion estimation. It is obvious that applications like image registration, retrieval and recognition, etc. can be also tackled with a minor modification.

Similarity Function Under Complex Appearance Variations

Matching two images under complex appearance variations is challenging due to lacking an appropriate similarity function. Similarity functions proposed in the literature are mostly generic and inadequate for handling complex appearance variations. A motivating example is illustrated in Fig. 1.

Consider a stress echocardiographic video (stress echo) (Otto, 2004), a series of 2D ultrasound images of the human heart captured after the patient undergoes exercise or takes special medicine. We focus on wall motion analysis to characterize the functionality of the heart. To be specific, we measure the motion of the endocardium (or the inner border) of the left ventricle (LV). As shown in Fig. 1 the

Figure 1. A stress echo sequence with six consecutive frames and according annotations of the LV endocardium. Due to the rapid heart rate (177 beats per second), the LV appearance varies significantly within a short period of six consecutive frames. (From (Zhou et al. 2006) at IEEE 2006)

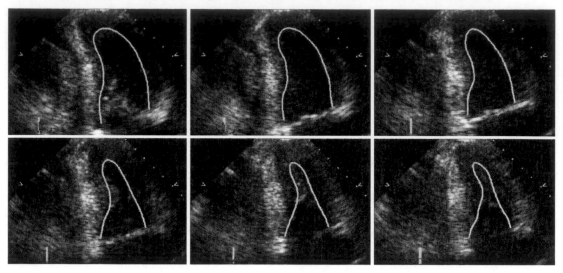

LV endocardium presents severe appearance changes over a cardiac cycle due to nonrigid deformation, imaging artifacts like speckle noise and signal dropout, movement of papillary muscle (which is attached to the LV endocardium but not a part of the wall), respiratory interferences, unnecessary probe movement, insufficient sampling for stress echo, etc.

For the above example of motion estimation, we will illustrate in later sections that the performances achieved by generic similarity functions are not satisfactory. To bridge the performance gap, we propose to learn a *discriminative similarity function* using the boosting framework (Freund & Schapire, 1997) (Friedman, Hastie, & Tibshirani, 2000). Our proposal is grounded on the following arguments:

- Albeit complex, the appearance variations manifest certain structures in an application-dependent fashion. In the stress echo example, the deformation of the LV endocardium is governed by the mechanical movement of the heart muscle, which, for example, is cyclic in nature. Therefore, it is possible to collect enough data to cover the structured appearance variations, thereby leading us to use *machine learning* tools to learn a similarity function.
- A good similarity function for image matching should possess the following two properties: its response map is both smooth and unimodal (ideally peaked at the correct location). In the chapter, we explore the second property. In the extreme, the similarity function operates like a *discriminative* function: *positive* if the centers of two paired image patches are in correspondence and *negative* if out of correspondence.

$$s(I, I') = \begin{cases} 1, & \text{if } (I, I') \text{ is a corresponding pair;} \\ 0, & \text{otherwise.} \end{cases} \qquad (3)$$

This fits the concept of discriminative learning. If we treat the image pairs in correspondence as positives and the rest as negatives (as shown in Fig. 2(a,d,e)), the similarity function becomes a discriminative function that separates two classes. Given an annotated video database, we can learn such a discriminative function using examples extracted from the database.

- In general, generic similarity functions, which will be briefly reviewed in Section II, work for certain imaging scenarios but break down for others, depending on the way in which the appearance changes. For example, the sum of squared distance (SSD) works best for isotropic Gaussian noise, the sum of absolute distance (SAD) for the Laplacian noise, and the CD_2 (Cohen & Dinstein, 2002) for fully developed speckle noise. On one hand, there is no such a *global* and generic similarity function universally good for all scenarios; on the other hand, it is very likely that different *local* regions of the image are best suited for different similarity functions. This strongly motivates us to take a *boosting* approach (Freund & Schapire, 1997) (Friedman, Hastie, & Tibshirani, 2000) that combines locally good similarity function (still weak though) into a globally strong similarity function that works best for the scenario exemplified by an annotated database.

Section III presents the issues related to learning such a discriminative similarity function. Among a variety of binary classification methods, we invoke the LogitBoost algorithm (Friedman, Hastie, & Tibshirani, 2000) to selectively combine weak learners into one strong similarity function. We associate a weak learner with a Haar-like local rectangle feature (Papageorglou, Oren, & Poggio, 1998) (Viola & Jones, 2001) to accommodate fast computation. The weak learner takes an image pair as input and uses the two feature responses collected from both images. We construct the weak learner as a nonparametric 2D piecewise constant function of the two feature responses in order to strengthen its modeling power, thereby bringing savings in both training speed and storage requirement.

Selecting negatives is crucial to the training accuracy and consequently influences the final performance. The negatives implicitly possess a location parameter measuring their closeness to the positives. To leverage the additional distance structure of the negatives, we present a location-sensitive cascade training procedure that bootstraps negatives for later stage of the classifier cascade from the regions closer to the positives. This allows not only viewing a large number of negatives as in the regular cascade training (Viola & Jones, 2001) but also steering the training process with respect to the desired final accuracy. Further, we empirically show that the location-sensitive cascade yields lower training and test errors than the regular one.

In Section IV, we present the so-called *BoostMotion* approach that experiments the boosted similarity function for motion estimation. We compare the discriminative similarity function with conventional similarity functions using the stress echo sequences and obtain improved performance when estimating the motion of the LV endocardium. We also contrast the BoostMotion approach, which takes a pair of images as input, with a learning-based detection algorithm, which takes a single image patch as input, and demonstrate the importance of temporal information in motion estimation. Then we insert the BoostMotion module into a naive tracker that estimates the motion vector frame by frame and hence is prone to drift. In the experiment of tracking regular echo sequences, we show that using the discriminative similarity function reduces drifting. We finally test the discriminative similarity function in general visual tracking. Section V summarizes the chapter.

GENERIC SIMILARITY FUNCTION

In this section, we briefly review similarity functions proposed in the literature. Because we focus on the applications like motion estimation, we refer the readers to (Santini & Jain, 1999) for a review of similarity functions used elsewhere. We first present a rough categorization of generic similarity function and then address the difficulty in applying them into real applications of motion estimation and image registration.

Categorization of Generic Similarity Function

The similarity functions for motion estimation proposed in the literature are generic in nature and mostly arise from the following two assumptions:

- The assumption of *constant brightness*. In a simplistic form, it assumes a probabilistic model as follows.

$$I_t(u + \delta u, v + \delta v) = I_{t-1}(u, v) + e_t(u, v), \tag{4}$$

where $e_t(u,v)$ is the observation noise.

- The assumption of *parametric noise model*, that is, the noise variable $e_t(u,v)$ in (4) is of certain parametric form. Often, the parametric noise model yields a parametric similarity function.

Depending on the noise model, similarity function can be roughly categorized as intensity-based, histogram-based, and modality-specific. Other similarity functions for motion estimation as well as image registration are available too.

Intensity-Based Similarity Function

Examples of intensity-based similarity function include sum of square distance (SSD) (Brox, Bruhn, Papenberg, & Wiecker, 2004) (Lucas & Kanade, 1981) (Shi & Tomasi, 1994), sum of absolute distance (SAD), etc.

The SSD similarity function takes the following form:

$$\text{SSD:} \quad s(I, I') = \|I - I'\|_2, \tag{5}$$

where the L_2 norm is used. The SSD is also equivalent to assuming an isotropic Gaussian noise model. The minimum value of the SSD is reached only when $I=I'$.

The SSD can be generalized in two ways. First, it can be based on images derived from the original ones. For example, if the gradient image (denoted by $\hat{I} = \partial I / \partial \alpha, \{\alpha \in x, y\}$) is used, this corresponds to the "gradient constancy" assumption (Brox, Bruhn, Papenberg, & Wiecker, 2004).

$$s(I, I') = \|\hat{I} - \hat{I}'\|_2 \tag{6}$$

Learning an affinity function using gradient information is also proposed in (Fowlkes, Martin, & Malik, 2003) (Lunqvist, Bengtsson, & Thurfjell, 2003). Second, the L_2 norm can be replaced by an L_p norm. If $p=1$, the similarity function becomes the SAD function, which is equivalent to assuming a Laplacian noise model.

SAD: $s(I,I') = \|I - I'\|_1$ (7)

Histogram-Based Similarity Function

Assuming that the histogram of I is given by $h(I)$, the Bhattacharyya distance (Comaniciu, Ramesh, & Meer, 2000) is defined as

BHA: $s(I,I') = \int \sqrt{h(I)h(I')}d\lambda.$ (8)

The Bhattacharyya distance $s(I, I')$ is always less than one because

$$\int \sqrt{h(I)h(I')}d\lambda \leq \frac{1}{2}\int (h(I) + h(I'))d\,\lambda = 1,$$ (9)

and achieves one only when $h(I)=h(I')$. The condition $I=I'$ is sufficient for $h(I)=h(I')$.

Other histogram-based similarity functions include the chi-square distance, earth moving distance, KL divergence, Jensen-Shannon distance, etc.

Modality-Specific Similarity Function

In the chapter, we focus on ultrasound images in the motion estimation experiment. The ultrasound-specific CD_2 similarity function proposed by Cohen and Dinstein (Cohen & Dinstein, 2002) is specially designed for handling a fully-developed speckle noise in an ultrasound image and shown to be effective by Boukerroui, Alison, & Brady (2003) for tracking ultrasound sequences.

The CD_2 function is defined as

CD_2: $s(I,I') = -\sum \log(\frac{i}{i'} + \frac{i'}{i}),$ (10)

where the pixels i and i' belong to I and I', respectively. The maximum of CD_2 is obtained only when $i=i'$ for all i (or equivalently, $I=I'$) because $\frac{i}{i'} + \frac{i'}{i} \geq 2$.

Other Similarity Function

We here also mention two similarity functions widely used in the literature: normalized cross correlation (NCC) and mutual information (MI).

The NCC is used to compensate an affine photometric variation and is defined as

NCC: $s(I,I') = -\dfrac{(I - \mu(I)) \bullet (I' - \mu(I'))/N}{\sigma(I)\sigma(I')},$ (11)

where $\bullet$ denotes the dot product, N is the number of pixel in the image I, and $\mu(.)$ and $\sigma(.)$ take the sample mean and standard deviation, respectively. The maximum is achieved only when $I=aI'+b$. Further to compensate the non-uniformity in the above linear model, the NCC is generalized to local normalized correlation coefficient (LNC). To calculate LNC, the image patch is first divided into several sub-regions whose NCC is computed. The mean of all NCC's is defined as LNC.

One popular similarity function used for medical image registration is the so-called mutual information (MI) (Viola & Welles, 1997) defined as:

$$\text{MI:} \quad s(I,I') = \int h(I,I') \frac{h(I,I')}{h(I)h(I')} d\lambda, \tag{12}$$

where $h(I,I')$ is the joint histogram. It is easy to prove that $MI \geq 0$; only when I and I' are independent, i.e., $h(I,I')=h(I)h(I')$, the MI reaches the minimum 0. Image registration is to find the maximum value of MI by deforming I'. Note that mutual information is not modality-specific, which makes it common for cross-modality registration.

Difficulty from Generic Similarity Function

One reason why the generic similarity functions are not working for real applications because the two assumptions are largely violated, that is, the brightness is not constant and/or the noise model is not parametric. For example, Fig. 2(a) shows a pair of consecutive frames in a stress echo sequence and Fig. 2(b) the cropped LV images from the two frames. When we take the difference of the LV images as in Fig. 2(b), we observe a lot of structures (mainly due to nonrigid deformation, disappearing papillary muscle) and speckles in Fig. 2(c). By learning the similarity function, we avoid any possibly unrealistic assumption.

DISCRIMINATIVE SIMILARITY FUNCTION

In this section, we address how to learn the discriminative similarity function (Zhou, Shao, Georgescu, & Comaniciu, 2006). We first review the LogitBoost algorithm and then proceed to the practical choice of weak functions used in boosting. Finally, we discuss how to deal with the numerous negative examples by leveraging their additional distance structure in terms of the closeness to the positives.

Boosting

We invoke the framework of boosting to learn the similarity function. Boosting iteratively selects weak learners to form a strong learner using an additive form:

$$F(x) = \sum_{f_m(x) \in \Omega} f_m(x), \tag{13}$$

where $F(x)$ is the strong learner, $f_m(x)$'s are the weak learners, and Ω is the *structural space* where the weak learners reside.

There exist many classifiers in the literature, such as multi-layer perceptron, support vector machine, Gaussian process, boosting, etc. Among them, support vector machine and boosting are probably the most influential ones due to their known large margin property or good generalization capability. We choose boosting over support vector machine mainly due to computational reasons. Using support vec-

Figure 2. (a) A pair of consecutive frames in a stress echo sequence. (b) The cropped LV images from the two frames. (c) The difference of the two LV images. (d) The positive pair for the left annulus point. (e) Four negative pairs for the left annulus point, i.e., the left end point on the contour.

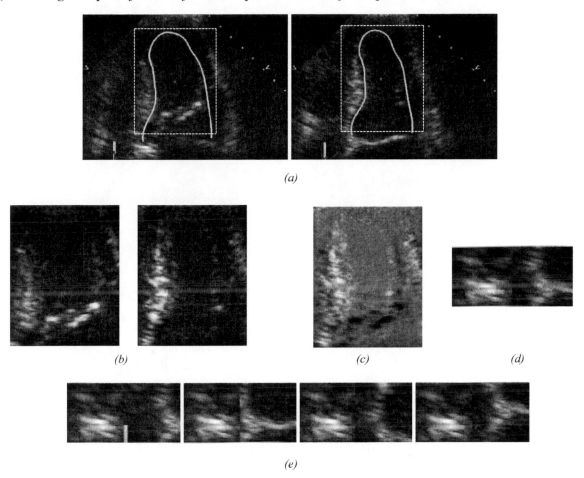

(a)

(b)   *(c)*   *(d)*

(e)

tor machine needs to store a lot of support vectors, which means a huge memory space, and to compare the query example with support vectors using some kernel function, which means a slow evaluation. In contrast, boosting combines weak learners that are based on local rectangle features into a strong learner and thus operates as a feature selector. As these features are calculated online, there is no need to store the training dataset in the memory and it is rapid to evaluate the boosted classifier.

Boosting has three key components: (1) structural space; (2) target/cost function; and (3) selection algorithm. Different variants of boosting are proposed in the literature depending on different choices of the key components. We decide to use the LogitBoost algorithm (Friedman, Hastie, & Tibshirani, 2000) summarized in Fig. 3. The LogitBoost algorithm differs from the commonly used AdaBoost algorithm approach (Freund & Schapire, 1997) in the following two aspects. First, they optimize different cost functions. The AdaBoost algorithm minimizes an upper bound of the target misclassification error; the LogitBoost algorithm directly minimizes a negative binomial log-likelihood, which is a natural choice for a binary classification problem. Second, the weak learner in the AdaBoost is a hard classifier while that in the LogitBoost is not: experimental evidence seems to favor the latter.

Figure 3. The two-class LogitBoost algorithm (Friedman, Hastie, & Tibshirani, 2000). (From (Zhou et al. 2006) at IEEE 2006)

Two-class Logit Boost Algorithm (positive $y=1$ and negative $y=0$)

1. Input: (i) Training data $\{x_i; i=1,2,...,N\}$ and their corresponding class labels $\{y_i; i=1,2,...,N\}$. (ii) The structural space Ω.
2. Start with weights $w_i=1/N$, $i=1,2,...,N$, $F(x)=0$, and probability estimates $p(x_i)=1/2$.
3. Repeat for $m=1,2,...,M$:
    a. Compute working responses and weights:

$$z_i = \frac{y_i - p(x_i)}{p(x_i)(1 - p(x_i))}; \quad w_i = p(x_i)(1 - p(x_i)). \qquad (14)$$

    b. Fit the function $f_m(x)$ by a weighted least-squares (LS) regression of z_i to x_i with weights w_i.

$$f_m(x) = \arg\min_{f \in \Omega} \varepsilon(f) = \sum_{i=1}^{N} w_i(z_i - f(x_i))^2 \qquad (15)$$

    c. Update $F(x)$ and $p(x)$ via

$$F(x) \leftarrow F(x) + \frac{1}{2} f_m(x), \qquad (16)$$

$$p(x) = \frac{\exp(F(x))}{\exp(F(x)) + \exp(-F(x))} . \qquad (17)$$

Output the classifier $sign[F(x)]$.

In our context, a data point x is an image pair $x=(I,I')$. One obvious choice for the boosted similarity function $s(I,I')$ is the probability of the class label $y(I,I')$ being 1, that is $s(I,I')=p(I,I')$.

$$s(I,I') = p(I,I') = \frac{\exp(F(I,I'))}{\exp(F(I,I')) + \exp(-F(I,I'))}, \qquad (18)$$

Using boosting to learn a similarity function has recently attracted attention. In (Jones & Viola, 2003), Jones and Viola learned a similarity function for face recognition. Even though the similarity function takes two image patches as input, it is the difference of the two images that are actually used, which is in the same spirit of constructing intrapersonal and interpersonal spaces (Moghaddam, Jebara, & Pentland, 2001), because the boosted local features are computed on top of the difference image. In (In, 2006 Yu, Amores, Sebe, & Tian independently proposed to boost a strong function by combining various generic similarity functions. The similarity function learned in such a way frees the assumption of parametric noise model, but is still affected by the constant brightness assumption.

Structural Space, Weak Learner, and Feature Selection

The structural space is the key to the performance of the learned classifier. In general, the space should be rich enough such that a simple additive function in (13) can characterize a complex decision boundary. In addition, the weak learners in the structural space should be robust to appearance variation and fast to evaluate.

As mentioned earlier, combining the generic similarity functions such as those listed in Section II into a strong committee (Yu, et al., 2006) is still limited. Since different similarity functions might be effective for different local regions, we construct the weak learners $f(I,I')$ based on Haar-like local rectangle features (Papageorgiou, Oren, & Poggio, 1998) (Viola & Jones, 2001), whose rapid evaluation is enabled via the use of integral image. As shown in (Viola & Jones, 2001), (1) it is easy to construct numerous local rectangle features, which renders a rich structural space, and (2) the local rectangle feature, whose response is normalized by the standard deviation of the image patch, is relatively robust to appearance variation.

A weak similarity function, based on a local rectangle feature, compares two local rectangle regions belonging to the two images I and I', respectively. As illustrated in Fig. 4(a), we parameterize the rectangle feature g by (r,c,dr,dc,t) where (r,c) is the starting point of the rectangle, (dr, dc) is the height and width, and t is the feature type. There are six feature types as shown in Fig. 4(a); other feature types can be used too. Given a rectangle feature g with a configuration (r,c,dr,dc,t) and an image pair (I,I'), we compute two feature responses $g(I|r,c,dr,dc,t)$ and $g(I'|r,c,dr,dc,t)$ from the two integral images associated with I and I', respectively. In principle, we can allow that two local rectangles have different parameters; however we refrain from doing this because empirically this shows no clear advantage but significantly increases training complexity.

We focus on the 2D feature space of the two feature responses $g(I)$ and $g(I')$ and model the weak learner $f(I,I')$ as a 2D piecewise constant function of $g(I)$ and $g(I')$, which has the following form:

$$f(I,I'\,|\,r,c,dr,rc,t,\{\alpha_{jk}\},\{T_j\},\{T_k{}'\}) = \sum_{j=1}^{J}\sum_{k=1}^{K}\alpha_{jk}[g(I)\in T_j]\wedge[g(I')\in T_k{}'], \tag{19}$$

where $[\pi]$ is an indicator function of the predicate π and α_{jk} is the constant associated with the region R_{jk}. In the above, we use a tessellation of the 2D feature space into non-overlapping regions $\{ R_{jk}= T_j \wedge T_k'; j=1,2,...,J, k=1,2,...,K\}$, where $\{T_j, j=1,2,...,J\}$ and $\{T_k', k=1,2,...,K\}$ are J and K non-overlapping intervals for the feature response $g(I)$ and $g(I')$, respectively.

The crucial step in the LogitBoost algorithm in Fig. 3 is step 3(b): fitting a weighted least square regression of z_i to x_i with weights w_i. It operates as a feature selection oracle: picking up from the structural space Ω the weak learner $f(I,I'|r,c,dr,dc,t,\{\alpha_{jk}\},\{T_j\},\{T_k'\})$ that minimizes the weighted least square cost $\varepsilon(f)$ defined in (15). Mathematically, we have the following optimization task:

$$f_m(I,I') = \arg\min_{r,c,dr,rc,t,\{\alpha_{jk}\},\{T_j\},\{T_k'\}} \sum_{i=1}^{N} w_i(z_i - \sum_{j=1}^{J}\sum_{k=1}^{K}\alpha_{jk}[g(I_i)\in T_j]\wedge[g(I_i')\in T_k'])^2, \tag{20}$$

where (I_i,I_i') is the ith training image pair.

This is a huge parameter space to search. The following three steps are used for efficiency.

1. First we empirically fix the T_j, T_k' for a given configuration (r,c,dr,dc,t) as follows: Calculate the feature responses from all training data points, determine the minimum and maximum response values, and uniformly divide them into the J (or K) intervals for image I (or image I').
2. We then find the optimal weights α_{jk}, given a weak learner f associated with a feature (r,c,dr,dc,t), by minimizing the weighted least square cost $\varepsilon(f)$ in (15). It is easy to show that the optimal weight α_{jk} is the weighted response z of all data points falling into the region R_{jk}.

$$\alpha_{jk} = \frac{\sum_{i=1}^{N} w_i z_i[g(I_i)\in T_j]\wedge[g(I_i')\in T_k']}{\sum_{i=1}^{N} w_i[g(I_i)\in T_j]\wedge[g(I_i')\in T_k']}. \tag{21}$$

Figure 4. (a) A weak similarity function compares two local rectangle regions belonging to images I and I', respectively. Panels from (b) to (d) illustrate the process of fitting a 2D piecewise constant function: (b) the field of w*z for all positives; (c) the field of -w*z for all negatives; and (d) the fitted 2D piecewise constant function. (From (Zhou et al. 2006) at IEEE 2006)

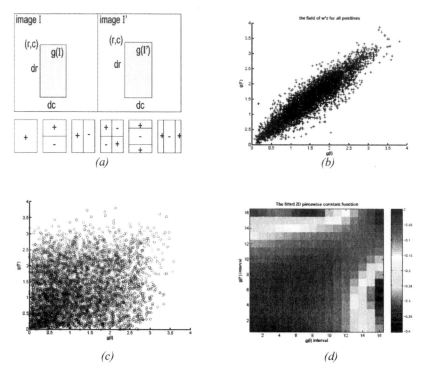

(a)   *(b)*

(c)   *(d)*

3.   Finally, we exhaust all possible configurations of (r,c,dr,dc,t) to find the smallest weighted least square cost $\varepsilon(f)$ for the step 3(b) in Fig. 3, which implements the feature selection. In other words, the weak function f based on the feature (r,c,dr,dc,t) with its optimal weights that yields the smallest weighted least square cost $\varepsilon(f)$ is selected.

Fig. 4 illustrates the process of finding the optimal weights in the piecewise constant function for a given feature. Fig. 4(b) visualizes the field of $w_i*z_i=y_i-p(x_i)=1-p(x_i)$ for all positives used in the first experiment of motion estimation in Section IV, where the color intensity corresponds to the value of $w*z$: the redder the plus sign is, the less likely the data point x is positive. The diagonal structure in Fig. 4(b) shows that the two feature responses of the positives are roughly same, which matches the intuition of motion estimation. Fig. 4(c) visualizes the field of $-w_i*z_i=p(x_i)$ for all negatives: the greener the circle sign is, the less likely the data point x is negative. As shown in Fig. 4(c), the negatives are characterized by a widely-dispersed nature. Fig. 4(d) shows the fitted 2D piecewise constant function: the constant coefficients α_{jk} along the diagonal lines are high, while off-diagonal ones are low.

Using nonparametric 2D piecewise constant functions as weak learners brings two extra benefits in terms of computation.

•   *Saving in training time.* Take the 1D case for example; 1D simple regression stumps (Viola & Jones, 2001) that `binarize' the feature response are often used as weak learners in the literature. It is easy to verify that any 1D piecewise constant function can be constructed by combining multiple 1D simple regression stumps. The similar holds for the 2D case. Such a combination strengthens the modeling power of weak learners and consequently accelerates the training process. Our empirical evidence shows that the learning time is almost inversely proportional to the number of thresholds used in the weak learner. One may argue that it brings the risk of overfitting. But boosting has the capability of combating the overfitting (in terms of classification though) even when the weak learner overfits; refer to the discussion part of (Friedman, Hastir, & Tibshirani, 2000). Further, in practice we smoothed the fields of $w*z$ and w before taking the division in (20) to ameliorate the overfitting of the weak learner itself.

- *Saving in memory requirement.* Boosting training requires calculating a matrix, whose row corresponds to the local rectangle feature and whose column to the training image pair. It is desired to store such a matrix in the memory in order to speedup the training process. Typically, the number of rectangle features is huge, e.g., more than 150K for a 24*24 image by an exhaustive construction (Viola & Jones, 2001). In one of our experiments, we kept about 40K rectangle features and about 10K training image pairs. To store the above matrix in a *float* precision, it consumes about 40K*10K*4* 2=3.2GB memory space, which exceeds the 2GB limit, the maximum contiguous block of memory of a 32-bit operating system. However, to learn the piecewise constant functions in our setting, we only need to store the interval index in the memory; refer to (20). In practice, we used 16 intervals, implying that an *unsigned char* precision is enough to store two indices, leading to a moderate memory requirement of about 400MB.

Location-Sensitive Cascade Training

Generating positives and negatives, which are pairs of images, from annotated videos is illustrated in Fig. 2(d,e) and Fig. 5(a). Given a pair of two successive frames (the left and right images in Fig. 5(a)), it contributes one positive by cropping two image patches centered at the target pixel (denoted by the red color) from the left and right frames, respectively. To generate negatives, we maintain the same image patch cropped from the left frame, i.e., centered at the target pixel, but force the center of the image patch cropped from the right frame away from the target pixel.

The negatives possess an additional location parameter that measures their distances to the target. Theoretically, the number of negatives is infinite if a non-integer pixel grid is used. To cover as many negatives as possible, we follow (Viola & Jones, 2001) to train a cascade of strong classifiers, which is a degenerate decision tree. After learning the strong classifier for the current stage using AdaBoost, the strong classifier threshold is tuned to pass all positives (or the majority of positives depending on the pre-specified detection probability). To train the strong classifier at a later stage, we maintain the same set of positives but bootstrap a new set of negatives that pass all previous strong classifiers (i.e., false positives). During scanning all test subwindows, the cascade structure is able to eliminate the negatives quickly.

The motion estimation or image registration accuracy is directly related to the selection of the negatives. On one hand, if the negatives are far away from the positives, it is easy to learn a perfect classifier but the accuracy is not guaranteed. On the other hand, if the negatives are too close to the positives, the accuracy is improved but it is hard to train a flawless classifier and might step into the zone of overfitting because the training positives and negatives are too confusing. Often in medical applications, different experts disagree with each other about the ground truth; thus, the performance only needs to be addressed

Figure 5. (a) Two successive frames and their corresponding positives and negatives. (b) Location-sensitive cascade training. (c) Performance comparison among location-sensitive cascade, regular cascade, and detection. (From (Zhou et al. 2006) at IEEE 2006)

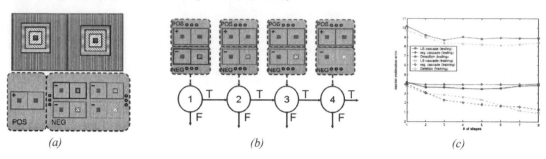

(a) (b) (c)

in a pre-specified precision, say the inter-user variability. To this end, we design a location-sensitive cascade training procedure that takes into account the location factor of the negatives.

As illustrated in Fig. 5(a), we divide all pixels into several negative regions according to their distances to the target pixel, where the target pixel is denoted by the red color and the negative regions are color-banded and with different strips. While preserving the features of the regular cascade training, we impose an additional constraint for the location-sensitive cascade training procedure: the negatives for several consecutive stages of the cascade are restricted to be from the same negative region. Further, the later stages use negatives closer to the positives; however, bootstrapping is still applied even across the boundary of the stages that are attached to different negatives regions. This procedure is graphically illustrated in Fig. 5(b). Refer to section IV (the first experiment of motion estimation) for a comparison between the location-sensitive cascade training and regular one, where we show that the location-sensitive cascade empirically yields lower training and test errors (also see Fig. 5(c)). Apart from the above performance improvement, location-sensitive cascade training enables steering the performance: If we find that the desired of accuracy is only 8 pixels instead of 5 pixels, the target achieved by the initial location-sensitive training, then we simply skip, during testing, the later stages of the cascade that is trained using the negatives less than 8 pixels away. But, the regular cascade training procedure does not enjoy such flexibility: The best guarantee is to retrain. Fig. 6 summarizes the proposed location-sensitive cascade training algorithm.

In practice, we need to convert the cascade output into a similarity function that measures the confidence of being positive. Suppose that the cascade consists of L stages and stage l has a strong classifier $F_l(I,I')$ that can be converted to posterior probability $s_l(I,I')$ using (18). Given the degenerate nature of the cascade, we approximate the final similarity function as:

$$s(I,I') \approx \prod_{l=1}^{L} s_l(I,I') = \prod_{l=1}^{L} \frac{\exp(2F_l(I,I'))}{\exp(2F_l(I,I'))+1}. \tag{22}$$

For the negatives rejected at an early stage $L'<L$, we stop evaluating them at later stages and simply set a dummy probability

$s_l(I,I')=e$ if $l>L'$, where $e<0.5$ is a small amount (we set $e=0.1$ in our experiments).

BOOSTMOTION

In this section, we investigate the use of the boosted discriminate similarity function in motion estimation (which is referred to BoostMotion). We first review the related literature on learning-based visual tracking and highlight our contribution. We then present our extensive experiments using echocardiographic and general tracking sequences.

Review of Learning-Based Visual Tracking

It should be emphasized that visual tracking is different from motion estimation. The latter concerns only two successive frames; while the former concerns the motion estimation of a whole video sequence. While a naive tracker estimates motion recursively frame by frame, tracking is more than motion estimation as the above naive tracker is prone to drift away. To overcome drifting, the tracking algorithm does the following: (1) updates the appearance model strategically and/or (2) performs temporal smoothing/fusion.

Underlying learning-based tracking algorithms lays a data-driven procedure. In most cases except (Lepetit, Pilet, & Fua, 2004), a binary classifier that discriminates the object of interest from the background is learned either offline or online. If the classifier is learned offline, this solves tracking as a detection problem. In (Mikolajczyk, Choudhury, & Schmid, 2001), temporal smoothing is enforced by casting the detector output as the observation likelihood in a particle filter setting. Avidan (2001) proposed a support vector tracking algorithm that learns a support vector machine (SVM) from the training data using the polynomial kernel. The SVM score, after the Taylor expansion, is analytically maximized for every frame. In 2003 Williams, Blake, & Cipolla built on the relevance vector machine to perform tracking, where temporal fusion is applied. In 2004 Lepetit, Pilet, & Fua artificially generated exemplars (using affine transform or 3D model) for each feature point that is treated as a class and used the 1-NN neighbor searching to determine the class label.

If the classifier is learned online, the appearance model updating is embedded into the classifier. In the work of Collins and Liu (2003) the appearance model is represented by a set of features that are selected online based on the variance ratio of the log likelihood function, which is empirically estimated. Ensemble tracking developed by Avidan (2005) invokes the AdaBoost to learn the classifier.

Figure 6. The location-sensitive cascade training algorithm

The location-sensitive cascade training algorithm
1.   Input: an annotated dataset of pairs of frames, K = the number of cascade stages, N_k = the number of weak classifiers for the kth stage, PD_k = the detection probability for the kth stage, $NREG_k$ = the negative region for the kth stage.
2.   For $k = 1:K$ /*loop over the number of stages*/

• Data preparation:
       Always keep the same set of positives.
       If ($k==1$) then random sample the negatives inside the $NREG_1$, otherwise bootstrap the negatives (e.g., the false positives from the previous stages up to $k-1$) from the range $NREG_k$. When sampling or bootstrapping, the number of negatives is kept almost the same to that of positives.

• Invoke the LogitBoost algorithm (e.g., Fig. 3) to learn a strong classifier. Stop training when the number of weak learners reaches N_k.
• Tune the strong classifier threshold to match the desired PD_k.
Output: a cascade of strong classifiers.

After tracking, the classifier is updated by adding the recently tracked results. Since the AdaBoost is a feature selection process, the ensemble tracker also represents the appearance model by features that are updated over time.

The approaches reviewed above commonly learn a classifier to differentiate the foreground object from the background. However, such a classifier gives no account of temporal information essential to motion estimation: No pairwise comparison along the temporal dimension is performed. In other words, the input to the classifier is always a single image patch not a pair of images. The proposed BoostMotion approach explores the possibility of using image pairs as inputs and embeds the temporal statistics into a learned similarity function. In (Viola, Jones, & Snow, 2003) the temporal difference images are used in boosting a pedestrian detector (again not a similarity function). Learning the spatial statistics of optical flow is addressed in (Roth & Black, 2005).

Experiments on Echocardiogram

The echocardiographic sequences are characterized by severe imaging artifacts and rapid appearance changes, which render traditional tracking algorithms that use conventional similarity functions ineffective. Here we address tracking the LV endocardial wall, which is parameterized by 17 landmark points along the contour as shown in Fig. 7(a) and then interpolated using a cubic spline.

Figure 7. (a) Two successive original frames and their ground truth landmarks and contours. (b) From left to right: the response maps of the similarity functions of NCC, CD2 and BoostMotion. (From (Zhou et al. 2006) at IEEE 2006)

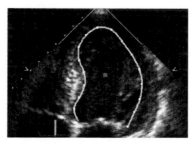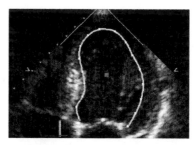

(a)

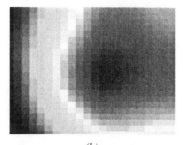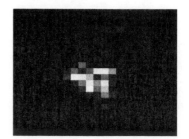

(b)

Motion Estimation

In the first experiment, we used the apical four chambers (A4C) view of stress echo sequences. Since an echocardiographic image is a 2D slice of 3D heart, different orientations of the ultrasound probe give different views of the heart. In clinical practices, standard cardiac views are captured, among which the A4C view is one such view that images all four heart chambers, namely left and right ventricles and left and right atria. We had 339 A4C sequences, providing 3162 frame pairs. The ground truth contour annotations for all 339 sequences were provided by one experienced sonographer. We randomly divided 339 sequences into two sets: the training set contains 270 sequences with 2543 pairs of frames and the test set 69 sequences with 619 pairs of frames. To reduce appearance variation, we aligned each video frame with respect to a mean shape using a rigid similarity transform and conducted experiments on the aligned domain.

We reported the results of estimating the motion vector of the left annulus point, *i.e.*, the left end point of the LV endocardium, which is characterized by drastic appearance changes mainly due to the valve movement. Given the correct left image patch, we exhaustively searched within a searching neighborhood the best right image patch that maximizes the similarity function. We estimated the motion vector for all test image pairs and measured the estimation error in terms of absolute displacement. For a pair of image patches, we set the patch size as 35 x 35 and the searching window W as [-21, 21] x [-21, 21].

We used the location-sensitive cascade training to learn a cascade of eight stages. We divided the whole search neighborhood into eight negative regions depending on their closeness to the center: specifically, they are $R_1=\{21,20,19\}$, $R_2=\{18,17,16\}$, $R_3=\{15,14,13\}$, $R_4=\{12,11\}$, $R_5=\{10,9\}$, $R_6=\{8,7\}$, $R_7=\{6,5\}$, $R_8=\{4,3\}$ pixels away from the center. To train the lth stage of the cascade, we bootstrapped negatives from the region R_l. For comparison, we also trained a regular cascade by randomly selecting out negatives at least three pixels away from the ground truth. Fig. 5(c) plots the curves of the training and test errors against the number of cascade stages. The location-sensitive cascade training consistently reduces the test error till overfitting is reached; while the regular cascade training saturates the performance even at the second stage.

We contrasted the BoostMotion approach, which uses pairs of images as inputs, with a detection algorithm, which uses single image patches as inputs. For the detection algorithm, we also trained a cascade of eight stages. From Fig. 5(c), even the training error of the detector is higher than that of the BoostMotion, which implies that the positives and negatives, which are single image patches, are very confusing even when they are far apart. Using the paired inputs significantly reduces the training and test errors. This is expected because motion estimation compares two images and thus temporal information is essential: Motion estimation based on one image is insufficient.

We compared the learned similarity function with the four conventional similarity functions reviewed in Section II. Table 1(a) reports the median and standard deviation of the estimation error. For the BoostMotion and detection approaches, we reported the minimum test error by varying the number of cascade stages. The BoostMotion approach yields the lowest training and test errors. In terms of test error, on average, it is only 3.47 pixels away from the ground truth, while the best among the others is the CD_2 similarity function whose estimation error is 4.38 pixels. The poor performance of the Bhattacharyya similarity function is probably due to the highly noisy nature of the ultrasound image and that only gray image is used. Fig. 7(b) displays the response maps of different similarity functions for the sample pair of frames in Fig. 7(a). The response map of the BoostMotion is peaked around the ground truth with a compact support region. Most of the off-center pixels are black because they are

Table 1. (a) Motion estimation training and test errors and (b) tracking performance based on the contour distances obtained using different similarity functions and a detector approach.

Approach	(a) Motion estimation training error	(a) Motion estimation test error	(b) Tracking error point-to-point	(b) Tracking error segmental Hausdorff
SSD	4.62 ± 2.48	4.54 ± 2.57	10.56 ± 2.37	5.63 ± 1.25
NCC	4.59 ± 2.38	4.49 ± 2.45	11.14 ± 2.45	5.84 ± 1.32
BHA	11.15 ± 6.66	11.40 ± 6.75	14.31 ± 3.19	7.22 ± 1.62
CD_2	4.39 ± 2.28	4.38 ± 2.17	7.32 ± 2.45	3.70 ± 1.30
Detection	8.34 ± 4.99	8.68 ± 5.07	NA	NA
BoostMotion	2.32 ± 1.72	3.47 ± 2.14	4.28 ± 1.24	2.16 ± 0.74

rejected by early stages of the cascade. In terms of computational time, the BoostMotion is slower than the generic similarity functions, because we used 654 weak learners.

Echocardiography Tracking

In the second experiment, we invoked the naive tracking algorithm that estimates motion vector frame by frame to perform echocardiography tracking (Cohen & Dinstein, 2002) (Boukerroui, Alison, & Brady, 2003) (Jacob, Noble, & Blake, 1998) (Mikic, Krucinski, & Thomas, 1998) (Zhou, Comaniciu, & Gupta, 2005). We used 445 regular echocardiographic sequences of apical two chambers (A2C) view where appearance changes are less pronounced than the stress echo. The A2C view is another canonical echo view used in clinical practices, where only left ventricle and left atrium are present. The ground truth annotations were provided by three experts, each annotating a non-overlapping subset of the whole dataset. We randomly divided the 445 sequences into a training set of 356 sequences and a test set of 89 sequences. The alignment is conducted in a recursive fashion.

To calibrate the contour tracking accuracy, we need to measure the proximity between two contours. We used two measures. The first is a simple point-to-point measure: the average distance of the landmark displacement defined as

$$\sum_{i=1}^{17} |p_i - g_i|^2 / 17,$$

where p_i and g_i are the ith landmark point on the probe and ground truth contours, respectively. The second is the so-called *segmental Hausdorff distance* (segHD) that allows certain degree of non-rigidity deformation during contour matching. The segHD between two corresponding landmark points x and x' on the two curves C and C', respectively, is defined as the Hausdorff distance between two segments $\omega(x)$ and $\omega(x')$, where $\omega(x)$ defines a segment around x on the curve C. We then take the mean of the segHD of all landmarks as the distance between C and C', denoted by $d_{segHD}(C, C')$.

$$shd(x,x') = HD(\omega(x),\omega(x')); \quad (d_{segHD} \ C,C') = \int_x shd(x,x')dC / \int_x dC. \qquad (23)$$

The tracking performances in terms of the above distances are listed in Table 1(b). Since each test sequence yields a contour distance, Table 1(b) documents its median and standard deviation. The segmental Hausdorff distance is about half smaller than the point-to-point distance as the former tolerates

Figure 8. Sample frames of two echocardiographic sequences with the ground truth (green) and tracking result (yellow) overlaid. (a,b) Frames 0, 5, 10, and 15 of the first sequence with results by (a) BoostMotion and (b) CD2. (c,d) Frames 0, 5, 10, and 15 of the second sequence with results by (c) BoostMotion and (d) CD2.

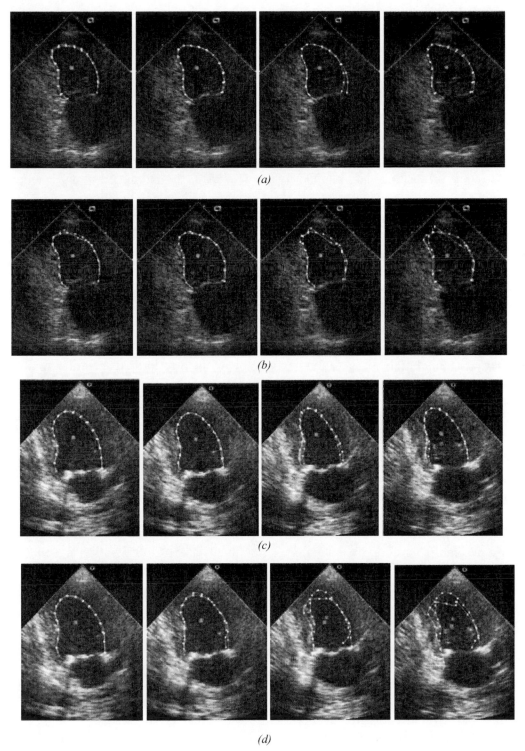

(a)

(b)

(c)

(d)

non-rigid deformation during contour matching and seems more compatible to our perception of contour difference. Using the discriminative similarity function substantially reduces the tracking error, with its corresponding point-to-point distance and segmental Hausdorff distance being 4.28 and 2.16 pixels, respectively; while the second best similarity function (CD_2) yields a tracking errors of 7.32 and 3.70 pixels, respectively. Therefore, utilizing the boosted similarity function greatly reduces drifting and produces a temporally smooth contour. Some tracking examples are presented in Fig. 8, which compares BoostMotion with CD_2, the second best similarity function.

Visual Tracking with Temporal Adaptation

In the previous two experiments, we assumed the existence of a large database that covers the appearance variances typically observed in the application of interest. While the above medical application provides such a database and hence is suitable for demonstrating the effectiveness of BoostMotion, it is not difficult to adapt the discriminative similarity function on the fly, making it appropriate for a general visual tracking problem. Here we present our experimental results along this line.

We experimented with our previous appearance-adaptive tracking approach reported in (Zhou, Chellappa, & Moghaddam, 2004), which is based on a state space model for an affine parameterization and a particle filter method. In the observation process of the state space model, the online appearance model, which is a generative mixture of a stable component and a wondering component (Jepson, Fleet, and El-Maraghi, 2003), is updated to absorb changing appearance; in the state transition process of the state space model, an adaptive velocity is predicted based on the incoming appearance and hence guides a better particle generation; the number of particles is made adaptive to the prediction error too. Because the main contribution of the chapter is on the similarity function itself, we simply replaced the generative online appearance model in the observation likelihood with the discriminative similarity function.

To initiate learning the similarity function, we manually annotated two starting frames with a bounding box. To generate positives, we perturbed the ground truth boxes in both frames by a small amount and cropped 20 images pairs. To generate negatives, we kept the image patches in the first frame within the positive perturbation region while cropping image patches in the second frames outside the positive perturbation region but within the particle sampling region. In total, we cropped 200 negative image pairs. We then learned a classifier of 25 weak learners.

To adapt the similarity function to incoming appearance, we proceeded as follows. Once the tracking is done on the current frame t, we augmented the training dataset by cropping positives and negatives based on tracking results of the current and previous frames and removed the training data generated from $t_0 = 5$ frames ago. Therefore, we maintained a training dataset of 100 positives and 1000 negatives except for the first 5 frames. During training, we controlled the number of local rectangle features to be around 1000. Overall, the tracker can handle a few frames per second on a PC with a 3GHz CPU and 3GB memory.

Fig. 9 displays the tracking results. Even though we displayed color image, we used the gray values (the average of RGB channels) as input. In the first example, we tracked a moving head in a surveillance video of 150 frames captured by PETS2001, which is available from http://www.cvg.rdg.ac.uk/PETS2001/. In the second example, we tracked a car driving in fog captured by researchers in Karlsruhe University. The sequence is from http://i21www.ira.uka.de/image/_sequences. In both examples, the challenges lie in small target size, dynamic foreground appearance, cluttered and changing background, etc. Despite all these challenges, our algorithm successfully tracks the target. We observe that the detector-based approach, which leverages no temporal information, yields more jittery results.

Figure 9. The top two rows are about tracking a moving head: frames 1, 30, 60, 90, 120, and 150. The bottom two rows are about tracking a driving car in fog: frames 1, 30, 60, 90, 120, and 150.

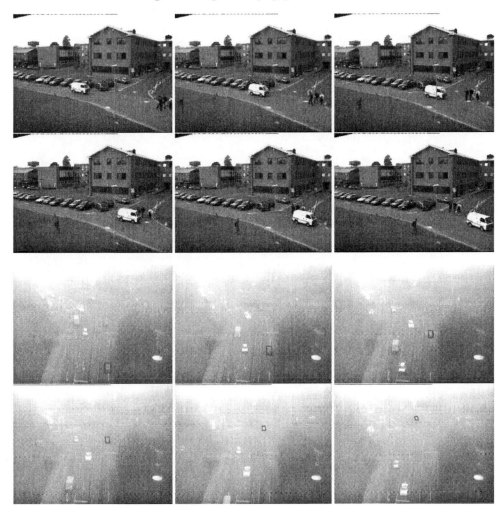

SUMMARY

We presented an approach to learning a similarity function for matching image under complex appearance changes, which are exemplified by an annotated video database. This type of similarity function is applicable to motion estimation. We used the LogitBoost algorithm to selectively combine weak learners into a strong similarity function. The weak learners were constructed as nonparametric 2D piecewise constant functions of the feature responses, which enhanced modeling power and brought savings in training time and storage requirement. Because the motion estimation accuracy is tied with the selection of negatives, which have an additional location parameter measuring their distances to the positives, we proposed to train a cascade structure in a steerable manner using a location-sensitive negative bootstrapping. Compared with the regular cascade, the location-sensitive cascade achieved lower training and test error. Finally, we tested the learned similarity function on motion estimation for echocardiographic sequences and general visual tracking: the learned similarity function outperformed conventional similarity functions.

REFERENCES

Otto, C. (2004). *Textbook of Clinical Echocardiography.* Saunders.

Freund, Y., & Schapire, R. (1997). A decision-theoretic generalization of online leaning and an application to boosting. *J. Computer and System Sciences, 55*(1), 119-139.

Friedman, J., Hastie, T., & Tibshirani, R. (2000). Additive logistic regression: a statistical view of boosting. *Ann. Statist., 28*(2), 337–407.

Cohen, B., & Dinstein, I. (2002). New maximum likelihood motion estimation schemes for noisy ultrasound images. *Pattern Recognition, 25,* 455-463.

Papageorgiou, C., Oren, M., & Poggio, T. (1998). A general framework for object detection. In *Proc. of ICCV.*

Viola, P., & Jones, M., (2001). Rapid object detection using a boosted cascade of simple features. In *Proc. of CVPR.*

Santini, S., & Jain, R. (1999). Similarity measures. *IEEE Trans. PAMI, 21*(9), 871–883.

Brox, T., Bruhn, A., Papenberg, N., & Wiecker, J., (2004). High accuracy optical flow estimation based on a theory of warping. *European Conf. Computer Vision,* (pp. 25–36).

Lucas,B., & Kanade, T. (1981). An iterative image registration technique with an application to stereo vision. In *Proc. DARPA IU Workshop,* (pp. 121–130).

Shi, J., & Tomasi, C. (1994). Good features to track. In *Proc. of CVPR,* (pp. 593–600).

Fowlkes, C., Martin, D., & Malik, J. (2003). Learning affinity functions for image segmentation: Combining patch-based and gradient-based approaches. In *Proc. of CVPR.*

Lundqvist, R., Bengtsson, E., & Thurfjell, L. (2003). A combined intensity and gradient-based similarity criterion for interindividual SPECT brain scan registration. *EURASIP Journal on Applied Signal Processing, 1,* 461 – 469.

Comaniciu, D., Ramesh, V., & Meer, P. (2000). Real-time tracking of non-rigid objects using mean shift. *Proc. of CVPR, 2,* 142–149.

Boukerroui, D., Alison, J.N., & Brady, M. (2003). Velocity estimation in ultrasound images: A block matching approach. *IPMI,* (pp. 586–598).

Viola, P., & Welles, W.M. (1997). Alignment by maximization of mutual information. *Int. J. Comp. Vision, 24*(2), 137–154.

Zhou, S., Shao, J., Georgescu, & Comaniciu, D. (2006). Boostmotion: Boosting a discriminative similarity function for motion estimation. *Proc. of CVPR, 2,* 1761–1768.

Jones, M., & Viola, P. (2003). Face recognition using boosted local features. In *Proc. of ICCV.*

Moghaddam, B., Jebara, T., & Pentland, A. (2001). Bayesian face recognition. *Pattern Recognition, 33,* 1771-1782.

Yu, J., Amores, J., Sebe, N., & Tian, Q. (2006). Toward robust distance metric analysis for similarity estimation. In *Proc. of CVPR.*

Lepetit, V., Pilet, J., & Fua, P., (2004). Point matching as a classification problem for fast and robust object pose estimation. In *Proc. of CVPR.*

Mikolajczyk, K., Choudhury, R., & Schmid, C. (2001). Face detection in a video sequence - a temporal approach. In *Proc. of CVPR.*

Avidan, S. (2001). Support vector tracking. *Proc. of CVPR, 1,* 184–191.

Williams, O., Blake, A., & Cipolla, R., (2003). A sparse probabilistic learning algorithm for real-time tracking. In *Proc. of ICCV,* 2003, 353–360.

Collins, R., & Liu, Y. (2003). On-line selection of discriminative tracking features. In *Proc. of ICCV.*

Avidan, S. (2005) Ensemble tracking. In *Proc. of CVPR, 2,* 494–501.

Viola, P., Jones, M., & Snow, D. (2003). Detecting pedestrians using patterns of motion and appearance. In *Proc. of ICCV,* (pp. 734– 741).

Roth, S., & Black, M.J. (2005). On the spatial statistics of optical flow. In *Proc. of ICCV.*

Jacob, G., Noble, A., & Blake, A. (1998). Robust contour tracking in echocardiographic sequence. In *Proc. Intl. Conf. on Computer Vision,* (pp. 408–413).

Mikic, I., Krucinski, S., & Thomas, J.D. (1998). Segmentation and tracking in echocardiographic sequences: Active contours guided by optical flow estimates. *IEEE Trans. Medical Imaging, 17,* 274–284.

Zhou, X.S., Comaniciu, D., & Gupta, A. (2005). An information fusion framework for robust shape tracking. *IEEE Trans. PAMI, 27*(1), 115–129.

Zhou, S., Chellappa, R., & Moghaddam, B. (2004). Visual tracking and recognition using appearance-adaptive models in particle filters. *IEEE Trans. Image Processing, 11,* 1434-1456.

Jepson, A.D., Fleet, D.J., & El-Maraghi, T.F. (2003). Robust online appearance models for visual tracking. *IEEE Trans. PAMI, 25,* 1296–1311.

Chapter VI
Active Learning for Relevance Feedback in Image Retrieval

Jian Cheng
National Laboratory of Pattern Recognition, Institute of Automation,
Chinese Academy of Sciences, China

Kongqiao Wang
Nokia Research Center, Beijing, China

Hanqing Lu
National Laboratory of Pattern Recognition, Institute of Automation,
Chinese Academy of Sciences, China

ABSTRACT

Relevance feedback is an effective approach to boost the performance of image retrieval. Labeling data is indispensable for relevance feedback, but it is also very tedious and time-consuming. How to alleviate users' burden of labeling has been a crucial problem in relevance feedback. In recent years, active learning approaches have attracted more and more attention, such as query learning, selective sampling, multi-view learning, and so forth. The well-known examples include Co-training, Co-testing, SVM_{active}, etc. In this literature, the authors will introduce some representative active learning methods in relevance feedback. Especially, they will present a new active learning algorithm based on multi-view learning, named Co-SVM. In Co-SVM algorithm, color and texture are naturally considered as sufficient and uncorrelated views of an image. SVM classifier is learned in color and texture feature subspaces, respectively. Then the two classifiers are used to classify the unlabeled data. These unlabeled samples that disagree in the two classifiers are chose to label. The extensive experiments show that the proposed algorithm is beneficial to image retrieval.

INTRODUCTION

Content-Based Image Retrieval (CBIR) has been one of the most active research topics in computer vision and pattern recognition fields since 1990's (Rui, Huang, & Chang, 1999; Smeulders, Worring, Santini, & Gupta, 2000; Datta, Li, & Wang, 2005). Most of existing CBIR systems adopted low-level features (color, texture, shape, etc) to represent images. However, it is inadequate to describe the semantic concepts with the low-level features of images, which is named *semantic gap*. The concept of semantic gap has been extensively used in the CBIR research community to express the discrepancy between the description of the low-level features extracted from the images and the semantic understanding of human.

To narrow the semantic gap, a straightforward way is to take human in the loop. As one of important ways of human-in-the-loop, Relevance Feedback (RF) is a query modification technique, which was initially developed in document retrieval and then introduced into CBIR during mid 1990's (Picard, Minka, & Szummer, 1996; Rui, Huang, Ortega, & Mehrotra, 1998). Relevance feedback attempts to capture the user's preference through iterative feedback and query refinement. In each round, the user is requested to provide feedbacks regarding the relevance or irrelevance of the current retrieval results. Then the classifier will be refined based on the feedback results. The pool of unlabeled images is classified as relevance or irrelevance by the learned classifier, and the relevant images are ranked and returned to user for next round labeling. With the interactive labeling and learning procedures, systems can learn user's preferences and improve the performance of image retrieval.

Many relevance feedback algorithms have been proposed for image retrieval in past years (Huang, & Zhou, 2001; Zhou, & Huang, 2003). The early work was mainly inspired by term-weighting and relevance feedback in document retrieval (Rocchio, 1971). Rui and Huang (1998) introduced the query refinement algorithm based on term-frequency and inverse-document-frequency in text retrieval into CBIR. Picard, et al. (1996) grouped the images or regions into hierarchical trees whose nodes were constructed through single-link clustering, and then weighted on grouping. These methods fall into heuristic-based formulation with empirical parameter adjustment. Later, there are more works focusing on learning-based strategy and many classic machine learning techniques are applied. Tieu and Viola (2000) assumed that an image was generated by a sparse set of visual cause and that images which were visually similar share causes. They proposed a mechanism for computing a very large number of highly selective features which captured some aspects of this causal structure, then used Boosting to learn a classification function which only relied on 20 features. In (Vasconcelos, & Lippman, 2000), Gaussian mixture model on DCT coefficient was used as image representation, then Bayesian inference was applied for image region matching and learning. Hong, et al. (2000) treated relevance feedback as a binary classification problem and incorporated Support Vector Machines (SVM) into the classification process. However, an inevitable issue in performing relevance feedback is the small sample size. The fact makes many learning methods inefficient, such as Bayesian, boosting, even SVM.

In general, more labeled data will result in higher accuracy. While the labeled data is limited, the unlabeled data is often abundant and easy to obtain. Therefore, the key issue addressing the small sample size is how to efficiently utilize the unlabeled data. Recently, the idea of semi-supervised learning (SSL), i.e. learning from both labeled and unlabeled data, has attracted much attention in information retrieval (Zhu, 2006). One recent approach is to apply Transductive SVM (TSVM) to exploit the unlabeled data (Joachims, 1999; Wang, Chan, & Zhang, 2003). However, some study challenged that TSVM might not be so helpful from unlabeled data in theory and in practice (Zhang, & Oles, 2000).

On the other hand, labeling is tedious and time-consuming and users do not have patience to provide enough feedbacks. So it is extremely necessary to significantly alleviate users' burden of labeling while achieve comparable performance. To address this issue, active learning, in contrast to passive learning, is introduced to image retrieval. The main difference between active learning methods and the regular passive methods lies in how to choose the unlabeled samples from a pool of unlabeled data. Active learning is to actively select samples in order to achieve the maximal information gain, or the minimized uncertainty in decision making. The earlier approaches of active learning take a constructive approach to query generation in the sense that each query is constructed by setting the values of the attributes so that the query is as informative as possible (Angluin, 1988).

Selective sampling is an alternative important approach of active learning (Freund, Seung, Shamir, & Tishby, 1997; Tong, & Koller, 2000). Selective sampling is typically applied to classification tasks in which the learner has access to a large number of unlabeled examples. There are two main schemes for sampling algorithms: stream-based and pool-based. The stream-based scheme assumes that unlabeled data are a stream and are presented in sequence to learner, while learner can go through the entire pool and select sample to label in pool-based condition. One of the most famous works in image retrieval is SVM_{Active} proposed by Tong and Chang (2001). SVM_{Active} is a pool-based algorithm. It employs SVM as learner and think that the samples lying beside the boundary can reduce the version space as fast as possible, i.e. eliminating the hypotheses. Therefore, in each round of relevance feedback, the images that are closest to the support vector boundary are returned to users for labeling.

A much recent approach of active learning is multi-view based learning. In multi-view method, the feature set is partitioned to several subsets (views) which are sufficient and compatible for learning the target concept. The seminal work was presented by Blum and Mitchell (1998), Co-training algorithm. After that, many multi-view algorithms appeared. The representative works are Co-EM (Nigam, & Ghani, 2000), Co-Boost (Collins, & Singer, 1999), Co-Testing (Muslea, Minton, & Knoblock, 2000). These multi-view learning algorithms exploit unlabeled examples to boost the performance of classifiers learned in each view by bootstrapping the views from each other, so they are semi-supervised algorithms in nature.

In this chapter, we will introduce some representative active learning methods in relevance feedback. Especially we will present a new active learning algorithm based on multi-view, named Co-SVM. In Co-SVM algorithm, color and texture are naturally considered as sufficient and uncorrelated views of an image. Two SVM classifiers are trained in color feature space and texture feature space, respectively. Then, the contention samples of two SVM classifiers in different feature representations are considered as the most informative samples and taken out to ask users to label. The extensive experiments show that the proposed algorithm can improve both efficiency and effectiveness of relevance feedback in content-based image retrieval.

ACTIVE LEARNING FOR RELEVANCE FEEDBACK

In relevance feedback, labeling is a troublesome task for users. Many learning methods fail due to most of users without patience to label sufficient sample. Active learning is a learning strategy designed to efficiently exploit the unlabeled data and reduce the labor cost of labeling. The basic idea of active learning is to select the most informative samples for labeling in each round feedback. Among the various active learning techniques, SVM based method and Multi-view based method are the most promising method. In the section, we will give a brief introduction to the two techniques.

Support Vector Machines Based Active Learning

Support Vector Machines (SVM) is built on structural risk minimization theory (Vapnik, 1998). With the labeled samples, SVM learns a hyper-plane (i.e., classification boundary) separating one class samples from the other class samples with maximum margin. Being an efficient binary classifier, SVM is particularly suitable for the classification task in relevance feedback of image retrieval (Joachims, 1999; Hong, Tian, & Huang, 2000). The task of learning user's preference can be regarded as one of learning a SVM binary classifier. An SVM captures the query concept by separating the relevant images from the irrelevant images with a hyper-plane in feature space. The samples on a side of hyper-plane are looked as relevance, and on the other side are looked as irrelevance. When the data set is not linear separable, the data usually need to be mapped into a high-dimensional feature space using an implicit function.

Given a set of labeled samples $(x_1, y_1),....,(x_n, y_n)$, x_i is the feature representation of sample in input space $x_i \in R^N$, $y_i \in \{-1, +1\}$ is the class label (-1 denotes negative and +1 denotes positive). The basic goal of SVM is to find a separating hyper-plane that separates the training data with a maximal margin. The primal form of SVM in linear separable case can be expressed as:

$$\min \quad \frac{1}{2}w^T w$$
$$subject\ to\ \ y_i(w^T x_i + b) \geq 1$$

Training SVM classifier leads to the following quadratic optimization problem:

$$\min W(\alpha) = \min\{-\sum_{i=1}^{n}\alpha_i + \frac{1}{2}\sum_{i=1}^{n}\sum_{j=1}^{n}y_i y_j\ \alpha_i\ \alpha_j k(x_i, x_j)\}$$

Subject to:

$$\sum_{i=1}^{n}y_i\alpha_i = 0$$
$$\forall i, 0 \leq \alpha_i \leq C$$

Where C is a constant, k is kernel function which is an identical function in case of linear separable. The hyper-plane (classification boundary) is

$$(w \cdot x) + b = 0.$$

Where

$$w = \sum_{i=1}^{n} \alpha_i x_i y_i$$

and

$$b = -\frac{1}{2} w \cdot [x_r + x_s],$$

here x_r and x_s are any support vectors satisfied α_r, $\alpha_s \geq 0$, $y_r = 1$, $y_s = -1$. The classification function can be written as:

$$f(x) = sign(\sum_i \alpha_i y_i \cdot k(x_i \cdot x) + b)$$

The earlier work generally applied SVM in relevance feedback using a randomly selected training set. Schohn and Cohn (2000) observed that they could achieve better performance from a small subset of the data than that achieved using all available data. They noticed that only unlabeled samples within the margin would have effect on classifier if the data was linearly separable, and stopped labeling data once the margin had been exhausted. Based on the assumption, they thought that the margin would exhaust when the sample closest to hyper-plane was support vector. At the same time, Tong and Koller (2000) also found this phenomenon in text classification. Taking advantage of the duality between parameter space and feature space, they arrived at three algorithms that attempted to reduce version space as much as possible at each query. These algorithms provide a guide to select better unlabeled samples, and lead to the same results as that Schohn and Cohn (2000) obtained. Tong and Chang further applied the idea to relevance feedback of image retrieval, i.e. SVM$_{active}$ algorithm (Tong, & Chang, 2001).

Before introducing the SVM$_{active}$ algorithm, the concept of version space must be addressed, as it is critical to SVM based active learning. If there exist a set of hyper-planes that can linearly separate the training data in the input space, this set of hyper-planes or hypotheses is called the version space (Mitchell, 1982). This can be defined as

$$v = \{f \in H \mid y_i f(x_i) > 0, i = 1, \cdots, n\}$$

or

$$v = \{w \in W \mid \|w\| = 1, y_i(w \cdot \varphi(x_i)) > 0, i = 1, \cdots, n\}$$

where H is the set of possible hypothesis and W is the parameter space for the unit vectors w. Note that the space H and W are dual, that is to say, points in the feature space correspond to hyper-plane in the parameter space and vice versa. The basic motivation of SVM$_{active}$ is that the query sample should split the current version space into two equal parts as much as possible. According to the duality, the query sample should be close to hyper-plane. The relevance feedback process using SVM$_{active}$ is comprised of the two steps:

1. SVM$_{active}$ learns the classifier quickly via active learning. The active part of SVM$_{active}$ selects the most informative samples, i.e. the samples closest to hyper-plane, to train the SVM classier.

2.   Once the classifier is trained, SVM_{active} returns the top-k most relevant samples. These are the k samples farthest from the hyper-plane on the query concept side.

Multi-View Based Active Learning

The traditional machine learning algorithms usually access to the entire set of domain features, which is called single-view learner. By contrast, in the multi-view setting one can partition the domain's features into subsets (views) that are sufficient for learning the target concept. Existing multi-view learning algorithms belong to semi-supervised algorithms. These algorithms exploit unlabeled data to boost the accuracy of the classifiers learned in each view by bootstrapping the views from each other. Blum and Mitchell (1998) presented the seminal work of multi-view based active learning. They provided the first formalization of learning in the multi-view framework, Co-training algorithm (Blum, & Mitchell, 1998). Co-training algorithm trains two classifiers separately on two sufficient and redundant views (feature subsets), and uses the predictions of each classifier on unlabeled samples to augment the training set of the other. Blum and Mitchell proved that two independent, compatible views could be used to PAC-learn a concept based on few labeled and many unlabeled samples.

After Co-training algorithm appeared, many types of extensions were proposed. Collins and Singer (1999) presented a boosting-like framework based on Co-training that was biased towards learning hypotheses that predicted the same label on most of the unlabeled samples. Collins and Singer's work give an explicit objective function that measures the compatibility of the learned hypotheses and use a boosting algorithm to optimize it. Dasgupta, et al. (2001) reported the theoretical justification for some aspects of Co-training algorithm, and gave a new PAC-style bound on generalization error. Intuitively, they showed that the ratio of contention points to unlabeled samples was an upper-bound on the error rate of the classifiers learned in the two views. The idea of Blum and Mitchell (1998) also has been extensively incorporated into other machine learning algorithms. Nigam and Ghani (2000) applied multi-view learning for EM algorithm, named Co-EM algorithm (Nigam, & Ghani, 2000). In Co-EM algorithm, two classifiers are trained in two views respectively, and then recommend prediction to each other by turns during the training process of EM. Zhou and Li (2005) extended the co-training to semi-supervised regression algorithm, i.e. COREG algorithm (Zhou, & Li, 2005). This algorithm employs two k-nearest neighbor regressors using different distance metrics. Like Co-training style, each regressor labels the unlabeled sample which can be most confidently labeled for the other regressor.

The above mentioned Co-training algorithm and its extensions are based on the idea of bootstrapping the views from each other, which utilize the compatibility of learned classifiers with different views. In contrast, as another important multi-view based active learning algorithms, Co-testing algorithm uses the multiple views to detect the contention points (Muslea, Minton, & Knoblock, 2000). Co-testing algorithm relies on the following observation: if the hypotheses learned in each view predict a different label for an unlabeled sample, at least one of predictions is wrong. By asking the user to label such contention points, Co-testing algorithm is guaranteed to provide useful information for the view that made mistake. Co-testing is an iterative algorithm that requires a few labeled and many unlabeled samples. First, Co-testing uses the few labeled samples to learn a hypothesis in each view. Then it applies the learned hypotheses to all unlabeled samples and detects the content points that are predicted different label by hypotheses. Finally, it ask user to label these content points and add the newly labeled samples to the training set. The original Co-testing algorithm also has been extended to a family of Co-testing algorithms (Muslea, Minton, & Knoblock, 2006). The major difference is the query selection strategies. There are three typical selection strategies: naïve, aggressive, and conservative. The naïve strategy chooses the contention points at random way; the aggressive strategy chooses the contention points that are the least confident of hypotheses makes the most confident prediction; the conservative strategy chooses the contention points on which the confidence of the predictions made by hypotheses is as close as possible.

CO-SVM ALGORITHM

For large-scale image database retrieval problem, labeled images are always rare compared with unlabeled images. It has become a hot topic how to utilize the large amounts of unlabeled images to improve the performance of the learning algorithms when only a small set of labeled images is available. Tong and Chang (2001) proposed an active learning paradigm for image retrieval, named SVM_{Active} algorithm (Tong, & Chang, 2001). SVM_{Active} considers the representation of an image as a single mixture view so that the least confident points are those which are the closest to the boundary. Usually, the feature representation of an image is a combination of diverse features, such as color, texture, shape, etc. For a specific image, the contribution of different features is significantly different. On the other hand, the importance of the same feature is also different for different images. For example, color is often more prominent than shape for a landscape image. However, the retrieval results are the averaging effort of all features, which ignores the distinct properties of individual feature.

The works mentioned above have suggested that multi-view learning could do much better than the single-view learning in eliminating the hypotheses consistent with the training set (Blum, & Mitchell,

Figure 1. The flowchart of Co-SVM algorithm

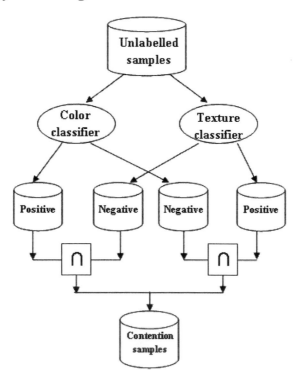

1998; Muslea, Minton, & Knoblock, 2000). In this chapter, from multi-view viewpoint, we propose a novel active learning algorithm by integrating the spirit of SVM_{Active} and Co-testing, which named Co-SVM algorithm (Cheng, & Wang, 2007).

Two-View Scheme

It is natural and reasonable to assume that color features and texture features are two sufficient and uncorrelated views of an image. In each round, the contention samples which disagree in the two views are returned to user to label.

Assume that $x = \{c_1,...,c_i, t_1,...,t_j\}$ is the feature representation of an image, where $\{c_1,...,c_i\}$ and $\{c_1,...,c_j\}$ are color attributes and texture attributes, respectively. For simplicity, we define the feature representation $V = V_C \times V_T$, and $\{c_1,...,c_i\} \in V_C$, $\{t_1,...,t_j\} \in V_T$.

In order to find relevant images as much as possible, like the general relevance feedback methods, SVM is used to learn a classifier h on these labeled samples with the combined view V at the first stage. The unlabeled set is classified into positive and negative. Then m positive images are returned to user to label. At the second stage, SVM is used to learn two classifiers h_C and h_T on labeled samples with color view V_C and texture view V_T, respectively. A set of contention samples that disagree in the two views is recommended to user to label. That is, the contention samples are classified as positive by h_C (CP) while are classified as negative by h_T (TN), or are classified as negative by h_C (CN) while are classified as positive by h_T (TP). In each classifier, the distance between sample and the hype plane (support vector boundary) can be looked as the confidence degree. The larger the distance, the higher the confidence degree is. In order to makes sure that user can label the most informative samples, these samples which are close to hype plane in both views are recommended to user to label. In summary, the flowchart of Co-SVM algorithm is described in figure1.

In Co-SVM algorithm, the relevance feedback procedure is divided into two stages. The aim is to improve not only the efficiency but also effectiveness of feedback. At the first stage, in order to insure users finding relevant images as much as possible, we rank the images by their similarity to the query on the combined view V like most of common relevance feedback algorithms. That is for effectiveness. The second stage let users to get the most informative images to label so that maximally reduce user's burden. This is for efficiency. The Figure 2 depicts the simple steps of Co-SVM algorithm applied to relevance feedback.

Multi-View Scheme

The proposed algorithm in two-view case is easily extended to multi-view scheme. Assume the feature representation of a color image is defined as $V = V_1 \times V_2 \times ... \times V_k$, each V_i, $i = 1,...,k$ correspond to different view of the color image. Then k SVM classifiers h_i can be individually learned on each view. All unlabelled data are classified as positive (+1) or negative (-1) by k SVM classifiers, respectively. Define the confident score:

$$S(x) = \left| \sum_{i=1}^{k} sign(h_i(x)) \right|$$

The confident score can reflect the consistency of all classifiers on a specified example. Higher the confident score, more consistent the classification is. Inversely, the lower score indicates that the classification is uncertain. The labeling on these uncertain samples will results in maximum improvement of performance. So the unlabelled samples whose confident scores are the lowest are considered as the contention samples.

EXPERIMENTS

To validate the effectiveness of the proposed algorithm on improvement of performance, we compare it with Tong&Chang's SVM_{Active} and the traditional relevance feedback algorithm using SVM (Hong, Tian, & Huang, 2000). Experiments are performed on a subset selected from the Corel image CDs. There are 50 categories in our subset. Each category contains 100 images, 5000 images in all. The categories have different semantic meanings, such as animal, building, landscape, etc.

In our experiments, the main purpose is to verify if the learning mechanisms of Co-SVM are useful, so we only employed simple color and texture features to represent images. The color features include

Figure 2. The pseudo-code of Co-SVM algorithm

Active learning with Co-SVM:

Input: a query image.

    Step 1.   Ranking the database in descending order of similarity to the query.

If user is unsatisfied; **repeat** the follows

    Step 2.   Training a SVM classifier h with the entire view V and classifying $Set_{\{unlabeled\}}$. Labeling the top m images as $Set^*_{\{relevant\}}$ or $Set^*_{\{irrelevant\}}$
        $Set_{\{relevant\}} = Set_{\{relevant\}} \cup Set^*_{\{relevant\}}$
        $Set_{\{irrelevant\}} = Set_{\{irrelevant\}} \cup Set^*_{\{irrelevant\}}$
        $Set_{\{unlabeled\}} = Set_{\{unlabeled\}} - \{Set^*_{\{relevant\}} \cup Set^*_{\{irrelevant\}}\}$

    Step 3.   Training a SVM classifier h_C with color view V_C and classifying $Set_{\{unlabeled\}}$
        $Set_{\{unlabeled\}} = \{CP \cup CN\}$
    Training a SVM classifier h_T with texture view V_T and classifying $Set_{\{unlabeled\}}$
        $Set_{\{unlabeled\}} = \{TP \cup TN\}$

    Step 4.   Finding contention samples
        $Set_{\{contention\}} = \{CP \cap TN\} \cup \{CN \cap TP\}$

    Step 5.   Ranking $Set_{\{contention\}}$ by their similarity to the query calculated in step 1, and labeling the least confident n samples as $Set^*_{\{relevant\}}$ or $Set^*_{\{irrelevant\}}$.
        $Set_{\{relevant\}} = Set\{relevant\} \cup Set^*_{\{relevant\}}$
        $Set_{\{irrelevant\}} = Set_{\{irrelevant\}} \cup Set^*_{\{irrelevant\}}$
        $Set_{\{unlabeled\}} = Set_{\{unlabeled\}} - \{Set^*_{\{relevant\}} \cup Set^*_{\{irrelevant\}}\}$

End of repeat

Output: the relevant images.

125-dimensional color histogram vector and 6-dimensional color moment vector in RGB. The color mean and color variance in Red, Green and Blue are calculated to form the 6-dimensional color moment vector. The texture features are extracted using Discrete Wavelet Transformation (DWT). Each wavelet decomposition results in 4 subimages: down-sampled image and wavelets in three orientations. In total, we perform 3-level wavelet decomposition and obtain 10 wavelet subbands. The mean and variance averaging on each of 10 subbands are arranged to a 20-dimensional texture feature vector. RBF kernel is adopted in SVM classifiers. The kernel width is learnt by cross-validation approach.

The first 10 images of each category, 500 images in total, are selected as query images to probe the retrieval performance. In each round, only the top 10 images are labeled and 10 most confident images selected from contention set are labeled. All accuracy in the following text is the averaging accuracy of all test images. Figure 3 is the accuracy vs. scope curve of the three algorithms after the third and fifth rounds of relevance feedback, respectively. From the comparison results we can see that the proposed algorithm (Co-SVM) is better than SVM_{Active} (Active SVM) and the traditional relevance feedback method (SVM). Furthermore, we investigate the accuracy of the three algorithms within top 10 to top 100, and with 5 rounds feedback. The results of top-30 and top-50 are depicted in figure 4. The detailed results are summarized in table 1. The results reported in table 1 show that Co-SVM achieves higher performance than that of SVM_{Active} and the traditional relevance feedback algorithm.

Figure 3. The accuracy of image retrieval with 3 feedbacks (left) and 5 feedbacks (right)

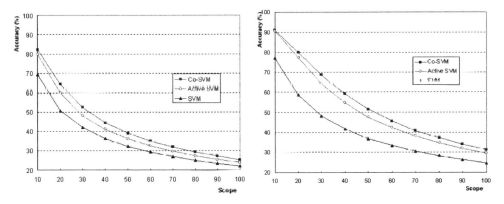

Figure 4. The accuracy of image retrieval averaging on top-30 (left) and top-50 (right)

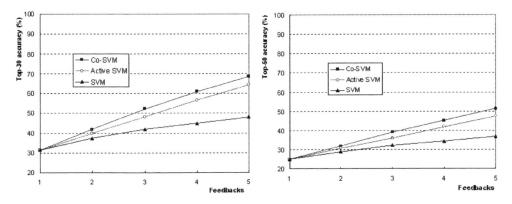

Table 1. Comparison among the proposed algorithm (Co-SVM), the traditional feedback algorithm (SVM) and Tong and Chang's SVMActive(Active SVM)

(%)	Top 60			Top 70			Top 80			Top 90			Top 100		
	SVM	Active SVM	Co-SVM	SVM	Active SVM	Co-SVM	SVM	Active SVM	Co-SVM	SVM	Active SVM	Co-SVM	SVM	Active SVM	Co-SVM
FB1	23.17	23.17	23.17	21.53	21.53	21.53	20.14	20.14	20.14	19.02	19.02	19.02	17.97	17.97	17.97
FB2	26.5	27.89	28.82	24.54	25.69	26.41	22.83	23.85	24.35	21.42	22.32	22.69	20.14	20.88	21.22
FB3	29.39	32.49	34.99	27.06	29.67	31.91	25.06	27.35	29.36	23.47	25.48	27.16	22.03	23.79	25.25
FB4	31.32	37.55	40.23	28.79	34.18	36.31	26.66	31.43	33.1	24.84	29	30.51	23.26	26.91	28.22
FB5	33.42	42.31	45.51	30.57	38.25	40.83	28.31	34.92	37.2	26.35	32.07	34.04	24.63	29.53	31.27

(%)	Top 10			Top 20			Top 30			Top 40			Top 50		
	SVM	Active SVM	Co-SVM	SVM	Active SVM	Co-SVM	SVM	Active SVM	Co-SVM	SVM	Active SVM	Co-SVM	SVM	Active SVM	Co-SVM
FB1	51.4	51.4	51.4	37.4	37.4	37.4	31.55	31.55	31.55	27.64	27.64	27.64	25.09	25.09	25.09
FB2	62.28	67.46	71.6	44.93	48.64	51.88	37.33	39.89	41.87	32.54	34.43	35.87	28.99	30.64	31.8
FB3	69.34	79.92	82.24	50.59	59.88	64.47	41.88	48.19	52.38	36.43	40.98	44.41	32.35	36.11	39.06
FB4	73.72	86.84	87.96	55.10	69.57	73.09	44.99	56.65	61.1	38.84	48.07	52.1	34.55	42	45.3
FB5	77.10	90.58	91.04	58.59	77.27	79.98	48.10	64.41	68.69	41.61	54.80	59.11	36.87	47.65	51.48

DISCUSSIONS

Active learning has been well-studied in data mining. The representative algorithms include Co-training and Co-Testing both created from multi-view viewpoint. Co-training algorithm adopts cooperative learning strategy. Two classifiers are separately learned on two different views of the labeled data. Then the training set is enlarged for each classifier by taking in the most confident unlabelled samples from another classifier. Co-training algorithm requires that the multiple views of data are compatible and redundant. In fact, we have attempted to augment the performance of both color and texture classifiers by adding the most confident unlabelled samples to complement the labeled set, but the results were worse. Considering the condition of co-training, it is not surprise to find that color attribute and texture attribute are not compatible but uncorrelated for a color image. In contrast, co-testing requires that the views should be sufficient and uncorrelated which makes the classifiers more independent for classification. The deficiency of co-testing is that it does not increase in itself any information except what given by users through labeling.

Like the previous works, Co-SVM algorithm selects the unlabeled samples in batch way. Intuitively, the uncertainty should be propagated to neighbors once an unlabeled sample is labeled. Therefore, uncertainty of each unlabeled sample should be dynamically updated during the feedback process. However, the update will brings mass increase in computational cost. How to balance the uncertainty update and computational cost is what we must consider. The further Investigations are conducting and partial of recent results have been reported in (Zhang, Cheng, Lu, & Ma, 2007, 2008).

CONCLUSION

In this chapter, we proposed a novel active learning algorithm for selective sampling in relevance feedback, Co-SVM algorithm. In order to obtain the maximal improvement of performance, the relevance feedback is divided into two stages. At the first stage, we rank the unlabeled images according to their similarity to the query and let user to label the top images like the common relevance feedback algorithms. In order to reduce the labeling requirement, a set of additional informative samples are selected by Co-SVM to label at the second stage. The experimental results show that the Co-SVM achieves obvious improvement compared with SVM_{Active} and the traditional relevance feedback algorithm without active learning.

REFERENCES

Angluin, D. (1988). Queries and concept learning. *Machine Learning, 2*, (4), 319-342.

Blum, A., & Mitchell, T. (1998). Combining labeled and unlabeled data with co-training. In *Proceedings of the 11th Annual Conference on Computational Learning Theory*, (pp. 92-100).

Cheng, J., & Wang, K.Q. (2007). Active learning for image retrieval with Co-SVM. In *Pattern Recognition, 40*(1), 330-334.

Collins, M., & Singer, Y. (1999). Unsupervised models for named entity classification. In *Proceedings of the Empirical NLP and Very Large Corpora Conference* (pp. 100-110).

Datta, R., Li, J., & Wang, J.Z. (2005). Content-based image retrieval – approaches and trends of the new age. In *Proceedings of the 7th ACM SIGMM workshop on Multimedia Information Retrieval* (pp. 253-262).

Dasgupta, S., Littman, M., & McAllester, D. (2001). PAC generalization bounds for co-training. In *Proceedings of 14th Neural Information Processing Systems* (pp. 375-382).

Freund, Y., Seung, H.S., Shamir, E., & Tishby, N. (1997). Selective sampling using the query by committee algorithm. *Machine Learning, 28*(2-3), 133-168.

Hong, P., Tian, Q., & Huang, T.S. (2000). Incorporate support vector machines to content-based image retrieval with relevance feedback. In *Proceedings of IEEE International Conference on Image Processing* (pp. 750-753).

Huang, T.S., & Zhou, X.S. (2001). Image retrieval with relevance feedback: from heuristic weight adjustment to optimal learning methods. In *Proceedings of International Conference on Image Processing* (pp. 2-5).

Joachims, T. (1999). Transductive inference for text classification using support vector machines. In *Proceedings of the 16th International Conference on Machine Learning* (pp. 200-209).

Mitchell, T. (1982). Generalization as search. *Artificial Intelligence, 28*, 203-226.

Muslea, I., Minton, S., & Knoblock, C.A. (2000). Selective sampling with redundant views. In *Proceedings of the 17th National Conference on Artificial Intelligence* (pp. 621-626).

Muslea, I., Minton, S., & Knoblock, C.A. (2006). Active learning with multiple views. *Journal of Artificial Intelligence Research, 27*, 203-233.

Nigam, K., & Ghani, R. (2000). Analysis the effectiveness and applicability of co-training. In *Proceedings of Information and Knowledge Management,* (pp. 86-93).

Picard, R.W., Minka, T.P., & Szummer, M. (1996). Modeling user subjectivity in image libraries. In *Proceedings of International Conference on Image Processing,* (pp. 777-780).

Rocchio Jr., J.J. (1971). Relevance feedback in information retrieval. In G. Salton (Eds.), *The SMART Retrieval System: Experiments in Automatic Document Processing,* (pp. 313-323). New Jersey: Prentice-Hall.

Rui, Y., Huang, T. S., & Chang, S. F. (1999). Image retrieval: current techniques, promising directions and open issues. *Journal of Visual Communication and Image Representation, 10*(1), 39-62.

Rui, Y., Huang, T.S., Ortega, M., & Mehrotra, S. (1998). Relevance feedback: a power tool in interactive content-based image retrieval. *IEEE Transactions on Circuits and Systems for Video Technology, 8*(5), 664-655.

Schohn, G., & Cohn, D. (2000). Less is more: active learning with support vector machines. *Proceedings of the 7th International Conference on Machine Learning* (pp. 839-846).

Smeulders, A.W.M., Worring, M., Santini, S., Gupta, A., & Jain, R. (2000). Content-based image retrieval at the end of the early years. *IEEE Transactions on Pattern Analysis and Machine Intelligence, 22*(12), 1349-1380.

Tieu, K., & Viola, P. (2000). Boosting image retrieval. In *Proceedings of IEEE Conference on Computer Vision and Pattern Recognition* (pp. 228-235).

Tong, S., & Chang, E. (2001). Support vector machine active learning for image retrieval. In *Proceedings of the 9th ACM International Conference on Multimedia,* (pp. 107-118).

Tong, S., & Koller, D. (2000). Support vector machine active learning with applications to text classification. In *Proceedings of the 7th International Conference on Machine Learning,* (pp. 999-1006).

Vapnik, V. (1998). *Statistical learning theory.* New York: Wiley.

Vasconcelos, N., & Lippman, A. (2000). Bayesian relevance feedback for content-based access of image and video libraries. In *Proceedings of IEEE Workshop on Content-based Access of Image and Video Libraries* (pp. 63-67).

Wang, L., Chan, K.L., & Zhang, Z. (2003). Bootstrapping SVM active learning by incorporating unlabelled images for image retrieval. In *Proceedings of IEEE Computer Vision and Pattern Recognition,* (pp. 629-634).

Zhang, T., & Oles, F. (2000). A probability analysis on the value of unlabeled data for classification problems. In *Proceedings of the 17th International Conference on Machine Learning,* (pp. 1191-1198).

Zhang, X.Y., Cheng, J., Lu, H.Q., & Ma, S.D. (2007). Weighted Co-SVM for image retrieval with MVB strategy. In *Proceedings of IEEE International Conference on Image Processing,* (pp. 517-520).

Zhang, X.Y., Cheng, J., Lu, H.Q., & Ma, S.D. (2008). Selective sampling based on dynamic certainty propagation for image retrieval. In *Proceedings of the 14th International Multimedia Modeling Conference,* (pp. 425-435).

Zhou, X.S., & Huang, T.S. (2003). Relevance feedback in image retrieval: A comprehensive review. *Multimedia Systems, 8*(6), 536-544.

Zhou, Z.H., & Li, M. (2005). Semi-supervised regression with Co-training. In *Proceedings of the International Joint Conference on Artificial Intelligence* (pp. 908-913).

Zhu, X. (2006). *Semi-supervised learning literature survey.* Wisconsin University, http://pages.cs.wisc.edu/~jerryzhu/pub.

Chapter VII
Visual Data Mining Based on Partial Similarity Concepts

Juliusz L. Kulikowski
Polish Academy of Sciences, Poland

ABSTRACT

Visual data mining is a procedure aimed at a selection from a document's repository subsets of documents presenting certain classes of objects; the last may be characterized as classes of objects' similarity or, more generally, as classes of objects satisfying certain relationships. In this chapter attention will be focused on selection of visual documents representing objects belonging to similarity classes.

INTRODUCTION

In numerous scientific research, medical examination, technological applications, education, artistic activity, and other areas visual data play a substantial, sometimes irreplaceable role. Intensive progress in image acquisition, recording, enhancement and storage technology in the last decades caused a dramatic increase in total volume of visual documents stored in archives and repositories of various types over the world. However, because of legal or organizational difficulties and low effectiveness of available remote data access and visual information retrieval methods only a small part of useful information from visual documents can be mined and effectively used in new investigations, decision making and/or in application tasks solution. This is why the interest to new methods of data mining from visual documents is still actual.

A visual document is here considered as an electronic digital file consisting of a textual and a graphical part, the last being, in fact, a digital representation of a graph or an image. The textual part of the document may contain some formal characteristics of the document as a whole (numerical identifier, emission date, source, accessibility conditions, etc.) as well as of its graphical part: image contents characteristics (string of key words, a semantic classification code, etc.), code of image modality, technical parameters, quality characteristics, and so forth. The graphical part of a visual document is assumed to present graphs or images in one of admissible standard forms that makes it possible to be displayed and visualized in order to be manually or automatically processed.

Image processing means here image selection, enhancement, compression/decompression, transmission, visualization as well as any type of image analysis: functional transformation, parameters extraction, recognition, contents' interpretation, application value assessment, and so forth.

Visual data mining is a procedure aimed at a selection from a documents' repository subsets of documents presenting certain classes of objects; the last may be characterized as classes of objects' similarity or, more generally, as classes of objects satisfying certain relationships. In this chapter attention will be focused on selection of visual documents representing objects belonging to similarity classes.

GENERAL CONCEPT OF *SIMILARITY*

Observing the surrounding world as an extremely sophisticated variety of objects, relationships between them and processes we try to put order on it for making it more comprehensible. One of ways to reach this is establishment of similarities between objects or processes which make it possible to apply some statements about individual objets or processes to the members of their similarity classes. This way of action is not only a human discovery. A wild animal first-time testing an apple and finding it good fixes in its mind a pattern of similar size, form, color and scent objects. In its later experiences the pattern may be corrected by exclusion the small size and dark-green color objects which finally leads to a fixation in the mind a pattern (a concept) of "good for being eaten" objects. Establishment of similarity concepts and detection of similarities in individual cases in many living beings is thus a capability of fundamental importance. Non less important seems explaining what, in general, does the *similarity* mean.

Strong similarity. In the forthcoming, the notion *object* will be assigned to any formal representative (geometrical point, vector, string of symbols, etc.) of a real or abstract being, characterizing its features and identifying it among other beings. Similarity is a property of a class C of objects that in the simplest case can be described by a formal *similarity relation* [Rasiowa H., Sikorski R. ,1968]:

1^0 reciprocal (each object a is similar to itself),
2^0 symmetrical (if object a is similar to object b then b is similar to a), and
3^0 transitive (if a is similar to b and b is similar to c then a is similar to c).

For the reasons that will be explained below, the above-defined similarity can be called a *strong similarity* concept. Similarity of triangles is a well known example of similarity in the above-given sense: two triangles on an Euclidean plane are similar if angular measures of the pairs of respective angles are equal. This property can easily be extended on any set of triangles. Similarity of polygons on a plane can also be based on the concept of pair-wise equality of angular measures of the pairs of respective angles.

Strong similarity can be based on various similarity criteria assigning different sense of similarity to the objects under consideration. For example, it is possible to assume that in the set C of triangles "*similar*" are the triangles of the same surface measure, of the same sum of lengths of edges, etc.

Figure 1. Similarity classes of a set of printed characters

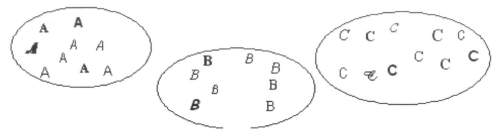

Figure 2. Example of non-transitiveness of similarity

It can be shown that if the above-given similarity relation is described in a class C of objects then C can be divided into a family F_C of mutually disjoint subclasses $C^{(1)}$, $C^{(2)}$,..., etc., called *similarity classes*, such that any two objects belonging to the same similarity class are similar in the sense of the relation and no two objects belonging to different similarity classes do so. In the above-mentioned case of similarity of triangles each similarity class consists of the triangles described by the same triple of fixed angular measures (admitting their permutations).

Example 1.

Let us consider a set of printed characters shown in Fig. 1.

The characters form three subsets constituting similarity classes established by assigned to them phonetic values, independent of their typeface.

Weak similarity. The above-presented concept of similarity, as it has been shown above, suits well to establishment of similarity between well defined, standardized objects. However, in the case of visual objects analysis such situation occurs rather exceptionally. A difficulty lies in the similarity transitiveness condition which in practice is not always satisfied. For example, if D (a daughter) is in a certain sense similar to F (her father) then also, in the same sense, F is similar to D. Moreover, D may be also similar to M (her mother). However, it does not imply that F is similar to M.

Example 2.

A sequence of characters shown in Fig. 2 has been ordered so that each character is approximately similar to its closest neighbors in the row. However, it is evident that similarity does not hold between the extreme characters, A and B. As a consequence, the notion of similarity classes has lost an exact sense in this case.

For image processing and pattern recognition purposes one should thus distinguish between the above-defined, *strong-sense similarity*, and a *weak sense similarity* being a sort of a neighborhood, reciprocal and symmetrical but not transitive relation. More exactly speaking, in the weak similarity case transitiveness holds in a limited degree that can be characterized by a notion of *similarity measure* [Kulikowski J.L., 2002].

Similarity measure. Let C be a class of objects and let a, b, c be some of its members. Then it can be defined a function:

$$\sigma: C \times C \to [0,\ldots,1] \tag{1}$$

assigning to any pair of objects belonging to C a number from the (continuous or discrete) closed interval $[0,\ldots,1]$ so that the conditions:

$$
\left.
\begin{array}{ll}
\text{I.} & \sigma(a,a) \equiv 1, \\
\text{II.} & \sigma(a,b) \equiv \sigma(b,a \\
\text{III.} & \sigma(a,b) \cdot \sigma(b,c) \leq \sigma(a,c).
\end{array}
\right\} \tag{2}
$$

are satisfied.

The I and II conditions correspond, respectively, to the reciprocity and symmetry of similarity. The III condition reminds the well known "triangle inequality" of a distance measure. If C is a metric space (a space in which a notion of *distance measure* $d(a,b)$ between its elements has been introduced) then a *distance-type similarity measure* $\sigma(a,b)$ between the objects on the basis of $d(a,b)$ can be defined as:

$$\sigma(a,b) = exp[-h \cdot d(a,b)] \tag{3}$$

where h is a real positive scaling coefficient. Then, taking into account that according to the "triangle inequality": $d(a,c) \leq d(a,b) + d(b,c)$ for any $a, b, c \in C$, the property III from (2) follows directly. It thus establishes lower bounds for similarity measures of objects linked by chains of other objects whose similarity measures pair-wise have been assessed. Therefore, the III condition plays a role of a weakened transitivity condition. It can easily be proven that in the above-given case $\sigma(a,a) \equiv 1$ and $\sigma(a,b) = 0$ when $d(a,b) = \infty$. The distance-type similarity measure is widely used in the *k-nearest-neighbors* (*kNN*) pattern recognition algorithms [Kulikowski J.L., 2002].

The conditions I, II and III hold also in other types of similarity measures, two of them being of particular interest in image processing. Let $a, b, \ldots$ be the elements of a multi-dimensional linear vector space. An angular measure of the angle between the vectors a and b will be denoted by $ang(a,b)$. Then, an *angular-type similarity measure* $\sigma(a,b)$ can be defined as

$$\sigma(a,b) = 1 - sin[ang(a,b)]. \tag{4}$$

Let us remark that in certain applications (pattern recognition, signal detection, etc.) the function $cos[ang(a,b)]$ is often used as a correlation measure between a and b., However, this function, satisfying the (2).I and II, does not satisfy the (2).III condition.

The right-hand side of (4) can be calculated if an *inner product* (a,b) of the vectors is known. If the vectors have the form: $a = [a_1, a_2,\ldots, a_i,\ldots]$, $b = [b_1, b_2,\ldots, b_i,\ldots]$, $a_1,\ldots, a_i,\ldots,b_1,\ldots, b_i\ldots$ being some their real components, then their inner product is given by the formula [3]:

$$(\boldsymbol{a},\boldsymbol{b}) = \sum_{(i)} a_i \cdot b_i \qquad\qquad (5)$$

(the sum being taken over all components of the vectors). In particular, the *norm* $|\boldsymbol{a}|$ of the given vector being used as its length's measure is given by the formula:

$$|\,a\,| = \sqrt{(a,a)} \qquad\qquad (6)$$

The angular *similarity measure* can be thus calculated as:

$$\sigma(a,b) = 1 - \sqrt{1 - \frac{[(a,b)]^2}{|a|^2 \cdot |b|^2}} \qquad\qquad (7)$$

The formula is based on the assumption that vectors $\boldsymbol{a}$, $\boldsymbol{b}$ have finite non-zero norms. It can be proven that for the angular similarity concept $\sigma(\boldsymbol{a},\boldsymbol{b}) = 1$ when $\boldsymbol{a} = \gamma \cdot \boldsymbol{b}$, where γ is a real coefficient, while $\sigma(\boldsymbol{a},\boldsymbol{b}) = 0$ if $\boldsymbol{a}$ is perpendicular to $\boldsymbol{b}$. Independence of the length of vectors is another property of the angular similarity measure, the property being important in certain types of applications.

Example 3

Let us denote by C a 3-dimensional vector space of colors coded in RGB system. Using an angular-type similarity measure means in this case that $\sigma(\boldsymbol{a},\boldsymbol{b}) = 1$ corresponds to a pair of spots coded, respectively, by $\boldsymbol{a}$ and $\boldsymbol{b}$, being of the same color despite a difference between their brightness levels.

Let us suppose that three spots, whose colors can be roughly described as *light green, vivid green* and *sea-green* have been coded, respectively, in the RGB system by the vectors:

$\boldsymbol{a} = [145, 247, 172]$, $\boldsymbol{b} = [14, 120, 63]$, $\boldsymbol{c} = [40, 120, 118]$.

We shall calculate the angular-type similarity measure of the pairs of colors. For this purpose it is necessary to calculate the norms and inner products of the vectors, using the formulae (6) and (5). For example:

$|\boldsymbol{a}|^2 = 145^2 + 247^2 + 172^2 = 111\,618$, $|\boldsymbol{a}| = 334.0928$,
$|\boldsymbol{b}|^2 = 14^2 + 120^2 + 63^2 = 18\,565$, $|\boldsymbol{b}| = 136.2534$,
$(\boldsymbol{a},\boldsymbol{b}) = 145 \cdot 14 + 247 \cdot 120 + 172 \cdot 63 = 42\,506$.

In similar way we obtain:

$|\boldsymbol{c}|^2 = 29\,924$, $|\boldsymbol{c}| = 172.9855$,
$(\boldsymbol{a},\boldsymbol{c}) = 55\,736$, $(\boldsymbol{b},\boldsymbol{c}) = 22\,394$.

Finally, using formula (7) we obtain:

$$\sigma(a,b) = 1 - \sqrt{1 - \frac{42506^2}{111618 \cdot 18565}} = 0.6421$$

In similar way it can be obtained:

$\sigma(a,c) = 0.7345, \quad \sigma(b,c) = 0.6881.$

Let us remark that the similarity measures will be different if another color coding system is used.

Similarity measure based on qualitative features of objects (called below a *logical-type similarity*) is another case of the weak similarity concept. Let for the given set C of objects it has been defined a set of K *logical tests* given in a functional form:

$$\tau_k : C \times C \to [0, 1] \quad \text{for } k = 1, 2, \ldots, K, \tag{8}$$

i.e. such that to any pair of objects a symbolic value *0* (*false*) or *1*(*true*) is assigned. Assigning *1* means that the given pair of objects satisfies a condition of coincidence of a qualitative property represented by the corresponding tests. For example, $\tau_k (a, b) = 1$ may mean that two mammograms, a and b, have been acquired by the same type of X-ray devices, two fingerprints belong to the same person, two aerial photos have been taken in the same season, etc.

For a given set of K logical tests to each pair of objects $a, b,$ it can be thus assigned a binary vector $v(a,b)$ consisting of components representing the coincidence of selected qualitative properties of the objects. So defined vectors can be taken as a basis of a *logical similarity measure*. Formally, the measure will be given by the formula:

$$\psi : [0, 1]^K \to [0, \ldots, 1] \tag{9}$$

where ψ is a function assigning to any vector v a real number from the interval $[0, \ldots, 1]$, and such that:

1. $\psi(\mathbf{0}) = 0, \; \psi(\mathbf{1}) = 1, \mathbf{0}$ and $\mathbf{1}$ denoting, correspondingly, a K-component vector consisting of *0*s or *1*s only;

2. ψ is a monotonically non-decreasing function, i.e. for any K-component binary vectors p, q, such that $q \neq \mathbf{0}$, it is $\psi(p \oplus q) \geq \psi(p)$.

The operation $\oplus$ is interpreted above as *maximum*, i.e. $0 \oplus 0 = 0, \; 1 \oplus 1 = 1 \oplus 0 = 0 \oplus 1 = 1.$ Condition 1 seems evident; condition 2 means that the logical similarity measure value should not be decreased by any additional positive results of logical tests. A function ψ satisfying the above-given conditions can be chosen in many ways. Two particular situations arise when: a/ $\psi(v) = 1$ if $v = \mathbf{1}$ and $\psi(v) = 0$ otherwise, and b/ $\psi(v) = 0$ if $v = \mathbf{0}$ and $\psi(v) = 1$ otherwise. Situation a/ means that two objects are determined similar when all logical tests are satisfied by their features. On the contrary, situation b/ means that one positive value of tests is sufficient the objects to be recognized similar. Among the above-mentioned extremities a variety of other solutions is possible. One of them can be based on the concept of weighed sum of tests. Let for the given set of tests it will be arbitrarily chosen a K-component vector w of normalized non-negative weight coefficients:

$$\sum_{\kappa=1}^{K} w_\kappa = 1,$$

(10)

where w_κ denotes a relative weight assigned to the importance of the tests τ_κ, $\kappa = 1,2,\dots,K$, in total similarity assessment. Then one can put:

$$\psi[v(a,b)] = \frac{1}{K}\sum_{\kappa+1}^{K} w_\kappa \cdot \tau_\kappa(a,b)$$

(11)

The following example should illustrate the above-described concept of logical-type similarity measure.

Example 4.

Let us assume that it is given a set Ω of microscopic images representing liver biopsy histologic specimens. To each image additional description is attached containing the following data: 1/ image identifying code, 2/ donor's personal identifying code, 3/ donor's age, 4/ date of image acquisition, 5/ laboratory's identifying code, 6/ type of microscope, 7/ type of specimen staining. For certain investigations it is necessary to select a subset of images satisfying the following conditions: a/ donors of the corresponding specimens are of an age kept within a fixed time-interval, b/ date of image acquisition is limited to several fixed years, c/ images have been acquired in a given group of laboratories and using several types of microscopes, d/ specimens have been prepared using a fixed type of staining. In addition, it is desired that conditions a/ and b/ are strongly satisfied, while c/ and d/ should be taken into account with fixed weights corresponding to their relative importance level.

For this purpose logical test-functions for the features 3/ - 8/ should be established, feature 1/ being not important for comparing the images and feature 2/ - not substantial for image selection. The tests may be then chosen as follows:

$$\tau_1 = \begin{cases} 1 \text{ if both donors' age belong to the given time-interval,} \\ 0, \text{ otherwise;} \end{cases}$$

$$\tau_2 = \begin{cases} 1 \text{ if the dates of acquisition of both images belong to the given time-interval,} \\ 0, \text{ otherwise;} \end{cases}$$

$$\tau_3 = \begin{cases} 1 \text{ if images have been examined in the laboratories of a given group,} \\ 0, \text{ otherwise;} \end{cases}$$

$$\tau_4 = \begin{cases} 1 \text{ if image examinations have been performed using microscopes of a given group,} \\ 0, \text{ otherwise;} \end{cases}$$

$$\tau_5 = \begin{cases} 1 \text{ if images have been examined after the given type of specimen staining,} \\ 0, \text{ otherwise;} \end{cases}$$

Finally, the logical similarity measure will be defined as follows:

$$\psi(a,b) = \tau_1(a,b) \cdot \tau_2(a,b) \cdot \frac{1}{3} \sum_{\kappa=3}^{5} \tau_\kappa(a,b)$$

So-defined similarity measure means that images a, b are recognized similar only if age of specimens' donors and image acquisition time are kept in strongly fixed intervals while type of laboratory, type of microscope and type of specimen staining are taken into consideration with weights equal 1/3.

Multi-aspect similarity measures. In the above-given example the following important property of similarity measures has been used:

Property 1.

If $\sigma_1, \sigma_2, ..., \sigma_n$ are similarity measures described on a given set C of objects, then their product:

$$\sigma = \sigma_1 \cdot \sigma_2 \cdot ... \cdot \sigma_n \tag{12}$$

also satisfies the general similarity measure conditions.

The proof of this property is very simple and will be omitted. The Property 1 makes it possible to construct a large variety of multi-aspect similarity measures as products of the single-aspect ones. In particular, combinations of distance-, angular-, and logical-based similarity measures are possible. This possibility can be useful in visual data mining, where logical similarity measures suit well to formal characterization of visual documents while other similarity aspects, directly concerning the graphical documents' part, can be evaluated and compared using any types of similarity measures. The next property extends this possibility.

Property 2.

If σ is a similarity measure satisfying the conditions (2).I, II, III, then σ^γ, where $\gamma, \gamma > 0$, is also a similarity measure such that for any pair of objects a, b it is $\sigma^\gamma(a,b) \leq \sigma(a,b)$ if $\gamma \geq 1$ and $\sigma^\gamma(a,b) < \sigma(a,b)$ if $0 < \gamma < 1$.

This property follows from the fact that: 1/ x^γ is a non-negative function such that for any $\gamma > 0$ it is $0^\gamma = 0$, $1^\gamma = 1$, 2/ for $0 \leq x \leq 1$ it is $x^\gamma \leq x$ if $\gamma \geq 1$ and $x^\gamma \geq x$ if $\gamma \leq 1$ and 3/ from (2).III it follows that for any objects a, b it is $log\ \sigma(a,b) + log\ \sigma(b,c) \leq log\ \sigma(a,c)$; therefore: $\gamma \cdot log\ \sigma(a,b) + \gamma \cdot log\ \sigma(b,c) \leq \gamma \cdot log\ \sigma(a,c)$ what leads to the conclusion $\sigma^\gamma(a,b) \cdot \sigma^\gamma(b,c) \leq \sigma^\gamma(a,c)$.

Property 2 makes it possible to relatively support some terms in the expression (12) by using them in power $\gamma < 1$ or to suppress them by using in power $\gamma > 1$. Therefore, a more general expression for multi-aspect similarity measure is:

$$\sigma = (\sigma_1)^{\gamma 1} \cdot (\sigma_2)^{\gamma 2} \cdot ... \cdot (\sigma_n)^{\gamma n} \tag{13}$$

where $\gamma_1, \gamma_2, ... \gamma_n$ are some strengthening coefficients.

Weak similarity classes. Similarity measure makes possible to extend the concept of objects' similarity classes. However, unlike the strong similarity, in the weak similarity case similarity classes, as it will be shown below, cannot be determined in an unique way. Let us assume that C is a countable set of objects on which a similarity measure σ has been defined. Let us take into consideration the set $C \times C$ (a Cartesian product) of all possible pairs (a,b) of objects of C and a set S of the values of similarity measures $\sigma(a,b)$ of the pairs. Let σ_1, $\sigma_1 \leq 1$, be the maximum value in S. One can select the pairs of objects whose similarity measure is σ_1. Let us denote by $C^{(1)}$, where $C^{(1)} \subseteq C$, a subclass of objects belonging to such pairs; $C^{(1)}$ will be called the *1st similarity level* of the objects. There may exist in $C^{(1)}$ subsets of objects similar each to each other one with the maximum similarity measure σ_1. The largest (i.e. not extendable) subsets having this property will be called *1st-level similarity classes*. So, the 1st similarity level will be decomposed into a certain number of 1st-level similarity classes; however, it should be remarked that some of the 1st-level similarity classes may consist of single objects. Then, for the rest of objects forming a subset $C \setminus C^{(1)}$ the above-described procedure can be repeated: if σ_2 is the maximum similarity measure among its members then a 2nd similarity level $C^{(2)} \subseteq C \setminus C^{(1)}$ can be selected and *2nd-level similarity classes* can be defined in the above-described manner. The procedure should be continued up to the moment when all objects of C are included into some similarity classes. Each so-defined similarity class consists of objects whose similarity to other members of the same similarity class is strongly fixed, but not obviously equal 1. Therefore, similarity measure can also be interpreted as *inner similarity compactness* measure of the classes of various levels.

The above-described procedure of selection of similarity levels was based on the assumption that a maximum number in the set S of values of similarity measures can be found. However, this assumption can be not true if the class C is countable and the similarity measure is continuous. In such case the scale of similarity measure values should be discretized (divided into a finite number of sub-intervals) and then the corresponding number of similarity levels can be delimited.

The partition of the similarity levels $C^{(1)}$, $C^{(2)}$, etc. into weak similarity classes is not unique, as it will be shown by the following example.

Example 5.

Let us assume that at i-th level of the above-described procedure of partition of the objects into similarity classes a subclass $C^{(i)}$, $C^{(i)} \subseteq C$, of objects corresponding to the similarity measure σ_i has been selected. In order to find similarity classes on this level $C^{(i)}$ will be represented by a graph whose nodes have been assigned to the objects and edges connect pairs of nodes corresponding to the pairs of objects whose similarity measure is exactly equal to σ_i. An example of a graph of this type is shown in Fig. 3

Then we are looking for maximum subsets of nodes in the graph such that each pair of nodes is connected within the subset by an edge. This problem is well known in the graph theory as a problem of finding cliques in the graph; several algorithms of solution of the problem have been described in the literature [5,6]. Fig. 3 A, B, C show that in general there may be several different partitions of a graph into cliques (the cliques are bordered by plotted lines); however, the number of cliques and their size (number of nodes) are strongly fixed. In our case each clique represents a similarity class of objects, the inner similarity compactness level in all similarity classes generated by the given graph being the same.

It thus can be concluded that there are many possibilities to define a similarity measure satisfying the general conditions and adjust it to a given application problem. Weak similarity can be considered as a reciprocal and symmetrical fuzzy relation imposed on a set of objects, the fuzziness being determined by a similarity measure satisfying the conditions (2). I, II and III. It leads to a partition (in general, in

Figure 3. Different partitions of a subclass of objects into weak similarity subclasses

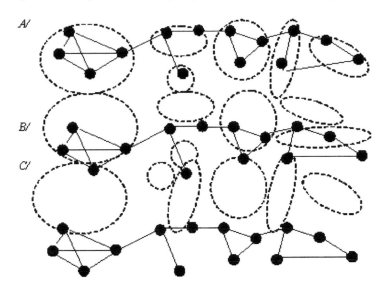

Figure 4 Partition of a class of objects into weak similarity subclasses

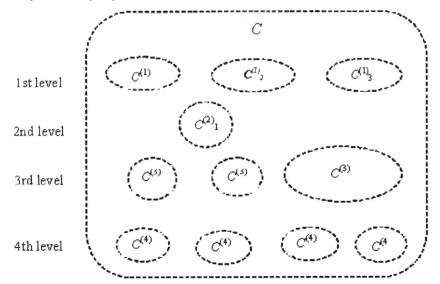

several possible ways) of the given class C of objects into weak similarity subclasses which can be arranged in a hierarchical structure as shown in Fig. 4. Subclasses belonging to a fixed level of the hierarchy are characterized by a fixed inner similarity compactness. The higher is the level index (the lower is the level position on the scheme), the lower is the inner similarity compactness of the subclasses on this level. Similarity of any two objects belonging to similarity subclasses on two consecutive levels is lower than the inner similarity compactness on the higher level. Such partition of the class of objects into subclasses according to their descending similarity to other objects plays an important role in image retrieval and selection, as it will be shown next.

DETECTION OF PARTIAL SIMILARITY OF IMAGES

It is well known that a natural language has a composite, multi-level structure. On the lowest level of a speech language organization phonemes can be distinguished. Morphemes, words, phrase structures, sentences, statements, etc. are the elements of higher levels of the speech language structure. Similar, multi-level composition holds also in images, including those stored in the form of visual documents in archives, data bases, etc. On the lowest level separate pixels or their simple combinations can be distinguished; basic geometrical details (primitives) or morphological forms on the higher level can be detected; more sophisticated structures as combinations of some simpler ones on the next levels can be observed, etc. On the top level a total scene as a composition of lower-level objects can be recognized. Hierarchical structure of visual data makes the problem of visual data management a very difficult one. The above-described concepts of strong or weak similarity suit well to image analysis if they are related to image features on a strongly defined composition level. This can be illustrated by the graphical structures shown in Fig. 5.

There are no differences between the structures on the 1st (pixel) and 2nd (geometrical primitives in the form of short line segments) composition levels. On the 3rd level two types of geometrical details in the form of upright standing and reversed small triangles can be recognized. Similarly, on the 4th level there are two upright standing and one reversed triangle. The patterns a/ and b/ are similar on the 3rd composition level and dissimilar on the 4th level. On the other hand, the patterns a/ and c/ are similar on the 4th level and dissimilar on the 3rd one. Patterns b/ and c/ represent an interesting case of a cross-similarity.

Figure 5. Examples of similarity on various image composition levels

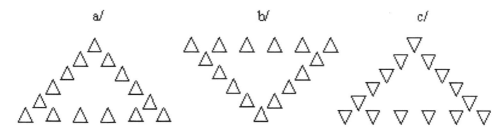

Figure 6. Example of partial similarity of two images': the centers of similarity in image a/ and b/ are marked by rectangles

(a)	*(b)*

Another example is shown in Fig. 6a,b representing two landscape photos. On the top image composition level no similarity between the images exists. However, on the lower level a certain sort of similarity between some architectural and natural objects can be observed. On the basic levels a lot of similar local details also can be detected.

The examples show that it may happen, in general, that two or more images totally dissimilar on a higher composition level still contain similar details on some lower levels. Similarity on the basic (1st or 2nd) levels is rather frequently observed; however, usually it is of no practical interest. Different situation may arise on the middle image composition levels where detection of some details may be of great practical importance for the user. This, for example, may concern detection of similarity of specific details hidden in large collections of astronomic, biological, medical, criminological etc. images. For this purpose a concept of partial similarity of images may be useful.

Two (or more) images will be called *partially similar* if on a given composition level in both (or more) images there can be detected objects satisfying a given criterion of similarity. Such objects will be called *centers of similarity*. Two examples of such centers have been marked in Fig. 6 a/ and b/ by rectangles.

A subset $\Xi^{(j)} \subseteq \Xi$ consisting of all partially similar images taken from a set Ξ and such that their partial similarity is based on a fixed set of centers of similarity, will be called a *class of partial similarity* of the images. It is evident that the class of partial similarity is also strongly connected with a given criterion of similarity. Finding the classes of partial similarity in a given set Ξ will be called, generally, a partial similarity-based retrieval problem. Two kinds of such problems can be distinguished:

1. When one or several strongly fixed *reference objects* are indicated and the problem consists in finding the classes of partial similarity based on the given set of centers of similarity;
2. When, instead of several reference objects, only a strong similarity class of objects is indicated as the one whose members should be taken into consideration as possible reference objects; the task consists in finding in the set of images all classes of partial similarity based on the centers of similarity belonging to the given similarity class.

The first case corresponds, e.g., to a situation when in a set of fingerprints the ones containing a strongly fixed configuration of fingerprint minutes are searched. For this purpose the set is looked through in order to select the regions of interest (ROI) where the fingerprint minutes can be found, then the minutes are recognized, their similarity to those of the reference fingerprints is assessed and their configuration is compared with this of the reference fingerprint. The class of partial similarity of images in this case is assumed to correspond, on a certain probability level, to the same fingerprint donor.

The second case arises when, e.g., in a set of photos presenting groups of persons the subsets of photos on which the same (however, individually not indicated) person(s) can be recognized. The class of partial similarity of images consists in this case of photos on which at least one, primarily not indicated, person is visible on at least two photos. Detection of images in the second case is more difficult than in the first one. First photo for the analysis can be randomly taken from the given set. Then, the ROIs corresponding to the persons in the photo should be selected. Each well visible person in the ROIs is taken into consideration as a reference object for finding similar to it objects in the ROIs selected in other photos. When finding the members of the classes of similarity based on the reference objects taken from the first photo is finished, additional reference objects from the second, third, etc. photos can be taken in order to continue the above-described procedure. It is evident that a solution of the second-type of partial similarity-based retrieval problem is much more time-consuming than the first type one. However, effective solution of the first type retrieval problems can be taken as a basis of a solution of the second-type ones.

For a given set of visual documents a partial similarity measure $s(V_i, V_j)$ of any pair V_i, V_j of images belonging to some documents can be defined. For this purpose, first, a class C of objects (e.g. fingerprint minutes, human faces, architectural details, tumors in radiological images, etc.), which should be taken into consideration as a basis of partial similarity of images assessment, should be specified. Let $G_i = [g_i^1,...,g_i^m]$, $G_j = [g_j^1,...,g_j^n]$ be local visual objects of the given class C primarily selected for analysis in V_i and V_j, respectively. Then all pairs of the type $[g_i^\mu, g_j^\nu]$ for $\mu = 1,2,...,m$, $\nu = 1,2,...,n$, should be taken into account. Each pair contributes to the partial similarity measure of $s(V_i,V_j)$ if the similarity $\sigma(g_i^\mu, g_j^\nu)$ of the objects satisfies the following logical condition (objects' *concordance* test):

$$t(g_i^\mu, g_j^\nu) = \begin{cases} 1 \text{ if } 0 \le \sigma_0 \le \sigma(g_i^\mu, g_j^\nu), \\ 0 \text{ otherwise,} \end{cases}$$

where σ_0 is a fixed threshold level, $0 \le \sigma_0 \le 1$. A partial similarity function then can be defined as:

$$s(V_i,V_j) = \frac{\sum_{\mu=1}^m \sum_{\nu=1}^n t(g_i^\mu, g_j^\nu)}{mn}$$

Using this function it is possible, for example, to evaluate partial similarity of mammograms according to the number of pairs of calcifications of similar size and form detected in the analyzed images. However, assessment of partial similarity of images is a time-consuming operation depending on the number of different pairs of the analyzed objects. This dependence becomes linear in the individual reference objects based similarity task solution case, when the set of reference objects is strongly limited.

The time consumption of partial similarity of images assessment can be reduced if a significant part of non-perspective objects within a procedure based on simplified selection criteria is rejected. For this purpose it can be established a sequence of objects' multi-aspect similarity measures:

$$\sigma^{(1)}(a, b), \sigma^{(2)}(a, b), \ldots, \sigma^{(k)}(a, b).$$

Let $\Sigma^{(\kappa)}$, $\kappa = 1,2,...,k$, denote the subset of single-aspect similarity measures on which $\sigma^{(\kappa)}(a, b)$ has been based. If the $\Sigma^{(\kappa)}$ s are chosen so that the inclusions $\Sigma^{(1)} \subset \Sigma^{(2)} \subset \ldots \subset \Sigma^{(k)}$ hold then the above-given sequence represents step-by step strengthened similarity criteria. Each next similarity formula is given there as a product of the preceding formula and some additional partial similarity measures. For a given reference object $a = g^*$ and a threshold level $\sigma_0^{(1)}$ using $\sigma^{(1)}(g^*,b)$ and based on them concordance test a subset $C^{(1)}$, $C^{(1)} \subseteq C$, of objects can be selected. The elements of $C^{(1)}$ are the first-step candidates for a class of objets similar to g^*. Then, taking into account the similarity measure $\sigma^{(2)}(g^*, b)$ and a threshold level $\sigma_0^{(2)}$ and applying them to the elements of $C^{(1)}$ a subset $C^{(2)}$, $C^{(2)} \subseteq C^{(1)}$, can be selected, etc. Repetition of such procedure leads to a descending sequence of subsets $C \supseteq C^{(1)} \supseteq C^{(2)} \supseteq \ldots \supseteq C^{(k)}$. Finally, $C^{(k)}$ consists of the most similar to g^* objects. Images containing the elements of $C^{(k)}$ are the searched ones, forming a class of partial similarity defined by g^*. The calculation-time reduction is achieved due to the fact that the initial selection steps are based on simplified concordance test, while the next selections are applied to reduced subsets of visual objects.

RELATIVE PARTIAL SIMILARITY

In the most general partial similarity detection cases non-numerical objects' similarity assessment is admissible. Instead of the above-described concordance tests $t(g^\mu_i, g^\nu_j)$ whose logical values are expressed in a binary scale (0 = "*false*", 1 = "*true*") the following statements:

$h(a, b; \sigma)$: "*a* is similar to *b* in the sense of σ",

for any $a, b, \dots \in C$ then can be taken into consideration and their logical values in a more general sense can be evaluated. This leads to the concept of partial similarity assessment based on relative (topological) logic [Hempel C.G. 1937, Kulikowski J.L. 1986, Vessel Ch.A. 1970]. In such case, instead of using any a priori fixed logical scale it is assumed that for any two statements, e.g. $h(a,b)$ and $h(c,e)$, (the argument σ being here neglected for the sake of simplicity) the following logical relationships are admitted:

1. $h(a,b) \preceq h(c,e)$, i.e. "*h(a,b) is not more logically valuable than h(c,e)*";
2. $h(a,b) \succeq h(c,e)$, i.e. "*h(a,b) is not less logically valuable than h(c,e)*";
3. $h(a,b) \preceq h(c,e)$ AND $h(a,b) \succeq h(c,e)$, i.e. "*h(a,b) AND h(c,e) are equally logically valuable*", which also can be denoted as $h(a,b) \approx h(c,e)$;
4. *NEITHER* $h(a,b) \preceq h(c,e)$, *NOR* $h(a,b) \succeq h(c,e)$, i.e. "*h(a,b) AND h(c,e) are logically incomparable*", which also can be denoted by $h(a,b) \; ? \; h(c,e)$.

In particular, it can be assumed that: 1st $h(a,b; \sigma) \preceq h(c,e; \sigma)$ if for a given similarity measure $\sigma(a, b)$ it is $\sigma(a,b) \leq \sigma(c, e)$, 2nd $h(a,b; \sigma') \preceq h(a,b; \sigma'')$ if $\sigma'(a, b) = \sigma''(a,b)$ and σ' and σ'' are such that $\Sigma' \subset \Sigma''$. If $a = g^*$ is a reference object for which similar objects in a set of images are searched then for any other objects g^μ, g^ν a situation $h(g^*, g^\mu) \approx h(g^*, g^\nu)$ means that the statements about the similarity of g^μ to g^* as well as of g^ν to g^* are logically equivalent; therefore, g^μ and g^ν belong to the same class of similarity to g^*. However, the above-mentioned relationships $\preceq, \succeq, \approx, ?$ among the statements can be established, as well, in any less-formalized way (e.g. suggested by human experts).

For a given reference object g^* and a set C of visual objects a *relative similarity class* (*RSC*) H' can be defined as a subset $H' \subseteq C$ of all objects $b, c, d, \dots$ for which the relationships $h(g^*, b) \approx h(g^*, c) \approx h(g^*, d) \approx \dots$ etc. hold and no such relationship occurs between two statements, say, $h(g^*, e), h(g^*, f)$ if e and f belong to different *RSCs*. The last condition implies that if H' and H'' are any two disjoint subsets of visual objects selected, at the first step of analysis, as candidates to form two different *RSCs*, then for any $a, b \in H'$ and any $c, d \in H''$ simultaneous relationships $h(g^*, a) \preceq h(g^*, c)$ and $h(g^*, b) \succeq h(g^*, d)$ for the sake of logical consistency should be detected and excluded. Let H' and H'' be, at the

Figure 7. Example of a Hasse diagram

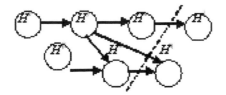

first step, two different subsets of visual objects that by the experts have been indicated as similar to a reference object g^* from the point of view of two different similarity criteria. Then they can be taken as the first approximation of the candidates to form two *RSC*s. For this purpose all pairs of statements $[h(g^*, a_m), h(g^*, c_n)]$ such that $h(g^*, a_m) \in H'$, and $h(g^*, c_n) \in H''$ should be taken into consideration and one of the relationships $\preceq$, $\succeq$ or $\approx$ to each of them by the experts should be assigned. However, if for certain pairs it is impossible to be done, the relationship $?$ to them should be assigned. Then, a possible logical inconsistency between H' and H'' can be corrected according to the following rules: 1st if between the elements of H' and those of H'' any of the relationships $\preceq$, $\succeq$ or $?$ prevails then it should be extended on all remaining pairs of the elements of H' and those of H''; 2nd if between the elements of H' and those of H'' the relationship $\approx$ prevails then it should be extended on all remaining pairs of the elements of H' and of H''; in such situation H' and H'' should be merged in a common *RSC*. According to the established dominating type of logical relationship between the statements in different *RSC*s H' and H'' a similar relationship: $\preceq$, $\succeq$, $\approx$ or $?$ between H' and H'' can be established. In similar way logical consistency between all initially selected candidates for *RSC*s can be established. The correction procedure leads thus to semi-ordering of the family F of *RSC*s: between any two *RSC*s H' and H'' one of the relationships (i.e. $H'' \succeq H'$) or $H' ? H''$ may occur. This semi-ordering relation can be represented by a directed contourless graph, called a Hasse diagram G. The nodes of G are assigned to the *RSC*s and an arc (ordered edge) between any ordered pair $[H', H'']$ of them exists if $H' \preceq H''$ and no other *RSC* H satisfies both $H' \preceq H$ and $H \preceq H''$. Example of a Hasse diagram illustrating a semi-ordering of a family of *RSC*s is shown below.

Two *RSC*s: are separated by a dotted line from the rest of the graph. They satisfy $H^\lambda ? H^\eta$, however, they are such that no other *RSC* H exists such that even $H^\lambda \preceq H$ or $H^\eta \preceq H$; such *RSC*s form a subset of maximally logically valuable statements. As a result, the corresponding subset of visual objects $C^\lambda \cup C^\eta$ should be taken into consideration as this of relatively the most similar ones to g^*. Visual data mining based on relative partial similarity concepts may be, in general, less effective than this, based on strongly defined similarity criteria. However, in certain application areas partial similarity measures cannot be precisely evaluated. In such case relative similarity is the only possible way to use information given in a suggestion like: *"From the facial expression point of view B seems to be more similar to A than C"* into a computer-aided decision process.

CONCLUSION

Visual data mining is a tool of extraction useful visual data dispersed in large repositories of visual documents and hidden among other visual data of lower value for the users. This goal can be reached in two ways: by direct indication of a reference pattern (visual object) that should be found in a set of visual documents or by rough indication of a class of objects expected to occur (maybe, not in identical form) in two or more documents. In both cases a general notion of similarity and/or similarity measure and based on them partial similarity can be used to solve the problem. These notions admit, in particular, using various image features to define multi-aspect similarity criteria. An extension of the visual data mining methods on the case of non-numerical similarity criteria is also possible. In particular, when similarity of selected visual objects to the reference objects without clearly defined formal backgrounds are suggested by the experts, selection of the subsets of the visual objects (and, consequently, of containing them partially similar visual documents), satisfying the requirement of similarity to the given reference object, can be reached due to the relative similarity concepts. The last approach puts a bridge between formalized and traditional (manual) visual data similarity assessment and based on them visual documents retrieval methods.

REFERENCES

Hempel, C.G. (1937). A Purely Topological Form of Non-Aristotelian Logic. *Journ. Symb. Logic, 2*(3).

Kulikowski, J.L. (1986). *Decision Making in a Modified Version of Topological Logic. Proceedings of the Seminar on "Non-conventional Problems of Optimization"*. *Prace IBS PAN, Part I*, 134, Warsaw: IBS PAN, 24-44.

Kulikowski, J.L. (2002). From Pattern Recognition to Image Interpretation. *Biocybernetics and Biomedical Engineering, 22*(2-3), 177-197.

Rasiowa, H., & Sikorski, R. (1968). *The Mathematics of Metamathematics*. Warsaw: PWN.

Vessel, Ch.A. (1970). On the Topological Logic (in Russian). *Non-Classical Logic*. Moscow: Nauka.

Section III
Semantic Analysis

Chapter VIII
Image/Video Semantic Analysis by Semi-Supervised Learning

Jinhui Tang
National University of Singapore, Singapore

Xian-Sheng Hua
Microsoft Research Asia, China

Meng Wang
Microsoft Research Asia, China

ABSTRACT

The insufficiency of labeled training samples is a major obstacle in automatic semantic analysis of large scale image/video database. Semi-supervised learning, which attempts to learn from both labeled and unlabeled data, is a promising approach to tackle this problem. As a major family of semi-supervised learning, graph-based methods have attracted more and more recent research. In this chapter, a brief introduction is given on popular semi-supervised learning methods, especially the graph-based methods, as well as their applications in the area of image annotation, video annotation, and image retrieval. It is well known that the pair-wise similarity is an essential factor in graph propagation based semi-supervised learning methods. A novel graph-based semi-supervised learning method, named Structure-Sensitive Anisotropic Manifold Ranking (SSAniMR), is derived from a PDE based anisotropic diffusion framework. Instead of using Euclidean distance only, SSAniMR further takes local structural difference into account to more accurately measure pair-wise similarity. Finally some future directions of using semi-supervised learning to analyze the multimedia content are discussed.

INTRODUCTION

Digital image and video collections are growing rapidly in recent years, accompanied with the decreased cost of storage devices, high transmission rates and improved compression techniques. The demand for solutions to manage image/video database is increasing tremendously. It is a common theme to develop automatic analysis techniques for deriving metadata to describe the visual content at semantic level (Smith & Schirling, 2006). Thus, automatically annotating image and video at the semantic concept level has emerged as an important topic in the multimedia research community as it is an elementary step for obtaining these metadata. The concepts of interest include a wide range of categories such as scenes (e.g., urban, sky, mountain.), objects (e.g., airplane, car, face, etc.), events (e.g., explosion-fire, people-marching, etc.) and certain named entities (e.g. person, place, etc.) (Naphade, et al., 2006; Snoek, et al., 2006). As manually annotating large image or video archive is labor-intensive and time-consuming, efficient automatic annotation methods are highly desired. To this end, generally statistical models are built from manually pre-labeled samples, and then the labels are automatically assigned to the unlabeled samples using these models. However, this process has a major obstacle: frequently the labeled data is limited so that the distribution of the labeled data typically cannot well represent the distribution of the entire data set (including labeled and unlabeled), which usually leads to inaccurate annotation results.

Semi-supervised learning, which attempts to learn from both labeled and unlabeled data, is a promising approach to deal with the above issue. As a major family of semi-supervised learning, graph based method is becoming one of the most active research area in semi-supervised learning community in recent years. Many works on this topic are reported in the literature of machine learning community (Carreira-Perpinan & Zemel, 2005; Seeger, 2001) and some of them have been applied to multimedia semantic analysis.

In Section II, we briefly introduce several semi-supervised learning techniques, including self-training, co-training and transductive SVM, and then we focus on graph-based methods (Zhu, 2005a). The graph-based methods define a graph with each vertex corresponding to each sample in the dataset, and the weighted edges reflect the similarity between neighboring samples. The objective of most graph-based methods is estimating a prediction function on the graph. Zhu, Ghahramani, & Lafferty (2003) have made two assumptions for this function: (1) the predicted scores on the unlabeled data should be close to the given labels of the unlabeled data; (2) the function should be smooth on the whole graph. These two assumptions directly lead to the Gaussian random field method, in which the *graph combinatorial Laplacian* is used as a regularizer. Besides these two assumptions, Zhou, Bousquet, Lal, Weston, & Scholkopf (2003) further made the *structural assumption*: points on the same structure (typically referred to as a cluster or a manifold) are likely to have the same label. This leads to the local and global consistency method, which uses the *normalized Laplacian* as the regularizer. Some more sophisticated regularization frameworks are also briefly introduced in this section, e.g., local learning regularization (Wu & Scholkopf, 2007), Tikhonov regularization (Belkin, Matveeva, & Niyogi, 2004) and manifold regularization (Belkin, Niyogi, & Sindhwani, 2006). In Section III, we present some applications of semi-supervised learning in video/image semantic analysis.

Obviously a key-point in graph based semi-supervised learning is the pair-wise similarity as it is the basis of the label propagation. However, one basic assumption, *structural assumption*, which is an essential of graph-based methods, is not embedded into the pair-wise similarity measure. Meanwhile, it is shown that the same results of normal graph-based methods can be deduced from the partial differential equation (PDE) based isotropic diffusion (Sapiro, 2001). Accordingly, a novel graph-based method, named Structure-Sensitive Anisotropic Manifold Ranking (SSAniMR) (Tang, Hua, Qi, Wang, Mei, & Wu, 2007), is derived from a PDE based anisotropic diffusion framework (Perona & Malik, 1990), by embedding the structural assumption into the similarity measure.

Finally, we will discuss some future directions for graph-based semi-supervised learning in the multimedia applications, including multi-label semi-supervised learning (Wu & Jing, 2006), multi-instance semi-supervised learning (Rahmani & Goldman, 2006) and multi-graph learning (Tong, et al., 2005).

SOME SEMI-SUPERVISED LEARNING METHODS

In this section, we briefly introduce semi-supervised learning methods, including self-training (Yarowsky, 1995), co-training (Blum & Mitchell 1998), transductive SVM (Joachims, 1999) and graph-based methods (Zhu, 2005a).

Self-Training and Co-Training

Self-training is a basic semi-supervised learning method. In self-training, a classifier is initially trained with a small number of labeled samples, and this classifier is used to predict the labels of unlabeled samples. Then, the most confident unlabeled samples (include both positive and negative ones) are added into the training set to retrain the classifier. The procedure repeats until some conditions are satisfied, and this is the so-called self-training method (as the classifier tries to teach itself with its own predictions, this method is also called self-teaching or bootstrapping).

In co-training, features are split into two sets which are conditionally independent given the class. Each sub-feature set is assumed to be sufficient to train a good classifier. Co-training uses the predicted samples to retrain the classifiers. This is analogous to self-training, and the difference is that the classifier in self-training teaches itself while co-training uses the predictions of one classier to teach the other classifier. Two classifiers are trained initially with the labeled samples on the two sub-feature sets respectively. Then each classifier predicts the labels of unlabeled samples. The most confident unlabeled samples from each classifier are added into the training set for the other classifier. Afterwards, the two classifiers are retrained and the procedure repeats.

There are several noteworthy issues in co-training (Zhu, 2005a). The sub-features must be good enough so that the labels predicted by each learner on the unlabeled samples can help improve the performance of the other classifier. And the sub-features sets should be conditionally independent so that one classifier's high confident predicted samples are *iid* samples for the other classifier.

Transductive Support Vector Machines (TSVM)

Transductive support vector machine (TSVM) is an extension of standard support vector machine (SVM). Regular SVM tries to induce a general decision function for a learning task. It only uses labeled data to find a maximum margin linear boundary in the Reproducing Kernel Hilbert Space (RKHS). TSVM takes into account a particular test set and tries to minimize misclassifications of just those particular examples (Joachims, 1999). So, it tries to find a linear boundary which has the maximum margin on both the labeled samples and the unlabeled samples. The decision boundary has the smallest generalization error bound on unlabeled data (Vapnik, 1998). In many practical tasks, TSVM can achieve

Figure 1. The difference between SVM and TSVM

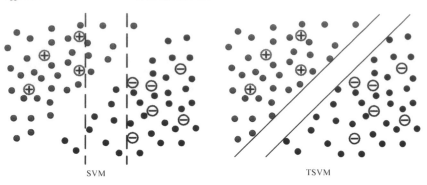

a better performance than normal SVM, especially when only a small training set is available. SVM works on $p(y|x)$ directly. This brings up the danger of leaving $p(x)$ outside of the parameter estimation loop, if $p(x)$ and $p(y|x)$ do not share parameters (Zhu, 2005a). It is worth noticing that since we can only get information about $p(x)$ from unlabeled data, semi-supervised learning cannot help if $p(x)$ and $p(y|x)$ do not share parameters (Seeger, 2001). To build the connection between $p(x)$ and the discriminative decision boundary, TSVMs do not allow putting the boundary in high density regions. The differences between SVM and TSVM are shown in Fig. 1. The maximum margin boundary for SVM is shown in the left figure (plotted with dashed lines) while the maximum margin boundary is shown in the right figure (plotted with solid lines). In the cases like the one shown in the figure, TSVM will get better results than SVM. However, finding the optimal TSVM solution is NP-hard. Several algorithms (Joachims, 1999; Bennett & Demiriz, 1999; Chapelle & Zien 2005; Fung & Mangasarian 1999) have been proposed for approximation.

Graph-Based Methods

As a major family of semi-supervised learning, graph-based methods have attracted more and more recent research. Many works on this topic are reported in the literature of machine learning community (Chapelle, Zien, & Scholkopf, 2006; Zhu, 2005a). Graph-based methods define a graph with the nodes representing the samples (including labeled and unlabeled ones) in the dataset while the edges reflecting the pair-wise similarity between samples. Graph based methods are nonparametric, discriminative, and transductive in nature.

Some basic notations for the graph-based semi-supervised learning are defined as follows: let $X=\{x_1;$ $\ldots ; x_l; x_{l+1}; \ldots ; x_n\}$ be a set of n samples (i.e., video shots for our application) in R^m (feature space with m dimensions). The first l points are labeled as $\mathbf{y}_L = [y_1; y_2; \ldots ; y_l]^T$ with $y_i \in \{0, 1\}$ ($1 \le i \le l$) and the remained points x_u ($l + 1 \le u \le n$) are unlabeled. The vector of the predicted labels of all samples is represented as $\mathbf{f}$, which can be split into two blocks after the l-th row:

$$\mathbf{f} = \begin{bmatrix} \mathbf{f}_L \\ \mathbf{f}_U \end{bmatrix}$$

(1)

Consider a connected undirected graph $G = (V, E)$ with the vertex set V corresponding to the n data points. Here $V = L \cup U$, where the vertex set $L = \{x_1; \ldots; x_l\}$ contains labeled points and the vertices in set U = $\{x_{l+1}; \ldots; x_{l+u}\}$ are unlabeled ones. The edges E are weighted by the $n{\times}n$ pair-wise similarity matrix.

Most graph-based methods can be viewed as an estimation of a decision function f on the graph. The function f is required to satisfy two conditions: (1) it should be close to the given labels $\mathbf{y}_L$ on the labeled nodes, and (2) it should be smooth on the whole graph. This can be expressed in a regularization framework where the first term is a *loss function* (also called *fit term*), and the second term is a *regularizer*.

Min-Cut

Blum & Chawla (2001) formulate semi-supervised learning as a graph *min-cut* problem. Let G be the undirected edge-weighted graph with nonnegative weights. A cut C of G is any nontrivial subset of V, and the weight of the cut is the sum of weights of edges crossing the cut. A mincut is then defined as a cut of G of minimum weight. The problem is polynomial time solvable as a series of network flow problems or using the algorithm of Stoer & Wagner (1994). It is a binary case, that is to say, $f_i \in \{0,1\}$. Equivalently mincut is the mode of a *Markov random field* with binary labels (Boltzmann machine). The loss function can be viewed as a quadratic loss with infinity weight, i.e.,

$$\infty \sum_{i \in L} (f_i - y_{i \in L})^2 ,$$

and the regularizer is

$$\frac{1}{2} \sum_{i,j} w_{ij} (f_i - f_j)^2 .$$

From the fit term, we can see that the labels of the training samples will not change in the entire process. Putting the fit term and regularizer terms together, mincut can be seen as an optimization problem by minimizing:

$$\frac{1}{2} \sum_{i,j} w_{ij} (f_i - f_j)^2 + \infty \sum_{i \in L} (f_i - y_{i \in L})^2 \tag{2}$$

subject to the constraint $f_{i \in V} \in \{0, 1\}$.

Gaussian Random Fields and Harmonic Functions Method

Zhu, Ghahramani, & Lafferty (2003) propose a Gaussian random fields and harmonic function method with a regularizer of *graph combinatorial Laplacian*. It will be abbreviated to GRF method in this chapter. It is a continuous relaxation to the discrete Markov random fields. The optimal prediction function f is estimated by minimizing the energy:

$$\frac{1}{2} \sum_{i,j} w_{ij} (f_i - f_j)^2 + \infty \sum_{i \in L} (f_i - y_i)^2$$
$$= \mathbf{f}^{\mathrm{T}} \Delta \mathbf{f} + \infty \sum_{i \in L} (f_i - y_i)^2 \tag{3}$$

where $\Delta = \mathbf{D} - \mathbf{W}$ is the *combinatorial Laplacian*, $\mathbf{W}$ is the $n \times n$ similarity matrix and $\mathbf{D}$ is a diagonal matrix with $D_{ii} = \sum_j w_{ij}$.

The main difference between GRF method and *min-cut* is that $f_i \in R$ in GRF method and $f_{i \in V} \in \{0, 1\}$ in *min-cut*.

Local and Global Consistency Method

The local and global consistency method proposed by Zhou, Bousquet, Lal, Weston, & Scholkopf (2003) is another widely-applied method. It adopts a regularizer of the *normalized graph Laplacian* $\mathbf{D}^{-1/2}\Delta\mathbf{D}^{-1/2} = \mathbf{I} - \mathbf{D}^{-1/2}\mathbf{W}\mathbf{D}^{-1/2}$. We abbreviated this method to consistency method in this chapter. The optimal prediction function f^* is defined to minimize a cost function $Q(f)$:

$$f^* = \arg\min_f Q(f) = \arg\min_f \frac{1}{2}(\sum_{i,j=1}^n w_{ij} \left\| \frac{1}{\sqrt{d_i}} f_i - \frac{1}{\sqrt{d_j}} f_j \right\|^2 + \mu \sum_{i=1}^n \|f_i - f_j\|^2), \tag{4}$$

The first term of $Q(f)$ is a smoothness constraint, which indicates that a good predicting function should not change too much between neighboring points. The second term is a fit constraint, which means that a good classifying function should not change too much from the initial label assignment. The trade-off between these two competing constraints is captured by a positive parameter μ. Note that the regularization term contains both the labeled and unlabeled data.

Linear Neighborhood Propagation (LNP)

Instead of considering pair-wise similarity relationships in traditional graph-based methods, LNP (Wang & Zhang, 2006) attempts to use the neighborhood information of each point to construct the graph G. The reconstruction matrix $\mathbf{W}$ is constructed by minimizing

$$\begin{aligned}
\varepsilon_i &= \left\| x_i - \sum_{j:x_j \in N(x_i)} w_{ij} x_j \right\|^2 \\
&= \left\| \sum_{j:x_j \in N(x_i)} w_{ij}(x_i - x_j) \right\|^2 \\
&= \sum_{j,k:x_j,x_k \in N(x_i)} w_{ij} w_{ik}(x_i - x_j)^T(x_i - x_k) \\
&= \sum_{j,k:x_j,x_k \in N(x_i)} w_{ij} G_{jk}^i w_{ik}
\end{aligned} \tag{5}$$

subject to

$\sum_j w_{ij} = 1$ and $w_{ij} \geq 0$.

Once the **W** is constructed, the optimal prediction function f is obtained by minimizing

$$Q(f) = \frac{1}{2}\sum_{i=1}^{n}\sum_{j:x_j \in N(x_i)} w_{ij}(f_i - f_j)^2 + \gamma \sum_{i=1}^{n}(f_i - y_i)^2. \tag{6}$$

Local Learning Regularization (LL-Reg)

In (Wu & Scholkopf, 2007), the authors formulate the above graph based methods as a quadratic optimization problem,

$$\min_{\mathbf{f}\in\mathbb{R}^n} \mathbf{f}^\mathsf{T}\mathbf{R}\mathbf{f} + (\mathbf{f}-\mathbf{y})^\mathsf{T}\mathbf{C}(\mathbf{f}-\mathbf{y}), \tag{7}$$

where $\mathbf{R} \in \mathbb{R}^{n\times n}$ is the regularization matrix, $\mathbf{f} = [f_1,...,f_n]^\mathsf{T} \in \mathbb{R}^n$ is the vector of real valued solution, $\mathbf{y} = [y_1,...,y_l, 0, ...,0]^\mathsf{T} \in \mathbb{R}^n$ and $\mathbf{C} \in \mathbb{R}^{n\times n}$ is a diagonal matrix with the entry $C_{ii} = C_l > 0$ for $1 \leq i \leq l$, and $C_{ii} = C_u \geq 0$ for $l+1 \leq i \leq n$, where C_l and C_u are two parameters. We can see that $\mathbf{R} = \Delta$ in GRF method and $\mathbf{R} = \mathbf{D}^{-1/2}\Delta\mathbf{D}^{-1/2}$ in consistency method.

LL-Reg (Wu & Scholkopf, 2007) replaces the regularizer $\mathbf{f}^\mathsf{T}\mathbf{R}\mathbf{f}$ with

$$\sum_{i=1}^{n}(f_i - o_i(x_i))^2,$$

where $o_i(\cdot)$ denotes the output function of a model, trained locally with some supervised learning algorithms using the labeled data. Then the optimization problem becomes

$$\min_{\mathbf{f}\in\mathbb{R}^n} \|\mathbf{f}-\mathbf{o}\|^2 + (\mathbf{f}-\mathbf{y})^\mathsf{T}\mathbf{C}(\mathbf{f}-\mathbf{y}) \tag{8}$$

where

$$\mathbf{o} = [o_1(x_1),...,o_n(x_n)]^\mathsf{T}.$$

A solution for $o_i(x_i)$ is given as:

$$o_i(x_i) = \alpha^\mathsf{T}\mathbf{f}_i, \tag{9}$$

where $\mathbf{f}_i \in \mathbb{R}^{n_i}$ is the vector $[f_j]^\mathsf{T}$ for $x_j \in \mathcal{N}_i$ ($\mathcal{N}_i$ denotes the set of neighboring points of x_i, not including x_i, and n_i denotes $|\mathcal{N}_i|$), and

$$\alpha_i^\mathsf{T} = \frac{\mathbf{1}^\mathsf{T} - \mathbf{1}^\mathsf{T}\mathbf{X}_i^\mathsf{T}\mathbf{X}_i(\lambda\mathbf{I}+\mathbf{X}_i^\mathsf{T}\mathbf{X}_i)^{-1}}{n_i - \mathbf{1}^\mathsf{T}\mathbf{X}_i^\mathsf{T}\mathbf{X}_i(\lambda\mathbf{I}+\mathbf{X}_i^\mathsf{T}\mathbf{X}_i)^{-1}\mathbf{1}}, \tag{10}$$

where $\mathbf{1}$ is the vector of all 1's, $\mathbf{X}_i \in \mathbb{R}^{d\times n_i}$ denotes the matrix $[x_j - x_i]$ for $x_j \in \mathcal{N}_i$. Here $\mathcal{N}_i$ is independent of $\mathbf{f}_i$ and it is different for different x_i. Note that $\mathbf{f}_i$ is a sub-vector of $\mathbf{f}$, so equation (13) can be written in a matrix form as:

$$\mathbf{o} = \mathbf{Af} \tag{11}$$

where $\mathbf{o}$ is the same as in (8), while the matrix $\mathbf{A} = [a_{ij}] \in \mathbb{R}^{n \times n}$ is constructed as follows: $\forall x_i$ and x_j $1 \leq i, j \leq n$, if $x_j \in \mathcal{N}_i$, then a_{ij} equals the corresponding element of α_i in (10), otherwise a_{ij} equals 0. Similar as α_i, the matrix $\mathbf{A}$ is also independent of $\mathbf{f}$. Substituting (11) into (8), we can see that the regularizer in LL-Reg is

$$\mathbf{R} = (\mathbf{I} - \mathbf{A})^{\top}(\mathbf{I} - \mathbf{A}) \tag{12}$$

LNP can also be represented in this local learning regularization framework with $o_i(x_i) = \sum_{x_j \in \mathcal{N}_i} w_{ij} f_j$.

Other Regularizations

Belkin, Matveeva, & Niyogi (2004) propose a Tikhonov regularization algorithm by minimizing

$$1 / k \sum_{i=1}^{n} (f_i - y_i)^2 + \gamma \mathbf{f}^T \mathbf{Sf},$$

where $\mathbf{S} = \Delta$ or Δ^p with some certain integer p. The manifold regularization framework (Belkin, Niyogi, & Sindhwani, 2006) minimizes the cost function:

$$\frac{1}{l} \sum_{i=1}^{l} V(x_i, y_i, f) + \gamma_A \|f\|_K^2 + \gamma_I \|f\|_I^2, \tag{13}$$

wherein two regularization terms are employed. Here V is an arbitrary loss function; K is a 'base kernel', e.g. a linear or *RBF* kernel, and I is a regularization term induced by the labeled and unlabeled data.

Graph Construction

The construction of the graphs is "at the heart" of graph based semi-supervised learning methods (Zhu, 2005a). However, this issue has not been studied extensively. Balcan *et al.* (2005) build graphs for video surveillance using strong domain knowledge. The graph consists of time edges, color edges and face edges. Robust graphs are built in (Carreira-Perpinan & Zemel, 2005) from multiple minimum spanning trees by perturbation and edge removal. The graph construction may be domain specific as it needs prior knowledge embedded. Detailed discussions on this problem can be found in Chapter 3 and Chapter 7 of Zhu's PhD thesis (Zhu, 2005b).

Learning with Directed Graphs

Most of the graph-based semi-supervised learning methods are based on undirected graphs. There are few methods based on directed graphs. Zhou, Scholkopf, & Hofmann (2005) investigate how to exploit the link structure of the graph and proposed a regularization framework for classifications on the directed graphs. The fundamental assumption of this method is the category similarity of co-linked nodes in a directed graph. It assumes that nodes with highly overlapping parent sets are likely to have same category. This assumption is shown to be effective for Web classification. Zhou, Huang, & Scholkopf

(2005) further generalize their work to a general framework semi-supervised learning on directed graphs. It takes a transition matrix as input and gives a closed form solution on unlabeled data.

We have briefly introduced some common semi-supervised learning methods. All these methods can be categorized as manifold learning, which have a close relation to spectral graph theory (Chung, 1997). There are still many other related methods. A more comprehensive survey can be found in (Zhu, 2005a).

IMAGE/VIDEO SEMANTIC ANALYSIS BASED ON SEMI-SUPERVISED LEARNING

Generally the labeled samples in multimedia semantic analysis come from the users during an interactive session. Manual annotating is labor-intensive and time-consuming. To reduce the labor of users, lots of efforts have been made to obtain good results using a very small amount of labeled data. As unlabeled multimedia data are much easier to be obtained, many semi-supervised learning approaches have been applied for image/video annotation and content based image/video retrieval, by leveraging a large amount of unlabeled samples with certain assumptions. This section provides a brief introduction of these works. As there are lots of works on the applications of semi-supervised learning in the multimedia area, we do not give a complete survey here, only part of these works are introduced.

Co-training is often applied in the multimedia analysis. Song, Hua, Dai, & Wang (2005) adopt the co-training method to video annotation, and in (Song, et al., 2006) they further apply a semi-supervised ensemble method for video annotation. Yan & Naphade (2005) analyze the drawbacks of co-training in video annotation, and propose an improved co-training style algorithm named semi-supervised cross-feature learning. In (He, Zhang, Zhao, & Tong, 2005), a co-ranking framework is proposed to re-rank the retrieved images to move the irrelevant ones to the tail of the ranked list returned by a web image search engine. As web-based images possess both intrinsic visual contents and text annotations, Feng, Shi, & Chua (2004) propose to bootstrap the learning process for web image annotation by adopting a co-training approach involving classifiers based on two orthogonal set of features – visual and text. In (Wang, Hua, Song, Lai, Dai, & Wang, 2007), co-training is applied to annotate the video shot size. Zhou, Chen, & Dai (2006) enhance the relevance feedback for image retrieval by integrating the merits of co-training and active learning into the relevance feedback process.

Graph-based methods are the most popularly used semi-supervised learning techniques in multimedia area recently. He *et al.* (2004; 2006) propose manifold-ranking approaches to propagate the label information of image samples from positively-labeled ones to unlabeled samples. In (Yuan, et al., 2006), a manifold ranking method based on feature selection is proposed for video annotation. Wang, Jing, Zhang, & Zhang (2006) propose a method based on random walk with restarts to refine the results of image annotation. A method based on kernel density estimation is proposed in (Wang, Hua, Song, Yuan, Li, & Zhang, 2006) for video semantic detection, in which the authors show that this method has close relationship with the graph-based semi-supervised learning. In (Tang, Hua, Qi, Song, & Wu, 2008), the authors analyze the limitation of linear neighborhood propagation (Wang & Zhang, 2006) for video annotation and propose a kernel-mapped linear neighborhood propagation method. In (Tong, et al., 2005), Tong *et al.* propose an image retrieval method to deal with two modalities in graph-based semi-supervised learning scheme. Motivated by this, Wang, Hua, Yuan, Song, & Dai (2007) propose a method OMG-SSL to integrate multiple graphs into a regularization and optimization framework to sufficiently explore their complementary nature for video annotation. A PageRank-like multi-graph fusion method is proposed in (Liu, Lai, Hua, Huang, & Li, 2007) to simultaneously leverage textual relevancy, semantic concept relevancy, and low-level-feature-based visual similarity for video search re-ranking. In (Rui, Yuan, & Yu, 2006), a model based on semi-supervised clustering with semantic soft constraints is proposed for image annotation, in which both visual features and semantic meanings are utilized.

Some graph-based methods try to analyze the image/video data with existed domain specific knowledge or context information. Tang, Hua, Mei, Qi, & Wu (2007) embed the temporal consistency of video data into the graph-based semi-supervised learning and propose a temporally consistent Gaussian random field method for video annotation. Liu, Li, Ma, Liu, & Lu (2006) propose a novel automatic image annotation method based on manifold ranking, in which the visual and textual information are well integrated, and the word-to-word correlations obtained from WordNet and the pair-wise co-occurrence are taken into consideration to expand the annotations and prune irrelevant annotations for each image. A context reranking approach (Hsu, Kennedy, & Chang, 2007) is proposed to leverage the recurrent patterns to improve the initial text search results for content based video search. This approach is formulated as a random walk problem along the context graph, where video stories are nodes and the edges between them are weighted by multimodal contextual similarities.

Graph-based methods are also combined with other learning method to handle the image/video analysis problem. A semi-supervised framework for image retrieval is proposed in (Hoi & Lyu, 2005) through a fusion of graph-based semi-supervised learning and support vector machines. In (Tang, Hua, Qi, & Wu, 2007), a two-stage semi-supervised multiple-instance learning based typicality ranking scheme is proposed for natural scene annotation.

Besides co-training and graph-based methods, there are few other semi-supervised learning techniques applied to multimedia area. In (Li & Sun, 2006), a semi-supervised conditional random field method is proposed to image annotation. This method can effectively capture the spatial dependency between the neighboring labels while exploit the unlabeled data to improve the joint classification performance. Although TSVM has shown superior performance in many applications, it is hardly used in multimedia analysis due to the large computational cost.

Table 1 gives a summarization of these works. From this table, we can see the popularity of graph-based semi-supervised learning, which is the topic this chapter focuses on.

STRUCTURE-SENSITIVE ANISOTROPIC MANIFOLD RANKING

We have introduced several semi-supervised learning methods and their applications in multimedia semantic analysis. As an example, in this section we will detail a novel graph-based method SSAniMR (Tang, Hua, Qi, Wang, Mei, & Wu, 2007), which is applied to annotate the video semantics.

Motivation

The basic assumption used in graph-based semi-supervised learning is: nearby points are likely to have the same label. It is referred to as *neighborhood assumption* in this chapter. Meanwhile, pair-wise similarity measure is a key point for graph-based methods, as it is the basis of label propagation, which

Table 1. A summarization of several works on the applications of semi-supervised learning in multimedia area

Approach	Learning method	Application
"Semi-supervised cross feature learning for semantic concept detection in videos" (Yan & Naphade, 2005)	Co-training	Video annotation
"Semi-automatic video annotation based on active learning with multiple complementary predictors" (Song, Hua, Dai, & Wang, 2005)	Co-training	Video annotation
"Efficient semantic annotation method for indexing large personal video database" (Song, et al., 2006)	Co-training	Video annotation
"Boosting web image search by co-ranking" (He, Zhang, Zhao, & Tong, 2005)	Co-training	Image retrieval
"A bootstrapping framework for annotating and retrieving WWW images" (Feng, Shi, & Chua, 2004)	Co-training	Image annotation
"An efficient automatic video shot size annotation scheme" (Wang, Hua, Song, Lai, Dai, & Wang, 2007)	Co-training	Video annotation
"Enhancing relevance feedback in image retrieval using unlabeled data" (Zhou, Chen, & Dai, 2006)	Co-training	Image retrieval
"Semi-supervised learning for image annotation based on conditional random fields" (Li & Sun, 2006)	Semi-supervised CRF	Image annotation
"Manifold-ranking based image retrieval" (He, et al., 2004)	Graph-based	Image retrieval
"Generalized manifold-ranking based image retrieval" (He, et al., 2006)	Graph-based	Image retrieval
"Manifold-ranking based video concept detection on large database and feature pool" (Yuan, et al., 2006)	Graph-based	Video annotation
"Image annotation refinement using random walk with restarts" (Wang, Jing, Zhang, & Zhang, 2006)	Graph-based	Image annotation
"Video annotation based on temporally consistent Gaussian random field" (Tang, Hua, Mei, Qi, & Wu, 2007)	Graph-based	Video annotation
"Automatic video annotation by semi-supervised learning with kernel density estimation" (Wang, Hua, Song, Yuan, Li, & Zhang, 2006)	Graph-based	Video annotation
"Video Annotation Based on Kernel Linear Neighborhood Propagation" (Tang, Hua, Qi, Song, & Wu, 2008)	Graph-based	Video annotation
"Typicality ranking via semi-supervised multiple-instance learning" (Tang, Hua, Qi, & Wu, 2007)	Graph-based	Image annotation
"A semi-supervised active learning framework for image retrieval" (Hoi & Lyu, 2005)	Graph-based	Image retrieval
"An adaptive graph model for automatic image annotation" (Liu, Li, Ma, Liu, & Lu, 2006)	Graph-based	Image annotation
"Image annotations based on semi-supervised clustering with semantic soft constraints" (Rui, Yuan, & Yu, 2006)	Graph-based	Image annotation
"Video search reranking through random walk over document-Level context graph" (Hsu, Kennedy, & Chang, 2007)	Graph-based	Video search
"Graph-based multi-modality learning" (Tong, et al., 2005)	Graph-based	Image retrieval
"Optimizing multi-graph learning: towards a unified video annotation scheme" (Wang, Hua, Yuan, Song, & Dai, 2007)	Graph-based	Video annotation
"Video search reranking via multi-graph propagation" (Liu, Lai, Hua, Huang, & Li, 2007)	Graph-based	Video search

is an essential technique in most of the graph-based methods. Neighborhood assumption can be easily enforced into the pair-wise similarity as

$$w_{ij} = \begin{cases} \exp(-\|x_i - x_j\|^2 / 2\sigma^2) & i \neq j \\ 0 & i = j \end{cases} \qquad (14)$$

where x_i is the low-level feature vector of sample i. This assumption is very useful and widely applicable. However, it sometimes is too weak, since most real-world dataset (especially the image or video dataset) has more complex structures than this assumption can capture (Bousquet, Chapelle, & Hein, 2003), such as the samples clustered in a certain region may have the same labels. This can be formulated as *structural assumption* or *global consistency assumption* (Zhou, Bousquet, Lal, Weston, & Scholkopf, 2003): points on the same structure (typically referred to as a cluster or a manifold) are likely to have the same label. Unfortunately, like the one defined in (14), typical similarity definitions do not take the *structural assumption* into account. Instead, this assumption is generally combined into most methods through an iterative label propagation process. Though weighted by distance, the label propagation is still isotropic, which will be shown later. This means the direct labeling contribution (i.e. the propagation coefficient which will be discussed later) from one sample to another, which is proportional to the pair-wise similarity, neglects the influence of the structural difference.

It is believed that embedding the *structural assumption* into the pair-wise similarity will furthermore improve the performance of the general graph-based methods (Tang, Hua, Qi, Mei, & Wu, 2007). An exemplary case is shown in Fig. 2, in which each point represents a sample in the feature space. The distance between A and C is equal to the distance between A and B, that is, w_{AC} equals to w_{AB} according to the normal similarity measure. However, it is more reasonable if the similarity w_{AB} is larger than w_{AC}, as A and B are on the same structure while A and C are on different structures. So we need to enhance the propagation between the samples in the same structure while weakening the counterpart between the samples in the different structures, according to the *structural assumption*.

Accordingly, *Structure-Sensitive Anisotropic Manifold Ranking* (SSAniMR) (Tang, Hua, Qi, Wang, Mei, & Wu, 2007) is derived from a Partial Differential Equation (PDE) based anisotropic diffusion framework (Perona & Malik, 1990; Sapiro, 2001), by embedding the *structural assumption* into the similarity measure. From the view of PDE-based diffusion, we can see that the label propagation in SSAniMR is anisotropic, which is intrinsically different from the isotropic label propagation process in general graph-based methods. That is why this method is named using "anisotropic".

Structure-Sensitive Anisotropic Manifold Ranking

In this section, we first introduce related graph-based methods, then analyze the influences of the point probability density on general graph-based approaches, and finally detail the SSAniMR.

Figure 2. Example for the influence of structure assumption

Related Graph-Based Semi-Supervised Learning Methods

As aforementioned, graph-based semi-supervised learning methods have attracted lots of interests in machine learning community recently. Many methods have been proposed, such as the well-used Gaussian random fields and harmonic function based method (GRF method) (Zhu, Ghahramani, & Lafferty, 2003), and the local and global consistency method (consistency method) (Zhou, Bousquet, Lal, Weston, & Scholkopf, 2003).

Most graph-based semi-supervised learning methods have a label propagation procedure; a key point in which is the propagation coefficients (also can be seen as transition probability or pseudo-transition probability). Pair-wise similarity measure is the basis of propagation coefficient. In (Zhu, Ghahramani, & Lafferty, 2003), the similarity between samples i and j is defined as:

$$w_{ij} = \exp(-\sum_{d=1}^{m} \frac{(x_{id} - x_{jd})^2}{\sigma_d^2}) \tag{15}$$

if $i \neq j$, and $w_{ii} = 0$. Here x_{ik} is the k-th component of sample i (represented as a vector $x_i \in R^m$), and σ_1, ..., σ_m are scale hyper-parameters for each dimension. This definition has a large number of parameters, which are not optimally learned in terms of difficulty. Therefore, the pair-wise similarity in (14), which is defined on the normalized features, is commonly applied in practice.

Based on the similarity measure (14), the propagation coefficient from vertex j to vertex i is defined in GRF method (Zhu, Ghahramani, & Lafferty, 2003) and consistency method (Zhou, Bousquet, Lal, Weston, & Scholkopf, 2003) respectively as:

$$s_{ij} = w_{ij} / d_i \tag{16}$$

and

$$\hat{s}_{ij} = w_{ij} / \sqrt{d_i d_j} \tag{17}$$

where

$$d_i = \sum_j w_{ij}.$$

It is obvious that $s_{ij} \geq 0$, $\sum_{j=1}^{n} s_{ij} = 1$ and $\hat{s}_{ij} \geq 0$, $\sum_{j=1}^{n} \hat{s}_{ij} \neq 1$.

Influences of Probability Density

The knowledge of the joint probability density $p(x; y)$ is enough to achieve the optimal classification in supervised learning (taking $argmax_y p(x; y)$ as decision function), while in semi-supervised learning, even if one knows the density distribution $p(x)$ of the samples, there is no unique or optimal way of using $p(x)$ (Bousquet, Chapelle, & Hein, 2003). Here the influences of point probability density on the normal graph-based semi-supervised learning methods are discussed.

A most popular density estimation method is the Parzen window density estimation (Duda, Stork, & Hart, 2000), by which the probability density of a sample i is estimated by

$$p_i = \frac{1}{N_i} \sum_{j \sim i} k(x_i - x_j) \tag{18}$$

where N_i is the number of samples connect to sample i, and $k(x)$ is a kernel function that satisfies $k(x) > 0$ and $\int k(x)dx = 1$.

If we use Gaussian kernel, that is,

$$k(x_i - x_j) = \frac{1}{\sqrt{2\pi}\sigma} \exp(-\frac{\| x_i - x_j \|^2}{2\sigma^2}) \tag{19}$$

we can see that

$$p_i = \frac{1}{\sqrt{2\pi}\sigma N} d_i, \tag{20}$$

since

$$\frac{1}{\sqrt{2\pi}\sigma N}$$

is a constant, so d_i can be seen as a measure of density for sample i. This demonstrates that both s_{ij} and $\hat{s}_{ij}$ have intrinsically taken the influence of density into account.

The propagation coefficient in (16) can be seen as the transition probability from j to i. However, this coefficient just considers the influence of the individual density but neglects the influence of density difference between samples. Rewrite the propagation coefficient in (17) as:

$$\hat{s}_{ij} = w_{ij} / \sqrt{d_i d_j} = \frac{w_{ij}}{d_i} (\frac{d_j}{d_i})^{-1/2} = s_{ij} (\frac{d_j}{d_i})^{-1/2} \tag{21}$$

The term d_j/d_i can be regarded as a measure of density difference between samples j and i. We can extend (17) to a general case:

$$\hat{s}_{ij} = s_{ij} \cdot g(\frac{d_j}{d_i}) \tag{22}$$

where $g(x)$ is a strictly decreasing function of x. That is to say, for a fixed vertex i, the propagation coefficient from its nearby vertex j to itself strictly decreases accompanied with the increment of the density difference d_j/d_i. Therefore, the propagation coefficient in (17) takes the influence of density difference into account. However, there are two drawbacks of this coefficient definition. First, we can see that

$$\sum_j \hat{s}_{ij} \neq 1,$$

which means it cannot be seen as a transition probability. We call this propagation coefficient pseudo-transition probability. Second, a fixed $g(x)$, that is, $g(x) = (x)^{-1/2}$, may not be the optimal degradation function, since frequently the optimization objectives vary with different real-world applications. Recall the example in Fig. 2, the density d_C is smaller than the density d_B. According to (17), the propagation coefficient from B to A will be smaller than the counterpart from C to A, which obviously violates the *structural assumption*.

From PDE-Based Diffusion to Structure-Sensitive Anisotropic Manifold Ranking

In this subsection, we first discuss the connection between normal graph-based semi-supervised learning and isotropic heat diffusion. And then the SSAniMR is deduced from an anisotropic diffusion framework.

The discrete version of the heat diffusion equation (Sapiro, 2001),

$$\frac{\partial f}{\partial t} = \Delta f,$$

where Δ is the *combinatorial Laplacian*, can be written as:

$$f_i^{(t)} - f_i^{(t-1)} = \frac{1}{\sum_{j \neq i} w_{ij}} \sum_{j \neq i} w_{ij}(f_j^{(t-1)} - f_i^{(t-1)}). \tag{23}$$

Notice that

$$w_{ii}(f_i^{(t-1)} - f_i^{(t-1)}) \equiv 0,$$

that is to say, the value of w_{ii} does not affect the result, so we can set $w_{ii} = 0$. Let

$$d_i = \sum_{j=1}^{n} w_{ij},$$

equation (23) can be rewritten as:

$$
\begin{aligned}
f_i^{(t)} - f_i^{(t-1)} &= \frac{1}{d_i} \sum_{j=1}^{n} w_{ij}(f_j^{(t-1)} - f_i^{(t-1)}) \\
&= \frac{1}{d_i} \sum_{j=1}^{n} w_{ij} f_j^{(t-1)} - f_i^{(t-1)}
\end{aligned}
\tag{24}
$$

Represent it with matrix form, we have

$$\mathbf{f}^{(t+1)} - \mathbf{f}^{(t)} = (\mathbf{D}^{-1}\mathbf{W} - \mathbf{I})\mathbf{f}^{(t)}, \tag{25}$$

and therefore

$$\mathbf{f}^{(t+1)} = \mathbf{D}^{-1}\mathbf{W}\mathbf{f}^{(t)} = \mathbf{S}\mathbf{f}^{(t)}, \tag{26}$$

where $\mathbf{f}(t)$ is the label vector at iteration point t. $\mathbf{W} = [w_{ij}]_{n \times n}$ is the similarity matrix with $w_{ii} = 0$, $\mathbf{S}$ is the normalization of $\mathbf{W}$ with the entries

$$s_{ij} = \frac{w_{ij}}{d_i}$$

and $\mathbf{D} = diag(d_i)$ is the diagonal matrix with entries $d_i = \sum_{j=1}^{n} w_{ij}$.

Split the matrix $\mathbf{S}$ after the *l-th* row and *l-th* column, we have

$$\mathbf{S} = \begin{bmatrix} \mathbf{S}_{LL} & \mathbf{S}_{LU} \\ \mathbf{S}_{UL} & \mathbf{S}_{UU} \end{bmatrix}, \tag{27}$$

and split the vector $\mathbf{f}(t)$ like in (1), then (26) can be rewritten as:

$$\begin{cases} \mathbf{f}_L^{(t)} = \mathbf{S}_{LL}\mathbf{f}_L^{(t)} + \mathbf{S}_{LU}\mathbf{f}_U^{(t)} \\ \mathbf{f}_U^{(t)} = \mathbf{S}_{UL}\mathbf{f}_L^{(t)} + \mathbf{S}_{UU}\mathbf{f}_U^{(t)} \end{cases} \tag{28}$$

Enforce the constraint that the labels of the labeled samples will not change in the diffusion procedure, that is $\mathbf{f}_L^{(t)} \equiv \mathbf{y}_L$, into the second equation in (28), we get:

$$\begin{aligned} \mathbf{f}_U^{(t)} &= \mathbf{S}_{UL}\mathbf{f}_L^{(t-1)} + \mathbf{S}_{UU}\mathbf{f}_U^{(t-1)} \\ &= \mathbf{S}_{UL}\mathbf{f}_L^{(t-1)} + \mathbf{S}_{UU}(\mathbf{S}_{UL}\mathbf{f}_L^{(t-2)} + \mathbf{S}_{UU}\mathbf{f}_U^{(t-2)}) \\ &= \dots \\ &= (\sum_{i=0}^{t-1} \mathbf{S}_{UU}^i)\mathbf{S}_{UL}\mathbf{y}_L + \mathbf{S}_{UU}^t\mathbf{f}_U^{(0)} \end{aligned} \tag{29}$$

It is obvious that $s_{ij} \geq 0$, $s_{ii} = 0$ and

$$\sum_{j=1}^{n} s_{ij} = 1,$$

$\mathbf{S}$ and $\mathbf{S}_{UU}$ are both non-negative matrices. When we connect each vertex to all other vertices (the case with a sparse representation of the matrix will be discussed in the section of experiments), every vertex $j \in L$ will satisfy $s_{ij} > 0$ when $j \neq i$, which results in that $\sum_{j \in L} s_{ij} > 0$.

Therefore

$$\sum_{j \in U} s_{ij} = \sum_{j=1}^{n} s_{ij} - \sum_{j \in L} s_{ij} \leq 1 - \sum_{j \in L} s_{ij} < 1. \tag{30}$$

According to the spectral diameter bound for the non-negative matrix in the matrix theory (Chung, 1997):

$$\rho(\mathbf{A}) \leq \max_{1 \leq i \leq n} \sum_{j=1}^{n} a_{ij}. \tag{31}$$

We have:

$$\rho(\mathbf{S}_{UU}) \leq \max_{l+1\leq i\leq n} \sum_{j\in U} s_{ij} < 1. \tag{32}$$

Therefore

$$\lim_{t\to\infty}\sum_{i=0}^{t-1}\mathbf{S}_{UU}^{i} = \lim_{t\to\infty}(\mathbf{I}-\mathbf{S}_{UU})^{-1}(\mathbf{I}-\mathbf{S}_{UU}^{t}) = (\mathbf{I}-\mathbf{S}_{UU})^{-1}$$

and

$$\lim_{t\to\infty}\mathbf{S}_{UU}^{t} = \mathbf{0},$$

where $\mathbf{0}$ is a $(n-l)\times(n-l)$ matrix with each entry equals to 0. Through iterations until convergence, the optimal result will be obtained:

$$\begin{aligned}
\mathbf{f}_{U}^{*} &= \lim_{t\to\infty}\mathbf{f}_{U}^{(t)}\\
&= \lim_{t\to\infty}\left\{(\sum_{i=0}^{t-1}\mathbf{S}_{UU}^{i})\mathbf{S}_{UL}\mathbf{y}_{L} + \mathbf{S}_{UU}^{t}\mathbf{f}_{U}^{(0)}\right\}\\
&= (\mathbf{I}-\mathbf{S}_{UU})^{-1}\mathbf{S}_{UL}\mathbf{y}_{L}
\end{aligned} \tag{33}$$

This result is the same as the result of a normal graph-based method: Gaussian Random Field (GRF) (Zhu, Ghahramani, & Lafferty, 2003). Since the heat diffusion is isotropic, the label propagation procedure in this method is isotropic though weighted by distance, which does not accord with the *structural assumption* of graph-based methods.

As aforementioned, we need to enhance the label propagation within a cluster while weakening the counterpart through different clusters according to *structural assumption*. In general, the density variation within a cluster will be smaller than the density variation between different clusters. From this, *structural assumption* encourages propagating label information within a region with uniform or close density in preference to propagating across the density boundaries. In the example shown in Fig. 3, we want to enhance the direct propagating strength from B to A while suppressing the counterpart from C to A. Accordingly we consider an anisotropic diffusion equation:

$$\frac{\partial f}{\partial t} = div(g(|\nabla p|)\nabla f) \tag{34}$$

This is a higher dimensional generalization of the anisotropic diffusion equation in (Perona & Malik, 1990), in which $g(x)$ is a nonnegative decreasing function and p is the density distribution. Discretize the equation like the Perona-Malik Discrete Formulation (Sapiro, 2001; Perona & Malik, 1990), we have

$$f_{i}^{(t)} - f_{i}^{(t-1)} = \frac{\gamma_{i}}{\sum_{j\neq i}w_{ij}}\sum_{j\neq i}w_{ij}g_{ij}(f_{j}^{(t-1)} - f_{i}^{(t-1)}) \tag{35}$$

where w_{ij} is the distance weighted similarity and g_{ij} is the density similarity.

Figure 3. Left figure shows the direct propagating strength from B to A equals to the counterpart from C to A. In the right figure we enhance the direct propagating strength from B to A while suppressing the counterpart from C to A.

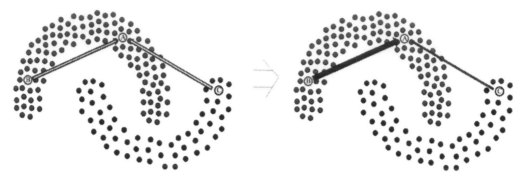

Notice that $w_{ii} = 0$ and set $\gamma_i = \sum_{j=1}^{n} w_{ij} / \sum_{j=1}^{n} w_{ij} g_{ij}$,

we have:

$$f_i^{(t)} - f_i^{(t-1)} = \frac{1}{\sum_{j=1}^{n} w_{ij} g_{ij}} \sum_{j=1}^{n} w_{ij} g_{ij} (f_j^{(t-1)} - f_i^{(t-1)}) \tag{36}$$

Let $\tilde{d}_i = \sum_{j=1}^{n} w_{ij} g_{ij}$ and represent (36) using matrix form:

$$\mathbf{f}^{(t)} - \mathbf{f}^{(t-1)} = (\tilde{\mathbf{D}}^{-1}(\mathbf{W} \cdot \mathbf{G}) - \mathbf{I})\mathbf{f}^{(t-1)} \tag{37}$$

therefore

$$\mathbf{f}^{(t)} = \tilde{\mathbf{D}}^{-1}(\mathbf{W} \cdot \mathbf{G})\mathbf{f}^{(t-1)} = \tilde{\mathbf{S}}\mathbf{f}^{(t-1)} \tag{38}$$

where $\tilde{\mathbf{S}}$ represents the matrix whose entry in i-th row and j-th column is $(g_{ij} w_{ij}) / \sum_{j=1}^{n} (g_{ij} w_{ij})$ and $\tilde{s}_{ii} = 0$,

which takes both the pair-wise distance and density difference into account. Then the predicted label vector of unlabeled data will be obtained:

$$\mathbf{f}_U^{(t)} = \tilde{\mathbf{S}}_{UL}\mathbf{f}_L^{(t-1)} + \tilde{\mathbf{S}}_{UU}\mathbf{f}_U^{(t-1)}. \tag{39}$$

It is worth noticing that, although (39) has similar form with (29), they have different intrinsic meanings: the label propagation in (29) is distance weighted isotropic while the propagation in (39) is structure-sensitive anisotropic.

Enforce the constraint $\mathbf{f}_L^{(t)} = \mathbf{y}_L$, similar to the iterative process above we can obtain the result:

$$\mathbf{f}_U^* = \lim_{t \to \infty} \mathbf{f}_U^{(t)} = (I - \tilde{\mathbf{S}}_{UU})^{-1} \tilde{\mathbf{S}}_{UL} \mathbf{y}_L. \tag{40}$$

This iterative method deduced from anisotropic diffusion is named as *Structure-Sensitive Anisotropic Manifold Ranking* (SSAniMR) (Tang, Hua, Qi, Wang, Mei, & Wu, 2007).

The Semi-Supervised Learning View of SSAniMR

In this subsection, we can see that SSAniMR is actually a graph-based semi-supervised learning method based on a structure- sensitive similarity measure.

As aforementioned, the similarity measure will be more accurate if the *structural assumption* is embedded into it and the density variation within a cluster generally will be smaller than the density variation between different clusters. We assume that the similarity between two samples not only decreases with respect to the increment of their distance in the feature space, but also decreases with the increment of their density difference. This pair-wise similarity is more consistent with the *structural assumption*.

Define a density similarity between x_i and x_j as:

$$g_{ij} = \exp(-\frac{(p_i - p_j)^2}{2\sigma_p^2}) \tag{41}$$

where p_i is the probability density of sample x_i. The new structure-related pair-wise similarity is defined as:

$$\tilde{w}_{ij} = w_{ij} \cdot g_{ij} = \exp(-\frac{\|x_i - x_j\|^2}{2\sigma^2}) \cdot \exp(-\frac{(p_i - p_j)^2}{2\sigma_p^2}) \tag{42}$$

while $i \neq j$ and $\tilde{w}_{ii} = 0$. The first term in the right side of (42) shows that the similarity between two samples decreases with respect to the increment of their distance in the feature space. The second one demonstrates that the similarity decreases with the increment of the density difference. That is to say, this similarity definition not only considers the neighborhood assumption, but also takes the *structural assumption* into account.

Motivated by the two basic assumptions, we can infer the real-valued labels for the unlabeled samples by minimizing the energy function

$$Q(f) = \frac{1}{2} \sum_{i,j=1}^{n} w_{ij} g_{ij} (f_i - f_j)^2 + \infty \sum_{i \in L} (f_i - y_i)^2 \tag{43}$$

Then the prediction function is $f^* = \text{argmin}_f Q(f)$. Intuitively, the first term of $Q(f)$ describes the total variation of the data labels with respect to the local structures, also called smoothness term. This term means that a good prediction function should not change too much between nearby density-similar points. The second term enforces the invariant constraint for the labels of labeled data $f_i^* = y_i$ ($i \in L$), also called fit term.

Differentiate $Q(f)$ with respect to f and represent it with matrix form:

$$\frac{\partial Q}{\partial f}\bigg|_{\mathbf{f}=\mathbf{f}^*} = \mathbf{f}^* - \tilde{\mathbf{S}}\mathbf{f}^* + \infty(\mathbf{f}_L^* - \mathbf{y}_L) = 0 \tag{44}$$

which can be transformed into

$$\mathbf{f}^* = \tilde{\mathbf{S}}\mathbf{f}^*$$
$$s.t. \quad \mathbf{f}_L^* = \mathbf{y}_L$$

(45)

where $\tilde{\mathbf{S}} = \tilde{\mathbf{D}}^{-1}(\mathbf{W} \cdot \mathbf{G})$ and $\cdot$ represents the component-wise *Hadamard product* (Duda, Stork, & Hart, 2000). $\mathbf{W}$ is the normal similarity matrix with entries w_{ij} defined in (1) and $\mathbf{G}$ is the density similarity matrix with entries g_{ij} defined in (12). $\tilde{\mathbf{D}} = diag(\tilde{d}_i)$ is the diagonal matrix with entries

$$\tilde{d}_i = \sum\nolimits_{j=1}^{n} w_{ij} g_{ij}.$$

That is to say, the propagation coefficient in SSAniMR is

$$\tilde{s}_{ij} = \frac{\tilde{w}_{ij}}{\tilde{d}_i} = \frac{w_{ij} g_{ij}}{\sum\nolimits_{j=1}^{n} w_{ij} g_{ij}}$$

(46)

It is obvious that $\tilde{s}_{ij} \geq 0$, $\tilde{s}_{ii} = 0$ and $\sum\nolimits_{j=1}^{n} \tilde{s}_{ij} = 1$.

So it can be seen as a transition probability. And the g_{ij} incorporate the influence of density difference while the parameter σ_p controls the significance of the influence.

Split the matrix $\tilde{\mathbf{S}}$ after the *l-th* row and *l-th* column, like in (28), then (45) can be rewritten as:

$$\mathbf{f}_U^* = \tilde{\mathbf{S}}_{UL}\mathbf{f}_L^* + \tilde{\mathbf{S}}_{UU}\mathbf{f}_U^*$$
$$s.t. \quad \mathbf{f}_L^* = \mathbf{y}_L$$

(47)

Solve this linear equation, consequently the optimal solution for $\mathbf{f}_U$ is obtained:

$$\mathbf{f}_U^* = (I - \tilde{\mathbf{S}}_{UU})^{-1}\tilde{\mathbf{S}}_{UL}\mathbf{y}_L.$$

(48)

Consequently, the same results of SSAniMR are deduced from two different viewpoints. The deep research in PDE-based diffusion (Sapiro, 2001) will give us new insights for graph-based semi-supervised learning.

Experiments

SSAniMR is evaluated on a widely used benchmark video dataset by comparing it with the Columbia374 SVM detectors (Yanagawa, Chang, Kennedy & Hsu, 2007) and two popularly used graph-based methods.

Experimental Settings

Experiments are conducted on the benchmark video corpus of the TRECVID 2005, which is consisted of about 170 hours of TV news videos from 13 different programs in English, Arabic and Mandarin (TRECVID, http://www-nlpir.nist.gov/projects/trecvid). The development (DEV) set of TRECVID05 is used in our experiments. After automatic shot boundary detection, the DEV set contains 137 broadcast

Figure 4. Comparisons of results using color moments

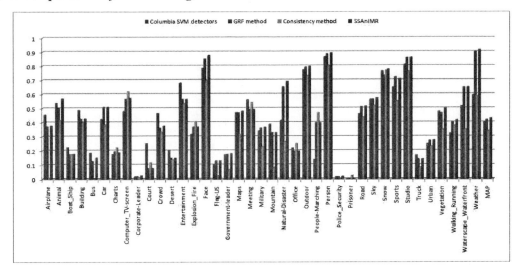

news videos with 43,907 shots. Some shots are further segmented into sub-shots, and there are 61,901 sub-shots for the DEV set. For each sub-shot, 39 semantic concepts are labeled according to LSCOM-Lite annotations (Naphade, et al., 2006). These annotated concepts consist of a wide range of genres, including program category, setting/scene/site, people, object, activity, event, and graphics. The DEV set is separated into four partitions with 90 videos as training subset, 16 videos as validation subset, 16 videos as fusion subset, and 15 videos as test subset. Here training subset is used to train models, validation subset is used to validate the optimal parameters, fusion subset is used to choose the linear fusion coefficients and test subset is used for testing. More details about the dataset separation can be found in (Yanagawa, Chang, Kennedy & Hsu, 2007).

For each concept, systems are required to return ranked-lists of up to 2000 sub-shots, and system performance is measured by the official performance metric Average Precision (AP) (Trec-10 proceedings appendix on common evaluation measures. http://trec.nist.gov/pubs/trec10/appendices/measures. pdf) in the TRECVID tasks. The AP corresponds to the area under a non-interpolated recall/precision curve and it favors highly ranked relevant sub-shots. The APs over all the 39 concepts are averaged to create the Mean Average Precision (MAP), which is the overall evaluation result.

Two low-level feature sets are used in the experiments: the first one is 225-D block-wise color moments in LAB color space, which are extracted over 5×5 fixed grid partitions, each block is described by a 9-D feature; and the second one is 75-D edge distribution layout. Experiments are conducted on the two feature sets respectively and then the two results are combined through linear fusion.

Implementation Issues

When implementing the SSAniMR algorithm, we need to calculate the inversion or the multiplication of the large-scale matrices in (40) or in the iterations of (39), which are difficult to be implemented subject to the limitation of both the computing ability and the memory quantity. For example, the video data set typically is very large (e.g., the DEV set in TRECVID05 has 61,901 sub-shots); it is difficult to storage the similarity matrix and compute its inversion. To deal with this issue, the graph is simplified by only

Figure 5. Comparisons of results using edge distribution layout

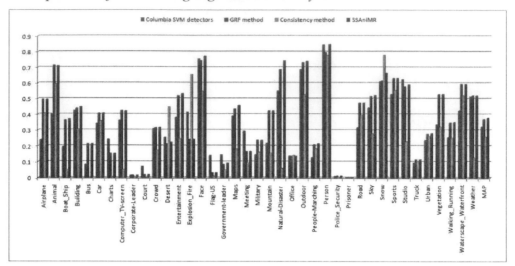

connecting neighboring points, and thus matrices $\tilde{\mathbf{W}}$ and $\tilde{\mathbf{S}}$ are sparse. Moreover, we can also calculate it offline. In this way, the quantity of memory and the processing time requested are greatly reduced.

There are two methods to find appropriate set of neighboring points for calculating the sparse representation of the matrices $\tilde{W}$ and $\tilde{\mathbf{S}}$ (Duda, Stork, & Hart, 2000): (a) k-NN: find the k nearest neighbors for each point; and (b) ε-NN: find nearest neighbors in the super-sphere centered at current point with radius of ε.

Another issue is to guarantee the convergence of the iterations. As mentioned before, for each sample x_i,

$$\sum\nolimits_{j \in U} \tilde{s}_{ij} < 1$$

is a necessary condition to ensure the convergence of the iteration process (39). But when using k-NN or ε-NN to choose the connecting neighbors, this requirement may not be satisfied since the chosen neighbors may all belong to the unlabeled set U, thus

$$\sum\nolimits_{j \in U} \tilde{s}_{ij}$$

will equal to 1. That is to say, the convergence of the iterative process cannot be ensured in this case.

To tackle this difficulty, a degradation factor λ ($\lambda = 1 - \delta$, where δ is a small arithmetic number) is introduced into (38) as

$$\mathbf{f}^{(t+1)} = \lambda \tilde{\mathbf{S}} \mathbf{f}^{(t)}. \tag{49}$$

Subject the invariant constraint $\mathbf{f}_L^{(t)} \equiv \mathbf{y}_L$, we obtain

Figure 6. Comparisons of results after linear fusion

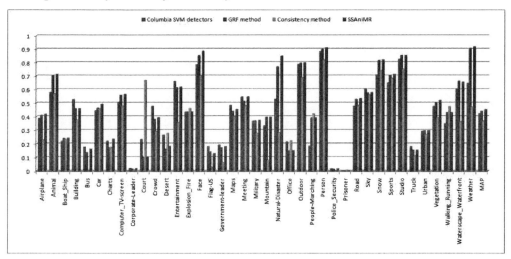

$$\mathbf{f}_U^{(t)} = \lambda \tilde{\mathbf{S}}_{UL} \mathbf{f}_L^{(t-1)} + \lambda \tilde{\mathbf{S}}_{UU} \mathbf{f}_U^{(t-1)}$$

$$= \sum_{i=0}^{t-1} (\lambda \tilde{\mathbf{S}}_{UU})^i (\lambda \tilde{\mathbf{S}}_{UL}) \mathbf{y}_L + (\lambda \tilde{\mathbf{S}}_{UU})^t \mathbf{f}_U \qquad (50)$$

It has been shown that $\sum_{j \in U} \tilde{s}_{ij} \leq 1$ and $0 < \lambda < 1$, which easily result in $\rho(\lambda \tilde{\mathbf{S}}_{UU}) < 1$. This leads to $\lim_{t \to \infty} (\lambda \tilde{\mathbf{S}}_{UU})^t = 0$ and

$$\lim_{t \to \infty} \sum_{i=0}^{t-1} (\gamma \tilde{\mathbf{S}}_{UU})^i = (I - \gamma \tilde{\mathbf{S}}_{UU})^{-1}.$$

Therefore:

$$\mathbf{f}_U^* = \lim_{t \to \infty} \mathbf{f}_U^{(t)} = (I - \gamma \tilde{\mathbf{S}}_{UU})^{-1} (\gamma \tilde{\mathbf{S}}_{UL}) \mathbf{f}_L. \qquad (51)$$

In applications with large-scale data, we can use (50) to replace (39) to implement SSAniMR.

Experimental Results

In (Tang, Hua, Qi, Wang, Mei, & Wu, 2007), k-NN is adopted to find the neighboring points (k is set to 30 empirically). This process is relatively time-consuming. It needs about 15 hours (with Intel P4 3.0G and 2G memory). However, this process is also required in other graph-based methods and can be calculated offline. The density is estimated by the distance-weighted Parzen window (Duda, Stork, & Hart, 2000). Once the nearest neighbors are obtained, the density estimation is very fast. The parameters in these methods are all tuned to be nearly optimal through validations while λ is empirically set to 0.99. Time costs of GRF method and consistency method are both about one minute, and SSAniMR costs about two minutes, all after the nearest neighbors are obtained. Although SSAniMR is a little slower than the other two methods, it is computationally effective as the processing time is always a challenging problem in TRECVID tasks.

For performance evaluation, SSAniMR is compared with the Columbia374 SVM detectors (Yanagawa, Chang, Kennedy & Hsu, 2007) and two popularly used graph-based methods: GRF method (Zhu, Ghahramani, & Lafferty, 2003) and consistency method (Zhou, Bousquet, Lal, Weston, & Scholkopf, 2003). The experimental results are shown in Fig. 4 (using color moments), Fig. 5 (using edge distribution layout), and Fig. 6 (for fused results) respectively. Comparing these results, we can see that SSAniMR performs the best on 21 of the all 39 concepts using color moments and performs the best on 25 of the all 39 concepts using edge distribution layout. After linear fusion, SSAniMR performs the best on 22 of the all 39 concepts. So SSAniMR is better than other methods for detecting most of these concepts.

At the same time, we can see that SSAniMR's performance on some of these concepts is worse than the other three algorithms. This may be caused by the following reasons: (1) the structural assumption (i.e. manifold assumption) may not be well satisfied for these concepts in the low-level feature space SSAniMR adopted; (2) the regularization framework of SSAniMR (which is similar to GRF) is not as good as that of consistency method for detecting some concepts; (3) the parameter validation process of SSAniMR in this paper is not as subtle as other three algorithms.

The MAP of SSAniMR is 0.427801 using color moments, which has an improvement of 6.26%, 2.01% and 25.57% over SVM, GRF method and consistency method, respectively. It has a MAP of 0.377531 using edge distribution layout, which respectively has an improvement of 17.09%, 2.08% and 46.72% over SVM, GRF method and consistency method. Through linear fusion, SSAniMR obtains a MAP of 0.450665, which has an improvement of 6.80% over SVM, 2.36% over GRF method and 22.25% over consistency method. All these comparisons demonstrate that SSAniMR is more appropriate than other semi-supervised learning methods and is effective for video semantic annotation.

DISCUSSION AND EXTENSIONS

In this chapter we have introduced the popular semi-supervised learning methods and their applications in image/video content analysis. Besides, we have shown that the normal graph-based semi-supervised learning method can be deduced from PDE based diffusion. Accordingly, a novel semi-supervised learning algorithm named Structure-Sensitive Anisotropic Manifold Ranking is derived from PDE based anisotropic diffusion. Experiments conducted on the TRECVID dataset have demonstrated its effectiveness.

It is worth noting that although many semi-supervised methods have been applied to image/video semantic analysis and have shown encouraging performance, their effectiveness on larger-scale dataset still need further validation. For example, in TRECVID high-level feature extraction, the best results are still obtained by purely supervised methods (TRECVID, http://www-nlpir.nist.gov/projects/trecvid). This may be attributed to several reasons, such as the high complexity of visual data and semantic concepts. Thus, semi-supervised learning based semantic analysis is still a challenging issue. There is also huge room for improvement of the existing methods. Here we briefly highlight several possible future works on similarity metric and graph-based learning:

1. Region-level features can be incorporated into the pair-wise similarity metric, instead of only using frame-level features. Most of existing approaches are using frame-level features to model concepts. However, it is observed that actually concepts often more closely related to regions. Semi-Supervised Multiple Instance Learning (SSMIL) is a promising solution to this issue, where

a pioneer work has been reported in (Rahmani & Goldman, 2006). However, how to make it work for large-scale high-diverse video concepts is still not studied.

2. Pair-wise similarity metrics are the same for all concepts in existing approaches. However, low-level features and local structures may have different influences for different concepts. To learn a specific similarity measure optimized for each concept, for example, parameterized by the choice of features, distance metrics, and structure differences, is promising to improve the performance. In other words, we may construct a concept-sensitive similarity measure, which take concepts into consideration in the similarity measure.

3. Concepts are correlated rather than isolated. Leveraging label correlations in graph-based semi-supervised learning to simultaneously model multiple concepts may have better performance than modeling them separately.

REFERENCES

TRECVID: TREC Video Retrieval Evaluation. http://www-nlpir.nist.gov/projects/trecvid.

Trec-10 proceedings appendix on common evaluation measures. http://trec.nist.gov/pubs/trec10/appendices/measures.pdf

Balcan, M.-F., Blum, A., Choi, P.P., Lafferty, J., Pantano, B., Rwebangira, M.R., & Zhu, X. (2005). Person identification in webcam images: An application of semi-supervised learning. In *Proc. ICML Workshop on Learning with Partially Classified Training Data.*

Belkin, M., Matveeva, I., & Niyogi, P. (2004). Regularization and semi-supervised learning on large graphs. In *Proc. Workshop on Computational Learning Theory.*

Belkin, M., Niyogi, P., & Sindhwani, V. (2006). Manifold regularization: A geometric framework for learning from labeled and unlabeled examples. *Journal of Machine Learning Research, 7,* 2399-2434.

Bennett, K., & Demiriz, A. (1999). Semi-supervised support vector machines. *Advances in Neural Information Processing Systems, 11.* MIT Press.

Blum, A., & Chawla, S. (2001). Learning from labeled and unlabeled data using graph mincuts. In *Proc.18th International Conference on Machine Learning.*

Blum, A., & Mitchell, T. (1998). Combining labeled and unlabeled data with co-training. In *Proc. Workshop on Computational Learning Theory.*

Bousquet, O., Chapelle, O., & Hein, M. (2003). Measure based regularization. *Advances in Neural Information Processing Systems, 15.* MIT Press.

Carreira-Perpinan, M.A., & Zemel, R.S. (2005). Proximity graphs for clustering and manifold learning. *Advances in neural information processing systems, 17.* MIT Press.

Chapelle, O., Zien, A., & Scholkopf, B. (Eds.). (2006). *Semi-supervised learning.* MIT Press.

Chapelle, O., & Zien, A. (2005). Semi-supervised classification by low density separation. In *Proc.Tenth International Workshop on Artificial Intelligence and Statistics.*

Chung, F. (1997). *Spectral graph theory*. American Mathematical Society.

Duda, R., Stork, D., & Hart, P. (2000). *Pattern classification*. JOHN WILEY, 2nd edition.

Feng, H., Shi, R., & Chua, T.-S. (2004). A bootstrapping framework for annotating and retrieving WWW images. In *Proc. ACM Multimedia*.

Fung, G., & Mangasarian, O. (1999). Semi-supervised support vector machines for unlabeled data classification. *Technical Report 99-05*. Data Mining Institute, University of Wisconsin Madison.

He, J., Li, M., Zhang, H.-J., Tong, H., & Zhang, C. (2004). Manifold-ranking based image retrieval. *Proc. ACM Multimedia*.

He, J., Li, M., Zhang, H.-J., Tong, H., & Zhang, C. (2006). Generalized manifold-ranking based image retrieval. *IEEE Transaction on Image Processing*, *15*(10).

He, J., Zhang, C., Zhao, N., & Tong, H. (2005). Boosting web image search by co-ranking. In *Proc. International Conference on Acoustics, Speech, and Signal Processing*.

Hoi, S.C.H., & Lyu, M.R. (2005). A semi-supervised active learning framework for image retrieval. In *Proc. IEEE Conference on Computer Vision and Pattern Recognition*.

Hsu, W.H., Kennedy, L. S., & Chang, S.-F. (2007). Video search reranking through random walk over document-level context graph. In *Proc. ACM Multimedia*.

Joachims, T. (1999). Transductive inference for text classification using support vector machines. In *Proc. International Conference on Machine Learning*

Li, W., & Sun, M. (2006). Semi-supervised learning for image annotation based on conditional random fields. In *Proc. International Conference on Image and Video Retrieval*.

Liu, J., Li, M., Ma, W.-Y., Liu, Q., & Lu, H. (2006). An adaptive graph model for automatic image annotation. In *Proc. ACM International Workshop on Multimedia Information Retrieval*.

Liu, J., Lai, W., Hua, X.-S., Huang, Y., & Li, S. (2007). Video search reranking via multi-graph propagation. In *Proc. ACM Multimedia*.

Naphade, M., Smith, J.R., Tesic, J., Chang, S.-F., Hsu, W., Kennedy, L., Hauptmann, A. G., & Curtis, J. (2006). Large-scale concept ontology for multimedia. *IEEE Multimedia*, *16*(3).

Perona, P., & Malik, J. (1990). Scale-space and edge detection using anisotropic diffusion. *IEEE Transaction on Pattern Analysis and Machine Intelligence*, *12*(7).

Rahmani, R., & Goldman, S. (2006). Multiple-instance semi-supervised learning. In *Proc. International Conference on Machine Learning*.

Rui, X., Yuan, P., & Yu, N. (2006). Image annotations based on semi-supervised clustering with semantic soft constraints. In *Proc. Pacific-Rim Conference on Multimedia*.

Sapiro, G. (2001). *Geometric partial differential equation and image analysis*. Cambridge University Press.

Seeger, M. (2001). Learning with labeled and unlabeled data. *Technical Report*. University of Edinburgh.

Smith, J.R., & Schirling, P. (2006). Metadata standards roundup. *IEEE Multimedia, 13*(2).

Snoek, C.G.M., Worring, M., Gemert, J.C.V., Geusebroek, J.-M., & Smeulders, A.W.M. (2006). The challenge problem for automated detection of 101 semantic concepts in multimedia. In *Proc. ACM Multimedia*.

Song, Y., Hua, X.-S., Dai, L., & Wang, M. (2005). Semi-automatic video annotation based on active learning with multiple complementary predictors. In *Proc. ACM International Workshop on Multimedia Information Retrieval*.

Song, Y., Hua, X.-S., Qi, G.-J., Dai, L., Wang, M., & Zhang, H.-J. (2006). Efficient semantic annotation method for indexing large personal video database. In *Proc. ACM International Workshop on Multimedia Information Retrieval*.

Stoer, M., & Wagner, F. (1994). A simple min cut algorithm. *Algorithms--ESA '94, LNCS 855*, 141-147.

Tang, J., Hua, X.-S., Qi, G.-J., Mei, T., & Wu, X. (2007). Anisotropic manifold ranking for video annotation. In *Proc. IEEE International Conference on Multimedia & Expo*.

Tang, J., Hua, X.-S., Mei, T., Qi, G.-J., & Wu, X. (2007). Video annotation based on temporally consistent Gaussian random field. *Electronics Letters, 43*(8).

Tang, J., Hua, X.-S., Qi, G.-J., Wang, M., Mei, T., & Wu, X. (2007). Structure-sensitive manifold ranking for video concept detection. In *Proc. ACM Multimedia*

Tang, J., Hua, X.-S., Qi, G.-J., & Wu, X. (2007). Typicality ranking via semi-supervised multiple-instance learning. In *Proc. ACM Multimedia*.

Tang, J., Hua, X.-S., Qi, G.-J., Song, Y., & Wu, X. (2008). Video annotation based on kernel linear neighborhood propagation. *IEEE Transactions on Multimedia, 10*(4).

Tong, H., He, J., Li, M., Zhang, C., & Ma, W.-Y. (2005). Graph based multi-modality learning. In *Proc. ACM Multimedia*.

Vapnik, V. (1998). *Statistical learning theory*. Springer.

Wang, C., Jing, F., Zhang, L., & Zhang, H.-J. (2006). Image annotation refinement using random walk with restarts. In *Proc. ACM Multimedia*.

Wang, F., Zhang, C., Shen, H. C., & Wang, J. (2006). Semi-supervised classification using linear neighborhood propagation. In *Proc. IEEE Conference on Computer Vision and Pattern Recognition*.

Wang, F., & Zhang, C. (2006). Label propagation through linear neighborhoods. In *Proc. 23th International Conference on Machine Learning*.

Wang, M., Hua, X.-S., Song, Y., Yuan, X., Li, S., & Zhang, H.-J. (2006). Automatic video annotation by semi-supervised learning with kernel density estimation. In *Proc. ACM Multimedia*.

Wang, M., Hua, X.-S., Song, Y., Lai, W., Dai, L., & Wang, R. (2007). An efficient automatic video shot size annotation scheme. In *Proc. International Multimedia Modeling Conference*.

Wang, M., Hua, X.-S., Yuan, X., Song, Y., & Dai, L. (2007). Optimizing multi-graph learning: towards a unified video annotation acheme. In *Proc. ACM Multimedia*.

Wu, M., & Jing, R. (2006). A graph-based framework for relation propagation and its application to multi-label learning. In *Proc. ACM Conference on Research & Development on Information Retrieval*.

Wu, M., & Scholkopf, B. (2007). Transductive classification via local learning regularization. In *Proc. 11th International Conference on Artificial Intelligence and Statistics*, (pp. 624-631).

Yan, R., & Naphade, M. (2005). Semi-supervised cross feature learning for semantic concept detection in videos. In *Proc. IEEE Conference on Computer Vision and Pattern Recognition*.

Yanagawa, A., Chang, S.-F., Kennedy, L., & Hsu, W. (2007). Columbia University's baseline detectors for 374 LSCOM semantic visual concepts. *Columbia University ADVENT Technical Report #222-2006-8*.

Yarowsky, D. (1995). Unsupervised word sense disambiguation rivaling supervised methods. In *Proceedings of the 33rd Annual Meeting of the Association for Computational Linguistics*.

Yuan, X., Hua, X.-S., Wang, M., & Wu, X. (2006). Manifold-ranking based video concept detection on large database and feature pool. In *Proc. ACM Multimedia*.

Zhou, Z.-H., Chen, K.-J., & Dai, H.-B. (2006). Enhancing relevance feedback in image retrieval using unlabeled data. *ACM Transactions on Information Systems, 24*(2), 219–244.

Zhou, D., Bousquet, O., Lal, T.N., Weston, J., & Scholkopf, B. (2003). Learning with local and global consistency. *Advances in Neural Information Processing Systems, 15*. MIT Press.

Zhou, D., Scholkopf, B., & Hofmann, T. (2005). Semi-supervised learning on directed graphs. *Advances in Neural Information Processing Systems, 17*. MIT Press.

Zhou, D., Huang, J., & Scholkopf, B. (2005). Learning from labeled and unlabeled data on a directed graph. In *Proc. 22nd International Conference on Machine Learning*.

Zhu, X., Ghahramani, Z., & Lafferty, J. (2003). Semi-supervised learning using Gaussian fields and harmonic function. *Proc. International Conference on Machine Learning*.

Zhu, X. (2005a). Semi-supervised learning literature survey. *Technical Report 1530*, Department of Computer Sciences, University of Wisconsin, Madison.

Zhu, X. (2005b). S*emi-supervised learning with graphs*. PhD Thesis, CMULTI-05-192.

Chapter IX
Content–Based Video Semantic Analysis

Shuqiang Jiang
Chinese Academy of Sciences, China

Yonghong Tian
Peking University, China

Qingming Huang
Graduate University of Chinese Academy of Sciences, China

Tiejun Huang
Peking University, China

Wen Gao
Peking University, China

ABSTRACT

With the explosive growth in the amount of video data and rapid advance in computing power, extensive research efforts have been devoted to content-based video analysis. In this chapter, the authors will give a broad discussion on this research area by covering different topics such as video structure analysis, object detection and tracking, event detection, visual attention analysis, and so forth. In the meantime, different video representation and indexing models are also presented.

INTRODUCTION

In recent years, digital equipments such as digital camera and digital video camera have become very popular, which makes the digital video data growing in an exponential speed. Information in the Internet has also changed from one-fold text information to multimedia information such as graphs, image, music and particularly video. Broadly speaking, the Internet can be regarded as a database which contains a big size of video data. Digital video is playing more and more important role in human's life in terms of working, education, entertainment, and so on.

The increasing amount of digital video brings up a lot of problems which are never met before. For example, it is time-consuming and labor-intensive to manually manage the large scale, rapidly increasing digital video collection. As a result, it is more difficult for users to find the desired video contents from the large scale video database. Therefore it is crucial in nowadays to automatically understand digital video data and make them convenient for people to access. During the recent two decades, video content analysis and understanding has been an active research area, and a whole range of models and methods have been proposed. One of the most famous achievements is the Content Based Video Retrieval (CBVR). CBVR firstly extracts the low-level visual and/or acoustical features of videos, and then finds videos that have low-level features similar to those of the query example. As this technology needs little human intervention and does not take human's perception into consideration, it is not satisfactory in most real applications. In fact, human often judge the similarity of videos according to the objects they describe, the events they contain, and the feeling they express, rather than the video features such as color, shot, motion intensity. This difference between the low-level features and high level understanding is referred to as *semantic gap*, which in fact has become an important barrier of natural communication between computer and human. In order to bridge the semantic gap, lots of methods have been proposed, including relevance feedback, object recognition, event detection, and so on.

In this chapter, we will outline the structure for content-based video semantic analysis and discuss some related technologies from low-level content analysis such as feature extraction, structure analysis, object detection and tracking, to high-level semantic analysis such as event detection, attention analysis and video mining.

LOW LEVEL VIDEO FEATURE EXTRACTION AND REPRESENTATION

Generally speaking, low-level feature representation includes visual feature extraction, description, dimension reduction and indexing. After the video is segmented and key frames are chosen, low-level image features can be extracted from these key frames. Low-level visual features such as color, texture, edge and shapes can be extracted from the key frame set in video and represented as feature descriptors. After post-processing on the feature descriptors such as dimension reduction, they can be stored in the database using indexing models for future queries. There are two categories of visual features: global features that are extracted from a whole image, and local or regional features that describe the chosen patches of a given image.

Global Features

In the sense of human perception, an image can be characterized from various aspects, consequently leading to different image feature extraction methods. Typically, three categories of these methods are commonly used: color-based, texture-based and shape-based (especially edge-based) methods.

Color: Color is the most widely used feature for its close relationship with the objects and the scene in the image and its little dependence with the image scale, view direction and view point. Due to these properties, color-based methods are often able to generate robust representations of an image. In general, three main problems should be taken carefully into account in color-based methods: (a) Which is the proper color space according to the application; (b) how to quantitatively quantize the color feature into a vector for future indexing and similarity comparison; (c) how to properly measure the vector distance in the color feature vector space. Typical color feature representations include color histogram, color moments (Stricker & Orengo, 1995), color set (Smith & Chang, 1995), color correlogram (Vetterli, 1995), and color coherence vector (Pass & Zabih, 1996). Among them, color histogram is the oft-used one which describes the relative quantity of each color in the image while overlooking the spatial relationships between different colors.

Texture: Texture is common vision phenomenon, which is, as stated by David A. Forsyth, "easy to recognize and hard to define" (Forsyth & Ponce, 2003). Smith and Chang (2003) defined texture as a color and illumination independent visual feature which reflects the homogeneity of an image. Some others say that texture is a densely and evenly arranged pattern of visible elements and a texture element is a repeated uniform intensity region of simple shape. Clearly, texture is an important part of an image and many methods are developed to extract texture features (Smith & Chang, 2003).

Shape: Shape is another important visual feature in images. However, since shape features are extracted by using image segmentation which is still a hard problem with little progress in achieving accurate and robust results, shaped-based methods are usually applied to salient objects in images (Aslandogan &Yu, 1999). There are many shape feature representations, such as Fourier shape descriptors, moment invariants, finite element method, and turning function and wavelet descriptor.

Local Features

The local feature extraction process can be roughly divided in two phases: region detection and region description. The feature detector is firstly used to detect a stable and characteristic region, and then the feature descriptor is used to describe the detected region in a precise, concise and robust way. In the two phases, one primary tackling issue is how to carry out the corresponding mission in a scale, rotation, illumination and noise invariant way.

Detectors: In order to obtain a robust detection result, the feature detectors should take into consideration the factors such as the affine transformation, photometric transformation and scale differences. Harris proposed a corner detector which is well known as Harris Detector (Harris &Stephens, 1988). Harris corner is not scale and affine invariant, but it contributes as the bases for many detectors. For example, Mikolajczyk and Schmid (2004) extended Harris detector to a scale and affine invariant detector. Lowe (2004) proposed a SIFT (Scale Invariant Feature Transform) detector which detects extremum in the DoG (Difference of Gaussian) space.

Descriptors: The raw pixel information of the detected region is sensitive to the illumination change, rotation and noise, thus is not a robust feature description. SIFT (Lowe, 2004) descriptor rotates the region according to the main intensity direction of the region, divides the region into several equal area sub-regions and uses the orientation histograms of all the sub-regions as the feature description. Ke and Sukthankar (2004) applied principal component analysis (PCA) on the intensity gradient map of a 41*41 patch on the detected region to get a lower dimensional descriptor. Other techniques such as Gabor filters and wavelets, steerable filters and generalized moment invariants are also used in the regional feature description.

VIDEO STRUCTURE ANALYSIS

To efficient access of video data, parsing video structures at different granularities is the first step. Generally speaking, videos can be hierarchically represented by five levels: key frame, shot, scene, story unit and video, as illustrated in Fig.1. The following are some of the definitions, and detailed discuss them thereafter:

- **Video frame:** The basic components of video stream. Video data is made up of continuous frames. Every frame is an independent image. Different video standard may have different frame rate. In PAL standard, the frame rate is 25 per second, while in NTSC standard, it is 30 per second.
- **Key frame:** The most representative frames in the video stream.
- **Video shot:** An unbroken sequence of frames recorded from a single camera, which is the minimal physical unit of video structure analysis. A video shot normally represents a continuous action in both space and time.
- **Video scene:** A collection of shots whose content are similar. It is a median representation of video content and contains some semantic information. With the help of video scene, we can analyze higher-level video content better.
- **Story units:** Story unit generally represents a whole event at a higher level. It is made up of several continuous shots which may belong to different scenes.

Key Frame Extraction

In order to understand the content of a video, there need to first decompose the video into a set of scenes, and then extract some key frames that most represent the content of each scene. Compared with the

Figure 1. A hierarchical video representation

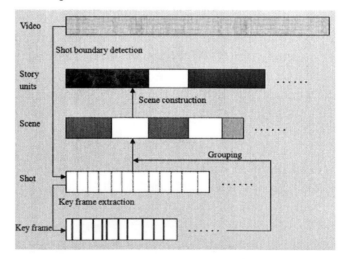

original video data, key frames can represent the scene more concise and are more adequate for video indexing, browsing and retrieval.

There are many works on the area of key frame extraction. We can briefly categorize the related work into 4 classes: sampling-based, shot-based, segment-based, and others (Li, Zhang, & Tretter, 2001). The following are detailed introductions.

Since shot is a video segment with a continuous period on certain scenario, shot based key frame extraction methods are natural. And it is the dominating way among the current solutions. A very simple method is to extract the first frame of every shot as the key frame. However, more sophisticated and powerful methods have been developed. In work (Zhang, Wu, Zhong, &Smoliar, 1997), the first frame is always chosen as the key frame. Then the color histogram distance between the subsequent frames and the latest key frame is computed. If the distance exceeds a threshold, a new key frame will be chosen. In (Wolf, 1996), the frames at the local minima of motion features are selected as key frames. Mosaic based approach can be employed to generate a synthesized panoramic image that can represent the entire content in an intuitive manner. This method is especially useful for the camera tilting/panning sequences.

A video segment is a higher-level video unit, which can be a scene, an event, or even the entire sequence. In (Uchihashi, Foote, Girgensohn, & Boreczky, 1999), a video is segmented into some segments. The segments may be clusters clustered using some distance metrics. Then the centers of clusters are extracted as key frames.

Other works (Campisi, Longari, & Neri, 1999), (Kim & Hwang, 2000) used techniques, such as wavelet transformation, face detection, etc. to fulfill the task. The first work (Campisi, Longari, & Neri, 1999) proposed a progressive multi-resolution method based on wavelet transformation to extract key frames. The draw back of this method is that the computation complexity is too high. In the second work, Kim & Hwang (2000) made the frames containing people and faces with a high likeliness to be key frames

In conclusion, key frame extraction is an important step to structure the whole video. Many people take great effort to find effective method for key frame extraction. There are many different approaches. But a general metric to evaluate the approaches is not proposed yet, because key frame extraction is a relatively subjective action. Different persons may regard different frames as key frames, and different applications tasks may require different kinds of key frames.

Shot Boundary Detection

To better facilitate the user's access requirement such as browsing and retrieval, video content must be structuralized by some schemes. Video shot is the fundamental element above the frame level. Video shot is defined as an unbroken sequence of frames recorded from a single camera (Rui, Huang, & Mehrotra, 1999). It is a physical entity and is delimited by shot boundaries. Therefore, to build up the semantic table-of-content structure for the video, the first step is to locate every shot by finding its beginning and end, what we call the task shot boundary detection (SBD for short) (TRECVID website, 2008).

The video creators may use a variety of editing types to transfer from one shot to another. 99% of them will fall into one of the following three types: (1) hard cut, (2) fade, and (3) dissolve. Related works on this topic will mainly focus on these three categories.

The simplest way to find the hard cut is measuring the pair-wise difference of consecutive frames is to compute the mean absolute change of intensity. A modification of this technique is only counting the pixels that change considerably from one frame to another (Otsuji, Tonomura, & Ohba, 1991). The problem of this kind of approaches is the sensitivity to the camera motion. To reduce this influence, a 3×3 low pass filter is applied to each pixel before the computing of pair-wise difference (Zhang, Kankanhalli, & Smoliar, 1993). Block matching based approach further alleviates the influence of motion. The algorithm in (Shahraray, 1995) computes the discontinuity between one block on frame i with the block in frame $i+\Delta$ that matches most with the former within a certain adjacent area, where Δ is the step size. Then the difference between frames can be computed.

A popular alternative to the pixel-wise and block-wise approaches is the color histogram difference (Boreczky & Rowe, 1996). Experimental results show that the color histogram difference is very robust in detecting the hard cut, where the only problem lies in the manual setting of the threshold. Zhang, Kankanhalli and Smoliar (1993) proposed a twin threshold color histogram method to detect fades and dissolves. Since histograms ignore spatial changes within a frame, this feature is considerably more insensitive to object motion than pixel-wise comparisons. However, a histogram difference remains sensitive to camera motion, such as panning, tilting, or zooming (Zhang, Kankanhalli, & Smoliar, 1993), which bring false alarms in shot detection for certain video files.

To detect more types of shot boundary, the edge change ratio (ECR) is used as a feature in (Zabih, Miller, & Mai, 1995). This is because when shot boundary occurs, there will be new edge appearing at the position far away from the former position, and the former will disappear gradually. According to the method in (Zabih, Miller, & Mai, 1995), hard cuts, fades, dissolves and wipes exhibit a characteristic pattern in the ECR time series.

The standard deviation of pixel intensity proposed by (Lienhart, Kuhmünch, & Effelsberg, 1997) detects fade-in and fade-out respectively. The fades are modeled as a linearly increasing or decreasing pattern along the time axis. The algorithms check the slope of pixel intensities by computing a line of regression repeatedly, when the absolute slope is larger than the predefined threshold, a fade-in or fade-out is detected.

Arman, Hsu and Chiu (1993) extracted the feature of compressed domain to detect the shot boundary. The differences of DCT coefficients of two frames are computed as the distance measure. Camera zoom/pan is likely effect the detection performance. To reduce the influence, Ueda, Miyatake and Yoshizawa (1991) computed the feature of motion vector by block matching, and detect the camera pan/zoom to precisely find the shot boundary.

In this part, we describe the problem of shot boundary detection; discuss some difficulties that may influence the detection performance. The best detection rate of hard cut could reach 90% or so, and the detection rate of gradual transition is not satisfactory, and the false alarm is high compared with hard cut solutions. After all, the SBD problem still need to be investigated since the gradual transition of shot remains a hard problem that has not been solved well until recently.

Scene Analysis and Story Unit Segmentation

Scene analysis and story unit segmentation play an important role in video analysis. Usually scene and story unit contains intact events that happen in the video. Users are mostly interest in the important event in the video and are more intend to see a complete story than uncompleted one. And scene and story unit have more exact event boundaries and complete event descriptions than shot. So the scene analysis and story unit are the important for semantic analysis of video content.

Many researchers have worked in this area. Lin, et al. (2001) and Huang, et al. (1998) try to develop a method for all types of videos. A technique for shot content representation and similarity measure using sub-shot extraction and representation is presented in (Lin & Zhang, 2001), that paper employs dominant color histograms and spatial structure histograms to measure content variation and to represent sub shots. Huang, Liu and Wang (1998) worked on joint audio-visual segmentation, and employs decision curve formulation mechanism to detect the story boundary. In fact, developing a general method for scene analysis and story unit segment is a very difficult task. In many times, it cannot become true due to the differences in different domains. The more we know about the domain knowledge of the video data, the better techniques we can develop about it. So researchers are mainly focused on specific domain, such as movies (Hanjalic, Lagendijk, & Biemond, 1999) (Sundaram & Chang, 2000), news (Zhu, et al., 2001) (Iurgel, et al., 2001) (Hsu & Chang, 2003), and sports (Kijak, Gravier, & Gros, 2003) (Kijak, Oisel, & Gros, 2003) (Nitta, Babaguchi, & Kitahash, 2002) (Wang, Liu, & Yang, 2005).

Hanjalic, et al. (1999) used the visual features to analyze the movie video; it divides the image into blocks and subsequently uses block-matching to compute the similarity between shots. Then it uses the overlapping links method to extracting candidate boundaries. Sundaram, et al. (2000) combined the features of visual and audio, including color histogram, spectral flux, and multi-channel cochlear decomposition and spectral vectors. It uses temporal distance and shot duration measures to compute the similarity between shots. Then memory model (Sundaram & Chang, 2000) is employed to segment scenes.

In news video analysis, Zhu, et al. (2001) employed visual and text features for scene analysis. Then it uses rules regarding anchorperson shots and captions as the main mechanism for identifying news topics. Iurgel, et al. (2001) used audio and semantic features to segment the story units; the semantic feature used here is the anchorperson shot. When segmenting the story unit, it employs not only the rules similar to (Zhu, et al., 2001), but also HMM model for boundary detection. The video, text, audio and semantic features is employed in (Hsu & Chang, 2003); the text feature here is the key-phrases in the introduction and conclusion of a news topic. These features are combined together for better segmenting story units. It uses the maximum entropy model (ME) to systematically fuse separate candidate story boundary sets, which are produced by mid-level features of various types.

Many researchers have devoted to sports video structure analysis. Statistical models such as the Hidden Markov Models have been used to analysis the structure of the video (Kijak, Gravier, & Gros, 2003) (Kijak, Oisel, & Gros, 2003). Especially in (Kijak, Gravier, & Gros, 2003), E. Kijak, et al. used both the visual and audio features. Nitta, et al. (2002) focused on grasping the story from the speech transcript by using a probabilistic framework based on Bayesian networks. Recently, Wang, et al. (2005) used templates based method to detect repetitive patterns in sport video.

In summary, story unit detection is an important and meaningful work in video analysis. However because this task is a high level concept, compared with shot boundary detection, it is a more challenging work. But specific domain knowledge of the video content can be used to develop some specific method on extracting story units.

OBJECT BASED VIDEO UNDERSTANDING AND REPRESENTATION

Object Detection

Objects detection is the first step in many video analysis and understanding applications, including object tracking, event detection, semantic annotation and retrieval of videos. Recently, video objects detection have received an increasingly attention in the literature. However, this is not an easy task.

The main problem in object detection is the amount of variation in visual appearance such as shape, pose, size, color and surrounding environment. An object detector must accommodate all these variations and distinguish the objects from other patterns that may occur in the visual world. Computing efficiency is also an important problem. Fast algorithm should be developed in order for detection in real-time.

Related Works

Many approaches have been proposed for object detection in video streams. Generally speaking, these algorithms can be classified as two categories: global appearance-based approaches and component-based approaches.

Global appearance-based approaches take an object as a unit and perform classification on features generated from the entire object. Many statistical learning mechanisms are explored to identify object patterns. For example, Neural networks are used to detect general objects (Garcia & Delakis, 2004); Support Vector Machines (SVM) (Osuna, Freund & Girosi, 1997) and Naive Bayes classifiers (Schneiderman & Kanade, 2000) are used to locate human faces and cars; boosting algorithms (Viola & Jones, 2001) are widely applied to detect objects, such as faces and text.

Component-based methods treat an object as a collection of parts. These methods first extract some object components, and then detect objects by using geometric information among object parts. Mohan, et al. (2001) proposed an object detection approach by components. In their approach, a person is represented by components such as head, arms, and legs, and then SVM classifiers are used to detect these components and to decide whether a person is present or not. Naquest and Ullman (2003) used fragments as features and perform object recognition with informative features and linear classification. Agarwal, et al. (2004) extracted a part vocabulary of side-view cars using an interest operator and learned a Sparse Network of Winnows classifier to detect side-view cars. Fergus, et al. (2003) and Leibe, et al. (2004) also used interest operators to extract objects' parts and perform detection by probabilistic representation and recognition on many object classes, such as motorbikes, human faces, airplanes, and cars.

In another point of view, object detection problem is typically solved by two stages: candidate generation and candidate verification (Ye, et al., 2005). Candidate generation generates regions of an image that may contain an object, and candidate verification further determines whether the candidate region is an object or not. To generate candidate, "Exhaustive search" and "Selective search" are two commonly used methods. The first one considers all the windows in an image as candidates while "selective" methods consider only the specific regions with specific features. In the verification procedure, supervised learning are normally used method to detect objects, classifiers may include Support Vector Machines (SVMs), Bayesian networks, Neural Networks (NNs), and boosting models. This method may require a large training data set to achieve a reasonably good performance.

A Technical Solution

We will introduce a solution of text detection for example. Text detection is a classical problem in the field of object detection. Text in images and video frames carries important information which is a very compact and accurate clue for video summarization and retrieval.

Based on the features selected, text detection algorithm can be classified into three kinds: (1) color and connected component based algorithm, (2) video temporal information based algorithm, and (3) edge/texture based algorithm. The first class is based on the analysis of homogeneous color and grayscale components that belong to characters (Jain &Yu, 1998). The second class is used to detect video captions by considering that the appearance of a caption will bring difference in successive frames (Tang, et al., 2002). Precise shot boundary detection is required before identifying the appearance of a text line. Furthermore, if a text line appears on a shot boundary, temporal information will fail to detect it. Edge and texture features (Wu, et al., 1999) (Kim, et al. 2003) are the most popular features and work well in many cases. It is based on the idea that text region may contain a lot of edges and textures.

Most text detection algorithms follow a coarse-to-fine framework. In the coarse-detection section, candidate text regions are detected. In order to locate candidate regions, candidate pixels are first detected. In this step, some filters are usually used, such as Sobel edge filter, Canny edge filter, Harr wavelet filter, etc. Then candidate pixels are selected according to these highlighted pixels. Candidate regions can be located using moving window algorithm. A fixed size window is defined (for example: 10*5) and moves all over the image. Some statistical information is calculated in the box and is used to identify if it is a candidate region. Candidate pixels density information and local dynamic threshold are the most simple and popular way. The size of the window is very important. Different sizes will generate different results. Another way called density-based region growing algorithm, is also useful to locate candidate text regions. This algorithm calculates the density information of every pixel and achieves better result. But it is time consuming. Once the text region is located, it is separated into text lines according to projection information; thus the position of the space can be found.

In the fine-detection section, candidate regions are identified by classifiers. In this procedure, two things are the most important: features and classifiers. Based on the review of previous methods, we know that edge and texture features are most frequently used. Text can be regarded as a kind of texture pattern, but the texture properties such as regularity and directionality are weak. It just contains some character strokes that form a text line in a special orientation. Then, only one kind of texture feature is insufficient to model text's texture pattern., A lot of texture feature are usually extracted, including: moments features, histogram features (energy histogram and direction histogram), co-occurrence features, scan line features, etc. Sometime some approaches (such as PCA, forward search algorithm) are used to decrease the feature dimensions. Compared with other classifiers such as neural network and decision tree, SVM is easier to train, needs fewer training samples and has better generalization ability. So it is the most popular classifier in text detection. Adaboost has also been used and be proved to be effective. Training data is also important. The number of the samples is depended on the dimensions of the feature. Whatever, false samples should be more than true samples to get a better interface in the feature space.

Short Summary

Object detection is a difficult problem. Although a lot of work has been done, we still have a long way to go. Maybe better features and better machine learning tools can achieve better results in the future. We are also looking forward to new framework which can make a revolutionary progress.

Object Tracking

Moving object tracking is a major issue in many video analysis systems. Tracking means to locate the object from frame to frame, in other words, to find out the trajectory of the moving object. It enables several important applications such as: (1) security and surveillance to recognize people, to provide better sense of security using visual information; (2) medical therapy – to improve the quality of life for physical therapy patients and disabled people; (3) retail space instrumentation – to analyze shopping behavior of customers, to enhance building and environment design; (4) video abstraction – to obtain automatic annotation of videos, to generate object-based summaries; (5) traffic management – to analyze flow, to detect accidents; (6) sports strategy analysis- to analyze the trajectory of the players; (7) human-computer interaction – to recognize gesture, track eye gaze for data input to computers.

In its simplest form, tracking can be defined as the problem of estimating the trajectory of an object in the image plane as it moves around a scene. In other words, a tracker assigns consistent labels to the tracked objects in different frames of a video. Additionally, depending on the tracking domain, a tracker can also provide object-centric information, such as orientation, area, or shape of an object.

Related Works

Object tracking methods can be divided into three categories: kernel tracking, silhouette tracking and point tracking (Yilmaz, et al., 2006). Next, a concise introduction and some representative work for each method will be provided.

Kernel tracking. Kernel can be regarded as the shape and appearance of the object. So kernel can be a template of a geometry shape or an ellipse with feature histograms. Apparently, for object's feature, every pixel's contribution is not equal. So we assign different weights to pixels according a function, which is named as "kernel". For example, an isotropic kernel

$$k(x) = \begin{cases} 1 - |x|, |x| \le 1 \\ 0, |x| > 1 \end{cases}$$

assigns larger weight to pixels nearer to the center and the object's feature histogram can be computed as

$$q(u) = C \sum_{i=1}^{n} k(\|x_i\|^2) \delta[b(x_i) - u], u = 1, .., m,$$

where n is the number of pixels of the object, $b(x)$ is function that associates to the pixel at location x_i the index $b(x_i)$ of its bin, m is the number of bins and C is the normalization constant, which is derived by imposing constraint

$$\sum_{u=1}^{m} q(u) = 1.$$

Next, in the current frame, we want to find the region that most similar to the object model or evaluate the object's motion. The popular methods are mean-shift, KLT and eigentracking.

Point Tracking. Objects can be represented by a number of points. In this case, tracking can be performed by finding the correspondence points. So point detection algorithms are needed. Then we should match these detected points with points that used to represent the object in the previous frame. Point correspondence methods can be divided into two classes: deterministic (e.g. Hungarian algorithm, Greedy algorithm) and statistical methods (e.g. Kalman filter, Particle filter (Isard &Blake, 1998)). The statistical methods explicitly take the object measurement and consider uncertainties in correspondence while deterministic methods use qualitative motion heuristics to constrain the correspondence problem.

Silhouette tracking. Some objects such as hand, body and shoulder have complex shapes and silhouette representations provide an explicit shape descriptor for those objects. Silhouettes have many different representations and the most popular representation is binary (0/1) mask, which mask the object region with 1 and non-object region with 0. Silhouette tracker is designed to find the object region in current frame according to the model generated in the previous frame. It uses the information (e.g. appearance density, shape model) of the object region and is performed through either shape matching or contour evolution. The goal of shape matching is to find out the object silhouette in the current frame. On the other hand, contour tracking want to get object's new position by evolving an initial contour. The main evolving methods are state space (e.g. HMM) and direct minimization of some energy function (e.g. gradient descent). Apparently, silhouette tracking can deal with various complex shapes.

A Technical Solution

In this part, we will introduce a well know tracking method: Particle filtering (Isard &Blake, 1998). Given an object, we want to use some points to represent it. Then how to select points or samples? Usually, different sub-region of the object region plays different roles. That is, some sub-regions are very important while some are not. For those important sub-regions, more samples (particle) should be selected. Those particles are not equal. Some are more important while some are less. How to get their weights or posterior probabilities?

In order to develop the details of the algorithm, let x_t^i represents the state (e.g. position) of the *i'th* particle at time t, and let w_t^i denotes the weight of the particle at time t. So $\{x_{0:k}^i, w_{0:k}^i\}_{i=1}^N$ denote a random measure that characterizes the posterior *pdf* $p(x_{0:k} \mid z_{1:k})$, where $x_{0:k}$ is the total states of all the particles up to time k. The weights are normalized such that

$$\sum_i w_k^i = 1.$$

Then, the posterior density at k can be approximated as:

$$p(x_{0:k} \mid z_{1:k}) \approx \sum_{i=1}^{N_t} w_k^i \delta(x_{0:k} - x_{0:k}^i) \tag{1}$$

How to get the weights? If the samples are drawn from an importance density $q(x_{0:k} \mid z_{1:k})$, then

$$w_k^i \propto \frac{p(x_{0:k}^i \mid z_{1:k})}{q(x_{0:k}^i \mid z_{1:k})} \tag{2}$$

$$p(x_{0:k} \mid z_{1:k}) = \frac{p(x_{0:k}, z_{1:k})}{p(z_{1:k})} = \frac{p(z_k \mid x_{0:k} \mid z_{1:k-1}) p(x_{0:k} \mid z_{1:k-1}) p(z_{1:k-1})}{p(z_k \mid z_{1:k-1}) p(z_{1:k-1})} = \frac{p(z_k \mid x_{0:k} \mid z_{1:k-1}) p(x_{0:k} \mid z_{1:k-1})}{p(z_k \mid z_{1:k-1})}$$

$$= \frac{p(z_k \mid x_{0:k} \mid z_{1:k-1}) p(x_k \mid x_{0:k-1} \mid z_{1:k-1})}{p(z_k \mid z_{1:k-1})} \times p(x_{0:k-1} \mid z_{1:k-1})$$

$$= \frac{p(z_k \mid x_k) p(x_k \mid x_{k-1})}{p(z_k \mid z_{1:k-1})} p(x_{0:k-1} \mid z_{1:k-1}) \propto p(z_k \mid x_k) p(x_k \mid x_{k-1}) p(x_{0:k-1} \mid z_{1:k-1}) \tag{3}$$

So

$$w_k^i \propto \frac{p(z_k \mid x_k^i) p(x_k^i \mid x_{k-1}^i)}{q(x_k^i \mid x_{0:k-1}^i, z_{1:k})} w_{k-1}^i . \tag{4}$$

If importance density satisfies the equation:

$$q(x_k \mid x_{0:k-1}, z_{1:k}) = q(x_k \mid x_{k-1}, z_k),$$

only a filtered estimate of $p(x_k \mid z_{1:k})$ is required at each time step.

After a few iterations, it is possible that few particles have too large weights and others have negligible weights. This is the degeneracy phenomenon which is an undesirable effect in particle. One method is selecting a very large number of particles, but this is impractical. Good choice of importance density and resampling are two effective solutions. Particle filtering approximates the density directly as a finite number of samples. A number of different types of particle filter exist, and some have been shown to outperform others when used for particular applications. However, when designing a particle filter for a particular application, it is the choice of importance density that is critical.

Short Summary

In this part, we first give a simple introduction to object tracking. Then we briefly introduce some main tracking methods. Last, a popular tracking method, particle filter, is introduced as a technical solution. There are many other solutions such as mean shift, condensation, eigentracking and so on.

Object Representation and Indexing

Object representation and indexing is the way to describe objects, by which objects can be easily retrieved, classified and detected in image or video dataset. So this method should be distinctive and efficiently computed. Imagine that you are standing beside a car (Fig.2) and you want to describe it to an auto-navigation robot, so that it can recognize cars in real-time. Thus, how to describe or represent cars? Should we only use color, shape or other features? Generally, objects can be represented by their shapes and appearances. The object shape representations mainly include points, primitive geometric shapes, silhouette and contour, articulated shape and skeletal models. Common appearance representations in the context of object can be divided into: (1) probability densities of object appearance, (2) templates, (3) active appearance models, (3) multi-view appearance models, and (4) integral image, etc.

Indexing is something that serves to guide, point out, or otherwise facilitate reference, especially in video dataset. According to the type of data being stored, video indexes can be classified into the following categories that have been discussed before: key frame, video shots, video story and video summary.

Object representations are the basis for high level stage process, such as detection, classification and tracking. So the right representation plays a critical role in multi-media computing. Some representative method will be described in the following according to examples illustrated in Fig.3:

- **Points-based method:** The object is represented by the centroid (Fig.3 (a), in tracking) or by a set of points-based patch, such as SIFT (Lowe, 2004), MSEA (Matas, et al. 2002) (Fig. 3(b), in classification context). In general, the point representation is suitable for representing and tracking objects that occupy small regions.
- **Primitive geometric shapes:** Object shape is represented by a rectangle, ellipse (Fig.3 (c), (d)), etc. Object motion for such representations is usually modeled by translation, affine, or projective transformation. Though primitive geometric shapes are more suitable for representing simple rigid objects, they are also used for non-rigid ones.

Figure 2. Different cars in different view points

Figure 3. Object representations. (a)point or centroid, (b) multi points, (c) rectangular patch, (d) elliptical patch, (e) part-based multiple patches, (f) object skeleton, (g) complete object contour, (h) control points on object contour, (i) object silhouette.

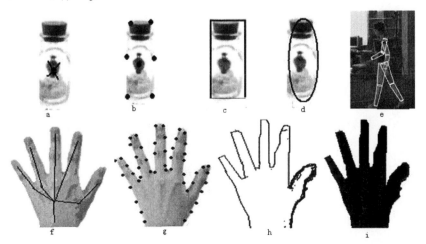

- **Object silhouette and contour:** Contour representation defines the boundary of an object (Fig. 3 (g), (h)). The region inside the contour is called the silhouette of the object (Fig.3 (i)). Silhouette and contour representations are suitable for indexing complex non-rigid shapes, such as human motion and hand motion analysis. The silhouette or contour can be described as shape context (Thayananthan, et al., 2003), or histogram of gradient (Xu & Li, 2002).
- **Articulated shape and models:** Articulated objects are composed of body parts that are held together with joints. For example, the human body is an articulated object with torso, legs, hands, head, and feet connected by joints. The relationship between the parts is governed by kinematics motion model, ex. joint angle, etc. In order to represent an articulated object, one can model the constituent parts using cylinders or ellipse as show in Fig.3 (e).
- **Skeletal models:** Object skeleton can be extracted by applying medial axis transformation to the object silhouette. This model is commonly used as a shape representation for objects recognition. Skeleton representation can be used to model both articulated and rigid objects (Fig.3 (f)). Chamfer matching (Thayananthan, et al., 2003) is also used for comparing the skeletal model.
- **Probability densities of object appearance:** The probability density estimates of the object appearance can either be parametric, such as Gaussian and mixture of Gaussians, or nonparametric, such as Parzen windows and histograms. The probability densities of object appearance features (color, texture) can be computed from the image region.
- **Templates:** Templates are formed using simple geometric shapes or silhouettes. An advantage of a template is that it carries both spatial and appearance information. Templates, however, only encode the object appearance generated from a single view. Thus, they are only suitable for view invariant objects whose poses do not vary considerably during the course (Comaniciu & Meer, 2002).
- **Integral image:** An integral image I is an intermediate representation for the image and contains the sum of gray scale pixel values of image N with height y and width x, i.e.,

$$I(x, y) = \sum_{x'=0}^{x} \sum_{y'=0}^{y} N(x', y').$$

The integral image is computed recursively, by the formulas:

$$I(x, y) = I(x, y-1) + I(x-1, y) + N(x, y) - I(x-1, y-1)$$

with

$$I(-1, y) = I(x, -1) = I(-1, -1) = 0,$$

therefore it requires only one scan over the input data. This intermediate representation $I(x,y)$ allows the computation of a rectangle feature value at (x,y) with height and width (h,w) using four references

$$F(x, y, h, w) = I(x, y) + I(x+w, y+h) - I(x, y+h) - I(x+w, y).$$

This representation is widely used in object detection for fast computing object statistic features in (Viola & Jones, 2000).

Generally speaking, there is strong relationship between the object representations and the application algorithms, such as detection, tracking *et al*, and object representations are usually chosen according to the application domain. Video indexing is a category representation for fast retrieval of the video information.

HIGH LEVEL VIDEO SEMANTIC ANALYSIS AND UNDERSTANDING

In order to understand and analysis the visual data, some high level semantic information should be extracted such event information, perceptual attention information and mining information. In the following, we will have a detailed introduction on these areas.

Event Detection

Video events are normally defined as the interesting or important events which capture user attentions. For example, a soccer goal event is defined as the ball passing over the goal line without touching the goal posts and the crossbar. With the advances of storage capabilities, computing power and multimedia technology, the research on semantic event detection become more and more active in recent years, such as video surveillance, sports highlight detection, TV/Movie abstraction and home video retrieval etc. Through event detection, consumers can retrieve specific video segments quickly from the long videos and save much time in browsing. Moreover, event detection makes it possible to deliver the video clips into mobile devices or webs. However, semantic event detection is still a challenging problem due to the large semantic gap and the difficulty of modeling temporal and multimodality characteristics of video streams.

In visual surveillance for example, after successfully tracking the moving objects from one frame to another in an image sequence, the problem of understanding object behaviors from image sequences appears naturally. Behavior understanding involves the analysis and recognition of motion patterns, and the production of high-level description of actions and interactions. In fact, event detection is based on the correct recognition of human behavior and object movement. Events scratched from the scene under surveillance could be divided into two large categories: normal events and abnormal events. Naturally, abnormal behavior or event detection after behavior understanding and description of behaviors would be more important, for it's wildly utilization.

Related Works

In the past few years, significant research has been devoted to the video event detection. Haering, et al. (2000) proposed a three-level video event detection method and apply it to animal-hunt detection in wildlife documentaries. Three levels are feature level; neural network based classifier level; and shot descriptor level respectively. A three-level video event detection method is also applied in (Wang, et al. 2006). The authors employed Conditional Random Fields (CRFs) to fuse temporal multi-modality cues for event detection. Ekin, et al. (2003) combined object-based features and cinematic features to develop an event detection algorithm and a summarization system for soccer videos. Shot are classified into four view (shot) types according to the dominant color features. Then high-level events such as goal, referee and penalty box are detected based on object-based features from the specific views. Bai, et al. (2007) also presented an event detection model for sports video; this model is based on perception concepts and finite state machines (PC-FSMs). PC-FSMs are described formally in terms of state graphs, then a graph matching method is used to discover semantic event automatically. Xie, Shyu, and Chen (2007) proposed a video event detection method which utilizes both the distance-based and rule-based data mining techniques; they try to provide a domain independent solution for rare event detection in video streams.

An important application in event detection is visual surveillance, where abnormal detection and behavior prediction are significant in practice. In applications of visual surveillance, not only should visual surveillance systems detect abnomalies such as traffic accidents and car theft etc, according to requirements of different functions, but also predicts what will happen according to the current situation and raise an alarm for a predicted abnormal behavior. Implementations are usually based on one or other of the following two methods.

1. *Probability reasoning and prior rules combined methods.* A behavior with small probability or against the prior rules would be regarded as an anomaly (Owens & Hunter, 2000) (Lou, Liu, Tan, & Hu, 2002).
2. *Behavior-pattern-based methods.* We can predict an object behavior by matching the observed sub-behavior of the object with the learned patterns (Johnson &Hogg, 1996) (Sumpter & Bulpitt, 2000). Generally, patterns of behaviors in a scene can be constructed by supervised or unsupervised learning of each object's velocities and trajectories, etc.

A Technical Solution

In this part, we introduce a method of exciting event detections in broadcast soccer video as an example (Ye, et al., 2005). Framework of the proposed method is described in Fig.4.

First, for each of the video frame, the playfield area is classified based on low-level features, and frames are hierarchically classified into defined views. Finally, view label, camera motion and shot boundary descriptions together with temporal relationship are fed into an SVM classifier to identify events. In our implementation, "shoot on goal", "placed kick", "break by offence" are selected for experiments.

To segment playfield, training models are automatically built by Gaussian Mixture Models (GMMs) (Jiang, et al., 2004). The model is updated online by an incremental procedure. Then three kinds of mid-level descriptions are extracted to represent the soccer video content. For each of the soccer frame, we can semantically assign a view label to them by a hierarchical classification procedure. The views are:

Figure 4. The framework of exciting event detection in soccer video

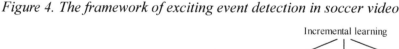
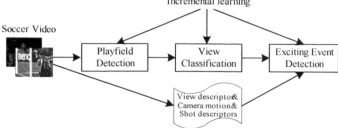

"goal mouth view", "corner view", "middle field view", "player close-up view" and "out-field view". For each of the level we extract low-level features of playfield ratio, projection profile of non playfield, and shape for classification. SVM classifiers are employed to perform the classification task on extracted features. An incremental scheme is adopted to improve the extensibility.

Short Summary

We have reviewed the state-of-the-art of event detection in video content analysis and visual surveillance. Although a large amount of work has been done in this scope, many issues are still open and deserve further research.

Visual Attention in Video Analysis

Visual attention is one of the most important features of Human Visual System (HVS). It can filter the signals received by the HVS and select the important ones to be processed. Visual attention has two mechanisms, bottom-up and top-down, correspond to stimulus-driven and object-driven respectively. The bottom-up mechanism is closely related to human sensory system, which is sensible to the contrast including both global effect and contextual difference. The top-down mechanism is closely related to human brain, which is a much complex mechanism.

Computational attention model enables computers to understand images and videos in the manner of HVS. It has been a hot research point for years and has been successfully applied in many fields including image compression, video summarization, image and video browsing on small displays and so on.

Limited by the capacity of human information processing system, only a small part of the information received by sensory system should have the chance to be processed by brain. The ability of human visual system to concentrate mental effort on sensory or mental events is referred as attention. Before being processed by brain the information should be filtered twice. The first one happens before pattern recognition, which is a stimulus driven process, referred as bottom-up attention. The second one happens after pattern recognition, which is a task driven process, referred as top-down mechanism. Computational visual attention can also be classified into the above two types similarly. The task of attention analysis is to detect the Region of Interest of images and the frames of interest of videos (Solso, et al. 2003).

Bottom-up attention analysis: Saliency map based attention model is the earliest and the most popular approach for bottom-up attention analysis. Till now all the proposed methods are saliency map based. The method is different in the following four aspects: the choice of the perceptive unit, the mechanism to compute saliency, the feature combination method, and extraction of the region of interest through saliency map.

Saliency map is the representation of the saliency of each perceptive unit. Here perceptive unit is defined as a set of pixels perceived as a union in attention analysis. A perceptive unit can be a pixel, a block, or a region. A region can be of any size, any scale, and contain much more perceptive information compared with a pixel or a block (Liu, et al., 2007).

For the center-surround structure of receptive field of human eye, a perceptive unit with large contrast will attract more attention. So contrast is widely used in attention analysis. Itti, et al. (1998) proposed a "center-surround" method, in which the "center" is the blocks at low level of Gaussian pyramid, and "surround" is the corresponding ones at high levels. The distance between different scales is used to generate saliency maps. Ma and Zhang (2003) used the contrast between an image block and its neighborhood to represent its saliency. Global contrast and statistical information (Zhai & Shah, 2006) are also used to obtain the saliency map.

In attention analysis, all of the features of the image can be used, including color, texture, intensity, orientation and so on. Each of the features will generate a saliency map and the fusion mechanism may affect the result heavily. Feature fusion can be both linear and nonlinear. Linear fusion is much easier by calculating the weighted average of the saliency maps. The weights of each feature can be predefined empirically or by machine learning (Itti & Koch, 1999). While nonlinear fusion is more complex but is more suitable from the point of view of perception (Hua & Zhang, 2004).

The final work in attention analysis is to extract the region of interest from the saliency map. Itti, et al. (1998) used a winner-take-all mechanism; Ma and Zhang (2003) used fuzzy growing method to extract the attentive region.

All the above is about attention analysis of images. For videos, another important feature should be considered: motion. This is because people always draw attention to the objects with distinct motion. In addition, there is an important property of human perception that it is affected strongly by knowledge context. According to this property, some object may catch more attention such as human face, text and so on. So face detection and text detection are often used in visual attention analysis (Ma, et al., 2005). Another kind of region which would draw people's great attention in an image is human face. So if an attention unit belongs to a part of human face, most work will give a high saliency value to it. Some work proposed a model based on camera motion. It considers the motion of camera will lead the audience to pay attention to the certain area. For example, if the camera pans left, people will always pay attention to the left part of the video frame; if the camera zooms in, people will always pay attention to the center part of the video frame.

Top-down attention analysis: The bottom-up method uses only low level features and does not need any prior knowledge. So it is simple and could satisfy most general applications. But the perception of human is always based on some certain prior knowledge. For example people always pay some attention to the objects and events which are meaningful. Top-down model is adequate for evaluating the attention caused by people's prior knowledge. Some work learns to pair the low-level signatures from a series of video clips with the corresponding eye positions (Peters & Itti, 2007). Machine learning methods are also used in top-down attention model to detect specific objects and events (Peters & Itti, 2007) (Navalpakkam & Itti, 2006).

In summary, visual attention model is an effective way to extract the essential content from the redundant video data. Now people are developing many new methods to extract the attentive parts in pictures and videos.

Video Mining

Data mining is the process of finding useful patterns or extracting previously unknown knowledge from a massive set of data (Oh, Lee, & Hwang, 2005). Different from textual information which has been studied for a long time, video contents have special characteristics: they are continuous sequences with temporal relations among them, and each video segment normally contains abundant information itself. Mining useful statistical information from the whole video content to help users have a better understanding of it is a relatively difficult task and has not been fully explored yet. Compared with object-, structure- or event-based video semantic information as discussed before, statistical mining information is hard to be acquired by human labeling.

Due to the semantic gap between human perception and computer-centered low-level features, many video understanding techniques such as shot boundary detection and event extraction remain open problems. Thus investigation on video mining is at its early stage as mining solutions normally need the extracted semantic information. In fact, the current status of video mining is still at the pre-processing stage, such as video clustering (Tavanapong & Zhou, 2004). The main motivation of video mining is to find undiscovered knowledge from the stream based on visual and audio cues. The knowledge may typically include structure information within a video clip or association information among various clips, as well as trend information based on the analysis for a massive size of video set. Xie, et al. (2003) provided a solution to find temporal structures of sports video by an unsupervised multi-scale statistical Hidden Markov method without employing domain knowledge. To find topic associations among news videos, Pan and Faloutsos (2002) proposed a tool called "GeoPlot" to provide the information of correlation of news events occurrence. Mining undiscovered video information is usually based on apparent semantic concept extraction techniques in video clips, such as object concept, scene concept and event concept. In the authors' mind, video mining need a long way to go to explore the full potential of this topic as most of the video understanding problems are still unsolved yet.

SUMMARY

Psychological and biological experiments show that more than 80% percent of the information we receive is chaptered by the visual system. As an important information carrier, Visual media which contains both images and videos, has lots of attractive features such as visualization, data carrying capacity for large amount of data, easier for understanding, and so on. It is common to us that video can easily and naturally express complicated information, which can be hardly matched by the traditional text based media. From the view point of the psychological study, the main reason why the video is more informative is because the content we get from the video can be easily mapped as semantic concepts. In the multimedia analysis field, we are trying to let computers imitate human's mapping from low level data to high level video content understanding, which can be seen as bridging the "Semantic Gap". Criterions of human's judgments for video media are different from the ones of computer vision system. For example, the objects in the real world are 3-dimensional, while the objects captured by the cameras are mapped into 2-dimensional space, and the real object contains many concepts for human while the digital images are just gathering of pixels for computers. This difference is always referred as "Sensory Gap". Consequently, one of the most urgent tasks of video analysis is conquering "Semantic Gap" and extracting high level information from the video. Video content analysis and understanding is proposed aiming at solving this problem. Although more and more researchers have engaged in this research and more and more methods have been proposed, the work on video semantic analysis and understanding is still not good enough and lots of problems need to be further investigated.

ACKNOWLEDGMENT

The authors are supported by grants from Chinese NSF under contract No. 60702035 and 60773136, National Hi-Tech R&D Program (863) of China under contract No. 2006AA01Z117 and 2006AA010105, and National Key Technology R&D Program under contract No. 2006BAH02A10. We would like to sincerely appreciate the help and valuable input provided by Shiliang Zhang, Xuekan Qiu, Guorong Li, Shuhui Wang, Xiaojun Li, Lei Hu, Lingfang Li, Shugao Ma, Shaojie Cai, Yu Gong and Chunxi Liu, Huiying Liu, etc.

REFERENCES

Agarwal, S., Awan, A., & Roth, D. (2004). Learning to detect objects in images via a sparse, part-based representation. *IEEE Transactions on Pattern Analysis and Machine Intelligence, 26*(11), 1475–1490. doi: 10.1109/TPAMI.2004.108.

Arman, F., Hsu, A., & Chiu, M.Y. (1993). Image processing on compressed data for large video database, *ACM international conference on Multimedia,* (pp. 267-272). doi: 10.1145/166266.166297.

Aslandogan, Y.A., & Yu, C.T. (1999). Techniques and systems for image and video retrieval. *IEEE Transactions on Knowledge and Data Engineering, 11*(1), 56-63. doi: 10.1109/69.755615.

Bai, L., Lao, S.Y., Jones, G., & Smeaton, A.F. (2007). A semantic content analysis model for sports video based on perception concepts and finite state machines. *IEEE International Conference on Multimedia and Expo,* (pp. 1407-1410). doi: 10.1109/ICME.2007.4284923.

Boreczky, J.S., & Rowe, L.A. (1996). Comparison of video shot boundary detection techniques. *In Proc. IS&T/SPIE Storage and Retrieval for Still Image and Video Databases IV, 2664,* 170-179.

Campisi, P., Longari A., & Neri, A. (1999). Automatic key frame selection using a wavelet based approach. In *Proc. of SPIE, 3813,* 861-872.

Comaniciu, D., & Meer, P. (2002). Mean shift: a robust approach toward feature space analysis. *IEEE Transactions on Pattern Analysis and Machine Intelligence, 24*(5), 603-619. doi: 10.1109/34.1000236.

Ekin, A., Tekalp, A. M., & Mehrotra, R. (2003). Automatic soccer video analysis and summarization. *IEEE Trans. on Image Processing, 12*(7), 796-807. doi: 10.1109/TIP.2003.812758.

Fergus, R., Perona, P., & Zisserman, A. (2003). Object class recognition by unsupervised scale-invariant learning. In *Proceedings of the Ninth International Conference on Computer Vision and Pattern Recognition, 2,* 264–271.

Forsyth, D.A., & Ponce, J. (2003). Computer vision: A modern approach. *Prentice Hall.*

Garcia, C., & Delakis, M. (2004). Convolutional Face Finder: A Neural Architecture for Fast and Robust Face Detection. *IEEE Translations on Pattern Analysis And Machine Intelligence, 26*(11), 1408–1423. doi: 10.1109/TPAMI.2004.97.

Haering, N., Qian, R.J., & Sezan, M.I. (2000). A semantic event detection approach and its application to detecting hunts in wildlife video. *IEEE Trans. on Circuits and Systems for Video Technology, 10*(6), 857–868. doi: 10.1109/76.867923.

Hanjalic, A., Lagendijk, R., & Biemond, J. (1999). Automated high-level movie segmentation for advanced video retrieval systems. *IEEE Transactions on Circuits and Systems for Video Technology, 9*(4), 580–588. doi: 10.1109/76.767124.

Harris, C., & Stephens, M. A. (1988). A combined corner and edge detector. *In Alvey Vision Conference*, (pp. 147–151).

Hsu, W., & Chang, S.F. (2003). A statistical framework for fusing mid-level perceptual features in news story segmentation. *IEEE International Conference on Multimedia and Expo*, (pp. 413-416).

Hua, X.S., & Zhang H.J. (2004). An attention-based decision fusion scheme for multimedia information retrieval. *Proceedings of Pacific-Rim conference on Multimedia.*

Huang, J., Liu, Z., & Wang, Y. (1998). Integration of audio and visual information for content-based video segmentation. *IEEE International Conference on Image processing,* (pp. 526-530). doi: 10.1109/ICIP.1998.727252.

Isard, M., & Blake, A. (1998). CONDENSATION—Conditional density propagation for visual tracking. *International Journal of Computer Vision, 29*(1), 5–28.

Itti, L., Koch, C., & Niebur, E. (1998). A model of saliency-based visual attention for rapid scene analysis. *IEEE Trans on Pattern Analysis and Machine Intelligence, 20*(11), 1254-1259. doi: 10.1109/34.730558.

Itti, L., & Koch, C. (1999). A Comparison of feature combination strategies for saliency-based visual attention systems. *SPIE Human Vision and Electronic Imaging IV (HVEI'99), 3644*, 73 82

Iurgel, U., Meermeier, R., Eickeler, S., & Rigoll, G. (2001). New approaches to audio-visual segmentation of TV news for automatic topic retrieval. *IEEE International Conference on Acoustics, Speech, and Signal Processing.* (pp. 1397-1400). doi: 10.1109/ICASSP.2001.941190.

Jain, A.K., & Yu, B. (1998). Automatic text location in images and video frames. *Pattern Recognition, 31,* 2055–2076.

Jiang, S.Q., Ye, Q.X., Gao, W., & Huang, T.J. (2004). A new method to segment playfield and its applications in match analysis in sports video, *ACM International Conference on Multimedia*, (pp. 292-295). doi: 10.1145/1027527.1027594.

Johnson, N., & Hogg, D.C. (1996). Learning the distribution of object trajectories for event recognition. *Image and Vision Computing, 14,* 609-615.

Ke, Y., & Sukthankar, R. (2004). PCA-SIFT: A more distinctive representation for local image descriptors. In *Proc. Conf. Computer Vision and Pattern Recognition, 2*, 511-517. doi: 10.1109/CVPR.2004.1315206.

Kijak, E., Gravier, G., Gros, P., Oisel, L., & Bimbot, F. (2003), HMM based structure of tennis videos using visual and audio cues. *IEEE International Conference on Multimedia and Expo*. doi: 10.1109/ICME.2003.1221310.

Kijak, E., Oisel , L., & Gros, P. (2003). Hierarchical structure analysis of sport video using HMMS. *IEEE International Conference on Image Processing, 2,* II-1025-8.

Kim, C., & Hwang, J.N. (2000). An integrated scheme for object-based video abstraction. *ACM international conference on Multimedia,* (pp. 303 – 311).

Kim, K.I., Jung, K., & Kim, H. (2003). Texture-based approach for text detection in images using support vector machines and continuously adaptive mean shift algorithm. *IEEE Transactions on Pattern Analysis and Machine Intelligence, 25,* 1631–1639. doi: 10.1109/TPAMI.2003.1251157.

Leibe, B., Leonardis, A., & Schiele, B. (2004). Combined object categorization and segmentation with an implicit shape model. *ECCV2004 Workshop on Statistical Learning in Computer Vision*, (pp. 17-32).

Li, Y., Zhang, T., & Tretter, D. (2001). An Overview of Video Abstraction Techniques. *HP Labs Technical Report*, HPL-2001-191, 20010809. Retrieved from http://www.hpl.hp.com/techreports/images/pdf.

Lienhart, R., Kuhmünch, C., & Effelsberg, W. (1997). On the detection and recognition of television commercials. In *Proceedings of the International Conference on Multimedia Computing and Systems*, Ottawa, Ontario, Canada, (pp. 509-516).

Lienhart, R. (1999). Comparison of automatic shot boundary detection algorithms. In *Proc. IS&T/SPIE Storage and Retrieval for Image and Video Databases VII*, 3656, 290–30.

Lin, T., & Zhang, H. (2001). Video content representation for shot retrieval and scene extraction. *International Journal of Image Graphics, 3*(1), 507–526.

Liu, H., Jiang, S., Huang, Q., Xu, C., & Gao, W. (2007). Region-based visual attention analysis with its application in image browsing on small displays. *ACM International Conference on Multimedia*, (pp. 305-308). 10.1145/1291233.1291298.

Lowe, D. (2004). Distinctive image features from scale-invariant key points. *Int'l J. Computer Vision, 2*(60), 91-110. doi: 10.1023/ B:VISI.0000029664.99615.94.

Lou, J., Liu, Q., Tan, T., & Hu, W. (2002). Semantic interpretation of object activities in surveillance algorithms in the area of computer vision and machine system. *Pattern Recognition, 3*, 777-780.

Ma, Y.F., & Zhang, H.J. (2003). Contrast-based image attention analysis by using fuzzy growing. *ACM international conference on Multimedia*, (pp. 374-381). doi: 10.1145/957013.957094.

Ma, Y.F., Hua, X.S., Lu, L., & Zhang, H.J. (2005). A generic framework of user attention model and its application in video summarization. *IEEE Trans on Multimedia, 7*(5), 907- 919. doi: 10.1109/ TMM.2005.854410.

Matas, J., Chum, O., Urban, M. & Pajdla, T. (2002). Robust wide baseline stereo from maximally stable extremal regions. *British Machine Vision Conference*, (pp. 384-393).

Mikolajczyk, K., & Schmid, C. (2004). Scale & affine invariant interest point detectors. *Int. J. Computer. Vision, 60*(1), 63-86. doi: 10.1023/ B:VISI.0000027790.02288.f2.

Mohan, A., Papageorgiou, C., & Poggio, T. (2001). Example-based object detection in images by components. *IEEE Transactions on Pattern Analysis and Machine Intelligence, 23*(4), 349–361. doi: 10.1109/34.917571.

Naquest, M.V., & Ullman, S. (2003). Object recognition with informative features and linear classification. *Ninth International Conference on Computer Vision, 1*, 281–288. doi: 10.1109/ICCV.2003.1238356.

Navalpakkam, V., & Itti, L. (2006). An integrated model of top-down and bottom-up attention for optimizing detecting speed. *IEEE Conference on Computer Vision and Pattern Recognition, 2*, 2049-2056. doi: 10.1109/CVPR.2006.54.

Nitta, N., Babaguchi, N., & Kitahashi, T. (2002). Story based representation for broadcasted sports video and automatic story segmentation. *IEEE International Conference on Multimedia and Expo*, 1, pp. 813-816. doi: 10.1109/ICME.2002.1035906.

Oh, J.H., Lee, J. K., & Hwang, S. (2005) Video data mining: current status and challenges. In J. Wang (Eds.) *Encyclopedia of Data Warehousing and Mining*, (pp. 104-107). Idea Group Inc. and IRM Press. doi: 10.1002/sam.10003.

Osuna, E., Freund, R. & Girosi, F. (1997). Training Support Vector Machines: an Application to Face Detection. *International Conference on Computer Vision and Pattern Recognition*, (pp. 130–136). doi: 10.1109/CVPR.1997.609310.

Otsuji, K. Y., Tonomura, & Ohba, Y. (1991). Video browsing using brightness data. *in Proc. SPIE/IS&T VCIP'91, 1606*, 980–989.

Owens, J., & Hunter, A. (2000). Application of the self-organizing map to trajectory classification. In *Proc. Third IEEE Visual Surveillance Workshop*, (pp. 77-83). doi: 10.1109/VS.2000.856860.

Pan, J., & Faloutsos, C. (2002). GeoPlot: Spatial data mining on video libraries. *Int'l Conf. Information and Knowledge Management*, (pp. 405-412).

Pass, G., & Zabih, R. (1996). Histogram refinement for content-based image retrieval. *IEEE Workshop on Applications of Computer Vision*, (pp. 96-102). doi: 10.1109/ACV.1996.572008.

Peters, RJ., & Itti, L. (2007). Beyond bottom-up: Incorporating task-dependent influences into a computational model of spatial attention. *IEEE Conference on Computer Vision and Pattern Recognition*, (pp. 1-6). doi: 10.1109/CVPR.2007.383337.

Rui, Y., Huang, T.S., & Mehrotra, S. (1999) Constructing Table-of-Content for videos, *ACM Multimedia System*, 7(5), 359–368. doi: 10.1007/s005300050138.

Schneiderman, H., & Kanade, T. (2000). A Statistical Method for 3D Object Detection Applied to Faces and Cars. *IEEE Conference on Computer Vision and Pattern Recognition*, 1, 746-751. doi: 10.1109/CVPR.2000.855895.

Shahraray, B. (1995). Scene change detection and content-based sampling of video sequences. *In Proc. IS&T/SPIE, 2419*, 2–13.

Smith, J.R., & Chang, S. F. (1995). Tools and techniques for color image retrieval. In *Proc. SPIE: Storage and Retrieval for Image and Video Database, 2670*, 426-437.

Smith, J.R., & Chang, S.F. (1996). Automated binary texture feature sets for image retrieval. *In Proc IEEE Int Conf Acoust, Speech and Signal Proc*, May, (pp. 2239-2242). doi: 10.1109/ICASSP.1996.545867.

Solso, R.L., Maclin, M.K. & Maclin, O.H. (2003). Cognitive psychology. *Perception and Attention*, (pp. 70-103). Pearson Education.

Stricker, M.A., & Orengo, M. (1995). Similarity of color images. In *Proc. SPIE: Storage and Retrieval for Image and Video Database, 2420*, 381-392.

Sumpter, N., & Bulpitt, A.J. (2000). Learning spatio-temporal patterns for predicting object behavior. *Image and Vision Computing, 18*(9), 697-704.

Sundaram, H., & Chang, S.F. (2000). Video scene segmentation using video and audio features. *IEEE International Conference on Multimedia and Expo, 2*, (pp. 1145-1148). doi: 10.1109/ICME.2000.871563.

Tang, X., Gao, X.B., Liu, J., & Zhang, H. (2002). Spatial-temporal approach for video caption detection and recognition. *IEEE Transactions on Neural Networks, 13*, 961–971.doi: 10.1109/TNN.2002.1021896.

Tavanapong, W., & Zhou, J. (2004). Shot clustering techniques for story browsing, *IEEE Transaction on Multimedia, 6*(4), 517-527. doi: 10.1109/TMM.2004.830810.

Thayananthan, A., Stenger, B., Torr, P., & Cipolla, R. (2003) Shape context and chamfer matching in cluttered scenes. *International Conference on Computer Vision and Pattern Recognition, 1*, 127-133. doi: 10.1109/CVPR.2003.1211346.

The TRECVID conference website. (2008). Retrieved June 6, 2008, from http://www-nlpir.nist.gov/projects/trecvid/.

Uchihashi, S., Foote, J., Girgensohn, A., & Boreczky, J. (1999). Video manga: Generating semantically meaningful video summaries. *ACM international conference on Multimedia*, (pp. 383–392).

Udea, H., Miyatake, T., & Yoshizawa, S. (1991). IMPACT—An integrated natural-motion-picture dedicated multimedia authoring system. *New York. ACM Press*, (pp. 343-250).

Vetterli, J.K.M. (1995). *Wavelets and subband coding*. Prentice Hall.

Viola, P., Jones, M. (2001). Robust Real Time Object Detection. *IEEE ICCV Workshop on Statistical and Computational Theories of Vision, 2*, II- 465-8. doi: 10.1109/ICME.2003.1221654.

Viola, P., & Jones, M. (2001). Rapid object detection using a boosted cascade of simple features. *IEEE Conference on Computer Vision and Pattern Recognition, 1*, 511-518. doi: 10.1109/CVPR.2001.990517.

Wang, T., Li, J., Diao, Q., Hu, W., Zhang, Y., & Duolong, C. (2006). Semantic event detection using conditional random fields. *Computer Vision and Pattern Recognition Workshops*, (pp. 109-109). doi: 10.1109/CVPRW.2006.190.

Wang, P., Liu, Z., & Yang, S. (2005). A probabilistic template-based approach to discovering repetitive patterns in broadcast videos. *ACM international conference on Multimedia*, (pp. 407-410). doi: 10.1145/1101149.1101238.

Wolf, W. (1996). Key Frame Selection by motion analysis. *IEEE International Conference on Acoustics, Speech, and Signal Processing, (ICASSP'96), 2*, 1228-1231. doi: 10.1109/ICASSP.1996.543588.

Wu, V., Manmatha, R., & Riseman, E.M. (1999). Textfinder: an automatic system to detect and recognize text in images, *IEEE Transactions on Pattern Analysis and Machine Intelligence, 20*, pp. 1224–1229. doi: 10.1109/34.809116.

Xie, L., Chang, S.F., Divakaran, A., & Sun, H.(2003). Unsupervised mining of statistical temporal structures in video. In A. Rosenfeld, D. Doremann, & D. Dementhon (Eds.), *Video Mining*. Kluwer Academic Publishers.

Xie, Z. X., Shyu, M.L., & Chen, S.C. (2007). Video event detection with combined distance-based and rule-based data mining techniques. *IEEE International Conference on Multimedia and Expo*, (pp. 2026-2029). doi:10.1109/ICME.2007.4285078.

Xu, X., Li. B. (2002). Head tracking using particle filter with intensity gradient and color histogram. *Journal of Computer Science and Technology, 17*(6), 859-864.

Ye, Q.X., Huang, Q.M., Gao, W., & Jiang, S.Q.(2005). Exciting event detection in broadcast soccer video with mid-level description and incremental learning. *ACM International Conference on Multimedia,* (pp. 455-458). doi: 10.1145/1101149.1101250.

Ye, Q.X., Huang, Q.M., Gao, W., & Zhao D.B. (2005). Fast and robust text detection in images and video frames. *Image and Vision Computing, 23,* (6), 565-576. doi: 10.1016/j.imavis.2005.01.004.

Yilmaz, A. Javed, O., & Shah, M. (2006). Object Tracking: A Survey. *ACM Computing Surveys, 38*(4), doi:10.1145/1177352.1177355.

Zabih, R., Miller, J., & Mai, K. (1995). A feature-based algorithm for detecting and classifying scene breaks. *ACM international conference on Multimedia,* (pp. 189-200). doi: 10.1145/217279.215266.

Zhang, H. J., Wu, J., Zhong, D., & Smoliar, S. W. (1997). An integrated system for content based video retrieval and browsing. *Pattern Recognition, 30*(4), 643-658.

Zhang, H., Kankanhalli, A., & Smoliar, S. W. (1993). Automatic partitioning of full-motion video. *Multimedia System, 1* 10–28. doi: 10.1007 /BF01210504.

Zhai, Y., & Shah, M. (2006). Visual attention detection in video sequences using spatio-temporal cues. *ACM international conference on Multimedia,* (pp. 815-824). doi: 10.1145/1180639.1180824

Zhu, X., Wu, L., Xue, X., Lu, X., & Fan, J. (2001). Automatic scene detection in news program by integrating visual feature and rules. *The second IEEE Pacific-Rim conference on multimedia, 2195,* 837–842.

Chapter X
Applications of Semantic Mining on Biological Process Engineering

Hossam A. Gabbar
University of Ontario Institute of Technology, Canada

Naila Mahmut
Heart Center - Cardiovascular Research Hospital for Sick Children, Canada

ABSTRACT

Semantic mining is an essential part in knowledgebase and decision support systems where it enables the extraction of useful knowledge form available databases with the ultimate goal of supporting the decision making process. In process systems engineering, decisions are made throughout plant / process / product life cycles. The provision of smart semantic mining techniques will improve the decision making process for all life cycle activities. In particular, safety and environmental related decisions are highly dependent on process internal and external conditions and dynamics with respect to equipment geometry and plant layout. This chapter discusses practical methods for semantic mining using systematic knowledge representation as integrated with process modeling and domain knowledge. POOM or plant/process object oriented modeling methodology is explained and used as a basis to implement semantic mining as applied on process systems engineering. Case studies are illustrated for biological process engineering, in particular MoFlo systems focusing on process safety and operation design support.

INTRODUCTION

The recent challenges of industrial, medical, and social systems are focused on how to provide intelligent learning systems that can deal with increasing complexity and multidimensional knowledge structures. The problem became worse when dealing with different scales of domain knowledge in multimedia formats. Researchers and professionals from industry are seeking practical approaches to extract useful knowledge to support decisions throughout process / system life cycle. Recent advances in semantic mining motivated researchers and industry in different system disciplines to adopt and apply semantic mining techniques for traditional and multimedia databases and knowledgebase systems. This chapter will discuss problems and solutions related to application of advanced semantic mining using formal representation of domain knowledge for process systems. The proposed approach can be divided into the following major stages:

- Model construction of process systems
- Knowledge structuring and representation of process models
- Construction of formal meta-language and language to represent domain knowledge and activities of process models
- Knowledge acquisition and validation (qualitative and quantitative)
- Semantic mining for decision support of process life cycle activities

The management of these stages requires robust modeling methodology, which facilitated the integration between nano, micro, and macro process levels. Each process level is abstracted using building blocks in three basic views: static, dynamic, and operation (Gabbar et al., 2001; 2003; 2004). In view of the proposed modeling and simulation methodology, control layer is used to support the design and operation of the underlying system as integrated with simulation environment. The proposed system engineering approach supports change management, HSE (health, safety, and environment), recycling, energy, and sustainability. Planning and scheduling are analyzed and managed for the different hierarchical levels i.e. nano, micro, and macro. For example, process of reconstruction of human cell functions includes MoFlo cell sorter systems.

Figure 1. Process engineering framework

OVERVIEW OF SEMANTIC MINING FOR PROCESS ENGINEERING

Almost all efforts made in semantic mining was directed towards discovering new knowledge or search for important knowledge within large number of data elements, databases, or knowledgebases in any form, e.g. html pages, multimedia, text, etc. Semantic mining is always associated with process where primitive data is collected, updated, and manipulated. Such process involves organizational and behavioral changes. For example, semantic mining for biological processes is associated with basic biological data, e.g., samples, and phenomena linked with such biological data such as cell separation, transformation, or demolishing. In order to effectively apply and benefit from knowledge obtained from semantic mining, it is essential to define clearly how the knowledge is created, maintained, and managed with respect to process model in terms of structure, behavior, and operation. The concept of process based semantic mining is the ultimate approach for successful semantic mining. In other words, the construction of database / knowledgebase is considered as part of the semantic mining where meta-data are constructed about domain knowledge that supports semantic mining process. There are several approaches that have been done in the area of semantic mining for process engineering. Among these approaches are those that have been directed towards operating procedures representation, synthesis, and verification.

Semantic Mining for Process Operation Design

To meet the ever-increasing market requirements, production and manufacturing plants are becoming more complex. The design of efficient operating procedures for complex production plants faces different challenges and tends to be impractical without providing clear, structured, and complete operating procedures for normal and abnormal operation. Providing structured and modular way to describe operating procedures will facilitate the operation design and management, will reduce operator errors, and will make it easier for operator to understand and follow operating procedures with less time and efforts.

Different attempts are made to structure operating procedures and provide automated solutions to design and synthesize operating procedures. ANSI/ISA-S88 is one the developed standards by ANSI, which proposed a structured way to define operating procedures for batch plants in hierarchical way (ANSI/ISA). It proposed mapping between plant structure hierarchy and operating procedures of batch plants. Many researchers have based their automated solutions of operating procedures synthesis on the framework described by ANSI/ISA-S88. However, the way operating procedures are represented varies from one approach to another. Viswanathan (1998), Johnsson (1998), and Arzen (1994) used Graphchart to represent operating procedures in graphical way. Such approach provides operator with friendly user interface to visualize operating procedures hierarchically. However it requires quite long preparation stage to define the different classes, objects, and definitions of operating procedures, so that they can be mapped to graph symbols. To overcome the limitations expressed by the graphical representations methods, formal methods are introduced. Gabbar (2003) proposed recipe formal definition language, or RFDL, to represent operating procedures in formal way as mapped to domain knowledge. In his solution, editor and parser are used to validate the syntax of operating procedures using set of predefined RFDL statements. The proposed method is used to design automated solution, called AOPS to synthesize master and control recipe of batch plants. However, there was major limitation in dealing with the semantics of the underlying plant operation due to the lack of robust integration with domain knowledge. In addition, the proposed approach requires further methods to validate the generated operating procedures.

To overcome these limitations and in order to provide general purpose operating procedure synthesis solutions for batch, continuous, as well as discrete production plants, this research work proposes an engineering formal language (called EFL), which is used to synthesize standard operating procedures (or SOP) in accurate and effective manner. To simplify complex operations, the concept of generic or meta-operation is introduced where operation libraries are defined as building blocks to define and represent SOP for complex plants, with less errors and time.

Operation engineering approach is proposed based on robust modeling methodology of the underlying plant process. Operation is structured and mapped to plant structure and generic definition of plant operation is proposed along with intelligent topology analysis methodology. Engineering formal language is proposed and used to represent standard operating procedures of different case studies from batch and oil & gas plants. Integrated automated solution for operation engineering is described to automate the synthesis of SOP and meta-operation, and to manage operation execution.

Plant operation is sets of instructions that are executed by operator and/or system to produce target products. Standard operating procedures are commonly used to describe plant operation with the required details to ensure quality, safety, steady, optimum and other life cycle factors while operating the plant.

Operation engineering is the process to manage SOP throughout its life cycle, which typically includes SOP design, validation, execution, and control. SOP design is a complex process that is usually done starting from the process design stage. In order to overcome such complexity, it is essential to structure operation according to the associated structure area. This requires hierarchical partitioning of the underlying plant structure (i.e. topology) and the definition of operation for each structure area in different hierarchical levels.

Operation: Structure Hierarchy

ANSI/ISA-S88 is one useful standard for chemical batch plants that proposed hierarchical definitions of plant structure and the associated operation hierarchy, as shown in figure 2.

Figure 2. ANSI/ISA-S88 structure (Modified by Gabbar 2004)

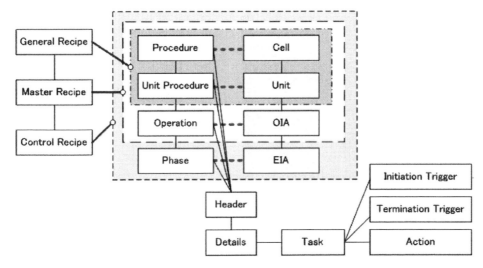

In figure 2, structure hierarchy is defined as cell, unit, OIA (or operation isolation area), and EIA (or equipment isolation area). OIA is defined as the topological area that is surrounded by flow control devices such as valves. EIA is defined as the topological area that includes the underlying process equipment (i.e. reactor), which is surrounded by flow control devices. Previously, the terms OIA and EIA were used in case of batch plants (Gabbar et al., 2004). However, in order to provide general solution that suits batch, continuous, and discrete manufacturing processes, the concepts of OIA and EIA are proposed.

MOFLO BIOLOGICAL PROCESS ENGINEERING

The recent advancement in biological and medical research mobilized biotechnology and biomedical manufacturers to provide advanced systems to automate different critical and functions in the biology and biomedical fields. One critical process is the separation of cells or biological elements, which is essential for many research experiments and biotechnology production. There are a variety of cell separation technologies, which are used by biological, clinical, pharmaceutical, and medical research labs. Among the latest of the cell sorting technologies is MoFlo, which is high-performance cell sorter used for precision analysis and sorting of cells, bacteria, chromosomes, macromolecular particles, and other similar sized particles. Most of the recent research is based primarily on the separation process, which provides the required biological elements to analyze, measure, reconstruct human body elements i.e. pancreas, liver, etc. The separation process is developed primarily using cell sorter technology. Currently, and for the coming few years, MoFlo machine, which is one type of Fluorescence Activated Cell Sorter, or FACS, is one of the latest and reliable cell sorter and biological particles separation system that is used widely in biological, medical, pharmaceutical research labs as well as in biotechnology industry. The operation of such system is relatively complex and costly, where it requires doing many experiments till achieving the required accurate cell sorting results. Each experiment is quite expensive where it might cost around US$100 for one experiment (i.e. one day). It takes quite long time, up to 6 months, till it can produce the required cell colony, which is the maximum grouping of the desired cells. In addition, the operation of MoFlo is associated with high risk where it contains some dangerous / hazardous operation scenarios. MoFlo manufacturers and makers are investigating system and bioengineering approaches

Figure 3. Modeling of typical MoFlo-based biological process

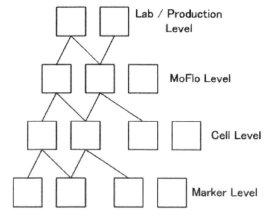

to improve the operation of such critical equipment and to assure cost and risk reduction of R&D and production systems of the underlying bio-process.

To support MoFlo makers as well as users, this research proposes knowledge-based system engineering approach, which is used to analyze MoFlo operation, and propose systematic way to design efficient operation with reduced operational cost and risks.

In the following section, proposed system engineering approach will be presented. In section three, MoFlo system model will be presented. In section four, the proposed operation model and engineering environment will be presented along with some hazardous operation scenarios and its analytical view.

Biological Research Process Hierarchy

MoFlo as part of the integrated biological research system includes different levels of interests: (a) nano level, which includes marker materials used to mark and separate cells; (b) micro level, which includes cells (around 50 micro meter); and (c) macro level, which includes components of the MoFlo system. The link between MoFlo machine and other machines and devices within the lab / production process is shown in the higher level of interest, which requires process engineering as well. Figure 3 shows the different levels of processing and control for MoFlo systems.

MoFlo Process Model Formalization

Lifecycle engineering is based on robust modeling methodology, which enables the construction of process design model in different hierarchical levels and link them together while designing the operation of MoFlo system with the considerations of lifecycle assessment of different factors such as health, safety, energy, cost, maintenance, etc. Model building blocks are used to construct model of complex processes / systems, where object-oriented modeling concepts i.e. inheritance, polymorphism, encapsulation are used to systematically construct process models. The proposed modeling methodology (called POOM or plant/process object-oriented modeling) enabled the design of the MoFlo operation and the whole process where operation model elements are defined in each building block, while operation knowledge are associated and accumulated during the design stage. Control layer includes control elements that ensure safe, steady, and optimized operation. This can be modeled as control rules and logic associated with the different building blocks of process model of the underlying MoFlo process.

Figure 4 shows the proposed iterative modeling mechanism, which is used to construct the underlying MoFlo process model. It starts with design of model elements: static, i.e. structure; dynamic, i.e. behavior; and operation, i.e. methods / recipe. Using these design model elements, and in view of the target functions, operation is designed in terms of methods and recipe (i.e. operation steps) for the different operation scenarios. Each operation scenario is simulated and evaluated in view of the required performance indicators such as cost, accuracy, time, etc. In view of the simulated results, tuning can be made to design model elements, operation model elements, and/or operation scenarios.

Figure 5 shows the links between the three different views of equipment (i.e. MoFlo), product (i.e. sorted cells), and process (i.e. human reconstruction) models. The integration among these models with business and system models is essential for lifecycle assessment and high performance MoFlo operation.

Figure 4. Based process modeling

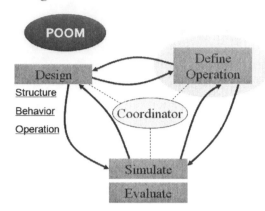

Figure 5. System engineering approach

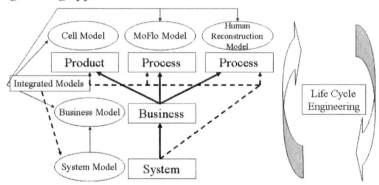

MoFlo Cytomation System

MoFlo is high precision, high performance, and modular Fluorescence Activated Cell Sorter, FACS, system used for research and clinical purposes to sort or separate cells, bacteria, and/or other macro-molecular particles. Using MoFlo Cell Sorter, multiple parameters can be analyzed for heterogeneous samples, which can be sorted in four separate collecting tubes at speed approaching 70,000 events per second. It can analyze up to 16 parameters for each particle, while with the newest technology of MoFlo DSP it can analyze up to 32 parameters.

MoFlo System Components

Figure 6 shows the system components of MoFlo system, which has around 27 components.

The MoFlo system is composed of three major components: Summit Workstation, Electronic Console, and Optical Bench. Figure 6 shows the basic elements of each component in hierarchical manner, reflecting the function decomposition.

Figure 6. MoFlo system architecture

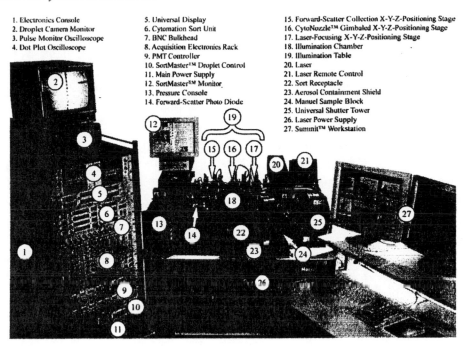

Figure 7. MoFlo function modeling

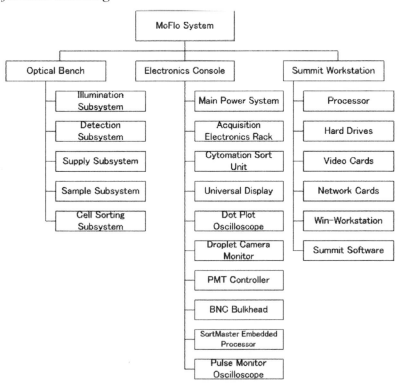

MoFlo System Modeling

The proposed modeling methodology is used to model MoFlo in three views: static, dynamic, and operation. SU or structure unit is used to model each structural element such as component, subassembly, or subsystem. The connection among the different SU's is defined as a port. Ports are information port, control port, sensor port, material port, or energy port. Each port could be input, output, or input/output. The different behaviors are defined for each SU so that control layer can select the most advantageous behavior to achieve the target operation. This can be determined in view of state variables, which include goal variables, control variables, disturbance variables, and other state variables that represent the behavior of each component. Operation recipe and instructions are synthesized / defined within each SU where they are defined with the use of simulation to ensure the limits of the values of each process variable. Details about the proposed POOM modeling methodology are explained by Gabbar (2001; 2002; 2004). Computer-aided modeling environment (called CAPE-ModE) on the basis of POOM has been proposed and developed by Gabbar (2004).

Figure 8 shows example structure model of MoFlo where three SU's are defined for one main SU "Optical Bench". Ports are defined as a connection between these SU's. Ports transfer energy such as electricity, process variable information such as sensor port, etc.

Each of the three SU components, defined in figure 8, has set of state variables i.e. process variables and set of behaviors as well as operating procedures. In addition, control rules / constraints and logic are defined within each SU and its detailed structural elements so that they can execute the defined operating procedures. The proposed control layer will be enable the resolution of conflicts among control rules and logic in the same hierarchical level and coordinate with upper and lower hierarchies.

KNOWLEDGE-BASED PROCESS MODELING APPROACH

One of the major difficulties that face lifecycle engineering is the definition of flexible structure to support the acquisition and management of lifecycle data and knowledge. This problem is more difficult when addressing engineering systems where business and engineering data are required to be linked and maintained in systematic way to support lifecycle activities. It is widely known that the key success factor to engineering enterprises is the robust data and knowledge modeling and management, which satisfy life cycle activities requirements. Standards, such as STEP, provided unified structure to manage engineering data, however, the realization of such approach requires more efforts to be unified and practically implemented. ANSI/ISA S95 provided better model and practice which can effectively be

Figure 8. POOM-based hierarchical structure unit model

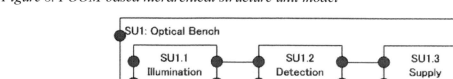

used to manage life cycle data with respect to product / process design. The proposed data and knowledge modeling approach is based on defining knowledge structure hierarchy based on domain ontology, which is used to define data elements within each building block class. This enabled linking domain knowledge with the different model elements in all hierarchical levels. For example, cell class will be associated with attributes such as type, category, status, etc. While marker class will be associated with attributes such as function, maker, limitation, working condition, etc. These classes will be linked to domain knowledge where cell types and sorting criteria will be defined.

In higher levels, MoFlo system can be linked to functions related to human cell reconstruction process where separated cells are linked to the requirements initiated from regenerative medicine or reconstruction of human cells. This requires integrated computer-aided modeling environment that facilitates the integration between domain knowledge and model elements in different hierarchies.

Based on the proposed modeling framework for MoFlo system, operation engineering approach is presented on the basis of formal methods. In the following section, formal methods are explained.

ENGINEERING FORMAL LANGUAGE (EFL)

Formal Methods Overview

The proposed system approach is based on proposed formal method to represent process design model and define operation in systematic and formal manner that enable the automatic design and synthesis of the operation of such complex and critical equipment.

Formal Methods

What is formal method? Fischer (1998) stated that formal methods are used to specify processes and systems, such as formal description techniques (FDT's) such as Estelle and SDL. Astesiano (2002) stated that formal method could be used to support activities in the development process, such as: support & validate engineering requirements and process design specifications; validate intermediate specifications against initial and final specification; provide smooth code generation with the validation against design/intermediate specifications; check the quality of some specification/code; reuse (replay) a part of the development process (single activity) by changing something in the inputs (scenario evaluation); and produce a new version of the already developed end-product (maintenance). In addition, formal methods can be used to design and validate the operation of the underlying system, especially for complex systems. This has been shown in different applications such as the use of formal methods to synthesis operating procedures of chemical plants (Gabbar, 2004).

Wide and narrow definitions of formal methods can be found in the literature. For example, Nancy Leveson states: A broad view of formal methods includes all applications of (primarily) discrete mathematics to software engineering problems. This application usually involves modeling and analysis where the models and analysis procedures are derived from or defined by an underlying mathematically- precise foundation.

The gaps between users' intentions and formal specifications and between physical implementations and abstract proofs create inherent limitations to formal methods, no matter how much they may be developed in the future.

Benefits of Using Formal Methods to Engineering Design & Operation

These are some reported benefits of using formal methods in engineering design & operation:

- Formal methods are directly applicable during the requirements, design, construction, and operation of engineering systems.
- Formal methods provide means for validation, verification, and the application of design rationales.
- Formal methods enable the management of change throughout the different stages of engineering and system lifecycle.
- Formal methods can be used as the base to develop robust software engineering solutions for engineering applications.
- Formal methods are entwined with lifecycle models that may provide an alternative to the Waterfall model, namely rapid prototyping, the Cleanroom variant on the spiral model, and "transformational" paradigms.
- Formal methods support precise and rigorous specifications of those aspects of a computer system capable of being expressed in the language. Since defining what a system should do, and understanding the implications of these decisions, are the most troublesome problems in software engineering, this use of formal methods has major benefits. In fact, practitioners of formal methods frequently use formal methods solely for recording precise specifications, not for formal verifications (Hall, 2001).

Formal Methods Examples

Some of the most well known formal methods consist of or include specification languages for recording a system's functionality. These methods include:

- Z (pronounced "Zed")
- Communicating Sequential Processes (CSP)
- Vienna Development Method (VDM)
- Larch
- Formal Development Methodology (FDM)

Formal methods can include graphical languages. Data Flow Diagrams (DFD's) are the most well known graphical technique for specifying the function of a system. DFD's can be considered a semi-formal method, and researchers have explored techniques for treating DFD's in a completely formal manner. Petri nets provide another well-known graphical technique, often used in distributed systems (Peterson, 1977). Petri nets are a fully formal technique. Finally, finite state machines are often presented in tabular form. This does not decrease the formalism in the use of finite state machines. So the definition of formal methods provided earlier is quite encompassing.

Limitations of Formal Methods

Given the applicability of formal methods throughout the lifecycle, and their pervasive possibilities for almost all areas of software and systems engineering, why are they not more widely visible? Part of the problem is educational. Revolutions are not made by conversion, but by the old guard passing away. More recent university graduates tend to be more willing to experiment with formal methods.

On the other hand, the only barrier to the widespread transition of this technology is not lack of knowledge on the part of practitioners. Formal methods do suffer from certain limitations. Some of these limitations are inherent and will never be overcome. Other restrictions, with research and practice, will be removed as formal methods are transitioned into wider use.

Empirical evidence does suggest, however, that formal methods can make a contribution to the problem of adequately capturing requirements. The discipline of producing a formal specification can result in fewer specification errors. Furthermore, implementers without an exceptional designer's knowledge of the application area commit fewer errors when implementing a formal specification than when relying on hazy knowledge of the application (Goel, 1991). These benefits may exist even when the final specification is expressed in English, not a formal language (Meyer, 1985). A specification acts as a "contract" between a user and a developer. The specification describes the system to be delivered. Using specifications written in a formal language to complement natural language descriptions can make this contract more precise. Finally, developers of automated programming environments, which use formal methods, have developed tools to interactively capture a user's informal understanding and thereby develop a formal specification (Zeroual, 1991).

Still, formal methods can never replace deep application knowledge on the part of the requirements engineer, whether at the system or the software level. The application knowledge of the exceptional designer is not limited to one discipline. For example, an avionics application might require knowledge of flight control, navigation, signal processing, and electronic countermeasures. Whether those drawing on interdisciplinary knowledge in developing specifications come to regard formal methods as just another discipline making their life more complicated, or an approach that allows them to simply, concisely, and accurately record their findings, will only be known with experience and experimentation.

From the above detailed explanations about formal methods, it has been proved that formal methods-based approach is the best choice to design and represent operation of complex systems such as MoFlo. The following section will highlight the proposed human-centered operation engineering approach and how formal methods can be used effectively to design the operation of MoFlo.

Engineering Formal Language

Formal representation provides a systematic framework to construct and validate the syntax of the underling system towards building standard representation approaches. Formal languages are used in most of the engineering applications to reduce the time and efforts required to communicate and manage the underling system or process. Formal language implies absolutely accurate and precise definitions of the underling system, which can be used to validate the system / process and can be used as a base for computer-aided solutions. One can say that the use of formal languages will help overcoming major engineering problems.

Operating procedures, as one element in engineering applications, is used to describe plant operation, e.g. operation of chemical batch plants. For efficient operating procedures synthesis, a structured way is required to represent the syntax and semantics of operating procedures as mapped to domain knowledge.

The construction of domain knowledge can be systemized if a robust model formalization methodology is used. Many researchers have investigated the construction of process and plant models, and proposed modeling methodologies to build the corresponding domain knowledge. Most of these modeling methodologies showed that plant model includes three views: structure, behavior, and operation (Gabbar et al., 2000; Lu et al., 1995, 1997). Utilization of formal representation of operating procedures facilitates the integration between operation, structure and behavior views, which will have a positive impact on the synthesis process of operating procedures. From the other side, formal representation will provide means to build and organize domain knowledge more efficiently.

Many researchers are motivated to use computer languages such as HTML, XML, or even build their own languages on the basis of these computer languages to describe their systems or processes. For example, world batch forum proposed the use of XML to represent batch recipe (WBF). However, it is essential to define engineering language in a higher layer, which can deal with the syntax and semantics of operating procedures as linked to plant model (structure and behavior), before addressing the implementation issues using computer languages such as XML, HTML, etc. It will be practical if two separate layers are defined to represent operating procedures. The higher layer will enable designers and engineers to define operating procedures in standard and formal way as mapped to the underling system, regardless of the implementation way. This will enable them to think freely without the limitations of any computer language. Based on the higher layer, the lower layer can be designed or selected for implementation. In general, the process of designing operating procedures requires flexible way to define and maintain the syntax and semantics of operating procedures as it involves different participants with different views. It is relatively easy to maintain the syntax of the defined higher layer language, as it doesn't involve modifications to any computer program. This can be transferred (i.e. translated) into computer language, which is relatively easy and can be implemented for any destination (i.e. host) computer language in the lower layer (e.g. HTML, XML, etc.).

As described by Carre (1989) and reported by Toyn (1998), formal language should be logically sound and unambiguous and the semantics must not be too complex, otherwise formal reasoning will become impractical. The proposed recipe formal language is based on the definition of simple and clear English-like statements, which are composed of keywords that are mapped to domain knowledge. The structure of the statements defines the syntax while the mapping to domain knowledge defines the semantics. The proposed recipe formal language fulfills the basic requirements of any formal language where hierarchical definitions are used to simplify the representation of complex procedures. For example, one can say: "material-movement is move material from area to area". This can be further explained as: "material is gas or liquid or solid fluid", while area could be "area is equipment or cell or unit"

As a conclusion, the use of formal representation will facilitate the definition of complex operation in structured way as mapped to domain knowledge. In addition, using formal language to represent operating procedures will facilitate the development of automated solutions to synthesis operating procedures.

Operation Engineering of MoFlo

As mentioned earlier, the operation of MoFlo system is quite complex and requires few months before being able to produce reliable results. This is due to complex operation and limited understanding of operators/users of MoFlo who are mainly biological or medical researchers / technicians, or industrial workers. In addition, the written operating procedures are relatively abstract and not well organized. Moreover, it requires many steps to be done manually, and many parameters to be defined and tuned, which requires good and enough training for MoFlo operators. In addition, it requires providing automation for the different manual operation tasks. This section describes the proposed human-centered operation design framework, which is used to cover the above mentioned limitation in current MoFlo operation.

MoFlo Operation Synthesis

Operation synthesis has mainly two sides, designer side, which goes from operation designer till it reaches computer format operating procedures, and the operation side, which links operation instructions from MoFlo to the user. Operation can be viewed as set of microinstructions that are stored within MoFlo, which will be triggered by button or condition. These microinstructions are stored within each subsystem individually as they can work independently. Operation design is usually made during the design stage where the condition of the MoFlo is simulated and the different state variables are calculated at each time step in view of the selected operation. The resulted sets of microinstructions are stored within each subsystem. This process is usually done through computer where microinstructions are synthesized and stored within computer, till final test, then transferred into machine either on chips or any sort of memory devices. During operation, these operation instructions are executed and resulted data are displayed to operator / user as a visual language, i.e. voice, light, number, test, image, etc.

Figure 9 shows proposed operation synthesis cycle, starting from operation designer, where operation is converted from natural language into formal language. Such formal language is translated into computer language, which is used to represent microinstructions. XML is proposed as a neutral language to represent operation instructions. The proposed operation synthesis framework provides an answer to the following major issues:

- Easy and understandable configuration of microinstructions with intelligent human interface
- User friendly design of visual language for easy human interactions
- Synthesis of microinstructions so that it can be mapped easily to understandable visual language

Figure 9. Operation design framework

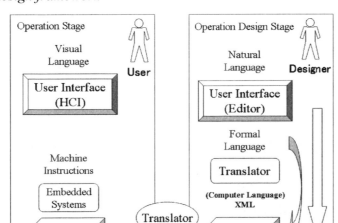

- Smooth mapping between operating procedures with microinstructions
- Considerations of malfunction and recovery operations and their conversion into microinstructions and visual language for safe operation

Proposed Approach Summary

The following are summary of the proposed operation synthesis approach:

- Synthesize microinstructions and map to visual language for intelligent human interface.
- Construct domain knowledge of biomedical equipment design & operation
- Design formal language (meta-language) to be used to synthesize microinstructions
- Develop editor and parser to capture the meta-language and to synthesize (generate) microinstructions for define operation as per the design spec of the medical equipment and functions (operation)
- Map microinstructions to visual language and propose intelligent human interface
- Define set of possible malfunctions and define recovery procedure, and synthesize the corresponding microinstructions and visualization.

Figure 10 shows the process flow for operation design and execution where designer creates and maintains design knowledge, which will be reflected into formal language in the computer system, then embedded instructions within MoFlo system. Operator will be maintaining operation knowledge, which is accumulated from the design stage.

Gabbar (2003) proposed useful formal representation called RFDL or recipe formal definition language, which was used for batch plants. Such solution enabled the systematic definition of batch recipe

Figure 10. Operation design execution system architecture

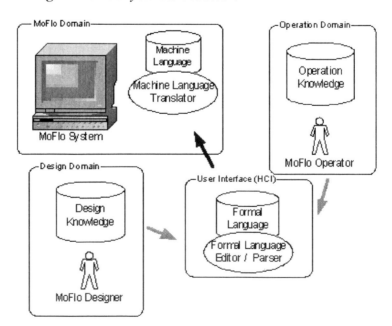

using keywords and predefined statements. However, RFDL was limited to batch plants and did not cover issues such as concurrent operation and logic handling for behavior generation and operation control decisions. In this research, and in order to overcome these limitations, engineering formal language, or EFL, is proposed to express engineering knowledge including vocabulary from domain knowledge and associated rules for control and process constraints. The proposed formal language is in the form of English-like statements. Each EFL statement is composed of keywords called tokens. The standard form of EFL statement is:

LHS-token :: token_1 token_2 .... token_n [S1]

Where LHS-token is the left hand side token that will be assigned to the sequence of tokens in the right hand side of "IS". Tokens are classified as shown in table 1. Among these token classifications is the "input" token: which is used to inform operation management system to acquire input from user, such as operating parameters. Another token type is "variable" token: which means that such token will be further defined using another EFL statement (i.e. in the left hand side). Another token type called "operator" is used to represent all operators for EFL statements such as "and". These operators are used by the EFL editor to understand and check the syntax of EFL statements, such as nested statements. Another token type called "lookup" is used to retrieve list of corresponding values from lookup table (i.e. in the database). Another token class is "constant", which is used as it is within EFL statements.

EFL statements are defined hierarchically. In other words, EFL statements are used as a meta-language to define SOP. The complete set of EFL statements should have at least one EFL statement for each variable token (i.e. variable token to appear in the left hand side of EFL statement). For example, operation actions are classified as: Operator-Action, System-Action, Procedure_Action, Material_Action, Topology_Action, External_Action, Control_Action, and Time_Action. Such operation action can be expressed as the following EFL statement [S2]:

Operation-Action :: Operator-Action | System-Action | Procedure_Action | Material_Action | Topology_Action | External_Action | Control_Action | Time_Action [S2]

Figure 11. Operation ontology structure

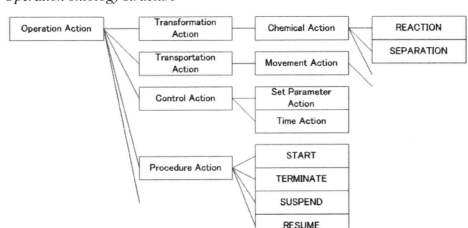

The above SOPFL statement can be further explored using other SOPFL statements. For example, procedure action can be expressed as per EFL statement S3 where "START", "TERMINATE", and "RESUME" constant tokens are used to express the primitive procedure action statement, while "procedure_id" is a lookup token, which is used to display all possible values of procedures defined within the system.

Procedure_Action :: (START | TERMINATE | SUSPEND | RESUME) procedure_id   [S3]

EFL statements (meta-language) and SOP statements are composed of vocabulary and rules. The vocabulary is described using ontology where concepts of the domain knowledge are classified. Figure 11 shows sample of the concepts classified using ontology. The developed ontology model is used as a base to construct EFL statements and to validate the semantics of operating procedures. Currently, base ontology model has been developed using ontology editor and converted into database repository, which is used by the proposed automated solution to design plant operation. Domain operation ontology can be used to construct EFL statements. For example, S2 can be constructed using parts of the ontology described in figure 3, where operation action can be classified as transportation action, control action, etc.

Similarly, master and control recipe statements can be defined on the basis of EFL where keywords are linked to domain knowledge such as plant design model, material, functions, products, recipe formula, etc. For example, master recipe statement (MOVE material1 FROM t1 TO t2) is derived from EFL statements S4 & S5.

Transportation_Action :: MOVE material FROM Topology_Area TO Topology_Area   [S4]

Topology_Area :: cell_id | unit_id | oid_id | ([class_function] [class_material] equip_class) | equipment_id   [S5]

Where material1 is selected from a lookup list of all materials defined within the domain knowledge of the used plant model. "FROM" and "TO" are constant keywords, while t1 and t2 are equipment id's, which are selected from lookup list of all equipments defined in the plant model.

The proposed EFL statements can be used within EFL-based editor to synthesize operating procedures with complete syntax and semantic validations. However, during the definition of SOP of complex plant, there are varieties of repeated operations that are used in different topological areas and for different functions. These repeated operations are defined independently, although they are almost the same. In addition, complex operation is usually composed of set of simpler operations, which are also repeated in different operations. The following section describes the concept of meta-operation, which is proposed to overcome such situation.

Mapping Operation Structure to MoFlo Structure Model

In order to design and synthesize MoFlo system operation, it is essential to define hierarchical structure model and to identify corresponding control levels, as shown in figure 2. Similar to ANSI/S88, which defined mapping between control levels (i.e. cell, unit, equipment) and operation levels (procedure, unit procedure, operation, and phase). In MoFlo, structure levels are defined as subsystem, unit, equipment, and component. The proposed operation hierarchy can be shown in figure 12.

Figure 12. Operation – Structure hierarchical mapping

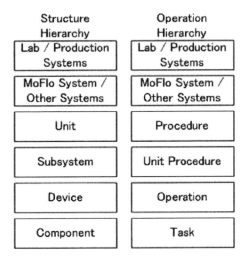

EFL for MoFlo

Keywords are extracted from domain knowledge and classified as per the meta-classes of the design knowledge. For example, set of keywords is extracted from the sample subsystem i.e. "Tilt Block", "Agitation", etc. Editor and parser are used to define the operation of the underlying MoFlo as follows:

Startup and Alignment

The following is the Ignite Laser startup operation:

1. Open cooling water valves (if applicable)
2. Turn key on laser power supply
3. Switch ON remote console to ignite laser
4. Allow laser to warm up and stabilize
5. Set laser to appropriate power and aperture
6. Record information in MoFlo System Log

The above operating procedures can be defined using formal language statement ML1.

OPEN <control-device>   [ML1]

In this example, <control-device> is a list of all possible control devices in the MoFlo system such as valves of (cooling-water, PMT Controller, Pulse Monitor Oscilloscope, etc.)
Similarly, control setting can be defined using ML2.

Set <device> to <setting-value>   [ML2]

In this statement, <device> is lookup token that is linked to a list of devices such as Laser.

Example Laser Alignment Operation

Single Laser Alignment operation can be viewed as:

1. Check switch setting on ADC and Dot Plot boards
2. Ensure stream is vertical using pinhole image and camera
3. Check laser beam for max diffraction & just below nozzle tip
4. Using appropriate calibration particles, establish an appropriate event rate. Coarsely align the instrument by placing the bead-flash over the image of the top pinhole
5. Visualize acquired data by selecting channels 1 vs 2 and 3 vs 4 on the dot plot oscilloscopes
6. Optimize fluorescence intensity, then optimize %CV
7. Optimize forward light scatter intensity, then %CV
8. Toggle the drop drive on and off while turning to verify the absence of any optical noise while drop drive is on
9. Repeat steps: 3 through 6, if necessary
10. If necessary, align dichroic mirrors in front of PMTs

Set of meta-language of SOPFL can be defined for all operating procedures, which will be reflected into the computer-aided engineering environment to synthesize and validate the operating procedures of the underlying MoFlo.

Figure 13. MoFlo Operation. (a) Fluorochrome-tagged cells or particles leave the CytoNozzle traveling single file in a charged stream. (b) A laser beam excites the fluorochromes, which fluoresce and emit photons at specific wavelengths. (c) Charged droplets, each containing one cell or particle, break away from the stream and pass between two charged plates. (d) The electric field created by the charged plate directs each cell or particle to a designated receptacle, e.g. – or +. The receptacle at center is waste i.e. unrecognized.

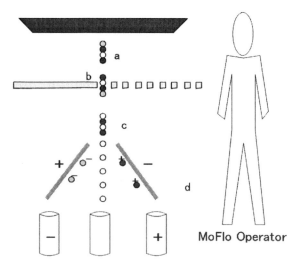

MoFlo Operator

Operation Reliability

Algorithm is proposed to measure the operation reliability in terms of purity, recovery, and yield. This will be the base to evaluate different operation scenarios to select the operation scenario with highest reliability factor. Sorting definitions are shown in Appendix 1.

Hazardous Operation Scenarios of MoFlo Cell Sorter

To avoid the scattering of the biological particles, which might be dangerous to operators and humans, a very high voltage of 3000 Volts, is used in the cylinder around the sample probe. This high voltage is controlled by switch and lamp. If, for any reason, the operator forgot the lamp and tries to touch the sample, it might cause death cases. This requires some design changes in the current system, to either switch off the high voltage once human hands or body is close, or by providing surrounding isolator to protect operator or humans.

Another hazardous situation might occur when the laser beam, which is used to excite the fluoro-chromes, hits the body or eyes of human. It causes harmful effect on human body. To avoid such cases, design changes might be recommended and/or operation regulations must be specified to restrict operators to avoid the direction of the laser beams while operation, as shown in Figure 13.

Operation engineering environment is proposed to design and ensure failsafe operation using the concept of formal methods, which links system design with microinstructions of the underlying MoFlo system.

Another example of safety requirements is in the illumination chamber. Illumination table houses the illumination chamber, which contains risk on operator and environment. System design and operation design are required.

Figure 14. Modeling framework of multimedia objects

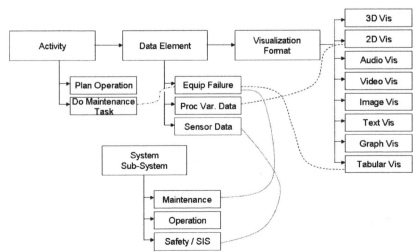

MULTIMEDIA MODELING AND VISUALIZATION

Figure 14 shows the mappings between activities within the operational systems and the associated data elements. Data elements include operational data, maintenance data, etc. Operational data elements include SOP (or standard operating procedures), sensor, alarm, simulation data, etc. These data elements can be visualized in different formats based on predefined preferences such as textual format, 2D, 3D, etc. For example, SIS or safety instrumented system is linked with data elements such as sensor data which can be visualized in 2D or 3D.

PROPOSED SYSTEM DESIGN

Computer-Aided Operation Engineering Environment

Computer-aided operation engineering environment CAPE-ModE (Gabbar et al., 2002) is proposed to capture MoFlo system model and associate data and knowledge elements related to: structure, function, behavior, and operation model elements.

Figure 15 shows the system topology and function modeling editor within the proposed computer-aided engineering environment. User menus are developed to enable the designer, engineer, and operator to analyze the different lifecycle views for the underlying MoFlo.

Figure 15. MoFlo process design within computer-aided process engineering environment

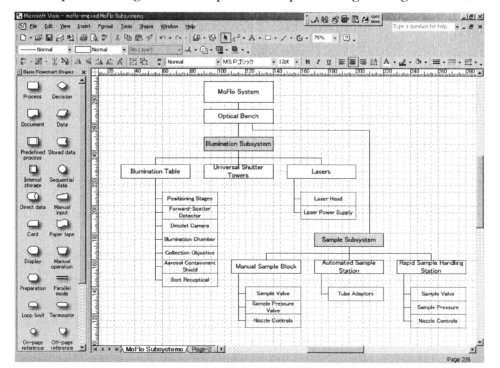

Operator Interface System

Operator interface can be first modeled using task-activity-data-system relationship, as shown in figure 16. In such approach, different operator activities are defined and modeled using basic activity model symbols. For each activity, set of tasks are defined in more details along with the associated data elements and linked systems. There are several systems that usually used by operator. For example, ERP or enterprise resource planning is used for resource planning and management such as human resources, tools, etc. CAD is computer-aided design which is usually used by engineers. MOC or management of changes is a system used to trace and manage the required authorization for different changes during plant operation. CAPE-SAFE is an integrated enterprise safety management system (Gabbar, 2001), which is proposed to manage safety activities throughout plant life cycle.

The proposed modeling approach will enable understanding different activities and map to the different automated systems that appear within operator interface. For example, operator activities can be defined for cases where fault or abnormal situation is detected. In such cases, operator validates sensor data, simulation data, operation history, and use incident / accident data to confirm possible root causes and consequences. FDS or fault diagnostic system was proposed by Gabbar (2006) to do such task and provide list of possible fault propagation scenarios. For each activity, list of tasks are identified and related information elements are listed along with the reference systems that owns / maintains such information elements. For example, sensor data can be detected from DCS system. Providing such list will enable the reengineering of operator interface systems. Also it will enable the engineering of virtual plant environment with suitable visualization and interaction mechanisms, such as 2D / 3D diagrams, voice, animation, textual, video, images, etc.

Figure 16. Proposed interface system modeling

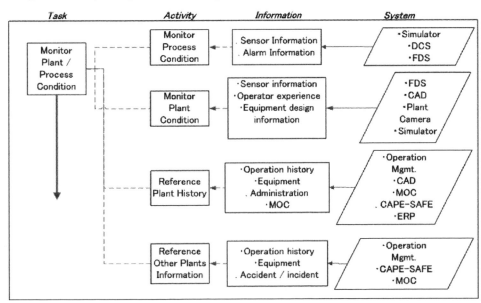

Modeling Human Factors

One critical factor to the design of virtual plant is the analysis of human factors that are related to the different activities of plant operation (Dyke, 1988; Nachreiner, 2006). The proper analysis of human factors will ensure practical design of virtual plant environment. The proposed approach is based on considering list of human factors that affect each operation activity, as shown in the activity-task-information model in figure 3. Such approach will enable building complete repository of all related human factors that affect the different activities of plant operation. For example, operation tasks that require visualization and interaction mechanisms should be supported with suitable virtual plant elements that reduce human errors related to failure to recognize, failure to percept, or failure to interact. List of human factors are gathered from literature, industrial reports, and previous research work and classified and linked with operation tasks and activities, as shown in table 1 (Nishiyama, 2006; Naval Safety Center, n.d.; Sasou, n.d.). Such classification can be evaluated qualitatively and quantitatively, which will support the selection of different design features of the target virtual plant. Detailed quantitative human performance analysis is described in several references (Khan, 2006).

Based on human factor analysis, essential design features of the target virtual plant are identified so that it can reduce risks and ensure process safety. The different human errors are mapped to operator activities, data elements, and visualization format, as shown in figure 17. Human factors are used to define and select data visualization, which is essential to design any user interface (Hall, 2001). In addition to

Table 1. Human factor classifications

Human Errors with Alarms / Equipment / Simulator / Interface Systems:
A: Failure to read / cognize data / messages / measures
B: Failure to take right decision / link information from different windows
C: Wrong response to emergency
D: Improper procedure executed
E: Physical stress of using mouse / keyboard / eye movement, i.e. switch among different windows
F: Loss of situation awareness
G: Failure to backup data
H: Failure to conduct an adequate brief
I: Inadequate supervision errors, inappropriate or absent supervision
J: Failure to track performance measures
K: Inadequate documentation from different systems / windows

Figure 17. Knowledge structure of human-based interface systems

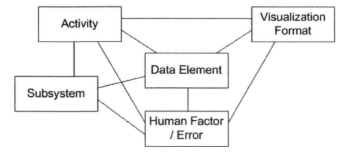

the visualization of operator activities, operator awareness and intention can also be considered (Feibush, 2000; Overbye, 1997). For example, to overcome the human error of "failure to read" during recovery operation a suitable visualization format can be selected such as sound/image. Similarly, when failure to read is associated with upper pressure limit, sound or bell should be used to ensure safe operation.

Based on the described virtual plant modeling approach, the following section describes the proposed integrated operator interface, which includes human factors and process requirements, with the ultimate goal of enabling operator to comprehend plant and process conditions in real time basis.

CONCLUSION

Semantic mining is the current and future approach to achieve intelligent systems. During the last era several techniques are proposed to structure domain knowledge using ontological engineering methods and practices. The logical next step is to seek advanced techniques to learn from such constructed knowledge via data mining. One more advanced step is to extract meta-knowledge via semantic mining where it is essential to construct intermediate level of meta-knowledge that is used to facilitate the learning practices. On the other hand, process engineering has been tightly linked with semantic mining in two aspects: (1) the analysis, design, and implementation of semantic mining support systems are best designed by considering the analysis of semantic mining process and constructing corresponding process models; (2) semantic mining is used to support process engineering for different applications, such as chemical, petrochemical, biological, social, and service processes. This chapter explained techniques and methods to deal with both tracks with examples from biological process using MoFlo cell sorter advanced equipment. The selection of cell sorter as a case study is critical which was motivated by the fact that biological data are in large numbers and lack of adequate meanings to basic data elements. This requires construction of meta-data and meta-rules about basic data elements which facilitate the semantic mining process. The proposed POOM or process object-oriented modeling methodology offers comprehensive yet simple way to construct detailed process models while structuring domain knowledge in systematic way that facilitates decision making related to life cycle activities. In order to realize practical computer-aided process engineering environment it is essential to formally define meta-language and language (called engineering formal language or EFL) that adequately describe process models and activities. In addition, meta-rules and rules are constructed to completely describe the underlying process models. Parser and editors are developed in view of EFL and rules / meta-rules to facilitate the semantic mining of the underlying process. The proposed semantic mining framework can be applied to processes from different disciplines to manage and support life cycle activities.

ACKNOWLEDGMENT

This work is implemented with the support of University of Toronto (Canada) and Okayama University (Japan).

REFERENCES

ANSI/ISA-TR84.00.02, Part 1 Safety Instrumented Functions (SIF).

ANSI/ISA-S88.01, 1995. Batch Control. Part 1. Models and terminology.

Arzen, K.E. (1994). Grafcet for intelligent supervisory control applications. *Automatica, 30*(10), 1513-1525.

Astesiano, E. & Reggio, G. (2000). Formalism and method. *Theoretical Computer Science, 236*, 3-34.

Chadha, H.S., Baugh Jr, J.W. & Wing, J.M. (1999). Formal specifications of concurrent systems. *Advances in Engineering Software, 30*, 211-224.

Dyke, F.H. (1988). The human dynamics of operator interfaces. *IEEE Conference Record of 1988 Fortieth Annual Conference of Electrical Engineering Problems in the Rubber and Plastics Industries* (pp. 36-39).

Eason, G., Noble, B., & Sneddon, I. N. (1955). On certain integrals of Lipschitz-Hankel type involving products of Bessel functions. *Phil. Trans. Roy. Soc.,* A247, 529-551.

Falla, M. (n.d.) Results and Achievements from the DTI/EPSRC R&D Programme in Safety Critical Systems.

Feibush, E., Gagvani, N., & Williams, D. (2000). Visualization for situational awareness. *IEEE Computer Graphics and Applications, 20*(5), 38- 45.

Gabbar, H.A. (2005). FDS: Fault Diagnostic System, Technical Notes, Okayama University. Retrieved from, http://syslab2.mech.okayama-u.ac.jp/staff/gabbar/fds.html.

Gabbar, H.A. (2006). *Design of Integrated Fault Diagnosis System (FDS)*. Paper presented at International Conference of IEEE SMC, Taiwan.

Gabbar, H.A., Aoyama, A., & Naka, Y. (2004a). Model-Based Computer-Aided Design Environment for Operational Design. *Journal of Computers & Industrial Engineering, 46*(3), 413-430.

Gabbar, H.A., Aoyama, A., & Naka, Y. (2004b). Recipe Formal Definition Language For Operating Procedures Synthesis. *Journal of Computers & Chemical Engineering, 28*(9), 1809-1822.

Gabbar, H.A., Chung, P.W.H., Suzuki, K., & Shimada, Y. (2000). Utilization of unified modeling language (UML) to represent the artifacts of the plant design model. In *Proceedings of "PSE Asia 2000" International Symposium on Design, Operation and Control of Next Generation Chemical Plants, PS5* (pp. 387-392). Kyoto-Japan.

Gabbar, H.A. & Naka, Y. (2003, August). *Computer-Aided Operation Design Environment for Chemical Production Plants*. Paper presented at ICCTA'2003 – IEEE, 12th International Conference on Computer Theory and Applications, Alexandria, Egypt.

Gabbar, H.A., Shimada, Y. & Suzuki, K. (2002). Computer-Aided Plant Enterprise Modeling Environment (CAPE-ModE) – Design Initiatives. *Computers in Industry, 47*(1), 25-37.

Gabbar, H.A., Yamashita, H., & Suzuki, K. (2006). Integrated Plant Maintenance Management Using Enhanced RCM Mechanism. *International Journal of Performability Engineering, 2*(4), 369-381.

Hall, S.K., Cockerham, K.J., & Rhodes, D.J. (2001). Applying human factors in graphical operator interfaces. In *2001 Conference Record of Pulp and Paper Industry Technical Conference* (pp. 241-246).

Huang, H.M.. (1996). Operator interface and situation perception in hierarchical intelligent control: a case study. In *Proceedings of the 1996 IEEE International Symposium on Intelligent Control* (pp. 68-73).

Human Factor Analysis and Classification System Presentation Preview. Naval Safety Center. Retrieved from, http://www.safetycenter.navy.mil/PRESENTATIONS/aviation/hfacs.htm

IEC 61508. Proposed framework for addressing human factors in IEC 61508.

Jamieson, G.A. & K.J. Vicente (2005). Designing effective human-automation-plant interfaces: A control-theoretic perspective. *Human Factors, 47*, 12-34.

Johnsson, C. & Arzen, K.E. (1998). Grafchart for recipe based batch control. *Computers & Chemical Engineering, 22*, 1811-1228

Khan, F.I., Amyotte, P.R., & DiMattia. D.G. HEPI: A new tool for human error probability calculation for offshore operation. *Safety Science, 44*(4), 313-334.

Kirkwood, R.L., Locke, M.H., & Douglas, J.M. (1988). A prototype expert system for synthesizing chemical process flowsheets. *Computers & Chemical Engineering, 12*(4), 329-343.

Lakshmanan, R. & Stephanopoulos, G. (1990). Synthesis of operating procedures for complete chemical plants – I Hierarchical, structured modelling for nonlinear. *Computers & Chemical Engineering, 14*(3), 301-317.

Meliopoulos, A.P.S., Cokkinides, G., Beker, B., & Dougal, R. (2000). A new tool for visualization and animation of power component and system operation System Sciences. In *Proceedings of the 33rd Annual Hawaii International Conference on System Sciences* (pp. 4022).

Nachreiner, F. Nickel, P., & Meyer, I. (2006). Human factors in process control systems: The design of human–machine interfaces. *Safety Science, 44*(1), 5-26.

Nishitani, H., Kawamura, T., & Suzuki, G. (2000). University-industry cooperative study on plant operations. *Computers and Chemical Engineering, 24*, 557-567.

Nishiyama, K. (2005). *Development of human factor analysis system for human errors prevention.* Unpublished Master Thesis, Okayama University, Japan.

Overbye, T.J., Gross, G., Laufenberg, M.J., & Sauer, P.W. Visualizing power system operations in an open market. Computer Applications in Power, *10*(1), 53-58.

Rao, M., Sun, X, & Feng, J. (2000). Intelligent system architecture for process operation support. *Expert Systems with Applications, 19*, 279-288.

Sasou, K. Human factor analysis on criticality accident, Human Factors Research Center, CRIEPI, Japan.

APPENDIX (1)

These are the detailed equations of calculating performance parameters of MoFlo systems.

$$\text{Purity (\%)} = \frac{Number - of - particles - of - \text{int} erest - in - sorted - sample}{Total - number - of - particles - in - sorted - sample}$$

Recovery (%) =

$$\frac{Number - of - particles - of - \text{int} erest - in - sorted - sample}{Number - of - particles - of - \text{int} erest - sorted - as - indicated - on - sort - counter}$$

$$\text{Yield (\%)} = \frac{Number - of - particles - of - \text{int} erest - in - sorted - sample}{Number - of - particles - of - \text{int} erest - in - original - sample}$$

Chapter XI
Intuitive Image Database Navigation by Hue–Sphere Browsing

Gerald Schaefer
Aston University, UK

Simon Ruszala
Teleca, UK

ABSTRACT

Efficient and effective techniques for managing and browsing large image databases are increasingly sought after. This chapter presents a simple yet efficient and effective approach to navigating image datasets. Based on the concept of a globe as visualisation and navigation medium, thumbnails are projected onto the surface of a sphere based on their colour. Navigation is performed by rotating and tilting the globe as well as zooming into an area of interest. Experiments based on a medium size image database demonstrate the usefulness of the presented approach.

INTRODUCTION

Efficient and effective ways for managing and browsing large image databases are increasingly sought after. This is due to the sheer explosion of availability of digital images in the last few years. Nowadays, the sizes of home user's image collections are already typically in the 1,000s while professional image providers overlook databases in excess of 1,000,000 images. Common tools display images in a 1-dimensional linear format where only a limited number of thumbnail images are visible on screen at any one time, thus requiring the user to search back and forth through thumbnail pages to view all images and locate the relevant ones. Obviously, this constitutes a time consuming, impractical and exhaustive way of searching for images, especially in larger catalogues. Furthermore, the order in which the pictures are displayed is based on attributes like file names and does not reflect the actual image contents and hence cannot be used to speed up the search.

Recently, several approaches have been introduced which provide a more intuitive interface to browsing and navigating through image collections (Ruszala & Schaefer, 2004). The basic idea behind most of these is to place images which are visually similar, as established through the calculation of image similarity metrics based on features derived from image content, also close to each other on the visualisation screen, a principle that has been shown to decrease the time it takes to localise images of interest (Rodden et al., 1999). One of the first approaches was the application of multidimensional scaling (MDS) (Kruskal & Wish, 1978) used to project images being represented by high dimensional feature vectors to a 2-dimensional visualisation plane (Rubner, Guibas, & Tomasi, 1997). In the PicSOM system (Laaksonen et al., 2000) tree-structured self organising maps are employed to provide both image browsing and retrieval capabilities. In (Krishnamachari & Abdel-Mottaleb, 1999) a hierarchical tree is employed to cluster images of similar concepts while the application of virtual reality ideas and equipment to provide the user with an interactive browsing experience was introduced in (Nakazato & Huang, 2001).

In this chapter we present a simple and fast approach to image database navigation. All images are projected onto a spherical globe; navigation through the image collection is performed by rotation of the sphere and zooming in and out (Schaefer & Ruszala, 2005). The use of a spherical object is not a coincidence, rather it stems directly from the type of features that are used for navigation. We utilise the median hue and median brightness (in HSV colour space) to calculate a pair of co-ordinates for each image in the database. As hue describes a circular quantity ($0°=360°$) whereas brightness is not, a sphere is a natural choice of geometrical body to encapsulate the combination of these two. The proposed method hence provides an effective, intuitive and efficient interface for image database navigation as is demonstrated on a medium sized image collection (Schaefer & Stich, 2004).

RELATED WORK

Several approaches which provide a more intuitive interface for image database navigation, compared to the traditional linear display of thumbnails, have been recently introduced in the literature. Rubner *et al.* were among the first (Rubner, Guibas, & Tomasi, 1997) and suggested the application of multidimensional scaling (MDS) (Kruskal & Wish, 1978) to calculate the locations of images and displaying them in a global 2-dimensional view on a single screen. Using this method, all images in a database are (initially) shown simultaneously; their locations are dependent on their visual similarity (based on features such as colour, texture or shape descriptors) compared to all other images features in the database. If two images are very similar in content they will also be located close to each other on the screen and vice versa. The user can browse the database easily from a top-down hierarchical point of view in an intuitive way.

The main disadvantage of the MDS approach is its computational complexity. First a full distance matrix for the complete database, i.e. all pairwise distances between any two images in the collection, needs to be calculated. MDS itself is then an iterative process which successively re-arranges the locations of each image minimising the distances between images on screen and their actual (feature-based) database distances. Interactive visualisation of a large number of images is hence difficult if not impossible to achieve. Furthermore, adding images to the database requires re-computation of (part of) the distance matrix and re-running MDS.

A computationally more attractive approach was presented by Krishnamachari and Abdel-Mottaleb (1999). They employed a hierarchical structure derived through a clustering process to access the images in a database. The user can navigate the images by traversing the tree structure. Unfortunately the user experience is limited by the fact that it is not possible to gain an overview of the whole database as for example MDS provides. In addition, at any particular level of the tree the child nodes are just displayed in a linear fashion without taking into account their relative similarities.

In (Laaksonen et al., 2000) the authors employ self organising maps (SOMs) for establishing image similarity. A hierarchical version of SOM, namely a tree structured self organising map is used both for retrieval and for visualisation purposes where the map itself can be navigated.

3D MARS (Nakazato & Huang, 2001) represents a virtual reality approach to image database navigation. Images are displayed on four walls in an immersive CAVE environment where browsing the database is done using a special wand to select images and make queries. While being an interesting novel idea it requires specialist equipment not available to the average user wanting to explore their personal collections. Although there exists also a desktop version called ImageGrouper which can be used with ordinary CRT displays, using this program is fairly difficult as there is no option for global browsing; only searching for an image first and then browsing from that location in the database is possible.

IMAGE DATABASE VISUALISATION ON A HUE-SPHERE

Our aim is to provide a simple yet effective interface for image database visualisation and navigation. It should allow fast and intuitive browsing of large image collections and not rely on any specialised equipment not available to the average user.

We separate our approach into two tasks: selection of suitable features and visualisation of the image collection. Among typical features used for image retrieval those describing the colour content are certainly the most popular ones (Smeulders et al., 2000). We follow this and describe each image by its median colour. However, rather than employing the standard RGB colour space we use the HSV space (Sangwine & Horne, 1998). Of this we take only the hue and value attributes as the saturation descriptor is deemed less important for describing image content. Value, which describes the brightness of a colour is defined in HSV as (Sangwine & Horne, 1998)

$$V = \frac{R+G+B}{3}$$

(1)

where *R*, *G*, and *B* are red, green and blue pixel values. *V* ranges between 0 and 1 where 0 corresponds to pure black and 1 to pure white. Hue "*is the attribute of a visual sensation according to which an area appears to be similar to one of the perceived colours, red, yellow, green and blue, or a combination of two of them*" (CIE, 1989) and is the attribute that is usually associated as 'colour'. Hue in HSV is defined as (Sangwine & Horne, 1998)

$$H = \cos^{-1} \frac{0.5\left[(R-G)+(R-B)\right]}{\sqrt{(R-G)(R-G)+(R-B)(G-B)}} \tag{2}$$

It is apparent that hue constitutes an angular attribute; H goes from red to yellow to green to blue back to red and is also often referred to as hue circle.

We now want to find a geometrical body that can be used to derive a co-ordinate system for placing thumbnails of the images contained in a database as well as to serve as the actual surface onto which those thumbnails are projected. Looking at the two attributes we have selected, H and V, we almost naturally end up with the body of a sphere, or a spherical globe. The hue circle describes one dimension of the sphere. As all colours with high V values are similar i.e. close to white and the same holds true for those colours with low V which become similarly close to black, and as black and white by definition don't have a hue quality, the two points $V=0$ and $V=1$ describe the poles of the globe.

The use of a globe not only comes naturally with the choice of features, it also has other clear advantages. The concept of a globe will almost certainly be familiar to the average user as it is a direct analogy of the earth globe. It therefore provides a very intuitive interface to the user who will have experience on how to navigate and find something on its surface. Furthermore it allows us to employ a familiar co-ordinate system based on latitude and longitude. Longitude describes the circumference of the globe (i.e. the east-west co-ordinate) and lies in the interval $[0°;360°]$. Latitude describes the north-south direction from pole to pole and ranges from $-90°$ at the south pole to $+90°$ at the north pole. Clearly each point on the surface of the globe can be uniquely described by a pair of longitude/latitude co-ordinates.

Our approach to visualising image databases is simple and straightforward. It also provides a very fast method for accessing the image collection. Images are transformed to an HSV representation and the median hue and value attributes are calculated. We make use of the median rather than the mean in order to provide some robustness with regards to the image background. Also, we actually calculate the median R, G, and B values and transform those to HSV which is computationally more efficient and results only in a slight deviation in terms of accuracy. From these the co-ordinates on the globe are then determined (see also Figure 1), where H directly translates to longitude and V is rescaled to match the latitude range ($V=0.5$ corresponds to $0°$ latitude, i.e. a position on the equator). A thumbnail of the

Figure 1. Hue-value co-ordinate system used

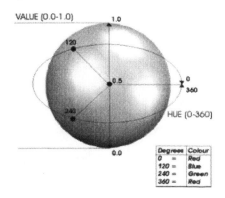

image is then projected onto the surface of sphere at the calculated co-ordinates (since those thumbnails are distorted more towards the poles we actually remap all images to be located between the great circles with ±80° latitude). Once the locations for all images have been calculated and their thumbnails projected, the system shows an initial view of the globe and is ready for navigation. Figure 2 shows the initial view of our image database globe based on the UCID (Schaefer & Stich, 2004) image database which contains some 1300 images.

Since the co-ordinates are extracted directly from the images, our approach is very fast and hence much more efficient than methods such as MDS which rely on a comparably slow and computationally expensive iterative convergence procedure. Also does the addition of images to the database require only the computation of its median hue and brightness with no further calculations necessary as is the case for MDS and similar approaches. In addition the features that we employ are intrinsically suitable for query-based image retrieval (Stricker & Orengo, 1995). Furthermore, the axes of the co-ordinate system are well defined and meaningful which is in contrast to those obtained by MDS or other similar techniques (such as principal components analysis) where axes are not associated with attributes. Finally, as the database globe is displayed on an ordinary CRT monitor no specialist equipment is necessary.

IMAGE DATABASE NAVIGATION

As mentioned above the interface starts with an initial view such as the one shown in Figure 2 (which has a central point of 30° longitude, i.e. an average reddish/yellowish hue, and 0° latitude, i.e. medium brightness). From Figure 2 we can also see the controls the user has at his/her disposal for navigation purposes. As these are kept fairly simple and again due to the average user's familiarity of localising places on an earth globe, navigation is straightforward and intuitive.

Figure 2. Initial globe view of the UCID dataset

The controls allow rotation of the globe around both the vertical and the horizontal axis and zooming in and out of a region of interest. The user can perform these operations using the keyboard where the cursor keys are translated to rotation of the sphere and the + and − keys are available for zooming. Similarly the mouse can be used for navigation: moving the mouse prompts a rotation whereas the scroll wheel (or the left and right mouse buttons) are responsible for zoom operations. Especially attractive is the application of a trackball: here the ball itself corresponds directly to the image globe, hence rotating the track ball rotates the sphere on screen whereas the two buttons are again used for zooming in and out.

From the previous section it becomes clear that a rotation around the vertical axis will focus on a different average hue of the displayed images. In Figure 3 we show the resulting view after a clock-wise rotation by 90° which causes the average hue of the shown images to shift from red/yellow to greenish.

Further rotation reveals images of the remaining hues as shown in Figure 4 which displays the results of two further 90° rotations exhibiting images of bluish and magenta hues respectively. Rotation around the horizontal axis will either shift the display to images that are darker (rotation towards south pole) or brighter pictures (rotation towards north pole).

While the global view of the sphere allows for easy selection of a general hue/brightness area, it is clear that in this view single images are hard to make out. Therefore a zoom function is provides which allows to user to restrict their attention to a smaller, more localised area of interest. In Figure 5 we show an example of a zoomed-in area where the user was interested in images with a beach/ocean view. It is clear that further zoom operation(s) can be applied to localise single images of interest.

We note, that for none of the operations used for browsing the images, i.e. neither for rotation nor for changing the zoom factor, any additional calculations need to be performed (in contrast to e.g. MDS which will re-calculate all co-ordinates for a zoomed-in area (Rubner, Guibas, & Tomasi, 1997)) as the co-ordinates at which the pictures are placed do not change. We are therefore able to provide an image browsing environment that can operate in real time. Furthermore, while we provide a dedicated appli-

Figure 3. Database view after a rotation around the hue axis by 90°

Figure 4. Globe view with central hue of 210° (left), and 300° (right)

Figure 5. Zoomed-in area displaying beach/ocean images

cation for image database navigation we can also export our image globe to a VRML model (VRML Consortium, 1997) which can then be used and browsed with a suitable viewer.

CONCLUSION

We have introduced an efficient and effective approach to visualise and browse large image collections. Thumbnails of images are projected onto a spherical globe which acts as the medium the user interacts with. Navigation is simple, intuitive, and fast as has been demonstrated on a medium sized image dataset. While we have used colour features to determine the position of the thumbnails on the sphere's surface, the method is generic and other types of features can be equally employed.

REFERENCES

CIE. (1989). *International Lighting Vocabulary.* CIE Publications 17.4, Commission International de L'Eclairage, 4th edition, 1989.

Krishnamachari, S., & Abdel-Mottaleb, M. (1999). Image browsing using hierarchical clustering. In *4th IEEE Symposium on Computers and Communications.*

Kruskal, J.B., & Wish, M. (1978). *Multidimensional scaling.* Sage Publications.

Laaksonen, J., Koskela, M., Laakkso, P., & Oja, E. (2000). PicSOM – content-based image retrieval with self organising maps. *Pattern Recognition Letters,* 21:1197-1207.

Nakazato, M., & Huang, T.S. (2001). 3D MARS: Immersive virtual reality for content-based image retrieval. In *IEEE Int. Conference on Multimedia and Expo.*

Rodden, K., Basalaj, D., Sinclair, D., & Wood, K. (1999). Evaluating a visualization of image similarity as a tool for image browsing. In *IEEE Symposium on Information Visualization,* pages 36-43.

Rubner, J., Guibas, L., & Tomasi, C. (1997). The earth mover's distance, multi-dimensional scaling, and color-based image retrieval. In *Image Understanding Workshop,* pages 661–668.

Ruszala, S.D., & Schaefer, G. (2004). Visualisation models for image databases: A comparison of six approaches. In *Irish Machine Vision and Image Processing Conference,* pages 186–191.

Sangwine, J., & Horne, R.E.N. (1998). *The Colour Image Processing Handbook.* Chapman & Hall.

Schaefer, G., & Ruszala, S. (2005). Image database navigation: A globe-al approach. In Int. Symposium on Visual *Computing,* volume 3804 *of Springer Lecture Notes on Computer Science,* pages 279-286.

Schaefer, G., & Stich, M. (2004). UCID - An Uncompressed Colour Image Database. In *Storage and Retrieval Methods and Applications for Multimedia 2004,* volume 5307 of Proceedings of SPIE, pages 472–480.

Smeulders, A.W.M., Worring, M., Santini, S., Gupta, A., & Jain, R. (2000). Content-based image retrieval at the end of the early years. *IEEE Trans. Pattern Analysis and Machine Intelligence,* 22(12):1249–1380.

Stricker, M., & Orengo, M. (1995). Similarity of color images. In *Conf. on Storage and Retrieval for Image and Video Databases III,* volume 2420 of Proceedings of SPIE, pages 381–392.

VRML Consortium. (1997). *The Virtual Reality Modeling Language.* ISO/IEC IS 14772-1.

Section IV
Multimedia Resource Annotation

Chapter XII
Formal Models and Hybrid Approaches for Efficient Manual Image Annotation and Retrieval

Rong Yan
IBM T.J. Watson Research Center, USA

Apostol Natsev
IBM T.J. Watson Research Center, USA

Murray Campbell
IBM T.J. Watson Research Center, USA

ABSTRACT

Although important in practice, manual image annotation and retrieval has rarely been studied by means of formal modeling methods. In this chapter, the authors propose a set of formal models to character- ize the annotation times for two commonly-used manual annotation approaches, that is, tagging and browsing. Based on the complementary properties of these models, the authors design new hybrid ap- proaches, called frequency-based annotation and learning-based annotation, to improve the efficiency of manual image annotation as well as retrieval. Both our simulation and experimental results show that the proposed algorithms can achieve up to a 50% reduction in annotation time over baseline methods for manual image annotation, and produce significantly better annotation and retrieval results in the same amount of time.

INTRODUCTION

Recent increases in the adoption of devices for capturing digital media along with the ever-greater ca- pacity of mass storage systems have led to an explosive amount of images and videos stored in personal collections or shared online. To effectively manage, access and retrieve these data, a widely adopted solution is to associate the image content with semantically meaningful labels, a.k.a. image annotation (Kustanowitz & Shneiderman, 2004). Two types of image annotation approaches are available: automatic and manual. Automatic image annotation, which aims to automatically detect the visual keywords from image content, have attracted a lot of attention from researchers in the last decade (Barnard et al., 2002; Jeon et al., 2003; Li & Wang, 2006; Griffin et al., 2006; Kennedy et al., 2006). For instance, Barnard et al. (2002) treated image annotation as a machine translation problem. Jeon et al. (2003) proposed an annotation model called cross-media relevance model (CMRM), which directly computed the probability of annotations given an image. The ALIPR system (Li & Wang, 2006) used advanced statistical learning techniques to provide fully automatic and real-time annotation for digital pictures. Kennedy et al. (2006) considered using image search results to improve the annotation quality. These automatic annotation approaches have achieved notable success, especially when the keywords have frequent occurrence and strong visual similarity. However, it remains a challenge to accurately annotate other more specific and less visually similar keywords. For example, the best algorithm for the CalTech-256 benchmark (Griffin et al., 2006) reported a mean accuracy of 0.35 for 256 categories with 30 examples per category. Similarly, the best automatic annotation systems in TRECVID 2006 (Over et al., 2006) produced a mean average precision of only 0.17 on 39 concepts.

Along another direction, recent years have seen a proliferation of manual image annotation systems for managing online/personal multimedia content. Examples include PhotoStuff (Halaschek-Wiener et al., 2005) and Aria (Lieberman et al., 2001) for personal archives, Flickr.com and ESP Game (von Ahn & Dabbish, 2004) for online content. This rise of manual annotation partially stems from its high annotation quality for self-organization/retrieval purpose, and its social bookmarking functionality in online communities. Manual image annotation approaches can be categorized into two types as shown in Figure 1 (details in Section III). The most common approach is tagging, which allows users to annotate images with a chosen set of keywords ("tags") from a vocabulary. Another approach is browsing, which requires users to sequentially browse a group of images and judge their relevance to a pre-defined keyword. Both approaches have strengths and weaknesses, and in many ways they are complementary to each other. But their successes in various scenarios have demonstrated the possibility to annotate a massive number of images by leveraging human power.

However, manual image annotation can be tedious and labor-intensive. Therefore, it is of great importance to consider using automatic techniques to speed up manual image annotation. In this work, we assume users will drive the annotation process and manually examine each image label in order to guarantee the annotation accuracy, but in addition we use automatic learning algorithms to improve the annotation efficiency by suggesting the right images, keywords and annotation interfaces to users. This is different from automatic image annotation, which aims to construct accurate visual models based on low-level visual features. But from another perspective, efficient manual annotation can bring benefits to automatic annotation algorithms, because they are typically built on manually annotated examples.

To quantitatively analyze and optimize manual annotation, it is necessary to start with some annotation time/efficiency models that formulate the annotation process. In the absence of existing studies, we propose two annotation time models to describe the process for two popular manual annotation approaches, i.e., tagging and browsing. To the best of our knowledge, this is the first attempt to quantify the manual image annotation process, and it serves as a theoretical foundation to analyze large-scale manual annotation without time-consuming user studies. Based on the time models, we further propose two hybrid annotation algorithms – frequency-based annotation and learning-based annotation – by

Figure 1. Examples of manual image annotation systems. Left: tagging (Flickr and ESP Game), Right: browsing (EVA and XVR).

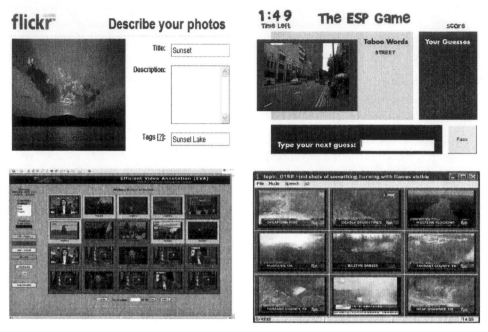

merging tagging and browsing into a unified framework. They can automatically learn from low-level features and adaptively chooses browsing/tagging interfaces for the right set of keywords/images. Both our simulation and empirical results on the TRECVID'05 (Over et al., 2006) and Corel (Barnard et al., 2002) collections confirm the validity of the time models, as well as demonstrate that the proposed algorithms can achieve an up to 50% reduction in annotation times and can consistently outperform the baseline methods in the entire annotation process. By extending similar mechanism to the interactive retrieval task on TRECVID'07 collection, we also observed a considerable improvement on the retrieval effectiveness under the same amount of retrieval time.

RELATED WORK

Applying automatic processing methods to assist manual image annotation is related to a large body of previous work. For example, existing systems have leveraged speech recognition, external semantic networks or time/location information to facilitate the manual annotation process (Kustanowitz & Shneiderman, 2004). However, since these systems require support from additional sources, their applicability is more restricted than the automatic methods that only use information from image content.

From the learning perspective, relevance feedback also explores the idea of using learning algorithms to refine the ranking results. MARS (Rui et al., 1997) is one of the first image retrieval systems using relevance feedback. Recent relevance feedback approaches have applied more advanced machine learning tools such as SVMs and kernel biased discriminant analysis (Zhou & Huang, 2001). MiAlbum (Wenyin et al., 2001) uses such a feedback mechanism to iteratively improve annotation quality for personal images. But in contrast to relevance feedback, which needs to work on one query at a time, learning-based annotation should be able to simultaneously operate across multiple keywords and dynamically switch to any keywords or interfaces in the learning process.

The idea of active image/keyword/interface selection is also related to the methods of active learning (Tong & Chang, 2001), which iteratively asks a user to review and provide the correct labels for some selected unlabeled data. Typically, the unlabeled examples can be selected by means of either minimization of the learner's expected error or maximization of information gain (Tong & Chang, 2001). The effectiveness of active learning for reducing annotation cost in automatic image annotation has been demonstrated by previous work (Yan & Hauptmann, 2004). Despite the connections on active image selection, learning-based annotation has some fundamental differences with active learning, because it mainly aims to collect a maximal number of annotations based on the time models, instead of attempting to build accurate visual models on low-level features. This leads to several implementation differences, such as image selection strategies, base learning models and so on. Moreover, learning-based annotation needs to investigate how the learning algorithm can be applied in a hybrid annotation environment, but this is rarely discussed in active learning.

MANUAL IMAGE ANNOTATION METHODS AND TIME MODELS

In this section, we introduce and discuss two types of manual image annotation approaches, i.e., tagging and browsing. We also propose two models to measure their annotation efficiency, which offers the foundation for the rest of our discussions. Formally, let us suppose we have to annotate a set of images $I=\{I_l\}_{l=1..L}$ with a set of keywords $W=\{W_k\}_{k=1..K}$.[1] Without loss of generality, we sort $\{W_k\}$ in a descending order of their frequency. So W_1 is the most frequent word and W_K is the least frequent one. L_k is the number of relevant images for W_k, and K_l is the number of keywords associated with I_l. The goal of manual annotation is to identify the relevance between each pair of image I_l and keyword W_k, or equivalently, annotate image I_l with keyword W_k. Once the relevance between I_l and all the keywords have been identified, we say I_l is annotated, otherwise I_l is unannotated.

Tagging

Tagging allows the users to annotate images with a chosen set of keywords("tags") from a controlled or uncontrolled vocabulary. This type of approaches is the basis for most of the current image annotation/tagging systems, although it can be implemented in a variety of ways with respect to interface designs and user incentives. For example, Flickr encourages users to create free-text tags for each uploaded image. It views tags as the central component for sharing, retrieval and discovery of the user-generated content. ESP Game (von Ahn & Dabbish, 2004) motivates users to annotate photos with freely chosen keywords in a gaming environment. PhotoStuff (Halaschek-Wiener et al., 2005) provides a domain-independent tool that facilitates creating and publishing annotations for image content. One advantage for tagging is that annotators can use any keywords in the vocabulary or freely choose arbitrary words to annotate the target images. However, this flexibility might result in a "vocabulary problem" (Furnas et al., 1987), which means multiple users or a single user in a long period can come up with different words to describe the same concept. Moreover, it can be more time-consuming for users to type new keywords, as compared with simply browsing and judging the relevance between images and pre-defined keywords.

In order to quantitatively analyze the efficiency of tagging approaches, we must design a formal model to represent its expected annotation time for each image. To begin, we can assume that the more keywords users annotate, the larger the annotation time is. Our user study described in Section VII-A confirmed that this assumption is reasonable, but it also shows that the annotation time is not exactly proportional to the number of keywords. This is because, for each image, users always need additional time up-front to understand the image content in order to make their decisions. The above observations suggest modeling the tagging time T_l for the lth image as a function of four major factors, i.e., the number of image keywords K_l, the average time for designing/typing one word t_f, the initial setup time for annotation t_s and a noise term ε, which follows a zero-mean probability distribution. Based on our user study, we find it is sufficient to adopt a linear time model to represent the annotation time for each image, i.e., $T_l = K_l t_f + t_s + \varepsilon$. Its mean can be derived as $t_l = K_l t_f + t_s$. For a total of L images, the overall expected annotation time is

$$t = \sum_{l=1}^{L} K_l t_f + L t_s \quad or \quad t = \sum_{k=1}^{K} L_k t_f + L t_s \tag{1}$$

These two formulations are equivalent because

$$\sum_{l=1}^{L} K_l = \sum_{k=1}^{K} L_k,$$

but they compute the total number of keywords from two orthogonal dimensions. We mainly consider the second formulation in the following analysis. Note that we assume users can find all relevant keywords – or equivalently, annotate every keyword – in one tagging step. It might be more reasonable to consider the possibility of missing keywords in the tagging process. This issue could be mitigated, however, by using keyword auto-completion interfaces and specific-to-general label propagation techniques. Moreover, due to a lack of statistics to support the modeling of missing keywords, we will pursue this direction in the future. Another point worth mentioning is that this time model does not require the parameters t_e and t_f to be constant in all the annotation scenarios. Instead, they can be affected by a number of factors, such as interface design, input device, personal preference and so on. For example, annotation on cell phones (Wilhelm et al., 2004) can have a much larger t_f than annotation on desktop computers. Therefore, rather than attempting to estimate fully accurate parameters for any specific settings, this paper mainly focus on examining the correctness of the proposed time models, and use them as a foundation to develop better manual annotation algorithms. We expect the proposed time models and the following analysis will generalize over a wide range of settings. Our experiments also evaluate the sensitivities of annotation performance over these parameters. Meanwhile, it is useful to re-estimate these coefficients for either a new user or a new environment.

Browsing

Another type of annotation approach, browsing, requires users to browse a group of images, so as to judge the relevance of each image to a given keyword. The number of images per group can vary from 1 to a large number such as 20. Because browsing annotation needs to start with a controlled vocabulary defined by domain experts or a seeded keyword manually initialized by users, it is not as flexible and as widely applied as tagging. However, browsing has advantages on several aspects. For instance, it allows users to provide more complete annotation outputs than tagging (Volkmer et al., 2005), because users only focus on one specific keyword at a time and they do not need to remember all possible keywords over a long period. Moreover, the time to annotate one keyword by browsing is usually much shorter than that in tagging, since users have a relatively simple binary judgment interface and a stable annotation context in the entire process. Therefore, recent years have seen more and more browsing annotation systems being developed. One such example is the Efficient Video Annotation (EVA) system (Volkmer et al., 2005), which allows multiple users to collaboratively annotate the same image collection by browsing and identifying keywords from a controlled vocabulary. Extreme video retrieval (XVR) (Hauptmann et al., 2006), although motivated by video search, follows a similar idea by asking users to quickly browse the automatic search results to judge their relevance.

Similar to tagging, we design a formal model to quantify the efficiency of browsing. First, the overall annotation time should be related to the number of images and the number of unique keywords. According to Section VII-A, we also find that the time for annotating a relevant image is significantly larger than the time for skipping an irrelevant image, because users tend to spend more time in examining the correctness on relevant images. Thus we model the browsing annotation time T_k for the kth keyword using four major factors, i.e., the number of relevant images L_k, the average time to annotate a relevant image t_p, the average time to annotate an irrelevant image t_n and a zero-mean noise term ε. The number of irrelevant images is simply $L^-_k = L - L_k$ and hence a reasonable linear time model is $T_k = L_k t_p + (L - L_k)t_n + \varepsilon$. For a total of K keywords, the overall expected annotation time is

$$t = \sum_{k=1}^{K} \left[L_k t_p + (L - L_k)t_n \right].$$

(2)

To summarize, these two annotation approaches are essentially complementary from many perspectives. For example, tagging has fewer limitations on the choice of words and users only need to consider relevant keywords for each image. But the annotated words must be re-calibrated due to the vocabulary problem. It also requires more time to determine and input the given keyword. On the contrary, browsing must work with one pre-defined keyword at a time and requires users to judge all possible pairs of images/keywords. But the effort to determine image relevance by browsing is usually much less than that by tagging, i.e., t_p, t_n is typically much smaller than t_p, t_s. Therefore, tagging is more suitable for infrequent keywords such as specific person/location names, and browsing works better for frequent keywords such as "person"/"face".

FREQUENCY-BASED ANNOTATION

The complementary properties of tagging and browsing provide an opportunity to develop more efficient algorithms for manual image annotation by merging their strengths. Because our analysis suggests that tagging/browsing is suitable for infrequent/frequent keywords respectively, we develop a hybrid annotation algorithm called frequency-based annotation, which first partitions the keyword space into two sets based on word frequency and then applies the best annotation strategy to label each set of words. To illustrate the basic idea, we can view the image annotation task as a problem of filling binary relevance information in an empty matrix of size $K \times L$. In this case, tagging is equivalent to annotating the matrix row by row, as shown in Figure 2(a), and browsing is equivalent to annotating column by column, as shown in Figure 2(b). However, since neither of these approaches are always ideal for the entire keyword space, it is useful to split the keywords into two disjoint sets shown in Figure 2(c). In order to reduce the annotation time, we can apply browsing for the frequent (or general) keywords in the left set, and apply tagging for the infrequent (or specific) keywords on the right set. By doing so, users can quickly browse through the frequent words in a short time and leave the rest of keywords to be picked up by tagging.

To estimate the best boundary to split the keyword space, we can minimize the total expected annotation time as a function of the boundary B. The annotation time consists of two parts including the browsing annotation cost for the words more frequent than w_B, and the tagging annotation cost for the words less frequent. Based on the time models presented in Eqn(1) and Eqn(2), we have the total expected time as follows,

$$t(B) = \sum_{k=1}^{B}\left[L_k t_p + (L - L_k)t_n\right] + \sum_{k=B+1}^{K} L_k t_f + Lt_s = LBt_n + Lt_s + \sum_{k=1}^{B} L_k(t_p - t_n) + \sum_{k=B+1}^{K} L_k t_f. \quad (3)$$

Figure 2. Illustration of four image annotation approaches based on a matrix representation, where each row stands for one image, and each column stands for one unique keyword.

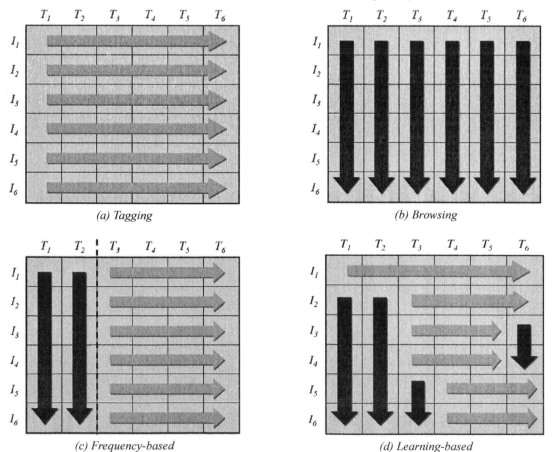

(a) Tagging

(b) Browsing

(c) Frequency-based

(d) Learning-based

To obtain the boundary that achieves the minimal annotation time, we can compute the largest B that satisfy $t(B) \leq t(B-1)$, or equivalently, the largest B satisfying

$$\frac{L_B}{L} > \frac{t_n}{t_f + t_n - t_p}. \tag{4}$$

Algorithm 1 summarizes the frequency-based annotation algorithm, where all the frequency information L_k is assumed to be known and the keywords W_k are sorted in the descending order of word frequency. The first step of this algorithm is to estimate the optimal boundary B based on either Eqn(4). The choice of the equations depends on whether the detailed frequency information is available, because Eqn(4) can provide a more accurate estimate, but it needs the exact frequency L_k as inputs. After B is determined, the algorithm requires users to annotate all the images via browsing for the top-B frequent keywords, followed by tagging all the images with the rest of the keywords. Finally, it outputs the annotations for all the images.

LEARNING-BASED ANNOTATION

The frequency-based annotation provides a simple hybrid framework to merge the advantages of tagging and browsing, but it requires all the frequency statistics to be available in order to determine the most frequent keywords. Unfortunately, accurate frequency statistics are not always available. Moreover, frequency-based annotation limits itself to use browsing annotation only for frequent keywords, which ignores the potential chance for improving efficiency on the other infrequent keywords. Therefore, we propose another approach called learning-based annotation which can automatically learn from visual features and adaptively choose annotation interface for the right set of keywords/images.

Figure 2(d) illustrates the basic idea of the learning-based annotation using the same annotation matrix as before. The algorithm starts by tagging some initial selected images. With more annotations collected, it attempts to dynamically find a batch of unannotated images for potential keywords and ask users to annotate them in a browsing interface. The algorithm will iterate until all the images are

---

Algorithm 1 The frequency-based annotation algorithm
___
Input: Images $\{I_l\}_{l=1..L}$, keywords $\{W_k\}_{k=1..K}$ and their frequency L_k, annotation parameters t_p, t_n, t_f, t_s

   1) Estimate optimal boundary B using Eqn(4)

   2) For k = 1 to B,

      a) Given the keyword W_k, ask user to annotate all images $\{I_l\}$ by browsing;

   3) For l = 1 to L,

      a) Ask user to tag image I_l using the other keywords;

   4) Output the annotations for all images.

___

shown in the tagging interface so as to guarantee none of the keywords is missing. This is in contrast to frequency-based annotation, which determines a fixed set of keywords for browsing before the annotation process. The advantages for the learning-based methods are two-fold: 1) it does not need to re-order the keyword space by frequency; 2) even for infrequent keywords, it can potentially discover a subset of images that are mostly relevant for them, and improve the annotation efficiency by switching to a browsing interface.

Analysis

To design the learning-based annotation algorithm, it is instructive to study when it can have a smaller annotation time than simple tagging/browsing. Let us first break down its total annotation time by keywords, or equivalently, column by column in the annotation matrix. Suppose the proposed algorithm has obtained L_k relevant labels for keyword W_k. Then we can assume $\beta_k L_k$ relevant labels come from browsing and the other $(1-\beta_k)L_k$ labels come from tagging, where β_k is called browsing recall. However, β_k is not enough to describe the total annotation time, because, based on the proposed time models, browsing irrelevant images will also introduce additional cost. Therefore we need to introduce browsing precision γ_k to represent the proportion of relevant images in all the browsed images. In this case, the number of irrelevant browsed images is $\beta_k L_k(1-\gamma_k)/\gamma_k$ and the total annotation time is,

$$t = \sum_{k=1}^{K}\left[\beta_k L_k\left(t_p + \frac{1-\gamma_k}{\gamma_k}t_n\right) + (1-\beta_k)L_k t_f\right] + Lt_s.$$

(5)

Our analysis in the Appendix shows that if an annotation algorithm is more efficient than tagging/browsing, its browsing recall and precision must satisfy

$$\beta_k \geq \max\left(0, \frac{1-ab_k}{1-a}\right), \gamma_k \geq \max\left(a, \frac{a\beta_k}{ab_k-(1-\beta_k)}\right)$$

(6)

where $a=t_n/(t_f+t_n-t_p)$, $b_k=L/L_k$. These inequalities offer us more insights to develop efficient annotation algorithms. Eqn(7) suggests that for keyword W_k, we should use browsing to annotate at least $(1-ab_k)L_k/(1-a)$ relevant images. Otherwise, simple browsing/tagging annotation can be a better choice in this case. Furthermore, it also indicates that the browsing precision should be larger than a lower bound related to a, b_k and β_k. To summarize, for a given keyword, an efficient annotation algorithm should be able to select a sufficient number of images for users to browse, and a sufficient proportion of these browsed images should be relevant to the predicted keyword.

Based on above analysis, we should switch to browsing interface if we expect the browsing precision can at least be higher than the lower bound $(1-ab_k)/(1-a)$. Therefore, the problem boils down to adaptively finding a set of unannotated images that are likely to be relevant for a given keyword based on the existing annotation. To this end, we translate manual annotation into an online learning problem, i.e., for keyword W_k, learn the visual model from available relevant images $I'_k=\{I'_j\}_{j=1...m}$, and use it to predict additional relevant images from the unannotated image pool $U'_k=\{I_l|I_l.I'_k\}$. To enable this learning process, we assume each image I is associated with a number of low-level features $\mathbf{x}$. Based on the annotation provided by users, we can learn their visual patterns by using kernel logistic regression, which aims to optimize the following empirical risk function for keyword W_k,

$$R(f) = \sum_{i=1}^{m'} \log(1 + e^{-y_i f(\mathbf{x}_i)}) + \lambda \|f\|_{H}^2 \tag{7}$$

where $\mathbf{x}_j$ is the feature for I'_j, $y_k \in \{-1,1\}$ is binary relevance label, and H denotes a reproducing kernel Hilbert space(RKHS) generated by an arbitrary positive definite kernel K. According to the representer theorem, the relevance of unannotated images can be estimated from the minimizer $f(x)$ with weights α_i for each training example,

$$f(\cdot) = \sum_{i=1}^{m'} \alpha_i K(\mathbf{x}_i, \cdot) \tag{8}$$

When users annotate an additional label $(y_m, \mathbf{x}_m)$, $m=m'+1$, the optimization function must be updated accordingly. To reduce the computational demand, only the weight for the new example is updated based on the Newton-Raphson method. Since the optimization function is convex, the Newton method can guarantee to find the global optimum. To be more specific, the gradient and Hessian of the risk function with respect to $\alpha_{\overline{m}}$ can be written as,

$$\frac{\partial R(\alpha)}{\partial \alpha_m} = \mathbf{K}_m^T \mathbf{p} + \lambda \mathbf{K}_m^T \alpha, \quad \frac{\partial^2 R(\alpha)}{\partial \alpha_m^2} = \mathbf{K}_m^T \mathbf{W} \mathbf{K}_m + \lambda K_{mm} \tag{9}$$

where $\mathbf{K}$ is the kernel Gram matrix, $\mathbf{K}_m$ is the vector of $\{K(x_m, \cdot)\}$, K_{mm} is the element of $K(x_m, x_m)$, $\mathbf{p}$ denote the logistic model $1/(1+\exp(-\mathbf{K}\alpha))$, and $\mathbf{W}$ denote the matrix $diag(\mathbf{p}_i(1-\mathbf{p}_i))$. The Newton updates can be straightforwardly derived from the gradient and Hessian function. These updates are iterated until the risk function converges or the iteration number is larger than a threshold.

In our implementation, we select the RBF kernel to model non-linear decision boundary between positive/negative examples. The kernel matrix is pre-computed before the annotation process in order to reduce online computational resources. Finally, after the optimal weight α_m is found, we can simply update the prediction function by $f(\cdot) \leftarrow f(\cdot) + \alpha_m K(x_m, \cdot)$.

Algorithm Details

The learning-based hybrid annotation is summarized in Algorithm 2. This algorithm starts with a number of unannotated images and a vocabulary of keywords. It first selects an image from the unannotated pool for tagging. After this image is completely tagged by the user, all the related variables are updated for its corresponding keywords W_k, i.e., the set of relevant images I'_k, the kernel weight α as well as the prediction function $f_k(\cdot)$ based on Eqn(8). By thresholding the prediction function, we generate the set of estimated relevant images R_k that represent the most potentially relevant images identified by the system. If the number of these images is larger than a pre-defined batch size S, the browsing interface is activated to annotate all the images in R_k. To avoid switching interfaces too frequently and disturbing the user experience, we typically set the batch size to be a large number and only invoke the browsing interface when there are a large number of relevant images available.

Algorithm 2 The learning-based annotation algorithm

Input: Images $\{I_l\}$, keywords $\{W_k\}$, browsing batch size S

1) Initialize adaptive threshold $\theta_k = 1$, browsing precision $\gamma_k = 1$, $\mathcal{I}'_k = \varnothing$, $\forall k = 1..K$ and $\mathcal{U} = \{I_l\}$, $\forall l = 1..L$;

2) While there are unannotated images left, i.e., $\mathcal{U} \neq \varnothing$,

    a) Ask user to tag the first image I_l in $\mathcal{U}$;

    b) For each keyword W_k associated with I_l;

        i) Add I_l into the labeled pool, $\mathcal{I}'_k = \mathcal{I}'_k \cup I_l$;

        ii) Update α and $f_k(\cdot)$ using Eqn(8);

        iii) Obtain the set of predicted relevant images
$$\mathcal{R}_k = \{I_l | f_k(\mathbf{x}_l) \geq \theta_k, I_l \notin \mathcal{I}'_k\};$$

        iv) If $|\mathcal{R}_k| \geq S$, then ask user to annotate $\mathcal{R}_k$ by browsing, update labeled pool $\mathcal{I}'_k$ and browsing precision γ_k, go to 2(b)ii;

        v) If $\gamma_k \geq \max(a, m'_k/m_k)$ (details below), then reduce θ_k to $\theta_k/2$, go to 2(b)iii;

    c) Remove I_l from $\mathcal{U}$, i.e., $\mathcal{U} = \mathcal{U} \setminus I_l$;

3) Output the annotations for all images.

Since the set of estimated images are not guaranteed to be relevant, we use the new image annotations to predict the browsing precision and update the learning parameters accordingly. As shown in Eqn(7), browsing precision needs to be sufficiently large for the proposed algorithm to improve efficiency. Therefore, in the next step, if we find the browsing precision is larger than a lower bound, we will reduce the adaptive threshold θ_k and thus the browsing interface can be used to annotate as many images as possible until the browsing precision is too low. The bound, i.e., $\max(a, m'_k/m_k)$, is derived from Eqn(7) with $\beta_k=1$ and m'_k/m_k to approximate the true frequency ratio L_k/L, where m'_k is the number of relevant images and m_k is the total annotated images for W_k so far. Above steps will be iterated until all the images are tagged.

APPLICATION TO INTERACTIVE RETRIEVAL

Although the aforementioned approaches are discussed in the context of manual image annotation, its idea and analysis can be simply extended to the interactive retrieval systems (Hauptmann & Witbrock, 1996; Snoek et al., 2004; Foley et al., 2004), which provide a means to help users to look up image/video using associated text and visual content in an interactive manner. Interactive retrieval can be categorized into three categories,

- A general class of users aims at browsing over a large number of videos from diversified sources, where users have no specific target except for finding interesting things.
- Another class of users wants to do arbitrary search by retrieving an arbitrary video satisfying his information need that can be presented by text keywords or visual examples.

- The third class of users, complete search/annotation, aims to discover every relevant video that belong to a specific information need. To support these users, the retrieval systems must possess more automatic processing power to reduce the huge manual annotation efforts.

Since the last paradigm is often time consuming and labor extensive, there are a number of interactive retrieval approaches that have been developed to reduce the overall retrieval effort in this case, such as Informedia (Hauptmann & Witbrock, 1996), MediaMill (Snoek et al., 2004), Fischlar (Foley et al., 2004) and so on. However, all of these interactive retrieval systems consider dealing with one query topic at a time. But it is not uncommon that users want to search for multiple related query topics simultaneously. For example, a security officer might want to search the surveillance video collection for a list of suspicious persons or a list of abnormal activities. Since multiple queries does not exist in isolation, it is possible to exploit the redundancy between queries so as to reduce the total retrieval time, or in other words, improve the retrieval performance within the same amount of time. In this sense, we can view multi-query retrieval as a manual image/video annotation task, which aims to annotate the entire collection with the given keywords/queries. Therefore, by treating the query topics as keywords, studies on manual image annotation approaches can bring us deeper insights on improving the performance of multi-topic interactive retrieval.

In the following discussions, we describe the interface design of the proposed multi-topic image/video retrieval system using hybrid learning-based annotation. The main components of the retrieval system consist of a single-image tagging interface and a single-query browsing interface. Figure 3 shows a screenshot of the tagging interface that aims to label one image simultaneously with 25 queries provided by TRECVID'07. The image browser in the middle displays the target image for users to label, where the target images are automatically selected based on the learning-based annotation algorithm in Algorithm 2. Users can use the mouse or the arrow keys on the keyboard to navigate the choice of images from the collection. On the right side, the query list shows all the query topics to retrieve. In this list, all the queries are denoted by a small number of keywords manually extracted from the query topic. For instance, "Dog_person_walk" means the query of "finding the video shots of person walking with

Figure 3. The tagging interface of the multi-topic retrieval system

Figure 4. The browsing interface of the multi-topic retrieval system

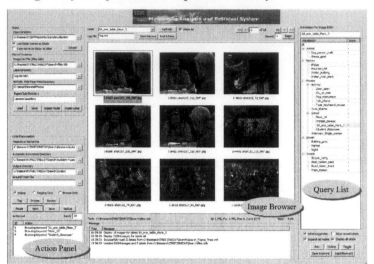

Figure 5. The shot information dialog of the multi-topic retrieval system

dogs". Also, all queries are categorized into multiple query groups, such as the group related to "people", "street" and "vehicle". Such a grouping is able to facilitate the manual judgment effort for the general users, and thus reduce the time for redundant decision on the same image. For example, if users are examining an image with no persons available, they can skip all the person-related queries at the same time. To classify the displayed image as relevant to one of the queries, user can input the related query keywords using the editor control on top of the query list, or double click the corresponding keyword to indicate its relatedness to the displayed image.

On the left side, the action panel automatically generates the interface switching actions suggested by the learning-based retrieval algorithm. Rather than fully controlling the interface selection by the system, we leaves the option of switching interface to users, who can choose to either keep using the current interface, or take the next action in the panel to switch to a new interface on the suggested queries or images. If the interface is switched, the system will then load the corresponding queries and images to the image browser.

Figure 4 shows a screenshot of the browsing interface that aims to retrieve a grid of images for a TRECVID'07 query "finding video shots of three or more people sitting on a table". This interface has a similar layout with the tagging interface, but with several key differences. For example, the selected images are organized in a 3x3 image grid in the image browser which allows users to quickly browse through. The selected queries suggested by the learning-based annotation algorithm is highlighted in the query list. Users can click a mouse button or press the space key on a specified image to toggle the relevance of the query to the image. The images that are judged relevant to the given queries are overlaid with a red border and the irrelevant images are overlaid with a yellow border. Similar to the tagging interface, the action panel lists all the interface switching actions automatically generated by the learning-based annotation algorithm. Users can decided to stay with the current query, change to a new query or switch back to the tagging interface.

In the case of video retrieval, users can invoke a separate shot information browser (Figure 5 so as to examine all the I-Frames in the selected video shot. The ability to browse individual video frames is important especially when the query topics are related to any temporal events/activities such as "people walking" or "people going up stairs".

EXPERIMENTS

Our experiments are carried out on three large-scale image/video collections. The first and the second collection is generally referred to as the TRECVID collection (Over et al., 2006), which is the largest video collection with manual annotations available to the research community. In the first collection, We use the TRECVID 2005 development set (TRECVID in short) which includes a total of 74,523 keyframes. This collection consists of broadcast news videos captured from 11 different broadcasting organizations across several countries. Each image is officially annotated with 449 semantic labels (Naphade et al., 2006). For each image, we generate a 150-dimensional color histogram as the visual features.

The second collection, i.e., the TRECVID 2007 collection (TRECVID'07 in short), includes a total of 22,084 keyframes from Netherlands Institute for Sound and Vision. They are fully labeled on 25 official queries. For each image, we generate a 166-dimensional color histogram and 108-dimensional co-occurrence texture as the visual features. In the following, we use both collections to simulate and examine the performance of the learning-based hybrid retrieval algorithm. We also report its real-world retrieval performance for searching both image collections.

Figure 6. Left: tagging interface. Right: tagging time statistics. The dash line is fitted based on the tagging model

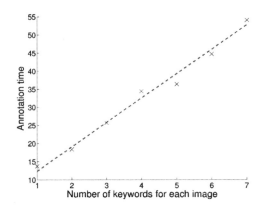

The third collection is compiled from the Corel image dataset (Corel in short) on 155 keywords and currently shared online by Barnard et al. (2002). The collection is organized into 10 different samples of roughly 16,000 images, where each image is associated with a vocabulary of 155 keywords such as "aircraft", "sky", "water" and so on. We use the first sample of the images which contains a total of 15,766 images. The low-level visual features are generated on image segments provided by N-Cuts. Each segment is associated with 46 features including size, position, color, oriented energy (12 filters), and a few simple shape features.

In the following discussions, we first present two user studies to confirm the validity of the tagging and browsing time models proposed in Section III-B. We use them to simulate and examine the efficiency of the learning-based hybrid annotation algorithm. Finally, we report the real-world annotation performance of hybrid annotation by asking a user to annotate the image collection in one hour.

Annotation Time Models

To examine whether the proposed tagging/browsing time models are reasonable in practice, we conducted user studies on two different types of annotation systems. To validate the tagging time model, we developed a keyword-based annotation system. Figure 6 shows the screenshot of the tagging system, together with the distribution of the average tagging time against the number of keywords. The TRECVID collection with its controlled vocabulary is used in this experiment. A total of 100 randomly selected images have been annotated by a user. The number of annotated keywords per image ranges from 1 to 7. We also generate a dashed line by fitting the time statistics with the tagging model. It can be observed that the average annotation time for an image has a clear linear correlation to the number of keywords. Another interesting observation is that the dashed line does not go across the origin after an extrapolation to zero keywords. This means it takes additional time for a user to start annotating a new image due to a switch of the annotated images. Based on the linear fitting, we can estimate the tagging model parameters for this user to be t_f=6.8 seconds and t_s=5.6 seconds.

To validate the browsing time model, we asked three different users to browse 25 keywords (extracted from 25 TRECVID'05 queries) in the TRECVID collection. The system screenshot is shown in Figure 7. In this study, we slightly rewrite the browsing model to be, $t_p + t_n L_k / L_k = t / L_k$, where L_k / L_k is the

Figure 7. Left: browsing interface. Right: browsing time statistics. Dash lines are fitted based on the browsing model

 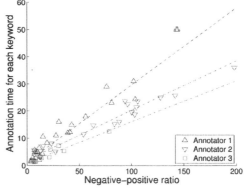

ratio between the number of irrelevant images and relevant images, or called negative-positive ratio, t/L_k is the average time for collecting one positive image. If the proposed browsing model is satisfied, we should be able to identify a linear relation between L_k/L_k and t/L_k. Figure 7 plots the distributions of these two factors for the three users. As we can see, the dashed lines estimated by linear regression fit the true distribution quite well, which confirmed the browsing time model is reasonable for the practical annotation environment. We estimate the model parameters by averaging all three users, i.e., $t_p=1.4$ seconds, and $t_n=0.2$ seconds.

Simulated Annotation Results

In this section, we evaluate the performance of the annotation algorithms in large-scale image collections. Similar to the typical experimental settings for active learning, we use the ground-truth image labels to simulate real user annotations in order to avoid spending prohibitive human resources for evaluation. The annotation time is obtained based on the time model parameters t_p, t_s, t_p and t_n estimated in the previous section. Note that these parameters only serve as a reasonable estimation for the annotation parameters in a desktop environment. It is possible for these parameters to change considerably for other interfaces, devices and annotators. But given the flexibilities of the proposed time models, we expect our analysis is generally applicable without being limited to specific settings. We also carry out additional experiments to study the sensitivities on the choice of time model parameters.

To illustrate how the learning-based annotation algorithm can automatically switch the annotation methods and select a batch of images to annotate by browsing, Figure 8 shows the initial 14 images which learning-based annotation asks for tagging in the TRECVID collection, and then the first batch of 30 images selected for browsing. The top of this figure lists all the initial tagged images and their associated keywords. After all the initial images are tagged, the algorithm found 5 of these images are annotated as "politicians" and predicted a large number of images can be potentially related to the key-

Figure 8. The images selected by learning-based annotation for the TRECVID collection. Top: the initial 14 images for tagging (with their keywords shown). Bottom: the first group of 30 images for browsing.

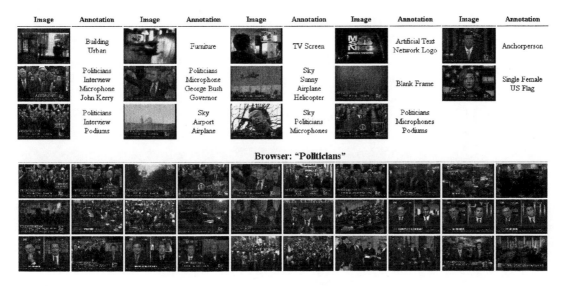

word "politicians" based on low-level visual features. Thus afterwards, it switched to present a batch of 30 images and ask the user to annotate keyword "politicians" by browsing. Because a significant faction of the browsed images are related to the keyword "politician", the user can save a lot of time without re-typing the same keyword again. This learning-based algorithm also helps to calibrate the annotated keywords, provide more complete annotations on each concept and make browsing annotation applicable even for an uncontrolled vocabulary.

Next, we present the annotation performance of frequency-based annotation (**FBA**) and learning-based annotation (**LBA**) together with two baseline algorithms, i.e., tagging (**Tag**) and browsing (**Browse**). All the algorithms are evaluated on the TRECVID collection and the Corel collection. For frequency-based annotation, we select the optimal boundary B using Eqn(4) by assuming the frequency of each keyword is known. For learning-based annotation, we set the RBF kernel parameter ρ to 1 and the batch size S in Algorithm 2 to 50 unless stated otherwise. Because we assume all the user annotations are correct, the widely-used accuracy-based performance measure is no longer applicable in the scenario of manual image annotation. Therefore, we propose three new measures – macro-recall, micro-recall and hybrid-recall – to evaluate the annotation quality. In this work, recall is defined as the ratio of the number of relevant images collected at a certain point of the labeling process, to the total number of relevant images. Similar to their counterpart in text classification (Yang & Pedersen, 1997), macro-recall r_a is the average of the recalls for each keyword, and micro-recall r_i is the recall on the entire image-keyword space. In some sense, macro-recall measures the annotation diversity and micro-recall measures the annotation completeness, where both of them are important to describe the annotation quality. Hybrid-recall is the harmonic mean of the macro-recall and micro-recall, $r_h=2r_a r_i/(r_a+r_i)$, designed using the same principle as the F1 measure (Yang & Pedersen, 1997). In addition, we also report the total annotation time when the annotation process is completed, or equivalently, when all three recalls become 1.

Figure 9 provides a detailed comparison between four annotation algorithms on the TRECVID collection and the Corel collection. All three recall measures are reported with a growing annotation time until the annotation process ends. It is obvious to see that both frequency-based annotation and learning-based annotation are superior to the baseline tagging/browsing methods in terms of the total annotation time. For example, in the TRECVID dataset, the time for frequency-based annotation to complete the labeling process is only 60% of the tagging annotation time and 36% of the browsing annotation time. Learning-based annotation further reduces the annotation time to be 50% of tagging time and 30% of browsing time. This is achieved without using any frequency information in contrast to frequency-based annotation. Their improvement in the Corel collection is also considerable, although it is relatively smaller than that in the TRECVID collection because of a lower number of keywords per image on average. A comparison between the curves on micro-recall and macro-recall shows that tagging is good at improving the macro-recall, while browsing does well in improving micro-recall. This is because tagging random images can bring a wide coverage of various keywords at the beginning, but browsing methods only focus on annotating the most frequent keywords at the early stage. This shows an important trade-off between micro-recall and macro-recall. Thus it is more impressive to observe that learning-based annotation is able to outperform tagging/browsing in terms of both macro-recall and micro-recall, as well as hybrid-recall. Our last observation is that learning-based annotation has a significantly higher hybrid-recall at the end of its labeling process. This indicates within the same amount of time, learning-based annotation allows us to collect much more image keywords with higher annotation diversity.

In order to gain deeper insight into the improvement of learning-based annotation, we plot the true browsing recall and browsing precision in Figure 10 in the TRECVID collection. The results on the 100 most frequent keywords are shown. For the purpose of comparison, we also show the minimal browsing recall required for learning-based annotation to outperform tagging/browsing, and the minimal precision given its true recall β_k. In the browsing recall curve, we can find that β_k for most keywords is higher than the lower bound except for the first 9 keywords. It is generally decreasing with the keyword frequency going down, which means, if the keyword is less frequent, a smaller proportion of the images will be covered by browsing. In the precision curve, the number of keywords that violate the minimal requirement increases to 20. It suggests that if the system knows the 20 most frequent keywords, it is better to use browsing alone to annotate them. For the other keywords, a large number of them produce a significantly higher precision over the minimal requirement, which finally leads to the overall

Figure 9. Annotation performance as a function of annotation time on the TRECVID and Corel collections

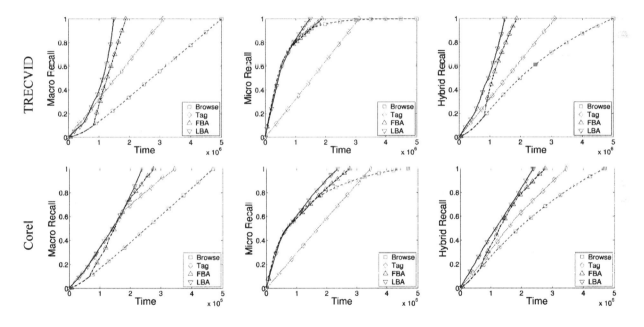

Figure 10. The distribution of browsing recall and browsing precision for the 100 most frequent keywords. Dashed lines show the minimum recall/precision to outperform tagging and browsing.

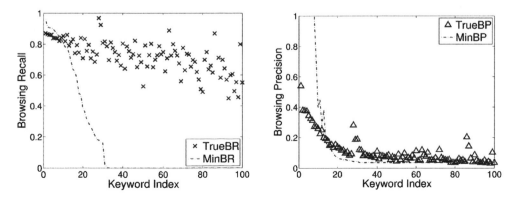

improvement for learning-based annotation. Some considerably improved keywords are 28-"Anchor", 29-"Interview", 30-"Overlayed Text", 86-"Soccer", 87-"George Bush", which clearly benefits from the common visual appearance in their relevant images.

To evaluate the sensitivity of learning-based annotation with respect to its parameters, we designed a series of experiments and report the learning curves in terms of total annotation time for the TRECVID collection.[2] Figure 11 compare the annotation time of three algorithms, i.e., Browse, Tag and LBA, with the model parameters t_a, t_b, t_e and t_f multiplied by a scaling factor from 0.5 to 1.5. It degrades to our previous results when the scaling factor is 1. As can be seen, the proposed algorithm can still obtain significant improvement over browsing/tagging with various time model parameters, especially when t_a, t_b is lower or t_f is higher than the default values. This confirms the insensitivity of our analysis. Figure 12(a) compares the annotation time with the browsing batch size S in Algorithm 2 varied from 10 to 200. With a larger batch size, the total annotation time always becomes higher. But since a smaller batch size might increase the cost for users by switching the annotation contexts more frequently, a user study is needed to determine the best batch size. Finally, because the observation in Figure 10 suggests using only browsing to annotate the most frequent concepts, we carry out the following experiments: before applying the learning-based annotation, we used browsing approaches to annotate a number of

Figure 11. Annotation time of LBA with scaled time model parameters on TRECVID collection

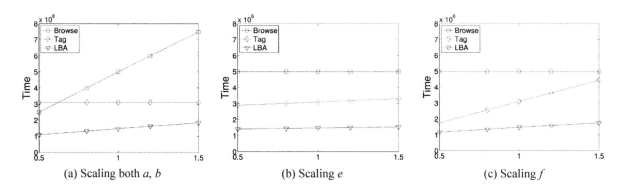

(a) Scaling both *a*, *b*   (b) Scaling *e*   (c) Scaling *f*

Figure 12. Annotation time of LBA with scaled learning parameters on TRECVID collection

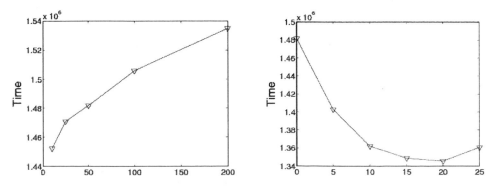

the most frequent keywords (assuming they are known) for all images. Figure 12(b) shows the learning curves with different number of browsed keywords. As we can see, if we can identify the 15 - 20 most frequent keywords, the total annotation time can be reduced by 10%. But identifying these keywords is still a challenge.

Empirical Annotation Results on TRECVID'05

To verify the simulation results, we implemented a hybrid annotation system and asked a user to manually annotate a subset of the TRECVID collection, which includes the keyframes of 10 randomly selected videos. We recorded the statistics for three annotation approaches, i.e., tagging, browsing and learning-based annotation, around every five seconds. Each annotation process lasted for one hour. The annotation parameters are re-estimated using linear regression on all 2142 annotation statistics. For this user, these parameters are set to t_p=1.16s,t_n=0.17s,t_f=4.01s,t_s=2.02s, which are slightly less than the value used in the simulation. Table I shows the number of tagged/browsed images at the end of the annotation process, and compares the estimated annotation time (based on time models) with the true annotation time recorded. It can be found that the estimated time closely approximates the true annotation time and the error is less than 4% in all three cases. This again confirms the correctness of the proposed time models in a large-scale annotation environment. Figure 13 shows the curve of hybrid recall as a function of annotation time.[3] The hybrid recall curves of tagging and browsing are similar to each other because

Figure 13. Comparing hybrid recall of three manual annotation approaches against the annotation time on the TRECVID collection

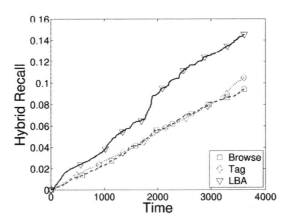

Table 1. Comparing estimated annotation time (T_{est}) with true annotation time (T_{true}). The number of annotated images are also shown (N_i: tagged images, N_t: tagged words, N_p: relevant browsed images, N_n: irrelevant browsed images)

Method	N_i	N_t	N_p	N_n	T_{est}	T_{true}
Tag	405	706	0	0	3649s	3600s
Browse	0	0	1393	11693	3603s	3608s
Hybrid	194	321	1009	3527	3478s	3601s

of their complementary properties on the macro-recall and micro-recall. The learning-based annotation, on the other hand, achieves a 50% improvement over tagging and browsing in terms of hybrid recall. This observation is in line with the simulation results presented before.

Retrieval Results on TRECVID'07

The last experiment describes the results and statistics of our TRECVID'07 interactive retrieval submission on 25 official queries using the proposed multi-topic hybrid retrieval system. The initial retrieval results are generated by an automatic retrieval system, of which the overall architecture was a combination of speech-based retrieval with automatic query refinement, model-based query retrieval and re-ranking based on automatic mapping of textual queries to semantic concept detectors, semantic

Figure 14. Comparing the mean average precision of the proposed method with the other TRECVID'07 submissions

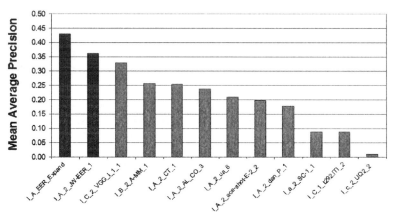

Figure 15. The number of relevant shots identified by tagging and browsing on the TRECVID'07 queries

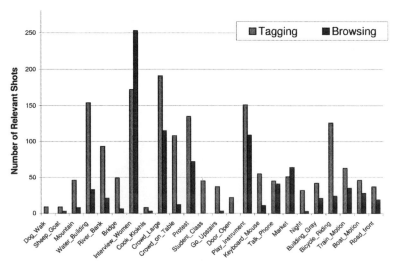

retrieval based on automatic mapping of visual query examples to concept detectors, and visual retrieval based on light-weight learning and smart pseudo-negative sampling. All processing was done at the sub-shot level based on the master shot boundary reference, where each sub-shot was represented by a single keyframe and a corresponding speech transcript segment. All ranking results were generated at the sub-shot level first and then aggregated at the shot level by taking the maximum confidence score across all sub-shots for each master shot. More details of the automatic retrieval system can be found in (Campbell et al., 2007).

The entire retrieval process lasted for 6 hours for 24 topics, which is translated into 15 minutes per query. We first examined the top 200 shots for each queries, iterate within each query until none of the unseen images are further suggested by the system. Then we switched back and forth on the tagging/browsing interfaces to retrieve multiple queries simultaneously. Our interactive system achieves a mean average precision of 0.36 on TRECVID'07 collection. With a simple temporal expansion at the end of the search result list, i.e., add discounted scores to the shots that are sufficiently close to the retrieved shots (within 3 shots) (Yan & Hauptmann, 2007), can boost the MAP to 0.43. Figure 14 compared the performance of the proposed system with other official interactive retrieval submissions in the TRECVID'07 evaluation. It can be seen that our system outperforms the other retrieval systems by a noticeable margin, which again confirms the effectiveness of the multi-topic retrieval approach. It is worthwhile to point out that since the other systems restrict the query time to be no more than 15 minutes, their performance might not directly comparable to ours. But from another perspective, this observation clearly demonstrates the advantages of multi-topic retrieval if we need to search for multiple query topics at the same time.

The statistics of our retrieval system shows that around 60% of the image-topic pairs in the entire video collection have been either browsed or tagged. Our system strikes a good balance on browsing and tagging the retrieved shots, where tagging produced 1726 retrieved shots and browsing produced 884. In contrast, according to our statistics, simple browsing interface can only label around 10% of the collection using the same amount of time. Simple tagging interface can label more image-topic pairs than browsing. However, it will miss most of the labeled shots provided by browsing. Figure 15 plots the breakdown of the number of browsed and tagged shots for each query. It shows that a larger proportion of the shots are retrieved by the tagging approach, but the browsing approach also contributes a comparable number of shots for each query. For two queries including "finding a women in the interview scene" and "finding market scene", the browsing approach offers a larger number of truth shots due to the visual similarity between the truth shots in these two queries.

CONCLUSION

In this paper we have presented two hybrid approaches for improving the efficiency of manual image annotation. This approach was inspired by our quantitative study of two widely used annotation approaches, i.e., tagging and browsing. We have proposed models to describe the processing time for tagging and browsing, and the validity of these models has been confirmed by our user studies. The quantitative analysis makes clear the complementary nature of tagging and browsing, and led us to propose a learning-based hybrid annotation algorithm which adaptively learns the most efficient annotation interface for selected keywords and images. Our simulation and empirical results on the TRECVID and Corel collections have shown that both proposed algorithms can achieve an up to 50% annotation time reduction compared with the baseline methods. In particular, learning-based annotation considerably outperforms the other approaches in terms of macro-recall, micro-recall and hybrid-recall in the entire annotation process. In the interactive retrieval experiments for TRECVID'07, the proposed method also enjoys a considerable improvement on the retrieval effectiveness under the same amount of retrieval time.

We expect this work to open up new research directions in modeling manual image annotation. For instance, the current annotation time models are by no means perfect. They can be refined to incorporate more user factors such as keyword missing rate, context switching cost, or vocabulary size. We can also consider other learning algorithms to support fast visual model updates. Finally, the interface design and user incentive for hybrid annotation algorithms can be further discussed.

ACKNOWLEDGMENT

This material is based upon work funded in part by the U. S. Government. Any opinions, findings and conclusions or recommendations expressed in this material are those of the author(s) and do not necessarily reflect the views of the U.S. Government.

REFERENCES

Barnard, K., Duygulu, P., Forsyth, D., de Freitas, N., Blei, D., & Jordan, M. (2002). Matching words and pictures. Journal of Machine Learning Research, 3.

Campbell, M., Haubold, A., Liu, M., Natsev, A. P., Smith, J.R., Tesic, J., Xie, L., Yan, R., & Yang, J. (2007). IBM research TRECVID-2007 video retrieval system. In Proceedings of NIST TRECVID-2007.

Foley, C., Gurrin, C., Jones, G., Lee, H., McGivney, S., O'Connor, N. E., Sav, S., Smeaton, A. F., & Wilkins, P. (2004). Trecvid 2005 experiments in dublin city university. In Proceedings of NIST-TRECVID. Gaitherberg, DC.

Furnas, G.W., Landauer, T.K., Gomez, L.M., & Dumais, S. T. (1987). The vocabulary problem in human-system communication. Communication of the ACM, 30, 964–971.

Griffin, G., Holub, A., & Perona, P. (2006). The caltech-256 (Technical Report). Caltech.

Halaschek-Wiener, C., Golbeck, J., Schain, A., Grove, M., Parsia, B., & Hendler, J. (2005). Photostuff - an image annotation tool for the semantic web. In Proceedings of the 4th international semantic web conference.

Hauptmann, A., & Witbrock, M. (1996). Informedia news on demand: Multimedia information acquisition and retrieval. In Intelligent multimedia information retrieval. Menlo Park, CA.

Hauptmann, A.G., Lin, W.-H., Yan, R., Yang, J., & Chen, M.-Y. (2006). Extreme video retrieval: joint maximization of human and computer performance. In Proceedings of the 14th ACM international conference on Multimedia (pp. 385–394). New York, NY, USA.

Jeon, J., Lavrenko, V., & Manmatha, R. (2003). Automatic image annotation and retrieval using cross-media relevance models. In Proceedings of the 26th annual international ACM SIGIR conference on Research and development in informaion retrieval (pp. 119–126). Toronto, Canada.

Kennedy, L.S., Chang, S.-F., & Kozintsev, I.V. (2006). To search or to label? predicting the performance of search-based automatic image classifiers. In Proceedings of the 8th ACM international workshop on Multimedia information retrieval (pp. 249–258). New York, NY, USA.

Kustanowitz, J., & Shneiderman, B. (2004). Motivating annotation for personal digital photo libraries: Lowering barriers while raising incentives (Technical Report). HCIL, Univ. of Maryland.

Li, J., & Wang, J. Z. (2006). Real-time computerized annotation of pictures. In Proceedings of the 14th ACM international conference. on Multimedia (pp. 911–920). Santa Barbara, CA, USA.

Lieberman, H., Rozenweig, E., & Singh, P. (2001). Aria: An agent for annotating and retrieving images. Computer, 34, 57–62.

Lin, W.-H., & Hauptmann, A. G. (2006). Which thousand words are worth a picture? experiments on video retrieval using a thousand concepts. In Proceedings of IEEE International Conference On Multimedia and Expo (ICME).

Naphade, M., Smith, J. R., Tesic, J., Chang, S.-F., Hsu, W., Kennedy, L., Hauptmann, A., & Curtis, J. (2006). Large scale concept ontology for multimedia. IEEE MultiMedia, 13, 86–91.

Over, P., Ianeva, T., Kraaij, W., & Smeaton, A.F. (2006). Trecvid 2006 overview. In Proceedings of NIST-TRECVID.

Rui, Y., Huang, T., & Mehrotra, S. (1997). Content-Based image retrieval with relevance feedback in MARS. In Proceedings of IEEE International Conference on Image Processing (pp. 815–818).

Snoek, C., Worring, M., Geusebroek, J., Koelma, D., & Seinstra, F. (2004). The MediaMill TRECVID 2004 semantic viedo search engine. In Proceedings of NIST-TRECVID.

Tong, S., & Chang, E. (2001). Support vector machine active learning for image retrieval. In Proceedings of the 9th ACM Intl. Conf. on Multimedia (pp. 107–118).

Volkmer, T., Smith, J.R., & Natsev, A. (2005). A web-based system for collaborative annotation of large image and video collections: an evaluation and user study. In Proceedings of the 13th ACM international conference on Multimedia. Hilton, Singapore.

von Ahn, L., & Dabbish, L. (2004). Labeling images with a computer game. In Proceedings of the SIGCHI conference on Human Factors in computing systems. Vienna, Austria.

Wenyin, L., Dumais, S., Sun, Y., Zhang, H., Czerwinski, M., & Field, B. (2001). Semi-automatic image annotation. In Proceedings of Interact: Conference on HCI.

Wilhelm, A., Takhteyev, Y., Sarvas, R., House, N.V., & Davis, M. (2004). Photo annotation on a camera phone. CHI '04 extended abstracts on Human factors in computing systems (pp. 1403–1406). Vienna, Austria.

Yan, R., & Hauptmann, A.G. (2004). Multi-class active learning for video semantic feature extraction. In Proceedings of IEEE International Conference on Multimedia and Expo (ICME) (pp. 69–72).

Yan, R., & Hauptmann, A.G. (2007). A review of text and image retrieval approaches for broadcast news video. Information Retrieval, 10, 445–484.

Yang, Y., & Pedersen, J.O. (1997). A comparative study on feature selection in text categorization. In Proceedings of the 14th International Conference on Machine Learning (pp. 412–420).

Zhou, X.S., & Huang, T.S. (2001). Comparing discriminating transformations and SVM for learning during multimedia retrieval. In Proceedings of the 9th ACM international conference on Multimedia (pp. 137–146). Ottawa, Canada.

APPENDIX. DERIVATION FOR EQN(7)

We analyze the annotation time for each keyword separately. For a given keyword T_k, the time of learning-based annotation should be lower than simply tagging or browsing T_k, otherwise either tagging or browsing should be used. When the learning-based annotation time is smaller than the tagging time for T_k, we can have

$$\beta_k L_k \left(t_p + \frac{1-\gamma_k}{\gamma_k} t_n \right) + (1-\beta_k) L_k t_f \leq L_k t_f$$

$$\Leftrightarrow \; t_p + \frac{1-\gamma_k}{\gamma_k} t_n \leq t_f \; \Leftrightarrow \; \gamma_k \geq \frac{t_n}{t_f + t_n - t_p} \tag{10}$$

Similarly, when the learning-based annotation time is smaller than the browsing time for T_k, we can have

$$\beta_k L_k \left(t_p + \frac{1-\gamma_k}{\gamma_k} t_n \right) + (1-\beta_k) L_k t_f \leq L_k t_p + (L - L_k) t_n$$

$$\Leftrightarrow (1-\beta_k)(t_f + t_n - t_p) + \frac{\beta_k}{\gamma_k} t_n - \frac{L}{L_k} t_n \leq 0.$$

By defining $a = t_n/(t_f + t_n - t_p)$ and $b_k = L/L_k$, we can simplify this inequality to be,

$$(1-\beta_k) + a \left(\frac{\beta_k}{\gamma_k} - b \right) \leq 0 \; \Leftrightarrow \; \frac{1}{\gamma_k} \leq \frac{ab + \beta_k - 1}{a\beta_k}.$$

The above inequality holds if and only if the following two conditions hold (since $\gamma_k \leq_l$),

$$\frac{\beta_k - 1 + ab}{a\beta_k} \geq 1, \; \gamma_k \geq \frac{a\beta_k}{ab + \beta_k - 1}. \tag{11}$$

Eqn(7) can be obtained by merging inequalities (10) and (11).

Chapter XIII
Active Video Annotation:
To Minimize Human Effort

Meng Wang
Microsoft Research Asia, China

Xian-Sheng Hua
Microsoft Research Asia, China

Jinhui Tang
National University of Singapore, Singapore

Guo-Jun Qi
University of Science and Technology of China, China

ABSTRACT

This chapter introduces the application of active learning in video annotation. The insufficiency of training data is a major obstacle in learning-based video annotation. Active learning is a promising approach to dealing with this difficulty. It iteratively annotates a selected set of most informative samples, such that the obtained training set is more effective than that gathered randomly. The authors present a brief review of the typical active learning approaches. They categorize the sample selection strategies in these methods into five criteria, that is, risk reduction, uncertainty, positivity, density, and diversity. In particular, they introduce the Support Vector Machine (SVM)-based active learning scheme which has been widely applied. Afterwards, they analyze the deficiency of the existing active learning methods for video annotation, that is, in most of these methods the to-be-annotated concepts are treated equally without preference and only one modality is applied. To address these two issues, the authors introduce a multi-concept multi-modality active learning scheme. This scheme is able to better explore human labeling effort by considering both the learnabilities of different concepts and the potential of different modalities.

INTRODUCTION

With rapid advances in storage devices, networks and compression techniques, large-scale video data is becoming available to more and more average users. The management of these data becomes a challenging task. To deal with this issue, it has been a common theme to develop techniques for deriving metadata from videos to describe their content at syntactic and semantic levels. With the help of these metadata, the manipulations of video data can be easily accomplished, such as delivery, summarization, and retrieval.

Video annotation is an elementary step to obtain these metadata. Ideally, video annotation is formulated as a classification task and it can be accomplished by machine learning methods. However, due to the large gap between low-level features and to-be-annotated semantic concepts, typically learning methods need a large labeled training set to guarantee reasonable annotation accuracy. But because of the high labor costs of manual annotation (experiments prove that typically annotating 1 hour of video with 100 concepts can take anywhere between 8 to 15 hours (Lin, Tseng, & Smith, 2003)), this requirement is usually difficult to meet.

Active learning has proved effective in dealing with this issue (Ayache & Quénot, 2007; Chen & Hauptmann, 2005; Cohen, Ghahramani, & Jordan, 1996; Panda, Goh, & Chang, 2006). It works in an iterative way. In each round, the most informative samples are selected and then annotated manually, such that the obtained training set is more effective than that gathered randomly. In this chapter, we discuss the application of active learning in video annotation, which mainly consists of two parts. In the first part, we provide a survey of the existing active learning approaches, especially their applications in image/video annotation and retrieval. We analyze the sample selection strategies in these methods and categorize them into five criteria: *risk reduction, uncertainty, positivity, density,* and *diversity.* Afterwards, we detail a widely-applied Support Vector Machine (SVM)-based active learning approach. In the second part, we analyze the deficiency of the existing active learning methods in video annotation, including: (1) the to-be-annotated concepts are treated equally without preference and (2) only a single modality is applied. To address these two issues, we introduce a multi-concept multi-modality active learning scheme, in which multiple concepts and multiple modalities can be simultaneously taken into consideration such that human effort can be more sufficiently exploited

The organization of the rest of this chapter is as follows. In Section II, we briefly review the related works, including video annotation and active learning. In Section III, we provide a survey of the sample selection strategies for active learning. In Section IV, we introduce the SVM-based active learning scheme. In Section V, we discuss the deficiency of the existing active learning approaches for video annotation, and then we present the multi-concept multi-modality active learning scheme in Section VI. Finally, we conclude the paper in Section VII.

RELATED WORKS

Video Annotation

Video annotation (also referred to as "video concept detection", "video semantic annotation" (Naphade & Smith, 2004a), or "high-level feature extraction" (TRECVID, http://www-nlpir.nist.gov/projects/trecvid)) is regarded as a promising approach to facilitating higher level manipulations of video data by bridging the semantic gap between low-level features and high-level users' needs (Hauptmann, 2005). As noted by Hauptmann (2005), *this splits the semantic gap between low level features and user information needs into two, hopefully smaller gaps: (a) mapping the low-level features into the intermediate semantic concepts and (b) mapping these concepts into user needs.* Annotation is exactly the step to accomplish the first mapping, as illustrated in Fig. 1. Typically video annotation can be accomplished by machine learning methods. First, videos are segmented into short units (such as shot and sub-shot). Then, low-level features are extracted from each unit (e.g., key-frames of each unit) to describe its content. Video annotation is then formalized to learn a set of predefined high-level concepts for each unit based on these low-level features. Figure 2 illustrates a typical learning-based video annotation scheme. Note that the concepts may not be mutually exclusive (such as "outdoor" and "building"), thus a general scheme is to conduct a binary classification procedure for each concept. Given a concept,

Figure 1. Video annotation bridges the semantic gap by mapping users' needs to semantic concepts

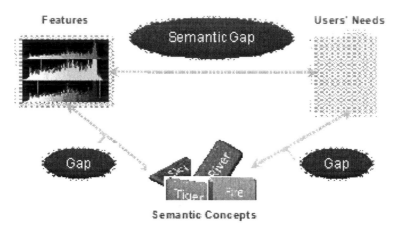

Figure 2. A typical learning-based video annotation scheme. Based on the models built upon training samples, a new sample is easily annotated with the concepts (or high-level features) of "lake", "mountain" and "sky".

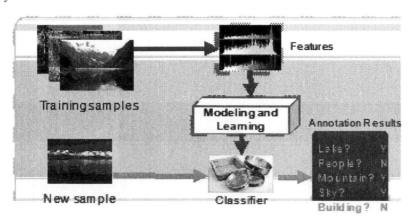

each unit is then labeled "positive" or "negative" according to whether it is associated with this concept. As shown in Fig. 2, a new video clip is annotated with "lake", "mountain" and "sky" since the corresponding concept classifiers/detectors output the "positive" results. Naphade and Smith (2004b) have given a survey on TRECVID high-level feature extraction benchmark, where a great deal of different algorithms applied in this task can be found.

Active Learning

Active learning, usually known as pool-based active learning, is an interactive learning technique designed to reduce human annotation effort. As previously mentioned, manual annotation is a labor-intensive and time-consuming process. Active learning aims to tackle this difficult by telling users to annotate only the most useful samples. A typical active learning system is composed of two parts, i.e., a learning engine and a selection engine. It works in an iterative way, as illustrated in Fig. 3. In each round, the learning engine trains a model based on the current training set. Then the selection engine selects a batch of the most informative unlabeled samples for manual annotation, and adds these samples to training set. In this way, the obtained training set is more informative than that gathered by random sampling.

It is obvious that the sample selection strategy plays a crucial role in an active learning scheme. Cohen, Ghahramani, & Jordan (1996) suggest that the optimized active learning approach should select the samples that minimize the expected risk. In (Cohen, et al., 1996; Roy & McCallum, 2001), the reduced risk is estimated with respect to each unlabeled sample, and then the most effective samples are selected. However, for most learning methods, it is infeasible to estimate the risk. Thus, practically most active learning methods adopt an uncertainty criterion, i.e., to select the samples closest to the classification boundary (Tong & Chang, 2001; Tong & Koller, 2000). Zhang et al. and Wu et al. further proposed to incorporate the density distribution of samples into the sample selection process (Zhang & Chen, 2003;

Figure 3. An illustration of active learning. It selects the most informative samples for manual labeling, such that the obtained training set is more effective than that gathered by random sampling.

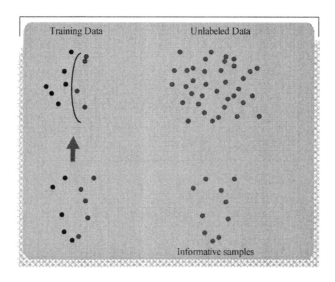

301

Wu, Kozintsev, Bouguet, & Dulong, 2006). Brinker et al. (Brinker, 2003) pointed out that the selected samples should be diverse. Several works also demonstrate that positive samples should be enhanced when applying active learning to image/video annotation or retrieval (Ayache & Quénot, 2007; Vendrig, Hartog, Leeuwen, Patras, Raaijmakers, Rest, Snoek, & Worring, 2002). In the next section, we will provide a more detailed survey of the existing sample selection methods for active learning.

Active learning techniques have been widely applied in image/video annotation and retrieval. In (Qi, Song, Hua, Zhang, & Dai, 2006), Qi et al. propose a video annotation framework with SVM-based active learning. In (Goh, Chang, & Lai, 2004), Goh et al. propose a concept-dependent active learning method for image annotation, so that different sample selection strategies are adopted for different concepts. Active learning is also frequently combined with Semi-Supervised Learning (SSL) methods[1] (Chapelle, Zien, & Schölkopf, 2006; Zhu, 2007). It is analyzed in (Muslea, Minton, & Knoblock, 2002) that combining active learning and semi-supervised learning is a stable approach to utilizing unlabeled data. In (Song, Hua, Dai, & Wang, 2005), Song et al. propose a video annotation scheme integrating active learning and a multi-view SSL method named co-training. In (Hoi & Lyu, 2005), Hoi et al. integrate active learning and a graph-based SSL method for image retrieval.

SAMPLE SELECTION STRATEGIES IN ACTIVE LEARNING

Obviously the sample selection strategy is crucial for an active learning method. In this section we provide a review of typical sample selection strategies.

Risk Reduction

Intuitively, the optimal sample selection strategy is consistent with the aim of the learner, i.e., minimizing the expected risk which can be denoted by

$$\int_x E[L(\hat{y}(x), y(x)) \mid x] p(x) dx \tag{1}$$

where $y(x)$ is the true label of sample x, $\hat{y}(x)$ is the classifier output, $p(x)$ is the probability density function of sample distribution, and L is a loss function that measures the difference between $y(x)$ and $\hat{y}(x)$. If the reduction of the expected risk of labeling each unlabeled sample can be estimated, then the optimal sample selection can be achieved. Cohen et al. (1996) have adopted such an approach for two different learners. But unfortunately, estimating the expected risk is not an easy task for most learning methods. Roy and McCallum (2001) have proposed to empirically estimate the reduced expected risk based on Monte Carlo sampling. But this approach is computationally intensive. Thus, many other heuristic sample selection strategies have been proposed. Here we categorize these strategies into the following four criteria, including *uncertainty*, *positivity*, *diversity* and *density*, as illustrated in Fig. 4.

Uncertainty

Applying *Uncertainty* criterion means that the most uncertain samples should be selected. This heuristic stems from the fact that in many learning algorithms the essential classification boundary can be preserved based solely on the nearby samples, and the sample that are far from the boundary can be regarded as redundant. For example, in a SVM model the hyperplane can be mainly constructed based on only the *support vectors* (i.e., the samples that lie closest to the hyperplane). Consider a binary classification problem. Denote by $\hat{P}(C_0 \mid x)$ the estimated posterior class probability of class k given x ($k = 0$ or 1). Then the uncertainty measure of a sample x can be simply denoted by

$$uncertainty(\boldsymbol{x}) = \left| \hat{P}(C_0 \mid \boldsymbol{x}) - 0.5 \right| \tag{2}$$

Note that there are also several other sample selection strategies that can be categorized into this criterion. For example, when multiple learners exist, the samples that have the maximum disagreement amongst them can be selected. This is the so-called query-by-committee method (Freund, Seung, Shamir, & Tishby, 1997; Seung, Opper, & Sompolinsky, 1992). Here the disagreement of multiple learners also can be regarded as an uncertainty measure, and thus this strategy is categorized into the *uncertainty* criterion as well.

Positivity

Positivity strategy is usually applied in image/video annotation and retrieval. In these tasks, samples are classified to be positive or negative according to whether they are relevant to the given concept or query. Of course the above *uncertainty* measure can also be applied in these tasks. But in many cases it is found that the using *positivity* criterion, i.e., directly selecting the samples that have the highest probabilities to be positive, is more effective (Ayache & Quénot, 2007; Gosselin & Cord, 2004; Vendrig, et al., 2002). This is due to the fact that positive samples are usually less than negative ones in these tasks, and the distribution of negative samples is usually in very broad domain. Thus, positive samples should contribute more than negative samples[2]. The *positivity* criterion can be simply denoted by

$$positivity(\boldsymbol{x}) = \hat{P}(C_0 \mid \boldsymbol{x}) \tag{3}$$

Density

Several works indicate that the samples within the regions of high density should be selected. From Eq. (1) we can also see the impact of the prior density distribution $p(x)$. Wu et al. define a "representativeness" measure for each sample according to its distance to nearby samples (Wu, et al., 2006). Zhang and Chen (2003) estimate data distribution $\hat{p}(x)$ by Kernel Density Estimation (KDE) (Parzen, 1962), and then utilize it in sample selection. Besides that, there are also several other clustering-based methods which first group the samples, and then only select the cluster centers in active learning (Nguyen & Smeulders, 2004; Qi, et al., 2006; Song, et al., 2005). Note that the cluster centers usually lie in the regions with high density. Thus, these works can also be regarded as applying a "density" strategy, i.e., trying to select samples in dense regions.

Here we introduce the approach proposed in (Zhang & Chen, 2003), by which the probability density function $\hat{p}(x)$ is estimated by

$$\hat{p}(\boldsymbol{x}) = \frac{1}{n} \sum_{j=1}^{n} K(\boldsymbol{x} - \boldsymbol{x}_j) \tag{4}$$

where n is the number of all samples (including both labeled and unlabeled samples) and $K(x)$ is a kernel function that satisfies $K(x) > 0$ and $\int K(x)dx = 1$. Consequently, the *density* measure can be defined by normalizing $\hat{p}(x)$ to [0, 1] as follows

$$density(x) = \frac{\sum_{j=1}^{n} K(x - x_j)}{\max_{i} \sum_{j=1}^{n} K(x - x_j)} \tag{5}$$

Diversity

Previous studies demonstrate that the selected samples should be diverse (Brinker, 2003; Wu, et al., 2006). This strategy can keep the variety of the selected samples, such that the selected samples will not be constrained in a more and more restricted area. Here we consider the method proposed in (Wu, et al., 2006). Given a kernel K, the angle between two samples x_i and x_j is defined as

$$\cos(<x_i, x_j>) = \frac{|K(x_i, x_j)|}{\sqrt{K(x_i, x_j)K(x_i, x_j)}} \tag{6}$$

Then the *diversity* measure can be estimated as

$$diversity(x_i) = 1 - \max_{x_j \in \mathcal{L}} \frac{|K(x_i, x_j)|}{\sqrt{K(x_i, x_j)K(x_i, x_j)}} \tag{7}$$

where $\mathcal{L}$ is the current labeled training set. There are also several variations for this criterion. In (Hoi, Jin, Zhu, & Lyu, 2006), Fisher information matrix is adopted for sample selection to keep the diversity of the selected samples, and in (Dagli, et al., 2006) an information-theoretic diversity measure is proposed based Shannon's entropy.

Up to now, we have discussed five typical sample selection criteria. But it is worth noting that these criteria are also frequently combined for sample selection. For example, in (Naphade and Smith, 2004b) the *uncertainty*, *density* and *diversity* criteria have been combined to form a sample selection strategy. In (Yuan, Zhou, Zhang, Wang, Zhang, Wang, & Shi, 2007), Yuan, et al. adopt the *uncertainty* criterion, and they also propose to shift the boundary such that more positive samples can be selected. So, this strategy also can be viewed as a combination of the *uncertainty* and the *positivity* criteria. Table 1 illustrates several works that adopt active learning in image/video annotation or retrieval. We have illustrated the description of the applications, the adopted learning methods and sample selection criteria.

SVM-BASED ACTIVE LEARNING

From Table 1 we can see that the SVM-based active learning scheme, in particular associated with the *uncertainty* sample selection criterion, is the most widely-applied approach. Thus, in this section we introduce this scheme in detail. From this scheme we can also see the main principle of active learning.

304

Figure 4. An illustration of the four sample selection criteria for active learning

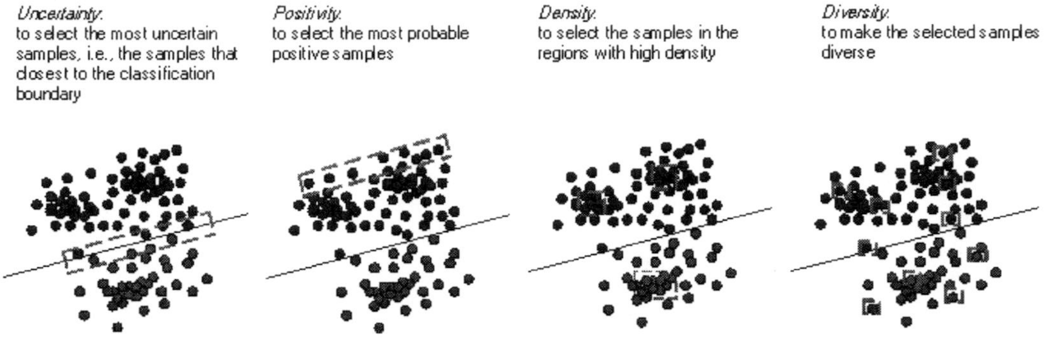

Uncertainty:
to select the most uncertain samples, i.e., the samples that closest to the classification boundary

Positivity:
to select the most probable positive samples

Density:
to select the samples in the regions with high density

Diversity:
to make the selected samples diverse

Table 1. Several existing works applying active learning in image/video annotation or retrieval

Works	Application	Adopted Learning Methods	Adopted Sample Selection Criteria
Ayache and Quénot (2007)	Video Annotation	SVM	Uncertainty; Positivity;
Chen, et al. (2005)	Video Annotation	SVM	Uncertainty
Dagli, et al. (2006)	Image Retrieval	SVM	Uncertainty; Diversity
Goh, et al. (2004)	Image Retrieval	SVM	Uncertainty; Positivity;
Gosselin, et al. (2004)	Image Retrieval	Bayes Classifier, k-NN; SVM	Uncertainty; Diversity
He, et al. (2004b)	Image Retrieval	SVM	Uncertainty
Hoi and Lyu (2005)	Image Retrieval	Graph-Based SSL (Zhu, Ghahramani, & Lafferty, 2003)	Risk Reduction
Naphade and Smith (2004a)	Video Annotation	SVM	Uncertainty
Panda, et al. (2006)	Image Retrieval	SVM	Uncertainty; Diversity
Qi, et al. (2006)	Video Annotation	SVM	Uncertainty; Density
Song, et al. (2005)	Video Annotation	Gaussian Mixture Model (Redner & Walker, 1984)	Uncertainty; Density
Sychay, Chang, & Goh (2002)	Image Annotation	SVM	Uncertainty
Tang, et al. (2007)	Video Typicality Ranking	Graph-Based SSL (Zhou, et al., 2004)	Uncertainty
Tong and Chang (2001)	Image Retrieval	SVM	Uncertainty; Diversity
Vendrig, et al. (2002)	Video Annotation	Maximum Entropy Classifier (Berger, Pietra, & Pietra, 1996)	Positivity
Wu, et al. (2006)	Personal Photo Retrieval	SVM	Uncertainty; Density; Diversity
Yuan, et al. (2006)	Image Retrieval	SVM	Uncertainty; Positivity; Diversity
Zhang and Chen (2003)	Object Categorization	Kernel Regression (Zhang and Chen, 2004)	Uncertainty; Density

Support Vector Machine

SVMs can be simply regarded as hyperplanes that separate the training samples with a maximal margin (Vapnik, 1995), as illustrated in Fig. 5. The training samples that lie closest to the hyperplane are called *support vectors*. Here we present a sketch introduction to the soft-margin SVM. For a binary classification problem, given a training data set which contains l labeled samples $(x_1, y_1), (x_2, y_2), ..., (x_l, y_l), x_i \in R^d, y_i \in \{0, 1\}$, the classification hyperplane is defined as

$$< w, \Phi(x) > +b = 0 \tag{8}$$

where $\Phi(.)$ is a mapping from R^d to a Hilbert Space $\mathcal{H}$, and $<., .>$ denotes the dot product in $\mathcal{H}$. Thus, the decision function $f(x)$ is

$$f(x) = sign(< w, \Phi(x) > +b) \tag{9}$$

SVM aims to find the hyperplane with the maximum margin between the two classes, i.e., the optimal hyperplane. This can be obtained by solving the following quadratic optimization problem

$$\min_{w,b,\xi} \frac{1}{2}\|w\|^2 + C\sum_{i=1}^{l}\xi_i \tag{10}$$

subject to $\quad y_i(< w, \Phi(x_i) > +b) \geq 1 - \xi_i$
$$\xi_i \geq 0, \forall i = 1, 2, ..., l$$

In the optimization process, the mapping $\Phi(.)$ will only appear in the dot product $<\Phi(x_i), \Phi(x_j)>$. Therefore, the mapping can be implicitly accomplished by defining a kernel $K(., .)$, i.e., $K(x_i, x_j) = <\Phi(x_i), \Phi(x_j)>$. The matrix **K** with components $K(x_i, x_j)$ is usually named Gram Matrix.

Figure 5. A simple example of SVM. The training samples that lie closest to the hyperplane are called support vectors.

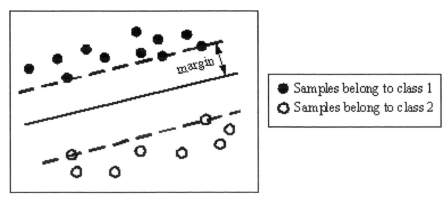

Active Learning with SVM

Here we only consider the *uncertainty* sample selection criterion. Previously we have mentioned that generally the *uncertainty* criterion is a heuristic strategy for sample selection, but in fact for SVM this strategy can also be derived from an optimization scheme, i.e., the minimization of the expected size of *version space*. Version space is defined to be the set of consistent hypotheses (Mitchell, 1982). It means that a hypothesis f is in version space if it satisfies $f(x_i) > 0$ if $y_i = 1$ and $f(x_i) < 0$ if $y_i = -1$ for every training sample x_i. For simplicity, we only consider an unbiased SVM model, i.e., the separating hyperplane that passes through origin. Then the version space can be denoted by

$$\mathcal{V} = \left\{ w \mid \; \|w\| = 1, \; y_i \langle w, \Phi(x_i) \rangle > 0, \; i = 1, 2, \ldots, n \right\} \tag{11}$$

In (Tong & Chang, 2001; Tong & Koller, 2000), it has been proved that selecting the samples closest to the current hyperplane in each round is an approximate approach to reducing version space in a fastest way. Detailed analysis and proof can be found in (Tong & Chang, 2001; Tong & Koller, 2000). Note that the samples closest to the hyperplane are exactly the ones with highest uncertainty measure. Thus, the *uncertainty* criterion is particularly suitable for SVM-based active learning. This partially explains why this combination has shown encouraging performance in many different learning tasks. The detailed implementation of SVM-based active learning scheme is illustrated in Fig. 6.

A DISCUSSION ON ACTIVE LEARNING-BASED VIDEO ANNOTATION

According to the previous introduction, we can see that many different active learning methods have already been applied in video annotation and encouraging results have also been reported. However, these methods are all studied in a relatively simple context. More specifically, in these methods the to-

Figure 6. The pseudo-code of SVM-based active learning approach with the uncertainty sample selection criterion

```
Input:
  L; /* labeled training set for a certain concept */
  U; /* unlabeled set for a certain concept */
  AT; /* the iteration time in active learning */
  h; /* the batch size for sample selection */

Output:
  f /* annotation results */

Functions:
  SVMTrain(L); /* SVM training algorithm */

Begin:
  for t = 1, 2, ..., AT
      f ← SVMTrain(L);
      Select h samples according to  arg min_{x_i ∈ U} |f_i|
      Manually label these samples, and move them from U to L;
  end
```

be-annotated concepts are usually sequentially annotated with fixed effort and only a single modality is applied. Consequently, these methods can be improved in two directions, i.e., considering the context of multi-concept annotation and multi-modality learning.

Multi-Concept Annotation

First, we consider the manual annotation for multiple concepts. Intuitively, there are two schemes, i.e., sequential annotation and simultaneous annotation. In the first scheme, each concept is exhaustively annotated for all samples before proceeding to the next, whereas in the second scheme each sample is simultaneously annotated with all concepts. In (Naphade & Smith, 2004a), a study once showed that simultaneously annotating multiple concepts may be more efficient. But recently a more detailed empirical evaluation has demonstrated that sequential annotation is superior to simultaneous annotation, in terms of both annotation accuracy and efficiency (Volkmer, Smith, & Natsev, 2005). Thus, here we only consider the sequential annotation approach.

When applying active learning to multi-concept annotation, the assignment of users' annotation effort becomes a problem. A most straightforward way is to equally assign the effort to all concepts. For example, suppose annotators may provide an effort of labeling s samples in all, and then s/c samples should be labeled for each concept, where c is the number of concepts. But this strategy may induce a waste of the annotation effort. For example, several concepts may be difficult to learn with existing features and some other concepts may already have accurate models, then labeling more samples for these concepts can hardly improve their performance. Thus, it is more rational to dedicate the annotation effort to other concepts.

Multi-Modality Learning

To differentiate or describe a variety of concepts, a large number of low-level features usually have to be applied. But a high-dimensional feature space frequently leads to the "curse of dimensionality" problem (Beyer, Goldstein, Goldstein & Shaft, 1999; Wu, Chang, Chang, & Smith) which may induce performance degradation. To deal with this issue, a natural method is to replace the high-dimensional learning task by multiple low-dimensional dimensional learning tasks, i.e., separately apply different modalities to learning algorithms and then fuse the results (Snoek, Worring & Smeulders, 2005). Here a modality is viewed as a description to video data, such as color, edge, texture, audio, and text. This method is usually called "multi-modality learning" or "multimodal fusion". Sometimes it is also named "late fusion" (Snoek, et al., 2005), whereas the method of using concatenated high-dimensional global feature vector is named "early fusion", as illustrated in Fig. 7. As demonstrated by a great deal of experiments, late fusion is able to improve video annotation performance compared with early fusion. But in most of the existing active learning methods only a single modality is applied. In (Chen & Hauptmann, 2005; Chen, et al., 2005), Chen et al. proposed a simple multi-modality active learning method with SVM, which selects a certain number of samples closest to the hyperplane of each sub-model (i.e., the model trained based on each individual modality). Although this method has shown better performance than single-modality-based active learning, it does not take the "discriminative abilities" of different modalities into account. For example, some features may not be discriminative enough for the concept to be annotated and some other sub-models may already have accurate models, and consequently the active learning process can only achieve very limited improvements for the these sub-models (this is analogous to the previously discussed deficiency of sequential multi-concept annotation).

Figure 7. A comparison of the early and late fusion schemes

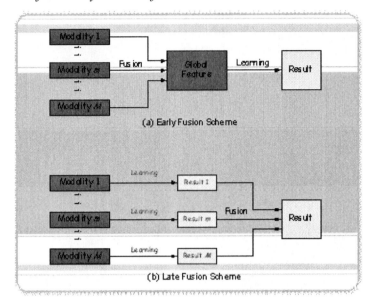

MULTI-CONCEPT MULTI-MODALITY ACTIVE LEARNING

In the above section, we have discussed the deficiency of the existing active learning-based video annotation approaches, i.e., the neglect of the context of multi-concept annotation and multi-modality learning. Now we introduce a multi-concept multi-modality active learning scheme which can simultaneously address the above two issues. The proposed method iteratively selects a concept and a batch of samples for manual annotation, as illustrated in Fig. 8. The concept is chosen to be the one that is expected to get the highest *performance gain*. Then a batch of samples is selected for annotation with

Figure 8. An illustration of multi-concept multi-modality active learning scheme

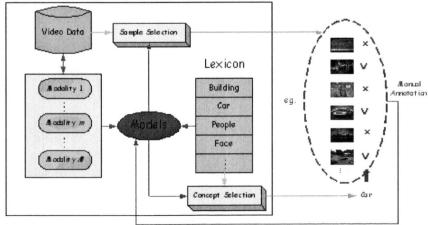

this concept. The numbers of the selected samples for different modalities are adapted according to the performance gains of their corresponding sub-models. In this way, the proposed approach can take both the learnabilities of multiple concepts and the discriminative abilities of multiple modalities into consideration. For a specific modality, four of the previously introduced criteria, including *uncertainty, positivity, density* and *diversity,* are combined to select samples. For the selected concept, a graph-based SSL algorithm named manifold-ranking (He, Li, Zhang, Tong, & Zhang, 2004a; Zhou, et al., 2004) is conducted on each modality with labeled samples for its effectiveness and efficiency.

As previously analyzed, the existing sequential multi-concept annotation does not take into account the impacts of the effort assigned to different concepts. To deal with this issue, in the proposed scheme an optimal concept is selected according to certain criterion for annotation in each round, such that the labeling effort can be most effectively utilized. The process is illustrated in Fig. 9. It can be viewed as a novel *exchangeable multi-concept annotation* approach, as opposed to the traditional sequential and simultaneous multi-concept annotation methods. We illustrate these three multi-concept annotation processes in Fig. 9 for comparison. In the proposed scheme, a concept and a batch of samples are selected for manual annotation in each round, and then manifold-ranking is employed to learn new sub-models of multiple modalities for the selected concept (although the manifold-ranking algorithm is adopted, we highlight that it can also be replaced by any other learning method, such as SVM and k-NN, when applying the multi-concept multi-modality active learning scheme). After several iterations, for each concept the results obtained from multiple sub-models are linearly fused with the weights decided by cross-validation based on labeled set. The detailed implementation is illustrated in Fig. 10.

Figure 9. A comparison of the three video annotation schemes

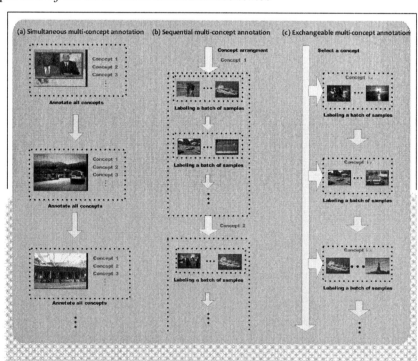

Figure 10. The pseudo-code of the proposed multi-concept multi-modality active learning approach

```
Input:
  𝓛ᵢ = φ, /* labeled training set for i-th concept, 1≤i≤c*/
  𝓤ᵢ = {x₁, x₂, …, xₙ}; /* unlabeled set for i-th concept, 1≤i≤c */
  AT; /* the iteration time in active learning */
  h; /* the batch size for sample selection */
  C; /* concept set */

Output:
  fᵢ /* annotation results for i-th concept, 1≤i≤c */

Functions:
  ConceptSelection(C); /* select a concept from C, see Section VI .A*/
  Manifold-Ranking(𝓛, 𝓤); /* manifold-ranking, see Section VI. B */
  SampleSelection(𝓛, 𝓤, h); /* select a batch of samples for the selected concept, see Section VI. C */

Begin:
  for t = 1, 2, …, AT
    k = ConceptSelection(C); /* select a concept */
    S = SampleSelection(𝓛ₖ, 𝓤ₖ, h); /* select a set of samples for this concept */

    Manually label samples in S, and move set S from 𝓤ₖ to 𝓛ₖ;

    fₖ = Manifold-Ranking(𝓛ₖ, 𝓤ₖ); /* obtain the annotation results for this concept */
  end
```

Concept Selection

To establish the concept selection strategy, firstly we have to define the evaluation of the performance of multi-concept annotation. Here a straightforward method is adopted, i.e., using the average of the performance of all concepts. It can be denoted by

$$perf_{ave} = \frac{1}{c}\sum_{i=1}^{c} perf_i,$$

where $perf_i$ is the performance of the i-th concept[3]. The Mean Average Precision (MAP) measure, which is widely applied in TRECVID (TREC-10 Proceedings appendix on common evaluation measures. From http://trec.nist.gov/pubs/trec10/appendices/measures.pdf), can be viewed as an example of this approach. Based on this performance measurement, a greedy strategy can be adopted by keeping selecting the concept that is expected to get the highest *performance gain*. The expected performance gain for each concept is approximated by the performance variation between the latest two learning iterations, which can be estimated from the newly labeled sample batches.

It is noteworthy that more sophisticated performance measurements can also be applied by assigning different weights to the concepts, i.e.,

$$perf_{ave} = \sum_{i=1}^{c} \lambda_i perf_i \Big/ \sum_{i=1}^{c} \lambda_i.$$

This measurement can guarantee the annotation accuracies of those concepts with high weights. In this case, we only have to weight the expected performance gains by λ_i as well, and then implement the concept selection method accordingly.

Obviously the proposed method needs an initial stage such that the performance gains of all concepts can be initialized. In the implementation each concept can be annotated for two iterations in this stage, and then the performance gains of all concepts are initialized. After these iterations, a concept is selected in each round and only the performance gain for this selected concept has to be updated.

Manifold-Ranking

Manifold-ranking has already been widely applied in the field of image and video content analysis (He, et al., 2004a; Yuan, et al., 2006). Here it is adopted to learn a sub-model for each modality with the selected concept (note that the discussion about manifold-ranking and sample selection in these two sub-sections is based on a certain concept, i.e., the concept selected by the proposed concept selection method). This method is chosen due to the following two reasons:

1.   It is a graph-based SSL method which can leverage a large amount of unlabeled samples, and it is able to achieve promising performance even with very limited training samples.
2.   It has low computational cost as it can be implemented by an efficient iterative process.

Let $\mathcal{L} = \{x_1, x_2, ..., x_l\}$ and $\mathcal{U} = \{x_{l+1}, x_{l+2}, ..., x_n\}$ be the labeled set and unlabeled set for the given concept, respectively. Considering there are M modalities, each sample x_i is represented by $\{x_i^1, x_i^2, ..., x_i^M\}$ where x_i^m is the feature representation for x_i in the m-th modality. Define a vector $y^+ = \{y_1^+, y_2^+, ..., y_n^+\}$, where $y_i^+ = 1$ if x_i is a labeled positive sample, and $y_i^+ = 0$ otherwise. Conversely, define $y^- = \{y_1^-, y_2^-, ..., y_n^-\}$, where $y_i^- = -1$ if x_i is a labeled negative sample, and $y_i^- = 0$ otherwise. Then the manifold-ranking process can be implemented for the m-th modality as follows:

1.   Define a graph over all samples in m-th modality as follows: x_i^m and x_j^m are connected if x_i^m belongs to the N-nearest neighborhood of x_j^m, and vice versa.
2.   Define an affine matrix $\mathbf{W}^m$ by letting $W_{ij}^m = \exp(-||x_i^m - x_j^m||/2\sigma)$ if x_i and x_j are connected and $i \neq j$, and otherwise $W_{ij}^m = 0$.
3.   Construct a matrix $\mathbf{S}^m = \mathbf{D}^{-1/2}\mathbf{W}^m\mathbf{D}^{-1/2}$ in which $\mathbf{D}$ is a diagonal matrix with its (i, i)-element equals to the sum of the i-th row of $\mathbf{W}^m$.
4.   Initialize $[f^{m+}, f^{m-}]$ (the final results are independent of the initial values). Here f_i^{m+} and f_i^{m-} can be regarded as the positive score and negative score of x_i^m, respectively. Then iterate $[f^{m+}, f^{m-}] = \alpha\mathbf{S}\times[f^{m+}, f^{m-}]+(1-\alpha) [y^+, y^-]$ for T times, where α is a parameter in (0, 1).
5.   Combine f^{m+} and f^{m-} as $f^m = \beta f^{m+} + f^{m-}$ for output, where β is a positive weight.

The above manifold-ranking process is similar to the method adopted in (He, et al., 2004a). There are several issues that need to be addressed in the above process. The first one is that a sparse graph is adopted. This strategy is frequently applied in graph-based learning methods as it can significantly reduce computational and storage costs while retaining close performance (He, et al., 2004a). Another issue is that the L_1 distance metric is used in the construction of the affine matrix $\mathbf{W}$. This is because empirical experiments have demonstrated that L_1 distance better approximates the perceptual difference for many visual features (He, et al., 2004a; Stricker & Orengo, 1995). In step 5 the results are generated as $f^m = \beta f^{m+} + f^{m-}$. This is due to the fact that positive samples are believed to contribute more in concept learning (He, et al., 2004a). Accordingly, a weight β is used to modulate the effect of positive samples, and typically we set $\beta > 1$. The final results are obtained by linearly combining the results from M modalities, where the weights are decided by cross-validation on the newly labeled samples.

Sample Selection

First, a sample selection strategy for individual modality is established by integrating the four criteria introduced in Section III, including *uncertainty, positivity, density,* and *diversity.* According to the principles introduced in Section III, in this scheme the *uncertainty* and *positivity* measures are defined as

$$uncertanty(x_i^m) = 1 - \left| f_i^m \right| \tag{12}$$

$$positivity(x_i^m) = f_i^{m+} \tag{13}$$

Between the *uncertainty* and *positivity* criteria, we have analyzed that the *uncertainty* criterion is better when positive and negative samples are balanced, and contrarily the *positivity* criterion may be superior if positive samples are much less than negative ones. Thus, the *uncertainty* and *positivity* measures are first integrated to form an *informativeness* measure as follows

$$informativeness(x_i^m) = 2 \times frequency \times uncertanty(x_i^m) + (1 - 2 \times frequency) \times positivity(x_i^m) \tag{14}$$

where *frequency* measures the percentage of positive samples in a labeled training set, i.e.,

$$frequency = \frac{\sum y_i^+}{l} \tag{15}$$

If *frequency* is near 0, i.e., the positive samples are very scarce, and then they contribute much more than negative samples in the learning of the concept. In this case, f_i^{m+} has a weight near 1, and the samples more likely to be positive are selected. If *frequency* is high (say, near 0.5), then the positive and negative samples are balanced, and thus $1 - \left| f_i^m \right|$ has higher weight and the samples closer to classification boundary are selected.

For computing *density* and *diversity* measures, the Exponential kernel is adopted, i.e., $K(x) = \exp(-\|x\|/2\sigma)$. Then, from Eq. (5) and Eq. (7) we can obtain

$$density(\mathbf{x}_i^m) = \frac{\sum_{j=1}^{n} W_{ij}^m}{\max_i \sum_{j=1}^{n} W_{ij}^m} \tag{16}$$

$$diversity(\mathbf{x}_i^m) = 1 - \max_{x_j \in L} S_{ij}^m \tag{17}$$

Now these criteria are combined as

$$effectiveness(x_i^m) = \gamma \times density(x_i^m) \times informativeness(x_i^m) + (1 - \gamma) \times diversity(x_i^m) \tag{18}$$

where γ is a weight in [0, 1].

Up to now we have addressed the sample selection strategy for a single modality. A remained problem is how to select samples for multiple modalities. Chen et al. have analyzed that samples should be selected for each individual modality to keep the specificity of multiple feature sets (Chen & Hauptmann, 2005; Chen, et al., 2005). Thus they select equal number of samples for each modality. But this method does not take the potentials of different modalities into account. For several modalities that are not discriminative enough for the given concept, it will achieve a "saturation" state after several active learning iterations, and then more samples should be selected for other modalities. Thus, here the sample selection strategy is constructed based on the performance gains of these modalities. Analogous to that defined for concepts, the performance gain for a modality is defined as the performance variation of the modality between the latest two learning iterations. Denote by $\Delta perf^m$ the performance gain of m-th modality. Then the numbers of selected samples are set to be proportional to the performance gains of multiple modalities, i.e.,

$$h^m = \frac{\Delta perf^m}{\sum_{m=1}^{M} \Delta perf^m} \times h \tag{19}$$

where h is the batch size. The above strategy is based on an assumption that the performance gain of a modality is higher if the modality is further from saturation. If a modality has a high performance gain, then more samples are selected for its sub-model in the next iteration; otherwise, if a modality achieves saturation state, then few samples are selected for its sub-model. Experiments will demonstrate that this adaptive approach is better than selecting a fixed number of samples for each modality.

Discussion

In this scheme, there is an assumption that the effort of labeling a sample with a concept is fixed. But in fact the effort may vary across different concepts and samples. The study in (Volkmer, et al., 2005) shows that different concepts may lead to different average annotation times per sample. Annotating different samples also may cost different effort even with the same concept. For example, the time cost for annotating a frame may depend upon the typicality (Tang, et al., 2007) and recognizability of the objects in it (see (Volkmer, et al., 2005)). But if the costs for different samples and concepts can be obtained, the sample selection and concept selection methods in our proposed scheme can be easily adapted as well by taking these costs into consideration.

Experiments

To evaluate the performance of the multi-concept multi-modality scheme, experiments have been conducted following the guideline of TRECVID 2005 high-level feature extraction task. TRECVID 2005 dataset consists of 273 broadcast news videos and is about 160 hours in duration. The dataset is split into a development set and a test set. The development videos are segmented into 49532 shots and 61901 sub-shots, and the test videos are segmented into 45766 shots and 64256 sub-shots. A key-frame is selected for each sub-shot, and from the key-frame we extract the following six feature sets: (1) block-wise color moment based on 5-by-5 division of the image (225D); (2) HSV correlogram (144D); (3) HSV histogram (64D); (4) wavelet texture (128D); (5) co-occurrence texture (16D); and (6) lay-out edge distribution histogram (75D). Each feature set is regarded as a modality, and thus we obtain six modalities.

Ten predefined benchmark concepts are annotated, including "Walking_Running", "Explosion_Fire", "Maps", "Flag-US", "Building", "Waterscape_Waterfront", "Mountain", "Prisoner", "Sports", and "Car". Other experimental settings, including the values of the parameters in the algorithm and the computation of MAP, can be found in (Wang, Hua, Tang, Song, & Dai, 2007).

Experiments for Sample Selection

First, experiments are conducted to demonstrate the effectiveness of the proposed sample selection strategy. The following three schemes are compared:

Scheme 1:
Integrate a global *effectiveness* measure as *effectiveness*$(x_i) = \Sigma\{\Delta perf^m \times effectiveness(x_i^m)\}$, and then select h samples according to this measure.

Scheme 2:
Select h/M samples for each modality, i.e., the method proposed in (Chen & Hauptmann, 2005).

Scheme 3:
Randomly select samples.

Denote by s the number of samples to be annotated in all. It is equally divided and assigned to all concepts. The batch size h is set to 500. The results are illustrated in Fig. 11. From the figure we can see that the proposed approach remarkably outperforms the other three schemes. It can achieve about twice MAP compared with random sample selection when $s = 1 \times 10^5$.

Experiments for Concept Selection

To evaluate the performance of the proposed concept selection method, it is compared with the following three schemes:

Scheme 1:
Sequential annotation, i.e., equally assign the annotation effort to all concepts as described in the above sub-section.

Scheme 2:
Assign annotation effort according to the annotation performance of these concepts. More specifically, first we estimate the annotation performance of each concept regarding the full development set as training set (the detailed results can be found in (Wang, et al., 2007)), and then we let the numbers of the annotated samples to be proportional to the performance of these concepts. It implies that the concepts that are easier to learn will be assigned more effort in each round.

Scheme 3:
Random concept selection method, i.e., in each round a concept is randomly selected.

Figure 11. Performance comparison for different sample selection methods (h = 500)

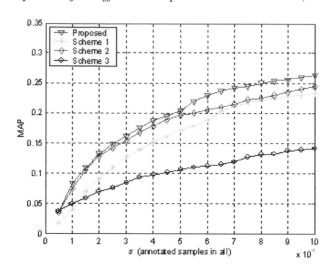

Figure 12. Performance comparison for different concept selection methods (h = 500)

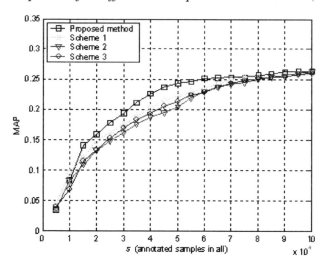

The experimental results are illustrated in Fig. 12. From the figure we can see that the performance of the proposed concept selection method increases much faster than those of Scheme 2 and Scheme 3 as the annotated samples grow. Now we compare the proposed approach with Scheme 1. It is worth noting that these two methods both have taken the learnabilities of the concepts into consideration. Scheme 1 statically assigns annotation effort according to the performance of different concepts, whereas the proposed approach dynamically selects the optimal concept in each round. From Fig. 12 we can clearly see the superiority of our proposed method.

Computational Cost

According to the previous description of the manifold-ranking method, it is easy to derive that the computational cost in each active learning iteration scales as $O(M \times T \times N \times n)$, where M is the number of

Table 2. The practical values of the notations

notation	description	practical value
n	number of samples	126157
M	number of modalities	6
N	neighborhood size	25
T	iteration time in manifold-ranking	20

modalities, T is the iteration time in the manifold-ranking process, N is the neighborhood size, and n is the number of samples. We illustrate the definitions of all these notations and their detailed values in the experiments in Table 2 for clarity. In practical experiments, the response time for interactive annotation is about 15 seconds (Pentium 1.8G Hz, 512M RAM). Thus, the proposed framework is quite efficient, and it is able to deal with large-scale datasets.

CONCLUSION AND DISCUSSION

In this chapter, we have discussed the active learning-based video annotation approach. We provide a brief survey of the existing active learning methods and categorize the sample selection strategies in these methods into the following five criteria: *risk reduction, uncertainty, positivity, density,* and *diversity.* We then analyze the deficiency of the existing active learning methods for video annotation, i.e., concepts are sequentially annotated without preference and only one modality is applied. We introduce a novel multi-concept multi-modality active learning scheme which can address these issues. By taken the learnabilities of the concepts and the potentials of different modalities into consideration, the proposed active learning scheme can better explore human effort.

There are also several challenging open issues in active learning-based video annotation. Since active learning involves the integration of human and computer, we categorize these issues into two problems: (1) the improvement of the efficiency of manual annotation and (2) better learning schemes.

Making Manual Annotation More Efficient

In active learning-based video annotation approach, users have to annotate the samples returned by the sample selection engine. The efficiency of manual annotation is thus an important issue, though it receives relatively less attention in research community. Obviously, by speeding up the manual annotation process, more training samples can be obtained in a fixed time. Several studies have been conducted on this issue (Lin, et al., 2003; Volkmer, et al., 2005; Yan, Natsev, & Campbell, 2007), and some conclusions have been obtained, such as the sequential annotation approach is better than the simultaneous annotation approach, and the annotation accuracy of a concept is correlated with its frequency (Volkmer, et al., 2005). But many issues are still worth further studying, for example, displaying and annotating only a few video clips per page without scrolling vs. scrolling and annotating many clips at a time, using mouse vs. using keyboard for navigation and annotation, and laying out the clips randomly vs. by grouping visually similar ones into clusters. A suitable tool will significantly facilitate users and improve the efficiency of manual annotation.

Applying Better Learning Schemes

The learning schemes can also be improved in several directions. In the existing active learning-based video annotation approaches, including the proposed multi-concept multi-modality active learning scheme, multiple concepts are learned separately. But concepts are correlated rather than isolated (Naphade, et al., 2006), and existing studies have shown that jointly learning multiple concepts can achieve better performance (Qi, Hua, Rui, Tang, Mei, & Zhang, 2007). Thus, the integration of correlative multi-concept learning and active learning methods is worth studying. Another interesting issue is incorporating active learning into multi-instance setting, since multi-instance learning[4] has already shown encouraging performance in video annotation, especially for annotating object concepts (Cohen, et al., 1996; Gu, Mei, Tang, Wu, & Hua, 2008).

REFERENCES

TRECVID: TREC Video Retrieval Evaluation. http://www-nlpir.nist.gov/projects/trecvid. In *TREC-10 Proceedings appendix on common evaluation measures.* From http://trec.nist.gov/pubs/trec10/appendices/measures.pdf.

Ayache, S., & Quénot, G. (2007). Evaluation of active learning strategies for video indexing. *Signal Processing: Image Communication, 22,* 692-704.

Berger, A., Pietra, S.D., & Pietra, V.D. (1996). A maximum entropy approach to natural language processing. *Computational Linguistics, 22*(1), 39-71.

Beyer, K., Goldstein, J., Ramakrishnan, R., & Shaft, U. (1999). When is "nearest neighbor" meaningful? In *Proceedings of International Conference on Database Theory,* (pp. 217-235).

Brinker, K. (2003). Incorporating diversity in active learning with support vector machines. In *Proceedings of International Conference on Machine Learning,* (pp. 59-66).

Chapelle, O., Zien, A., & Schölkopf, B. (Eds.). (2006). *Semi-supervised learning.* MIT Press.

Chen, M., & Hauptmann, A. (2005). Active learning in multiple modalities for semantic feature extraction from video. In *Proceedings of AAAI workshop on learning in computer vision.*

Chen, M., Christel, M., Hauptmann, A., & Wactlar, H. (2005). Putting active learning into multimedia applications: dynamic definition and refinement of concept classifiers. In *Proceedings of ACM Multimedia,* (pp. 902-911).

Chen, Y., & Wang, J.Z. (2005). Image categorization by learning and reasoning with regions. *Journal of Machine Learning Research, 5,* 913-939.

Cohen, D.A., Ghahramani, Z., & Jordan, M.I. (1996). Active learning with statistical models. *Journal of Artificial Intelligence, 4,* 129-145.

Dagli, C.K., Rajaram, S., & Huang, T.S. (2006). Leveraging active learning for relevance feedback using an information-theoretic diversity measure. In *Proceedings of International Conference on Image and Video Retrieval,* (pp. 123-132).

Dietterich, T.G., Lathrop, R.H., & Lozano-Pérez, T. (1997). Solving the multiple-instance problem with axis-parallel rectangles. *Artificial Intelligence, 89,* 31-71.

Freund, M., Seung, H.S., Shamir, E., & Tishby, N. (1997). Selective sampling using the query by committee algorithm. *Machine Learning, 28,* 133-168.

Goh, K. –S., Chang, E. Y., & Lai, W. –C. (2004). Multimodal concept-dependent active learning for image retrieval. In *Proceedings of International Conference on Machine Learning,* (pp. 564-571).

Gosselin, P.H., & Cord, M. (2004). A comparison of active classification methods for content-based image retrieval. In *Proceedings of International Workshop on Computer Vision Meets Databases,* (pp. 51-58).

Gu, Z., Mei, T., Tang, J., Wu, X., & Hua, X.–S. (2008). MILC^2: a multi-layer multi-instance learning approach for video concept detection. In *Proceedings of International Multimedia Modeling Conference,* (pp. 24-34).

Hauptmann, A.G. (2005). Lessons for the Future from a Decade of Informedia Video Analysis Research. In *Proceedings of ACM International Conference on Image and Video Retrieval,* (pp. 1-10).

He, J. R., Li, M., Zhang, H.–J., Tong, H., & Zhang, C. (2004a). Manifold-ranking based image retrieval. In *Proceedings of ACM Multimedia,* (pp. 9-16).

He, J. R., Li, M., Zhang, H–J., Tong, H., & Zhang, C. (2004b). Mean version space: a new active learning method for content-based image retrieval. In *Proceedings of ACM Workshop on Multimedia Information Retrieval,* (pp. 15-22).

Hoi, S. C.H., Jin, R., Zhu, J., & Lyu, M.R. (2006). Batch mode active learning and its application to medical image classification. In *Proceedings of International Conference on Machine Learning,* (pp. 417-424).

Hoi, S.C.H., & Lyu, M.R. (2005). A semi-supervised active learning framework for image retrieval. In *Proceedings of International Conference on Computer Vision and Pattern Recognition,* (pp. 302-309).

Lin, C., Tseng, B., & Smith, J. (2003). VideoAnnEx: IBM MPEG-7 annotation tool for multimedia indexing and concept learning. In *Proceedings of International Conference on Multimedia & Expo.*

Lin, C., Tseng, B., & Smith, J. (2003). Video collaborative Annotation forum: establishing ground-truth labels on large multimedia datasets. In *Proceedings of TRECVID Workshop.*

Mitchell, T. (1982). Generalization as search. *Artificial Intelligence,* (pp. 203-226).

Muslea, I., Minton, S., & Knoblock, C.A. (2002). Active + Semi-supervised learning = Robust multi-view learning. In *Proceedings of International Conference on Machine Learning,* (pp. 435-442).

Naphade, M., & Smith, J.R. (2004a). Active learning for simultaneous annotation of multiple binary semantic concepts. In *Proceedings of International Conference on Image Processing,* (pp. 77-80).

Naphade, M., & Smith, J.R. (2004b). On the detection of semantic concepts at TRECVID. In *Proceedings of ACM Multimedia,* (pp. 660-667).

Naphade, M., Smith, J.R., Tesic, J., Chang, S.–F., Hsu, W., Kennedy, L., Hauptmann, A.G., & Curtis, J. (2006). Large-scale concept ontology for multimedia. *IEEE Multimedia Magazine, 13*(3), 86-91.

Nguyen, H.T., & Smeulders, A. (2004). Active learning using pre-clustering. In *Proceedings of International Conference on Machine Learning*, (pp. 623-630).

Panda, N., Goh, K., & Chang, E.Y. (2006). Active learning in very large image databases. *Journal of Multimedia Tools and Applications Special issue on Computer Vision Meets Databases, 31*(3), 249-267.

Parzen, E. (1962). On the estimation of a probability density function and the mode. *Annals of Mathematical Statistics, 33(3), 1065-1076.*

Qi, G., Song, Y., Hua, X.–S., Zhang, H.–J., & Dai, L.–R. (2006). Video annotation by active learning and cluster tuning. In *Proceedings of Computer Vision and Pattern Recognition Workshop.*

Qi, G., Hua, X.–S., Rui, Y., Tang, J., Mei, T., & Zhang, H.–J. (2007). Correlative multi-label video annotation. In *Proceedings of ACM Multimedia, (pp. 17-26).*

Redner, R., & Walker, H. (1984). Mixture densities, maximum likelihood and the EM algorithm. SIAM review, 26(2), 195-239.

Roy, N., & McCallum, A. (2001). Toward optimal active learning through Monte Carlo estimation of error reduction. In *Proceedings of International Conference on Machine Learning.*

Seung, H.S., Opper, M., & Sompolinsky, H. (1992). Query by committee. In *Proceedings of Annual Workshop on Computational Theory*, (pp. 287-294).

Snoek, C.G.M., Worring, M., & Smeulders, A.W.M. (2005). Early versus late fusion in semantic video analysis. In *Proceedings of ACM Multimedia*, (pp. 399-402).

Song, Y., Hua, X.-S., Dai, L.-R., & Wang, M. (2005). Semi-Automatic Video annotation based on active learning with multiple complementary predictors. In *Proceedings of ACM Workshop on Multimedia Information Retrieval*, (pp. 94-104).

Stricker, M., & Orengo, M. (1995). Similarity of color images. In *Proceedings of SPIE 2420, Storage and Retrieval for Image and Video Databases*, (pp. 381-392).

Sychay, G., Chang, E.Y., & Goh, K. (2002). Effective image annotation via active learning. In *Proceedings of International Conference on Image Processing*, (pp. 209-212).

Tang, J., Hua, X.–S., Qi, G., Gu, Z., & Wu, X. (2007). Beyond accuracy: typicality ranking for video annotation. In *Proceedings of International Conference on Multimedia & Expo*, (pp. 647-650).

Tong, S., & Chang, E. Y. (2001). Support vector machine active learning for image retrieval. In *Proceedings of ACM Multimedia*, (pp. 107-118).

Tong, S., & Koller, D. (2000). Support Vector Machine Active Learning with Applications to Text Classification. In *Proceedings of International Conference on Machine Learning*, (pp. 999-1006).

Vapnik, V.N. (1995). *The nature of statistical learning theory.* New York: Springer Verlag.

Vendrig, J., den Hartog, J., Leeuwen, D., Patras, I., Raaijmakers, S., Rest, J. van, Snoek, C., & Worring, M. (2002). TREC feature extraction by active learning. In *Proceeding of Text Retrieval Conference (TREC)*.

Volkmer, T., Smith, J.R., & Natsev, A. (2005). A web-based system for collaborative annotation of large image and video collections. In *Proceedings of ACM Multimedia*, (pp. 829-901).

Wang, M., Hua, X.-S., Tang, J., Song, Y., & Dai, L.-R. (2007). Multi-concept multi-modality active learning for interactive video annotation. In *Proceedings of International Conference on Semantic Computing*, (pp. 321-328).

Wu, Y., Chang, E.Y., Chang, K.C.-C., & Smith, J.R. (2004). Optimal multimodal fusion for multimedia data analysis. In *Proceedings of ACM Multimedia*, (pp. 572-579).

Wu, Y., Kozintsev, I., Bouguet, J.-Y., & Dulong, C. (2006). Sampling strategies for active learning in personal photo retrieval. In *Proceedings of International Conference on Multimedia & Expo*, (pp. 529-532).

Yan, R., Natsev, A., & Campbell, M. (2007). An efficient manual image annotation approach based on tagging and browsing. In *Proceedings of ACM Multimedia Workshop on The Many Faces of Multimedia Semantics*, (pp. 13-20).

Yuan, J., Zhou, X., Zhang, J., Wang, M., Zhang, Q., Wang, W., & Shi, B. (2007). Positive sample enhanced angle-diversity active learning for SVM based image retrieval. In *Proceedings of International Conference on Multimedia & Expo*, (pp. 2202-2205).

Yuan, X., Hua, X.-S., Wang, M., & Wu, X. (2006). Manifold-ranking based video concept detection on large database and feature pool. In *Proceedings of ACM Multimedia*, (pp. 623-626).

Zhang, C., & Chen, T. (2003). Annotating retrieval database with active learning. In *Proceedings of International Conference on Image Processing*, (pp. 595-598).

Zhou, D., Bousquet, O., Lal, T.N., Weston, J., & Schölkopf, B. (2004). Learning with local and global consistency. In *Proceedings of Advances in Neural Information Processing Systems*, (pp. 321-328).

Zhou, Z.-H. (2004). *Multi-instance learning: a survey*. Technical Report, Department of Computer Science & Technology, Nanjing University, China.

Zhu, X. (2007). *Semi-supervised learning literature survey*. Technical Report (1530), University of Wisconsin-Madison, www.cs.wisc.edu/~jerryzhu/pub/ssl_survey.pdf.

Zhu, X., Ghahramani, Z., & Lafferty, J. (2003). Semi-supervised learning using Gaussian fields and harmonic functions. In *Proceedings of International Conference on Machine Learning*, (pp. 912-919).

ENDNOTES

[1]   Semi-Supervised Learning (SSL) is another approach to dealing with the difficulty of training data insufficiency. It attempts to leverage a large amount of unlabeled samples based on certain

assumptions, such that the obtained models can be more accurate than those that achieved by purely supervised methods. More details about semi-supervised learning can be found in (Chapelle, et al., 2006; Zhu, 2007).

[2] There may be another important reason, i.e., ranking performance rather than classification accuracy is usually adopted for evaluation in these tasks. For example, in TRECVID benchmark the Average Precision (AP) measure is adopted (TREC-10 Proceedings appendix on common evaluation measures. From http://trec.nist.gov/pubs/trec10/appendices/measures.pdf). This implies that finding more positive samples with high confidence is more important than correctly classifying the samples. So, the *positivity* criterion may outperform the *uncertainty* criterion since it is able to find more positive samples.

[3] To make notations consistent, the indices for concept and modality are denoted by subscripts and superscripts, respectively. But the sample indices are denoted by subscripts as well. We have tried to avoid the simultaneous occurrence of these three indices for clarity. For examples, the notation $Perf_i$ and $Perf^m$ indicate the performance of the i-th concept and the m-th modality respectively, and x_i^m indicates the feature representation for x_i in the m-th modality.

[4] Multi-Instance Learning (MIL) aims to handle the problems in which the labels are not available for each individual instance but only for *bags* of instances. A bag is labeled positive if it contains a positive instance, and it is labeled negative if all the instances in it are negative. It is suitable for annotating *object* concepts in images or video samples, since the samples will be labeled positive or negative only according to the existence of the objects. More details about MIL can be found in (Chen & Wang, 2005; Dietterich, Lathrop, Lozano-Pérez, 1997; Zhou, 2004).

Chapter XIV
Annotating Images by Mining Image Search

Xin-Jing Wang
Microsoft Research Asia, China

Lei Zhang
Microsoft Research Asia, China

Xirong Li
Microsoft Research Asia, China

Wei-Ying Ma
Microsoft Research Asia, China

ABSTRACT

Although it has been studied for years by computer vision and machine learning communities, image annotation is still far from practical. In this chapter, the authors propose a novel attempt of modeless image annotation, which investigates how effective a data-driven approach can be, and suggest annotating an uncaptioned image by mining its search results. The authors collected 2.4 million images with their surrounding texts from a few photo forum Web sites as our database to support this data-driven approach. The entire process contains three steps: (1) the search process to discover visually and semantically similar search results; (2) the mining process to discover salient terms from textual descriptions of the search results; and (3) the annotation rejection process to filter noisy terms yielded by step 2. To ensure real time annotation, two key techniques are leveraged – one is to map the high dimensional image visual features into hash codes, the other is to implement it as a distributed system, of which the search and mining processes are provided as Web services. As a typical result, the entire process finishes in less than 1 second. Since no training dataset is required, our proposed approach enables annotating with unlimited vocabulary, and is highly scalable and robust to outliers. Experimental results on real Web images show the effectiveness and efficiency of the proposed algorithm.

INTRODUCTION

The number of digital images has exploded with the advent of digital cameras which requires effective image search techniques. Although it is an intuitive way of image search since "a picture worths a thousand word", currently the Query-By-Example (QBE) scheme (i.e. using images as queries) is seldom adopted by commercial image search engines. The reasons are at least twofold: 1) the semantic gap problem. It is also the fundamental problem in Content-based Image Retrieval (CBIR) field. The techniques to extract low-level features, such as color, texture, and shape etc., are far from powerful to represent the semantics contained in an image, and hence given an image, its search results may be quite different conceptually to the query, although they possess same chromatic or textural appearances. 2) Computational expensiveness. It is well known that the inverted indexing technique ensures the practical and successful usage of current text search engines. This technique uses keywords as entries to index documents containing them, which also aligns seamlessly with the Query-by-Keyword (QBK) scheme adopted by text search engines. Thus given a number of query keywords, the search result can just be the intersection of documents indexed by these keywords separately (if no ranking functions applied). However, in the image search case, since images are 2D media, and the spatial relationship between pixels is critical in conveying the semantics of an image, how to define image "keyword" is still an open question. This prevents the inverted indexing technique from being directly used in image search, which creates a critical efficiency problem of using image visual features to search.

Due to the above reasons, there is a surge of interests on image auto-annotation and object recognition in recent years. Researchers try to define ways to automatically assign keywords onto images or image regions. While all the previous work build learning models to annotation images, in this chapter, we attempt to investigate how effective a modeless and data-driven approach, which leverages the huge amount of commented image data in the Web, could be.

This is reasonable because (1) to manually label images is a very expensive task (Naphade, Smith, Tesic, Chang, Hsu, Kennedy, Hauptmann, & Curtis, 2006), and in many cases, different people tend to have different explanations on a single image. Such inconsistency even makes image labeling a research topic that many questions should be addressed: What kind of images can be labeled consistently? What is the strategy of labeling images that can ensure the consistency, etc? All these obstacles lead to the lack of training data, which discourages researchers from learning a practically effective annotation model even if we have such a huge image data set in the Web. (2) Some researchers proposed very efficient and effective image encoding approaches (Fan, Xie, Li, Li, & Ma, 2005) which convert an image into an N-bit hash code so that image visual distance can be measured simply by the Hamming distance between the hash codes. This enables large-scale content-based image search in real-time and set a light on combining image visual appearance into the commercial search engines that are purely based on text search since both image indexing (e.g. matching the first n bits of two hash codes) and retrieval are of $O(1)$ complexity.

Imagine that an image set that is large enough is available, so that for each query image at least one duplication can be found in the image set, and then what we need to do is just to annotate the query by the comments or surrounding texts of the duplication. As analyzed above, this is applicable in real-time since each image is converted into a hash code so that large-scale image indexing is enabled.

This motivated us to leverage Web data and crawl Web images for a data-driven image annotation approach since the Web not only deposits huge amount of images but also they generally have human assigned comments or descriptions as their surrounding texts. Apparently the ideal case above is still far from what our current technique can achieve; however, we can retrieve a group of very similar images to the query, or the near-duplicate, instead of the duplications. These search results, intuitively, will cover the major semantics inside the query image. On the other hand, the textual descriptions of these near duplications are most often noisy and diverse which are far from optimal as annotations, so that intuitively, data mining techniques can successively be applied onto the search results to learn the common keywords or phrases in a majority voting sense, which can thus be assigned to the query image as the learned annotations. This is the key idea of our proposed modeless and data-driven approach in this paper. It not only investigates how much data can help us in recognizing an image as the saying "data is the king", but also demonstrates a way to support practical image annotation which can handle large-scale image data in real-time.

The paper is organized as follows. Section II gives a survey on the previous works on image annotation, which provides the reader a general picture on current art. Section III describes our insights of the image annotation problem, which motivate us the proposed modeless and data-driven approach as a novel and practical solution compared with the previous model-based ones. Section IV presents our modeless approach in detail and Section V provides experimental results. Several discussions are inspired in Section VI and the paper is concluded in Section VII with a few outlooks of possible improvements.

RELATED WORKS

In the early works on image annotation, many researchers sought to users' relevance feedback to assign labels to a given image. For example, Liu, Dumais, Sun, Zhang, Czerwinski, & Field (2001) asked the user to label a given image in the relevance feedback stage and then propagate these labels to all the positive images suggested by the retrieval system. Shevade and Sundaram (2006) made a further step. They attempted to propagate the image annotations by calculating the propagation likelihood based on WordNet (Fellbaum, 1998) synonym sets as well as image low-level features, and present only those images that are most ambiguous to the user for relevance feedback.

Due to the explosion of digital images and the semantic gap problem, image auto-annotation has become a hot research topic in recent years. And most of the researchers work on two major research directions. One attempt is to learn the joint probabilities between images and words. Most of this type of research tries to learn a generative model leveraging a training dataset and then infer the labels for the new-coming images according to the learnt correlations. For example, Blei et al. extended the Latent Dirichlet Allocation (LDA) model to the mix of words and images and proposed a so-called Correlation LDA model (Blei and Jordan, 2003). This model assumes that there is a hidden layer of topics, which are a set of latent factors and obey the Dirichlet distribution. And words and regions are conditionally independent given the topics. This work used 7,000 Corel photos and a vocabulary of 168 words for annotation.

Barnard, Duygulu, Freitas, Forsyth, Blei, & Jordan (2003) proposed a generative model and tested various statistical models to learn the joint probabilities of image regions and words. They used 16,000 Corel photos with 155 words and automatically annotated 10,000 test images.

Li and Wang (2003) proposed a two-dimensional multi-resolution hidden Markov model to connect images and concepts. They used 60,000 Corel photos with 600 concepts. In one of their recent work, they improved this model and propose a real-time annotation approach named Alipr which attracts attention from both academic and industry. Lavrenko, Manmatha, & Jeon (2003) proposed a continuous relevance model, a generative model which directly associates continuous features with words and achieved significant improvement in performance. Jeon, Lavrenko, & Manmatha (2003) and Jeon and

Manmatha (2004) extended this model to learn the joint probabilities between a set of words and image features. The training set they used were about 56,000 Yahoo! news images with noisy annotations and a vocabulary of 4,073 words. This is the largest vocabulary used in the previous work, and they discussed noisy-annotation filtering and speeding-up schemes.

The generative model proposed by Zhang, Zhang, Li, Ma, & Zhang (2005) added a hidden layer of semantic concepts to connect visual features and words. The concepts are discovered to explicitly exploit the synergy among the modalities.

All the approaches mentioned above suggest generative models. As a different approach, Pan, Yang, Faloutsos, & Duygulu (2004a) formulated this problem as learning a graph structure. They constructed a two-layer graph on training images and their associated captions, and used the random-walk-with-restarts algorithm to estimate the correlations between new images and the existed captions. In another work of Pan, et al. (2004b), they further extended the model into a three-layered graph by taking into consideration the image regions. Also, Monay and Gatica-Perez (2003, 2004) tested the performance of latent space models on this task.

Duygulu, Barnard, Freitas, & Forsyth (2002) and Barnard, Duygulu, Freitas, & Forsyth (2003) represented images by a group of blobs, and then used a statistical machine translation model to translate the blobs into a set of keywords.

Another group of researchers attempted to learn classifiers based on the training data. Chang, Kingshy, Sychay, & Wu (2003) started their process by manually labeling one caption for each image in a small training set, then train an ensemble of binary classifiers, each classifier for a specific label. Li, Goh, & Chang (2003) proposed a Confidence-based Dynamic Ensemble model which was a two-stage classification method. Carneiro and Vasconcelos (2005) attempted to establish a one-to-one mapping between semantic classes and the groups of database images that share semantic labels, and the criterion is to minimize the probability of errors. Mori, Takahashi, & Oka (1999) uniformly divided each image into sub-images with key words, and then used vector quantization of the feature vectors of sub-images to estimate which words should be assigned to a new image.

The work above generally requires a training stage to learn prediction models, thus the generalization capability should be a crucial assessment for practical effectiveness of the proposed approaches.

Recently, some researchers began to leverage Web-scale data for image understanding (Duygulu, et al., 2002, Yeh, Tollmar, & Darrell, 2004). An interesting work was proposed by Yeh, Tollmar, & Darrell (2004) which identifies locations by searching the Internet. Given a picture of an unknown place, it firstly obtains a small number of visually relevant Web images using content-based search, then extracts a few keywords from the descriptions of these images. A text-based search is successively performed and the search results are further filtered by visual features.

The disadvantages of (Yeh, et al. 2004) are that due to the efficiency problem, only a small number of relevant images can be retrieved as seeds which possibly degrades the performance, and the semantic gap problem will inevitably bias the final results. However, ignoring all these vulnerabilities, it is still an important work which pioneers a different point of view to investigate the image annotation problem.

THEORY BEHIND – THE MOTIVATION

This section provides our insights into the image auto-annotation problem, which directly inspired the idea of our modeless and data-driven image annotation approach.

Fundamentally, the aim of image auto-annotation is to find a group of keywords $\mathbf{w}^*$ that maximizes the conditional distributions $p(\mathbf{w} \mid I_q)$, as shown the first row in Eq.1, where I_q is the uncaptioned query image and $\mathbf{w}$ are keywords or phrases in the vocabulary. Applying the Bayes rule, we obtain Eq.1(a), where I_i denotes the ith image in the database. This corresponds to the generative model shown in Fig. 1(a), in which annotations are generated directly from the images. If we assume that there is a hidden layer of "topics", so that images are distributed w.r.t. a group of topics, and it is from these topics that words are generated, then we obtain a topic model as shown in Fig. 1(b), which corresponds to the function shown in Eq.1(b), where t_j represents the jth topic in the topic space.

$$
\begin{aligned}
\mathbf{w}^* &= \arg\max_{\mathbf{w}} p(\mathbf{w} \mid I_q) \\
&= \arg\max_{\mathbf{w}} \sum_i p(\mathbf{w} \mid I_i) \cdot p(I_i \mid I_q) \qquad \cdots (a) \\
&= \arg\max_{\mathbf{w}} \sum_i \left(\sum_j p(\mathbf{w} \mid t_j) \cdot p(t_j \mid I_i) \right) \cdot p(I_i \mid I_q) \quad \cdots (b)
\end{aligned} \tag{1}
$$

Most of the previous generative approaches can be categorized into these two formulations. Moreover, since the model of Eq.1(b) investigates the relationships between images and words in a more exhaustive way, it is generally reported as more effective in many previous works (Barnard, et al., 2003, Blei and Jordan, 2003, Monay and Gatica-Perez, 2004, Zhang, cta al. 2005).

However, in this paper we interpret Eq.1 in a different way. More specifically, we view Eq.1 from the angle of search and data mining.

Recall that the goal of a typical search process is to retrieve a set of images $\boldsymbol{I}^*$ given a query I_q such that for each $I_k \in \boldsymbol{I}^*$, we have

$$
I_q = \arg\max_{I_i \in \boldsymbol{I}^*} p(I_i \mid I_q) \tag{2}
$$

Moreover, contrary to traditional approaches which learn $p(\mathbf{w} \mid I_i)$ by defining either a generative model or discriminative model, we can just *mine* it out given a set of images, and such a mining process attracts interests recently, which is typically called label-based clustering techniques (Toda and Kataoka 2005, Zeng, He, Chen, & Ma, 2004).

Figure 1. Generative models for image auto-annotation

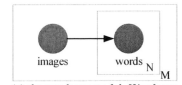

(a) the two-layer model. Words are directly generated from visual features

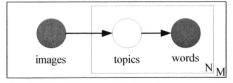

(b) the three-layer model. Words are generated from a hidden layer of "topics"

Different from the traditional document-based clustering approaches, e.g. k-means, which cluster documents based on the similarity of features and yield non-overlapped clusters, label-based approaches are typically applied to search results, which attempt to generate indicative and detailed descriptions to categorize the retrieved documents into clusters as well as to facilitate users' browsing, and generally yield overlapped clusters. The art is in learning the informative and classifiable words or phrases which summarize and categorize a subset of the documents. For example, Zeng, et al. (2004) defined five features to represent each n-gram and then learnt a linear regression model to rank the n-grams; the top-ranked n-grams were used as the corresponding clusters' names to differentiate the documents into clusters.

Note that a pre-requisition of label-based clustering approaches is that such techniques should be applied to search results. Since all the documents are retrieved given a single query, or say they are relevant in some sense, it reduces the noise and diversity. Hence the most important feature of the "cluster names", or the learnt indicative words or phrases, is to provide further details of a cluster of documents, and hence such techniques are typically used for improving the display of a search engine (Vivisimo, 2007).

This pre-requisition is automatically satisfied in our case, as stated in Section I. Instead of finding duplications for a query image (as is an excessive demand), we find each query image a group of near-duplications, or relevant images both visually and semantically (i.e. have similar textual descriptions), which are just the "search results" required by a label-based clustering technique, and hence we get to the solution of $p(\mathbf{w} \mid I_i)$.

Based on the analysis above, we propose a novel solution of image annotation by first retrieving a subset of similar images $\{I_i\}$ to the query (i.e. $p(I_i \mid I_q)$), and then mining annotations from this image subset $\{I_i\}$ leveraging a label-based clustering technique (i.e. $p(\mathbf{w} \mid I_i)$), which solves Eq.1(a).

THE MODELESS ANNOTATION APPROACH OF MINING SEARCH RESULTS

We have illustrated that the idea of annotating an image by those informative and distinctive phrases mined from its search results is reasonable. Here in this section we not only provide the detailed solution, but also show our ways of ensuring its effectiveness and efficiency simultaneously.

The Reformulation

Before the illustration, let us reformulate Eq.1 in a more "image" way. Let $\Theta_q = \bigcup_i I_i^q$ denotes the set of images relevant images $I_{i=1,\ldots,n}^q$ to query I_q, so that $p(\Theta_q \mid I_q)$ simulates the search process, and $p(\mathbf{w} \mid \Theta_q)$ simulates the mining process. The label-based clustering approach is then to discover topics such that

$$p(\mathbf{w} \mid \Theta_q) = \arg\max_{\mathbf{t}} p(\mathbf{w} \mid \mathbf{t}) \cdot p(\mathbf{t} \mid \Theta_q) \tag{3}$$

where $\mathbf{t}$ is approximated by the "cluster names" given by the clustering approach.

Hence we have

$$\mathbf{w}^* = \arg\max_{\mathbf{w}} p(\mathbf{w} \mid I_q)$$
$$= \arg\max_{\mathbf{w}} \sum_i p(\mathbf{w} \mid \Theta_q) \cdot p(\Theta_q \mid I_q) \qquad \cdots (a)$$
$$= \arg\max_{\mathbf{w}} \left[\arg\max_{\mathbf{t}} p(\mathbf{w} \mid \mathbf{t}) \cdot p(\mathbf{t} \mid \Theta_q) \right] \cdot p(\Theta_q \mid I_q) \quad \cdots (b) \qquad (4)$$

From Eq.4, we can see that there are three critical factors that affect the effectiveness of the proposed approach, namely the retrieval process $p(\Theta_q \mid I_q)$, the mining process $p(\mathbf{t} \mid \Theta_q)$, and the filtering process $p(\mathbf{w} \mid \mathbf{t})$.

We do not want to propose a label-based clustering technique here in this paper, but adopt an existing and proved-effective approach instead called Search Result Clustering (SRC) proposed by Zeng, et al. (2004) which is a released product by Microsoft Research Asia (SRC, 2006).

As for the filtering process, we propose a simple but effective *relevance ranking and annotation rejection* approach to select and rank the mined cluster names, and use the top ones as the output annotations. Intuitively, the preciseness of the identified annotations depends on the effectiveness of the SRC technique. However, since SRC is purely based on textual descriptions rather than taking image visual features into consideration as well, the effectiveness of SRC is thus degraded in our scenario. We will leave it as a future work and concentrate on the entire solution of a search and mining based image auto-annotation approach in this paper.

Figure 2. The flowchart of the modeless image annotation process of mining annotations from image search results. It contains three steps: the search stage (labeled by "(1)" in the figure), the mining stage ("(2)") and the filtering stage ("(3)"). The uncaptioned image and an initial keyword "sunset" assigned serve as the queries. The highlighted yellow block shows the output annotations.

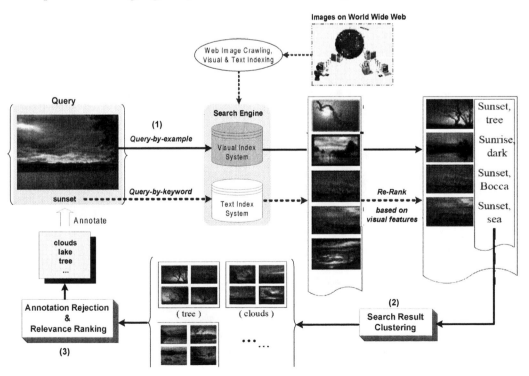

The retrieval process is a bit tricky in our current implementation, but we believe that it helps move a step forward in image understanding. It is well known that the semantic gap problem dooms the *Content-based Image Retrieval* (CBIR) approaches, which is thus called a fundamental problem in CBIR fields. It is caused by the gap between human semantics and the low-level visual features insufficiently effective given current feature extraction skills (Huang, Kumar, Mitra, Zhu, & Zabih, 1997). On the other hand, many researchers have proved that although individually the visual features and textual descriptions of images are ambiguous, e.g. both images labeled as "tiger lily" and "white tiger" are relevant to query keyword "tiger", they tend not to be when combined together (Barnard, Duygulu, Freitas, & Forsyth, 2001, Blei and Jordan, 2003, Li and Wang, 2003, Li and Wang, 2006).

Hence we suggest to divide-and-conquer the semantic gap problem. Suppose two steps: (1) given a query image, find *one* accurate[1] keyword (or phrase); and (2) given the image and the keyword, find more complementary keywords or phrases that detail the content of the image. The second step is easy to comprehend. By providing an initial keyword, we reduce the ambiguity of the image query and promise the search results to be relevant both visually and semantically at least to some extent. On the other hand, the requirement in the first step is not as lacking in subtlety as it may first seem. For example, for desktop images, users usually name the folders by locations or event names, and for Web images, generally there are plenty of textual descriptions from which the initial keyword can be chosen.

We shrink from discussing the first step and leave it as another future work, and start our approach from the second step, thus the image annotation approach formulate our current proposal is given in Eq.5 below:

$$\mathbf{w}^* = \arg\max_{\mathbf{w}} p(\mathbf{w} \mid I_q, w_q)$$
$$= \arg\max_{\mathbf{w}} \sum_i p(\mathbf{w} \mid \Theta_q) \cdot p(\Theta_q \mid I_q, w_q)$$
$$= \arg\max_{\mathbf{w}} \left[\arg\max_{\mathbf{t}} p(\mathbf{w} \mid \mathbf{t}) \cdot p(\mathbf{t} \mid \Theta_q) \right] \cdot p(\Theta_q \mid I_q, w_q) \tag{5}$$

Sketch of the Proposed Modeless Image Annotation Approach

The flowchart of the modeless image annotation process of mining annotations from image search results is shown in Fig. 2. It contains three steps: the search stage (labeled by "(1)" in the figure), the mining stage ("(2)") and the filtering stage ("(3)"). The uncaptioned image and an initial keyword "sunset" serve as the queries. The highlighted yellow block shows the output annotations.

As a pre-processing step, a large scale Web image dataset is firstly crawled and reserved as a pre-requisition of a data-driven approach, which will be illustrated in Section IV.C, and then visual and textual indices of the images are built up to support the real-time process, on which we give the details in Section IV.D.

Given the query image, we adopt the traditional Query-By-Example (QBE) method in CBIR to retrieve visually similar images. Intuitively, when the image database contains millions or billions of images, image retrieval based on pair-wise computation of the Euclidean distance is too time consuming and thus impractical, and we solve this problem by two means: Firstly, Query-By-Keyword (QBK) method is conducted before QBE retrieval, and thus we can leverage the inverted indexing technique[2] to retrieve the "semantically" similar images in real time (the time complexity is O(1)). Normally, the number of candidate images that are possibly relevant to the query will be greatly reduced in this step, and hence improves a great deal of the efficiency of the QBE retrieval step. Secondly, instead of calculating the Euclidean distances of two images based on the original low-level feature extracted, we encode each feature vector into a hash code which is binary bitwise, so that efficient distance measures such as the Hamming distance can be leveraged to greatly increase the search efficiency.

We detail this step in Section IV.D. In this way, we obtain a small subset of images that are both visually and semantically similar to the query image, which concludes the search stage.

The next step is to mine a number of terms (i.e. words or phrases) from the textual descriptions of the search results, which we adopt a previous work by Zeng et al. (Zeng, et al., 2004) named SRC (SRC, 2006), as described in Section III for this task. The cluster names output by SRC are assumed the topics in Eq.5.

Then an annotation rejection step which we call "filtering" is applied onto t to approximate $p(w \mid t)$ as annotation selection. The intention of this step is to further improve the precision of the output annotations for two reasons: (1) as aforementioned, the SRC technique (Zeng, et al., 2004) is based on textual features only and does not take visual features into consideration, hence the cluster names learnt may contain unsuitable terms for the query image. (2) Current SRC generates about 20 clusters[3], which is too large a number to promise high precision in our image annotation scenario. We detail this step in Section IV.E.

The user interface of our propose approach is shown in Fig. 3. It supports various query image suggestion schemes – the user can either upload a query image or select one from its QBE search results; s/he can type in a query term and select a query from its QBK results, or click the "Random" button to randomly select one.

The gray block highlights the query image and when clicking on the word "annotate," the annotation process begins. The statistical number of time cost in search and mining are shown in the blue bar below the query image. As for the real example in Fig. 3, 500 images are retrieved from the 2.4 million Web image database and the time cost in the search and mining process are 15 and 563 milliseconds respectively, which is in real time. The terms in blue are the output annotations, which are cluster names yielded by SRC (Zeng, et al., 2004) and separated with the sign "|". In Fig. 3, three terms survived the annotation filtering step. The underneath tab form displays a subset of the 500 relevant images retrieved in the search stage whose textual descriptions took part in the SRC mining.

In the following sections, we give the details of both technical and engineering designs which support effective data-driven annotation in real time.

Dataset Selection: One Factor to Ensure an Effective Data-Driven Approach

Since it is not only a very tedious and expensive task to manually label training data, but also very difficult to produce consistent labeling (Naphade, et al., 2006), the learning approaches always suffer from the small training data problem which degrades their power in handling outliers. For example, most previous works propose their researches based on Corel images, which contains only about 60 thousands high-quality images, and the images of the same category tend to be very similar visually.

On the other hand, recall that to ensure the effectiveness our modeless and data-driven approach of annotating images by mining search results, a basic assumption is that we can find near-duplicate images, or images that share semantics with the uncaptioned query image, so collecting a large scale image dataset is necessary. Due to these reason, we resort to the Web.

In fact, recently, some researchers have begun to investigate the usage of Web images and reported its effectiveness in many areas (Yeh, Tollmar, & Darrell, 2004, Weijer, Schmid, & Verbeek, 2006, Li, Wang, & Fei-Fei, 2007). However, since Web images are generally noisy and their surrounding text may

Figure 3. The interface of the proposed modeless and data-driven image annotation approach. The gray block highlights the query image. The blue bar below it gives the statistical number of the number of images retrieved from the 2.4 million Web images and the time cost in search and mining process respectively. The blue keywords show the learned annotations. They are actually three cluster names output by SRC (Zeng, et al., 2004) and "|" separates each name. The tab form displays the relevant images retrieved in the search stage which take part in the mining step.

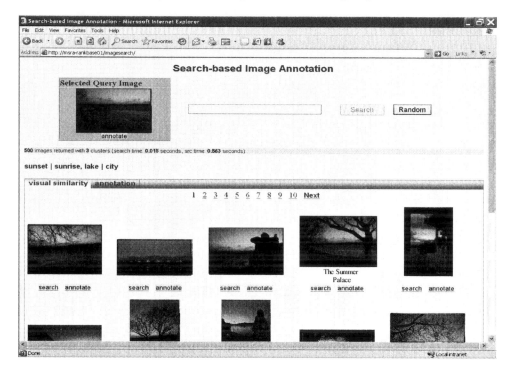

be of very low quality, it is not necessary that any Web images will help and hence post-processing is generally applied to ensure the quality of collected Web images (Weijer, et al., 2006, Li, et al., 2007).

Hence in our approach, we collect 2.4 million images from a few photo forums. The advantages are that (1) since these photos are taken by photographers, they generally have high resolution; (2) when uploading their works, the photographers will provide comments which more or less describe the photos; (3) most of the photos are nature images which have simpler semantics compared to artificial ones or portraits like the Corbis dataset; (4) there are plenty of images which are of the same semantic but with diverse appearance, which ensures a higher generalization ability of the proposed approach than using Corel images as the training data.

Three examples from the 2.4 million photo forum images are shown in Fig. 4. We can see that although the descriptions are noisy, more or less they hit a few contents in the corresponding images (e.g. "tiger" in the first example) or suggest keywords (e.g. "forest") that statistically co-occur with the central objects.

Table I provides statistics on the 2.4 million photos. The dictionary contains 362,669 words and each photo has 19.6 textual descriptions on average, which to our knowledge, is the largest database used in image annotation, without saying real-time annotation systems.

Table 1. Statistics on the 2.4 million database

No. of images indexed	2,409,609
No. of images having titles or comments	2,142,156
No. of distinctive words	362,669
No. of distinctive words with frequency $\geq$ 10	45,438
Average doc length of "title" field	2.3
Average doc length of "comment" field	17.3

The Promise of Real-Time

The obstacles to real-time annotation in our case include the content-based retrieval process and the handling of the 2.4 million images[4]. We solve the first problem by mapping image visual feature vectors into hash codes and the second one by setting up a distributed system.

Accelerating the Search Process by Mapping Visual Features to Hash Codes

Typically, the similarity of two images is measured in Euclidean space. However, since visual features are generally of high dimensional, measuring pair-wise Euclidean distance becomes a bottleneck in retrieval efficiency even if the search space is greatly reduced by text-based search given the query keyword. To accelerate the content-based search process, an effective way is to compress the images. Some previous works proposed vector quantization techniques, for example, Zhu, Zhang, Rao, & Srihari (2000) segments an image into regions, and quantizes the regions to obtain a few keyblocks. The widely used inverted index technique in text-based search field is thus naturally applied onto such a kind of keyblock-based discrete representation, and in this way, the content-based image retrieval problem is converted seamlessly into a text-based one which greatly improves the retrieval efficiency.

In this paper, we adopt another technique of image hash code generation (Fan, et al., 2005, Wang, Li, Li, & Ma, 2006) since it is more scalable than vector quantization methods (Zhu, et al., 2000) and hence is better fit for large-scale databases.

Related Works on Hash Encoding. The hash code generation algorithms (Fan, et al., 2005, Wang, et al., 2006) were originally proposed to detect duplicate images, i.e. images which are visually identical to each other. The basic idea is: suppose that visual features are mapped into bit streams, with higher bits representing more important contents of an image, and lower bits representing less important contents, thus duplicate images should have equal hash codes (i.e. the bit streams), and the equality is easily measured by the Hamming distance (i.e. the "AND" operation). This technique can also be applied to discover near-duplicates, by comparing only the higher bits of two hash codes. Intuitively, since the higher bits represent the more important contents, so that two images are more possibly alike if more highest bits match.

The hash code generation algorithm proposed in (Fan, et al., 2005) is shown in Fig. 5. Firstly, it transforms an input color image to gray scale and divides it evenly into 8x8 blocks. Each block is represented by the average intensity so that the original image is converted into an 8x8 matrix M with each element I_{ij} in Eq.6.

Figure 4. Three examples of the 2.4 million photos collected from a few photo forum websites. These photos are generally of high quality and have comments from the photographer.

Title	Tiger Grooming	Butterfly	Snowy Water Fall
Categories	Animal, Nature	Animal	Landscape, Nature
Descriptions	I saw this tiger grooming itself at the Miami Zoo. It reminded me of a giant pet cat.	Took this pic around Khaokeaw forest last week	It's Going on Three weeks now that i've had my camera and as time goes on my picture Quality is getting better...I think and Hope :)

Figure 5. The hash code generation process proposed in (Fan, et al., 2005), which is originally used for identical image search. This figure is adapted from (Fan, et al., 2005).

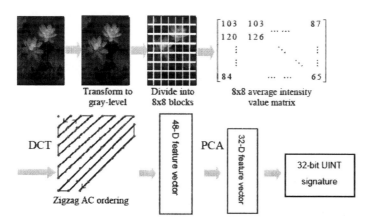

$$I_{ij} = \frac{\sum_{x=0}^{w-1}\sum_{y=0}^{n-1} Int(x, y)}{w \times h} \tag{6}$$

where $Int(x, y)$ is the intensity of the (i, j)-th matrix entry, and w, h denote the block width and height respectively.

2-D DCT transformation (Rao and Yip, 1990) is then applied to M. The DC coefficient, which is the average of M, is omitted to eliminate the effect of luminance. The remaining AC coefficients are zigzagged into a sequence, and the first 48 coefficients in lower frequencies are collected as the feature vector X_m of the original image, which is further mapped to a n-dimensional vector Y_n by a PCA (Joliffe, 1986) model P^T trained on 5,500 Web, as shown in Eq.7:

$$Y_n = P^T X_m \tag{7}$$

The hash code is thus generated from Y_n using the encoding function shown in Fig. 6.

Wang, et al. (2006) proposed a similar idea but is more efficient, as shown in Fig. 7. Images are hierarchically divided into blocks and average luminance is used as features. The projection model is still PCA trained from 11 million *iFind* (Chen, Liu, Hu, Li, & Zhang, 2001) images, and the 24 eigenvectors which correspond to the 24 largest eigenvalues are retained. The intuition behind using PCA for dimension reduction is that the PCA space is essentially a rotated version of the original feature space. If all the feature dimensions are kept, it draws the same conclusion on data points' distances as measured in the Euclidean space. Moreover, since PCA dimension reduction is achieved by cutting off the lower variance dimensions, the information loss is so small that can be ignored, while on the other hand, the hash code based matching can be significantly speeded up.

Mapping Visual Features to Hash Codes. Though it is proposed in duplicate finding, the same technique can be applied to accelerate search process with low information loss. Recall that since the higher bits represent the more important contents in an image, if some hash codes have equal n highest bits, they are thus indexed by the same key. Henceforth we can significantly speed up the search process in visual space by creating an inverted index based on the hash codes.

In our approach, we use 36-bin color Correlogram (Huang, et al., 1997) instead of intensity and luminance (Fan, et al., 2005, Wang, et al., 2006) as the original visual features. The reasons are two-fold: (1) the goal of (Fan, et al., 2005, Wang, et al., 2006) is to find duplicate images which are identical both in layout and contents, hence luminance of gray-scale images is an effective feature which is also efficient. However, our goal is to find relevant images — images that may not have the same layout and contents but share similar concepts. Hence to keep the color, texture and shape, etc., features is important in our case. Obviously Correlogram features keep more information than the gray-image based ones; and (2) Correlogram is also a widely used feature in content-based image retrieval (Rui, Huang, & Chang, 1999, Carson, Thomas, Belongie, Hellerstein, & Malik, 2002, Cox, Miller, Minka, Papathomas, & Yianilos, 2000).

Since 3-channel (e.g. RGB) features are used in our case, rather than the 1-channel one in (Fan, et al., 2005), 2-D DCT transformation is inapplicable here, and hence we adopt the hash code generation approach proposed by Wang, et al. (2006). However, we extract the 144-dimensional color Correlo-

Figure 6. The hash code generation algorithm proposed in (Fan, et al., 2005)

```
Input: feature vector Y = {y_i}: i ranges from 0 to n-1
For each element y_i
        If y_i >0, the ith bit of signature is set to 1
        Else the ith bit of signature is set to 0
End
Output: signature
```

Figure 7. The hash code generation process proposed in (Wang, et al., 2006)

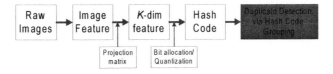

grams for each image and learn the 144x32 PCA projection model based on the same 11 million iFind images as in (Wang, et al., 2006). Then we use this model to offline map all the 2.4 million photos we collected into hash codes.

Hash Code Based Image Retrieval. Each image is now represented by a 32-dimensional bit streams, with the higher bits represent the major information while the lower bits describe the less informative ones. We design and compared four distance measures in our current implementation to check the effectiveness and efficiency of hash code based image retrieval, the results are given in Section V. The four distance measures are listed below:

- *Hash code filtering plus Euclidean distance*. If the highest n bits of an image exactly match those of the query image, then the Euclidean distance of these two images are measured based on their Correlograms. This measure is a tradeoff between search effectiveness and efficiency since the time consuming Euclidean distance computing is required only for a small set of images. On the other hand, mapping Correlograms to hash codes brings information loss, thus calculating image similarities based on the original features may ensure a better effectiveness. In our experiments, n = 20.
- *Hamming distance*. It measures the number of different bits of two hash codes. Obviously this is the most efficient measurement. Its effectiveness depends on that of the hash code generation approach.
- *Weighted Hamming distance*. Hamming distance assume all bits have equal weights. But intuitively, since the higher bits are more important, differences in higher bits should be larger-weighted. We propose a weighting function as below:
  Firstly, we evenly group a 32-bit hash code into 8 bins. From left to right, each bin contains 4-bits. Then we weight the Hamming distance on the ith bin by $2^{(8-i)}$, $1 \leq i \leq 8$. Obviously the weighting function magnifies the difference on the higher bits. It is simple but effective as proved in our experiments.
- *Euclidean distance*. The Euclidean distance based on original Correlogram features is also given as a baseline to assess the performance of the above hash code-based measurements.

We rank the images in the ascending order of the distances respectively and return the top N as search results.

Efficiently Handling the Large-Scale Database with Distributed Computing

In part 1), we demonstrate the method of supporting content-based search in real time and proposed a hash code generation approach as well as different distance measures. However this is not enough to support real time image annotation when the database contains millions or billions of images. In this subsection, we describe our design of a distributed system, which as shown in Fig. 3, finishes the search process in 15 milliseconds and the mining process in 563 milliseconds, based on 2.4 million images.

The system architecture is shown in Fig. 8. The key is that the content-base search engine, text search engine and SRC clustering engine are provided as Web services using C# Remoting technique. Each service register a distinct TCP port and listening to it, when there is a service request, the service accepts inputs, does its own work, and sends back outputs. Moreover, by building up this distributed system, both visual and textual features can be kept in memories of servers, and no disk I/O is requested, so obviously it is quite efficient and easily scalable.

The Control of SRC (Zeng, et al., 2004) Outputs

As mentioned in Section IV.A, we use the search result clustering technique named SRC (Zeng, et al., 2004) to learn the topics based on the visually and semantically similar search results.

A left problem is that SRC requires users to provide the number of clusters $|n_{src}|$ wanted, which is difficult to select without observing the data. We provide an experiential algorithm as Eq. 8 below to select $|n_{src}|$:

$$|n_{src}| = \max(|\Theta^{*}|/200, 4)$$ (8)

where $|\Theta^{*}|$ is the number of retrieved images. 200 is an empirical value of cluster size suggested by SRC to ensure the saliency of learned cluster names. On the other hand, if $|\Theta^{*}|$ is too small, SRC tends to group all images in one or two clusters and hence images in one cluster may be too diverse to produce meaningful cluster names. To avoid this, we force the algorithm to output at least 4 clusters, while 4 is another empirically selected parameter.

Moreover, because SRC extracts all n-grams $\Theta^{*}(n \leq 3)$ as its candidate key phrases, if Θ^{*} is too large, time cost of the SRC service may be very high. Hence, we set max $\Theta^{*} - 200$.

The final problem is annotation rejection. As aforementioned (refer to Section IV.B), it is unsuitable to output all cluster names yield by SRC as the annotations, hence to define criteria for annotation rejection is necessary to ensure the performance. Two criteria are compared in our current implementations:

- *Maximum cluster size criterion.* This is a very simple but effective annotation rejection method, which uses the size of each cluster, i.e. the number of images in each cluster, as the score to rank each cluster name, and the top ranked ones are assigned onto the query image as the final annotations. This is equivalent to the Maximum a Posteriori estimation (MAP) which assumes that "the majority speaks the truth" and is statistically reasonable since the cluster names are learned from search results which are assumed visually and semantically relevant to the query image.
- *Average member image score criterion.* The term "member image" of a cluster A indicates an image that is assigned to A, and the cluster score is measured as the average similarity of its member images to the query image. It is reasonable since the more relevant member images a cluster contains, the more probably the concepts learned from this cluster represents the content of the query image.

We keep the top ranked clusters, merge their cluster names by removing the duplicate words and phrases, and output as the learned annotations, which closes the entire system process.

EVALUATIONS

2.4 million photos from several online photo forums are collected as the database, from which the relevant images are retrieved to annotate the query image. These photos are not only of high quality, but also have rich descriptions, as discussed in Section IV.C.

In order to evaluate the effectiveness and efficiency of our proposed approach, we conducted a series of experiments based on two datasets. One is an open dataset, of which the images are collected from Google image search engine (Google, 2006). 30 Google images from 15 categories (as shown in Table II) were randomly selected. However, to give a more objective evaluation of the effectiveness, we deliberately selected a few vague query keywords, e.g. using "Paris" as the query keyword to annotate a photo of "Sacre Coeur". Because no ground truth labels are available, we manually evaluated the retrieval performance on this dataset.

The other testing dataset is a benchmark content-based image retrieval database provided by the University of Washington (UW)[5]. Images in this dataset have about 5 manually labeled ground truth annotations on average, and the UW folder names were used as the query keywords (see Table III). A problem with this dataset is that for many images, not all objects are annotated. For a fair evaluation, we manually revised the results to accept synonyms and correct annotations that do not appear in UW labels.

Experiments on Google Images

Evaluation Criterion

The evaluation of image auto-annotation approaches is still an open problem. Typically in many previous works (Blei, et al., 2003, Carneiro and Vasconcelos, 2005, Jeon and Manmatha, 2004), image retrieval technique is used for evaluation. Generally in these approaches, the entire dataset is separated into two parts, one for training and the other for testing such that images in these two datasets share almost the same vocabularies and data distributions, and ground truth annotations are available for the testing

Figure 8. System architecture of the proposed modeless and data-driven image annotation approach. The visual search engine, text search engine and SRC engine are implemented as services, which make up of a distributed system using C# Remoting technique.

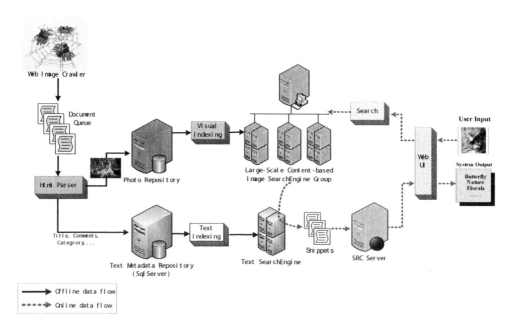

dataset. Thus in their evaluation, a number of keywords can be selected from the vocabulary to query the annotated testing dataset and the precision and recall are calculated for the returned images.

Let G be the ground truth relevant images and L be the retrieved images, retrieval precision and recall are defined as in Eq.9.

$$Precision = \frac{|L \cap G|}{|L|}, \quad Recall = \frac{|L \cap G|}{|G|} \tag{9}$$

i.e. precision evaluates the proportion of relevant images in the retrieval results, while recall calculates that of the relevant images in all the relevant images contained in the database.

However, Eq.9 suggests only the probability of identifying "correct" annotations. But for an annotation system, generally the output annotations belong to three categories: "perfect", "correct", and "wrong". The "perfect" annotations hit the specific objects inside an image, e.g. "tiger" for the first image in Fig. 4. The "correct" annotations are those that are not-wrong but also not perfect, e.g. "France" for an image about Eiffel tower. The "wrong" annotations are the incorrect outputs, which have nothing to do with the contents of the query image. We believe that a comprehensive evaluation should take all these three categories into consideration. Hence we propose Eq.10 to evaluate the performance. It modifies the normalized score measure (Barnard, et al., 2003, Li and Wang, 2006), which only categorizes the annotations into "right" or "wrong".

$$E = \frac{p + 0.5 \times r - w}{m} \tag{10}$$

where m denotes the number of annotations predicted. p, r, w are the number of "perfect", "correct", and "wrong" annotations respectively. Note that to emphasize the preference for "perfect" annotations, we punish the "correct" ones by a lower weight 0.5. Obviously when all the predictions are "perfect", $E = 1$, while if all are wrong, $E = -1$.

Since there are no ground truth annotations available for this dataset, it is impossible for us to evaluate the recall performance.

System Effectiveness

Fig. 9 shows how annotation precision varies as the similarity weight changes. This weight weights the average similarity of images retrieved in the content-based search stage, and the product serves as the threshold to filter out irrelevant images, i.e. images whose similarity to the query image is lower than

Table 2. Queries from google

Apple, Beach, Beijing, Bird, Butterfly, Clouds, Clownfish, Japan, Liberty, Lighthouse, Louvre, Paris, Sunset, Tiger, Tree

Table 3. Queries from U.washington

Australia, Campus, Cannon beach, Cherries, Football, Geneva, Green lake, Indonesia, Iran, Italy, Japan, San juan, Spring flower, Swiss mountain, Yellowstone

Figure 9. Annotation precision measured by Eq.10. It shows respectively the precision curve of using the four distance measures described in Section IV.D vs. the similarity weight as a threshold to control the number of image search results yield at the search stage.

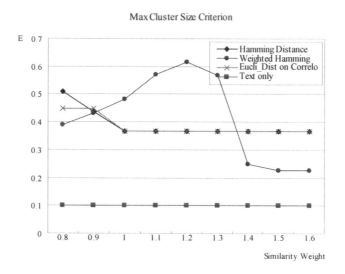

(a) Precision w.r.t. maximum cluster size criterion

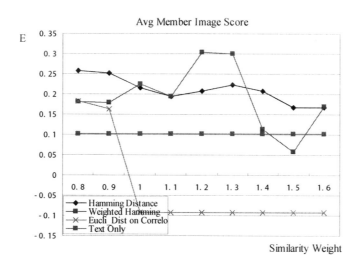

(b) Precision w.r.t. average member image score criterion

this threshold will not be delivered to the SRC mining stage. This parameter determines Θ^* in Eq.8 and thus directly affects the learned clusters and the predicted annotations.

The reason of proposing such a threshold strategy is that, since the similarity of images varies greatly; it is very difficult to select a hard threshold which can promise high system performance for any queries. On the contrary, our soft threshold is query-dependent, it leverages the information provided by content features of the image search results.

The green square curve in Fig. 9 represents the process without the content-based search step, i.e. it relies purely on text-based search to yield near duplicates, and SRC clustering is based on the images that are "semantically" similar but may not visually similar. It serves as the baseline method here. Also, since no visual features are available, annotations predicted by this method uses the maximum cluster size criterion (see Section IV.E).

Fig. 9(a) shows annotation precision curves of the four content-based search distance measures (refer to Section IV.D) under maximum cluster size criterion.

From this figure, we can see that the weighted Hamming distance measure performs the best. This is reasonable because it emphasizes the feature components that captures the important information in an image while at the same time de-emphasize the unimportant ones.

It is interesting that Euclidean distance measure based on the original Correlogram features performs comparatively to the Hamming distance measure in effectiveness. This shows that the information-loss of mapping original features into hash codes (refer to Section IV.D) can be ignored on this dataset, or say, the model for hash code generation is effective.

Another interesting result is that the hash code filtering plus Euclidean distance method performs badly. The reason may be that the higher 20 bits of hash codes learned are too coarse to distinguish relevant images from irrelevant ones.

All the distance measures perform much better than the baseline method. This shows that requiring the visual similarity of clustering images is necessary and important.

Fig. 9 (b) shows the performance with maximum average member image score criterion. It is generally worse than that with the maximum cluster size criterion. A possible reason is due to the semantic gap. Recall that SRC algorithm clusters images purely based on their surrounding texts and ignores image visual features. Thus images in one cluster may have very different visual features even if they belong to the same category. Obviously this will not affect the maximum cluster size criterion but only the average member image score criterion, because the latter one uses visual similarity to score the clusters. Another possible reason may be that the images which share similar descriptions vary greatly in their visual appearances.

Note that the system's performance jumps when the threshold is too large such that Θ^* is too small to ensure satisfying SRC clustering performance.

Fig.10 shows a few examples of the annotation results. The boldfaced keywords indicate the queries. It can be seen that our approach is able to find correct and most of the time perfect complementary annotations.

System Efficiency

We have give the readers a sense of the efficiency in Fig. 3, which shows that our annotation process is fulfilled in real time, although the database contains 2.4 million images, which is the largest till now to our knowledge.

In the subsection, we conduct one more experiment to evaluate the efficiency statistically. For all the queries, we collect their search results, which are about 24,000 images on average, and test the system efficiency according to the four distance measures: Hamming Distance, Weighted Hamming Distance, Hash code filtering plus Euclidean distance, and the traditional Euclidean distance based on original Correlogram features. The hardware environment is a computer with one Dual Intel Pentium 4 Xeon hyper-threaded CPU and 2G memory. The time cost for computing the pair-wise distance between each

Figure 10. A few examples of the annotation results yield by the modeless and data-driven image annotation approach

	Paris Las vegas, effel tower, love paris		**Paris** Sacre coeur, paris building, effel tower		**Paris** Eiffel tower, france, sky, paris nights
	Sunset Lake, tree, mountain, sky, beautiful, water		**Tiger** Whiter tiger, usa, zoo		**Tree** House, flower, snow, sky, tree trunk
	Apple Studio, kitchen, fruit, color		**Beach** South america, beautiful beach, beach house		**Butterfly** Flower, butterfly house, beautiful butterfuly
	Apple Fruit, apple tree		**Beach** Sky,island, sun beach, sunrise, beach island		**Butterfly** Yellow butterfly, swallowtail, nature
	Beach Morn, sand, south beach, sun beach		**Beach** beach resort, white beach South beach		**Clouds** National park, europe, south america, blue sky
	Clouds Dark clouds, sun, sky, sunrise, morn		**Clownfish** Anemone, reef, red sea		**Liberty** York, liberty statue, sun

Figure 11. Search efficiency vs. the four distance measures. Pair-wise distances are measured based on 24,000 images. It proves the efficiency of the proposed idea. Moreover, the Hamming distance is the most efficient, which is also reasonable.

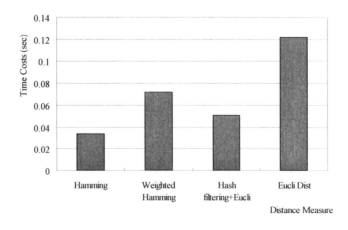

of the 24,000 images and the query image, as well as ranking the images accordingly, is shown in Fig. 11, which cost 0.034, 0.072, 0.051 and 0.122 seconds respectively. We can see that computing Euclidean distance is nearly 4 times slower of calculating Hamming distance.

The hash code filtering plus Euclidean distance measure is the second efficient. The reason is that the hash codes here serve as the inverted indices to identify the relevant images which is of O(1) computation complexity. Time cost for this measure is consumed by the Euclidean distance calculation afterwards.

Note that the above evaluations were conducted with all features loaded into memory. If disk access is required, we can imagine that hash code-based measures will be even faster than the original visual feature-based ones.

Experiments on UW Dataset

In this subsection, we evaluate the performance of our proposed approach based on the benchmark U.Washington database.

Because ground truth is available and this dataset is comparably small, we use precision and recall as the evaluation criteria. Fig. 12 shows the maximum precision and recall of our approach w.r.t. the two annotation rejection criteria vs. the four distance measures. All images in the database are used for the evaluation. Again the weighted Hamming distance measure performs the best.

An interesting point is that the average member image score criterion now works better. This is because few images in our 2.4 million photograph database are visually similar to the UW images, while

Figure 12. Precision and recall yielded corresponding to the four distance measure given the two annotation rejection criteria based on all the images in UW dataset.

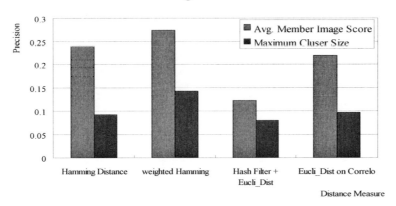

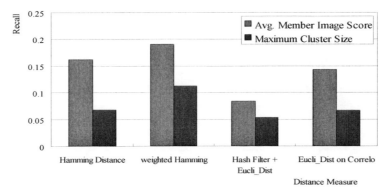

the UW images of the same category share similar visual appearance. Moreover, the average image score strategy helps to rank higher the clusters whose member images are more visually relevant to the query thus is less biased by the irrelevant member image descriptions.

It is worth mentioning that the real performance of our system is actually much better than shown in Fig. 12. Since the evaluation shown in Fig.12 did not grant synonyms, e.g. "beach" and "coast", and semantically relevant keywords, e.g. "Geneva" and "Switzerland", as correct answers. Moreover, UW ground truth annotations may ignore some contents of an image, so that our current evaluation assumes them to be "wrong" even if the predicted annotations are correct, just because they do not appear in UW ground truth. To prove this, we manually examined the predicted annotations of 100 randomly selected queries. The corrected precision and recall are 38.14% and 22.95% respectively, nearly 12% precision improvement, with weighted Hamming distance measure, the average member image score criterion, and the similarity weight 1.2.

Fig. 13 show four examples of our output, which hit no UW ground truth labels and gives zero precisions in the strict evaluation but are indeed correct answers.

Moreover, since our method is a modeless one which has no supervised learning stage, and the UW images are "outliers" to our database from which few relevant images can be found, the task is thus much tougher for us than for the previous approaches. On the contrary, in most of the previous works, training data and testing data are selected from the same dataset and the training dataset is usually much larger than the testing dataset, e.g. (Barnard, et al., 2003, Blei and Jordan, 2003) use 4,500 Corel images for training and 500 images for testing, and the performance is around 20-30%. This shows that our system is more effective in predicting annotations, and is robust in handling outsiders.

DISCUSSIONS

Compared to the previous works, or traditional computer vision and machine learning ones which built up generative or discriminative annotation models, in this paper, we propose a novel attempt of modeless image annotation, which investigates how effective to a data-driven approach only can be, and suggest mining annotations for an uncaptioned image by mining its search results. It has at least three advantages: (1) no training dataset and supervised learning are required and hence is free from the problem of lack of training data; (2) since no training stage is available, and hence it requires no pre-defined vocabularies while vocabulary creation is still an open research topic (Naphade, et al., 2006); (3) by leveraging the Web data, we can obtain diverse images for the same semantics which ensure a

Figure 13. Four examples of output annotations produced by our approach based on UW database, which hit no UW ground truth labels but are indeed correct answers.

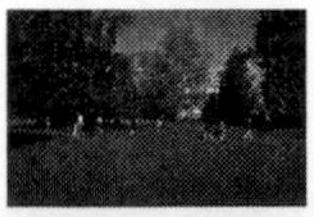	**Campus** college, campus life, center, tree	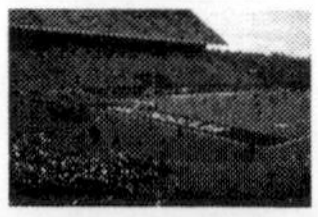	**Football** stadium, school football, football game, football player
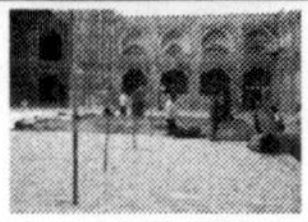	**Iran** mashhad, kish island, esfahan	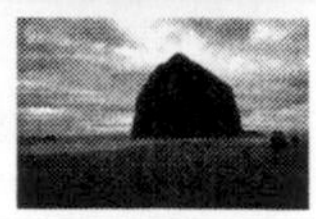	**Cannon Beach** haystack rock

high generalization capability or say the practical usage of the proposed annotation approach. This is a noticeable advantage to using the Corel Stock-style database in which images of the same concept have similar visual appearances with clean descriptions. Moreover, our approach is highly scalable and very robust to outsider queries.

CONCLUSION

Compared to the previous annotation approaches which build up generative or discriminative annotation models, in this paper, we propose a novel attempt of modeless image annotation, which investigates how effective a data-driven approach can be, and suggest mining annotations for an uncaptioned image by mining its search results. We collected 2.4 million images with their surrounding texts from a few photo forum websites.

The entire process contains three steps: (1) the search stage, which yields visually and semantically search results given the uncaptioned images as queries; (2) the mining stage, which applies a label-based clustering technique to mining topic labels from the textual descriptions of the search results as candidate annotations; (3) the annotation rejection stage, which filtered the candidate annotations to ensure the preciseness of the final outputs.

Compared with the previous works, our method saves labor both in training data collection and vocabulary creation, and is highly scalable and robust to outliers. And as to our knowledge, it is a real-time approach that handles the largest number of images.

To ensure real time annotation, two key techniques are leveraged—one is to map the high dimensional image visual features into hash codes, the other is to implement it as a distributed system, of which the search and mining processes are provided as Web services. As a typical result, the entire process finishes in less than 1 second.

Experiments conducted on both an open database (Google images) and a benchmark database (UW CBIR database) proved the effectiveness and efficiency of this proposed approach.

There are much room to improve our proposed approach, e.g. as mentioned in Section IV.B, to propose label-based clustering technique which takes also image visual features into consideration is necessary and important for further performance improvement. And we would like to investigate how much performance gain we can obtain by embedding learning approaches into our current implementation.

ACKNOWLEDGMENT

The authors would like to thank Feng Jing, Hua-Jun Zeng, Kefeng Deng, Bin Wang and Le Chen for their sincere helps on technical discussions, assistances, as well as system implementations. Many thanks should also be given to the volunteers that help in manually evaluating our experimental results.

REFERENCES

Barnard, K., Duygulu, P., Freitas, N., Forsyth, D., Blei, D., & Jordan, M. (2003). Matching words and pictures. *Journal of Machine Learning Research*, (pp. 1107-1135).

Barnard, K., Duygulu, P., Freitas, N., & Forsyth, D. (2003). Recognition as translating images into yext. *Internet Imaging IX, Electronic Imaging.*

Barnard, K., Duygulu, P., Freitas, N., & Forsyth, D. (2001). Clustering art. *Computer Vision and Pattern Recognition*, (pp. 434-439).

Blei, D., & Jordan, M.I. (2003). Modeling annotated data. *Annual International ACM SIGIR Conference*, Toronto, Canada.

Cai, D., He, X., Li, Z., Ma, W.-Y., & Wen, J.-R. (2004). Hierarchical clustering of WWW image search results using visual, textual and link information. *ACM International Conference on Multimedia*, (pp. 952-959).

Carneiro, G., & Vasconcelos, N. (2005). A database centric view of semantic image annotation and retrieval. In *Proceedings of ACM SIGIR Conf. on Research and Development in Information Retrieval.*

Carson, C., Tomas, M., Belongie, S., Hellerstein, J.M., & Malik, J. (2002). Blobworld: image segmentation using expectation-maximization and its application to image querying. *IEEE Transactions on Pattern Analysis and Machine Intelligence, 24*(8), 1026-1038.

Chen, Z., Liu, W.Y., Hu, C., Li, M., & Zhang, H.J. (2001). iFind: a web image search engine. *Proc. of the 24th Annual International ACM SIGIR Conference on Research and Development in Information Retrieval,* (pp. 450-458).

Chang, E., Kingshy, G., Sychay, G., & Wu, G. (2003). CBSA: content-based soft annotation for multimodal image retrieval using Bayes Point Machines. *IEEE Trans. on CSVT, 13*(1), 26-38.

Cox, I.J., Miller, M.L., Minka, T.P., Papathomas, T.V., & Yianilos, P.N. (2000). The Bayesian image retrieval system, PicHunter: theory, implementation, and psychophysical. *IEEE Transactions on Image Processing, 9*(1), 20-37.

Duygulu, P., Barnard, K., Freitas, N., & Forsyth, D. (2002). Object recognition as Machine Translation: Learning a Lexicon for a Fixed Image Vocabulary. In *Seventh European Conference on Computer Vision, 2002,* (pp. 97-112).

Fan, X., Xie, X., Li, Z., Li, M., & Ma, W.-Y. (2005). Photo-to-search: using multimodal queries to search the Web from mobile devices. *ACM SIGMM International Workshop on Multimedia Information Retrieval.*

Fan, J.P., Gao, Y.L., & Luo, H.Z. (2004). Multi-level annotation of natural scenes using dominant image components and semantic concepts. In *Proc. ACM International Conference on Multimedia.*

Fan, J.P., Gao, Y.L., Luo, H.Z., & Xu, G.Y. (2004). Automatic image annotation by using concept-sensitive salient objects for image content represent. In *27th Annual International ACM SIGIR Conference.*

Fellbaum, C. (Ed.) (1998). *WordNet: an electronic lexical database.* MIT Press, Cambridge, Massachusetts.

Ghoshal, A., Ircing, P., & Khudanpur, S. (2005). Hidden Markov models for automatic annotation and content-based retrieval of images and video. In *28th Annual International ACM SIGIR Conference.*

Google image. (2008). *http://images.google.com.*

Huang, J., Kumar, S.R., Mitra, M., Zhu, W.-J., & Zabih, R. (1997). Image indexing using color correlograms. *IEEE Conf. on Computer Vision and Pattern Recognition*, San Juan, Puerto Rico.

Jeon, J., Lavrenko, V., & Manmatha, R. (2003). Automatic image annotation and retrieval using cross-media relevance models. In *Proc. of the Annual Int. ACM SIGIR Conf. on Research and Development in Information Retrieval.*

Jeon, J., & Manmatha, R. (2004). Automatic image annotation of news images with large vocabularies and low quality training data. *ACM International Conference on Multimedia.*

Joliffe, I.T. (1986). *Principal component analysis.* New York: Springer-Verlag.

Lavrenko, V., Manmatha, R., & Jeon, J. (2003). A model for learning the semantics of pictures. *NIPS.*

Li, B.T., Goh, K., & Chang, E. (2003). Confidence-based dynamic ensemble for image annotation and semantics discovery. In *Proc. ACM International Conference on Multimedia*, (pp. 195-206).

Li, J., Wang, G., & Fei-Fei, L. (2007). OPTIMOL: automatic Object Picture collecTion via Incremental MOdel Learning. *IEEE Computer Vision and Pattern Recognition.*

Li, J., & Wang, J. (2003). Automatic linguistic indexing of pictures by a statistical modeling approach. *IEEE Transactions on Pattern Analysis and Machine Intelligence, 25*(9), 1075-1088.

Li, J., & Wang, J. (2006). Real-time computerized annotation of pictures. *ACM International Conference on Multimedia.*

Liu, W.Y., Dumais, S., Sun, Y., Zhang, H., Czerwinski, M., & Field, B. (2001). Semi-automatic image annotation. In *Proc. Of Interact: Conference on HCI*, (pp. 326-333).

Li, X., Wang, X.-J., Wang, C., & Zhang, L. (2007). SBIA: search-based image annotation by leveraging Web-scale images. *ACM International Conference on Multimedia.*

Monay, F., & Gatica-Perez, P. (2003). On image auto annotation with latent space models. In *Proc. ACM Int. Conf. on Multimedia.*

Monay, F., & Gatica-Perez, P. (2004). PLSA-based image auto-annotation: constraining the latent space". In *Proc. ACM InternationalConference on Multimedia.*

Mori, Y., Takahashi, H., & Oka, R. (1999). Image-to-word transformation based on dividing and vector quantizing images with words. In *First International Workshop on Multimedia Intelligent Storage and Retrieval Management.*

Naphade, M., Smith, J. ., Tesic, J., Chang, S.-F., Hsu, W., Kennedy, L., Hauptmann, A., & Curtis, J. (2006). Large-scale concept ontology for multimedia. *IEEE Multimedia Magazine, 13*(3).

Pan, J.-Y., Yang, H.-J., Faloutsos, C., & Duygulu, P. (2004). Automatic multimedia cross-modal correlation discovery. In *Proceedings of the 10th ACM SIGKDD Conference.*

Pan, J.-Y., Yang, H.-J., Faloutsos, C., & Duygulu, P. (2004). GCap: graph-based automatic image captioning. *International Workshop on Multimedia Data and Document Engineering.*

Rao, K.R. & Yip, P. (1990). *Discrete cosine transform: algorithms, advantages, applications.* New York: Academic.

Rui, Y., Huang, T.S., & Chang, S.-F. (1999). Image retrieval: current techniques, promising directions, and open issues. *Jounal of Visual Communication and Image Representation, 10*(1), 39-62.

Shevade, B., & Sundaram, H. (2006). Incentive based image annotation. *Technical Report, Arizona State University.* AME-TR-2004-02.

SRC (2006). Search result clustering toolbar in Microsoft Research Asia. *http://rwsm.directtaps.net/.*

Toda, H. & Kataoka, R. (2005). A search result clustering method using informatively named entities. *7th ACM Workshops on Web Information and Data Management .*

Vivisimo (2007). *http://www.vivisimo.com.*

Volkmer, T., Smith, J., Natsev, A., Campbell, M., & Naphade, M. (2005). A web-based system for collaborative annotation of large image and video collections. In *Proc. ACM International Conference on Multimedia M.*

Wang, B., Li, Z.W., Li, M.J., & Ma, W.-Y. (2006). Large-scale duplicate detection for Web image search. *IEEE International Conference on Multimedia & Expo.*

Wang, X.-J., Ma, W.-Y., Xue, G.-R., & Li, X. (2004). Multi-model similarity propagation and its application for Web image retrieval. *ACM International Conference on Multimedia,* (pp. 944-951).

Weijer, J., Schmid, C., & Verbeek, J. (2006). Learning color names from real-world images. *IEEE Computer Vision and Pattern Recognition.*

Yahoo News Search. (2006). *http://news.search.yahoo.com/news.*

Yeh, T., Tollmar, K., Darrell, T. (2004). Searching the Web with mobile images for location recognition. *IEEE Computer Society Conference on Computer Vision and Pattern Recognition,* (2), 76-81.

Zeng, H.J., He, Q.C., Chen, Z., & Ma, W.-Y. (2004). Learning to cluster Web search results. In *Proc. of the 27th Annual International Conference on Research and Development in Information Retrieval,* (pp. 210-217).

Zhang, R.F., Zhang, Z.F., Li, M.J., Ma, W.-Y., & Zhang, H.J. (2005). A probabilistic semantic model for image annotation and multi-modal image retrieval. In *Proc. of the IEEE International Conference on Computer Vision.*

Zhu, L., Zhang, A., Rao, A., & Srihari, R. (2000). Keyblock: an approach for content-based image retrieval. In *Proceedings of ACM Multimedia.*

ENDNOTES

[1]   Note that we do not require it to be perfect, at least in our approach, e.g. given an image about the Eiffel Tower, the "perfect" keyword is "Eiffel" but an accurate one can be "France".

[2]   This is a crucial technique for text search engines. It stores the keyword-document relationship into a so-called inverted index file, whose entries are keywords and values are the document ids

to represent which document is indexed by a given keyword, or say which document contains this keyword.

3   Although SRC accepts user-assigned number to indicate how many categories are preferred, it is a suggested number that statistically produces the highest performance.

4   We need to keep in mind that our system should be easily scale up, e.g. to support real-time annotation with billions of images.

5   http://www.cs.washington.edu/research/imagedatabase/groundtruth/

Chapter XV
Semantic Classification and Annotation of Images

Yonghong Tian
Peking University, China

Shuqiang Jiang
Chinese Academy of Sciences, China

Tiejun Huang
Peking University, China

Wen Gao
Peking University, China

ABSTRACT

With the rapid growth of image collections, content-based image retrieval (CBIR) has been an active area of research with notable recent progress. However, automatic image retrieval by semantics still remains a challenging problem. In this chapter, the authors will describe two promising techniques towards semantic image retrieval—semantic image classification and automatic image annotation. For each technique, four aspects are presented: task definition, image representation, computational models, and evaluation. Finally, they will give a brief discussion of their application in image retrieval.

INTRODUCTION

With the advance of multimedia technology and growth of image collections, content-based image retrieval (CBIR) is therefore proposed, which finds images that have low-level visual features (e.g., color, texture, shape) similar to those of the query image. However, retrieving images via low-level features has proven unsatisfactory since low-level visual features cannot represent the high-level semantic content

Figure 1. Examples of images for semantic image categorization.

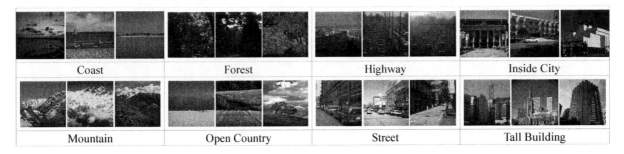

Coast	Forest	Highway	Inside City
Mountain	Open Country	Street	Tall Building

Figure 2. Examples of images for automatic image annotation.

Images					
Original manual annotations	sky jet Plane smoke	bear close-up face polar	cat rocks tiger water	flowers porcupine rodent	sky sun tree water
Automatic annotations	sky jet plane *water tree*	bear *snow* polar *grass water*	water cat tiger *people swimmers*	*leaf plants* flowers *garden*	*sunset* water *horizon* sun *clouds*

of images. To reduce the so-called *semantic gap* (Smeulders, Worring, Santini, Gupta, & Jain, 2000), a variety of techniques have been developed. In this chapter, we discuss promising techniques on two important aspects of CBIR — (a) semantic image classification, and (b) automatic image annotation. Each component plays an important role in the greater semantic understanding of images.

General speaking, the semantics of images can be categorized into four levels from the lowest to the highest (Wang, Li, & Wiederhold, 2001):

- *semantic types* (e.g., landscape photograph, clip art),
- *object composition* (e.g., a bike and a car parked on a beach, a sunset scene),
- *abstract semantics* (e.g., people fighting, happy person, objectionable photograph), and
- *detailed semantics* (e.g., a detailed description for a given picture).

In (Song, Wang, & Zhang, 2003), the image semantics can be further grouped into *local semantic level* and *thematic level* (or *global semantic level*). Currently, most works in image classification and annotation have been done in the first two levels. Good progress has been made at the first level, which corresponds closely to image's *physical* attributes such as indoor vs. outdoor. The second level of semantics seems more difficult to extract than the first. In this chapter, we pay our primary interest to the second level to investigate the problems of image classification and annotation.

Semantic image classification aims to classify images into (semantically) meaningful categories. Potentially, the categorization enhances image retrieval by permitting semantically adaptive searching methods and by narrowing down the searching range in a database. Fig. 1 shows several representative categories of images. Roughly speaking, two basic strategies can be found in the literature. The first uses low-level visual features, such as color, texture or shape. Then different classifiers are applied on these visual features (e.g., Szummer & Picard, 1998; Vailaya, Figueiredo, Jain, & Zhang, 2001; Wang, et al., 2001; Grauman & Darrell, 2005; Zhang, Berg, Maire, & Malik, 2006). The second strategy adds an intermediate representation between the low-level features and semantic concepts (e.g., Li & Perona, 2005; Wang, Zhang, & Li, 2006). In the context of Web images, additional features are also exploited by image classification algorithms, such as the text extracted from the page that contains an image (Cai, He, Li, Ma, & Wen, 2004) or the link information between images or pages (Tian, Huang, & Gao, 2005).

Automatic image annotation is the process of automatically assigning metadata in the form of captions or keywords to an image. Different with image categorization, annotated words for each image may exhibit a large variability in general (Monay & Gatica-Perez, 2007). That is, several words can describe one or more regions or even the whole image (see Fig. 2), which makes automatic image annotation a distinct research problem. There have been many works done in automatic image annotation, differentiated by the *auto-annotation* models such as word co-occurrence model (Mori, Takahashi, & Oka, 1999), translation model (Duygulu, Barnard, Fretias, & Forsyth, 2002), cross-media relevance model (Jeon, Lavrenko, & Manmatha, 2003; Feng, Manmatha, & Lavrenko, 2004), hierarchical aspect model (Barnard & Forsyth, 2001; Barnard, Duygulu, Freitas, Forsyth, Blei, & Jordan, 2003), probabilistic latent semantic analysis (pLSA) model (Quelhas, Monay, Odobez, Gatica-Perez, Tuytelaars, & Gool, 2005; Sivic, Russell, Efros, Zisserman, & Freeman, 2005; Monay & Gatica-Perez, 2007), latent Dirichlet allocation (LDA) model (Barnard, et al., 2003; Blei & Jordan, 2003), 2D multi-resolution hidden Markov model (2D-MHMM) (Li & Wang, 2003; Wang & Li, 2002), supervised multi-class labeling (Carneiro, Chan, Moreno, & Vasconcelos, 2006), relevant low-level global filters (Oliva & Torralba, 2001), and so on. In this chapter we shall only be able to summarize some of the various methods.

Up to this point in time, automatic image retrieval by semantics still remains a challenging problem due to the difficulty in object recognition and image understanding. However, automatic image categorization and annotation can be used to help generate meaningful retrieval. Thus in Section IV, we will give a brief discussion of image retrieval with the help of image annotation and categorization. Finally, Section V concludes this chapter.

SEMANTIC IMAGE CLASSIFICATION

In this section, we begin by formulating the problem of semantic image classification, and then describe the representation models and classification algorithms.

Problem Formulation

Semantic image classification is a technique for classifying images based on their semantics from a domain of some given predefined concepts, such as building, waterside, landscape, cityscape, and so forth. While semantic image classification is a limited form of image understanding, its goal is not to understand images by the way human beings do, but merely to assign images to semantic categories (Wang, et al., 2001). Nevertheless, classifying images is still not an easy task owing to their variability, ambiguity, and the wide range of illumination and scale conditions that may apply (Bosch, Zisserman, & Muyyoz, 2008).

Conventionally, semantic image classification is posed as a *single-label classification* problem where each image is classified into one mutually-exclusive category, such as indoor vs. outdoor (Szummer & Picard, 1998), or textured vs. non-textured (Wang, et al., 2001).

Single-label image classification. Consider a database $\mathbf{D} = \{d_1,...,d_N\}$ of images d_i and a set of labels $\mathbf{C} = \{c_1,...,c_L\}$. Let $\mathbf{H}$ be the set of classifiers for $\mathbf{D} \rightarrow \mathbf{C}$. Thus the goal is to find a classifier $h \in \mathbf{H}$ maximizing the probability of $h(d) = c$, where $c \in \mathbf{C}$ is the ground truth label of d, i.e., $c = \arg\max_i P(c_i \mid d)$.

In practice, different statistical learning approaches, such as Bayesian probability models (Vailaya, et al., 2001; Aksoy, Koperski, Tusk, Marchisio, & Tilton, 2005; Li & Perona, 2005), linear discriminant analysis (Pappas, Chen, & Depalov, 2007) and support vector machines (SVM) (Serrano, Savakis, & Luo, 2004; Zhang, et al., 2006), have been successfully employed for single-label image categorization.

In the image classification domain, however, it is likely that many images may belong to multiple semantic classes. Considering examples shown in Fig. 1, the three images of category *coast* may be also viewed as *sky* scenes, and some images of category *inside city* can be classified into category *street* or *building*. In this case, the base categories are non-mutually-exclusive and may overlap by definition. Correspondingly, semantic image categorization is formulated as a *multi-label classification* problem where each image can be described by multiple class labels (e.g., a coast scene with a sky in the background). As before, this problem can be formulated as follows (Boutell, Shen, Luo, & Brown, 2004):

Multi-label image classification. Let $\mathbf{H}$ be the set of classifiers for $\mathbf{D} \rightarrow \mathbf{B}$ where $\mathbf{B}$ is a set of C-dimensional binary vectors, each of which indicates membership in the categories in $\mathbf{C}$ (+1=member, -1=non-member). Thus the goal is to find the classifier $h \in \mathbf{H}$ that minimized a distance (e.g., Hamming)

Figure 3. Overview of semantic image classification approaches

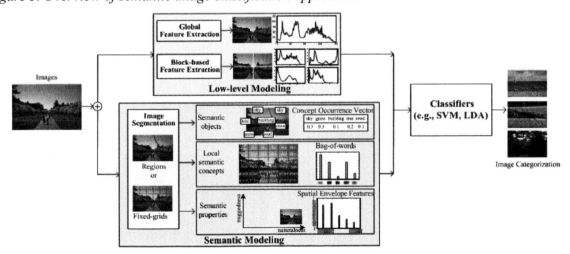

between h(d) and **b**$_d$ *for a new image d, or equivalently, to find one or more class labels in* **C** *and for a threshold δ such that P(c | d) > δ, ∀c ∈* **C**.

The mathematical formulation and its physical meaning are distinctively different from those used in the single-label image classification. Moreover, the multi-label classification models can be directly used for automatic image annotation (Goh, Chang, & Li, 2005; Carneiro, et al., 2006).

As noted in (Boutell, Brown, & Luo, 2002), the approaches for semantic image classification are divided into two main categories: *exemplar-based* and *model-based*. On one hand, most systems use an exemplar-based approach that employs statistical pattern recognition techniques on vectors of low-level features (such as color, texture, or edges) or semantic features (such as sky, faces or grass). On the other hand, model-based approaches use the expected configuration of a scene where the scene's configuration is the layout (relative location and sizes) of its objects created from expert knowledge of the scene. However, it is only possible to build a scene model for a constrained scene type and such a model is usually not generalizable to other scene types.

From a viewpoint of scene modeling and representation in images, Bosch, Muňoz, & Marti (2007) divided the approaches for semantic image classification into two basic strategies. The first uses low-level features such as global color or texture histograms, the power spectrum, and is normally used to classify only a small number of scene categories (indoor vs. outdoor, city vs. landscape etc.) (Szummer & Picard, 1998; Vailaya, et al., 2001; Wang, et al., 2001; Grauman & Darrell, 2005; Zhang, et al., 2006). The second strategy uses an intermediate representation before classifying scenes (Li & Perona, 2005; Wang, et al., 2006), and has been applied to cases where there are a larger number of scene categories. The two approaches are referred to as *low-level scene modeling* and *intermediate semantic modeling* respectively. The intermediate semantic modeling provides a potentially larger amount of information that can be exploited to achieve a higher performance on image classification.

Fig. 3 summarizes the semantic image classification approaches. Scene modeling and classifier are two main components in the procedure, which will be further discussed in the following subsections.

Scene Modeling

Scene modeling is necessary for a number of vision tasks, including classification and segmentation. In this subsection, we simply discuss two scene modeling approaches for image classification. More details can be found in (Bosch, et al., 2007).

Low-Level Modeling

The problem of low-level scene modeling has been studied in image and video retrieval for several years (e.g., Szummer & Picard, 1998; Vailaya, et al., 2001; Wang, et al., 2001; Grauman & Darrell, 2005; Zhang, et al., 2006). Color, texture and shape features have been widely used in combination with supervised learning methods to classify images into several semantic categories. The underlying assumption is that the type of scene can be directly described by the visual properties of the image. For instance, a *forest* scene presents highly textured regions (trees), or a *sunset* scene typically has saturated colors (mostly yellow and red). According to the way in which low-level features are extracted, it is possible to distinguish two trends of low-level modeling and representation approaches (Bosch, et al., 2007):

1. **Global approach:** Each scene is represented by low-level visual features from the whole image. In (Vailaya, et al., 2001), different global features are used at each level in the hierarchical classification of vacation images: indoor/outdoor (using spatial color moments); city/landscape (using edge direction histograms and coherence vectors); sunset/forest/mountain (using spatial moments, color histograms and coherence vectors), and so on. In (Zhang, et al., 2006), the image classification problem is addressed in the framework of measuring similarities based on global features such as shape and texture. Similarly, global features are used in (Chang, Goh, Sychay, & Wu, 2003) to produce a set of semantic labels by an ensemble of binary classifiers. Due to the complexity of visual content, good classification performance cannot be achieved by considering only a single type of features alone (Shen, Shepherd, & Ngu, 2005).

2. **Block-based approach:** The image is first partitioned into several blocks and then low-level visual features are extracted from each block. These blocks are then classified, and finally the scene is categorized from the individual classification of each block. This approach was originally used for indoor-outdoor classification problem in (Szummer & Picard, 1998). Similarly, an image is represented by a set of regions in the SIMPLIcity system (Wang, et al., 2001), each of which is characterized by color, texture, shape, and location. Then the system classifies images into semantic categories, such as textured-nontextured, graph-photograph. There are some other works (e.g., Paek & Chang, 2000; Serrano, et al., 2004) that use this approach for image classification, differentiated by the classifiers that are employed for blocks and the way how to infer the semantic category of the whole image from block classification results. For example, Paek and Chang (2000) developed a framework to combine multiple probabilistic classifiers in a belief network; while Serrano et al. (2004) used SVM for a reduction in feature dimensionality so that the block beliefs can be combined numerically.

Even good performance obtained by above proposals, the low-level modeling approach suffers several limitations (Bosch, et al., 2007). Firstly, this approach is normally used to classify only a small number of scene categories (indoor vs. outdoor, textured vs. nontextured, or city vs. landscape, etc). Secondly, it is often difficult to generalize theses methods using low-level visual features to additional image data beyond the training set. Finally, this approach lacks of an intermediate semantic image description that can be extremely valuable in determining the scene type.

Intermediate Semantic Modeling

The modeling of scenes by a semantic intermediate representation was next proposed in order to reduce the gap between low-level and high-level image processing, and therefore to match the scene model with the perception we humans have. Nevertheless, the semantic meaning of a scene is not unique, and different semantic representations of images have been proposed. Bosch et al. (2007) summarized three approaches of semantic modeling as follows:

1. **Semantic objects:** Objects of an image are detected and labeled by local classifiers as known semantic objects, and then the scene is represented by the occurrence of these semantic objects. This approach mainly relies on an initial segmentation of the image into meaningful regions that coarsely match objects or object parts. This assumption translates into several variations of image representation models. In (Aksoy, et al., 2005), scene representation is achieved by decomposing

the image into *prototype regions* and modeling the interactions between these regions in terms of their spatial relationships. Scene is also represented by regions in (Fredembach, Schröder, & Süsstrunk, 2004), but with the addition of *eigenregions* (the principal components of the intensity of the region). In (Mojsilovic, Gomes, & Rogowitz, 2002), the image is first segmented using color and texture information to find the semantic indicators (e.g. skin, sky, water), and then these objects are used to identify the semantic categories (i.e. people, outdoor, landscapes). Concept sensitive *salient objects* are detected in (Fan, Gao, Luo, & Xu, 2005) as the dominant image components for image classification. Moreover, some works (e.g. Luo, Savakis, & Singhal, 2005; Yang, Kim, & Ro, 2007) integrated the low-level and semantic features for classification by a general-purpose knowledge framework that employs a Bayesian Network (BN), or a two-layer SVM classifier. The limitation of this approach is that no automatic segmentation algorithm is currently capable of dividing an image into consistently meaningful objects or object parts.

2. **Local semantic concepts:** The semantic of an image is represented by intermediate properties extracted from local descriptors. In this case, a dictionary of visual words or local semantic concepts is first identified to define the semantics of images from local information (e.g., blue sky, mountain with snow). The visual words distribution can be learned for each scene category and then used for scene classification. This approach avoids object segmentation and detection by using a fixed-grid layout. Using this representation, three typical image descriptors can be found in the literatures.

The first type is the so-called *concept occurrence vector* (COV), which measures the frequency of different semantic concepts in a particular image. In (Vogel, 2004) and (Vogel & Schiele, 2004, 2007), each regular region is classified into semantic concept classes such as water, rocks, or foliage, and an image is then represented by a COV to measure the occurrence frequency of these local concepts. The average COV over all members of a category defines the category prototype. Scene classification is carried out by using the prototypical representation itself or Multi-SVM approaches.

Inspired by statistical text analysis, the second type of image descriptors is *bag-of-words* or *bag-of-visterms* (Mori, et al., 1999), formed by using a visual analogue of a word and vector-quantizing local

Figure 4. Illustration of four steps to compute the bag-of-words when working with image (quoted from Fig. 5 in (Bosch, et al., 2007))

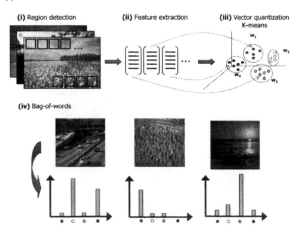

visual features. Recent works have shown that bags-of-words representation is suitable for scene classification, demonstrating impressive levels of performance (Li & Perona, 2005; Quelhas, et al., 2005; Bosch, Zisserman, & Muñoz, 2006; Perronin, 2007; Bosch, et al., 2008). As shown in Fig. 4, constructing the bag-of-words from images involves the following steps (Bosch, et al., 2007): (1) Automatically detect regions/points of interest, (2) compute local descriptors over those regions/points, (3) quantize the descriptors into words to form the visual vocabulary, (4) find the occurrences in the image of each specific word in the vocabulary in order to build the bag-of-words (histogram of words). Exiting works can be differentiated by the way how the features are used. Scale-Invariant Feature Transform (SIFT) (Lowe, 1999) features are computed on a regular grid (Li & Perona, 2005; Bosch, et al., 2006) or around an interest point (Quelhas, et al., 2005). Different with the above approaches that characterize an image with a single histogram, Perronin (2007) represented an image as a set of histograms, one *per* class describing whether an image is more suitably modeled by the universal vocabulary or a class-specific visual vocabulary. Using this bag-of-words representation, an image containing instances of several objects is modeled as a mixture of topics or object categories. This topics distribution over the images can be used to classify an image as belonging to a certain scene. Some probabilistic latent space models, such as probabilistic latent semantic analysis (pLSA) model (Quelhas, et al., 2005; Sivic, et al., 2005; Bosch, et al., 2006, 2008) and latent Dirichlet allocation (LDA) model (Li & Perona, 2005; Sivic, et al., 2005), have been adapted to model scene categories. In the next subsection, we will further discuss how pLSA and LDA are used for image categorization.

The third type is a variation of bag-of-words descriptor by using contextual knowledge like common spatial relationships between neighboring local objects or the absolute position of objects in certain scenes. The underlying assumption is that spatial structure could provide valuable information to achieve better results for scene classification. In (Lazebnik, Schmid, & Ponce, 2006), the spatial-pyramid is proposed as a simple computationally efficient extension of an orderless bag-of-words image representation by partitioning the image into increasingly finer sub-regions and computing histograms of local features found inside each sub-region. In (Fergus, Li, Perona, & Zisserman, 2005), pLSA is extended to include absolute position and spatial information in a translation and scale invariant manner respectively.

3. **Semantic properties:** The semantic of an image is described by a set of statistical properties/qualities of the image, including naturalness (vs. man-made), openness (presence of a horizon line), roughness (fractal complexity), expansion (perspective in man-made scenes), and ruggedness (deviation from the horizon in natural scenes) (Oliva & Torralba, 2001). Each feature corresponds to a dimension in the spatial envelope space, and all features together represent the dominant spatial structure of a scene. These properties may be reliably estimated using spectral and coarsely localized information. A significant advantage of this modeling approach is that the semantic is related to global configurations and scene structure, instead of local objects or regions, and consequently, neither segmentation nor the processing of local regions or objects is required (Bosch, et al., 2007).

In conclusion, the intermediate semantic modeling provides a potentially larger amount of information that must be exploited to achieve a higher performance on scene classification. However, it also makes more difficult the problem we are tackling because it habitually involves a local/region processing like (a not necessarily accurate) object recognition (Bosch, et al., 2007).

Classification Algorithms

Given the image representation, one primary tackling point is learning approach itself so that classifier realizes minimal bound of error in real tasks. In existing systems, many popular statistical learning approaches have been successfully used. In this subsection, we will describe several representative classification algorithms for images.

Hierarchical Image Classification with Low-level Scene Representation

In 2001, Vailaya et al. show that within a constrained domain, low-level features can successfully discriminate between many scene types arranged hierarchically. In the hierarchical classification task, each image is represented by a feature vector extracted from the image and different visual features are used at each level depending on the classification problem. Then the classification problem is addressed by using Bayesian decision theory. Formally, consider N training samples, each belonging to one class in $\mathbf{C} = \{c_1,...,c_L\}$. A vector quantizer is used to extract q codebook vectors, $\mathbf{v}_j$, from the N training samples. The class conditional density of a feature vector $\mathbf{y} = \{\mathbf{y}^{(1)},..., \mathbf{y}^{(m)}\}$ given the class $c \in \mathbf{C}$, i.e., $f(\mathbf{y} \mid c)$, is then approximated by a mixture of Gaussians (with identity covariance matrices), each centered at a codebook vector, resulting in:

$$f(\mathbf{y}|c) \propto \prod_{i=1}^{m}\sum_{j=1}^{q} m_j^{(i)} \exp\left(-\frac{\|\mathbf{y}^{(i)} - \mathbf{v}_j^{(i)}\|^2}{2\sigma^2}\right) \tag{1}$$

where $m_j^{(i)}$ is the proportion of training samples assigned to $\mathbf{v}_j$. The Bayesian classifier is then defined using the maximum a posteriori (MAP) criterion as follows:

$$\hat{c} = \arg\max_{c\in\mathbf{C}}\{p(c|\mathbf{y})\} = \arg\max_{c\in\mathbf{C}}\{f(\mathbf{y}|c)p(c)\} \tag{2}$$

where $p(c)$ represents the a priori class probability. Their system achieved a good performance at each level of the hierarchy over a set of 6931 vacation photographs.

Many other works also exploit low-level scene modeling for semantic image classification. For example, three kinds of classifiers, KNN, SVM and GMM, are used in (Shen, et al., 2005). SVM is also used in (Serrano,et al., 2004) for a reduction in feature dimensionality without compromising image classification accuracy. Due to the space limitation, the details are not included in this chapter.

Scene Classification Using Semantic Object Detection

The *salient objects* are defined as the dominant image components that are semantic to human being and are also visually distinguishable (Fan, et al., 2005). For example, the salient object "*sky*" is defined as the connected image regions with large sizes (i.e., dominant image components) that are related to the human semantics "*sky*". By detecting the concept-sensitive salient objects, an image classification technique was developed in (Fan, et al., 2005) to achieve automatic image annotation at the concept level. Thus here we use this approach as an example to illustrate how to detect salient objects in images and then how to exploit them for semantic image classification.

To detect the concept-sensitive salient objects, a set of 32 detection functions are learned in *one-against-all* manner from the labeled image regions, each for a specific type of these salient objects. A detection function consists of three steps: (1) automatic image segmentation by using mean shift algorithm, (2) binary region classification by using SVMs with an automatic scheme for searching the optimal model parameters and (3) label-based aggregation of the connected similar regions for salient object generation. This process is automatic and the human interaction is only involved in the procedure to label the training samples (i.e., homogeneous regions) for learning the detection functions. The semantic image classification system takes the following steps: (1) Given a specific test image d_i (which may consist of multiple types of different salient objects), the underlying salient objects $d_i = \{o_1,...,o_n\}$ are detected automatically. (2) The class distribution of the salient objects $d_i = \{o_1,...,o_n\}$ is then modeled as a finite mixture model (FMM) $P(\mathbf{y}, c_j | \kappa, \omega_{c_j}, \Theta_{c_j})$. (3) The test image d_i is finally classified into the best matching semantic image concept c_j with the maximum posterior probability.

$$P(c_j | \mathbf{y}, d_i, \Theta) = \frac{P(\mathbf{y}, c_j | \kappa, \omega_{c_j}, \Theta_{c_j}) \; (P_j)}{\sum_{j=1}^{N_c} P(\mathbf{y}, c_j | \kappa, \omega_{c_j}, \Theta_{c_j}) \; (P_j)} \qquad (3)$$

where $\Theta = \{\kappa, \omega_{c_j}, \Theta_{c_j} | j = 1, \cdots, L\}$ is the set of the mixture parameters (i.e., Θ_{c_j} and the mixture component number κ) and relative weights (i.e., ω_{c_j}) for the classifiers, $\mathbf{y}$ is the n-dimensional visual features for representing the relevant concept-sensitive salient objects, and $P(c_j)$ is the prior probability of the semantic concept c_j. An adaptive Expectation-Maximization (EM) algorithm is proposed to determine the optimal model structure and parameters simultaneously.

Similar scene classification algorithms can also be found in (Mojsilovic, et al., 2002; Fredembach, et al., 2004; Aksoy, et al., 2005; Luo, et al., 2005). The authors argue that with the more advances of automatic image segmentation, better classification could be achieved by using this approach.

Scene Classification with Latent Space Representation

Recently, the *bag-of-words* model has been widely used in image classification and made great progress. However it may suffer from two issues (Quelhas, et al., 2005): *polysemy* — a single visual word (i.e., *visterm*) may represent different scene content, and *synonymy* — several visterms may characterize the same image content. In order to disambiguate the representation, probabilistic latent space models, such as pLSA (Hofmann, 2001) and LDA (Blei, Ng, & Jordan, 2003), have been applied to capture co-occurrence information between visterms in a collection of images. Here we simply describe how these models are used to latent topic discovery in semantic image classification.

Suppose that we have an image set $\mathbf{D} = \{d_1,...,d_N\}$ with words from a visual vocabulary $\mathbf{W} = \{w_1,...,w_V\}$. The data is a $V \times N$ co-occurrence table of counts $N_{ij} = n(w_i, d_j)$, where $n(w_i, d_j)$ denotes how often the visterm w_i occurred in an image d_j. pLSA (Hofmann, 2001) assumes the existence of a latent variable $z \in \mathbf{Z}$ in the generative process of each word $w \in \mathbf{W}$ in an image $d \in \mathbf{D}$. As shown in Fig. 5(a), the observed variables w and d are conditionally independent given the latent variable z, thus a joint probability $P(w, z)$ over $V \times N$ is defined by the mixture:

$$P(w | d) = \sum_{z \in \mathbf{Z}} P(w | z) P(z | d) \qquad (4)$$

where $P(w \mid z)$ are the topic-specific distributions, and each image is modeled as a mixture of topics, $P(z \mid d)$. The equation expresses each image as a convex combination of $|\mathbf{Z}|$ topic vectors. This amounts to a matrix decomposition as shown in Fig. 5(b) with the constraint that both $P(w \mid z)$ and $P(z \mid d)$ are normalized to make them probability distributions. Given that both w and z are discrete variables, the conditional probability distributions $P(z \mid d)$ and $P(w \mid z)$ are multinomial. The parameters of these distributions are estimated by the EM algorithm (Hofmann, 2001). Given a new image d_{new}, $P(z \mid d_{new})$ can be inferred by using the *folding-in* method, which maximizes the likelihood of the image d_{new} with a partial version of the EM algorithm while keeping the learned $P(w \mid z)$ fixed. More details about pLSA can be found in (Hofmann, 2001).

pLSA is appropriate to disambiguate the bag-of-words representation because it provides a correct statistical model for clustering in the case of multiple object categories *per* image (Quelhas, et al., 2005). Consequently, pLSA can be used to generate a robust, low-dimensional scene representation. Given a new image d_{new}, the model determines the mixture coefficients $P(z \mid d_{new})$ for each image d_{new} where $z \in \mathbf{Z}$. The image d_{new} is then classified as the semantic category z according to the maximum of $P(z \mid d_{new})$ over $z \in \mathbf{Z}$. In (Quelhas, et al., 2005) and (Sivic, et al., 2005), pLSA is applied on sparse SIFT features for recognizing compact scene categories, where SIFT features are computed around an interest point. While in (Bosch, et al., 2006, 2008), pLSA is applied on dense SIFT features to obtain a better scene categorization, where SIFT features are computed on a regular grid and using concentric patches around each point to allow scale variance. Moreover, spatial information can also be exploited in the framework of pLSA to improve scene classification performance. In 2005, Fergus *et al.* develop two new models, ABS-pLSA and FSI-pLSA, by extending pLSA to include absolute position and spatial information in a translation and scale invariant manner respectively. For example, the ABS-pLSA model quantizes the location within the image into one of X bins. The joint density on the appearance and location of each region is then represented. Thus $P(w \mid z)$ in pLSA becomes $P(w,x \mid z)$, a discrete density of size $(V \times X) \times N$. Inspired by ABS-pLSA and spatial-pyramid matching (SPM) algorithm (Lazebnik, et al., 2006), Bosch, et al. (2008) proposed the SP-pLSA model by using the X bins at each resolution level l, weighting the bins for each level as in SPM. Thus $P(w \mid z)$ in pLSA becomes $P(w, x, l \mid z)$. The same pLSA update equations can be applied to these models in learning and recognition.

In contrast to pLSA, LDA treats the multinomial weights $P(z \mid d)$ over topics as latent random variables. The LDA model is extended by sampling those weights from a Dirichlet distribution, the conjugate prior to the multinomial distribution. This extension allows the LDA model to assign probabilities to data outside the training corpus and uses fewer parameters, thus reducing overfitting (Sivic, et al., 2005). Graphically, LDA is a three-level hierarchical Bayesian model, in which each item of a

Figure 5. (a) pSLA graphical model. Filled circles indicate observed random variables; unfilled are unobserved. (b) Graphical representation of the matrix decomposition form of pLSA. (c) LDA graphical model.

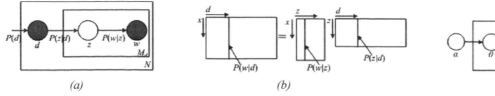

collection is modeled as a finite mixture over a set of latent aspects (Blei, et al., 2003). Each aspect is, in turn, modeled as an infinite mixture over an set of laten aspect probabilities. The LDA model is shown in Fig. 5(c). The goal is to maximize the following likelihood:

$$P(w|\alpha, \beta) = \int P(\theta|\alpha)\left(\sum_{z \in \mathbf{Z}} P(z|\theta)P(w|z, \beta)\right)d\theta \tag{5}$$

where θ is the multinomial parameter over the topics, and P($\theta \mid \alpha$) is Dirichlet distribution parameterized by the hyper-parameter α. As the figure makes clear, there are three levels to the LDA representation. The parameters α and β are collection-level parameters, assumed to be sampled once in the process of generating a collection. The variables θ_d are image-level variables, sampled once *per* image. Finally, the variables z_{d_n} and x_{d_n} are element-level variables and are sampled once for each element in each image. More details about LDA can be found in (Blei, et al., 2003).

In the LDA case, the unseen mixed-category images can be classified based on the topic mixture weights θ, which can be computed using the samples drawn by the Gibbs sampler (Sivic, et al., 2005). Li and Perona (2005) proposed two variations of LDA to represent and learn image categorization models, in which local regions are first clustered into different intermediate themes (local concepts) and then into categories. Probability distributions of the local regions as well as the intermediate themes are both learnt automatically, bypassing any human annotation apart from labeling a single category to the training images.

Web Image Classification

With the rapid growth of digital images on the Internet, Web image classification has become an important research topic. Web images have a lot of properties which are quite different from those images in small database such as Corel and family album (Cai, et al., 2004). For example, Web images are associated with text and link information. Many works (e.g., Hu & Bagga, 2004; Kalva, Enembreck, & Koerich, 2007) use the text content from the document that contains an image as the semantic features for classifying that image. In (Lempel & Soffer, 2002; Cai, et al., 2004; Wang, Ma, Xue, & Li, 2004), link information is also exploited to improve Web image retrieval. Here we will describe how to exploit visual, textual and link information for Web image classification by using our work (Tian, et al., 2005) as an illustrating example.

Fig. 6(a) illustrates the relational representation of images in the context of Web. Given a collection $\mathbf{D} = \{d_1,...,d_N\}$ of Web images, each image $d_i \in \mathbf{D}$ can be represented by a vector of global or local visual features, $\mathbf{f}_i^{(V)}$. By extracting the surrounding text (and other related text such as the filename and URL of the image), each image can also be represented by a textual term vector $\mathbf{f}_i^{(T)}$, in which each term can be weighted by its term frequency (TF) or term frequency inverse document frequency (TFIDF). Then in the joint visual-textual feature space, each image can be represented as $\mathbf{f}_i^{(C)} = \left[\mathbf{f}_i^{(V)}, \mathbf{f}_i^{(T)}\right]$. Moreover, with the assumption that images which are co-contained in pages are likely to be related to the same topic, and images which are contained in pages that are co-cited by a certain page are likely related to the same topic (Lempel & Soffer, 2002), we can derive the *image adjacency matrix* $\mathbf{A}_{I \sim I}$ among the images in $\mathbf{D}$. The matrix $\mathbf{A}_{I \sim I}$ naturally defines an image graph G_I, and can be used to derive semantically richer representation of linked images. The first representation is derived directly from the matrix $\mathbf{A}_{I \sim I}$, referred to as *linkage relationship vector (LRV)*. Namely, the link features of each image d_i can be represented by the i-th column $\mathbf{f}_i^{(L)}$ of $\mathbf{A}_{I-I}$. Alternatively, each image d_i can be represented by a class-based weighted vector

$$\ddot{\mathbf{f}}_i^{(L)} = \left[w_{i,1}, w_{i,2}, \cdots, w_{i,5L} \right], \tag{6}$$

where $w_{i,2}(1 \leq k \leq 5L)$ are the weighted frequencies of the five important link relations (i.e., co-containedness, in-link, out-link, co-citation and co-reference) between image d_i and its neighboring images of different classes, L is the number of the class labels $\mathbf{C} = \{c_1,...,c_L\}$. This representation is referred to as *class-based LRV (CLRV)*.

By extending SVM to the relational domain, a *relational support vector classifier* (*RSVC*) is proposed. If the vector $\acute{\alpha}$ and the scalar b are the parameters of the hyperplane learned from the training images, then the RSVC decision rule is defined as:

$$y_i = \text{sgn}\left(\sum_{j=1}^{l} \alpha_j y_j \left[(1-\beta)K(\mathbf{f}_i^{(C)}, \mathbf{f}_j^{(C)}) + \beta K(\mathbf{f}_i^{(L)}, \mathbf{f}_j^{(L)}) \right] + b \right)$$

$$\backsimeq \text{gn}\left(\beta \sum_{j=1}^{l} \alpha_j y_j K(\mathbf{f}_i^{(L)}, \mathbf{f}_j^{(L)}) + \theta_i \right), \tag{7}$$

where y_i is its class label indicator, $K(\mathbf{f}_i^{(C)}, \mathbf{f}_j^{(C)})$ and $K(\mathbf{f}_i^{(L)}, \mathbf{f}_j^{(L)})$ are the content kernels and linkage kernels respectively, β is the combination weight, and

$$\theta_i = (1-\beta) \sum_{j=1}^{l} \alpha_j y_j K(\mathbf{f}_i^{(C)}, \mathbf{f}_j^{(C)}) + b$$

is the decision function of a conventional SVM, and l denotes the number of support vectors (SVs). Given a new image d_{new}, the link feature of d_{new} is computed by adding d_{new} to the collection of the training and labeled test images $\mathbf{D}$, and then RSVC is used to classified the image d_{new}. On a sports Web image collection crawled from Yahoo!, RSVC yields significant improvement in accuracy over SVM using visual and/or textual features.

Figure 6. (a) The representation of Web images. (b) An example link graph of Web images

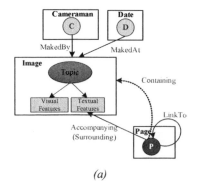

(a)

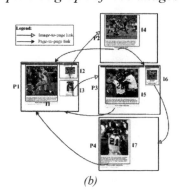

(b)

Discussion

This section is meant to capture the landscape of semantic image classification by clearly formulating the problem, and simply discussing recent representative works from the viewpoints of scene modeling and classification algorithms. We now discuss some research issues connected to the ideas discussed here. First, latest trends are using the bag-of-words representations jointly with different latent topic discovery techniques (Bosch, et al., 2007). However, bag-of-words representation should be further improved by using contextual knowledge. It's only a good start point that the spatial information is taken into account in this representation. Second, as mentioned in (Boutell, et al., 2004), seldom works address multi-label image classification. Such a problem poses challenges to the classic pattern recognition paradigm and demands a different treatment. Finally, in spite of progress, no semantic classification algorithm is currently capable of classifying images with complex scene into a very large number of classes with relatively high accuracy. Indeed, classifying images with complex scene is still a challenging task owing to their variability, ambiguity, and the wide range of illumination and scale conditions that may apply. Such image classification methods are extended for image annotation with the goal of approaching greater semantic understanding of images.

AUTOMATIC IMAGE ANNOTATION

In this section, we begin by presenting two typical tasks of image annotation. Then, we shall discuss two important aspects for automatic image annotation — image representation and auto-annotation models. Finally, we shall discuss how to evaluate the image annotation systems.

Task Definition

Typically, automatic image annotation systems take advantage of annotated images to link the visual and textual modalities by using machine learning techniques. Accordingly, they can be posed as a task of either supervised or unsupervised learning (Carneiro, et al., 2006).

Supervised Annotation

In the supervised annotation systems (Chang, et al., 2003; Li & Wang, 2003; Smith, Lin, Naphade, Natsev, & Tseng, 2003; Carneiro, et al., 2006), multi-label image classification algorithms are extended for image annotation: All training images are labeled different *concepts*, where each concept contains a group of semantically related keywords that describe different aspects of that concept. For example, the concept "*wild animal*" can be described as "*animal, wild life, grass, snow, rock*" (Li & Wang, 2003). Given these categorized images, one generative or discriminative classifier is trained for each concept and then applied to all test images which are annotated with respect to the presence or absence of the concept.

One important problem is how to statistically model images for each concept. In (Carneiro, et al., 2006), images are represented as bags of localized feature vectors, and the mixtures associated with all images annotated with a common concept pooled into a density estimate for the corresponding class. Annotation is then performed with a minimum probability of error rule, based on these class densities. In (Li & Wang, 2003), a 2D multi-resolution hidden Markov model (2D-MHMM) is learned on a fixed-grid segmentation of all category examples. The likelihood of a new image given each category's 2D-MHMM allows assigning words for this image. Similarly, one SVM is trained for each concept in the model vector indexing approach (Smith, et al., 2003) while a binary classifier (Bayes Point Machine and SVM) is trained for each word (totally 116 words) in Content-Based Soft Annotation (CBSA) system (Chang, et al., 2003).

The major advantage of supervised annotation is that models for different concepts can be independently trained and retrained. If images representing new concepts or new images in existing concepts are added into the training database, only the models for the involved concepts need to be trained or retrained. However, if the vocabulary size is very large, there are a relatively large number of models that need to be elaborately trained. Moreover, since a concept contains a group of keywords that have a related meaning, labeling an image by all keywords of the concept may produce incorrect annotations. For example, not all images of the concept "*wild animal*" have the visual content that corresponds to *snow* or *rock*. Automatic image annotation systems therefore tend to unsupervised learning approach in recent years.

Unsupervised Annotation

Most automatic image annotation systems (e.g., Mori, et al., 1999; Barnard & Forsyth, 2001; Duygulu, et al., 2002; Barnard, et al., 2003; Blei & Jordan, 2003; Jeon, et al., 2003; Feng, et al., 2004; Monay & Gatica-Perez, 2007) tend to solve the problem in greater generality by resorting to unsupervised learning. The basic idea is to introduce one auto-annotation model to characterize the relation between words and visual features. During training, a set of words is assigned to each image, and unsupervised learning techniques are run over the entire database to train one auto-annotation model for the whole vocabulary. Given a new image, visual features are extracted, and inference on the learned model is then used to assign annotations to the image.

A whole range of statistical assumptions about visual features and image annotations can lead to different auto-annotation models, from the simple empirical distribution estimation to complex generative or discriminative models. Typical unsupervised auto-annotation models include word co-occurrence model (Mori, et al., 1999), translation model (Duygulu, et al., 2002), cross-media relevance model (Jeon, et al., 2003; Feng, et al., 2004), multi-modal hierarchical aspect model (Barnard & Forsyth, 2001; Barnard, et al., 2003), pLSA model (Monay & Gatica-Perez, 2007), LDA model (Barnard, et al., 2003; Blei & Jordan, 2003), etc.

The main advantage of unsupervised annotation is that only one model is learned for all words in the vocabulary. Consequently, this approach is better suited for large vocabularies than the supervised learning approach. As mentioned in (Barnard & Forsyth, 2001), however, one major limitation is that this approach relies on semantically meaningful segmentation while automatic segmentation is still an open problem in computer vision (Shi & Malik, 2000).

Image Representation

All image annotation approaches use either a fixed-grid layout or an image segmentation algorithm to divide images into a number of irregularly-shaped regions. This entails that the features should be extracted from local image regions for annotation. To extract such local features and build the auto-annotation models, there are three kinds of image representations: *blob*-based, *grid*-based and *keypoint*-based. The first relies on large-scale image regions; while the two others are based on a larger number of smaller scale regions, uniformly extracted from a fixed grid or identified by a point detector. The three representations encode different image properties and are therefore expected to produce different effects on image annotation. Fig. 7 shows several examples of the three image representations.

Blob-Based Representation

Blobs were proposed by Duygulu et al. (2002) to capture the content of an image with a set of homogeneous regions. As shown in Fig. 7(b), each image can be represented as a certain number of blobs. These blobs may coarsely match objects or object parts. This naturally brings up an assumption that there is some implicit correspondence between regions and words in the annotated images. To build blobs, images are first segmented into regions using the normalized cut segmentation algorithm (Shi & Malik, 2000) which requires a maximum count of regions to avoid too small regions. Each region is represented by 36 features including color (18), texture (12), and shape/location (6). The K-means clustering algorithm is then applied to the region descriptors, quantizing them into a multi-dimensional blob representation. Let m denote the blob number in image d, then the image d can be represented by the corresponding histogram $b(d)$ of size m (Monay & Gatica-Perez, 2007)

$$b(d) = \{n(b_1), \cdots, n(b_i), \cdots, n(b_m)\} \tag{8}$$

where $n(b_i)$ denotes the number of regions in image d that are quantized into the blob b_i. Similar to the word-by-document matrix in text mining, the *blob-by-image* matrix representation is also proposed in (Pan, Yang, Duygulu, & Faloutsos, 2004) by weighting with the TFIDF scheme.

Blob-based image representation has been widely used in automatic image annotation and retrieval, such as (Barnard & Forsyth, 2001; Duygulu, et al., 2002; Barnard, et al., 2003; Jeon, et al., 2003; Pan, et al., 2004). However, the effect of blobs depends on the automatic segmentation algorithms which haven't achieved human-like results. Moreover, as mentioned in (Feng, et al., 2004), the match between the segmented regions and objects in images is relatively poor in general.

Grid-Based Representation

Instead of the use of a segmentation algorithm, some works (e.g. Mori, et al., 1999; Wang & Li, 2002; Li & Wang, 2003; Feng, et al., 2004) use the grid-based representation for image annotation with the help of a fixed-grid layout (as shown in Fig. 7(c)). Compared with blob-based representation, grid-based representation provides a number of advantages (Feng, et al., 2004), including significant reduction in the computational time, simplified parameter estimation, and the easier ability to incorporate context (e.g., relative position) into the auto-annotation model. One major limitation of this representation is that grid regions lack of significant semantic correspondence with objects or object parts.

Using grid-based representation, local visual features can be extracted and quantized for every grid region. In (Wang & Li, 2002) and (Li & Wang, 2003), every image is characterized by a set of wavelet feature vectors extracted at multiple resolutions and spatially arranged on a pyramid grid. In (Mori, et al., 1999), the color and texture representations of all training image blocks are quantized into a finite set of visual terms (*visterms*). As mentioned in the previous section, this quantization form is called

Figure 7. Examples of image representations for annotation

(a) Original images   (b) Images with blobs   (c) Images with fixed-grids   (d) Images with keypoints

bag-of-visterms or directly *bag-of-words*. Bag-of-visterms ignores the spatial relationship between regions in an image. However, recent research results show that regions are spatially relevant and not independent of the global meanings of images. For example, the neighboring regions may have a strong recommendation of visual content (Ghoshal, Ircing, & Khudanpur, 2005). By incorporating spatial relationship, the auto-annotation models can obtain comparable annotation performance.

Keypoint-Based Representation

Keypoints (also as salient points) refer to a set of local features detected in images such Harris corner points. Numerical feature vectors can be extracted from these keypoints such as Scale-Invariant Feature Transform (SIFT) (Lowe, 1999). SIFT transforms an image into a large collection of local feature vectors, each of which is invariant to image translation, scaling, and rotation, and partially invariant to illumination changes and affine or 3D projection. Recently, this representation has been successfully combined with probabilistic latent space models and has shown good performance in scene modeling (Li & Perona, 2005; Quelhas, et al., 2005) and image annotation (Monay & Gatica-Perez, 2007).

The construction of the SIFT feature vector from an image involves the steps illustrated in Fig. 8. In this process, the image is first sampled with the difference-of-Gaussians (DoG) point detector at different scales and locations. SIFT descriptor is then computed on affine covariant region around the interest point. Each SIFT descriptor consists of a histogram of edge directions at different locations. All SIFT descriptors are then quantized by the K-means clustering algorithm to obtain a discrete set of local image-patch indexes. As a result, an image is represented by the histogram of its constituting local patches. The details of SIFT descriptor computation can be found in (Lowe, 1999).

Auto-Annotation Models

Independent of what features are chosen, the question is how to model the relation between textual and visual features to achieve the best textual indexing. As the pioneering work, the co-occurrence model (Mori, et al., 1999) uses a fixed-grid image segmentation and a vector quantization step to transfer a set of words assigned to the whole image to each image part (i.e., visterm) and then model the co-occurrence of words with visterms. As pointed out by Feng, et al. (2004), however, the approach tends to annotate unknown images with high frequency words and requires large number of training samples to estimate the correct probabilities. Thereafter, a whole range of models and methods have been proposed in the literature, offering a large variety of approaches. In this subsection, we will describe four main models — translation model, cross-media relevance model, probabilistic latent space model and 2D-MHMM model.

Translation Model

In 2002, Duygulu et al. proposed the *translation model* by treating image annotation as the task of translating from a vocabulary of blobs to a vocabulary of words. In this model, the word and blob modalities are considered as two languages. Given a set of training images, a classical machine translation model is used to annotate a test set of images:

$$p(w \mid b) = \prod_{n=1}^{N} \prod_{i=1}^{M_n} \sum_{i=1}^{L_n} p(a_{nj} = i) t(w = w_{nj} \mid b = b_{ni}),$$

(9)

where N is the number of images, M_n and L_n are the numbers of words and blobs in the n-th image respectively, a_n denotes the assignment $a_n = \{a_{n1}, \cdots, a_{nM_n}\}$ such that $a_{nj} = i$ if blob b_{ni} translates to word w_{nj}, $p(a_{nj} = i)$ is the assignment probability, and $t(w \mid b)$ is the probability of obtaining instance of word w given instance of blob b. An EM procedure is then proposed to estimate the probability distributions linking words and blobs. Once the model parameters are learned, words can be attached to a new image region. This *region naming* process is analogous with learning a lexicon from an aligned vocabulary.

The translation model is a substantial improvement over the co-occurrence model. However, this model can capture the correlation between blobs and words but the dependencies between them are not captured. Moreover, the training stage with the EM algorithm requires a high computational effort and is very time-consuming when dealing with large datasets.

Cross-Media Relevance Model

Also relied on a quantized blob image representation, the *cross-media relevance model* was proposed by Jeon, et al. (2003) to capture the complex dependency between blobs and words in images (not a

Figure 8. SIFT feature extraction and quantization framework

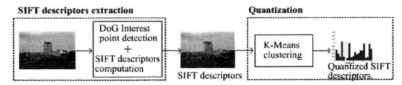

simple one-to-one correspondence). Consider an example. In the image context, "*tigers*" are more often associated with "*grass, water, tree or sky*" and less often with man-made objects such as "*car*" or "*computer*". Therefore, it is assumed that for each image $d_i = \{w_{i1}, w_{iM_i}, b_{i1}, b_{iL_i}\}$ there exists some underlying probability distribution $P(\bullet \mid d_i)$ (called the relevance model of d_i). The relevance model can be thought of as an urn that contains all possible blobs that could appear in image d_i, as well as all words that could appear in the caption of d_i. To annotate a test image d_i, we need estimate the probability $P(w \mid d_i)$ for every word w in the vocabulary,

$$P(w \mid d_i) \approx P(w \mid b_{i1}, \cdots, b_{iL_i}) = \frac{P(w, b_{i1}, \cdots, b_{iL_i})}{\sum_w P(w, b_{i1}, \cdots, b_{iL_i})} \tag{10}$$

Then the joint distribution can be computed as an expectation over the training image set **T**,

$$P(w, b_1, \cdots, b_m) = \sum_{d_k \in \mathbf{T}} P(d_k) P(w \mid d_k) \prod_{i=1}^{m} P(b_i \mid d_k) \tag{11}$$

Here the conditional probability of a word w (or blob b_i) given a training image d_k, i.e., $P(w \mid d_k)$ (respectively, $P(b_i \mid d_k)$), is estimated by the count of word w (respectively, blob b_i) in image d_k smoothed by the average count of word w (respectively, blob b_i) in the training set **T**. An extended version of this model uses the multiple Bernoulli distribution for modeling image annotation (Feng, et al., 2004). Compared to the translation model, the cross-media relevance model performs much better on the same dataset (with the same training and test images and the same features).

Probabilistic Latent Space Models

More recently, *probabilistic latent space models* have attracted much attention in image annotation. A hidden variable (latent aspect) is assumed in the data generative process, which links the textual and visual modalities through conditional relationships. Under this assumption, an image is modeled as a mixture of latent aspects that generates the image regions (or features). A subset of these latent aspects is then selected to generate the text caption, which intuitively corresponds to the natural process of image annotation. In practice, this assumption translates into several model variations, including pLSA (Monay & Gatica-Perez, 2007) and LDA (Barnard, et al., 2003; Blei & Jordan, 2003).

pLSA. Under the framework of PLSA, an image is modeled as a mixture of latent aspects that generates both image features and text words. To learn a pLSA model for the co-occurrence of visual and textual features in annotated images, the simplest method is a direct application of pLSA to the early integration of visual and textual modalities (Monay & Gatica-Perez, 2003). An asymmetric PLSA learning algorithm is proposed in (Monay & Gatica-Perez, 2007) to allows choosing between the textual and visual modalities to estimate the conditional distributions of latent aspects given the training images. Their experiments show that the best performance is achieved when the mixture of latent aspects is learned from the text words.

LDA. Several variations of LDA have been proposed for image annotation, including correspondence LDA (Corr-LDA) (Blei & Jordan, 2003), Multi-modal LDA (MoM-LDA) (Barnard, et al., 2003). Corr-LDA is depicted in Fig. 9(a). This model can be viewed in terms of a generative process that first generates L region descriptions b_i and subsequently generates the caption words. That is, for each of the M words, one of the regions is selected from the image and a corresponding word w_j is drawn, conditioned on the factor that generated the selected region. The distribution over words conditioned on a region an image is approximated by (Blei & Jordan, 2003)

$$p(w \mid b) = \sum_{i=1}^{L} \sum_{z_i \in Z} q(z_i \mid \varphi_i) p(w \mid z_i, \beta), \tag{12}$$

where $q(z_i \mid \phi_i)$ is the approximate posterior distribution over the latent variables given a particular image/caption, ϕ_i are L K-dimensional multinomial parameters. Experimental results show that the additional constraint on word generation improves the overall annotation performance over less constrained LDA-based models.

As shown in Fig. 9(b), MoM-LDA is another multi-modal extension to LDA. Given an image and a MOM-LDA, we can compute both an approximate posterior over mixture components and, for each mixture component, an approximate posterior Dirichlet over latent aspects. Using these parameters, we can perform image-based word-prediction by finding the corresponding distribution over words. Let φ denote the approximate posterior over mixture components, and γ_α denote the corresponding approximate posterior Dirichlet. The distribution over words given an image (that is, a collection of blobs) is:

$$p(w \mid b) = \sum_{\alpha} p(\alpha \mid \phi) \sum_{z_i \in Z} p(w \mid z_i) \int p(z_i \mid \theta) p(\theta \mid \gamma_\alpha) d\theta. \tag{13}$$

One of the advantages of LDA-based mixture models is that they provide well-defined inference procedures for previously unseen images (Blei, et al., 2003). Thus they are expected to have more applications in the area of image annotation in the future.

2D Multi-Resolution Hidden Markov Model

By adopting a supervised learning strategy, Li and Wang (2002; 2003) introduced a statistical modeling approach to the problem of automatic linguistic indexing of pictures. To model the stochastic process of associating an image with the textual description of a concept, a 2D-MHMM is learned on a fixed-grid segmentation of all category examples. In this model, every image is characterized by a set of wavelet feature vectors extracted at multiple resolutions and spatially arranged on a pyramid grid. Given each category's 2D-MHMM, the likelihood of a new image allows selecting words for this image. As mentioned before, the major advantages of this model are (1) models for different concepts can be independently trained, stored and retrained, and (2) spatial relation among image pixels within and across resolutions is taken into consideration.

Figure 9. Graphical representation of different variations of LDA models for automatic image annotation

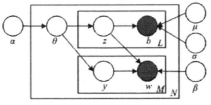
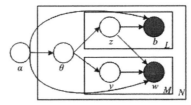

(a) CORR-LDA model   *(b) MoM-LDA model*

Evaluation

Data Sets

Corel image dataset is the *de facto* benchmark dataset used in the evaluation of image annotation. This set of 60,000 images consists of 600 CD-ROMs, each of which corresponds to a semantic concept or topic (e.g., *beach, buildings, buses, dinosaurs*) and typically contains about 100 images. Each image is described by several keywords from a controlled vocabulary. The Corel dataset was originally used in (Duygulu, et al., 2002) with a subset with 5,000 annotated images (denoted by *Corel5K*). Corel5K has been widely used as an evaluation standard by a number of research groups (e.g., Jeon, et al., 2003; Feng, et al., 2004; Carneiro, et al., 2006; Zhang, et al., 2006). Another oft-used Corel subset, denoted by *Corel16K*, consists of 16,000 annotated images (Barnard, et al., 2003; Monay & Gatica-Perez, 2007) and is an extension of Corel5K. By the adoption of such *de facto* standard datasets, significant progress has been accomplished in the recent past.

However, the Corel image collection has been criticized because the annotations are nouns selected from a relatively small vocabulary and is relatively simple from an image retrieval point of view (Barnard, et al., 2003; Zhang, et al., 2006). Caltech101 is another widely used dataset for image annotation. Recently, the authors of Caltech101 have released a new version of their dataset, called Caltech256, including 256 picture categories. Some new image sets are also introduced in recent years for the evaluation of image annotation, by downloading real-world images from Internet (Chang, et al., 2003; Zhang, et al., 2006).

Performance Measures

A whole range of performance measures for automatic image annotation systems has been discussed in the literature. Roughly speaking, they can be grouped into two categories.

Intuitively, the annotation performance can be measured by comparing the words predicted by various models with words actually present for held-out data. The first measure is annotation accuracy (Barnard, et al., 2003; Pan, et al., 2004), defined as the ratio of the correctly predicted words *per* image (i.e., $m_{correct}$) divided by the number m of words in the ground-truth annotation, i.e., $E = m_{correct}/m$. Alternatively, another measure for annotation is the Normalized Score (Barnard, et al., 2003)

$$E_{NS} = \frac{m_{correct}}{m} - \frac{m_{incorrect}}{(M_{voc} - m)}, \tag{14}$$

where M_{voc} is the vocabulary size. This measure depends on the number of predicted words and allows estimating the optimal number of words to predict.

All image annotation approaches provide a confidence value for each word, which can be used for ranking all images in a collection and enabling the construction of an image index for text-based image retrieval (Monay & Gatica-Perez, 2007). Therefore, evaluating annotation performance by retrieval became consensual for image annotation (e.g., Jeon, et al., 2003; Smith, et al., 2003; Feng, et al., 2004; Pan, et al., 2004; Monay & Gatica-Perez, 2007). In this way, the precision and recall values of the retrieved image sets for a number of given queries are widely used. In (Monay & Gatica-Perez, 2007), a mean average precision (mAP) for a set of queries is used to measure the retrieval performance, as follows

$$mAP = \frac{\sum_{q=1}^{N_q} AP(q)}{N_q}, \text{ where} \tag{15}$$

$$AP(q) = \frac{\sum_{i \in relevant} precision(i)}{rel(q)}. \tag{16}$$

Here *precision*(*q*) denote the precision of the correctly retrieved images at rank *i*, and *rel*(*q*) denote the total number of relevant images for query *q*. The AP measure of a query is thus sensitive to the entire ranking of images. The mean of the APs of N_q queries summarizes the performance of a retrieval system in one mAP value.

Discussion

Automatic image annotation given a large image dataset and a large vocabulary is widely recognized as an extremely difficult task. The difficulty of image segmentation and general object recognition presents a significant challenge to the development of an automatic image annotation system. Consequently, the annotation performance of the state-of-the-art models still remains a relatively low level (Monay & Gatica-Perez, 2007).

Without considering the difficulty of image segmentation, how to model the cross-modal correlation between textual and visual features is the most crucial issue to achieve the best textual indexing. Obviously, words and image features are of different nature and carry quite distinct levels of semantics. Moreover, there may not be simple correlations between the visual features and text captions. Nevertheless, their difference and correlation have not yet been fully investigated and exploited. Although how exactly our brain does this correlation is unclear, researchers in automatic image annotation could take a pragmatic stand to design models and build systems of practical significance (Datta, Ge, Li, & Wang, 2007).

One may also investigate refinement algorithms or exploit various context constraints to refine the automated annotations. Some pioneering refinement algorithms (e.g., Jin, Khan, Wang, & Awad, 2005; Wang, Jing, Zhang, & Zhang, 2006, 2007) were proposed to refine the initial candidate annotations by re-ranking the candidate annotations and reserving the top ones. Li, Chen, Zhang, Lin, & Ma (2006) also proposed an image annotation approach by searching for similar images from a large-scale image database and mining key phrases from the descriptions of the resultant images. Notwithstanding, there is still much room for improvement in annotation performance.

Finally, modest performance guarantees and limited adaptability often restrict the applicability of current automatic image annotation systems to real-world settings. Traditionally, these systems have been trained on fixed image collections tagged using fixed vocabularies. Therefore, a realistic application of such a system in an online setting must tackle three main issues (Datta, Joshi, Li, & Wang, 2007): (a) Current state-of-the-art in annotation is far to being reliable on real-world data. (b) Image collections in online systems are dynamic in nature, which poses a challenge for the training of current annotation models. (c) While a solution may be to re-train the annotation engine with newly acquired images, most proposed methods are too computationally intensive to re-train frequently. How to answer these questions clearly requires for a lot more research efforts.

APPLICATIONS

Up to this point in time, automatic image retrieval by semantics still remains a challenging problem due to the difficulty in object recognition and image understanding (Song, et al., 2003). However, automatic image categorization and annotation can be used to help generate meaningful retrieval. We denote this section to simply discussing their application in image retrieval.

Potentially, semantic image categorization enhances retrieval by permitting semantically adaptive searching methods and by narrowing down the searching range in a database. Often, image categorization can be treated as a pre-processing step for speeding up image retrieval and improving accuracy in large databases. Domain-specific collections such as medical image databases, remotely sensed imagery, and art and cultural image databases are examples where categorization can be beneficial. For example, semantic classification methods are used in the SIMPLIcity system to categorize images into semantic classes including *"graph," "photograph," "textured," "nontextured," "benign," "objectionable," "indoor," "outdoor," "city," "landscape," "with people,"* and *"without people,"* so that semantically-adaptive searching methods applicable to each category can be used (Wang, et al., 2001).

On the other hand, automatic image annotation can be directly used as a means to generate semantic retrieval. If the resultant automated mapping between images and annotated words can be trusted, text-based image searching can be semantically more meaningful than search in the absence of any text. When images are sought using these annotations, such retrieval is known as annotation-driven image retrieval (ADIR) (Datta, et al., 2007). Ultimately, the desire of ADIR is to be able to use keyword queries for all images regardless of any manual annotations that they may have. To this end, a recent attempt at bridging the retrieval-annotation gap has been made (Datta, et al., 2007). More recently, some annotation engines have also been made public for people to try online and have their pictures annotated, including ALIPR.com — an real-time image annotation and visual search engine (http://www.ALIPR.com), Behold (http://photo.beholdsearch.com) — an image search engine that indexes over 1 million Flickr images using automatically generated tags, and Illustrator (http://www.ulib.org.cn/) — an illustration search engine over more than 8.7 million illustrations using automatically extracted descriptions from electronic books. As part of ALIPR search engine, an effort to automatically validate computer generated tags with human collaborative annotation is being made to build a very large collection of searchable images.

SUMMARY

In this chapter, we have described two promising techniques related to semantic image retrieval — semantic image categorization and automatic image annotation. For each technique, four aspects were presented: task definition, image representation, computational models, and evaluation. We also simply discussed their application in image retrieval.

This chapter is only meant to capture the landscape of a field that is still young and still evolving. Many of the works discussed in this chapter are deemed by the authors as good representatives of existing semantic image classification and annotation techniques. For a long-term perspective, semantic annotation and retrieval of images is an interesting issue that currently requires for a lot more research efforts.

ACKNOWLEDGMENT

The authors are supported by grants from Chinese NSF under contract No. 60605020, National Hi-Tech R&D Program (863) of China under contract No. 2006AA01Z320 and 2006AA010105, and National Key Technology R&D Program under contract No. 2006BAH02A10.

REFERENCES

Aksoy, S., Koperski, K., Tusk, C., Marchisio, G., & Tilton, J.C. (2005). Learning Bayesian classifiers for scene classification with a visual grammar. *IEEE Transactions on Geoscience and Remote Sensing, 43*(3), 581-589. doi: 10.1109/TGRS.2004.839547.

Barnard, K., & Forsyth, D.A. (2001). Learning the semantics of words and pictures. In *Proc. Int'l Conf. Computer Vision,* 408-415. doi: 10.1109/ICCV.2001.937654.

Barnard, K., Duygulu, P., Freitas, N., Forsyth, D., Blei, D., & Jordan, M.I. (2003). Matching words and pictures. *Journal of Machine Learning Research, 3,* 1107-1135. doi: 10.1162/jmlr.2003.3.4-5.1107.

Blei, D., Ng, A., & Jordan, M. (2003). Latent Dirichlet allocation. *Journal of Machine Learning Research, 3,* 993-1022. doi: 10.1162/jmlr.2003.3.4-5.993.

Blei, D., & Jordan, M. (2003). Modeling annotated data. *Proc. Int'l Conf. Research and Development in Information Retrieval,* (pp. 127-134). doi: 10.1145/860435.860460.

Bosch, A., Zisserman, A., & Muñoz, X. (2006). Scene classification via plsa. *Proc. European Conf. Computer Vision, 4,* 517-530. doi: 10.1007/11744085_40.

Bosch, A., Muñoz, X., & Marti, R. (2007). A review: Which is the best way to organize/classify images by content? *Image and Vision Computing, 25*(6), 778-791. doi: 10.1016/j.imavis.2006.07.015.

Bosch, A., Zisserman, A., & Muyyoz, X. (2008). Scene classification using a hybrid generative/discriminative approach. *IEEE Transactions on Pattern Analysis and Machine Intelligence, 30*(4), 712-727. doi: 10.1109/TPAMI.2007.70716.

Boutell, M., Brown, C., & Luo, J. (2002). *Survey on the state of the art in semantic scene classification* (Technical Report 799). Rochester, NY: University of Rochester.

Boutell, M., Shen, X.P., Luo, J., & Brown, C. (2004). Learning multi-label semantic scene classification. *Pattern Recognition, 37*(9), 1757-1771. doi: 10.1016/j.patcog.2004.03.009.

Cai, D., He, X.F., Li, Z.W., Ma, W.Y., & Wen, J.R. (2004). Hierarchical clustering of WWW image search results using visual, textual and link analysis. In *Proc. 2th ACM Int'l Conf. Multimedia,* (pp. 952-959). doi: 10.1145/1027527.1027747.

Carneiro, G., Chan, A.B., Moreno, P., & Vasconcelos, N. (2006). Supervised learning of semantic classes for image annotation and retrieval. *IEEE Transactions on Pattern Analysis Machine Intelligence, 29*(3), 394-410. doi: 10.1109/TPAMI.2007.61.

Chang, E.Y., Goh, K., Sychay, G., & Wu, G. (2003). CBSA: Content-based soft annotation for multimodal image retrieval using Bayes Point Machines. *IEEE Transactions on Circuits System Video Technology, 13*, 26-38. doi: 10.1109/TCSVT.2002.808079.

Datta, R., Joshi, D., Li, J., & Wang, J.Z. (2007). Tagging over time: Real-world image annotation by lightweight meta-learning. In *Proc. 15th Ann' ACM int'l Conf. Multimedia*, (pp. 393-402). doi: 10.1145/1291233.1291328.

Datta, R., Ge, W., Li, J., & Wang, J. Z. (2007). Toward bridging the annotation-retrieval gap in image search. *IEEE Multimedia, 14*(3), 24-35. doi: 10.1109/MMUL.2007.67.

Duygulu, P., Barnard, K., Fretias, N., & Forsyth, D. (2002). Object recognition as machine translation: Learning a lexicon for a fixed image vocabulary. In *Proc. European Conf. Computer Vision,* 97-112. doi: 10.1007/3-540-47979-1_7.

Fan, J., Gao, Y., Luo, H., & Xu, G. (2005). Statistical modeling and conceptualization of natural images. *Pattern Recognition, 38*, 865-885. doi: 10.1016/j.patcog.2004.07.011.

Feng, S., Manmatha, R., & Lavrenko, V. (2004). Multiple Bernoulli relevance models for image and video annotation. *Proc. IEEE Conf. Computer Vision and Pattern Recognition*, (pp. 1002-1009). doi: 10.1109/CVPR.2004.1315274.

Fergus, R., Li, F.-F., Perona, P., & Zisserman, A. (2005). Learning object categories from Google's image search. *Proc. Int'l Conf. Computer Vision, II*, 1816-1823, 2005. doi: 10.1109/ICCV.2005.142.

Fredembach, C., Schröder, M., & Süsstrunk, S. (2004). Eigenregions for image classification. *IEEE Transactions on Pattern Analysis Machine Intelligence, 26*(12), 1645-1649. doi: 10.1109/TPAMI.2004.123.

Ghoshal, A., Ircing, P., & Khudanpur, S. (2005). Hidden Markov models for automatic annotation and content-based retrieval of images and video. In *Proc. 28th Ann. Int'l ACM SIGIR Conf.*, (pp. 544-551). doi: 10.1145/1076034.1076127.

Goh, K.-S., Chang, E.Y., & Li, B.T. (2005). Using one-class and two-class SVMs for multiclass image annotation. *IEEE Transactions on Knowledge and Data Engineering, 17*(10), 1333-1346. doi: 10.1109/TKDE.2005.170.

Grauman, K. & Darrell, T. (2005). Pyramid match kernels: Discriminative classification with sets of images features. In *Proc. Int'l Conf. Computer Vision, 2*, 1458-1465. doi: 10.1109/ICCV.2005.239.

Hofmann, T. (2001). Unsupervised learning by probabilistic latent semantic analysis. *Machine Learning, 42*, 177-196. doi: 10.1023/A:1007617005950.

Hu, J., & Bagga, A. (2004). Categorizing images in Web documents. *IEEE Multimedia, 11*(1), 22-30. doi: 10.1109/MMUL.2004.1261103.

Jeon, J., Lavrenko, V., & Manmatha, R. (2003). Automatic image annotation and retrieval using cross-media relevance models. In *Proc. ACM SIGIR Conf. on Research and Development in Information Retrieval*, (pp. 119-126). doi: 10.1145/860435.860459.

Jin, Y., Khan, L., Wang, L., & Awad, M. (2005). Image annotations by combining multiple evidence & wordNet. In *Proc. 13th Ann. ACM int'l Conf. Multimedia*, (pp. 706-715). doi: 10.1145/1101149.1101305.

Kalva, P., Enembreck, F., & Koerich, A. (2007). Web image classification based on the fusion of image and text classifiers. In *Proc. 9th Int'l Conf. Document Analysis and Recognition, 1*, 561-568. doi: 10.1109/ICDAR.2007.4378772.

Lazebnik, S., Schmid, C., & Ponce, J. (2006). Beyond bags of features: Spatial pyramid matching for recognizing natural scene categories. In *Proc. IEEE Conf. Computer Vision and Pattern Recognition, II*, 2169-2178. doi: 10.1109/CVPR.2006.68.

Lempel, R., & Soffer, A. (2002). PicASHOW: pictorial authority search by hyperlinks on the web. *ACM Transactions on Information Systems, 20*(1), 1-24. doi: 10.1145/503104.503105.

Li, F.-F., & Perona, P. (2005). A Bayesian hierarchical model for learning natural scene categories. *Proc. IEEE Int'l Conf. Computer Vision and Pattern Recognition, II*, 524- 531. doi: 10.1109/CVPR.2005.16.

Li, J., & Wang, J.Z. (2003). Automatic linguistic indexing of pictures by a statistical modeling approach. *IEEE Transactions on Pattern Analysis and Machine Intelligence, 29*(9), 1075-1088. doi: 10.1109/CVPR.2005.16.

Li, X.R., Chen, L., Zhang, L., Lin, F.Z., & Ma, W.-Y. (2006). Image annotation by large-scale content-based image retrieval. *Proc. Int'l Conf. Multimedia*, (pp. 607-610). doi: 10.1145/1180639.1180764.

Lowe, D. (1999). Object recognition from local scale-invariant feature. *Proc. Int'l Conf. Computer Vision (ICCV 1999)*, (pp. 1150-1157). doi: 10.1109/ICCV.1999.790410.

Luo, J., Savakis, A.E., & Singhal, A. (2005). A Bayesian network-based framework for semantic image understanding. *Pattern Recognition, 38*, 919-934. doi: 10.1016/j.patcog.2004.11.001.

Mojsilovic, A., Gomes, J., & Rogowitz, B. (2002). Isee: Perceptual features for image library navigation. In *Proc. SPIE Human Vision and Electronic Imaging, 4662*, 266-277. doi: 10.1117/12.469523.

Monay, F., & Gatica-Perez, D., (2003). On Image Auto-Annotation with Latent Space Models. In *Proc. ACM Int'l Conf. Multimedia*, 275-278. doi: 10.1145/957013.957070.

Monay, F., & Gatica-Perez, D., (2007). Modeling semantic aspects for cross-media image indexing. *IEEE Transactions on Pattern Analysis and Machine Intelligence, 29*(10), 1802-1917. doi: 10.1109/TPAMI.2007.1097.

Mori, Y., Takahashi, H., & Oka, R. (1999). Image-to-word transformation based on dividing and vector quantizing images with words. In *Proc. Int'l Workshop Multimedia Intelligent Storage and Retrieval Management*. From http://citeseer.ist.psu.edu/368129.html.

Oliva, A., & Torralba, A. (2001). Modeling the shape of the scene: a holistic representation of the spatial envelope. *International Journal of Computer Vision, 42*, 145-175. doi: 10.1023/A:1011139631724.

Paek, S., & Chang, S.-F. (2000). A knowledge engineering approach for image classification based on probabilistic reasoning systems. In *Proc. IEEE Int'l Conf. Multimedia and Expo, II*, 1133-1136. doi: 10.1109/ICME.2000.871560.

Pan, J. Y., Yang, H.-J., Duygulu, P., & Faloutsos, C. (2004). Automatic image captioning. *Proc. 2004 IEEE Int'l Conf. Multimedia and Expo (ICME'04), III*, 1987-1990. doi: 10.1109/ICME.2004.1394652.

Pappas, T. N., Chen, J.Q., & Depalov, D. (2007). Perceptually based techniques for image segmentation and semantic classification. *IEEE Communications Magazine, 45*(1), 44-51. doi: 10.1109/MCOM.2007.284537.

Perronin, F. (2007). Universal and adapted vocabularies for generic visual categorization. *IEEE Transactions on Pattern Analysis and Machine Intelligence, 30*(7), 1243-1256.doi: 10.1109/TPAMI.2007.70755.

Quelhas, P., Monay, F., Odobez, J.-M., Gatica-Perez, D., Tuytelaars, T. & Gool, L.V. (2005). Modeling scenes with local descriptors and latent aspects. In *Proc. IEEE Int'l Conf. Computer Vision, I,* 883-890. doi: 10.1109/ICCV.2005.152.

Serrano, N., Savakis, A., & Luo, J. (2004). Improved scene classification using efficient low-level features and semantic cues. *Pattern Recognition, 37,* 1773-1784. doi: 10.1016/j.patcog.2004.03.003.

Shen, J., Shepherd, J., & Ngu, A.H.H. (2005). Semantic-sensitive classification for large image libraries. In *Proc. Int'l Multimedia Modeling Conf.,* (pp. 340-345). doi: 10.1109/MMMC.2005.66.

Shi, J., & Malik, J. (2000). Normalized cuts and image segmentation. *IEEE Transactions on Pattern Analysis and Machine Intelligence, 22*(8), 888-905. doi: 10.1109/34.868688.

Sivic, J., Russell, B.C., Efros, A.A., Zisserman, A., & Freeman, W. T. (2005). Discovering objects and their locations in images. In *Proc. Int'l Conf. Computer Vision,* (pp. 370-377). doi: 10.1109/ICCV.2005.77.

Smeulders, A. W.M., Worring, M., Santini, S., Gupta, A., & Jain, R. (2000). Content-based image retrieval at the end of the early years. *IEEE Transactions on Pattern Analysis and Machine Intelligence, 22*(12), 1349-1380. doi: 10.1109/34.895972.

Smith, J., Lin, C., Naphade, M., Natsev, A., & Tseng, B. (2003). Multimedia semantic indexing using model vectors. In *Proc. IEEE Int'l Conf. Multimedia and Expo, II,* 445-448. doi: 10.1109/ICME.2003.1221649.

Song, Y. Q., Wang, W., & Zhang, A. D. (2003). Automatic annotation and retrieval of images. *World Wide Web, 6,* 209-231. doi: 10.1023/A:1023674722438.

Szummer, M.,& Picard, R. W. (1998). Indoor-outdoor image classification. In *Proc. ICCV Workshop on Content-based Access of Image and Video Databases,* 42-50. doi: 10.1109/CAIVD.1998.646032.

Tian, Y.H., Huang, T.J., & Gao, W. (2005). Exploiting multi-context analysis in semantic image classification. *Journal of Zhejiang University SCIENCE, 6A*(11), 1268-1283. doi: 10.1631/jzus.2005.A1268.

Vailaya, A., Figueiredo, A., Jain, A., & Zhang, H. (2001). Image classification for content-based indexing. *IEEE Transactions on Image Processing, 10,* 117-129. doi: 10.1109/83.892448.

Vogel, J. (2004). Semantic scene modeling and retrieval. *No. 33 in Selected Readings in Vision and Graphics,* Houghton Hartung-Gorre Verlag Konstanz, from http://www.vision.ethz.ch/vogel/documents/diss_final_neu.pdf.

Vogel, J., & Schiele, B. (2004). Natural scene retrieval based on a semantic modeling step. *Proc. Int'l Conf. Image and Video Retrieval, LNCS, 3115,* 207-215. doi: 10.1007/b98923.

Vogel, J., & Schiele, B. (2007). Semantic modeling of natural scenes for content-based image retrieval. *International Journal of Computer Vision, 72*(2), 133-157. doi: 10.1007/s11263-006-8614-1.

Wang, C., Jing, F., Zhang, L., & Zhang, H. J. (2006). Image annotation refinement using random walk with restarts. In *Proc. 14th Ann' ACM int'l Conf. Multimedia*, (pp. 647-652). doi: 10.1145/1180639.1180774.

Wang, C., Jing, F., Zhang, L., & Zhang, H. J. (2007). Content-based image annotation refinement. In *Proc. IEEE Computer Vision and Pattern Recognition*, (pp. 1-8). doi: 10.1109/CVPR.2007.383221.

Wang, J.Z., Li, J., & Wiederhold, G. (2001). SIMPLIcity: Semantics-sensitive Integrated Matching for Picture Libraries. *IEEE Transactions on Pattern Analysis and Machine Intelligence*, *23*(9), 947-963. doi: 10.1109/34.955109.

Wang, J.Z., & Li, J. (2002). Learning-based linguistic indexing of pictures with 2-D MHMMs. In *Proc. ACM Multimedia*, (pp. 436-445). doi: 10.1145/641007.641104.

Wang, G., Zhang, Y., & Li, F.-F. (2006). Using dependent regions for object categorization in a generative framework. In *Proc. IEEE Conf. Computer Vision and Pattern Recognition*, (pp. 1597-1604). doi: 10.1109/CVPR.2006.324.

Wang, X.J., Ma, W.Y., Xue, G.R., & Li, X. (2004). Multi-model similarity propagation and its application for Web image retrieval. In *Proc. 12th ACM Int'l Conf. Multimedia*, (pp. 944-951). doi. 10.1145/1027527.1027746.

Yang, S., Kim, S.-K., & Ro, Y.M. (2007). Semantic home photo categorization. *IEEE Transactions on Circuits System and Video Technology*, *17*(3), 324-335. doi: 10.1109/TCSVT.2007.890829 .

Zhang, H., Berg, A.C., Maire, M., & Malik, J. (2006). Svm-knn: Discriminative nearest neighbor classification for visual category recognition. In *Proc. IEEE Conf. Computer Vision and Pattern Recognition*, 2126-2136. doi: 10.1109/CVPR.2006.301.

Section V
Other Topics Related to Semantic Mining

Chapter XVI
Association–Based Image Retrieval

Arun Kulkarni
The University of Texas at Tyler, USA

Leonard Brown
The University of Texas at Tyler, USA

ABSTRACT

With advances in computer technology and the World Wide Web there has been an explosion in the amount and complexity of multimedia data that are generated, stored, transmitted, analyzed, and accessed. In order to extract useful information from this huge amount of data, many content-based image retrieval (CBIR) systems have been developed in the last decade. A Typical CBIR system captures image features that represent image properties such as color, texture, or shape of objects in the query image and try to retrieve images from the database with similar features. Recent advances in CBIR systems include relevance feedback based interactive systems. The main advantage of CBIR systems with relevance feedback is that these systems take into account the gap between the high-level concepts and low-level features and subjectivity of human perception of visual content. CBIR systems with relevance feedback are more efficient than conventional CBIR systems; however, these systems depend on human interaction. In this chapter, we describe a new approach for image storage and retrieval called association-based image retrieval (ABIR). The authors try to mimic human memory. The human brain stores and retrieves images by association. They use a generalized bi-directional associative memory (GBAM) to store associations between feature vectors that represent images stored in the database. Section I introduces the reader to the CBIR system. In Section II, they present architecture for the ABIR system, Section III deals with preprocessing and feature extraction techniques, and Section IV presents various models of GBAM. In Section V, they present case studies.

INTRODUCTION

The rapid growth in the number of large-scale image repositories in many domains such as medical image management, multimedia libraries, document archives, art collection, geographical information the systems, law enforcement management, environmental monitoring, biometrics, and journalism has brought the need for efficient mechanisms for managing the storage and retrieval of images. Effective retrieval of image data is an important building block for general multimedia information management. DataBase Management Systems (DBMSs) typically have a wide variety of features and tools supporting various aspects of data management. Two such features, however, are essential. A DBMS must be able to store information about data objects efficiently, and it must facilitate user-driven searching and retrieval of that information. It follows, then, that a MultiMedia DataBase Management System (MMDBMS) must provide similar capabilities while handling images and other types of multimedia data, such as audio and video. Unlike traditional simple textual data elements, images are considered to have content when they are displayed to users. Consequently, one of the goals of an MMDBMS is to allow users to search the database utilizing that visual content. This goal is commonly referred to as Content-Based Image Retrieval (CBIR). The key idea from the above goal, called Content-Based Image Retrieval (CBIR), is that searches are performed on the visual content of the database images rather than the actual images themselves. So, for an image to be searchable, it has to be indexed by its content. This goal is nontrivial for an MMDBMS to achieve because of the difficulties associated with representing the visual content of an image in a searchable form. Consequently, one of the most critical issues for any MMDBMS supporting CBIR user queries is deciding how to best represent and extract that content. Many ideas from fields including computer vision, database management, image processing, and information retrieval are used to address this issue.

Many systems connect text-based keywords with each image in the database so that users can search the database by submitting simple text queries (Yoshitaka & Ichikawa, 1999). However, text-based keywords have to be attached manually, which is not only time-consuming but often leads to having incorrect, inconsistent, and incomplete descriptions associated with the images in the system. Text-based image retrieval using keyword annotation can be traced back to the 1970s. The keyword annotation method involves a large amount of manual effort. Furthermore, the keyword annotation depends upon human interpretation of image content, and it may not be consistent. In the early 1990s, because of the emergence of large-scale image collections, the difficulties faced by the manual annotation approach became more and more acute, and to overcome these difficulties, content-based image retrieval (CBIR) was proposed. In CBIR instead of being manually annotated by keyword, images are indexed by their own visual content.

Because it is often difficult to describe the visual content of an image with only textual keywords and phrases, a user may not be able to accurately describe his or her desired content solely using a text-based query. As an alternative, the system should provide facilities for a user to indicate the desired content visually. One method of achieving this is to support a Query-By-Example (QBE) interface where a user presents an image or a sketch to the system as a query object representing an example of his or her desired content. The system should search for images within its underlying database that have matching content. Unfortunately, it is not realistic for the user to expect to find database images that have identical content to the query object. So, the typical environment is for a user to present a query object, Q, to the MMDBMS requesting the system to search for and retrieve all images in the database that are similar to Q. Queries of this type are called similarity-based searches or similarity searches, for short. Note that after executing one of these queries, some of the retrieved images can be used as the bases for subsequent queries allowing the user to refine his or her search.

Typically, an MMDBMS will process each image in the database and generate a signature for it which will then be used for searching. The signature is typically a collection of features of the image that represents its content. Several systems extract low-level features such as color, texture, and shape because they can be extracted automatically, and they can be used to support searching images from a broad, heterogeneous application domain (Aslandogan & Yu, 1999; Yoshitaka & Ichikawa, 1999). However, low-level features by themselves are usually not adequate for representing higher-level content, leading to a "semantic gap" between the extracted features of an image and the visual content humans perceive in it (Smeulders et al., 2000). As a result, the system may fail to satisfactorily retrieve images when responding to user queries. For example, given a query image of a landscape photo, a system that represents content using color features may retrieve images that are primarily blue and green. Consequently, the retrieved set would contain any image that has several blue and green objects, which was not what the user wanted. In addition, the retrieved set would miss landscape photos that contained large amounts of other colors, such as a photo of a landscape taken at sunset. When an MMDBMS supports an application operating on a specific image domain, the system can use knowledge about that domain to extract higher-level features. For example, consider applications that perform facial recognition. Since these types of applications are only expected to manage photos of faces, a system supporting one of them can represent the content of each image using high-concept features relevant only to faces such as nose length or eye color (Zhao et al., 2003). The use of high-level or low-level features does not prevent an MMDBMS from also using free-form textual descriptions to represent the content of images. The descriptions allow the systems greater flexibility in representing high level content. They also allow the systems to represent information that may be impossible to extract from an image without human intervention, such as identifying the name of a geographic region displayed in a landscape photo. In order to combat the problem of having humans review each database image manually, some systems attempt to automatically generate text descriptions of database images from previously known descriptions of images with similar content (Datta, Li, & Wang, 2005).

Many CBIR systems with low-level features such as color, texture, and shape have been developed (Flickner et al., 1995; Smeulders et al., 2000; Wan & Kuo, 1998; Wang et al., 2003). Krishnapuram et al. (2004) proposed a fuzzy approach for CBIR. It may be noted that CBIR does not rely on describing the content of the image in its entirety. It may be sufficient that a retrieval system presents similar images in some user-defined sense. Smeulders et al. (2000) considered the description of image content in two steps. The first step deals with image processing operations that transpose the image data array into another spatial data array that can include methods over local color, local texture, or local geometry. The second step is to extract invariant features. The aim of invariant description is to identify objects no matter how and where they are observed. The strategy for earlier CBIR systems is to find the "best" representation for visual features, and based on the selected features to find images that are similar to the query image. While this approach establishes the basis for CBIR, the performance is not satisfactory due to two reasons a) the gap between the high-level concepts and b) the subjectivity of human perception. In order to overcome these drawbacks, Rui et al. (1998) proposed a relevance feedback based interactive retrieval approach. In their approach during the retrieval process, the user's high-level query and subjectivity are captured by dynamically updated weights based on the user's feedback. Given that each image in an MMDBMS is associated with a feature signature, they can be used to respond to a user's QBE similarity search. The first step, typically, is for the system to identify and extract a feature signature from the query image using the same extraction process applied to the database images when they were initially inserted. The query image's signature can then be compared to the signatures of the database images. If a database image's signature is similar to the query image's signature, then the MMDBMS considers the two images to be similar to each other. All such database images are returned as by the MMDBMS as the result of the user's query.

Stages of a CBIR system include preprocessing, feature extraction, annotation, and indexing. A dataflow diagram for a typical CBIR system is shown in Figure 1. There are two data paths in the system. One deals with storing a set of images in the database, while other path deals with a query image. All images stored in the database are passed through the preprocessing and feature extraction stages. The preprocessing stage deals with geometric and radiometric corrections. The preprocessing stage may also include edge detection and transforms such as the Fourier transform. Extracted features represent color, texture, and shape characteristics of object in the image. The indexing stage deals with creating index table that contains feature vectors and pointers to the corresponding image locations. For faster retrieval, images in the database can be grouped in predefined categories. In order to store an image it is first annotated. In the feature extraction stage, features based on characteristics such as the color, texture, or shapes are extracted. Most CBIR systems use color histograms to compare the query image with images in the database. Often color histograms alone are not sufficient to retrieve desired images from the database, because a single color histogram may represent multiple images in the database. Many CBIR systems use texture or shape features in conjunction with color features. In order to retrieve similar images from the database the feature vector obtained from the query image is compared with feature vectors in the database. The query image goes through the same processing as the stored image in the database. The database contains stored images along with their feature vectors. Each row in the index table represents an image in the database, and it contains information such as the feature vector, pointer to the location of the image, and annotation for the image.

Just as there is a wide variety of features that can be used to represent images, there is a wide variety of methods to measure the similarity between two feature vectors (Santini & Jain, 1999). These methods rely on the image retrieval system to contain a distance function that accepts two feature vectors as

Figure 1. Schematic diagram of a CBIR system

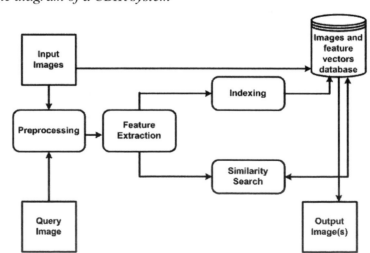

input and returns a scalar value as output. The scalar value represents the similarity between the two feature vectors. It is often restricted to the range [0, 1] where the value of 1 indicates the vectors have maximum dissimilarity, and the value of 0 indicates that the vectors are identical. Note that this latter case implies that the system would also consider their corresponding images to be identical. In many of these distance functions, each feature vector is treated as a point in a multidimensional data space. Thus, a vector with k values is typically treated as a multidimensional data value $<x_1, ..., x_k>^T$. The distance between two such vectors corresponds to the distance between them as points in that multidimensional space. For example, if we represent the vectors of images X and Y as $\mathbf{x} = (x_1,...,x_k)^T$ and $\mathbf{y} = (y_1,...,y_k)^T$, respectively, common methods of computing the distance, d, between them utilize the Lp-distances

$$d(\mathbf{x},\mathbf{y}) = \left(\sum_{i=1}^{k} (x_i - y_i)^p \right)^{\frac{1}{p}} \qquad (1)$$

When p is 1, this formula represents the city-block distance, and when p is 2, this formula represents the Euclidean distance. Note that these formulae consider each dimension of a feature vector to be equally different from each of the other dimensions, which is not always desirable. For example, consider a system that generates feature vectors from images so that each vector's dimension represents the percentage of the image's pixels that are of a different color. Such a system may want to define that the two dimensions of the feature vector corresponding to the colors red and blue, respectively, are more different than the two dimensions corresponding to the colors red and orange, respectively. To allow this flexibility in comparing features when computing the distance formula, a common method is computing the distance between X and Y as

$$d(\mathbf{x},\mathbf{y}) = \mathbf{x}^T \mathbf{A} \mathbf{y} \qquad (2)$$

where $\mathbf{A}$ is a k×k matrix such that each a_{ij} represents the similarity, if any, between dimension i and dimension j. If $\mathbf{A}$ is the identify matrix, then all dimensions are considered to be equally different from all other dimensions.

Having a representation of each image's content as a set of feature values, and a distance function that measures the similarity between two such vectors allows an MMDBMS supporting CBIR to process several different types of queries based on an example query image, Q. One such type includes range queries which request all database images, X, so that the distance between Q and X is less than some input threshold. Another type includes nearest-neighbor queries which request the k database images that are the most similar to Q for some integer k. This type is related to the third query type which requests the k database images that are the least similar to Q for some integer k.

While it is feasible to retrieve a desired image from a small collection by exhaustive search, techniques that are more effective are needed with a large database. Many indexing techniques have been proposed for efficient retrieval. Just as databases and information retrieval systems utilize indexes or other types of access methods to speed up processing of retrieval queries for traditional alphanumeric and text data, an MMDBMS supporting CBIR should utilize indexes to speed up retrieval of image data. Traditional indexes, such as the B-tree and its many variants (Comer, 1979), typically operate on a single value. Consequently, when creating an index in a traditional database management system, users typically specify the collection of data they are indexing as well as the search key on which people are likely use when searching for information. In contrast, queries submitted to an MMDBMS are processed using the feature vectors of the database images, so, the index or access method must operate using those vectors. Each feature vector, as described earlier, will have some number of dimensions, k. It is insufficient to simply concatenate each of the k values of a feature vector into a single value for a traditional index since the dimensions at the end would be virtually unusable for searching. Consequently, an MMDBMS supporting CBIR should utilize multidimensional indexes for searching. There are a wide variety of multidimensional indexes that have been proposed in the literature (Gaede & Günther, 1998). One common type includes tree-based indexes (Brown & Gruenwald, 1998), which contain nodes in a hierarchical structure where the root contains a collection of <region, pointer> pairs. Each region in the pair logically corresponds to a section of the multidimensional feature vector space. Each pointer associated with a region references a child of the node that contains its own collection of <region, pointer> pairs. The tree is structured so that a region logically associated with a node is a subregion of the region associated with the node's parent. Examples of these trees include the R-tree (Guttman, 1984) and the numerous variants proposed after it. Query processing in these trees typically start at the root where the each region of multidimensional space contained in the node is compared to the space representing the user's query. The system then follows the pointers associated with regions that overlap the space of the user's query. Thus, the system traverses down the tree starting from the root to its leaves which ultimately point to the actual data images contained within the database. Several algorithms for processing nearest-neighbor searches on these types of indexes have been proposed (Cheung & Fu, 1998; Hjaltason & Samat, 1999; Roussopoulos, Kelley, & Vincent, 1995). Other features of a CBIR system include defining the query feature space and displaying query results. The first component of the query space is the selection of a subset of images from the large image archive. In order to reduce the query space, images in the database can be clustered into a small number of categories. Some illustrative examples of retrieval with a CBIR system are presented in Section V.

The use of the above techniques to process CBIR queries is limited by the ability of visual features to represent high-level information. Often, people attach information to objects in an image that cannot be extracted through visual features alone. For example, a person may remember that a vase captured in a photo was purchased in Italy on a recent trip. Thus, all of the memories of Italy and the trip as well are associated to the simple photo of the vase. Building an MMDBMS that has the ability to associate, and therefore retrieve, this type of information from an image represents the next step in processing image retrieval queries. In this chapter, we propose a new approach for image retrieval called association-based image retrieval (ABIR). We try to mimic the human brain. Association is one of the fundamental characteristics of the human brain. The human memory operates in an associative manner; that is, a portion of recollection can produce an associated stream of data from the memory. The human memory can retrieve a full image from a partial or noisy version of the image as the query image. Furthermore, given a query image as the input, the human brain can recall associated images that have been stored in the past. The human memory can respond to abstract queries. For example, if we see an image of a person, we can recall images of his house, spouse, and car. The associative storage and retrieval mechanism is not explored in the present CBIR systems. The main disadvantage of the current CBIR systems is their inability to respond to abstract queries. This ability, Associative-Based Image Retrieval (ABIR), is described in more detail in the following sections beginning with the next section which describes the architecture for the proposed ABIR system.

ARCHITECTURE FOR AN ABIR SYSTEM

The architecture for the ABIR system is shown in Figure 2. As in Figure 1, there are two data paths in the system. One deals with storing a set of images in the database, while the other path deals with a query image. The stages of the proposed ABIR system include preprocessing, feature extraction, indexing, database that stores images and feature vectors, and the GBAM. The preprocessing and feature extraction stages are similar to that of a CBIR system. All images stored in the database are passed through the image-processing block that deals with preprocessing and feature extraction. The preprocessing stage deals with geometric and radiometric corrections, mapping the image from the red, blue, green (RGB) color space to hue, saturation, and intensity (HSI) color space. The preprocessing stage may also include edge detection and transforms such as the Fourier transform. Extracted features represent color, texture, and shape characteristics of object in the image. The indexing stage deals with creating an index table that contains feature vectors and pointers to the corresponding image locations. For faster retrieval, images in the database can be grouped in predefined categories. The user can select a query image via the user interface. The query image undergoes the same processing as the stored images. The feature vector obtained from the query image is used as the input to the GBAM, which produces the feature vectors of the associated images as the output. The corresponding images are then retrieved from the databases and presented to the user via the user interface. The most important feature of the ABIR system is that we use associative memory for storage and retrieval of images. The GBAM is used to store associations between feature vectors of associated images. The basic functions of the GBAM are to store associative pairs through a self-organizing process and to produce an appropriate response pattern on receipt of the associated stimulus input pattern. The stimulus and response patterns represent feature vectors that correspond to the query image and output images.

Figure 2. Architecture for an ABIR system

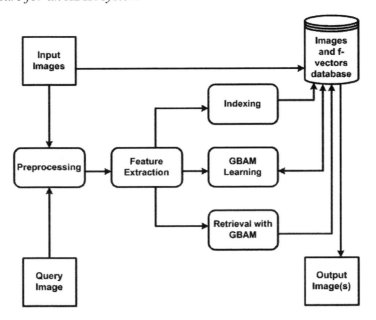

PREPROCESSING AND FEATURE EXTRACTION

An ABIR system can be viewed as the step beyond a CBIR system in that it can utilize associations between images during query processing that cannot be established through the sole use of visual properties. Since it builds upon a CBIR system, however, the architecture of an ABIR system has some of the same components as a CBIR system. Specifically, an ABIR system will have the same preprocessing and feature extraction modules of a CBIR system. This section describes the extraction process employed by these modules for the commonly used features of color, texture, and shape, while the next section describes the modules that are unique to an ABIR system.

Color Features

The color feature is one of the most widely used visual features in CBIR. As with the other low-level features of shape and texture, color-based features are commonly used in CBIR systems because they are easy to extract from most images. Examples of application types in which color-based features are closely connected to the content of an image include road sign recognition applications, where the color of the sign yields information about its content, and consumer catalogs, where consumers are often looking for a specific color of automobile or piece of clothing. Alternatively, applications such as fingerprint matching systems would not be expected to extract color-based features since the color of a fingerprint is usually immaterial in identifying the person who made it. When using color-based features, a global color histogram can be extracted from a database or query image by simply counting the number of pixels in the image that are of each different color recognized by the system. To normalize the histogram, each total should be divided by the total number of pixels in the image so that each value in the histogram represents the percentage of pixels that are of a particular color. A simplified example of global color histograms is displayed in Figure 3 which displays possible histograms extracted from several images of flags when a system identifies pixels that are black, blue, red, yellow, and white. These and other colors will be represented as values in the color space of some model such as RGB. Note that, as demonstrated in this figure, the locations of pixels are not taken into account when extracting a global color histogram from an image. In order to consider locations, a system may divide an image into multiple regions and then identify a localized histogram for each region.

Swain and Ballard (1991) used color histograms for indexing images. Huang et al. used color correlograms instead of color histograms (Huang et al., 1997). The interest in color is due to the discrimination potentiality of a three dimensional domain compared to the single dimensional domain of gray level images. The commonly used color space is the red, blue, green (RGB) color space. The RGB-color space is not a perceptually uniform color space. A significant improvement over the RGB-color space (at least for image retrieval applications comes from the use of an opponent color representation, which uses opponent color axes (R-G, 2B-R-G, R+G+B). Other color spaces such as hue, saturation, intensity (HSI) have also been used. The HSI-color space is perceptually uniform color space, and its design reflects the way human see colors. The RGB-color space to HSI-color space transformation is given by the following equations (Gonzalez & Woods, 2002).

The intensity component I is given by

$$I = \frac{1}{3}(R + G + B) \tag{3}$$

Figure 3. Examples of global color histograms associated with images

	Black	Blue	Yellow	Red	White
	0.0	0.33	0.0	0.33	0.33
	0.0	0.0	0.0	0.25	0.75
	0.0	0.30	0.0	0.33	0.34
	0.33	0.0	0.33	0.33	0.0

The saturation component S is given by

$$S = 1 - \frac{3}{(R+G+B)}\left[\min(R,G,B)\right] \tag{4}$$

The hue component H is given by

$$H = \begin{cases} \theta & \text{if } B \leq G \\ 2\pi - \theta & \text{if } B > G \end{cases} \tag{5}$$

where $\theta = \cos^{-1}\left[\dfrac{\frac{1}{2}\left[(R-G)+(R-B)\right]}{\left[(R-G)^2+(R-B)(G-B)\right]^{1/2}}\right]$

Another issue associated with color histograms identifying the different colors that a system will use when it extracts them. This involves selecting both a color model such as RGB or HSI, and selecting the method for grouping similar colors in the model. To illustrate the importance of the latter selection, consider that the typical approach of representing a RGB color as a collection of three values each in the range [0, 255] means that there are $(2^8)^3 = 16M$ different colors in the model. Without grouping similar colors, each histogram extracted from an image would have 16M different bins. Typically, the groups are obtained by uniformly quantizing the color model using a prespecified number of divisions along each of the model's dimensions. For example, a system may divide each RGB axis in half yielding 8 separate groups of colors that loosely correspond to the general colors of black, blue, green, cyan, red, magenta, yellow, and white, respectively. Unfortunately, there is no universal standard for selecting a color model of the number of divisions, so the choices vary from system to system. When evaluating the similarity between pairs of color histograms, commonly distance functions include the city-block or Euclidean distances as described earlier. Another function was proposed specifically for color histograms called the Histogram Intersection (Swain & Ballard, 1991). The intersection between two n-dimensional histograms X and Y is presented in the following equation.

$$\mathbf{x} \cap \mathbf{y} = \sum_{i=1}^{n} \min(x_i, y_i) \tag{6}$$

In image retrieval, the color histogram is the most commonly used color feature representation. Statistically, it denotes the joint probability of the intensities of the three color channels. Several alternatives or variants to color histograms have been proposed and used in CBIR systems over the years. These include color coherence vectors which distinguish pixels based on whether or not they are part of a larger connected group of pixels of the same color (Pass, Zabih, & Miller, 1996). The idea is that a large group of connected pixels with the same color represents an object in the image, so for each color, the system should differentiate between the number of pixels that are part of objects, and the number of pixels that are not. The result is that instead of having a single value for each color recognized by a system as in a histogram, a color coherence vector would have two. Another alternative includes recording only the largest values that appear in a histogram bin (Gong, Y. et al., 1994). Several other color representations have been applied for image retrieval including color moments and color sets (Rui, Huang, & Chang, 1999). With color sets, the system only records the colors that appear most frequently in an image instead of extracting and saving its entire histogram. Smith and Chang (1997) first transformed the RGB-color space into a perceptually uniform color space and then quantized the transformed color space into some number, *M*, of bits. Finally, color correlograms are another alternative which focus on identifying how often different pairs of colors appear within various distances from one another (Huang et al., 1997).

Texture Features

Texture is generally recognized as being fundamental to perception. Chang and Kuo (1993) proposed the use of texture features via the wavelet transform. The taxonomy of problems encountered within the context of texture analysis could be that of classification, description, and segmentation. There is no precise definition or characterization of texture available in practice. Texture has been described in a variety of ways. Intuitively, texture descriptors provide measures of properties such as smoothness, coarseness, and regularity. One way to describe texture is to consider it as being composed of elements of texture primitives. Texture can also be defined as mutual relationship among intensity values of neighboring pixels repeated over an area larger than the size of the relationship. The task of extracting texture features from the input image is critical. If one could model and quantify the process by which the human recognizes texture, one could construct a highly successful recognition system. Unfortunately, the process by which we recognize texture is not really understood, and researchers left to consider some ad hoc techniques such as statistical, structural, and spectral methods as well as neural network models. Human observers are capable of performing some image segmentation and discrimination tasks under conditions (such as brief exposure of a test image) that prevent detailed scrutiny of the image. This ability is referred to as "effortless" or "preattentive" visual discrimination. In a sense two images (which do not portray particular objects or forms) are said to have the same "texture" if they are not effortlessly discriminable to a human observer. Many texture feature extraction and recognition algorithms are available in practice (Ballard & Brown, 1982; Coggins & Jain, 1985; Daugman, 1988; Haralick et al., 1973; O'Toole & Stark, 1980; Rosenfeld & Kak, 1982). Conventional approaches for extracting texture features can be grouped into three classes: structural, statistical, and spectral. Statistical approaches yield characterizations of textures as smooth, coarse, grainy, and so on. Statistical algorithms are based on the relationship between intensity values of pixels; measures include the entropy, contrast, and correlation based on the gray level co-occurrence matrix. Structural algorithms are based on the image primitives; they regard the primitive as a forming element to generate repeating patterns and describe rules for generating them. The notion of a primitive is central to texture analysis. A *texel* is (loosely) a visual primitive with certain invariant properties. Texels occur repeatedly in different positions, deformations, or orientations inside a given area. Texture primitives may be pixels or aggregates of pixels. One way of describing rules that govern texture is through a grammar. Structural approaches deal with the grammar rules to generate patterns by applying these rules to a small number of symbols. Spectral techniques are based on properties of the Fourier spectrum and are used primarily to detect global periodicity in the image by identifying high-energy narrow peaks in the spectrum.

In statistical methods, we describe features using a spatial gray level dependency (SGLD) matrix. For a two-dimensional image $f(x,y)$ with N discrete gray values, we define the spatial gray level dependency matrix $\mathbf{P}(d, \phi)$ for each d and ϕ. The element p_{ij} is defined as the relative number of times a gray level pair (i, j) occurs when pixels separated by the distance d along the angle ø are compared. Each element is finally normalized by the total number of occurrences giving the co-occurrence matrix $\mathbf{P}$. A spatial gray level dependency matrix is also called a co-occurrence matrix, and it is given by

$$\mathbf{P}(d,\phi)=\begin{bmatrix} p_{00} & p_{01} & \cdot & \cdot & p_{0,n-1} \\ p_{10} & p_{11} & \cdot & \cdot & p_{1,n-1} \\ & & & & \\ & & & & \\ p_{n-1,0} & p_{n-1,1} & \cdot & \cdot & p_{n-1,n-1} \end{bmatrix} \tag{7}$$

where p_{ij} is given by

$$p_{ij} = \frac{N_{ij}}{N_T}$$

Where N_{ij} represents the number of pairs with gray values i and j, and N_T is the total number of pairs.

Commonly used features that are obtained from the co-occurrence matrix are the energy, entropy, correlation, inertia, and local homogeneity (Haralick et al., 1973). These are given by the following expressions.

1. Angular second moment (a measure of picture homogeneity)

$$\phi_1 = \sum_{i=0}^{N-1} \sum_{j=0}^{N-1} p_{ij}^{\,2} \tag{8}$$

2. Contrast (measure of amount of intensity variation)

$$\phi_2 = \sum_{i=0}^{N-1} \sum_{j=0}^{N-1} (i-j)^2\, p_{ij} \tag{9}$$

3. Correlation (a measure of gray level dependencies)

$$\phi_3 = \sum_{i=0}^{N-1}\sum_{j=0}^{N-1} \frac{(1-\mu_x)(1-\mu_y)p_{ij}}{\sigma_x \sigma_y} \qquad (10)$$

where

$$\mu_x = \sum_{i=0}^{N-1}\sum_{j=0}^{N-1} ip_{ij}$$

$$\mu_y = \sum_{i=0}^{N-1}\sum_{j=0}^{N-1} jp_{ij}$$

$$\sigma_x^{\,2} = \sum_{i=0}^{N-1}\sum_{j=0}^{N-1} p_{ij}(i-\mu_x)^2$$

$$\sigma_y^{\,2} = \sum_{i=0}^{N-1}\sum_{j=0}^{N-1} p_{ij}(j-\mu_y)^2$$

4. Entropy (another homogeneity measure)

$$\phi_4 = -\sum_{i=0}^{N-1}\sum_{j=0}^{N-1} p_{ij}\log(p_{ij}+\varepsilon) \qquad (11)$$

where ε is a small positive constant to avoid overflow when p_{ij} equals zero. The basic idea here is to characterize the "content" of the cooccurrence matrix via these descriptors. Haralick et al. suggested a set of twenty-eight texture features based on the cooccurrence matrix (Haralick et al., 1973). These features characterize texture patterns. The angular moment feature (ϕ_1) is a measure of the homogeneity of the image. The contrast feature (ϕ_2) is a difference moment and is a measure of the amount of local gray tone variation present in the image. The correlation feature (ϕ_3) is a measure of gray tone linear dependencies in the image. These features have been used successfully in many image-processing applications.

Shape Features

Shape features based on Fourier descriptors, moment invariants also have been used in conjunction with color, and texture features in CBIR systems (Jain & Vailaya, 1998). Mehrotra and Gary have suggested a shape management system for retrieving similar shapes. One of the well-known methods for invariant feature extraction is the moment invariants (Mehrotra & Gary, 1995). Hu defined a set of seven moment-invariant functions that are invariant to translational, scale, and rotational differences in input patterns (Hu, 1962). The main disadvantage of the moment- invariant technique is that there is no guarantee that the invariant moments, which number exactly seven, form a complete set of descriptors. However, for most practical applications the set of seven invariants is adequate to distinguish between input patterns. The Fourier descriptors form a complete set of features; however extracted features are usually large in number and are unwieldy to use in classification unless they are grouped together by some grouping criterion. The seven moment invariants are described below.

Let $g(x, y)$ be an input image. The $(p + q)^{th}$ geometric moment for an image of the size $(2n + 1) \times (2n + 1)$ is given by

$$m_{pq} = \sum_{x=-n}^{n} \sum_{y=-n}^{n} x^p y^q g(x,y) \tag{12}$$

for $p, q = 0, 1, 2, 3,...$

To make these moments invariant to translation, one can define the central moment as

$$\bar{m}_{pq} = \sum_{x=-n}^{n} \sum_{y=-n}^{n} (x-\bar{x})^p (y-\bar{y})^q g(x,y) \tag{13}$$

where

$$\bar{x} = \frac{m_{10}}{m_{00}}, \ \bar{y} = \frac{m_{01}}{m_{00}}$$

The central moments in Equation (13) can be normalized for scale invariance as shown below:

$$\mu_{pq} = \frac{m_{pq}^{\gamma}}{m_{00}} \tag{14}$$

where

$$\gamma = \frac{(p+q)}{2} + 1.$$

Hu developed the following seven functions of central moments that are invariant to rotational and scale differences (Hu, 1962).

$$\phi_1 = (\mu_{20} + \mu_{02})$$

$$\phi_2 = (\mu_{20} + \mu_{02})^2 + 4\mu_{11}^2$$

$$\phi_3 = (\mu_{30} - 3\mu_{12})^2 + (3\mu_{21} - \mu_{03})^2$$

$$\phi_4 = (\mu_{30} + \mu_{12})^2 + (\mu_{21} + \mu_{03})^2$$

$$\phi_5 = (\mu_{30} - 3\mu_{12})(\mu_{30} + \mu_{12})\left[(\mu_{30} + \mu_{12})^2 - 3(\mu_{21} + \mu_{03})^2\right]$$
$$+ (3\mu_{21} + \mu_{03})(\mu_{21} + \mu_{03})\left[3(\mu_{30} + \mu_{12})^2 - (\mu_{21} + \mu_{03})^2\right]$$

$$\phi_6 = (\mu_{20} - \mu_{02})\left[(\mu_{30} + \mu_{12})^2 - (\mu_{21} + \mu_{03})^2\right]$$
$$+ 4\mu_{11}(\mu_{30} + \mu_{12})(\mu_{21} + \mu_{03})$$

$$\phi_7 = (3\mu_{21} - \mu_{03})(\mu_{30} + \mu_{12})\left[(\mu_{30} + \mu_{12})^2 - 3(\mu_{21} + \mu_{03})^2\right]$$
$$+ (\mu_{30} - 3\mu_{12})(\mu_{21} + \mu_{03})\left[3(\mu_{30} + \mu_{12})^2 - (\mu_{21} + \mu_{03})^2\right] \tag{15}$$

Hu showed analytically that moment invariants described by Equation (15) are insensitive to translational, rotational, and scale differences in input images (Hu, 1962). However, the values of these invariants are small, and they are very sensitive to round-off errors and noise, which makes recognition difficult. One of the solutions to the sensitivity problem is to consider the log values of the moment invariants.

Fourier Transform Domain Features

The Fourier transform (FT) is a well-known transform technique used in data compression. In order to process digital images we need to consider the discrete Fourier transform (DFT). If $\{x(n)\}$ denotes a sequence $x(n)$, $n = 0,\ 1,...,N-1$ of N finite valued real or complex numbers, then its discrete Fourier transform is defined as (Rosenfeld & Kak, 1982).

$$c(u) = \frac{1}{N}\sum_{n=0}^{N-1} x(n) e^{-\frac{2\pi jun}{N}}$$ (16)

for $u = 0,1,2,...N-1$ and $j = \sqrt{-1}$. The exponential functions in Equation (16) are orthogonal. The inverse discrete Fourier transform (IDFT) is defined as

$$x(n) = \sum_{n=0}^{N-1} c(u) e^{\frac{2\pi jun}{N}}$$ (17)

Equation (16) and (17) represent the DFT and IDFT for a one-dimensional data sequence. Images are inherently two-dimensional in nature, and we need to consider the two-dimensional Fourier transform. The two-dimensional discrete Fourier transform is given by

$$F(u,v) = \frac{1}{MN}\sum_{m=0}^{M-1}\sum_{n=0}^{N-1} f(m,n) e^{-2\pi j\left(\frac{mu}{M} + \frac{nv}{N}\right)}$$ (18)

for $u = 0,1,2,...M-1$ and $v = 0,1,2,...N-1$. The inverse discrete Fourier transform is given by

$$f(m,n) = \sum_{u=0}^{M-1}\sum_{v=0}^{N-1} F(u,v) e^{2\pi j\left(\frac{mu}{M} + \frac{nv}{N}\right)}$$ (19)

for $m = 0,1,2,...M-1$ and $n = 0,1,2,...,N-1$.

The double summation in Equation (18) can be written in a matrix form as

$$\mathbf{F_t} = \mathbf{PFQ}$$ (20)

where $\mathbf{Q}$ and $\mathbf{P}$ are nonsingular ortho-normal matrices of the size $M \times M$ and $N \times N$ respectively; $\mathbf{F}$ represents the input image matrix, and the elements of matrices $\mathbf{P}$ and $\mathbf{Q}$ are given by Equations (21) and (22), respectively.

$$q_{vn} = \frac{1}{N} e^{-\frac{2\pi jnv}{N}}$$ (21)

where $v = 0,1,2,...,N-1$ and $n = 0,1,2,...,N-1$.

$$p_{um} = \frac{1}{M} e^{-\frac{2\pi jmu}{M}}$$ (22)

where $u = 0,1,2,...,M-1$ and $m = 0,1,2,...,M-1$. The inverse Fourier transform is given by

$$\mathbf{F} = \mathbf{P}^{-1}\mathbf{F_t}\mathbf{Q}^{-1}$$ (23)

Some of the properties of the FT (that magnitudes of FT coefficients are shift invariant, high frequencies in input images correspond to large values further from the origin, and with a rotation of the input image the FT distribution also rotates) are used for invariant feature extraction. It can be seen that as input image rotates, its Fourier transform also rotates. It can be seen that smaller objects produce high values of FT coefficients that correspond to high spatial frequencies. In order to obtain invariant features, the FT plane is sampled with angular and radial bins. Feature extraction also results in significant data reduction. By sampling the FT plane with wedge-shaped elements, information on rotation can be captured in the extracted features. Similarly, by sampling the FT plane with angular or ring-shaped elements, information on scale can be captured in the extracted features. Since the FT coefficients are symmetrical in the FT plane, it is possible to use half of the FT plane for angular bins and half of the plane for radial bins. The radial bins are given by

$$V_{r1r2} = \iint F^2(u,v)\,dudv \tag{24}$$

where the limits of integration are defined by

$$r_1^2 \le (u^2 + v^2) \le r_2^2, 0 \le u, v \le n-1$$

Radial features are insensitive to rotational differences of input images, and they can be used for extracting rotation-invariant image recognition. The angular bins are given by

$$V_{\psi 1 \psi 2} = \iint F^2(u,v)\,dudv \tag{25}$$

where the limits of integration are defined by

$$\phi_1 \le \tan^{-1}\left(\frac{u}{v}\right) \le \phi_2$$

and $0 \le u, v \le n-1$. Angular features are insensitive to coarseness of input images, and they can be used for extracting scale invariant components.

ASSOCIATIVE STORAGE AND RETRIEVAL

The basic functions of the GBAM are to store associative pairs through a self-organizing process and to produce an appropriate response pattern on receipt of the associated stimulus input pattern. The stimulus and response patterns represent feature vectors that correspond to the query image and output images. Many associative memory models have been proposed to simulate human memory. However, the potential of these models has not been explored for CBIR. Linear associative memories have been studied extensively by Kohonen (1988). Bidirectional associative memories (BAMs) have been studied by Kosko (1988). A two-layer network with feedback that simulates a BAM is shown Figure 4. The network is designed to map stimulus vectors $\{x_1, x_2,...x_n\}$ to response vectors $\{y_1, y_2,...y_n\}$. In an auto-associative network, the response vector y_i and the corresponding stimulus vector x_i are the same. In a hetero-associative memory, the stimulus and the response vector are not identical. Associative memories are often able to produce correct response patterns even though stimulus patterns are distorted or incomplete. Conventional BAMs are used to store are retrieve pairs of stimulus and response patterns. However, if the number of associated inputs and/or outputs is more than two; that is, instead of pairs of vectors, if we want to store triplets or quadruplets of vectors, then we need to use generalized BAMs. Pairs of vectors $(\mathbf{x}_i, \mathbf{y}_i)$ can be stored with the BAM by summing bipolar correlation matrices. In a $m \times n$ BAM, n neurons in layer L_1 represent field $\mathbf{F}_x = \{\mathbf{x}_1, \mathbf{x}_2,..\mathbf{x}_n\}$, and m neurons in layer L_2 by $\mathbf{F}_y = \{\mathbf{y}_1, \mathbf{y}_2,.. \mathbf{y}_n\}$. The two fields are interconnected by a $m \times n$ synoptic weight matrix $\mathbf{W}$. The neuron states in field $\mathbf{F}_x$ and field $\mathbf{F}_y$ are the units of the short-term memory (STM). The connection matrix $\mathbf{W}$ is the unit of the long-term memory (LTM).

If the input vectors are orthonormal then the recall is perfect.

$$\mathbf{x}_i \mathbf{x}_j = \begin{cases} 1 \text{ for } i = j \\ 0 \text{ for } i \neq j \end{cases} \tag{26}$$

If the input vectors are not orthonormal, then the output vector may contain cross talk. In a dual BAM, feedback is achieved with $\mathbf{W}^\mathrm{T}$ and is given by

$$\mathbf{W}^\mathrm{T} = \sum_{i=1}^{N} \left(\mathbf{y}_i \mathbf{x}_i^\mathrm{T} \right)^\mathrm{T} = \sum_{i=1}^{N} \mathbf{x}_i \mathbf{y}_i^\mathrm{T} \tag{27}$$

If we assume a nonlinear transfer function for neurons in the BAM, then the recalled output is a nonlinear function of a transformed input vector and is given by

$$\mathbf{y}_i = F\left(\mathbf{W}\mathbf{x}_i\right) \tag{28}$$

With the feedback the input vector $\mathbf{x}_i$ can be estimated as

$$\mathbf{x}_i = F\left(\mathbf{W}^T \mathbf{y}_i\right) \tag{29}$$

The simplest transfer function for the BAM is a step function. The stable reverberation corresponds to the system energy local minimum. The stable reverberation corresponds to the system energy local minimum. When the BAM neurons are activated, the network quickly evolves to a stable state of two-pattern reverberation or a non-adaptive resonance. In order to improve recall accuracy, the output vector $\mathbf{y}_i$ can be synchronously fed back. The back-and-forth flow of distributed information quickly resonates on a fixed data pair. The sequence can be represented by

$$\mathbf{x}_i(0) \rightarrow \mathbf{W} \rightarrow \mathbf{y}_i(0)$$

$$\mathbf{y}_i(0) \rightarrow \mathbf{W}^T \rightarrow \mathbf{x}_i(1)$$

$$\mathbf{x}_i(1) \rightarrow \mathbf{W} \rightarrow \mathbf{y}_i(1)$$

$$\mathbf{y}_i(1) \rightarrow \mathbf{W}^T \rightarrow \mathbf{x}_i(2)$$

$$. \qquad . \qquad .$$

$$. \qquad . \qquad .$$

$$\mathbf{x}_i(n) \rightarrow \mathbf{W} \rightarrow \mathbf{y}_i(n)$$

$$\mathbf{y}_i(n) \rightarrow \mathbf{W}^T \rightarrow \mathbf{x}_i(n+1) \tag{30}$$

Linear associative matrices are in general not bidirectionally stable. Kosko (1988) showed that with a sigmoid transfer function all the matrices are bidirectionally stable. If the dimensions of the stimulus vector **x** and the response vector **y** are n and m, respectively, then an estimate of the BAM storage capacity for reliable recall is given by $p \leq \min(n, m)$, where p represents the number of data pairs to be stored.

Let us consider a simple example of a BAM construction and synchronous operation. Let the number of units in layer L_1 be eight ($n = 8$), the number of units in layer L_2 be five ($m = 5$), and the number of pairs of vectors to be encoded be four ($N = 4$). The stimulus and response vector pairs are given by Equation (31)

$$\mathbf{x}_1^T = (\text{-}1 \ \ 1 \ \ \text{-}1 \ \ 1 \ \ \text{-}1 \ \ 1 \ \ \text{-}1 \ \ 1)$$

$$\mathbf{x}_2^T = (\text{-}1 \ \ \text{-}1 \ \ 1 \ \ 1 \ \ \text{-}1 \ \ \text{-}1 \ \ 1 \ \ 1)$$

$$\mathbf{x}_3^T = (\text{-}1 \ \ \text{-}1 \ \ \text{-}1 \ \ 1 \ \ 1 \ \ 1 \ \ \text{-}1 \ \ \text{-}1)$$

$$\mathbf{x}_4^T = (\text{-}1 \ \ \text{-}1 \ \ \text{-}1 \ \ \text{-}1 \ \ 1 \ \ 1 \ \ 1 \ \ 1)$$

$$\mathbf{y}_1^T = (1 \ \ 1 \ \ \text{-}1 \ \ 1 \ \ 1)$$

$$\mathbf{y}_2^T = (\text{-}1 \ \ 1 \ \ 1 \ \ 1 \ \ \text{-}1)$$

$$\mathbf{y}_3^T = (\text{-}1 \ \ \text{-}1 \ \ 1 \ \ \text{-}1 \ \ \text{-}1)$$

$$\mathbf{y}_4^T = (\text{-}1 \ \ 1 \ \ \text{-}1 \ \ 1 \ \ \text{-}1) \tag{31}$$

The weights between the two layers are given by the correlation matrix **W**.

$$\mathbf{W} = \mathbf{y}_1\mathbf{x}_1^T + \mathbf{y}_2\mathbf{x}_2^T + \mathbf{y}_3\mathbf{x}_3^T + \mathbf{y}_4\mathbf{x}_4$$

$$\mathbf{W} = \begin{bmatrix} 2 & 4 & 0 & 0 & -2 & 0 & -2 & 0 \\ -2 & 0 & 0 & 0 & -2 & 0 & 2 & 4 \\ 0 & -2 & 2 & 2 & 0 & -2 & 0 & -2 \\ -2 & 0 & 0 & 0 & -2 & 0 & 2 & 4 \\ 2 & 4 & 0 & 0 & -2 & 0 & -2 & 0 \end{bmatrix} \tag{32}$$

The BAM convergence is quick and robust when W is constant. The neural network architecture for the BAM is shown in Figure 4. Here, the stimulus vector $\mathbf{x}_i$ is used as the input to layer L_1. Vector $\mathbf{y}_i$ represents the output or the response vector. The weights between layers L_1 and L_2 are represented by the elements of matrix W. The weights between layers L_2 and L_3 are given by the elements of matrix $\mathbf{W}^T$. The output of layer L_2 is used, iteratively, as the input to layer L_1. When the BAM neurons are activated, the network quickly evolves to a stable state of two-pattern reverberation or a non-adaptive resonance. In order to improve recall accuracy, the output vector $\mathbf{y}_i$ can be synchronously fed back. The back-and-forth flow of distributed information quickly resonates on a fixed data pair. Humpert has suggested generalization of the BAM that can store associated multiple input/output patterns (Humpert, 1990). We suggest three models of the GBAM with topologies such as the bus, ring, and tree. The GBAM with tree topology is shown in Figure 5, and GBAMs with ring and bus topologies are shown

Figure 4. Bi-directional associative memory

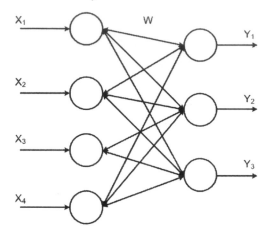

Figure 5. Generalized BAM- tree structure

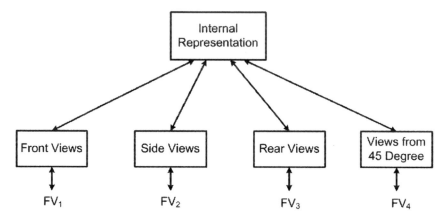

in Figures 6 and 7, respectively. The bus and tree topologies are suitable for retrieving temporal images or image sequences. The generalization of the BAM to several vector fields raises the questions regarding the updating process. In a BAM, all units in a field are synchronously updated. By contrast, the sequence of updating weights in a generalized BAM is not obvious. The generalization of a BAM to several fields also raises question of interconnections. The generalized BAMs are extremely useful in content-based image storage and retrieval for multimedia applications. In addition, one needs to consider the storage capacity of the GBAM.

CASE STUDIES

As part of our research in developing algorithms for CBIR components of multimedia database management systems, we have implemented a prototype system used to test the retrieval accuracy of CBIR

Figure 6. Generalized BAM- bus structure

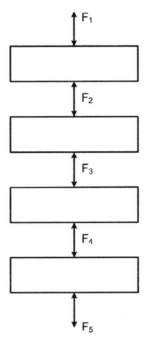

Figure 7. Generalized BAM-ring structure

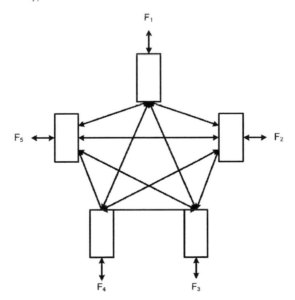

queries that focus on color-based retrieval using global color histograms (Brown & Gruenwald, 2001). The prototype was originally developed using the Perl language on a SUNSparc workstation on a Unix operating system. It is currently being rewritten in Java for a Windows-based environment. It does not use any commercial software for managing databases, but it does use utilities from the pbmplus package to convert jpg and gif images to and from ASCII text files (Pbmplus, 2003). The prototype was written to allow users to test a variety of color models and uniform quantization schemes when using global color histograms to represent image content. The implemented models include RGB, HSI, and Luv. The quantization schemes are indicated by specifying the desired number of dimensions along each axis of the selected model. The prototype supports QBE queries of the form *"Retrieve all images whose distance to query image q is less than threshold t"*, where q is a query image and t is a distance threshold; it supports nearest-neighbor queries of the form *"Retrieve the k images that are most similar to image q"*, where q again is a query image and k is a positive integer; and it supports queries on specific feature values of the form *"Retrieve all images with between m% and n% pixels of color b"*, where m is the minimum desired percentage, n is the maximum desired percentage, and b is the histogram bin representing a color produced by the system's quantization scheme.

The first example from this prototype demonstrates the retrieval of images of international road signs. The images were obtained from the Web (Signs, 2005). This data set was selected for two reasons. First, it was selected because color-based features are important to this application domain since the color of a sign reflects its purpose. Second, it was selected because the Web site presented classifications for the signs which provided a method of judging whether or not a database image was relevant to a given QBE query without relying on human observers. Specifically, all images that have the same classification as a query image are considered to be relevant to the query and are therefore expected to be retrieved. This allows the system to compute the classical information retrieval metrics precision and recall for determining the accuracy of the CBIR system. An example query image and set of images retrieved as a result of querying this data set are displayed in Figure 8.

The second example from this prototype demonstrates the retrieval of images of international flags from various countries, states, and provinces. As before, this data collection was obtained from the Web, and it was selected because color-based features are important when recognizing and identifying flags (Flags, 2003). An example query image and set of images retrieved as a result of querying this data set is displayed in Figure 9. The interface from the original Web-enabled version of the prototype for posing a query for specific feature values and the interface displaying the set of images retrieved as a result of the query are displayed in Figure 10a and Figure 10b, respectively.

The third example from this prototype demonstrates retrieving images of flags from U. S. states. Unlike the previous collections, this collection was obtained using the image retrieval component of Google. The collection contains 100 images for each U. S. state yielding a total of 5000 images. They were obtained using the following approach. For each state S, the top 100 results generated from the text-based query "State Flag of S" were added to the data collection. If this query did not produce 100 total images for the state, the query "S State Flag" was executed, and the top images were added to the data collection until the total of 100 was reached. This method of obtaining images served to classify the images in the data set so that the precision and recall could be computed for a given QBE query. An example query image and set of images retrieved as a result of querying this data set are displayed in Figure 11.

The final example from this prototype demonstrates retrieving images of helmets from U.S. collegiate football teams. Again, this collection was obtained from the Web because the color of helmets and uniforms are important when recognizing and identifying sports teams (Helmets, 2003). An example query image and set of images retrieved as a result of querying this data set is displayed in Figure 12. The interface from the original Web-enabled version of the prototype for selecting a query image by browsing the database and posing a nearest-neighbor query are displayed in Figures 13a and 13b.

Figure 8. Example query image submitted to prototype and results (road sign data set)

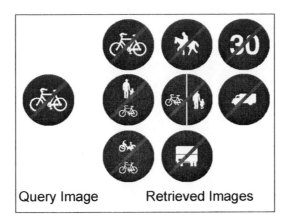

Figure 9. Example query image submitted to prototype and results (world flag data set)

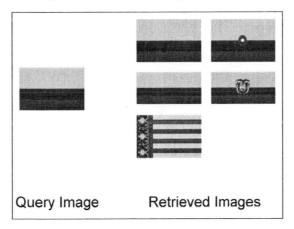

We have developed software to implement the ABIR system. In the first example we have considered three sets of images (Kulkarni, 2001). The first set contained images of numbers {1, 2, 3}, the second set contained images of characters {A, B, C}, and the third set contained images of Greek characters {α, β, γ}. Each character was represented by a 12x12 matrix. Each image was represented by a feature vector of 144 elements. These feature vectors are stored in the GBAM. During retrieval, any one image (partial or noisy) from any set was used as the query image, and the corresponding images from the other sets were retrieved. The retrieved images are shown in Figures 14 and 15. The first row shows the query images and subsequent rows show corresponding retrieved images. The GBAM stores and recalls feature vectors. We can use feature vectors that may represent color, texture and/or shape of objects in the image. In the present simulation, we used a tree topology for storing three sets of images.

In the second example, we use the system to store and retrieve multiple views of military vehicles. The system can be used for automatic target recognition. In this example, we have considered images of vehicles such as jeeps, tanks, and HUMVEES as shown in Figure 16. We have used the system to

Figure 10a. User interface for submitting queries for specific feature values

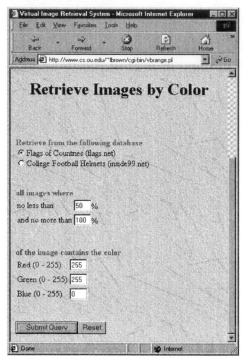

Figure 10b. User interface displaying results of Figure 10a

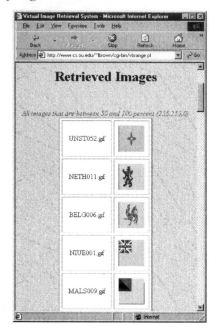

Figure 11. Example query image submitted to prototype and results (state flag data set)

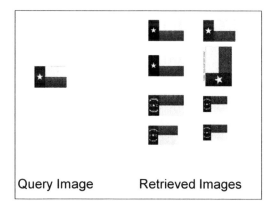

Query Image   Retrieved Images

store images four views of each vehicle such as side, rear, front, and at an angle. The system retrieves images similar to the human brain. For example, if we see a front view of a vehicle, our mind can retrieve side and rear views of the same vehicle. We have used the GBAM with a tree structure to store and retrieve these associations. The units in the root node represent the reference vectors, and the units in leaf nodes F_1, F_2, and F_3 represent front, side and rear views, respectively. Figure 17 shows the stimulus and output images.

Figure 12. Example query image submitted to prototype and results (helmet data set)

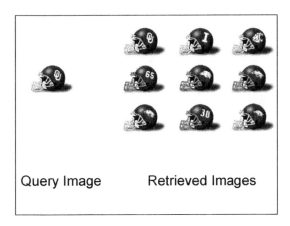

Query Image   Retrieved Images

Figure 13a. User interface for selecting a query image

Figure 13b. User interface for submitting a nearest-neighbor query

In the third example, there are three sets of images that represent flags, food items, and monuments of fifteen countries. These sets are shown in Figures 18 through 21. Three images that correspond to a flag, food dish, and monument of a country form a set of associative images. The association between these images is captured in the GBAM via their feature vectors. We have used the GBAM with a tree structure to store these associations. The common theme that links images of a flag, food dish, and monument is the country that they represent. We represent each country by a reference vector that is binary and generated with Walsh functions as basis functions. The units in the root node represent reference vectors, and units in leaf nodes F_1, F_2, and F_3 represent feature vectors corresponding to images

Figure 14. Partial input and recalled images

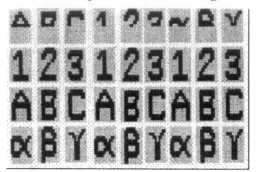

Figure 15. Noisy input and recalled images

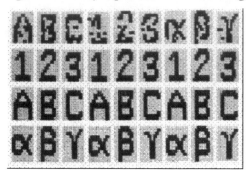

Figure 16. Sample image data sets

Figure 17. Query and output images (Example 2)

Figure 18. Images of flags

Figure 19. Images of food items

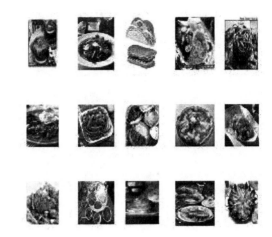

Figure 20. Images of monuments

Figure 21. Output images- Example1

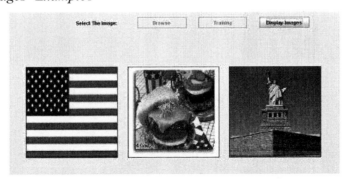

of flags, food dishes, and monuments, respectively. If we present an image of a flag as a query image, the system generates the corresponding feature vector that is used as the stimulus vector at field F_1. The stimulus vector at F_1 produces the corresponding reference vector at the root node as the output vector, which in turn produces the associated feature vectors at fields F_2 and F_3. The feature vectors are used to generate output images via the index table. Figure 19 shows the output images obtained with of a sample query. The image of a US flag was used as the query image and the corresponding retrieved images are displayed on the screen.

DISCUSSIONS AND CONCLUSION

We have proposed a new image storage and retrieval system called an ABIR system. We try to mimic human memory in that the human brain stores and retrieves images by association. We used a generalized bi-directional associative memory (GBAM) to retrieve images from a database. The method has been used successfully to retrieve associated images from the database. The generalization of a BAM to several fields also raises the question of interconnections. The GBAM is extremely useful for image storage and retrieval for multimedia applications. Our approach provides a new direction for CBIR. The main difference between the CBIR and ABIR systems is that in CBIR similar images are retrieved, whereas in ABIR the images are retrieved based on their associations.

REFERENCES

Aslandogan, Y.A., & Yu, C.T. (1999). Techniques and Systems for Image and Video Retrieval. *IEEE Transactions on Knowledge and Data Engineering, 11*(1), 56-63.

Ballard, D.H., & Brown, C.M. (1982). *Computer Vision.* Englewood Cliffs, New Jersey: Prentice Hall.

Brown, L., & Gruenwald, L. (1998). Tree-Based Indexes for Image Data. *Journal of Visual Communication and Image Representation, 9*(4), 300-313.

Brown, L., & Gruenwald, L. (2001). A Prototype Content-Based Retrieval System that Uses Virtual Images to Save Space. *Proceedings of the 27th International Conference on Very Large Databases (VLDB)* (pp. 693-694), Rome, Italy.

Chang, T., & Kuo, C. (1993). Texture analysis and classification with tree-structured wavelet transform. *IEEE Transactions on Image Processing, 2*(4), 429-441.

Cheung, K.L., & Fu, A.W. (1998). Enhanced Nearest Neighbour Search on the R-tree. *ACM SIGMOD Record. 27*(3), 16-21.

Coggins, J.M., & Jain, A.K. (1985). A spatial filtering approach to texture analysis. *Pattern Recognition Letters, 3*, 195-203.

Comer, D. (1979). The Ubiquitous B-Tree. *ACM Computing Surveys, 11*(2), 121-137.

Datta, R., Li, J., & Wang, J. Z. (2005). Content-Based Image Retrieval – Approaches and Trends of the New Age. In *Proceedings of Multimedia Information Retrieval 2005 (*pp. 253-262), Singapore.

Daugman, J.G. (1988). Complete discrete 2-D Gabor transforms by neural networks for image analysis and compression. *IEEE Transactions on Acoustics, Speech and Signal Processing, 36*, 1169-1179.

Flags (2003). Retrieved January 7, 2003, from http://www.flags.net

Flickner, M., et al. (1995). Query by image and video content: The QBIC system. *IEEE Computer, 9*, 23-32.

Gaede, V., & Günther, O. (1998). Multidimensional Access Methods. *ACM Computing Surveys, 30*(2), 170-231.

Gong, Y., et al. (1994). An Image Database System with Content Capturing and Fast Image Indexing Abilities. *IEEE Computer, 27*(5), 121-130.

Gonzalez, R.C., & Woods, R. (2002). *Digital Image Processing*. Reading, Massachusetts: Addison-Wesley.

Guttman, A. (1984). R-trees: A Dynamic Index Structure for Spatial Searching. In *Proceedings of the 1984 ACM SIGMOD International Conference on Management of Data* (pp. 47-57), Boston, Massachusetts.

Haralick, R.M., et al. (1973). Texture features for image classification. *IEEE Transactions on System, Man and Cybernetics, 3*, 610-620.

Helmets (2003). Retrieved January 7, 2003, from http://inside99.net/Helmet_Project/index.htm.

Hjaltason, G.R., & Samat, H. (1999). Distance Browsing in Spatial Databases. *ACM Transactions on Database Systems, 24*(2), 71-79.

Hu, M.K. (1962). Visual pattern recognition by moment invariants. *IRE Transactions on Information Theory, 8*, 28-32.

Huang, J., et al. (1997). Image indexing using color correlograms. In *Proceedings of Conference on Computer Vision and Pattern Recognition* (pp. 762-768), Puerto Rico.

Humpert, B. (1990). Bi-directional associative memory with several patterns. In *Proceedings of International Joint Conference on Neural Networks vol. 1* (pp. 741-750), San Diego, California.

Jain, A.K., & Vailaya, A. (1998). Shape-based retrieval: A case study with trademark image databases. *Pattern Recognition, 31*(9), 1369-1390.

Kohonen, T. (1988). *Self-Organization and Associative Memory*. Berlin: Springer-Verlag.

Kosko, B. (1988). Bi-directional associative memories. *IEEE Transactions on Systems, Man and Cybernetics, 18*, 49-60.

Krishnapuram, R., et al. (2004). Content-based image retrieval based on a fuzzy approach. *IEEE Transactions on Knowledge Engineering, 16*(10), 1185-1199.

Kulkarni, A.D. (2001). *Computer Vision and Fuzzy-Neural Systems*. Upper Saddle River, New Jersey: Prentice Hall.

Mehrotra, R., & Gary, J.E. (1995). Similar-shape retrieval in shape data management. *IEEE Computer, 9*, 57-62.

O'Toole, R.K., & Stark, H. (1980). Comparative study of optical vs. all digital techniques in textural pattern recognition. *Applied Optics, 19*, 2496-2506.

Pass, G., Zabih, R., & Miller, J. (1996). Comparing Images Using Color Coherence Vectors. In *Proceedings of the 4th ACM International Conference on Multimedia* (pp. 65-73), Boston, Massachusetts.

Pbmplus (2003). Retrieved January 7, 2003, from http://www.acme.com/software/pbmplus/

Rosenfeld, A., & Kak, A. (1982). *Digital Image Processing,* Volumes I and II. Orlando, Florida: Academic Press.

Roussopoulos, N., Kelley, S., & Vincent, F. (1995). Nearest-Neighbor Queries. In *Proceedings of the 1995 ACM SIGMOD International Conference on Management of Data* (pp. 71-79).

Rui, Y., Huang, T.S., & Chang, S.F. (1999). Image Retrieval: Current techniques, promising directions, and open issues. *Journal of Visual Communication and Image Representation, 10*, 39-62.

Rui, Y., et al. (1998). Relevance feedback: A power tool for interactive content-based image retrieval. *IEEE Transactions on Circuits and Systems for Video Technology, 8*(3), 644-655.

Santini, S., & Jain, R. (1999). Similarity Measures. *IEEE Transactions on Pattern Analysis and Machine Intelligence, 21*(9), 871-883.

Signs (2005). Retrieved September 7, 2005, from *http://www.geocities.com/jusjih/roadsigns.html#d*

Smeulders, A. W., et al. (2000). Content-based image retrieval at the end of the early years. *IEEE Transactions on Pattern Recognition and Machine Learning, 22*(12), 1349-1380.

Smith, J.R., & Chang, S. (1997). VisualSEEK: A Fully Automated Content-Based Image Query System. In *Proceedings of the 4th ACM International Conference on Multimedia* (87-98), Boston, Massachusetts.

Swain, M.J., & Ballard, D.H. (1991). Color indexing. *International Journal of Computer Vision, 7*(1), 11-32.

Wan, X., & Kuo, C.C.J. (1998). A new approach to image retrieval with hierarchical color clustering. *IEEE Transactions on Circuits and Systems for Video Technology, 8*(3), 628-643.

Wang, T., et al. (2003). Adaptive three similarity learning for image retrieval. *Multimedia Systems, 9*, 131-143.

Yoshitaka, A., & Ichikawa, T. (1999). A Survey on Content-Based Retrieval for Multimedia Databases. *IEEE Transactions on Knowledge and Data Engineering, 11*(1), 81-93.

Zhao, W., et al. (2003). Face Recognition: A Literature Survey. *ACM Computing Surveys, 35*(4), 399-458.

Chapter XVII
Compressed–Domain Image Retrieval Based on Colour Visual Patterns

Gerald Schaefer
Aston University, UK

ABSTRACT

Image retrieval and image compression have been typically pursued separately. Only little research has been done on a synthesis of the two by allowing image retrieval to be performed directly in the compressed domain of images without the need to uncompress them first. In this chapter the authors show that such compressed domain image retrieval can indeed be done and lead to effective and efficient retrieval performance. They introduce a novel compression algorithm – colour visual pattern image coding (CVPIC) – and present several retrieval algorithms that operate directly on compressed CVPIC data. Their experiments demonstrate that it is not only possible to realise such midstream content access, but also that the presented techniques outperform standard retrieval techniques such as colour histograms and colour correlograms.

INTRODUCTION

With the recent enormous increase in digital image collections there is no doubt that effective image retrieval techniques are desperately needed. Fortunately, this problem has been subject of extensive research for over a decade. In 1991 Swain and Ballard (1991) published results of their work on colour indexing. Their method of finding similar images - while being very simple - performed extremely well. They quantised colour space into bins, creating a 3-dimensional colour histogram. All pixels are scanned, allocated to the bins that they correspond to and then the number (or percentage) of pixels in each bin is extracted. Comparing two images is done by finding the L_1 norm between their respective histograms.

Although colour information is very important in object recognition, it is often not sufficient, especially if colour descriptors are extracted globally for a whole image. This was soon realised and techniques which also address texture and shape properties investigated (Smeulders et al., 2000). Although these methods are usually not as efficient as colour-based algorithms, incorporating several feature types provides improved performance.

All these methods have one common factor that can be regarded as their weakness. Storage space is very limited when compared to the enormous amount of images that we keep on producing. Moreover, the ability to transfer these pieces of information is still limited by bandwidths of networks (especially the Internet). Many different compression algorithms have been developed to enable us to store more data using less storage space. In fact, these highly effective techniques are now being used extensively and virtually all image data now exists in compressed form. Many of the original uncompressed images are not kept or indeed never existed as compression is typically performed on-the-fly inside digital cameras. Many others never even existed in their uncompressed form, because virtually all digital cameras compress images to increase their capacity. Despite the fact that almost all images are compressed, image retrieval techniques are based on the uncompressed pixel bitmap domain, meaning that two pictures have to be first uncompressed to enable comparing them on-line which clearly is a limitation. While features can be extracted off-line and stored separately, this conflicts with the original intention of compression as the features may require a significant amount of storage space. Despite these limitations, only relatively little research has been done in the area of retrieval in the compressed domain of images (Mandal, Idris, & Panchanathan, 1999).

In this chapter we show that so-called midstream content access (Picard, 1994) can indeed be achieved to provide effective and efficient image retrieval. Colour visual pattern image coding (CVPIC) is one of the first so-called 4th criterion image compression algorithms (Schaefer, Qiu, & Luo, 1999; Schaefer & Qiu, 2000). A 4th criterion algorithm allows - in addition to the classic three image coding criteria of image quality, efficiency, and bitrate - the image data to be queried and processed directly in its compressed form; in other words the image data are directly meaningful without the requirement of a decoding step (Picard, 1994). The data that are readily available in CVPIC compressed images is the colour information of each of the 4x4 blocks the image has been divided into, and information on the spatial characteristics of each block, including whether a given block is identified as a uniform block (a block with no or little variation) or a pattern block (a block where an edge or gradient has been detected).

We make direct use of this information and present several image retrieval algorithms that allow for retrieval directly in the compressed domain of CVPIC. Since both colour and shape (edge) information is pre-calculated and readily available in the CVPIC domain, a simple combined histogram of these can be obtained very efficiently. Exploiting these histograms allows for image retrieval based on both colour and shape contents (Schaefer & Lieutaud, 2004a). Similarly, the division into uniform and edge blocks permits us to calculate two distinct histograms similar to the colour coherence vector approach (Schaefer & Lieutaud, 2004b). Finally, a colour block co-occurrence matrix can be derived (Schaefer, Lieutaud, & Qiu, 2004). Experimental results obtained from querying the UCID (Schaefer & Stich, 2004) dataset show that these techniques not only allow efficient retrieval directly in the compressed domain but also clearly outperform popular techniques such as colour histograms, colour coherence vectors, and colour correlograms.

COLOUR VISUAL PATTERN IMAGE CODING (CVPIC)

The Colour Visual Pattern Image Coding (CVPIC) image compression algorithm introduced by Schaefer, Qiu, and Luo (1999) is an extension of the work by Chen and Bovic (Chen & Bovik, 1990). The underlying idea is that within a 4x4 image block only one discontinuity is visually perceptible.

CVPIC first performs a conversion to the CIEL*a*b* colour space (CIE, 1986) as a more appropriate image representation. As many other colour spaces, CIEL*a*b* comprises one luminance and two chrominance channels. CIEL*a*b* however, was designed to be a uniform representation, meaning that equal differences in the colour space correspond to equal perceptual differences. A quantitative measurement of these colour differences was defined using the Euclidean distance in the L*a*b* space and is given in ΔE units.

A set of 14 patterns of 4x4 pixels has been defined in (Chen & Bovik, 1990). All these patterns contain one edge at various orientations (vertical, horizontal, plus and minus 45°) as can be seen in Figure 1 where + and − represent different intensities. In addition a uniform pattern where all intensities are equal is being used.

The image is divided into 4x4 pixel blocks. Determining which visual pattern represents each block most accurately then follows. For each of the visual patterns the average L*a*b* values μ+ and μ− for the regions marked by + and − respectively (i.e. the mean values for the regions on each side of the pattern) are calculated according to

$$\mu_{+} = \frac{\sum\limits_{i \in +} p_i}{\sum\limits_{i \in +} i} \qquad \mu_{-} = \frac{\sum\limits_{j \in -} p_j}{\sum\limits_{j \in -} j} \tag{1}$$

where p_i and p_j represent the pixel vectors in L*a*b* colour space.

The colour difference of each actual pixel and the corresponding mean value is obtained and averaged over the block

$$\varepsilon = \frac{\sum\limits_{i \in +} \left\| p_i - \mu_{+} \right\| + \sum\limits_{j \in -} \left\| p_j - \mu_{-} \right\|}{16} \tag{2}$$

The visual pattern that leads to the lowest ε value (given in CIEL*a*b* ΔE units) is then chosen. In order to allow for the encoding of uniform blocks the average colour difference to the mean colour of the block is also determined according to

Figure 1. The 14 edge patterns used in CVPIC

++++	++++	++++		---+	--++	-+++	
----	++++	++++		---+	--++	-+++	
----	----	++++		---+	--++	-+++	
----	----	----		---+	--++	-+++	
--++	-+++	++++	++++	----	----	---+	--++
---+	--++	-+++	++++	----	----	--++	-+++
----	---+	--++	-+++	---+	--++	-+++	++++
----	----	---+	--++	--++	-+++	++++	++++

$$\sigma = \frac{\sum_{\forall i} \|p_i - \mu\|}{16} \quad \text{where} \quad \mu = \frac{\sum_{\forall i} p_i}{\sum_{\forall i} i} \tag{3}$$

A block is coded as uniform if either its variance in colour is very low, or if the resulting image quality will not suffer severely when coded as a uniform rather than as an edge block. To meet this requirement two thresholds are defined. The first threshold describes the upper bound for variations within a block, i.e. the average colour difference to the mean colour of the block. Every block with a variance below this value will be encoded as uniform. The second threshold is related to the difference between the average colour variation within a block and the average colour difference that would result if the block were coded as a pattern block (i.e., the lowest variance possible for an edge block) which is calculated by

$$\delta = \sigma - \min_{\forall \, patterns} (\varepsilon) \tag{4}$$

If this difference is very low (or if the variance for a uniform pattern is below those of all edge patterns in which case σ is negative) coding the block as uniform will not introduce distortions much more perceptible than if the block is coded as a pattern block. Hence, a block is coded as a uniform block if at least one of the following criteria is met (Schaefer, Qiu, & Luo, 1999):

(i) $\sigma < 1.75$

(ii) $\delta < 1.25$

For each block, one bit is stored which states whether the block is uniform or a pattern block. In addition, for edge blocks an index identifying the visual pattern needs to be stored. Following this procedure results in a representation of each block as 5 bits (1 + 4 as we use 14 patterns) for an edge block and 1 bit for a uniform block describing the spatial component, and the full colour information for one or two colours (for uniform and pattern blocks respectively).

In contrast to (Schaefer, Qiu, & Luo, 1999) where each image is colour quantised individually, the colour components are quantised to 64 universally pre-defined colours (we adopted those of (Qiu, 2003)). Each colour can hence be encoded using 6 bits. Therefore, in total a uniform block takes 7 (=1+6) bits, whereas a pattern block is stored in 17 (=5+2*6) bits. We found that this yielded an average compression ratio of about 1:30. We note, that the information could be further encoded to achieve lower bitrates. Both the pattern and the colour information could be entropy coded. In here however, we refrain from this step as we are primarily interested in a synthesis of coding and retrieval.

CVPIC RETRIEVAL BY COLOUR AND SHAPE

We can see from above that for each image block in CVPIC, both colour and edge information is readily available in the compressed form: each block contains either one or two colours and belongs to one of 15 edge classes. We can make direct use of this information for the purpose of image retrieval. In a sense our approach is similar to the work by Jain and Vailaya (1996) where image retrieval is performed based on colour and shape (edge) information. However, our method differs in two important aspects. In stark contrast to their work, our method runs directly in the compressed domain without any further need for calculating these descriptors. Furthermore due to the low dimensionality of our features we are able to build a combined colour and shape histogram rather than two separate descriptors that need to be re-integrated in the retrieval process.

It is well known that colour is an important cue for image retrieval. In fact, simple descriptors such as histograms of the colour contents of images (Swain & Ballard, 1991) have been shown to work well and have hence been used in many CBIR systems such as QBIC (Niblack et al., 1993) or Virage (Bach et al., 1996). A colour histogram is built by (uniformly) quantising the colour space into a number of bins (often 8x8x8) and counting how many pixels of the image fall into each bin. From the description of the CVPIC algorithm it can be easily deduced how a colour histogram can be efficiently calculated there. First, CVPIC colour histograms need only 64 entries since there are only 64 colours in the palette used during the encoding. This in turn means that the dimensionality is lower compared to traditional colour histograms which again implies that the comparison of these histograms requires fewer computations. Since each block contains one or two colour indices and an edge index an exact colour histogram can be calculated by weighing the respective two colours by the number of pixels they occupy. While this method requires fewer computations than are needed for obtaining histograms in the pixel domain we propose a yet more efficient approach. Instead of applying weights according to the layout of each pattern we simply increment the relevant histogram bins for each block (we note that by doing so we put more emphasis on the colour content of edge blocks compared to uniform blocks).

While image retrieval based on colour usually produces useful results, integration of this information with another paradigm such as texture or shape will result in an improved retrieval performance. Shape descriptors are often calculated as statistical summaries of local edge information such as in (Jain & Vailaya, 1996) where the edge orientation and magnitude is determined at each pixel location and an edge histogram calculated. Exploiting the CVPIC image structure an effective shape descriptor can be determined very efficiently. Since each (pattern) block contains exactly one (pre-calculated) edge and there are 15 different patterns, a simple histogram of the edge indices could be built. However, since both colour and shape features are of low dimensionality we propose to integrate them into a combined colour/shape histogram rather than building two separate descriptors as in (Jain & Vailaya, 1996). We further reduce the dimensionality by considering only 5 edge classes: horizontal and vertical edges, edges at plus and minus 45°, and no edge (uniform blocks). Thus, we end up with a 64x5 colour/shape histogram $H_{CS}(I)$ for an image I:

$$
\begin{array}{lll}
H_{CS}(I)(i,1) = \Pr((c_1 = i \vee c_2 = i) \wedge p \in \{1,2,3\}) & \text{horizontal} \\
H_{CS}(I)(i,2) = \Pr((c_1 = i \vee c_2 = i) \wedge p \in \{4,5,6\}) & \text{vertical} \\
H_{CS}(I)(i,3) = \Pr((c_1 = i \vee c_2 = i) \wedge p \in \{7,8,9,10\}) & -45° \\
H_{CS}(I)(i,4) = \Pr((c_1 = i \vee c_2 = i) \wedge p \in \{11,12,13,14\}) & +45° \\
H_{CS}(I)(i,5) = \Pr(c_1 = i \wedge p = 15) & \text{uniform} \quad (5)
\end{array}
$$

where c_1, c_2, and p are the colour and pattern indices (the patterns are numbered according to Figure 1, going from left to right, top to bottom) of a block.

It should be pointed out that these CVPIC colour/shape histograms $H_{CS}(I)$ can be created extremely efficiently. In essence, per 4x4 image block only 1 addition is needed (to increment the relevant histogram bin). This makes it unnecessary to store any information alongside the image as the indices can be created online with hardly any overhead to reading the image file. As thus it automatically lends itself to online retrieval e.g. of the web which - due to the dynamic structure of the Internet - is impossible to achieve with traditional index-based approaches.

Two CVPIC colour/shape histograms $H_{CS}(I_1)$ and $H_{CS}(I_2)$ obtained from images I_1 and I_2 are compared using the histogram intersection measure introduced in (Swain & Ballard, 1991)

$$s_{CS}(I_1, I_2) = \sum_{i=1}^{64} \sum_{j=1}^{5} \min(H_{CS}(I_1)(i,j), H_{CS}(I_2)(i,j)) \qquad (6)$$

which provides a similarity score between 0 and 1 (for normalised histograms).

CVPIC RETRIEVAL WITH UNIFORM/NON-UNIFORM COLOUR HISTOGRAMS

Pass and Zabih (1996) introduced colour coherence vectors (CCV) as a method of introducing spatial information into the retrieval process. Colour coherence vectors consist of two histograms: one histogram of coherent and one of non-coherent pixels. Pixels are considered to be coherent if they are part of a continuous uniformly coloured area and the size of this area exceeds some threshold (usually defined as 1% of the overall area of an image). The L_1 norm is used as the distance metric between colour coherence vectors.

Stehling, Nascimento, and Falcao (2002) took a similar approach to that of coherence vectors with their border interior pixel (BIP) algorithm. Pixels are classified as either interior or border pixels. A pixel is an interior pixel if (after a quantisation step) it has the same colour as its 4-neighbourhood, otherwise it is a border pixel. We see that in contrast to colour coherence vectors here the classification process is much simplified. Two histograms for border and interior pixels are created and again histogram intersection is used as a similarity measure.

Based on CVPIC it is possible to follow an approach similar to CCV and BIP by exploiting the information that is readily available in the CVPIC compressed format. CVPIC information is directly visually meaningful. While on the one hand, the colour information is readily available, on the other hand information on the spatial content, i.e. shape-based information is also pre-calculated in the form of uniform and edge blocks.

The division into uniform and pattern blocks creates an automatic classification of image pixels. Pixels that are part of a uniform area (i.e. 'coherent' or 'interior' pixels) will more likely be contained within a uniform block. On the other hand pixels that form part of an edge (i.e. 'border' pixels) will fall into pattern blocks. We can therefore immediately distinguish between these two types of pixels without any further calculation (as would need to be done for CCV or BIP calculations). We hence create two colour histograms: a uniform histogram H^u by considering only uniform blocks and a non-uniform histogram H^n calculated solely from edge blocks. While exact histograms could be calculated by simply adding the appropriate number of pixels to the relevant colour bins while scanning through the image we suggest a simpler, less computationally intensive, method. Instead of weighing the histogram increments by the relative pixel proportions we simply increment the affected colour bins (two for an edge block, one for a uniform block) by 1 (we note that this puts more weight on the non-uniform histogram than on the uniform one). We also wish to point out that the resulting histograms are *not* normalised as is often the case with histogram based descriptors. The reason for this is that by not normalising we preserve the original ratio between uniform and pattern blocks - an image feature that should prove important for distinguishing between images with similar colour content.

Having calculated H^u and H^n which can be done efficiently enough on-line, two images can then be compared by calculating the L_1 norm between their histograms

$$d_{UN} = \sum_{k=1}^{n} \left(\left| H_1^u(k) - H_2^u(k) \right| + \left| H_1^n(k) - H_2^n(k) \right| \right) \tag{7}$$

CVPIC RETRIEVAL WITH BLOCK COLOUR CO-OCCURRENCE MATRIX

In our third approach we also make use of the fact that for each image block in CVPIC both colour and edge information is readily available in the compressed form as each block contains either one or two colours and belongs to one of 15 edge classes (14 for edge blocks, and one for uniform blocks).

Our approach to exploit the colour information that is readily available in CVPIC - block colour co-occurrence matrix - is similar to that of colour correlograms (Huang et al., 1997) which are histograms that record the probabilities that a pixel with a certain colour is a certain distance away from another pixel with another colour. However, in contrast to those it is very efficient to compute. We define the block colour co-occurrence matrix BCCM as

$$BCCM(c_i, c_j) = Pr(p_1 = c_i \wedge p_2 = c_j) \tag{8}$$

In other words for each CVPIC 4x4 sub-block we increment the histogram bin that is defined by the two colours on each side of the edge in the block. We note, that for uniform blocks the bins along the 'diagonal' of the (64x64) histogram get incremented, i.e. those bins that essentially correspond to the auto correlogram (Huang et al., 1997).

Two BCCMs are compared by

$$d_{BCCM}(I_1, I_2) = \frac{\sum_{i=1}^{64} \sum_{j=1}^{64} \left| BCCM_1(i,j) - BCCM_2(i,j) \right|}{1 + \sum_{i=1}^{64} \sum_{j=1}^{64} BCCM_1(i,j) + \sum_{i=1}^{64} \sum_{j=1}^{64} BCCM_2(i,j)} \tag{9}$$

As pointed out above, exploiting the CVPIC image structure an effective shape descriptor can be determined very efficiently. Since each (pattern) block contains exactly one (pre-calculated) edge and there are 14 different patterns we simply build a 1x14 histogram of the edge indices. We decided not to include a bin for uniform blocks, since these give little indication of shape (rather they describe the absence of it). Block edge histograms BEH_1 and BEH_2 are compared analogous to BCCMs by

$$d_{BEH}(I_1, I_2) = \frac{\sum_{k=1}^{14} \left| BEH_1(k) - BEH_2(k) \right|}{1 + \sum_{k=1}^{14} BEH_1(k) + \sum_{k=1}^{14} BEH_2(k)} \tag{10}$$

Having calculated the distances $d_{BCCM}(I_1,I_2)$ and $d_{BEH}(I_1,I_2)$ between two images I_1 and I_2 these two can be combined in order to allow for image retrieval based on both colour and shape features. Obviously, the simplest method of doing that would be to just add the two measures which is indeed what we did for the experiments presented in the next section. However, dependent on the database or task at hand, it is also possible to weigh them, i.e. to put more emphasis on one of the two measures.

EXPERIMENTAL RESULTS

We evaluated the presented algorithms using the UCID dataset (Schaefer & Stich, 2004). UCID (available from http://vision.cs.aston.ac.uk), an Uncompressed Colour Image Database, consists of 1338 colour images all preserved in their uncompressed form which makes it ideal for the testing of compressed domain techniques. UCID also provides a ground truth of 262 assigned query images each with a number of predefined corresponding matches that an ideal image retrieval system would return.

We compressed the database using the CVPIC coding technique and performed image retrieval using the 3 techniques detailed above, based on the queries defined in the UCID set. As performance measure we used the modified average match percentile (AMP) from (Schaefer & Stich, 2004) and the retrieval effectiveness from (Faloutsos et al, 1994). The modified AMP is defined as

$$MP_Q = \frac{100}{S_Q} \sum_{i=1}^{S_Q} \frac{N - R_i}{N - i} \tag{11}$$

with $R_i < R_{i+1}$ and

$$AMP = \frac{1}{Q} \sum MP_Q \tag{12}$$

where R_i is the rank the ith match to query image Q was returned, S_Q is the number of corresponding matches for Q, and N is the total number of images in the database. A perfect retrieval system would achieve an AMP of 100 whereas an AMP of 50 would mean the system performs as well as one that returns the images in a random order.

The retrieval effectiveness is given by

$$RE_Q = \frac{\sum_{i=1}^{S_Q} R_i}{\sum_{i=1}^{S_Q} I_i} \tag{13}$$

where R_i is again the rank of the ith matching image and I_i is the ideal rank of the ith match (i.e., $I = \{1,2, ...,S_Q\}$). The average retrieval effectiveness ARE is then taken as the mean of RE over all query images. An ideal CBIR algorithm would return an ARE of 1, the closer the ARE to that value (i.e. the lower the ARE) the better the algorithm.

In order to relate the results obtained, we also implemented colour histogram based image retrieval (uniformly quantised 8x8x8 RGB histograms with histogram intersection) according to (Swain & Ballard, 1991), colour coherence vectors (Pass & Zabih, 1996), border/interior pixel histograms (Stehling, Nascimento, & Falcao, 2002) and colour (auto-)correlograms (Huang et al., 1997). Results for all methods are given in Table 1. From there we see that our compressed domain approaches are not only capable of achieving good retrieval performance, but that they also clearly outperforms all other methods.

While the border/interior pixel approach achieves an AMP of 91.27 and all other methods perform worse, CVPIC colour/shape histograms provide an average match percentile of 93.70, that is more than 2.50 higher than the best of the other methods. This is indeed a significant difference as a drop in match percentile of 2.5 will mean that 2.5% more of the whole image database need to be returned in order to find the images that are relevant; as typical image database nowadays can contain tens of thousands to hundreds of thousands images this would literally mean additional thousands of images. CVPIC uniform/non-uniform colour histograms perform similarly, with an AMP of 93.28. The overall best retrieval performance is achieved by the combined BCCM and shape histogram approach which reaches an AMP of 94.23 and an ARE of 53.43.

The superiority of the CVPIC based techniques is especially remarkable so as it is based on images compressed to a medium compression ratio, i.e. images with a significantly lower image quality compared to uncompressed images whereas for all other methods the original uncompressed versions of the images were used. Compressing these images to a size similar to the CVPIC images using a standard coding technique such as JPEG would result in a further performance drop as has been shown in (Schaefer, 2008), hence the results for the pixel domain algorithms here are based on a best case scenario. Furthermore, methods such as colour histograms, colour coherence vectors and colour correlograms are known to work fairly well for image retrieval and are hence among those techniques that are widely used in this field.

An example of the difference in retrieval performance is illustrated in Figure 2 which shows one of the query images of the UCID database together with the five top ranked images returned by all methods. Colour histograms, colour coherence vectors, and border/interior pixel histograms manage to retrieve only two of the targets in the top five while retrieval based on colour correlograms returns three. The two CVPIC techniques based on colour & shape histograms, and based on uniform/non-uniform colour histograms both do better and retrieve four. The best result is again achieved by the combined BCCM and shape algorithm where all of the top five retrievals are relevant images (as indeed is the 6th ranked image not shown in Figure 2).

Table 1. Retrieval results based on the UCID database

	AMP	ARE
Colour histograms	90.47	90.83
Colour coherence vectors	91.03	85.88
Border/interior pixel histograms	91.27	82.49
Colour correlograms	89.96	95.61
CVPIC colour & shape histograms	**93.70**	**57.82**
CVPIC uniform/non-uniform histograms	**93.28**	**62.40**
CVPIC BCCM & shape histograms	**94.23**	**53.43**

Figure 2. Sample retrieval from the UCID database

Query image

Colour histograms

Colour coherence
vectors

Border/interior
pixel histograms

Colour
correlograms

CVPIC colour &
shape

CVPIC uniform/
non-uniform
histograms

CVPIC BCCM &
shape histograms

CONCLUSION

In this chapter we have shown that it is possible to perform effective and efficient image retrieval in the compressed domain. Based on a 4th criterion image compression algorithm, CVPIC, three different retrieval techniques were developed that utilise the visually meaningful information of CVPIC compressed images. Extensive experimental results have demonstrated that these techniques are not only capable of performing compressed domain image retrieval, but also that the retrieval performance achieved is significantly better than those of popular pixel domain based retrieval algorithms such as colour histograms and colour correlograms.

REFERENCES

Bach, J., Fuller, C., Gupta, A., Hampapur, A., Horowitz, B., Humphrey, R., & Jain, R. (1996). The Virage image search engine: An open framework for image management. In *Storage and Retrieval for Image and Video Databases, volume 2670 of Proceedings of SPIE,* (pp. 76–87).

Chen, D., & Bovik, A. (1990). Visual pattern image coding. *IEEE Trans. Communications, 38,* 2137–2146.

CIE. (1986). Colorimetry. *CIE Publications 15.2,* Commission International de L'Eclairage, 2nd edition.

Faloutsos, C., Equitz, W., Flickner, M., Niblack, W., Petkovic, D., & Barber, R. (1994). Efficient and effective querying by image content. *Journal of Intelligent Information Retrieval, 3*(3/4), 231–262.

Huang, J., Kumar, S.R., Mitra, M., Zhu, W-J., & Zabih, R. (1997). Image indexing using color correlograms. In *IEEE Int. Conference Computer Vision and Pattern Recognition,* (pp. 762–768).

Jain, A.K., & Vailaya, A. (1996). Image retrieval using color and shape. *Pattern Recognition, 29*(8), 1233–1244.

Mandal, M., Idris, F., & Panchanathan, S. (1999). A critical evaluation of image and video indexing techniques in the compressed domain. *Image and Vision Computing, 17*(7), 513-529.

Niblack, W., Barber, R., Equitz, E., Flickner, M.D., Glasman, D., Petkovic, D., & Yanker, P. (1993). The QBIC project: Querying images by content using color, texture and shape. In *Conf. on Storage and Retrieval for Image and Video Databases, volume 1908 of Proceedings of SPIE,* (pp. 173–187).

Pass, G., & Zabih, R. (1996). Histogram refinement for content-based image retrieval. In *3rd IEEE Workshop on Applications of Computer Vision,* (pp. 96–102).

Picard, R.W. (1994). Content access for image/video coding: The fourth criterion. *Technical Report 195,* MIT Media Lab.

Qiu, G. (2003). Colour image indexing using BTC. *IEEE Trans. Image Processing, 12*(1), 93–101.

Schaefer, G., & Qiu, G. (2000). Midstream content access based on colour visual pattern coding. In *Storage and Retrieval for Image and Video Databases VIII, volume 3972 of Proceedings of SPIE,* (pp. 284–292).

Schaefer, G., Qiu, G. & Luo, M.R. (1999). Visual pattern based colour image compression. In *Visual Communication and Image Processing 1999,* volume 3653 *of Proceedings of SPIE,* (pp. 989–997).

Schaefer, G., & Lieutaud, S. (2004a). CVPIC compressed domain image retrieval by colour and shape. *Springer Lecture Notes in Computer Science, LNCS Vol. 3211,* (pp. 778-786).

Schaefer, G., & Lieutaud, S. (2004b). CVPIC based uniform/non-uniform colour histograms for compressed domain image retrieval. In *7th Int. Conference on VISual Information Systems,* (pp. 344-348).

Schaefer, G., Lieutaud, S., & Qiu, G. (2004). CVPIC image retrieval based on block colour co-occurance matrix and pattern histogram. In *IEEE Int. Conference on Image Processing,* pages 413-416.

Schaefer, G. (2008). Does compression affect image retrieval performance? *Int. Journal of Imaging Systems and Technology, 18*(2-3), 101-112.

Schaefer, G., & Stich, M. (2004). UCID - An Uncompressed Colour Image Database. In *Storage and Retrieval Methods and Applications for Multimedia 2004, volume 5307 of Proceedings of SPIE*, (pp. 472–480).

Stehling, R.O., Nascimento, M.A., & Falcao, A.X. (2002). A compact and efficient image retrieval approach based on border/interior pixel classification. In *11ᵗʰ Int. Conf. on Information and Knowledge Management*, (pp. 102–109).

Smeulders, A.W.M., Worring, M., Santini, S., Gupta, A., & Jain, R. (2000). Content-based image retrieval at the end of the early years. *IEEE Trans. Pattern Analysis and Machine Intelligence, 22*(12), 1249–1380.

Swain, M.J., & Ballard, D.H. (2001). Color indexing. *Int. Journal Computer Vision, 7*(11), 11–32.

Chapter XVIII
Resource Discovery Using Mobile Agents

M. Singh
Middlesex University, UK

X. Cheng
Middlesex University, UK
Beijing Normal University, China

X. He
Reading University, UK

ABSTRACT

Discovery of the multimedia resources on network is the focus of the many researches in post semantic web. The task of resources discovery can be automated by using agent. This chapter reviews the current most used technologies that facilitate the resource discovery process. The chapter also the presents the case study to present a fully functioning resource discovery system using mobile agents.

INTRODUCTION

Resource discovery is one of the main issues in the today's networks. The main target for any resource sharing system is to make available it resources to all other users. This can only be achieved if there is a service that allows discovering or matching of the attributes or the multi-attributes across heterogeneous domains. Such service is defined as resource discovery service (Paolo Trunfio, June 2007) (Miguel Castro, 2004). Typically, such system after matching the attributes will return a list of possible resource location where the resource is available. Peer-to-Peer (P2P) systems have been used for sharing resources (Miguel Castro, 2004). As nodes share resource a diverse set of techniques have been developed for discovering of the resource provider, assuming initial heuristics are available. The P2P systems are distinguished from other systems based on the fact of decentralization. There is not central authority that maintains the networks. Nodes can join the network and leave the network without destroying the resource network. The communication between two peers is a direct connection (Clip2, 2002). There has been multiple ways that have been devised to enhance the scalability of such networks.

Semantic Web addresses the navigation as compared to World Wide Web by creating a new approach in knowledge representation and different way of representing information on the Internet (McGuinness, March 2001). The Semantic Web is a network of information that could be easily processed by machines, on a global scale. It empowers the human user to employ agent software for searching as well as it enables the agent to act as the user's representative and that can enter transaction on behalf of the human user (McGuinness, March 2001) (Siderean Software, 2003).

A mobile agent is an autonomous and intelligent entity executing in computer environments. In addition to the characteristics inherited from the fixed agent, mobility is the most important attribute, which greatly improves the flexibility in multi-agent systems. As a fundamental building block of the mobile computing paradigm, the mobile agent has many potential applications in e-commerce and e-business (Yang, April, 2006). As a replacement of the traditional Remote Process Call (RPC) mode in which clients communicate with a non-local server with a static client-server interface, mobile agent enables the execution of the server side services within the server by travel to the local server host and interacts with it. After the completion of tasks, mobile agent will travel back to the client (service requester) with the service results. This reduces the need for bandwidth, as mobile agent can be very small in size (but can grow dynamically as needed to accommodate more data) (Dunne, 2001). In addition, there is no need for the centralized and real-time control of mobile agents. After a mobile agent is sent to the server (or other hosts), the creator of the mobile agent does not need to keep an eye on it until it travels back. The tasks are performed asynchronously. Also, users can create more than one agent for a specific task, and thereby enables the parallel processing of tasks. (Mobile agents are assigned to different sites to perform subtasks in parallel, and return the results of the sub tasks to the user. The user then would be able to make final decisions according to the returned results.)

The purpose of this chapter is provide a review of various technologies that have been applied in the field of resource discovery, so that a qualitative comparison of existing approaches can be performed and the conclusions can drawn to design an algorithm that can be applied to resource discovery using mobile agents. We will also depict what mobile agents are, and why they are in particular suitable for resource discovery.

A sample mobile agent system, demonstrating how resource discovery is achieved in a mobile agent system will be illustrated as well.

TECHNOLOGIES USED IN EXISTING RESOURCE DISCOVERY SYSTEMS

There are diverse set of solutions that are available for resource discovery. The solutions have been characterized through the routing strategies that have been applied by them. The main categories are algorithms that are used by unstructured networks and algorithms that are used by the overlay network between peers (Mordacchini, 2007).

In the unstructured networks the first technology that was applied was that of central servers. The technology was refined to get decentralized system for example GNUtella like systems, where the search message were routed using flooding techniques throughout the network that lead to saturation in the networks (Clip2, 2002) (Napster). The techniques were improvised to introduce data indexing that was further improvised with introduction of distributed hashing table (M. Castro, 2003). In this technique the node is associated with the keys and their values. When the query is presented it is changed in changed into the search for the key. The hash table passes the query forward to other node that is numerically closer to requested key (Miguel Castro, 2004) (I. Stoica, 2001) (Sylvia Ratnasamy, 2001). The examples of structured systems are Chord (I. Stoica, 2001) and CAN (Sylvia Ratnasamy, 2001). In hybrid systems like Pastry (Druschel, 2001) and Peer Discovery System the routing structure is comparatively more fluid as compared to Chord as the routing table can suggest the routing of the query to any node that is part of the defined subspace (Paolo Trunfio, June 2007).

Unstructured

The unstructured networks organize the nodes into a random graph and use floods to discover resource on the nodes. The nodes that are visited during the floods are checked against the query (Paolo Trunfio, June 2007) (Miguel Castro, 2004). This approach does not impose any constraints on the node graph. Any node can join any other node in the network and will only be discovered during flooding process. The centralized resource discovery queries the central server for node address that can provide certain resource, and will then connect to it directly as opposed to the decentralized approach where the nodes are peers and will query for resource through decentralized means of flooding the network (Y. Chawthe, 2003).

Centralized System

The famous example that describes the centralised systems is that of Napster. The Napster is not pure P2P system, since it requires the centralised servers and hence the category of the centralised systems. The central servers are used to keep the index of the resource that is owned by the certain peer on the network. The resource is located by querying the central server that after finding the matching resource will provides the IP address of the resource owner to the resource requestor. The IP address makes provision of direct connect between the two peers for the download of the resource (Mordacchini, 2007) (Napster). See Figure 1 for details of working.

The downloads take place in the P2P fashion; however the resource discovery is centralised. The fact that the resource discovery is centralised introduces the issue of the single point of failure. In case of central index failure the resources will not be available to any peers. Hence, the scalability of the centralised systems for resource discovery is very low (Y. Chawthe, 2003).

Decentralized System

In decentralized unstructured P2P systems, every peer maintains the connection with minimal set of the other peers. This leads to an overlay structure of the network. The famous example is that of GNUtella and Bearshare where there is no centralized index for the resources. The process of resource discovery is started by the peer's query that is broadcasted through this overlay network of peers, through the process called flooding (Clip2, 2002) (Mordacchini, 2007). When the query is received by the peer, it broadcasts it further to the peers that are connected to it, other than the peer from where the query was received. All the matching responses of the query are sent to the originating peer. This broadcasting of

Figure 1. A typical scenario of the centralised system. The peer A1, peer B1 and peer C1 are sharing resources 8, 9; 1,8,10 and 1, 2, 3 respectively. The central server, "Napster.com" that keeps the index of all resources shared by the peers. The central server is queried by the peer A1 and peer B1 for the resource 10 and resource 3 respectively. The central server replies by providing the IP address of the resource providers to each of the peers. The direct connection is established between two peers for downloading of the resource.

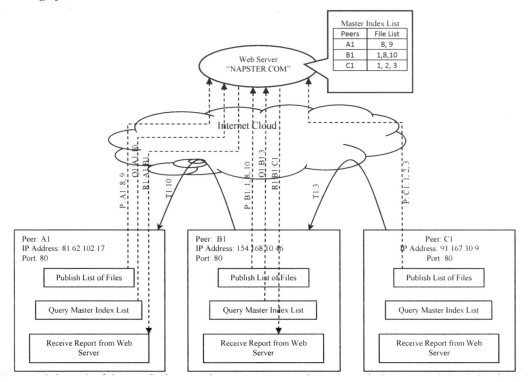

the query from one peer to all the other peers clearly results in unnecessary traffic on the network. To reduce the flooding, TTL (time to live) is associated with every query. Every time the query is received by a certain peer, in addition to providing the results for the query, it also reduces the TTL by one and then broadcasts it to all the downstream peers until the TTL drops to zero. This results in scalable flooding where the query will only reach certain depth and hence reduces the network coverage (Paolo Trunfio, June 2007). See Figure 2 and Figure 3 for workings.

The implication of the small TTL is that the resource may not be located by covering only little percentage of the network, when the resource may actually exist on the perimeters of the P2P network (Clip2, 2002) (Y. Chawthe, 2003).

There are number of ways have been devised to reduce the flooding. One of the controlled flooding mechanisms is called Dynamic Querying (Y. Chawthe, 2003). In order to reduce the flooding using dynamic query, the peer broadcasts the query to the other peers with very small TTL. If the matching results are found in the responses, then the connection between that node and the originating node are established. This reduces the cost of flooding dramatically. However, if the response for the query is not found then the TTL is dynamically increased in relation to the results obtained. This process continues

Figure 2. The diagram illustrates the flooding process. When the search begins from id=1, it is broad-casted to all the peers that are connected to the node with TTL=3. The TTL is decreased by 1 after every hop until TTL drops to zero. If the matching resource is found it is responding through the reverse path until it reaches to the originating node id=1. (Duncan Aitken, 2002)

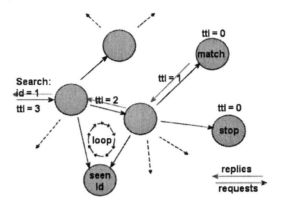

Figure 3. To download a file the client creates a direct connection to the client with the file it wants and sends a HTTP packet requesting the file. The client with the file interprets this and sends a standard HTTP response. (Duncan Aitken, 2002)

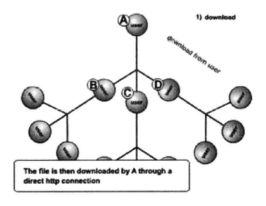

until the satisfactory results are obtained or until all the peers have been queried (Y. Chawthe, 2003).

Experiments further demonstrate that the peers that are connected to the network with low bandwidth saturate very quickly under flooding circumstances (Paolo Trunfio, June 2007) (Miguel Castro, 2004) (Mordacchini, 2007). This results in poor performance for the resource discovery. The solution to that is by isolating such peers with low bandwidth while routing. The peers with low bandwidth connect to the super peers which are have high bandwidth and will also keep the index of resources that are being shared by the low bandwidth. When the query is received by the super peer, it checks it against its and low bandwidth peers file index, if the result is found the connection between the originating peer and the peer with resource is established else the broadcast continues until TTL=0 (Y. Chawthe, 2003).

Structured

The structured system imposes constraints on node in network and data placement to enable efficient resource discovery (Paolo Trunfio, June 2007) (Mordacchini, 2007) (M. Castro, 2003). Each resource becomes a key and nodes are organized into structured graph that maps key to the node. The resource's address is stored at the node responsible for the key (Miguel Castro, 2004).

Chord

Chord (I. Stoica, 2001) is the structured P2P system that uses the distributed indexing based on hashing - distributed hash tables. In Chord, the peers are ordered in a virtual one-dimensional circle. The ordering is based on the IDs that are assigned to every peer based on their resources through a hash function (I. Stoica, 2001). Hence, peers and resources are mapped to a key. Each peer on the circle has knowledge of its successor in circle and it also maintains a routing table also called as finger table (Paolo Trunfio, June 2007) (I. Stoica, 2001).

In simple key location, every peer has knowledge of only one successor. When the peer n is presented with the key id, it checks the key against the finger table. If the key is found it returns the successor that is publishing the key id else it forwards the request to its successor to find the key id. This process will iterate until the key id is found or the all the nodes are exhausted (I. Stoica, 2001). See Figure 4.

In the scalable key location, a peer with a key z is connected to the peers with keys $(z+2i)$ mod N, where i is the entry in the finger table and the value of i ranges between $0 <= I < \log(N)$, N is the size of the key space. Therefore the finger table will have a maximum of log N entries in it (I. Stoica, 2001). See Figure 5 for details.

Figure 4. Simple key location. One dimensional circle where the nodes are evenly distributed on the circle. When the lookup is made for key id – 54 on node 8, it iterates through all active nodes to find the key id-54.

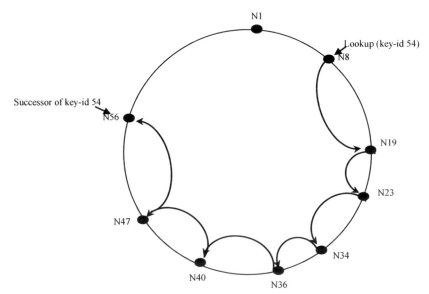

Figure 5. The finger table for node N8 that has knowledge about peers with keys (N8+2i) mod N for 0 ≤ i < log N.

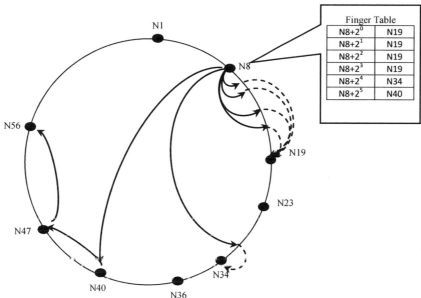

To speed the lookup process, when a peer Z is queried about the resource with key R, it uses the finger table to route the request to the node Z' whose ID is numerically closet to the ID of key R. This process of routing will iterate until the node ZR that publishes the resource R is reached. Lastly the node ZR contacts the node Z (Miguel Castro, 2004) (I. Stoica, 2001). See Figure 6 for details.

Using scalable lookup for key location the lookup latency is reduced as the routing is one for the nodes that are numerically close in underlying network (I. Stoica, 2001).

When a new peer N wants to join the Chord network, first of all the hash function is used to calculate the hash value for the peer and its resources. Following to this calculation, it contacts the peer N' that is already part of the Chord network, that will use its finger table to find the immediate successor N'' for the node N. N' will then return the ID of the successor N'' for the new node N. Clearly, the predecessor of the node N is old predecessor of N'' and the predecessor for N'' is the new node N. The finger table has to be up to date for the routing process to continue successfully and also to find the resource published by certain node. This process is schedules periodically through stabilization, where the nodes make checks about the entries in the table and their predecessors and successors. All new nodes are added in this process too. In case of removal of node N on the Chord network, it passes the keys that it has in its finger table to the successor N' and informs the predecessor N'' about the new successor N' (Mordacchini, 2007) (I. Stoica, 2001).

Content Addressable Network – CAN

CAN (Sylvia Ratnasamy, 2001) uses the basic principle from Chord by mapping the peer's key and the resources to a key space. The key space for the peers is seen as d-dimensional Cartesian space. This d-dimensional space is divided into all the available peers and each peer is responsible for all resources keys corresponding to points in its own Cartesian space. When a query is passed to the peer P, the query

Figure 6. Scalable key location. When the node N8 is queried for the key id - 54, it uses the finger table in the Figure 5 to locate the successor that is numerically closest or whose ID immediately precedes the key id - 54; i.e. the node N40. The node N40 uses its finger table route to N56 which has key K54.

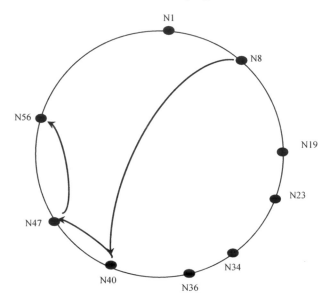

is translated into a d-dimensional space coordinate using the hash function that is used to place the keys in this space. If the peer P does not have any information about the requested coordinate, it passes the query to another node that is among its known nodes, and is geometrically close to the coordinate that is being searched. The process continues until the node that controls the zone to which searched item belong is reached (Paolo Trunfio, June 2007) (Sylvia Ratnasamy, 2001). See Figure 7 for details.

When the new node F wants to join the CAN network, it request randomly to a node E. The zone is then splitted into half assigned to the new node F. The routing table for the E and all the nodes in the routing table update their routing tables for this change. In case the node leaves the CAN network, it passes its region to the neighbour that splitted its space into half for this node. The update messages are also sent like Chord, to each of the neighbours reporting the zone coordinates, list of neighbours and their zone coordinates (Sylvia Ratnasamy, 2001).

Semantic Vector Space

Semantic vector space model is based on the Content Addressable Network – CAN that is based on distributed hashing table (S. Kang, 2007). CAN is used because of its support for d-dimensional space (Sylvia Ratnasamy, 2001). The resources are organised on their semantic vectors, that is, the more similar two resource's semantics, the closer the location of resolver registered in space. Each resolver is assigned a distinct zone. Zones are split as new resolvers join the Cartesian space. The semantic vector for resources is based on the ontology tree, which means the coordinates that are closer in this Cartesian space are similar to each other (S. Kang, 2007).

Figure 7. CAN – 2 dimensional space partitioned between 5 CAN nodes and coordinate space after F joined. If dimension d =2, then the available keys N are between (0,0) and ($N^{1/2}$, $N^{1/2}$). Hence the resource can be located in 2* $N^{1/2}$ hops.

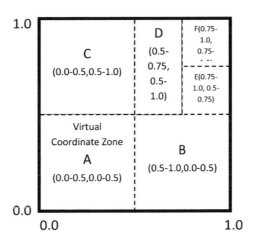

The registration message for resource R1 is routed to resolver N8, that manages the zone including R1's corresponding point PR1. When a query message for resource R2 with semantic distance d_{R2} is routed to N8 that is responsible for the zone containing R2's corresponding coordinate P_{R2}. In case N8 leaves the network the query is routed through the neighbour (for example N7 or N9), as long as their zones intersect search region, the circle whose radius is d_{R2} from P_{R2} (S. Kang, 2007). See Figure 8. for details.

Hybrid Systems

The hybrid systems impose the resource placement and the nodes in the graph like structured networks (Mordacchini, 2007). However as opposed to structured networks, the routing table can suggest the routing of the query to any node that is part of the defined subspace (Miguel Castro, 2004) (Mordacchini, 2007) (M. Castro, 2003).

Pastry

Pastry (Druschel, 2001) also shares its working principles with Chord. Each peer is mapped to a 128 bit random ID also called as Node Identifier, NodeID. All the nodes are placed in order on the one dimensional circle. Pastry node M maintains three tables for network and routing purposes; leaf set, routing table and neighbourhood set. The leaf set has L set of nodes, out of which mod(L)/2 number of nodes have nodeIDs less than and mod(L)/2, higher than that of nodeID of M. The routing table for nodeID of M contains one entry for each address assigned to it. These address blocks are calculated by recursively dividing the nodeID by b bits of length. Number of rows and columns for the routing table are given by log2bN and (2b-1) respectively. Each entry in row x and column y shares a prefix of length x with the present node. The x+1 digit of the node in row x is equal to the digit of the corresponding column y. The nodes in the neighbourhood set table are chosen based on the network proximity metric for example

Figure 8. CAN based semantic vector space model (S. Kang, 2007)

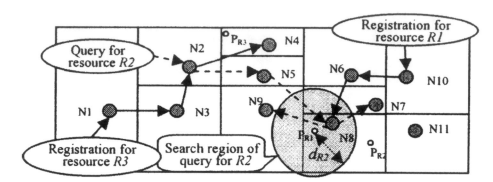

Figure 9. Pastry node with nodeID 10323201 and b=2. The shaded cells in each row of routing table shows the corresponding digit of the present node's nodeID. The nodeIDs in each entry splits recursively to show the common prefix with 10323201-next-digit-rest of the nodeID.

NODE ID 10323201			
Leaf Set	Smaller (<)	Larger (>)	
10323001 1	0323199	1032351 1 1	0323250
10323100 1	0323151	10323300 1	0323202
Routing Table			
-0-1121201	1	-2-2345678 -	3-1234567
0	1-1-311267 1	-2-234567	1-3-456202
10-0-49631 1	0-1-26911	12-2-45672	3
103-0-4321 1	02-1-4321	2	103-3-0121
1033-0-999 1	020-1-816	1032-2-101	3
10331-0-01 1	0231-1-01	2	
0	102312-1-6		
	1		
Neighbourhood Set			
01121201 1	0311267	10322101 3	1234567
10323100 1	0323199	10323300 3	1203210

Side notes:
|L|/2 numerically closest smaller node Ids

|L|/2 numerically closest larger node Ids

Number of rows = $\log_2^b N$

Each entry in row n shares prefix of length n with current node

Proximity metric to choose nodes

|M| closest nodes (based on proximity metric)

the number of IP routing hops. If no node is known with suitable nodeID, then the routing table entry is left empty (Paolo Trunfio, June 2007) (Druschel, 2001). See Figure 9. for details.

Given a message, the node N first checks to see of the key K is within the range of keys in the leaf set. The node in the leaf set that is numerically closet to the key receives the message. Else if the key is not within the range of leaf set then it passed on the routing table. The node than shares a common prefix with the key and at least one more digit is selected as destination node and the message is passed to this nodeID. In case the entry of such node is missing in routing table, the message is passed to the node that shares the common node that has prefix equal to N and is closer to Key K (Druschel, 2001). See Figure 10 for details.

In case node A wants to join the Pastry network, it connects to the node N that is already a part of this network. Node A receives a unique nodeID and asks N to route it to the correct zone of the one-

Fig.10. The route taken based on the routing table in Figure 9 for finding nodeID-31323110 from nodeID-10323201. The pseudo code shows the algorithm applied for finding the key D. Line 1-3 checks if the key D is covered by the leaf set $\pm|L|/2$, if so the message is forwarded to that node numerically closest to key D. Line 4-9 checks the routing table for node that shares the prefix with key D and one more extra digit, if so message is forwarded to that nodeID. Line 10-15 informs in case that no such node is found in routing table the prefix of D is matched against current node and also numerically closer to key D.

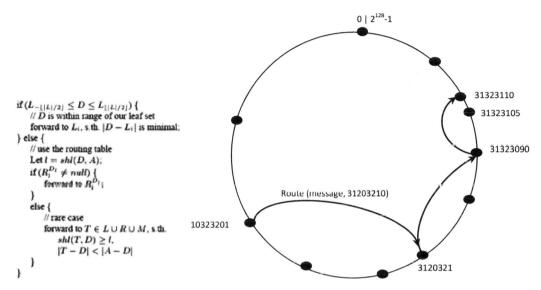

dimensional circle. Node A initializes the table, when it reaches the node Z that is numerically closest to A, with nodes that it routed during this phase. Node A also initializes its leaf set with that of Z. The routing table for A is filled with first row that contains nodes that do not share prefix with A. The second row of the node A routing table contains the second node that it encountered when joining the network, and so on. Finally the updated state information about the table is sent to set of known nodes (Druschel, 2001). See Figure 11 for details.

Mobile Agent System

The term agent has been widely used in different areas such as philosophy, linguistics, law, science, economics, and finance, with a distinct meaning in each of the areas. According to (YunYong Zhong, 2003), in computer science, agent can be classified into Human agent, Hardware agent, and Software agent. Software agent is a piece of code or software which is supposed to know how to make decisions and cope with difficulties independently (Wooldridge, 2002). Agents are intelligent individuals that have the characteristics of autonomy, reactivity, communication, pro-activity / goal oriented learning/adaptation, cooperation, coordination etc. In key areas of computer science such as web services, semantic grid and network security, agent technology has either been proved or is expected to improve the system performance and intelligence.

Software agent can be further classified according to the functions, attributes, and special types, as Figure 12 shows.

Figure 11. The route taken for inserting the new node d46a1c. The new node contacts a known node of Pastry network; 65a1fc that routes the request to the node that is closest numerically to the request node with one prefix matching d. This nodes routes in to the node d4213f with two matching prefixes and so on until the requested node is ordered in one dimensional circle.

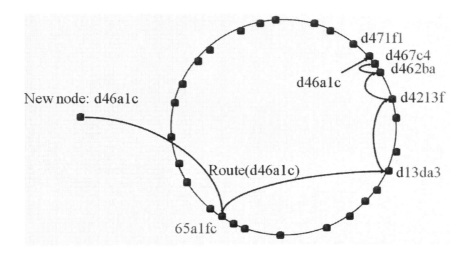

Figure 12. Software agent classification (YunYong Zhong, 2003)

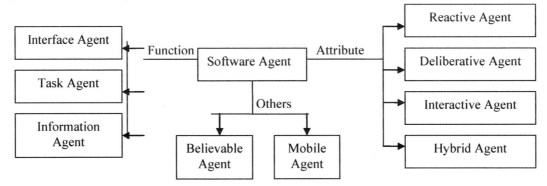

The following merits make mobile agents in particular suitable for resource discovery (Dunne, 2001):

- Asynchronous: After a mobile agent is dispatched, there is no need for the source peer to keep an eye on the mobile agent. The thread can be completely released. The original peer does not even need to remain connected to the network. The mobile agent will perform the given tasks completely in parallel with the original peer as a separate thread. After all of the tasks have been fulfilled, the mobile agent will return to the original peer (when it is connected to the network).

- Autonomous: The mobile agents decide the travel route as it progresses through the network. When a mobile agent is in a network peer, it is able to choose the next stop according to the network conditions it is learnt about, and the history of the visited peers and the current peer. Mobile agents may also visit peers that were unknown when it was originally dispatched, which in particular suits network based resource discovery.

- Information is being disseminated: Both the peer that a mobile agent visits and the mobile agent itself will benefit from accepting the mobile agent as they may receive either new or more recent information about resources. Although this accepting and hosting mobile agents results in the consumption of physical resources such as the computing resources and memory, it is manageable by the peer as the peer can easily refuse further requests to accept mobile agents when the physical resources become critical.

- Tasks are being performed in parallel: Tasks can be easily divided into sub-tasks and be performed by multi-mobile agents. Mobile agents may easily be cloned and dispatched in different directions, which allows them to function in parallel and thereby result in the earlier completion of work.

- Fault tolerant: Even if one mobile agent is destroyed by mistake or in purpose, all surviving ones will still have a positive impact. And the destroyed ones will have benefited every peer up to the point where they were destroyed.

- Compatibility: Agent based systems can be combined with successful features from other resource discovery systems.

The followings are the available architecture standard for mobile agent systems (Schoeman, 2003):

Foundation for Intelligent Physical Agent (FIPA) standard FIPA is the standards organization for agents and multi-agent systems who promotes agent-based technology and the interoperability of its standards with other technologies (Vieira, 2001). A collection of specifications have been provided, which are intended to promote the interoperation of heterogeneous agents and the services they represents. However these specifications are focussed on agent communication languages, agent management, message transport and the support for the use of ontologies in general. Many features that are specific to mobile agents are excluded from FIPA (Vieira, 2001).

Mobile Agent System Interoperability Facility (MASIF) standard OMG organization defined a standard named as MAF (later on changed to MASIF), which is aimed at promoting the interoperability of JAVA based mobile agent systems developed by different vendors (YunYong Zhong, 2003). MASIF presents a set of definitions and interoperable interfaces for mobile agent systems. The MAFAgentSystem interface and the MAFFinder interface are the two primary ones which are designed towards the following interoperability concerns (Schoeman, 2003): (1) management of agent, including creation, suspension, resumption and termination; (2) commonly accepted mobility infrastructure that enabling the communications between different mobile agent systems and the transport of mobile agents; (3) a standardised syntax and semantics for naming services; and (4) a standardised location syntax for finding agents. MASIF also excludes the following important architectural components in its standardisation attempts (Schoeman, 2003): (1) it only addresses interoperability between agent systems written in Java, thus brings the obstacle of the interoperability between non-java based systems and MASIF compliant systems; (2) it does not address local agent operations such as agent interpretation and execution; (3) some conventional issues of inter-agent communication are excluded (Dejan Milojicic, August 25, 2006).

The followings are the most popular mobile agent platforms (Schoeman, 2003):

Voyager (Voyager) is a commercial mobile agent platform supporting dynamic aggregation feature. The basic idea behind Voyager and dynamic aggregation feature is to reuse existing java classes and make objects of such classes mobile by means of incorporating those objects as its attachments (known as facets) and move from one site to another hence moving those objects with itself. The objects will retain their internal state upon moving from one host to another (Johnny Wong, 2001).

Scalable Mobile and Reliable Technology (SMART) SMART (Johnny Wong, 2001) is a MASIF specification compliant client-server based mobile agent platform. As Figure 13 shows, there are four main components in smart architecture (Johnny Wong, 2001): Region administrator, which uses a finder model to provide naming services to the region administrator and also to the agent system; Agent system, enables mobile agents to create, migrate and destroy themselves; Place, forms the execution environment; and Agent proxy, provides the mobile agent API for applications written in SMART.

D'Agents (Robert S. Gray) is a general purpose mobile agent system which was developed to support distributed information retrieval and to support for strong mobility and multi-agent languages. Using D'Agent, several information-retrieval applications, ranging from searching three-dimensional drawings of mechanical parts for a needed part to supporting the operational needs of a platoon of soldiers have been implemented. The architecture of D'Agent is shown in Figure 14 TCP/IP is used to provide transport mechanism. Server layer is a multi-threaded process and runs multiple mobile agents as threads inside a single process. The Generic C/C++ core layer holds shared C++ libraries used by agent threads. The upper layer provides the execution environment for Java, Tcl, or Scheme. The agents themselves are defined on the top layer (Schoeman, 2003).

Grasshopper is an OMG MASIF and FIPA-conformant agent platform, which consists of a Distributed Agent Environment (DAE) and a Distributed Processing Environment, as Figure 15 shows.

A host in the distributed agent environment include an agency that has access to the services including execution, transport, management, communication, security, naming mechanism, adapter interfaces for external hardware/software, task control functions, and application-specific GUIs (Schoeman, 2003). The distributed processing environment is composed of following components: Regions, facilitates the management of the distributed components (agencies, places, and agents) in the Grasshopper environment; Places, provides a logical grouping of functionality inside an agency; Agencies, as well as their places can be associated with a specific region by registering them within the accompanying region registry; and Different types of agents – mobile agents and stationary agents. Mobile agents move from one platform to another, whereas stationary agents reside on one platform permanently (Grasshopper Mobile Agent Platform).

Figure 13. The SMART architecture (Johnny Wong, 2001)

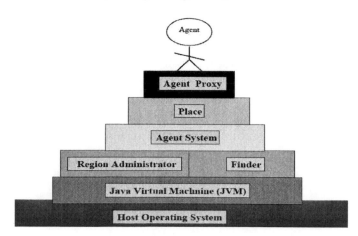

Figure 14. The D'Agent architecture

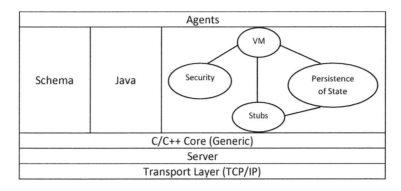

Figure 15. The simplified version of Grasshopper Architecture. The basic services include MASIF and Core Services. MASIF includes agent creation, destruction, suspend, activate and location services and Core services include agent execution, transport, management, communication, security and naming. The enhanced services include APIs, GUIs and task control features.

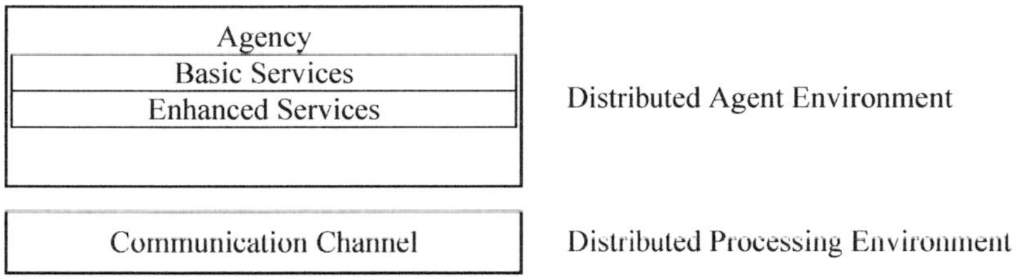

Agency
Basic Services
Enhanced Services

Distributed Agent Environment

Communication Channel

Distributed Processing Environment

Aglets (Aglet) is a well known java based mobile agent platform, which contains libraries for developing mobile agent based applications. As Figure 16 shows, Aglets' architecture consists of two layers: Runtime layer, consists of a core framework and sub-components to provide services such as serialization/de-serialization, class loading and transfer, reference management and garbage collection, persistence management, maintenance of byte code, and protecting hosts and agents from malicious entities; and Communication layer, defines the methods for creating and transferring agents, and tracking and managing agents in an agent-system-and-protocol-independent way (Schoeman, 2003).

The detailed features of existing mobile agent platforms are shown in Table 1.

Peer Discovery Algorithm using Mobile Agent

This algorithm is hybrid algorithm that uses some of the techniques from unstructured and other from structured resource discovery. The set of nodes N are connected to each other using graph. The heuristics for node are defined as graph G =(V,E), where V is set of nodes in G and E is the set of edges that are available for the mobile agent. Each node is identified using its nodeID based in the 128 bit IP address assigned to it. Each node publishes its resource as semantic information formally as ontology (S. Ding, 2005).

Figure 16. The Aglets architecture (Schoeman, 2003)

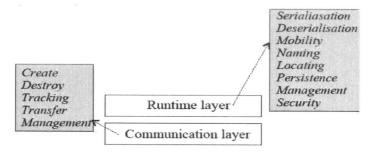

Table.1. Comparative table for P2P based systems and the mobile agent system

	Number of Rounds	Pointer Communication	Connection Communication	Payload
Structured and Unstructured Systems	Initial hypothetical number	Every pointer is sent over edge during algorithm	There are at least initial rounds during which each node opens up connection with all hypothetical neighbors	Message based payload increased due to initial rounds
Mobile agent based	Initial hypothetical number	Pointer sent to only two nodes	There are at least two nodes that open connection	Minimal as the mobile agent is sent as package.

Each node X is provided the hypothetical set of ±5 IP addresses (I), which are numerically close to the IP address of the node X. When the query Q is presented to the node X, an attempt is made to contact the nodes I. The two nodes that reply in earliest possible time are chosen for querying by the mobile agent A1 and A2, about the semantic information they publish and the matchmaking algorithm is applied. Each agent is assigned a TTL, when the node is captured by agents, TTL is reduced by one. This process iterates until the TTL is reduced to zero. The replies from other prospective nodes that have delayed reply are nullified. The neighbourhood table is updated with the state of captured nodes. The next hop for the agent is done based on the set nodes I on node X that are free. The central repository on node X ensures that latency is minimal and network saturation is kept to minimal. This process iterates until the TTL has dropped to zero or all the set of nodes available have been exhausted (M. Singh, 2006). The most important decisions that are outcome of this resource discovery algorithm are as follows:

- Those nodes that are online and have server host and fall in the category of search query.
- Those nodes that are online and have server host, but not fall in the category of search query.
- Those nodes that are online and have no ontology server
- Those nodes that not online

For query

Initialize set nodes I

    If I are in state "available"

        Issue to agent for querying

    Else

        Initializes I

Agent requesting for more nodes

Find Sender S

    If repository contains an item I that has sender S

        Set item I as invaded

    Else

        Issue the set of items I' from repository that have state available

The algorithm for the resource discovery using mobile agent suggested can be model as a non-autonomous differential equation. The rate of depletion of nodes that are unknown is directly proportional to the mobile agent size which know the nodes and also to the size of unknown nodes and inversely proportional to the change in size of nodes (B. Kegan, 2005). If the factor β is used as constant then it can be expressed as

$$\frac{du}{dt} = -\beta \frac{u(n'(t) - u)}{n'(t)} \text{ (B. Kegan, 2005)} \tag{1}$$

The rate of depletion of unknown nodes in equation 1 is inspired for logistic differential equation (B. Kegan, 2005).

The function can be plotted to shows that after time z a node becomes aware of almost all nodes in the network at that moment in time. However, the asymptotic behavior of this curve informs the unknown nodes may never know about the all known nodes as number of nodes is changing randomly. The actual time z and depletion factor $- \beta$ can be found through simulations.

Findings from Various Algorithms

The structured systems perform better than unstructured systems with respect to scalability, as DHT has many advantages, such as scalability, load balancing, logarithmic hop routing, fault tolerance, and a self organizing nature. Although self-organizing works as the advantage but as each peer must periodically update all its neighbours and hence result in increased traffic (C. Mastroianni, 2005). When the nodes leave or join the network the updated index need to be redistributed and hence the tables need to restructure. Although, the nodes involves is this restructuring may be very few, however the periodic updates can sum up to significant traffic on network (Mordacchini, 2007). This is not the case in unstructured systems as node can leave or join the network without sending stabilization message. Unstructured systems have provided many strategies for reducing traffic like dynamic querying, routing indices, and super-peers architectures (Y. Chawthe, 2003). The structured systems have advantage over unstructured systems as these systems provide the ability to route the queries in very small number of hops. Both Chord and Pastry resolve the queries in O(log N), while CAN requires O(N1/d) steps,

Table 2. Comparative table for various algorithms

System	Architecture	Routing	Load Balancing	Periodic Updates
Centralized Systems	Not Pure P2P	Query to Central Server	No	No
Decentralized Systems	P2P	Flooding	Super peers will index resources for peers with low bandwidth. And TTL	No
Chord	Distributed Hash Table	Finger table	Exchange of load between neighbours	Stabilization process
Content addressable network - CAN	Distributed Hash Table	Calculation of coordinates in d-dimensional space for results that are intersecting with query.	Neighbour load exchange	Routing of updates periodically
Pastry	Distributed Hash Table	Leaf set, Routing table and Neighbourhood set	Leave and join protocol.	Stabilization Process
Matchmaking	Semantic Based	NA	NA	NA
Semantic Vector Space	Distributed Hash Table for Semantic Vectors	CAN	Neighbuor informed about joining and leaving	Routing of updates periodically
Resource Discovery using MA	Centralized Repository for Mobile Agent on parent node based Hash table	Mobile Agent, state of the hash table	No two agent will create traffic by visiting same node and in case of leaving the hash table is updated.	Hash table issues only the nodes that are free.

where N is number of nodes and d is number of dimensions in CAN. As the peers and the resources are based on the hash function – key generated by the hash function is very specific (I. Stoica, 2001) (Sylvia Ratnasamy, 2001). As the queries may not be exact, some times it may be difficult to find the resource in the structured network (C. Mastroianni, 2005).

Both systems heavily rely on stationary agent. Stationary agents keep track of all resource discoveries. This will use the host computer resources and can potentially drain the local resources and may cause failure of host computer. The back bone of both approaches is P2P communication. P2P communication blurs the distinction between client and server computers. This can potentially saturate the network. Unstructured resource discovery - is a linear connection between computers where each computer (agent) knows the ping computer. Failure of any computer in the chain results to loss of all down stream resources. Furthermore, the issue of recoverability from failure in both architectures is very vulnerable against failure (Miguel Castro, 2004).

Semantic information based resource discovery is more precise (Siderean Software, 2003) (S. Kang, 2007). The SVS and Peer Resource Discovery are few agent based techniques using semantic information in service description that should be applied to P2P networks. The mobile agents for resource discovery require lesser bandwidth (Schoeman, 2003). As opposed to the multiple interactions between peers, mobile agent tends to pack these interactions and send them as discrete piece of traffic. Also mobile agents are much smaller in size and grow dynamically as they accommodate more data (Schoeman, 2003). In structured or unstructured systems, the communication is synchronous which is not the case with mobile agent which can encapsulate its state and carry on the execution on the different node asynchronously (Oshima, 1998).

Table 3 summarizes the structured, unstructured and semantic based systems described above in terms of architecture, routing, load balancing, and periodic updates.

SAMPLE MOBILE AGENT BASED RESOURCE DISCOVERY SYSTEM

The following system is illustrated to explain in a more intuitive way that how a resource discovery system functions using mobile agents. The system is fully implemented in Java.

Scenario

The query word "academic" is search item that needs to found in the university network. This means the mobile agent must find the node in the network that provides "academic" ontology. For the experimental reasons 31 node in the research room are used. The client computer plays the role of the host computer or node 1. The 30 nodes are potential ontology providers. The 30 nodes are queried by the mobile agent to make them fall into one of the following categories: nodes with platform service installed and "academic" resource published, Nodes with platform installed and "philosophy" resource published, Nodes with platforms but no ontology resource, and Nodes with no platform at all.

System Architecture

The system level architecture diagram (Figure 17) illustrates the node 1 where the client requests for information about the certain query and passes it to the platform. To perform the search; the platform initializes the agent to perform the task of searching. The task of searching is done by the mobile agent by migrating from one node to the other. These nodes are proximity metric closer to node 1. Since two agents performing same task created from same mother node (node 1) can visit the same node, the knowledge base is kept centrally, hence making the redundancy of agent equal to zero. The centrally available repository also keeps the state of every node that has been visited the agents. Every time the agents migrate, the request for new set of nodes is passed to node 1, which ensures collection of resource heuristics and stopping agents to visit nodes that have been already visited by other agents for same query or take the reverse path.

Platform Level Architecture

The platform level architecture (Figure 18) shows the system components that provide platform support to the mobile agents. Each node that is part of the resource discovery network must have the platform service so that the agents can execute and perform the various tasks that are assigned to them by clients. In order to publish the resource the node will use the components of ontology support. Furthermore, for migration to other nodes the agent will use the migration support and the knowledge base pack. These components put together act as mobility pack, as they will provide essential knowledge to the agent for the next migration and will also serialize and de-serialize the state of the agent for migration. Another important component is that of persistence that is used in conjunction with migration support this will

Table 3. Comparative table for various algorithms Table.3. The features of mobile agent systems (Robert S. Gray)

System	Languages	Thread migration	Data migration	Code migration	Multithreaded agents?
Aglets [LO98]	Java	weak, fixed entry	Java serialization	sender push or on-demand from server	no
Ara [PS97, Pei98]	C, C++, Tcl	strong	custom	sender push	no
Bond [BJP$^+$00]	Java, Python, Jess	weak, ?	custom	sender push?	yes?
Concordia [WPW$^+$97, WPW98]	Java	weak, itinerary	Java serialization in various ways	sender push or on-demand from sender	yes
D'Agents [GKCR98, BMcI$^+$00, KGN$^+$97]	Java, Tcl, Scheme	strong	custom	sender push	no
FarGo [HBSG99]	Java	weak, ?	Java serialization		
Grasshopper [BM98]	Java	weak, ?		on-demand from sender?	yes
Jumping Beans [AA98]	Java	weak; itinerary	Java serialization?	sender push	yes
Messengers [TDM$^+$94, TMN97, DMTH95, Muh98]	M0	weak	manual	sender push	no
Mole [BHRS98, SR99]	Java	weak, fixed entry	Java serialization	on-demand from code server	yes
μCODE [Pic98a, Pic98b]	Java	weak, ?		many ways	possible
NOMADS [SBB$^+$00]	Java (custom JVM)	strong	custom JVM	sender push	yes
[Visual] Obliq [Car95, BN97, BC95]	Obliq	weak	push desired objects	push desired procedure	
Tacoma [JvRS95, JSvR98]	v1.2: C+others. V2.0: C only	weak, ?	manual	sender push	yes
Telescript [Whi94b, Whi94a, Whi97]	Telescript	strong	custom	sender push	no
Voyager [OBJ97]	Java	weak	Java serialization		yes

continued on following page

Table 3. continued

System	Persistence?	Communication	Authentication	Access control	Resource control
Aglets [LO98]	yes	send object as message, via proxy	programmer signs code, user signs data	ACL based on sigs?	
Ara [PS97, Pei98]	yes	free-form via named rendezvous points	programmer signs code, user signs data	ACL based on sigs?	allowances based on sigs
Bond [BJP+00]	no?	KQML, XML messages			
Concordia [WPW+97, WPW98]	yes	send object as event, publish/subscribe	signed by user	ACL based on user	no
D'Agents [GKCR98, BMcI+00, KGN+97]	no	string messages	agent signed by user and sending machine	ACL based on user	limits on user; market-based control
FarGo [HBSG99]		method calls or events			
Grasshopper [BM98]		send object; various protocols	SSL, X.509		
Jumping Beans [AA98]	yes	CORBA method calls	central server authenticates all	ACL based on user	limits in ACL
Messengers [TDM+94, TMN97, DMTH95, Muh98]		local: shared memory and bulletin board; remote: none			market-based
Mole [BHRS98, SR99]	sophisticated rollbacks	send object; message, RPC, or publish/subscribe			no
µCODE [Pic98a, Pic98b]	no	send object	no	no	no
NOMADS [SBB+00]	no	raw messages	accounts and passwords	Java security, per-account policy file	mechanisms for limiting usage
[Visual] Obliq [Car95, BN97, BC95]		method invocation	no crypto	ACL	no
Tacoma [JvRS95, JSvR98]		raw message	relies on OS	relies on OS	no
Telescript [Whi94b, Whi94a, Whi97]	yes	method invocation or events	agent signed by user	"permits" assigned based on user	"permits" assigned based on user
Voyager [OBJ97]	yes	method call via proxy, or publish/subscribe			

enable collection of sensory information about physical movement and hence enabling the agent after migration is completed.

Class Diagram

Class diagram (Figure 19) provides the static view of the system. We feel that the figure is not very expressive because it does not show the agent communication faithfully. The location of the agent is

Figure 17. The system level architecture

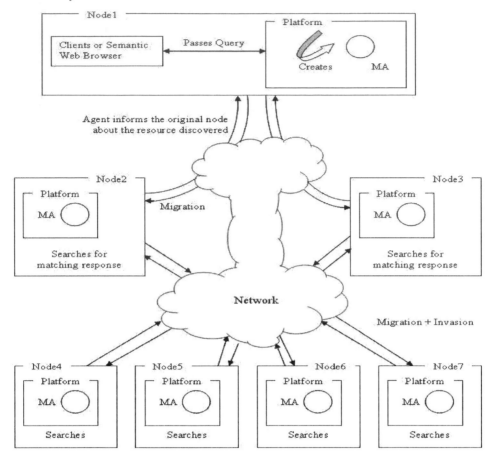

described in its relation to the host computer that is not shown in this diagram. Although class diagram is informing the abstract view of the system, still we believe that this diagram is too generic because of its inadequacy to inform the relation between the service and itself from remote and local perspective. However, the class diagram shows the general relationship of two main components; Platform and the MA of MAS regardless of location of host or agent. There two component in the MAS. One is the platform that provides host with functionality and the other is the Agent that offers the resource discovery functionality. In the following; first the classes that make platform will be discussed and then followed by the classes that make an agent.

Platform Classes

Ontology Interface

An interface is a pure virtual class that defines the methods and the arguments to the methods that will be available in a class that implements it. These methods will however be implemented by separate class. The design has been chosen in such a way because the object needs to be available to remotely. Rather than making a copy of the implementation object in the receiving Java virtual machine, RMI passes

Figure 18. The platform level architecture

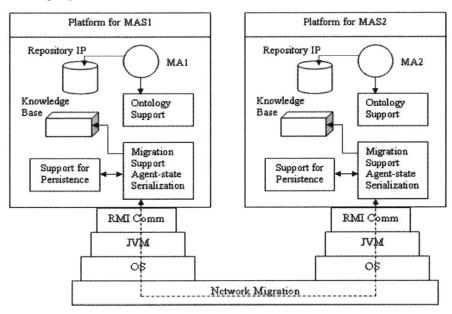

Figure 19. The class diagram

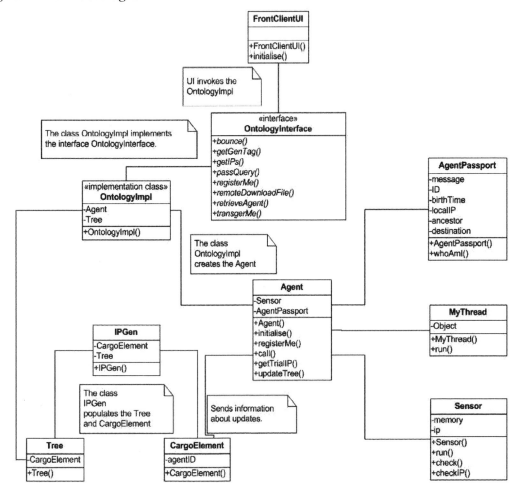

a remote stub for a remote object. The stub acts as the local representative, or proxy, for the remote object and to the client as the remote reference. The client invokes a method on the local stub, which is responsible for carrying out the method invocation on the remote object (M. Singh, 2006).

OntologyImpl Class

This class is the implementation of the OntologyInterface. This class provide functionality such as moving the agent providing central repository for agents, communication facility for agent to registering, retrieving agent after migration and creating the mobile agent. This class acts as the control class for the platform as it is responsible for all the binding the platform with an IPAddress, publish the resource and also creation of hypothetical list of nodes (M. Singh, 2006).

Tree Class

This class is a utility class that can only be accessed OntologyInterface. The instance of this class acts as a repository that hold a list of neighbourhood nodes in form of their IP addresses. This class holds the IP addresses as a binary tree. Tree class at the beginning of the search contains a hypothetical list of the nodes and by the end of the search it holds an actual map of heuristics of where the resource may exist. The process of resource discovery is done by the mobile agent that undergoes the migration based on the hypothesis provided by this repository. The repository also acts as knowledge base that accumulates the knowledge gathered by the mobile agent. This class provide an essential knowledge to mobile agent and helps mobile agents to synchronise their behaviour to avoid duplication and redundancy. As the mobile agents progress into the unknown environment, they always consult the Tree class and update it with their finding (M. Singh, 2006).

IPGen Class

IPGen is another utility class that take an IP address as base and generates hypothetical nodes based on the current node's IP. This class populates the Tree repository class (M. Singh, 2006).

CargoElement Class

This class is used for communication burst between agent and the platform (OntologyImpl). The information is loaded to this object as single object or as an array and send back and forth between agent and OntologyImpl (M. Singh, 2006).

OntologyServer Class

This class is responsible to create an instance for implementation of the OntologyInterface and registers it to RMI registry (M. Singh, 2006).

FrontClient Class

This class is used to pass the query search to Agent. In other word this class will initiate the search (M. Singh, 2006).

OntologyMole

This class provides the semantic web category. When an agent arrived in particular host, it will read the ontology category from this class (M. Singh, 2006).

Agent Classes

Agent Class

This threaded class is a main body of the agent component. It initializes other classes that belong to mobile agent components. It is responsible for communication with local and potential hosts. Agent is the owner of the segment of knowledge base and responsible for examining and updating it. Agent class is responsible for updating the central knowledge base (M. Singh, 2006).

AgentPassport Class

This class acts as identity provider for the Agent class. The persistence for agent's state after the migration will be provided through this class. It helps agent to know who it is; what is its goal; where is it at any given time and where is the home node (M. Singh, 2006).

Sensor Class

It is synchronised thread class that act as a sensor to agent. It helps the agent to react to the host change and reinitiate the Agent. It reads the local node from the Agent passport and updates it with current location. If it senses the current location is changed it calls the agent and causes the agent to renew its database for search based on new location (current host IP) (M. Singh, 2006).

Mythread Class

This class asynchronously contacts the other nodes by searching for platform in the destination nodes. This class contacts the destination node and waits for the reply. Based on the reply and the waiting time this thread will inform the agent. The analogy of this class can done to the another sensory device that looks to a location and try to find the whether the location under investigation fall into the search category or not (M. Singh, 2006).

Sequence Diagram

The sequence diagram (Figure 20) illustrates the movement of the agent with respect to the internal functions. The query is passed by the user through the implemented method passquery of the ontologyimpl class. This initialises the agent that in turn creates the agent passport and changes the state of the sensor thread. The agent then requests for the set of trial IPs through getTrialIP() method. The ontologyimpl further request the tree repository for the IPs through getip() and initiate cargoelement object for storing the IPs. The agent then uses the IPs and pass them to mythread object that initiate the method bounce() on the remote object of the remote nodes (possibly resources). If the nodes exists, it returns a reply through the call() method to the mother node passed during bounce(). The agent then compares the results for time proximity metric and requests the ontology interface for transferring it to the remote node through transferme() method. The ontologyimpl object calls the remote method remotedownloadFile() on the remote object that is chosen based on the time proximity metric. Before migration the state of agent is written into the agent passport and the agent passport object is serialized. On the next node, sensor detects the change in IP address through localIP() method and reinitiates the agent with its state from the deserialized agent passport. Agent the informs the mother node about the state of the resource and requests for more trialIPs through getTrialIP() method. This whole process is iterated until the TTL for the migration reduces to zero.

Figure 20. The sequence diagram (M. Singh, 2006)

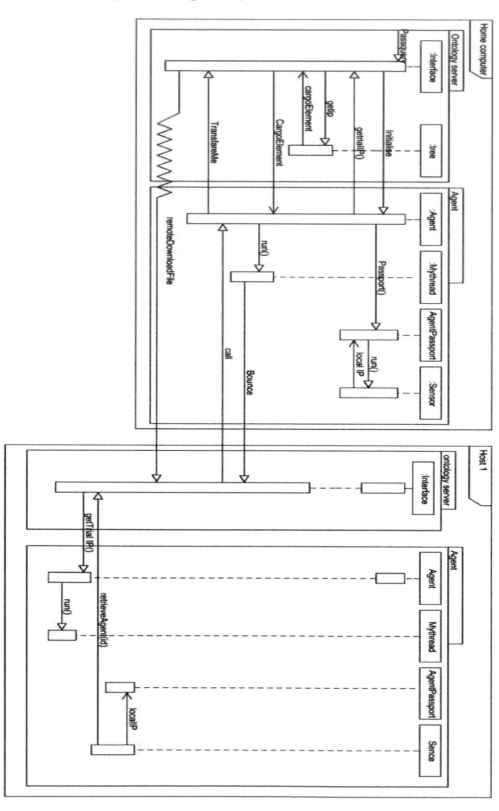

Figure 21. The activity diagram (M. Singh, 2006)

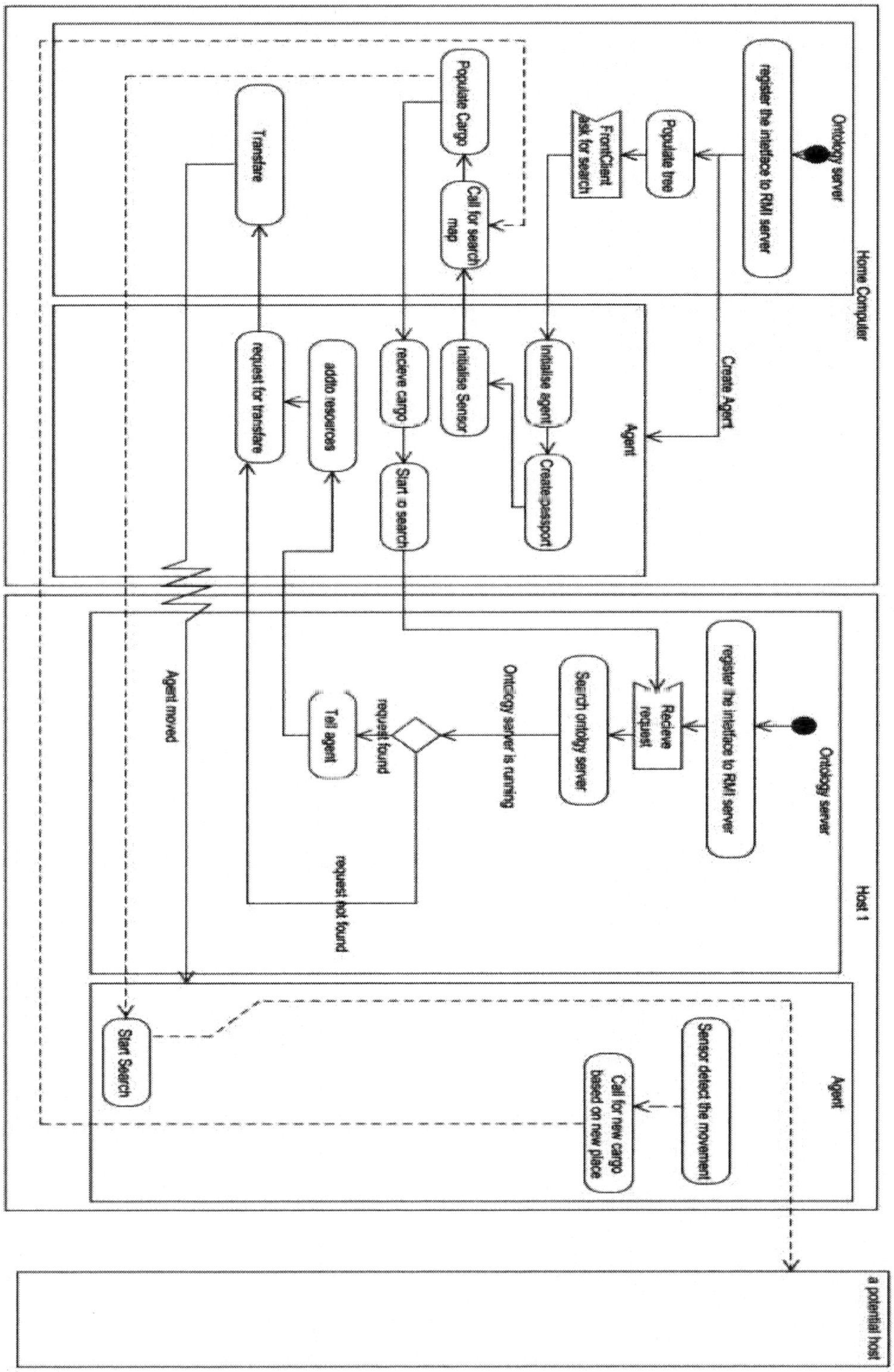

Activity Diagram

The activity diagram (Figure 21) for the MAS system depicts a typical scenario where the ontology server is initialized as a service which provides the platform where the agent can perform its task. This service is available on the all the potential host. The agent is created at this stage, however it is not initialized. The list for the potential destination hosts is created after initialization of the service and this list is saved in the tree data structure. When the query is passed by the front end client, it is passed to the agent by the ontology server, which makes agent active. Agent passport that acts as the memory for the agent is created with this initialization. The sensor for the stimuli of movement is also created at this stage. Agent requests the ontology server for list of hosts that it needs to visit. The server loads this information as cargo (payload) object and passes it to the agent. Following to these initial steps, the agent starts its task of contacting potential host provided to it by the cargo object. Agent waits for reply from the potential remote host (for instance Host 1 in above figure). If the agent does not receive any reply in finite period of time, it stops listening to that host. However, if the reply is received, it requests the ontology server to transfer it to the remote host. When the agent is at the remote host, the sensor informs the agent about movement after comparing its information against the passport. This mobility is strong mobility as agent can suspend its activity at any time, has its memory and can reinitialize it self on the new host and continue from the state where it suspended its control on the last host.

System Evaluation

The scenario has been implemented and works in an efficient manner. The results for the resource discovery are good as there is reduction in the redundancy of visited nodes. The authors are also experimenting with other resource discovery algorithms so as to have distributed knowledge base and having stabilisation process for periodic updates. This scenario describes how the mobile agent can be used for semantic data mining and resource discovery.

CONCLUSION

Using the mobile agent for resource discovery has advantage over the traditional approach. Mobile agents engage in gradual discovery process and respond to changing set of requirements. The mobile agents can change behaviour based upon the results of the inference process. When the agent needs detailed information about the system, the repository is used to dynamically provide based on the state of remote resources.

REFERENCES

Aglet. (2002). Retrieved from http://www.trl.ibm.com/aglets/

Castro, P.Y.M. (2003). *Proximity neighbor selection in tree-based structured peer-to-peer overlays*. Technical Report MSR-TR-2003-52.

Chawthe, S.R.Y. (2003). Making GNUtella-like P2P systems scalable. *Applications, Technologies, Architectures, and Protocols for Computer Communication.*

Clip2. (2002). *The GNUtella Protocol Specification v0.4 Document Revison 1.2.* Retrieved September 23, 2007, from Limewire: http://www9.limewire.com/developer/gnutella_protocol_0.4.pdf

Dejan Milojicic, M.B. (August 25, 2006). MASIF: The OMG Mobile Agent System Interoperability Facility. *Personal and Ubiquitous Computing* , (pp. 117-129).

Ding, J.Y.S. (2005). *A Heuristic Algorithm for Agent-Based Grid Resource Discovery.* Washington.

Druschel, A.R. (2001). Pastry: scalable decentralized object location, and routing for large scale peer-to-peer systems. In *Proceedings of IFIP/ACM Internation Conference on Distributed Systems Platforms*, Heidelberg, Germany.

Duncan Aitken, J.B. (2002). *Peer-to-Peer Technologies and Protocols.* Retrieved 2007, from NTRG: http://ntrg.cs.tcd.ie/undergrad/4ba2.02/p2p/index.html

Dunne, C.R. (2001). *Using Mobile Agents for Network Resource Discovery in Peer-to-Peer Networks*, *2*(3), 1-9.

Emerson F.A.L.,P.D. (2004, May). An Approach to Modelling and Applying Mobile Agent Design Patterns. *ACM SIGSOFT Software Engineering Notes* (pp. 1-8). New York: ACM Press.

Grasshopper Mobile Agent Platform. (n.d.). Retrieved 2007, from http://cordis.europa.eu/infowin/acts/analysis/products/thematic/agents/ch4/ch4.htm

Gray, G.C.R.S. (n.d.). *D'Agents: Applications and Performance of a Mobile-Agent System*, *35*(6), 543-573.

Hansen, K. (2003). *Lecture 11.* Retrieved 2007, from P2P Lectures: http://www.daimi.au.dk/~marius/p2p-course/lectures/11/talk.html

Kang, Y.L.S. (2007). A Landmark-Based Scalable Semantic Resource Discovery Scheme. *E90-D,* (6).

Kegan, R.W. (2005). Modelling the simple epidemic with differential equations and random initial conditions. *Mathematical Biosciences* , *197*(1).

Kusek, M.A. (2006). Extending UML Sequence Diagrams to Model Agent Mobility. In *Agent-Oriented Software Engineering, 7th International Workshop* (pp. 51-63). Hakodate, Japan: Springer Berlin/Heidelberg.

Mastroianni, D.T.C. (2005). A Super Peer Model for Building Resource Discovery Services in Grods: Design and Simulation Analysis. In *LNCS: Proceedings European Grid Conference (EGC 2005).*

McGuinness, N.F. (2001, March). *Ontology Development 101: A Guide to creating Your First Ontology.* Stanford: Stanford Knowledge Systems Laborartory technical report KSL-01-05 and Stanford Medical Informatics Technical Report SMI-2001-0880.

Miguel Castro, M.C. (2004). *Peer-to-peer overlays: structured, unstructured, or both?* Technical Report MSR-TR-2004-73. Cambridge.

Mordacchini, M. (2007). *Grid and Peer-to-Peer Resource Discovery Systems.* Universita Ca Foscari Di Venezia, PhD Thesis.

Mylopoulos, M.K. (2001). UML for Agent-Oriented Software Development: The Tropos Proposal. In *Lecture Notes in Computer Science* (pp. 422-441). *Proceedings of UML 2001.*

Napster. (n.d.). Retrieved September 12, 2007, from http://www.napster.com

Oshima, D.L. (1998). *Programming and Deploying Java Mobile Agents with Aglets.* Addison Wesley.

Paolo Trunfio, D.T. (June 2007). *Peer-to-Peer Models fot Resource Discovery on Grids.* Italy: Core Grid - Institute on System Architecture.

Ratnasamy, P.F.S. (2001). A Scalable Content-Addressable Network. In *Proceedings of the 2001 conference on applications, technologies, architectures, and protocols for computer communications.*

Schoeman, M.a. (2003). Architectural Components for the Efficient Design of the Mobile Agent Systems. *ACM International Conference Proceedings Series; Vol. 47* (pp. 48-58). South Africa: South African Institute for Computer Scientists and Information Technologies.

Siderean Software. (2003, January). *From Site Search to the Sematic Web.* Los Angeles, CA, USA.

Singh, M. & Zojajiy, H. (2006). *Infrastructure for Resource Discovery using Mobile Agents.* London.

Stoica, R.M. (2001). Chord: A Scalable Peer-to-Peer Lookup Service for Internet Applications. In *Proceedings of the 2001 ACM SIGCOMM Conference*, San Diego.

Vieira, S. (2001). *Foundation of Intelligent Agents - Agent Communication Language.* FIPA.

Voyager. (n.d.). Retrieved 2007, from http://www.recursionsw.com

Wong, G.H.J. (2001). SMART Mobile Agent Facility. *Journal of Systems and Software*, (pp. 9-22).

Wooldridge, M. (2002). *An Introduction of Multi Agent Systems.* John Wiley & Sons, Inc.

Yang, S. Z. (April, 2006). Verifiable Distributed Oblivious Transfer and Mobile Agent Security. 11 (2), 201-210

Zhong, J.L.Y.Z. (2003). *The Mobile Agent Technology.* ISBN 7-89494-143-3.

Chapter XIX
Multimedia Data Indexing

Zhu Li
Hong Kong Polytechnic University, Hong Kong

Yun Fu
BBN Technologies, USA

Junsong Yuan
Northwestern University, USA

Ying Wu
Northwestern University, USA

Aggelos Katsaggelos
Northwestern University, USA

Thomas S. Huang
University of Illinois at Urbana-Champaign, USA

ABSTRACT

The rapid advances in multimedia capture, storage and communication technologies and capabilities have ushered an era of unprecedented growth of digital media content, in audio, visual, and synthetic forms, and both individually and commercially produced. How to manage these data to make them more accessible and searchable to users is a key challenge in current multimedia computing research. In this chapter, the authors discuss the problems and challenges in multimedia data management, and review the state of the art in data structures and algorithms for multimedia indexing, media feature space management and organization, and applications of these techniques in multimedia data management.

INTRODUCTION

The 21st century is unique in human history in the sense that the amount of information produced and consumed by human being is unprecedented, especial those in the digital media forms, e.g., audio, image, video, email, web pages. This trend of rapid growth of digital content is unrelenting, as indicated by the amount of pictures and video clips hosted by the popular online image and video repository websites, e.g., Flickr (http://flickr.com), Snapfish (http://snapfish.com) and Youtube (http://youtube.com), as well as the amount of image/video clips generated every day by thousands of TV stations, millions of surveillance cameras, and billions of digital cameras. Without an efficient data management system to give all these data structure, and therefore make them searchable, they will become much less useful. Fortunately, with the advances in electronics and computing technology, the hardware has made significant advances in the past decade. Storage is getting larger and cheaper, roughly 1GB/$ for hard disk at this time, and the computing power available to both business and personal usage is unprecedented. Furthermore, the advances in networking technology makes distributed solution based on the sharing of storage and computing power available.

Data management research has a long history and has produced effective solutions like relational database engine for tabular data management, inverted file for information retrieval. The multimedia data management shares a lot of common philosophy and solutions with the traditional data management. However, due to the nature of media data, there also exist unique challenges. In this chapter, we review the problem of multimedia data representation, and the data structure and algorithms for multimedia data indexing in Section II, we discuss the problem of "curse of dimensionality" and feature space modeling and processing in section III. In Section IV, we discuss randomized solutions in indexing and searching, and in Section V, we present an example solution for video retrieval.

MULTIMEDIA DATA INDEXING AND MANAGEMENT

Media data like images, video clips, audio clips are often represented by their d-dimensional features, and each media object becomes a point in some feature space R^d. How to find a proper feature representation that captures necessary information for effective search and retrieval tasks is the active research topic in the multimedia analysis community. Industrial standard like MPEG-7 also captures the state of the art of image/video features and metrics for search and retrieval, including color, shape and texture features for images, as well as motion and camera features for video.

The purpose of multimedia data base system is to have structured storage and indexing such that the amount of I/O operations that load data into memory, and also the amount computation involved for a query request can be reduced and therefore achieving fast response time to end users. This is also a well studied field dates back to early days of computer science and with a rich set of tools and solutions. The multimedia data base present unique challenges in the sense that the typical feature data space dimensionality is high, and if this issue is not dealt with effectively, the retrieval performance of the traditional indexing and storage solutions degenerates quickly.

In this section, we discuss the multimedia data indexing and storage solutions, and the typical queries supported. The effect of dimensionality on retrieval performance is discussed in detail.

Multimedia Data Storage and Indexing Solutions

A set of multimedia objects can be viewed as a collection of data points in some d-dimensional feature space R^d. The most naive solution of storage and indexing would be just store the data in sequential order, e.g., timestamp of images, and allow sequential retrieval of data at query time. In fact, most people store their personal digital camera images this way. To locate a certain picture of interests, an exhaustive image loading and examination have to be performed. This involves amount of I/O operation and computing (examination) in order of $O(N)$, whereas N is the repository size. More sophisticated users will create file folders according to, for example, year and month to give it a better structure to support search of images by date. This intuitive approach precisely reflects the essence of data storage and indexing – to give the multimedia repository a hierarchical structure according to some key information (in this case, time stamp), such that the I/O and computation in searching can be reduced – instead of exhaustive search, people can look at folder timestamp and narrow the I/O to certain month, and then examine only images in certain folder.

The basic structure of multimedia data base is a tree that represents the hierarchical partition of data set. Each tree node contains a subset of data points in repository, and each node has a *key* that defines the region of feature space that data points in this node reside. There are two types of nodes, leaf node, or *data node*, which stores the actual data points and key values, while the non-leaf node, or *directory node*, stores key values and pointers to its child nodes. At the top of structure is the *root* node, which is the entry point of the whole structure. In practice, each node is a basic I/O unit that resides in permanent disk storage and need to be loaded into the memory for processing. The distance from root node to data node is called the *height* of the index, which roughly corresponds to the number of I/O operations needed to access the data page. The size of data node, i.e., number of data points M, will affect the computational complexity in feature matching for query processing. An example is illustrated in Figure 1. Node 1 is the root node, nodes 2~7 are directory nodes, while nodes 8 ~ 15 are leaf or data nodes. To access data points in node 10, for example, the number of node I/O operation is 4, which is also the height of node 10. The design of index tree and the size of data and directory node need to consider the computer system hardware and OS limitations, as well as balance the time complexity in I/O and feature space computing.

There are basically two approaches to create this tree structure, data partition based, which organize around data, and also feature space partition based, which organize data based on the region it resides. Examples of data partition approaches include R-tree (Guttman, 1984) and variations, R*-tree

Figure 1. Example of index tree structure

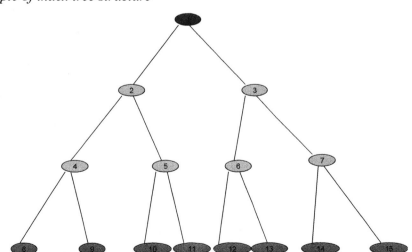

(Beckmann, Kriegel & Schneider, 1990), X-tree (Berchtold, Keim & Kriegel, 1996), while space partition approaches include kd-tree (Robinson 1981) and variations. We will have a discussion of both approaches, and present a video index solution that combines elements of both approaches to achieve high performance in retrieval.

Data Partition Based Approach

The basic idea of R-tree family of indexing solution is quite straightforward. Data points are represented by the axis parallel Minimum Bounding Rectangles (MBR), each MBR is the tightest rectangle approximation of data points, and therefore each surface of MBR must contain at least one data point. If not, this surface is not tight enough. Several MBRs can be combined to have a parent node with MBR encompassing all data points in child MBRs, and a hierarchical tree structure can be built as more data points are inserted into the repository. The key is to maintain a well behaving R-tree structure through a series of splits and merges of tree nodes to maintain the right balance of leaf node size and height.

As the directory node MBRs of R-tree can be overlapping, this complicates the insertion and query processing process. Consider the example below, at the time of point insertion, the MBRs of a directory node with 2 child nodes are shown in Figure 2a. If the new data point belongs to either child node, it is inserted into that child node, as demonstrated in Figure 2c. If the new data point residing in the overlapped region, as shown in Figure 2b, it is then inserted into the node with the smallest volume. If the new data point does not belong to any child node, it is added to the child node such that the new child node has the smallest volume increment, as shown in Figure 2d. Notice that in cases (b) and (c), the MBR of child node with new insertion does not change, while in case (d), the MBR is enlarged.

The insertion starts at root node, and progress until it reaches the leaf node. As leaf node data size grows with insertions, split need to be performed to prevent overflow. The heuristic of split is to create new child nodes with smallest volume possible, and there exist a number of algorithms with different complexity as discussed in (Gaede & Gunther, 1998) and (Beckmann et al, 1990). In summary R-tree

Figure 2. R-Tree insertion example

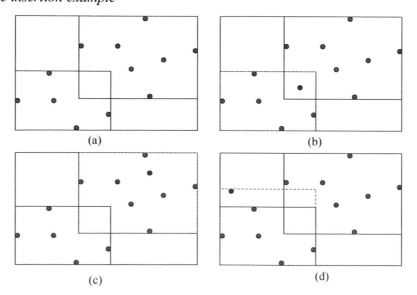

approaches organizes around data and create hierarchical structures with overlapping MBRs that does not necessary complete in feature space, i.e., the union of leaf node MBRs may have holes in feature space. The process of insertion and split has an objective to create MBRs that are tight with data points and have small volumes. This will have implications in query processing that is discussed later.

To minimizes the overlap of MBRs in R-tree, R*-tree is developed in (Beckmann et al, 1990). For the insertion operation criterion, in addition to minimum volume increase consideration, the increases in overlaps to the neighboring sibling MBRs are also minimized. The split of a node can also be avoided in some case by re-inserting certain portion of data points that reside far from the centroid of the MBR. This incurs a penalty in computation though.

To completely avoid overlaps in MBRs, non-overlapping variations of R-tree solutions also exists. Examples include R$^+$-tree (Stonebraker, Sellis & Hanson, 1986), whereas when an non-overlapping split is not possible, the child nodes are further cut up to avoid overlapping. X-tree (Berchtold et al, 1996) also achieves non-overlap MBRs by creating super node for those that cannot have overlap free splits.

Another interesting extension of R-tree approaches is to use sphere, instead, or in addition to the rectangles in representing data points in the index structure. This results in the SS-tree (White & Jain, 1996) solution, which is sphere based, and SR-tree (Katayama & Satoh, 1997), which is a combination of sphere and rectangles.

Space Partition Based Approach

Instead of organizing the index structure around data, the kd-tree family approaches build the indexing tree via a recursive partition of data space. In the simplest form, the d-dimensional feature space is first split along a chosen axis x_j at value v_j, which is the medium value of projection of all data points onto axis x_j. This gives us a left-right child partition of the root node. The key value of (x_j, v_j) is stored. This is a concise form of MBR description, which uses only a d-dimensional vector and an integer indicating which axis to split. Now the process is repeated for the feature spaces of the left and the right child, until desired leaf node height and data point size are achieved. The process is illustrated in Figure 3. After 3 splits, a height = 2 index tree is created.

Notice that the MBRs of leaf nodes are non-overlapping and complete, as compared with the R-tree solution. This eliminates the ambiguity at insertion time as indicated in Figure 2. The re-split of leaf nodes to avoid overflow is also straightforward. The MBRs for kd-tree does not necessarily have a data point on each surface, though. This may become a penalty in nearest neighbor search, in which the minimum and maximum distance of an MBR to a query point need to be estimated.

Multimedia Query Processing and the Curse of Dimensionality

Traditional database systems typically support two types of queries, 1) point query, for a given key value, e.g., a date, find all images that were taken on that day, or, 2), range queries, find all pictures taken in August last year. Given the index structure discussed in Section A, processing of these types of queries is quite straight. For the given query key value, the data nodes are quickly located typically in time complexity of O(N).

Figure 3. kd-Tree example

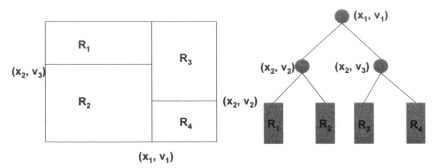

However for multimedia data base applications, key values of image features are typically without any interpretable meaning, e.g., a color histogram vector, or energies in the wavelet filter bank decomposition of texture images. A more useful query type is the k-Nearest Neighbor (NN) queries that supports Query-by-Examples (QbE), and related ranking queries, where for a given query object, for example an image, a list of similar images are returned in order of relevance to the query image.

For the given query point, q in R^d, and the database X with data points $\{x_1, x_2, ..., x_N\}$, the k-NN search problem is defined as,

$$kNN(q,X,k) = \{x_{(1)}, x_{(2)}, \cdots, x_{(k)} \in X \mid d(q,x_{(1)}) \le d(q,x_{(2)}) \le \cdots \le d(q,x_{(k)}) \le \cdots \le d(q,x_{(N)})\} \qquad (1)$$

The distance metric function d(q, xj) is defined from the multimedia feature space. Without an index structure, the complexity of k-NN search algorithm comprises of distance vector computing which has complexity O(N) and then a quick sort on the distances, which has complexity $O(N\log N)$. Obviously with index structure, we have much richer information on the data distribution and organization, better time complexity can be achieved.

The core idea of k-NN search with index structure is to limit the actual distance computation between query point and candidate data points. The MBR at each node gives an approximation of maximum and minimum distances w.r.t. the query point, and this can be exploited to prune the search and speed up the response.

Let us consider the Nearest Neighbor (NN) search (1-NN search). In the case of kd-Tree index structure, with non-overlapping hierarchical partition of feature space, this can be achieved with the following algorithm. First, the leaf node where the query point resides is located by traversing down the kd-tree. This is a very fast process since it involves only scalar computing at each node and generally have a complexity of O(log$N$). Then the nearest point within the leaf node is computed, and the distance is stored. Is this the NN we are looking for? Not necessarily. Consider the example in Figure 4 below, which has the same kd-tree as in Figure 3. The query point is located in leaf node R_3, and the NN point and the distance is computed as d_{min}. Apparently, the true NN point is actually in leaf node R_4. How to find the true NN without being exhaustive in search?

The solution lies in computing the minimum distance possible from query point to other nodes' MBRs. For a MBR defined by its lower and upper vector coordinates, v_0 and v_1, the minimum distance vector D_{min} to a query point q is computed as,

Figure 4. NN search with kd-tree

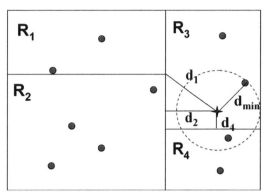

$$D_{\min} = \sqrt{\sum_i D_{\min}(i)^2}, \quad D_{\min}(i) = \begin{cases} q(i) - v_1(i), & q(i) > v_1(i) \\ 0, & v_0(i) \leq q(i) \leq v_1(i) \\ v_0(i) - q(i), & v_0(i) > q(i) \end{cases} \qquad (2)$$

If query point resides inside a MBR, the D_{min} is zero. The D_{min} to MBRs R_1, R_2 and R_4 are illustrated in Figure 4 as d_1, d_2, d_4. Obviously, if the D_{min} of a MBR is greater than the current d_{min}, which is the smallest distance achievable for all points inside, then this MBR can be pruned from the search. As shown in Figure 4, the algorithm will back track from leaf node up and examine the D_{min} for all sibling nodes MBR along the way. When examining sibling node R_4, we notice that $d_4 < d_{min}$, therefore R4 can potentially have a better NN point. This is indeed the case, and the d_{min} is updated. When moving up to root node, the D_{min} to R_1 and R_2 are all greater than d_{min}. The search is therefore over and the true NN is found.

Generally the NN search with kd-tree stops after a few nodes are examined. The complexity is O(*logN*) for a kd-tree with *N* nodes. But there could be also cases where all nodes need to be examined, depending on the data point distribution. Theoretical analysis and empirical results of NN search performance with kd-tree can be found in (Moore 1991).

For the R-tree family indexing structure, the NN search algorithm is very similar in spirit. The RKV algorithm reported in (Roussopoulos, Kelley & Vincent, 1995) and improvements in (Cheung & Fu, 1998) all operate in a similar fashion as the NN search with kd-tree outlined. When searching a node, all child node MBRs are sorted according to the potential of having a better NN candidates. This can be computed as sorting by the D_{min}, or a combination of D_{min} with other metrics. For real applications, heuristics like a good guess of initial d_{min} can also be used to cut down the amount of search.

For multimedia database applications, the feature space dimensionalities are typically high. The high-dimensional geometry is different from the lower dimensional intuitions we have and this may have unexpected consequences for indexing and NN searches (Bohm, Berchtold, & Keim, 2001). First consider the volume distribution in high dimensional space. The volume of a sphere or cube grows exponentially with dimension *d*, this also means that more and more volume of a given size sphere or cube will concentrate on the surface. This is illustrated for the cube case. The portion of cubic volume as the function of surface crust depth *z* is plotted in Figure 5a. Note that as the dimension *d* grows, larger portion of cubic volume will concentrate in a thinner crust on the surface. This effect has counter-intuitive impact on the indexing schemes and NN searches. For example, if we have a fixed height kd-tree, then the number of splits from the root to the leaf node is h. Assume that data has uniformly marginal distributions, and every axis is likely to be split equally, then as the dimension d goes up, the average number of splits per dimension goes down as h/d. This gives us a very coarse partition of the data along each axis.

The effect of high dimension on queries is also significant. Considering the range query, to cover the same portion of volume of the whole data space, the range radius has to grow exponentially and eventually reach the surface of data space. This is because of the concentration of volume to the surface. For an unit d-dimensional cube data space $[0\ 1]^d$, a cube of side 0.5 anchored at the origin can cover 1/4 of volume when $d=2$. But to cover the same volume in $d=16$, 64 and 128 dimensional spaces, the cubic side has to grow to 0.918, 0.979 and 0.990, respectively.

The effect of high dimension on NN search is even more interesting. It is established in (Beyer, Goldstein, Ramakrishnan & Shaft, 1999) that in the high dimensional space, the distance between query point and the NN point, d_{min}, converges with the distance between the query point and the fartherest point, d_{max}, under certain conditions. This means that a small change in query point will leads to totally

Figure 5. High dimensional space volume distribution

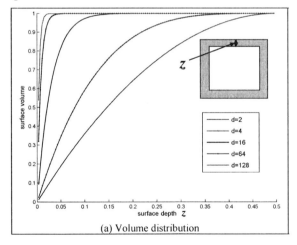

(a) Volume distribution

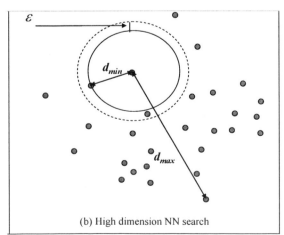

(b) High dimension NN search

different NN point returns. This is proved in (Beyer et al, 1999) by arguing that a small increase of hyper-sphere radius to $(1+\varepsilon)d_{min}$, will actually encompass all data points including the one with distance d_{max} to query point, for any given ε, if dimension d is large enough,

$$\lim_{d\to\infty} \Pr\{d_{max} \leq (1+\varepsilon)d_{min}\} = 1. \tag{3}$$

An intuitive understanding of this result can actually derive from the volume concentration along the surface as indicated in Figure 5a. As dimensionality is high, the ε–thin sphere surface actually has a very large volume that can eventually encompass all data points. Detailed proof and discussions can be found in (Beyer et al, 1999).

From the discussion we know that the aforementioned indexing and query processing techniques suffer performance degradation as feature space dimensionality grows large. The solution to deal with this "curse of dimensionality" is either through better feature space modeling, which will be discussed in Section III, or through approximate solutions as will be discussed in Section IV.

SUBSPACE MODELING AND DIMENSIONALITY REDUCTION

In computer vision and pattern recognition fields, the sensory inputs, such as images and videos, are often viewed as high-dimensional data with large percent of dimensionality redundancy. In practice, feature extraction is in great demand owing to the fact that the effective information often lies in a lower-dimensional feature space. To process those data for the purpose of management, feature extraction and dimensionality reduction is becoming fairly important (Yan et al, 2007), (Fu, Yan & Huang, 2008b), (Fu, Li, Huang & Katsaggelos, 2008).

Reflected in the theoretical domain, feature extraction and dimensionality reduction are often intertwined and realized by machine learning tools. A significant obstacle for the implementation of such approaches is the curse of dimensionality. The expression "curse of dimensionality" in statistics is to describe the problem caused by the exponential increase in volume associated with adding extra dimensions to a sample space (Bellman, 1961). This phenomenon directly complicates many real-world problems, which means limited number of training samples can not be sufficiently used to estimate the infinite distribution in a high-dimensional feature space. Moreover, the performance of a parametric model can be negatively affected in the small-sample case when the sample dimension is high (Fu, Yan & Huang, 2008a), (Fu, Yan & Huang, 2008b).

Subspace learning is a prevalent tool for feature extraction (Fu, Li, Yuan, Wu & Huang, 2008), especially for high-dimensional data feature extraction. A large family of subspace learning methods has been proposed in the last several decades motivated by different learning strategy: parametric or nonparametric.

Motivation: Parametric vs. Nonparametric Learning

Subspace learning can be performed by starting from either parametric or nonparametric model.

The basic idea of parametric model is using a parameterized family of probability distributions to describe the nature of a set of data (Moghaddam & Pentland, 1997). In this case, the data distribution is empirically assumed or estimated. The subspace learning is conducted by measuring a set of fixed parameters, such as mean and variance. This method is effective for the large-sample case when the training data is statistically sufficient. The basic theory can be self-contained with a probabilistic explanation. However, for the small-sample and high-dimensionality case which is more often in real-world, such kind of methods can degrade the performance due to the statistical insufficient. Moreover, for complicated data distribution, those methods may suffer from the high computational cost or model complexity since the parameter space has uncontrollable high dimensionality. Model selection is a difficult task since over-fitting and under-fitting may happen quite often. The representative methods can be Principal Component Analysis (PCA) (Turk & Pentland, 1991) and Linear Discriminant Analysis (LDA) (Belhumeur, Hepanha & Kriegman, 1997) which assume the Gaussian distribution for the data space.

The nonparametric model is distribution free as it does not rely on assumptions that the data are drawn from a given probability distribution (Li, Liu, Lin & Tang, 2005). In this case, the subspace learning is conducted by measuring the pair-wise data relationship in both global and local manners. This method is effective and robust due to the reliance on fewer assumptions and parameters. It especially works for small-sample and high-dimensionality case. For the complicated data distribution, this method can effectively capture the intrinsic manifold structure and model the nature of data. However, it may also suffer from the high computational cost for the large-sample case since the computational complexity is proportional to the second power of the number of training data. This method may also introduce parameters, such as the neighborhood size and distance metric for the measurement of local pair-wise data relationship. The representative methods can be Locally Linear Embedding (LLE) (Roweis & Saul, 2000) and ISOMAP (Tenenbaum, Silva & Langford, 2000), which assume the existence of low-dimensional manifold embedded in the data space.

Graph-Based Model

As summarized in Graph Embedding (Yan et al, 2007), most dimensionality reduction algorithms, in either parametric or nonparametric learning, can be unified into a general framework. Assume that the training set is represented as matrix form $\mathbf{X} = [\mathbf{x}_1, \mathbf{x}_2, ..., \mathbf{x}_n]$, where $\mathbf{x}_i \in \Re^D$ and n is the number of training data. The corresponding class label of $\mathbf{x}_i$ is denoted as $l_i \in \{1, ..., n_c\}$, where n_c is the number of classes. The corresponding low-dimensional representation set is represented as matrix form $\mathbf{Y} = [\mathbf{y}_1, \mathbf{y}_2, ..., \mathbf{y}_n]$, where $\mathbf{y}_i \in \Re^d$ ($d < D$).

Let $G = \{\mathbf{X}, \mathbf{S}\}$ be an undirected weighted graph with vertex set $\mathbf{X}$ and similarity matrix $\mathbf{S} \in \Re^{n \times n}$. Each element of the real symmetric matrix $\mathbf{S}$ measures the similarity between a pair of vertices. For a

Figure 6. Graph-based model (originally shown in (Fu, 2008)). LLE and its linear form LEA.

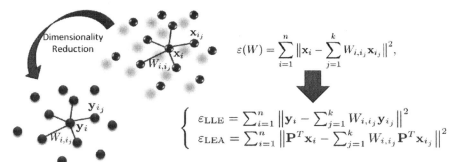

$$\varepsilon(W) = \sum_{i=1}^{n} \left\| \mathbf{x}_i - \sum_{j=1}^{k} W_{i,i_j} \mathbf{x}_{i_j} \right\|^2,$$

$$\begin{cases} \varepsilon_{\text{LLE}} = \sum_{i=1}^{n} \left\| \mathbf{y}_i - \sum_{j=1}^{k} W_{i,i_j} \mathbf{y}_{i_j} \right\|^2 \\ \varepsilon_{\text{LEA}} = \sum_{i=1}^{n} \left\| \mathbf{P}^T \mathbf{x}_i - \sum_{j=1}^{k} W_{i,i_j} \mathbf{P}^T \mathbf{x}_{i_j} \right\|^2 \end{cases}$$

specific dimensionality reduction algorithm, such as discriminant analysis, there may exist two graphs, the intrinsic graph $G_i = \{\mathbf{X}, \mathbf{S}_i\}$ and the penalty graph $G_p = \{\mathbf{X}, \mathbf{S}_p\}$. The intrinsic graph characterizes data properties that the algorithm favors and the penalty graph describes properties that the algorithm tries to avoid. The graphs are typically used to estimate the data distribution or manifold structure for subspace learning (Fu, Yan & Huang, 2008a), (Fu, 2008).

Nonlinear Methods

Most existing nonlinear methods are nonparametric learning. It is worthwhile to look into the family of those methods since they are the basis of many existing subspace learning methods. The representative nonlinear methods such as LLE, ISOMAP, Laplacian Eigenmaps (Belkin & Niyogi, 2003), and Semi-definite Embedding (SDE) (Weinberger& Saul, 2004), focus on preserving the topological structure which reflects the latent geometry of the low-dimensional manifold. For example, LLE formulates the manifold learning problem as a neighborhood-preserving embedding, which learns the global structure by exploiting the local symmetries of linear reconstructions. Isomap extends the classical Multidimensional Scaling (MDS) (Cox & Cox, 2001) by computing the pairwise distances in the geodesic space of the manifold. Based on the spectral decomposition of graph Laplacians, Laplacian Eigenmaps finds an approximation to the Laplace-Beltrami operator defined on the manifold. SDE uses semidefinite programming as a tool and suggests estimating angles and local distances to support the existence of rotation, reflection or translation for the local mapping between data points and their neighbors. The general objective of those methods is to directly learn $\mathbf{Y}$ from given $\mathbf{X}$. A graph preserving criterion for the nonlinear method is defined as

$$\mathbf{y}^* = \underset{\mathbf{y}^T \mathbf{C} \mathbf{y} = b}{\operatorname{argmin}} \sum_{i \neq j} \left\| \mathbf{y}_i - \mathbf{y}_j \right\|^2 \mathbf{W}_{ij}, \tag{4}$$

where similarity matrix $\mathbf{W}$ is a function of $\mathbf{X}$. b is a constant and $\mathbf{C}$ is a constraint matrix. Most nonlinear methods share the similar objective function but using different $\mathbf{W}$ and $\mathbf{C}$. Typically, $\mathbf{W}$ can be the intrinsic graph similarity matrix $\mathbf{S}_i$ and $\mathbf{C}$ can be the scale normalization matrix or the penalty graph Laplacian matrix, $\mathbf{C} = \mathbf{D}_p - \mathbf{S}_p$, where each diagonal element of diagonal matrix $\mathbf{D}_p$ is the sum of corresponding row of $\mathbf{S}_p$. In this case, Eq. (4) can be rewritten as

$$\mathbf{y}^* = \underset{\mathbf{y}^T \mathbf{C} \mathbf{y} = b}{\operatorname{argmin}} \mathbf{y}^T \mathbf{L} \mathbf{y}, \tag{5}$$

where $\mathbf{L} = \mathbf{D} - \mathbf{C}$ is the Laplacian matrix of $\mathbf{C}$. Eq. (5) can be easily solved in closed-form solution by SVD (Fu, Yan & Huang, 2008a), (Fu, 2008). A standard example is shown in Figure 6 for LLE where dimensionality reduction is performed by first learning $\mathbf{W}$ given $\mathbf{X}$ and finally learning $\mathbf{Y}$ given $\mathbf{W}$ (Roweis et al 2000).

Another work suggests looking into the most nonparametric methods with a kernel view (Ham, Lee, Mika & Schölkopf, 2004). It shows LLE, ISOMAP, and Laplacian Eigenmaps can all be considered as kernel PCA on particular Gram matrices.

Many of the existing nonlinear methods perform well for manifold visualization, but they still have some limitations. The nonlinear projection is defined only on the training data. There is no straightforward "bridge" connecting $\mathbf{X}$ and $\mathbf{Y}$. If we do not take an out-of-sample extension (Saul & Roweis, 2003), (Bengio, Paiement, Vincent & Delalleau, 2004) for new datum, the entire manifold embedding procedure has to be repeated. Moreover, even if out-of-sample extension is available, there is still a storage problem in real-world applications. The system needs to store all the training data for the testing usage, which costs more storage resource. An alternative way is to formulate the particular linearization forms for the nonlinear methods, in which case a "bridge" connecting $\mathbf{X}$ and $\mathbf{Y}$ is built by subspace learning.

Linear Methods

Linear methods can be either parametric or nonparametric. They bridge $\mathbf{X}$ and $\mathbf{Y}$ by a projection matrix $\mathbf{P} = [\mathbf{p}_1, \mathbf{p}_2, ..., \mathbf{p}_d]$ learned from subspaces, where $\mathbf{p}_i \in \Re^D$. Conventional subspace learning methods, such as PCA and LDA, assume the data are in Gaussian distribution. So, the subspaces are learned by measuring the sample mean, variance and scatter. PCA finds the embedding that maximizes the projected variance, while LDA works by maximizing the between-class scatter and at the same time minimizing the within-class scatter. These methods, widely adopted in many existing work, have the properties of simplicity and effectiveness. However, it is often the case that the data distribution is non-Gaussian and there often do not capture sufficient training samples. So, the conventional parametric methods may fail to discover the intrinsic structure of the training samples, if they are lying on or close to a submanifold of the ambient space.

Motivated by the objective of existing nonlinear methods, most popular manifold based linear dimensionality reduction methods, such as Locality Preserving Projections (LPP) (He & Niyogi, 2003) and Locally Embedded Analysis (LEA) (Fu & Huang, 2005), are derived from a nonparametric neighborhood graph modeling (Fu, 2008). The problem is constrained by noting that the data points should be closely related to the nearest neighbors and using a graph matrix to encode the manifold, thereby obtaining a linear mapping from the original data to the manifold by solving an eigen value decomposition problem. The general objective of those methods is to learn projection $\mathbf{P}$ from given $\mathbf{X}$. Then $\mathbf{Y}$ is calculated by $\mathbf{Y}=\mathbf{P}^T\mathbf{X}$ or $\mathbf{y}=\mathbf{X}^T\mathbf{p}$. A graph preserving criterion for the linear method is defined as

$$\mathbf{p}^* = \underset{\substack{\mathbf{p}^T\mathbf{XCX}^T\mathbf{p}=b \\ or\, \mathbf{p}^T\mathbf{p}\ b}}{\arg\min} \sum_{i \ne j} \left\| \mathbf{p}^T\mathbf{x}_i - \mathbf{p}^T\mathbf{x}_j \right\|^2 \mathbf{W}_{ij}, \tag{6}$$

where similarity matrix $\mathbf{W}$ and constraint matrix $\mathbf{C}$ are defined in the same way as nonlinear methods. If we define the Laplacian matrix as same as the nonlinear methods, Eq. (6) can be rewritten as

$$\mathbf{p}^* = \underset{\substack{\mathbf{p}^T\mathbf{XCX}^T\mathbf{p}=b \\ or\, \mathbf{p}^T\mathbf{p}\ b}}{\arg\min} \mathbf{p}^T\mathbf{XLX}^T\mathbf{p} \tag{7}$$

Figure 7. Discriminant simplex analysis (originally shown in (Fu 2008)). Note for subspace learning, here we have $\mathbf{y}=\mathbf{X}^T\mathbf{p}$

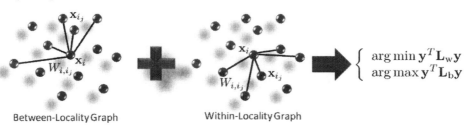

Between-Locality Graph   Within-Locality Graph

Eq. (7) can still be easily solved in closed-form solution by SVD. A standard example is shown in Figure 6 for LEA where dimensionality reduction is performed by first learning **W** given **X** and finally learning **P** given **W**, (Fu, 2008).

Despite the success of those algorithms in many applications, the general discriminating power cannot be guaranteed sufficiently high, since the real data distributions are often too complicated to faithfully measure and at the same time the classes of the data patterns may highly overlapped. In addition, these methods focus more on the manifold criterion which is not for the discriminating purpose. To boost the discriminating power, some recent discriminant learning methods, such as Marginal Fisher Analysis (MFA) (Yan et al 2007), Discriminant Simplex Analysis (DSA) (Fu, Yan & Huang, 2008a), Correlation Embedding Analysis (CEA) (Fu, Yan & Huang, 2008), Local Discriminant Embedding (Chen, Chang & Liu, 2005) and Locality Sensitive Discriminant Analysis (Cai, He, Zhou, Han, & Bao, 2007), combine the Fisher criterion with manifold criterion and explicitly aim at the classification capacity and discriminating efficiency of the embedding. They outperform the linear subspace learning methods conforming to either Fisher criterion or manifold criterion by taking both advantages. They still share the objective function in Eq. (7), but they model the intra-class compactness and inter-class separability of data distributions with intrinsic and penalty graphs. Figure 7 shows the example of DSA which builds between-locality graph and within-locality graph and uses Fisher criterion for subspace learning.

Extensions

As suggested by many existing work, the graph embedding based linear methods can all be extended to kernel form and tensor form (Yan et al 2007), (Fu & Huang, 2008), (Tao, Li, Wu & Maybank, 2007). The basic idea of kernel form is to map the data $\{x_i\}_{i=1}^n$ from the original input space, $\Re^D$, to a higher or even infinite dimensional feature space, $\Re^F$, by a nonlinear mapping function: $\Phi: \Re^D \rightarrow \Re^F$, $F > D$. Denote the $n \times n$ kernel matrix **K** in the feature space $\Re^F$ by $K[i,j] = \Phi(x_i) \cdot \Phi(x_j)$. The objective functions are changed by substituting **K** for **X** in the previous equations. For the tensor form, we assume there are high-order data structures appearing in the feature space. Assume the given high-dimensional data are denoted as a set of n mth-order tensors $\{X_i \,|\, X_i \in \Re^{D_1 \times D_2 \times \cdots \times D_m}\}_{i=1}^n$. Let $Y_i = X_i \times_1 U_1 \times_2 \cdots \times_m U_m$, where $U_j \in \Re^{D_j \times d_j}$ for $j=1$, 2, ..., m. So, our goal is to calculate all the optimal U_j.

Generalized Feature Extraction for Dimensionality Reduction

Formulation

In general case as we discussed in (Fu, Yan & Huang, 2008), (Fu, 2008), the purpose of feature extraction is to seek a mapping function, denoted as $f(x, P)$ where **P** represents the parameters, to map the datum **x** to the desired low-dimensional representation $y \in \Re^d$, namely, $y = f(x, P)$. Again, let's build the intrinsic graph $G_i = \{X, S_i\}$ and the penalty graph $G_p = \{X, S_p\}$. A generalized graph preserving criterion is imposed for these two objectives as

$$\begin{cases} \min_P \sum_{i \neq j} \left\| f(x_i, P) - f(x_j, P) \right\|^2 W_{ij}^{(i)} \\ \max_P \sum_{i \neq j} \left\| f(x_i, P) - f(x_j, P) \right\|^2 W_{ij}^{(p)}. \end{cases} \tag{8}$$

There exist several different formulations for this purpose (Yan et al, 2007), (Tao et al, 2007), Here, we consider the difference-form formulation in (Tao et al 2007), namely,

$$\underset{\mathbf{P}}{\operatorname{argmax}}\left\{F(\mathbf{P})=\sum_{i\neq j}\left\|f(\mathbf{x}_i,\mathbf{P})-f(\mathbf{x}_j,\mathbf{P})\right\|^2\cdot(\mathbf{W}_{ij}^{(p)}-\mathbf{W}_{ij}^{(i)})\right\}. \tag{9}$$

In the foregoing discussion, we discussed four types of mapping functions for $f(\mathbf{x},\mathbf{P})$, which correspond to four types of graph embeddings (Yan et al, 2007), (Fu, Yan & Huang, 2008):

a. Direct graph embedding with implicit mapping functions;
b. Linearization with linear mapping functions;
c. Kernelization with kernel-based nonlinear mapping functions;
d. Tensorization with multilinear mapping functions.

These four types of graph embeddings are widely used owing to their straightforward formulation and computational efficiency. But note that the possible mapping functions for $f(\mathbf{x},\mathbf{P})$ here are defined far beyond these four types. This is useful since real applications often demand more general solutions for the graph embedding.

Generalized Solution

We introduce the general solution (Fu, Yan & Huang, 2008b), (Fu, 2008) for the generalized graph embedding formulation. The solution is based on the assumption that the mapping function $f(\mathbf{x},\mathbf{P})$ is differentiable almost everywhere with respect to $\mathbf{P}$. In this case, a direct method is to utilize the gradient descent approach to search for the solution based on the derivative,

$$\frac{\partial F(\mathbf{P})}{\partial \mathbf{P}}=2\sum_{i\neq j}(\mathbf{W}_{ij}^{(p)}-\mathbf{W}_{ij}^{(i)})\cdot\sum_{k=1}^{d}\left(f_k(\mathbf{x}_i,\mathbf{P})-f_k(\mathbf{x}_j,\mathbf{P})\right)\cdot\left(\frac{\partial f_k(\mathbf{x},\mathbf{P})}{\partial\mathbf{P}}\bigg|_{\mathbf{x}_i}-\frac{\partial f_k(\mathbf{x},\mathbf{P})}{\partial\mathbf{P}}\bigg|_{\mathbf{x}_j}\right). \tag{10}$$

This formulation and solution for generalized graph embedding offer great flexibility for feature extraction. There is no constraint on the parameter $\mathbf{P}$, which means that for linear feature extraction, we can use general transformation matrix for feature extraction instead of the conventional column normalized matrix. Moreover, it is possible to constrain the value of $\mathbf{y}$, e.g., on a unit sphere, by properly designing the mapping function, $f(\mathbf{x},\mathbf{P})$. Some representative algorithm designs based on this generalized framework are Correlation Embedding Analysis (CEA) (Fu, Yan & Huang, 2008b), (Fu, 2008), Correlation Tensor Analysis (CTA) (Fu & Huang, 2008), Correlation Principal Component Analysis (CPCA) (Fu, Yan & Huang, 2008b), and Correlation Discriminant Analysis (CDA) (Ma, Lao, Takikawa & Kawade, 2007).

Discussion

Supervised and Unsupervised Learning

In the case of parametric modeling, conventional PCA is unsupervised since it focuses on data representation and dimensionality reduction. LDA is supervised since labels for the training data are used to learn a subspace that can differentiate different classes. Supervision is easily performed by labeling different classes in the training data to calculate the class means. In the case of nonparametric modeling, unsupervised learning is conducted to search nearest neighbors in the entire training data. There are two ways of supervised learning. If only manifold criterion is considered, the intrinsic graph is the only graph to build. Taking one training data, its nearest neighbors are searched within the same class of it. If Fisher criterion is also considered, the penalty graph is also considered. Taking one training data, its nearest neighbors are searched within the different class of it.

Parameters

The graph based subspace learning methods have several parameters that need to tune. When the nearest neighbor search is used to build the graphs, the numbers of nearest neighbors for both intrinsic graph and penalty graph are parameters. When the similarity matrices are defined, some methods may introduce parameters to scale the similarity weights. Sometimes a regularization term needs to be used for singular problem for SVD. Then a parameter may be introduced to balance the regularization term. If the generalized solution is used for generalized feature extraction, the number of iterations is an important parameter.

Summary

Based on the "no free lunch theorem" (Duda, Peter, & David, 2000), there is no method that can work for all the real application cases in reality. Different methods may be tailored to deal with particular cases. Either parametric method or nonparametric method for subspace learning can be adopted for feature extraction in real-world applications when data distribution is simple or complicated. But, in general they can be unified in the general way of graph based formulation. From this point of view, we can design new subspace learning algorithms by carefully tuning the graph modeling details and trying efficient similarity metric adapting to specific databases and scenario.

APPROXIMATE SOLUTION FOR INDEXING AND QUERYING HIGH-DIMENSIONAL SPACE

As Discussed in section II, tree-based index provides efficient solution for searching huge data collection by taking advantages of the tree structure (Robinson 1981). Given a query point, without comparing with all of the data samples in the data base, the closest point can be retrieved by efficiently browsing the tree. In the case of low-dimensional space, the search process is largely speeded up compared with the exhaustive search. However, tree-based index cannot be easily scaled to high-dimensional space, because the number of tree nodes can grow exponentially fast regarding to the number of dimensions of the feature space. For instance, when indexing a high-dimensional space based on a tree structure, it is possible that during the search process, the number of tree nodes required to be checked is as many as the total number of data points in the data base. As a result, tree-based index methods cannot perform significantly better than exhaustive search), both in theory and in practice (Bohm, et al, 2001), (Shakhn-arovich, Darrell & Indyk, 2007), when the dimensionality is higher than 30 to 50 dimensions.

To overcome the curse-of-dimensionality problem and to make the index and search methods scalable to high dimensions, approximate index and search solutions are proposed. We will discuss these methods in this section. Compared with tree-based index, these approximate solutions provide approximate answers instead of exact ones to the query, with the gain in efficiency. In the following, we will first review the concept of approximate nearest-neighbor (NN) search and explain how it can speed up the search process by sacrificing the accuracy. Besides indexing individual data point, we will also discuss the approximate and randomized solutions to index and search a collection of points (point-set).

Locality Sensitive Hashing (LSH) for Approximate Nearest Neighbor Search

Instead of performing exact NN query, locality sensitive hash (LSH) performs approximate NN query, where it retrieves approximate NNs which can be of high probability to be the exact NNs. By sacrificing the retrieval accuracy to some extent, LSH gains the speed significantly. Unlike tree-based index methods, it is scalable to high-dimensional space. The problem of approximate NN search is defined as follows:

Definition 1: *Approximate Nearest-Neighbor Search (Gionis, A., Indyk, P. & Motwani, 1999)*
For a data set DB={ W_p }swhich is composed of data points W_p, preprocessing DB to efficiently search for the approximate NNs of any given query Q. That is, to find $W_p \in DB$, such that $d(W_p, Q) < (1 + \varepsilon)d(W_{qnn}, Q)$ where $d(W_{qnn}, Q)$ denotes the distance of Q to its nearest neighbor W_{qnn} in DB.

By modifying the task of exact NN search, it is possible to provide efficient NN search through LSH. Suppose h is a function that maps R^d to some universe U, h is called locality sensitive hash function if it satisfies the following condition. Locality sensitive hash provides randomized index for approximate NN search.

Definition 2: *(p1, p2, r, cr)-sensitive hash functions*
According to (Indyk &Motwani, 1998), a family H of functions: h: $R^d \rightarrow$ U is called (p1,p2,r,cr)-sensitive, if for any W and Q in R^d:
        -- if $\|W-Q\| < r$, then Pr[h(W)=h(Q)] > p1;
        -- if $\|W-Q\| > cr$, then Pr[h(W)=h(Q)] < p2;
where h(.) denotes the hashing function and $\| W- Q\|$ denotes the distance measure between W and Q in R^d, for example, L1 or L2 norm. For the parameters, we have 1>p1>p2>0 and c>1.

Based on the (p1, p2, r, cr)-sensitive property of LSH functions, we can see the probability of collision is much higher for points that are close to each other than for those far apart. For example, if two points W and Q are close to each other (i.e., $\|W-Q\|<r$), it is of high probability to have hash collision (i.e., Pr[h(W)=h(Q)] > p1). On the other hand, if two points W and Q are further away (i.e., $\|W-Q\| > cr$), it is of low probability that hash collision happens (i.e., Pr[h(W)=h(Q)] < p2). As a result, the closer the two points W and Q, the more likely their hash values are identical. When many independent hash functions are provided, the distance between W and Q can be inferred from the number of times their hash functions collide.

Given the distance measure, it is important to find appropriate (p1, p2, r, cr)-sensitive hashing functions. For different distance measures, for example hamming or Euclidean distance, we need to propose different hash functions that satisfy the (p1, p2, r, cr)-sensitive conditions under the distance measure. A good survey of various hash functions under different distance measure can be found in (Andoni & Indyk, 2006). Here, we only discuss the most popular LSH under hamming and Euclidean distance, respectively.

LSH for Hamming Space

LSH is firstly proposed for approximate NN query with hamming distance (Gionis et al, 1999). Suppose W is a binary vector, the (p1, p2, r, cr)-sensitive hashing functions under hamming distance can be: h(W) = W(i), where W(i) is the i_{th} element of W. Given two binary vectors W and Q, the probability of collision is $\Pr[h(W)=h(Q)] = 1 - D_H(W,Q)/d$, where $D_H(W,Q)$ denotes hamming distance between W and Q, and d is the dimensionality of the hamming space. This hash function is (p1,p2,r,cr)-sensitive under hamming distance.

LSH for Euclidean Space

The LSH scheme that directly works for Euclidean distance is proposed in (Datar, Immorlica, Indyk, & Mirrokni, 2004). It embeds the high-dimensional points into real line (1-dimension) through random projection. Then by quantizing the real-line, it can index high-dimensional points by their quantized values. Each hash function h(·) is a random mapping from vector W_p to an integer h: $R^d \rightarrow N$,

$$h_{a,b}(W_p) = \left\lfloor \frac{a \times W_p + b}{r} \right\rfloor \tag{11}$$

where **a** is a random vector of *d*-dimension with each element **a**(i) independently generated through standard Gaussian distribution; b is a random variable chosen uniformly from [0, r]. With r fixed as a predefined parameter, each pair of **a** and b defines a unique hash function, which projects an original high-dimensional vector onto the real line, which is then quantized. The random variable $a \times W_p$ has the same distribution as $\|W_p\|$.

In order to find the nearest neighbors of the query point Q, it requires a collection of hash functions $g_i=(h_1, h_2, ..., h_k)$, i=1,2..., L. Each hash function has its own projection parameters **a** and b. All the points W_p are then hashed many times through random projections g_i, each time W_p corresponding to a hash bucket $g_i(W_p)$.

During the query phase, we search the nearest neighbors of Q based on the hash values, instead of in the original high-dimensional space. Based on the property of (p1, p2, r, cr)-sensitive hash function, the closer the two points W_p and Q, the more likely they will have the same hash value under the random projection h, because if W_p is the neighbor of Q, then W_p will be the neighbor of Q in the real line as well. This search process can be very efficient: under a specific hash function, two points W_p and Q are possible neighbors in the original space if their hash values are identical. Thus we can first retrieve the candidate points that have same hash values with the query point, from buckets $g_1(Q), g_2(Q), ..., g_L(Q)$. Then we can refine the search by only comparing the selected candidates, which is a much smaller subset of the whole data collection.. By pre-building a set of hashing functions for the database, each new query vector q can efficiently retrieve most of its neighbors in the features space by only comparing the hash values (*i.e.*, whether they are located in the same interval) instead of calculating the distance in high-dimensional space.

Besides random projection from high-dimensional space to real-line (1-dimension), the recent work of LSH (Andoni & Indyk, 2006) applies different types of hash functions which embed high-dimensional points into a lower k-dimensional space. Such a scheme is even more efficient compared with (Datar et al, 2004).

Indexing and Querying Point-Set

Although a lot of progresses have been achieved in indexing and searching individual data points in high dimensions, depending on the representation of multimedia objects such as images and videos, it is also of great interests to index and retrieve point-sets. For example, instead of using a single color histogram to represent an image, it can be characterized by a collection of interest points (feature vectors) (Grauman & Darrell, 2006), (Yuan, Wu & Yang, 2007a), (Xu, Cham, Yan & Chang, 2008). Similarly, instead of characterizing a video segment as an individual feature vector (Ferman, Tekalp & Mehrotra, 2002), (Kashino, Kurozumi, & Murase, 2003), (Yuan, Duan, Tian & Xu, 2004), a video query can be represented by many shots or key-frames (Xu & Chang, 2007), which is a collection of features when each key-frame contributes an individual feature vector. In these cases, the objects we need to index and query are point-sets instead of individual points. The target database contains a collection of such point-sets and task is to search for similar matches of the query point-set from all candidates.

Before we can address the point-set query problem, it is essential to define the distance or similarity between two point sets. It is a challenging problem as two point-set being compared can contain different number of points. In many applications, the matching is formulated as a partial matching problem (Grauman & Darrell, 2005), (Yuan et al, 2007a), where the exact solution involves high computational cost. For example, given two sets both containing m points, the solution of the partial matching is of complexity $O(m^3 log m)$ (Rubner, Tomasi, & Guibas, 2000). Similar to indexing and searching individual point, to speed up the search, one possibility is to provide approximate solution. In the following, we will discuss three different approximate solutions in indexing and matching the point-sets.

Bag of Words Method

The "bag of words" method is popularly applied in visual object categorization (Dance, Willamowski, Fan, Bray, & Csurka, 2004), image retrieval (Sivic & Zisserman 2008) and image pattern discovery (Yuan et al, 2007a), (Yuan, Wu & Yang, 2007b). First of all, an image is described by a collection of local features, where each one corresponds to a small image patch. After collecting many such local features from images, a visual vocabulary can be built through clustering local features into a few clusters. Each cluster contains local features of similar characteristics and corresponds to one "visual word" in the vocabulary. Through such a visual vocabulary, an image can be translated into a collection of visual words and can be represented as a "document." As each document can be characterized by a word histogram, the similarity between two images can be determined by the similarity between two word histograms. Compared with the original partial matching formulation between two point sets, such a histogram matching provides an efficient yet approximate solution. Although matching two histograms is easier than matching two point sets, it cannot provide the accurate matching result. For instance, although two local features are close to each other in the feature space, they could be two different "words" if they happen to belong to two different clusters. As a result, the quantization error introduced in the "bag of words" process inevitably affects the accuracy of the matching.

Pyramid Matching

The pyramid matching method proposed in (Grauman & Darrell, 2005) is an approximate solution for matching two point-sets in high-dimensional space. It applies a multi-resolution histogram pyramid in the feature space to perform feature matching implicitly. Such a novel approximate solution is very efficient. Give two sets of size m, the complexity of pyramid matching is of linear time complexity $O(m)$, which is a significant improvement compared with the exact solution which can is of complexity $O(m^3 log m)$. Moreover, the matching is insensitive to outlier feature points, thus is suitable for matching two images, where noisy feature points can be introduced due to variations of image patterns. Pyramid matching requires the quantization of each feature point into several buckets, under various quantization resolutions. As a result, the approximate is introduced when it performs matching based on the quantization value instead of performing distance measure in the original high-dimensional space. In pyramid matching, by gaining the efficiency, the matching accuracy is sacrificed due to quantization.

Approximated Matching

In (Yuan, Li, Fu, Wu & Huang, 2007), another approximate solution for matching two point-sets is provided, with upper bounded estimation of the exact matching score. Instead of quantizing local features into words (bag of words method) or buckets (pyramid matching), it firstly performs NN query for each local feature. Each local feature finds its own best matches. As a result, quantization error is *not* introduced in matching local features. Instead, the approximation happens during matching two point sets, where an upper bounded estimation of the similarity matching is given.

In terms of indexing an image collection, a randomized index method called spatial random partition is proposed in (Yuan & Wu, 2007), with application of mining common patterns from images. The proposed index scheme partitioned each image randomly many times to form a pool of sub-images. Each sub-image contains a collection of local features and is treated as a point set. All sub-images are queried and matched against the pool, and then common patterns can be localized by aggregating the set of matched sub-images. According to the asymptotic property of the proposed algorithm, it can automatically discover multiple common patters without knowing the total number *a priori*, and is robust to pattern variations like rotations, scale changes and partial occlusion.

APPLICATIONS AND SUMMARIES

Effective lower dimensional feature representation of multimedia object combined with an efficient indexing structure can achieve very high performance in multimedia retrieval accuracy and speed. In this section we present a LUminance Field Trajectory (LUFT) representation (Li, Katsaggelos & Gandhi, 2005) of video sequences and its Query by Example (QbE) search solution based on kd-Tree indexing (Li, Gao & Katsaggelos, 2006).

Video sequences F_k with frame size w x h pixels can be viewed as some temporal trajectory in R^{wxh}. The dimensionality of this feature space is very high, take for example QCIF sized sequences, the dimension would be 176x144=25344. This will serious degrade the nearest neighbor search performance. Instead, we compute the lower dimensional approximation of F_k via a scaling and PCA projection process, as illustrated in Figure 8.

Figure 8. LUFT computation

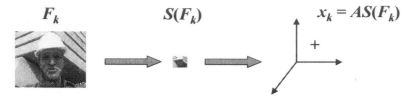

F_k $S(F_k)$ $x_k = AS(F_k)$

By careful selection of the scaling factor s, which produces an icon image vector of dimension $d_s = \dfrac{wxh}{s^2}$, and training of PCA projection matrix, A of $d \times d_s$, we obtain a d-dimensional trajectory representation of video, x_k. Examples of 3-dimensional LUFT trajectory of various video sequences are illustrated in Figure 9 below. The trajectory in red is the "foreman" sequence, while others are randomly chosen clips from TRECVID (http://www-nlpir.nist.gov/projects/trecvid) clips. Notice that different video sequences have different trajectories in this LUFT space, and this can be used as a robust feature for the Query-by-Example problems (Yuan et al, 2004).

Consider an m-frame query clip Q with trajectory $\{ q_1, q_2, \ldots ,q_m\}$, and an n-frame video repository T with trajectory $\{ t_1, t_2, \ldots ,t_n \}$, the QbE problem is to answer if query clip exists in the repository, and if exists, return the location. The problem has wide applications in video content management applications. In fact TRECVID 2008 has a competition on this specific problem. In the context of LUFT features, the problem can be formulated as finding the minimum projection distance problem. Let the minimum average projection distance between Q and T be,

$$d(Q,T) = \frac{1}{m} \min_{k_1,k_2,\cdots,k_m} \sum_{j=1}^{m} \| q_j - t_{k_j} \| \tag{12}$$

which is a function of projection locations $k_1, k_2, \ldots k_m$. Since video repository is different from image repository by having this temporal coherence constraint, that is, the matching clip should have the same order of frames, the variables on projection location actually have only one degree of freedom, since $k_{t+1}=k_t + 1$. Therefore, the problem can be re-written as,

$$d(Q,T) = d(k;Q,T) = \frac{1}{m} \min_{k} \sum_{j=1}^{m} \| q_j - t_{k+j-1} \| \tag{13}$$

In solving the QbE problem, a projection distance threshold d_{min} is used to determine if query clip Q exists,

$$k^* = \begin{cases} \arg\min_{k} d(k;Q,T), & if \ \min_{k}\{d(Q,T_k)\} \le d_{min} \\ not\ found, & else \end{cases} \tag{14}$$

Notice that the choice of d_{min} controls the precision-recall performance tradeoff of the QbE system, as will be illustrated later.

The LUFT feature is a robust feature for video clip QbE applications as indicated in (Li, Katsaggelos & Gandhi, 2005). However, when the video repository size grows, an exhaustive search is not

Figure 9. LUFT examples

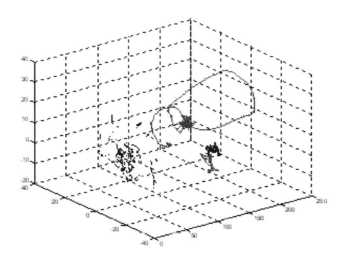

Figure 10. LUFT space kd-tree partition with height 12

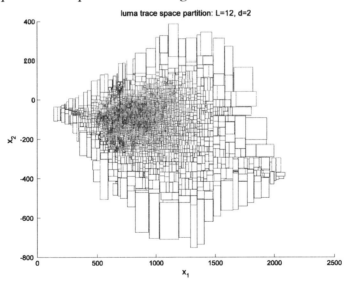

practical. Instead, we apply the kd-tree space partition with split axis decision based on the variance of data projection, i.e., at each split, the variances of projection of data onto each axis are sorted, and the split axis is chosen to be the one with largest variance. To further improve retrieval efficiency, we also compute MBR for each node. An example of kd-tree partition of 2-d LUFT space with 5 hours of video from TRECVID and resulting leaf node level MBRs are shown in Figure 10.

The kd-tree height is $L=12$, this results in 2048 leaf level MBRs. This gives a non-overlapping but can be disjoint partition of LUFT feature space. To process the QbE query, the temporal coherence feature of video repository is utilized. Instead of performing NN search for each query clip frame, we first

Table 1. Indexing efficiency and retrieval speed

d_{indx}	m	t_{search} *(ms)*	t_{match} *(ms)*
2	15	0.93	27.45
2	30	1.61	48.53
2	60	2.78	91.11
4	15	0.65	12.38
4	30	1.23	21.65
4	60	2.08	41.91
8	15	**0.62**	**11.32**
8	30	1.20	20.82
8	60	1.87	41.15

Figure 11. Precision-recall performance

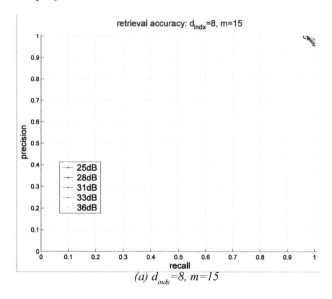

(a) d_{indx}=8, m=15

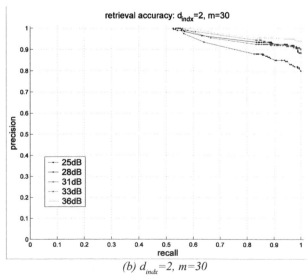

(b) d_{indx}=2, m=30

identify search localities by locating leaf nodes traversed by query clip. Then all clips in this locality are matched with the query clip by computing the minimum average projection distance as discussed. This approach significantly reduces the computational complexity by limiting the search to one degree of freedom and results in very good performance in both speed and accuracy.

For a video data base size of 5 hours, we set up simulations to test the speed and precision-recall performances. One hundred Query clips each of lengths 15, 30, 60 frames are randomly chosen from both the 5-hour repository (for positive tests) and other sources (for negative tests). The average response times for different clip lengths as well as LUFT feature space dimension, d, are tabulated in Table 1. The algorithms are implemented with Matlab and the computer is a desktop PC with 2.0 GHz Pentium processor and 1G Bytes of memory. t_{search} is the time needed to identify the matching repository locality, while t_{match} is the computation time for computing the average projection distance between query clips and repository locality.

Notice that the best performance in speed is achieved when choosing a feature dimension of $d_{indx}=8$, and query clip length of $m=15$, where the average response time for QbE against a 5-hour repository is only 0.012 seconds. The precision-recall performance for this set up is also quite good. For a range of additive noise in the query clips, as measured as PSNR (dB) in range of 25dB to 38dB, the precision-recall performance is outstanding. It achieves roughly 100% precision with a high recall in the range of 90%, as in Figure 11a. For a comparison, when $d_{indx}=2$, $m=30$, the loss of information in LUFT representation becomes severe, with corresponding degradation of performance in Figure 11b.

In summary, multimedia database applications typically require a high-dimensional feature space to have robust and effective representation of multimedia object for effective matching in search applications. However, the high dimensionality of the feature space presents this "curse-of-dimensionality" issue to the indexing and query processing, and good retrieval accuracy and speed can be achieved by striking a good balance between robust and effective feature representation and low dimensionality for effective indexing solution, as indicated in the aforementioned video clip QbE solution. Alternatively, approximate solution can be a viable solution as well, which make compromise in the accuracy of search to gain the speed.

REFERENCES

Andoni, A., & Indyk, P. (2006). Near-Optimal Hashing Algorithms for Approximate Nearest Neighbor in High Dimensions. In *Proc. of the Symposium on Foundations of Computer Science* (FOCS).

Beckmann, N., Kriegel, H.P., & Schneider, R. (1990). The R*-tree: An efficient and robust access method for points and rectangles. In *Proceedings of ACM SIGMOD*, (pp. 322-331).

Berchtold, S., Keim, D., & H.P. Kriegel, H.P. (1996). The x-tree: An index structure for high dimensional data. In *Proceedings of the 22nd Int'l Conf on VLDB*, (pp. 28-39).

Belhumeur, P.N., Hepanha, J.P., & Kriegman, D.J. (1997). Eigenfaces vs. Fisherfaces: Recognition Using Class Specific Linear Projection. *IEEE Trans. on Pattern Analysis & Machine Intelligence, 19*(7), 711-720.

Bellman, R. (1961). *Adaptive Control Processes: A Guided Tour*. Princeton University Press.

Belkin, M., & Niyogi, P., (2003). Laplacian Eigenmaps for Dimensionality Reduction and Data Representation. *Neural Computation, 15*(6), 1373-1396.

Bengio, Y., Paiement, J.F., Vincent, P., & Delalleau, O. (2004). Out-of-sample extensions for LLE, isomap, MDS, eigenmaps, and spectral clustering. In *Advances in Neural Information Processing Systems.* Whistler, BC: MIT Press.

Beyer, K.S., Goldstein, J., Ramakrishnan, R., & Shaft, U. (1999). When Is `Nearest Neighbor' Meaningful? In *Proceedings 7th International Conference on Database Theory* (ICDT'99), (pp. 217-235), Jerusalem, Israel.

Bohm, C., Berchtold, S., & Keim, D. A. (2001). Searching in High-Dimensional Spaces—Index Structures for Improving the Performance of Multimedia Databases. *ACM Computing Survey, 33*(3), 322-373.

Cai, D., He, X., Zhou, K., Han, J., & Bao, H. (2007). Locality sensitive discriminant analysis. In *Proceedings of Int'l Joint Conf. on Artificial Intelligence*, (pp. 708-713).

Chen, H.T., Chang, H.W., & Liu, T.L. (2005). Local Discriminant Embedding and Its Variants In *Proceedings of IEEE Conf. on Computer Vision & Pattern Recognition*, (pp. 846-853).

Cox, T.F., & Cox, M.A.A. (2001) *Multidimensional Scaling.* Chapman and Hall.

Cheung K., & Fu, A. (1998). Enhanced nearest neighbour search on the r-tree. *ACM SIGMOD Record, 27*(3).

Dance, C., Willamowski, J., Fan, L.X., Bray, C., & Csurka, G. (2004). Visual Categorization with Bags of Keypoints In *Proc. of ECCV International Workshop on Statistical Learning in Computer Vision.*

Datar, M., Immorlica, N., Indyk, P., & Mirrokni, V. (2004). Locality-Sensitive Hashing Scheme Based on p-Stable Distributions. *Symposium on Computational Geometry.*

Duda, R.O., Peter, E. H., & David, G.S., (2000). *Pattern Classification* (2nd ed.). Wiley Interscience.

Ferman, A.M., Tekalp, A.M., & Mehrotra, R. (2002). Robust color histogram descriptors for video segment retrieval and identification. *IEEE Trans. on Image Processing, 1*(5), 497-508.

Fu, Y., & Huang, T.S. (2005). Locally linear embedded eigenspace analysis, *IFP Technical Report.* Dept of ECE, UIUC.

Fu, Y. Li, Z., Yuan, J., Wu, Y., & Huang, T.S. (2008). Locality vs. globality: Query-driven localized linear models for facial image computing. *IEEE Transactions on Circuits & System for Video Technology, 18*(12), 1741-1752.

Fu, Y., Yan, S., & Huang, T.S. (2008a). Classification and feature extraction by simplexization. *IEEE Trans. on Information Forensics and Security, 3*(1), 91-100.

Fu, Y., Yan, S., & Huang, T.S., (2008b). Correlation metric for generalized feature extraction. *IEEE Transactions on Pattern Analysis & Machine Intelligence, 30*(12), 2229-2235.

Fu, Y., & Huang, T.S. (2008). Image classification using correlation tensor analysis. *IEEE Trans. on Image Processing, 17*(2), 226-234.

Fu, Y., Li, Z., Huang, T.S., & Katsaggelos, A. K. (2008). Locally Adaptive Subspace and Similarity Metric Learning for Visual Clustering and Retrieval. *Computer Vision and Image Understanding* (CVIU), *110*(3), 390-402.

Fu, Y. (2008). *Unified discriminative subspace learning for multimodality image analysis*. Ph. D thesis, Dept of Electrical & Computer Engineering, University of Illinois at Urbana-Champaign.

Gaede, V., &. Gunther, O. (1998). Multidimensional access methods. *ACM Computing Survey, 30*(2), 170-231.

Gionis, A., Indyk, P., & Motwani, R. (1999). Similarity Search in High Dimensions via Hashing. In *Proceedings of 25th International Conference on Very Large Databases* (VLDB).

Grauman, K. & Darrell, T. (2005). The Pyramid Match Kernel: Discriminative Classification with Sets of Image Features, *Proceedings of the IEEE International Conference on Computer Vision* (ICCV), Beijing, China.

Grauman, K., & Darrell, T. (2006). Unsupervised learning of categories from sets of partially matching image features. In *Proceedings of IEEE Conf. on Computer Vision and Pattern Recognition.*

Guttman, A. (1984). R-trees:Adynamic index structure for spatial searching. In *Proc. ACM SIGMOD*, (pp.47-57). Boston.

Ham, J., Lee, D. D., Mika S., & Schölkopf, B., (2004). A kernel view of the dimensionality reduction of manifolds. In *Proc of Int'l Conf. on Machine learning.*

He, X., & Niyogi, P. (2003). Locality Preserving Projections. In *Proc. of NIPS.*

Kashino, K., Kurozumi, T., & Murase, H. (2003). A Quick Search Method for Audio and Video Signals Based on Histogram Pruning. *IEEE Trans. on Multimedia, 5*(3), 348-357.

Katayama N., & Satoh, S. (1997), SR-Tree: An Index Structure for Nearest Neighbor Searching of High-Dimensional Point Data, *Transactions of the Institute of Electronics, Information and Communication Engineers, J80-D-I*, (8), 703-717.

Indyk, P., & Motwani, R. (1998). Approximate Nearest Neighbors: Towards Removing the Curse of Dimensionality. In *Proc of 30th Symposium on Theory of Computing.*

Li, Z., Katsaggelos, A. K., & Gandhi, B. (2005). Fast video shot retrieval based on trace geometry matching. *IEE Proceedings on Vision, Image and Signal Processing, 152*(3), 367-373.

Li, Z., Liu, W., Lin, D., & Tang, X., (2005). Nonparametric subspace analysis for face recognition. In *Proc of IEEE Conf. on Computer Vision and Pattern Recognition*, (pp. 961-966).

Li, Z., Gao, L., & Katsaggelos, A. K. (2006). Locally Embedded Linear Spaces for Efficient Video Shot Indexing and retrieval. In *Proceedings of IEEE Int'l Conference on Multimedia & Expo*, Toronto, Canada.

Ma, Y., Lao, S., Takikawa, E., & Kawade, M. (2007). Discriminant analysis in correlation similarity measure space. In *Proc of Int'l Conf. on Machine Learning, 227*, 577-584.

Moghaddam, B., & Pentland, A. (1997). Probabilistic Visual Learning for Object Representation. In *IEEE Trans. on Pattern Analysis & Machine Intelligence, 19*(7), 696-710.

Moore, A. (1991). An introductory tutorial on kd-tree, extract from A. Moore's PhD Thesis. *Efficient Memorybased Learning for Robot Control,* University of Cambridge.

Robinson, J. (1981). The k-d-b-tree: A search structure for large multidimensional dynamic indexes. In *Proc. Of ACM SIGMOD,* (pp. 10-18).

Roussopoulos, N., Kelley, S., & Vincent, F. (1995). Nearest neighbor queries. In *Proc of ACM SIGMOD Int'l Conference on Management of Data,* (pp. 71-79).

Roweis, S. T., & Saul, L. K. (2000). Nonlinear Dimensionality Reduction by Locally Linear Embedding. *Science, 290*(5500), 2323-2326.

Rubner, Y., Tomasi, C., & Guibas, L. (2000). The Earth Mover's Distance as a Metric for Image Retrieval. *International Journal of Computer Vision, 40,* (2), 99-121.

Saul, L.K., & Roweis, S.T. (2003). Think Globally, Fit Locally: Unsupervised Learning of Low Dimensional Manifolds, *J. Machine Learning Research, 4,* 119-155.

Shakhnarovich, G., Darrell, T., & Indyk, P. (2007). *Nearest-Neighbor Methods in Learning and Vision: Theory and Practice,.* MIT Press.

Sivic, J., & Zisserman, A. (2008). Efficient Visual Search for Objects in Videos. *Proceedings of the IEEE, 96*(4), 548-566.

Stonebraker, M., Sellis, T., & Hanson, E. (1986). An analysis of rule indexing implementations in data base systems. *Proc. Intl. Conf. on Expert Database Systems.*

Tenenbaum, J.B., Silva, V., & Langford, J.C. (2000). A Global Geometric Framework for Nonlinear Dimensionality Reduction. *Science, 290,* 2319-2323.

Tao, D., Li, X., Wu, X., & Maybank, S.J. (2007). General tensor discriminant analysis and Gabor features for gait recognition, IEEE Trans. on Pattern Analysis & Machine Intelligence, *29*(10), 1700-1715.

Turk, M., & Pentland, A.P. (1991). Face Recognition Using Eigenfaces. In *Proc of IEEE Conf. Computer Vision and Pattern Recognition.*

Weinberger, K. Q., & Saul, L. K. (2004). Unsupervised Learning of Image Manifolds by Semidefinite Programming. *IEEE Conf. on Computer Vision & Pattern Recognition, 2,* 988-995.

White, D. & Jain, R. (1996). Similarity indexing with the SS-tree, *Proc of 12th Intl. Conf. on Data Egineering,* New Orleans.

Xu, D., & Chang, S.F. (2007). Visual Event Recognition in News Video using Kernel Methods with Multi-Level Temporal Alignment. *IEEE Int. Conf. on Computer Vision and Pattern Recognition.*

Xu, D., Cham, T.J., Yan, S., & Chang, S.F. (2008). Near Duplicate Image Identification with Spatially Aligned Pyramid Matching. *IEEE Int. Conf. on Computer Vision and Pattern Recognition.*

Yan, S. C., Xu, D., Zhang, B., Zhang, H., Yang, Q., & Lin, S. (2007). Graph Embedding and Extension: A General Framework for Dimensionality Reduction. *IEEE Trans. on Pattern Analysis & Machine Intelligence, 29*(1), 40-51.

Yuan, J., Duan, L., Tian, Q., & Xu, C. (2004). Fast and Robust Short Video Clip Search Using an Index Structure. In *Proc. of ACM Intl. Workshop on Multimedia Information Retrieval* (MIR).

Yuan, J., Wu, Y., & Yang, M. (2007a). From Frequent Itemsets to Semantically Meaningful Visual Patterns. In *Proc. of ACM. Knowledge Discover and Data Mining* (KDD).

Yuan, J., Wu, Y., & Yang, M. (2007b). Discovery of Collocation Patterns: from Visual Words to Visual Phrases. *IEEE Int. Conf. on Computer Vision and Pattern Recognition* (CVPR).

Yuan, J., Li, Z., Fu, Y., Wu, Y., & Huang, T.S. (2007). Common Spatial Pattern Discovery by Efficient Candidate Pruning. In *Proc. of IEEE Intl. Conference on Image Processing* (ICIP).

Yuan, J., &Wu, Y. (2007). Spatial Random Partition for Common Visual Pattern Discovery. In *Proc. of IEEE Intl. Conference on Computer Vision* (ICCV).

Compilation of References

Acton, S., & Mukherjee, D. (2000a). Image edges from area morphology. In *International Conference on Acoustics, Speech, and Signal Processing (ICASSP)* (pp. 2239–2242). Istanbul, Turkey.

Acton, S., & Mukherjee, D. (2000b, April). Scale space classification using area morphology. *IEEE Transactions on Image Processing, 9*(4), 623–635.

Adjeroh, D., & Lee, M. (2004). Scene-adaptive transform domain video partitioning. *Multimedia, IEEE Transactions on, 6*(1), 58-69.

Agarwal, G. (2005). *Presenting Visual Information to the User: Combining Computer Vision and Interface Design.* Master Thesis, Univseristy of Maryland, 2005.

Agarwal, G., Belhumeur, P., Feiner, S., Jacobs, D., Kress, J.W., Ramamoorthi, R., Bourg, N., Dixit, N., Ling, H., Mahajan, D., Russell, R., Shirdhonkar, S., Sunkavalli, K., & White, S. (2006). First Steps Toward an Electronic Field Guide for Plants. *Taxon, 55*(3), 597-610.

Agarwal, S., Awan, A., & Roth, D. (2004). Learning to Detect Objects in Images via a Sparse, Part-Based Representation. *IEEE Trans. on Pattern Analysis and Machine Intelligence, 26*(11), 1475-1490.

Agarwal, S., Awan, A., & Roth, D. (2004). Learning to detect objects in images via a sparse, part-based representation. *IEEE Transactions on Pattern Analysis and Machine Intelligence, 26*(11), 1475–1490. doi: 10.1109/TPAMI.2004.108.

Aglet. (2002). Retrieved from http://www.trl.ibm.com/aglets/

AhmedM, K. A. (1999). Video segmentation using an opportunistic approach. *Multimedia Modeling, Ottawa, Canada, 389*–405.

Aksoy, S., Koperski, K., Tusk, C., Marchisio, G., & Tilton, J.C. (2005). Learning Bayesian classifiers for scene classification with a visual grammar. *IEEE Transaction on Geoscience and Remote Sensing, 43*(3), 581-589. doi: 10.1109/TGRS.2004.839547.

Akutsu, A., Tonomura, Y., Hashimoto, H., & Ohba, Y. (1992). *Video indexing using motion vectors.* (pp. 1522-1530).

An Electronic Field Guide: Plant Exploration and Discovery in the 21st Century. (2008). Retrieved December 12, 2008, fromhttp://herbarium.cs.columbia.edu/.

Anastassopoulos, V., & Venetsanopoulos, A. (1991). The classification properties of the pecstrum and its use for pattern identification. *Circuits, Systems and Signal Processing, 10*(3), 293–326.

Andoni, A., & Indyk, P. (2006). Near-Optimal Hashing Algorithms for Approximate Nearest Neighbor in High Dimensions. In *Proc. of the Symposium on Foundations of Computer Science* (FOCS).

Angluin, D. (1988). Queries and concept learning. *Machine Learning, 2*, (4), 319-342.

ANSI/ISA-S88.01, 1995. Batch Control. Part 1. Models and terminology.

ANSI/ISA-TR84.00.02, Part 1 Safety Instrumented Functions (SIF).

Aptoula, E., & Lefèvre, S. (2006, September). Spatial morphological covariance applied to texture classification. In *International Workshop on Multimedia Content Representation, Classification and Security (IWMRCS)*, *4105*, 522–529. Istanbul, Turkey: Springer-Verlag.

Aptoula, E., & Lefèvre, S. (2007a, November). A comparative study on multivariate mathematical morphology. *Pattern Recognition, 40*(11), 2914–2929.

Aptoula, E., & Lefèvre, S. (2007b, October). On morphological color texture characterization. In *International Symposium on Mathematical Morphology (ISMM)* (pp. 153–164). Rio de Janeiro, Brazil.

Arman, F., Hsu, A., & Chiu, M.Y. (1993). Image processing on compressed data for large video database, *ACM international conference on Multimedia*, (pp. 267-272). doi: 10.1145/166266.166297.

Arzen, K.E. (1994). Grafcet for intelligent supervisory control applications. *Automatica, 30*(10), 1513-1525.

Asano, A., & Yokozeki, S. (1996). Multiresolution pattern spectrum and its application to optimization of nonlinear filter. In *IEEE International Conference on Image Processing (ICIP)* (pp. 387–390). Lausanne, Switzerland.

Asano, A., Miyagawa, M., & Fujio, M. (2000). Texture modelling by optimal grey scale structuring elements using morphological pattern spectrum. In *IAPR International Conference on Pattern Recognition (ICPR)* (pp. 475–478).

Aslandogan, Y.A., & Yu, C.T. (1999). Techniques and systems for image and video retrieval. *IEEE Transactions on Knowledge and Data Engineering, 11*(1), 56-63. doi: 10.1109/69.755615.

Aslandogan, Y.A., & Yu, C.T. (1999). Techniques and Systems for Image and Video Retrieval. *IEEE Transactions on Knowledge and Data Engineering, 11*(1), 56-63.

Astesiano, E. & Reggio, G. (2000). Formalism and method. *Theoretical Computer Science, 236*, 3-34.

Avidan, S. (2001). Support vector tracking. *Proc. of CVPR, 1*, 184–191.

Avidan, S. (2005) Ensemble tracking. In *Proc. of CVPR, 2*, 494–501.

Ayache, S., & Quénot, G. (2007). Evaluation of active learning strategies for video indexing. *Signal Processing: Image Communication, 22*, 692-704.

Ayala, G., & Domingo, J. (2001, December). Spatial size distribution: applications to shape and texture analysis. *IEEE Transactions on Pattern Analysis and Machine Intelligence, 23*(12), 1430–1442.

Ayala, G., Diaz, E., Demingo, J., & Epifanio, I. (2003). Moments of size distributions applied to texture classification. In *International Symposium on Image and Signal Processing and Analysis (ISPA)* (pp. 96–100).

Ayala, G., Diaz, M., & Martinez-Costa, L. (2001). Granulometric moments and corneal endothelium status. *Pattern Recognition, 34*, 1219–1227.

Bach, J., Fuller, C., Gupta, A., Hampapur, A., Horowitz, B., Humphrey, R., & Jain, R. (1996). The Virage image search engine: An open framework for image management. In *Storage and Retrieval for Image and Video Databases, volume 2670 of Proceedings of SPIE*, (pp. 76–87).

Baeg, S., Batman, S., Dougherty, E., Kamat, V., Kehtarnavaz, N., Kim, S., et al. (1999). Unsupervised morphological granulometric texture segmentation of digital mammograms. *Journal of Electronic Imaging, 8*(1), 65–73.

Bagdanov, A., & Worring, M. (2002). Granulometric analysis of document images. In *IAPR International Conference on Pattern Recognition (ICPR)* (pp. 468–471). Quebec City, Canada.

Bai, L., Lao, S.Y., Jones, G., & Smeaton, A.F. (2007). A semantic content analysis model for sports video based on perception concepts and finite state machines. *IEEE International Conference on Multimedia and Expo*, (pp. 1407-1410). doi: 10.1109/ICME.2007.4284923.

Balagurunathan, Y., & Dougherty, E. (2003). Granulometric parametric estimation for the random boolean model using optimal linear filters and optimal structuring elements. *Pattern Recognition Letters, 24*, 283–293.

Balcan, M.-F., Blum, A., Choi, P.P., Lafferty, J., Pantano, B., Rwebangira, M.R., & Zhu, X. (2005). Person identification in webcam images: An application of semi-supervised learning. In *Proc. ICML Workshop on Learning with Partially Classified Training Data*.

Ballard, D.H., & Brown, C.M. (1982). *Computer Vision*. Englewood Cliffs, New Jersey: Prentice Hall.

Bangham, J., Gibson, S., & Harvey, R. (2003). The art of scale-space. In *British Machine Vision Conference (BMVC)*.

Bangham, J., Ling, P., & Harvey, R. (1996, May). Scale-space from nonlinear filters. *IEEE Transactions on Pattern Analysis and Machine Intelligence, 18*(5), 520–528.

Barnard, K., & Forsyth, D.A. (2001). Learning the semantics of words and pictures. In *Proc. Int'l Conf. Computer Vision*, 408-415. doi: 10.1109/ICCV.2001.937654.

Barnard, K., Duygulu, P., Forsyth, D., de Freitas, N., Blei, D., & Jordan, M. (2002). Matching words and pictures. Journal of Machine Learning Research, 3.

Barnard, K., Duygulu, P., Freitas, N., & Forsyth, D. (2001). Clustering art. *Computer Vision and Pattern Recognition*, (pp. 434-439).

Barnard, K., Duygulu, P., Freitas, N., & Forsyth, D. (2003). Recognition as translating images into yext. *Internet Imaging IX, Electronic Imaging*.

Barnard, K., Duygulu, P., Freitas, N., Forsyth, D., Blei, D., & Jordan, M. (2003). Matching words and pictures. *Journal of Machine Learning Research*, (pp. 1107-1135).

Barnard, K., Duygulu, P., Freitas, N., Forsyth, D., Blei, D., & Jordan, M.I. (2003). Matching words and pictures. *Journal of Machine Learning Research, 3*, 1107-1135. doi: 10.1162/jmlr.2003.3.4-5.1107.

Barnich, O., Jodogne, S., & Droogenbroeck, M. van. (2006). Robust analysis of silhouettes by morphological size distributions. In *International Workshop on Advanced Concepts for Intelligent Vision Systems (ACIVS), 4179*, 734–745. Springer-Verlag.

Basri, R., Costa, L., Geiger, D., & Jacobs, D. (1998). Determining the Similarity of Deformable Shapes. *Vision Research, 38*, 2365-2385.

Batman, S., & Dougherty, E. (1997). Size distribution for multivariate morphological granulometries: texture classification and statistical properties. *Optical Engineering, 36*(5), 1518–1529.

Batman, S., Dougherty, E., & Sand, F. (2000). Heterogeneous morphological granulometries. *Pattern Recognition, 33*, 1047–1057.

Beckmann, N., Kriegel, H.P., & Schneider, R. (1990). The R*-tree: An efficient and robust access method for points and rectangles. In *Proceedings of ACM SIGMOD*, (pp. 322-331).

Bederson, B.B. (2001). PhotoMesa: A Zoomable Image Browser Using Quantum Treemaps and Bubblemaps. *ACM Symposium on User Interface Software and Technology, CHI Letters, 3*(2), 71-80.

Belhumeur, P., Hespanha, J., & Kriegman, D. (1996). Eigenfaces vs. Fisherfaces: recognition using class specific linear projection. In *Proc. Of European Conference on Computer Vision*, (pp. 45-58).

Belhumeur, P.N., Hepanha, J.P., & Kriegman, D.J. (1997). Eigenfaces vs. Fisherfaces: Recognition Using Class Specific Linear Projection. *IEEE Trans. on Pattern Analysis & Machine Intelligence, 19*(7), 711-720.

Belkin, M., & Niyogi, P., (2003). Laplacian Eigenmaps for Dimensionality Reduction and Data Representation. *Neural Computation, 15*(6), 1373-1396.

Belkin, M., Matveeva, I., & Niyogi, P. (2004). Regularization and semi-supervised learning on large graphs. In *Proc. Workshop on Computational Learning Theory*.

Belkin, M., Niyogi, P., & Sindhwani, V. (2006). Manifold regularization: A geometric framework for learning from labeled and unlabeled examples. *Journal of Machine Learning Research, 7*, 2399-2434.

Bellens, R., Martinez-Fonte, L., Gautama, S., Chan, J., & Canters, F. (2007). Potential problems with using reconstruction in morphological profiles for classification of remote sensing images from urban areas. In *IEEE International Geosciences and Remote Sensing Symposium (IGARSS)* (pp. 2698–2701).

Bellman, R. (1961). *Adaptive Control Processes: A Guided Tour*. Princeton University Press.

Belongie, S., Malik, J., & Puzicha, J. (2002). Shape Matching and Object Recognition Using Shape Context. *IEEE Trans. on Pattern Analysis and Machine Intelligence, 24*(24), 509-522.

Benediktsson, J., Pesaresi, M., & Arnason, K. (2003, September). Classification and feature extraction for remote sensing images from urban areas based on morphological transformations. *IEEE Transactions on Geoscience and Remote Sensing, 41*(9), 1940–1949.

Benediktsson, J., Pesaresi, M., & Arnason, K. (2005, March). Classification of hyperspectral data from urban areas based on extended morphological profiles. *IEEE Transactions on Geoscience and Remote Sensing, 43*(3), 480–491.

Bengio, Y., Paiement, J.F., Vincent, P., & Delalleau, O. (2004). Out-of-sample extensions for LLE, isomap, MDS, eigenmaps, and spectral clustering. In *Advances in Neural Information Processing Systems*. Whistler, BC: MIT Press.

Bennett, K., & Demiriz, A. (1999). Semi-supervised support vector machines. *Advances in Neural Information Processing Systems, 11*. MIT Press.

Berchtold, S., Keim, D., & H.P. Kriegel, H.P. (1996). The x-tree: An index structure for high dimensional data. In *Proceedings of the 22nd Int'l Conf on VLDB*, (pp. 28-39).

Berger, A., Pietra, S.D., & Pietra, V.D. (1996). A maximum entropy approach to natural language processing. *Computational Linguistics, 22*(1), 39-71.

Bertini, M., Del Bimbo, A., & Pala, P. (2001). Content-based indexing and retrieval of TV news. *Pattern Recognition Letters, 22*(5), 503-516.

Bescos, J., Cisneros, G., Martinez, J., Menendez, J., & Cabrera, J. (2005). A unified model for techniques on video-shot transition detection. *Multimedia, IEEE Transactions on, 7*(2), 293-307.

Beyer, K., Goldstein, J., Ramakrishnan, R., & Shaft, U. (1999). When is "nearest neighbor" meaningful? In *Proceedings of International Conference on Database Theory*, (pp. 217-235).

Beyer, K.S., Goldstein, J., Ramakrishnan, R., & Shaft, U. (1999). When Is 'Nearest Neighbor' Meaningful? In *Proceedings 7th International Conference on Database Theory* (ICDT'99), (pp. 217-235), Jerusalem, Israel.

Beymer, D. (1993). *Face recognition under varying pose*. Technical Report AIM-1461. MIT AI Laboratory.

Biederman, I. (1987). Recognition--by--components: A theory of human image understanding. *Psychological Review, 94*(2), 115-147.

Blanz, V., Rornhani, S., & Vetter, T. (2002). Face identification across different poses and illuminations with a 3D morphable model. In *Proc. of IEEE International Conference on Automatic Face and Gesture Recognition*, (pp. 202-207).

Blei, D., & Jordan, M. (2003). Modeling annotated data. *Proc. Int'l Conf. Research and Development in Information Retrieval*, (pp. 127-134). doi: 10.1145/860435.860460.

Blei, D., & Jordan, M.I. (2003). Modeling annotated data. *Annual International ACM SIGIR Conference*, Toronto, Canada.

Blei, D., Ng, A., & Jordan, M. (2003). Latent Dirichlet allocation. *Journal of Machine Learning Research, 3*, 993-1022. doi: 10.1162/jmlr.2003.3.4-5.993.

Blum, A., & Chawla, S. (2001). Learning from labeled and unlabeled data using graph mincuts. In *Proc.18th International Conference on Machine Learning*.

Blum, A., & Mitchell, T. (1998). Combining labeled and unlabeled data with co-training. In *Proceedings of the 11th Annual Conference on Computational Learning Theory*, (pp. 92-100).

Blum, A., & Mitchell, T. (1998). Combining labeled and unlabeled data with co-training. In *Proc. Workshop on Computational Learning Theory*.

Blum, H. (1973). Biological Shape and Visual Science. *J. Theor. Biol., 38*, 205-287.

Boccignone, G., De Santo, M., & Percannella, G. (2000). An algorithm for video cut detection in MPEG sequences. (pp. 523–530).

Bohm, C., Berchtold, S., & Keim, D. A. (2001). Searching in High-Dimensional Spaces—Index Structures for Improving the Performance of Multimedia Databases. *ACM Computing Survey, 33*(3), 322-373.

Bookstein, F. (1989). Principal Warps: Thin-Plate-Splines and Decomposition of Deformations. *IEEE Trans. on Pattern Analysis and Machine Intelligence, 11*(6), 567-585.

Boomgaard, R. van den, & Smeulders, A. (1994, November). The morphological structure of images: the differential equations of morphological scale-space. *IEEE Transactions on Pattern Analysis and Machine Intelligence, 16*(11), 1101–1113.

Boreczky, J.S., & Rowe, L.A. (1996). Comparison of video shot boundary detection techniques. *In Proc.*

IS&T/SPIE Storage and Retrieval for Still Image and Video Databases IV, 2664, 170-179.

Borg, I., & Groenen, P. (1997). *Modern Multidimensional Scaling: Theory and Applications.* Springer.

Bosch, A., Muňoz, X., & Marti, R. (2007). A review: Which is the best way to organize/classify images by content? *Image and Vision Computing, 25*(6), 778-791. doi: 10.1016/j.imavis.2006.07.015.

Bosch, A., Zisserman, A., & Muňoz, X. (2006). Scene classification via plsa. *Proc. European Conf. Computer Vision, 4*, 517-530. doi: 10.1007/11744085_40.

Bosch, A., Zisserman, A., & Muyyoz, X. (2008). Scene classification using a hybrid generative/discriminative approach. *IEEE Transaction on Pattern Analysis and Machine Intelligence, 30*(4), 712-727. doi: 10.1109/TPAMI.2007.70716.

Bosworth, J., & Acton, S. (2003). Morphological scale-space in image processing. *Digital Signal Processing, 13*, 338–367.

Boukerroui, D., Alison, J.N., & Brady, M. (2003). Velocity estimation in ultrasound images: A block matching approach. *IPMI*, (pp. 586–598).

Bousquet, O., Chapelle, O., & Hein, M. (2003). Measure based regularization. *Advances in Neural Information Processing Systems, 15*. MIT Press.

Boutell, M., Brown, C., & Luo, J. (2002). *Survey on the state of the art in semantic scene classification* (Technical Report 799). Rochester, NY: University of Rochester.

Boutell, M., Shen, X.P., Luo, J., & Brown, C. (2004). Learning multi-label semantic scene classification. *Pattern Recognition, 37*(9), 1757-1771. doi: 10.1016/j.patcog.2004.03.009.

Bouthemy, P., Gelgon, M., Ganansia, F., & IRISA, R. (1999). A unified approach to shot change detection and camera motioncharacterization. *Circuits and Systems for Video Technology, IEEE Transactions on, 9*(7), 1030-1044.

Braga-Neto, U., & Goutsias, J. (2005). Constructing multiscale connectivities. *Computer Vision and Image Understanding, 99*, 126–150.

Breen, E., & Jones, R. (1996, November). Attribute openings, thinnings, and granulometries. *Computer Vision and Image Understanding, 64*(3), 377–389.

Brinker, K. (2003). Incorporating diversity in active learning with support vector machines. In *Proceedings of International Conference on Machine Learning*, (pp. 59-66).

Brown, L., & Gruenwald, L. (1998). Tree-Based Indexes for Image Data. *Journal of Visual Communication and Image Representation, 9*(4), 300-313.

Brown, L., & Gruenwald, L. (2001). A Prototype Content-Based Retrieval System that Uses Virtual Images to Save Space. *Proceedings of the 27th International Conference on Very Large Databases (VLDB)* (pp. 693-694), Rome, Italy.

Brox, T., Bruhn, A., Papenberg, N., & Wiecker, J., (2004). High accuracy optical flow estimation based on a theory of warping. *European Conf. Computer Vision*, (pp. 25–36).

Bruno, E., & Pellerin, D. (2002). Video shot detection based on linear prediction of motion. *Multimedia and Expo, 2002. ICME'02. Proceedings. 2002 IEEE International Conference on, 1*

Cai, D., He, X., Li, Z., Ma, W.-Y., & Wen, J.-R. (2004). Hierarchical clustering of WWW image search results using visual, textual and link information. *ACM International Conference on Multimedia*, (pp. 952-959).

Cai, D., He, X., Zhou, K., Han, J., & Bao, H. (2007). Locality sensitive discriminant analysis. In *Proceedings of Int'l Joint Conf. on Artificial Intelligence*, (pp. 708-713).

Cai, D., He, X.F., Li, Z.W., Ma, W.Y., & Wen, J.R. (2004). Hierarchical clustering of WWW image search results using visual, textual and link analysis. In *Proc. 2th ACM Int'l Conf. Multimedia*, (pp. 952-959). doi: 10.1145/1027527.1027747.

Camara-Chavez, G., Precioso, F., Cord, M., Philipp-Foliguet, S., De, A., & Araujo, A. (2007). Shot boundary detection by a hierarchical supervised approach. (pp. 197-200).

Campbell, M., Haubold, A., Liu, M., Natsev, A.P., Smith, J.R., Tesic, J., Xie, L., Yan, R., & Yang, J. (2007). IBM research TRECVID-2007 video retrieval system. In Proceedings of NIST TRECVID-2007.

Campisi, P., Longari A., & Neri, A. (1999). Automatic key frame selection using a wavelet based approach. In *Proc. of SPIE, 3813*, 861-872.

Canny, J. (1986). *A computational approach to edge detection. IEEE Trans. Patt. Analysis and Mach. Intell.,* 8(6), 679-698.

Carneiro, G., & Vasconcelos, N. (2005). A database centric view of semantic image annotation and retrieval. In *Proceedings of ACM SIGIR Conf. on Research and Development in Information Retrieval.*

Carneiro, G., Chan, A.B., Moreno, P., & Vasconcelos, N. (2006). Supervised learning of semantic classes for image annotation and retrieval. *IEEE Transaction on Pattern Analysis Machine Intelligence, 29*(3), 394-410. doi: 10.1109/TPAMI.2007.61.

Carreira-Perpinan, M.A., & Zemel, R.S. (2005). Proximity graphs for clustering and manifold learning. *Advances in neural information processing systems, 17.* MIT Press.

Carson, C., Tomas, M., Belongie, S., Hellerstein, J.M., & Malik, J. (2002). Blobworld: image segmentation using expectation-maximization and its application to image querying. *IEEE Transactions on Pattern Analysis and Machine Intelligence, 24*(8), 1026-1038.

Castro, P.Y.M. (2003). *Proximity neighbor selection in tree-based structured peer-to-peer overlays.* Technical Report MSR-TR-2003-52.

Chadha, H.S., Baugh Jr, J.W. & Wing, J.M. (1999). Formal specifications of concurrent systems. *Advances in Engineering Software, 30,* 211-224.

Chang, E., Kingshy, G., Sychay, G., & Wu, G. (2003). CBSA: content-based soft annotation for multimodal image retrieval using Bayes Point Machines. *IEEE Trans. on CSVT, 13*(1), 26-38.

Chang, E.Y., Goh, K., Sychay, G., & Wu, G. (2003). CBSA: Content-based soft annotation for multimodal image retrieval using Bayes Point Machines. *IEEE Transaction on Circuits System Video Technology, 13,* 26-38. doi: 10.1109/TCSVT.2002.808079.

Chang, T., & Kuo, C. (1993). Texture analysis and classification with tree-structured wavelet transform. *IEEE Transactions on Image Processing, 2*(4), 429-441.

Chanussot, J., Benediktsson, J., & Pesaresi, M. (2003). On the use of morphological alternated sequential filters for the classification of remote sensing images from urban areas. In *IEEE International Geosciences and Remote Sensing Symposium (IGARSS).* Toulouse, France.

Chapelle, O., & Zien, A. (2005). Semi-supervised classification by low density separation. In *Proc.Tenth International Workshop on Artificial Intelligence and Statistics.*

Chapelle, O., Zien, A., & Scholkopf, B. (Eds.). (2006). *Semi-supervised learning.* MIT Press.

Chapelle, O., Zien, A., & Schölkopf, B. (Eds.). (2006). *Semi-supervised learning.* MIT Press.

Chawthe, S.R.Y. (2003). Making GNUtella-like P2P systems scalable. *Applications, Technologies, Architectures, and Protocols for Computer Communication.*

Chen, D., & Bovik, A. (1990). Visual pattern image coding. *IEEE Trans. Communications, 38,* 2137–2146.

Chen, H., Belhumeur, P., & Jacobs, D. (2000). In search of Illumination Invariants. *IEEE Conf. on Computer Vision and Pattern Recognition, 1,* 254-261.

Chen, H.T., Chang, H.W., & Liu, T.L. (2005). Local Discriminant Embedding and Its Variants In *Proceedings of IEEE Conf. on Computer Vision & Pattern Recognition,* (pp. 846-853).

Chen, M., & Hauptmann, A. (2005). Active learning In multiple modalities for semantic feature extraction from video. In *Proceedings of AAAI workshop on learning in computer vision.*

Chen, M., & Yan, P. (1989, July). A multiscale approach based on morphological filtering. *IEEE Transactions on Pattern Analysis and Machine Intelligence, 11*(7), 694–700.

Chen, M., Christel, M., Hauptmann, A., & Wactlar, H. (2005). Putting active learning into multimedia applications: dynamic definition and refinement of concept classifiers. In *Proceedings of ACM Multimedia,* (pp. 902-911).

Chen, Y., & Wang, J.Z. (2005). Image categorization by learning and reasoning with regions. *Journal of Machine Learning Research, 5,* 913-939.

Chen, Z., Liu, W.Y., Hu, C., Li, M., & Zhang, H.J. (2001). iFind: a web image search engine. *Proc. of the 24th Annual International ACM SIGIR Conference on Research and Development in Information Retrieval,* (pp. 450-458).

Cheng, J., & Wang, K.Q. (2007). Active learning for image retrieval with Co-SVM. In *Pattern Recognition, 40*(1), 330-334.

Cheng, S. C., & Wu, T. L. (2006). Scene-adaptive video partitioning by semantic object tracking. *Journal of Visual Communication and Image Representation, 17*(1), 72-97.

Cherfaoui, M., & Bertin, C. (1995). Temporal segmentation of videos: A new approach. *, 2419* 38.

Cheung K., & Fu, A. (1998). Enhanced nearest neighbour search on the r-tree. *ACM SIGMOD Record, 27*(3).

Cheung, K.L., & Fu, A.W. (1998). Enhanced Nearest Neighbour Search on the R-tree. *ACM SIGMOD Record. 27*(3), 16-21.

Chung, F. (1997). *Spectral graph theory.* American Mathematical Society.

CIE. (1986). Colorimetry. *CIE Publications 15.2*, Commission International de L'Eclairage, 2nd edition.

CIE. (1989). *International Lighting Vocabulary.* CIE Publications 17.4, Commission International de L'Eclairage, 4th edition, 1989.

Clip2. (2002). *The GNUtella Protocol Specification v0.4 Document Revison 1.2.* Retrieved September 23, 2007, from Limewire: http://www9.limewire.com/developer/gnutella_protocol_0.4.pdf

Coggins, J.M., & Jain, A.K. (1985). A spatial filtering approach to texture analysis. *Pattern Recognition Letters, 3*, 195-203.

Cohen, B., & Dinstein, I. (2002). New maximum likelihood motion estimation schemes for noisy ultrasound images. *Pattern Recognition, 25*, 455-463.

Cohen, D.A., Ghahramani, Z., & Jordan, M.I. (1996). Active learning with statistical models. *Journal of Artificial Intelligence, 4*, 129-145.

Collins, M., & Singer, Y. (1999). Unsupervised models for named entity classification. In *Proceedings of the Empirical NLP and Very Large Corpora Conference* (pp. 100-110).

Collins, R., & Liu, Y. (2003). On-line selection of discriminative tracking features. In *Proc. of ICCV.*

Comaniciu, D., & Meer, P. (2002). Mean shift: a robust approach toward feature space analysis. *IEEE Transactions on Pattern Analysis and Machine Intelligence, 24*(5), 603-619. doi: 10.1109/34.1000236.

Comaniciu, D., Ramesh, V., & Meer, P. (2000). Real-time tracking of non-rigid objects using mean shift. *Proc. of CVPR, 2*, 142–149.

Comer, D. (1979). The Ubiquitous B-Tree. *ACM Computing Surveys, 11*(2), 121-137.

Cootes, T., Wheeler, G., Walker, K., & Taylor, C. (2002). View-based active appearance model. *Image and Vision Computing, 20*, 657-664.

Cormen, T., Leiserson, T, Rivest, R., & Stein, C. (2001). *Introduction to Algorithms*, 2nd edition. The MIT Press.

Cox, I.J., Miller, M.L., Minka, T.P., Papathomas, T.V., & Yianilos, P.N. (2000). The Bayesian image retrieval system, PicHunter: theory, implementation, and psychophysical. *IEEE Transactions on Image Processing, 9*(1), 20-37.

Cox, T.F., & Cox, M.A.A. (2001) *Multidimensional Scaling.* Chapman and Hall.

Dagli, C.K., Rajaram, S., & Huang, T.S. (2006). Leveraging active learning for relevance feedback using an information-theoretic diversity measure. In *Proceedings of International Conference on Image and Video Retrieval,* (pp. 123-132).

Dance, C., Willamowski, J., Fan, L.X., Bray, C., & Csurka, G. (2004). Visual Categorization with Bags of Keypoints In *Proc. of ECCV International Workshop on Statistical Learning in Computer Vision.*

Dasgupta, S., Littman, M., & McAllester, D. (2001). PAC generalization bounds for co-training. In *Proceedings of 14th Neural Information Processing Systems* (pp. 375-382).

Datar, M., Immorlica, N., Indyk, P., & Mirrokni, V. (2004). Locality-Sensitive Hashing Scheme Based on p-Stable Distributions. *Symposium on Computational Geometry.*

Datta, R., Ge, W., Li, J., & Wang, J. Z. (2007). Toward bridging the annotation-retrieval gap in image search. *IEEE Multimedia, 14*(3), 24-35. doi: 10.1109/MMUL.2007.67.

Datta, R., Joshi, D., Li, J., & Wang, J.Z. (2007). Tagging over time: Real-world image annotation by lightweight meta-learning. In *Proc. 15th Ann' ACM int'l Conf. Multimedia*, (pp. 393-402). doi: 10.1145/1291233.1291328.

Datta, R., Li, J., & Wang, J. Z. (2005). Content-Based Image Retrieval – Approaches and Trends of the New Age. In *Proceedings of Multimedia Information Retrieval 2005 (pp.* 253-262), Singapore.

Datta, R., Li, J., & Wang, J.Z. (2005). Content-based image retrieval – approaches and trends of the new age. In *Proceedings of the 7th ACM SIGMM workshop on Multimedia Information Retrieval* (pp. 253-262).

Daugman, J.G. (1988). Complete discrete 2-D Gabor transforms by neural networks for image analysis and compression. *IEEE Transactions on Acoustics, Speech and Signal Processing, 36*, 1169-1179.

Dejan Milojicic, M.B. (August 25, 2006). MASIF: The OMG Mobile Agent System Interoperability Facility. *Personal and Ubiquitous Computing* , (pp. 117-129).

Demarty, C. H., & Beucher, S. (1999). Morphological tools for indexing video documents. *, 2*, 991-1002.

Dietterich, T.G., Lathrop, R.H., & Lozano-Pérez, T. (1997). Solving the multiple-instance problem with axis-parallel rectangles. *Artificial Intelligence, 89*, 31-71.

Ding, J.Y.S. (2005). *A Heuristic Algorithm for Agent-Based Grid Resource Discovery*. Washington.

Divakaran, A., Ito, H., Sun, H., & Poon, T. (2003). Scene change detection and feature extraction for MPEG-4 sequences, *3656*, 545.

Dougherty, E., & Cheng, Y. (1995). Morphological pattern-spectrum classification of noisy shapes: exterior granulometries. *Pattern Recognition, 28*(1), 81–98.

Dougherty, E., Newell, J., & Pelz, J. (1992, October). Morphological texture-based maximum-likelihood pixel classification based on local granulometric moments. *Pattern Recognition, 25*(10), 1181–1198.

Dougherty, E., Pelz, J., Sand, F., & Lent, A. (1992). Morphological image segmentation by local granulometric size distributions. *Journal of Electronic Imaging, 1*, 46–60.

Doulamis, A., Doulamis, N., & Maragos, P. (2001). Generalized multiscale connected operators with applications to granulometric image analysis. In *IEEE International Conference on Image Processing (ICIP)* (pp. 684–687).

Draper, B., Baek, K., Bartlett, M., & Beveridge, J. (2003). Recognising faces with PCA and ICA. *Comuter Vision and Image Understanding, 91*(1-2), 115-137.

Droogenbroeck, M. van, & Buckley, M. (2005). Morphological erosions and openings: fast algorithms based on anchors. *Journal of Mathematical Imaging and Vision, 22*, 121–142.

Droogenbroeck, M. van. (2002). Algorithms for openings of binary and label images with rectangular structuring elements. In *International Symposium on Mathematical Morphology (ISMM)* (pp. 197–207).

Druschel, A.R. (2001). Pastry: scalable decentralized obiect location, and routing for large scale peer-to-peer systems. In *Proceedings of IFIP/ACM Internation Conference on Distributed Systems Platforms*, Heidelberg, Germany.

Duda, R., Stork, D., & Hart, P. (2000). *Pattern classification*. JOHN WILEY, 2nd edition.

Duda, R.O., Peter, E. H., & David, G.S., (2000). *Pattern Classification* (2nd ed.). Wiley Interscience.

Dugad, R., Ratakonda, K., & Ahuja, N. (1998). Robust video shot change detection. (pp. 376-381).

Duits, R., Florack, L., Graaf, J. D., & Haar Romeny, B. ter. (2004). On the axioms of scale space theory. *Journal of Mathematical Imaging and Vision, 20*, 267–298.

Duncan Aitken, J.B. (2002). *Peer-to-Peer Technologies and Protocols*. Retrieved 2007, from NTRG: http://ntrg.cs.tcd.ie/undergrad/4ba2.02/p2p/index.html

Dunne, C.R. (2001). *Using Mobile Agents for Network Resource Discovery in Peer-to-Peer Networks, 2*(3), 1-9.

Duygulu, P., Barnard, K., Freitas, N., & Forsyth, D. (2002). Object recognition as Machine Translation: Learning a Lexicon for a Fixed Image Vocabulary. In *Seventh European Conference on Computer Vision, 2002*, (pp. 97-112).

Duygulu, P., Barnard, K., Fretias, N., & Forsyth, D. (2002). Object recognition as machine translation: Learning a lexicon for a fixed image vocabulary. In

Proc. European Conf. Computer Vision, 97-112. doi: 10.1007/3-540-47979-1_7.

Dyke, F.H. (1988). The human dynamics of operator interfaces. *IEEE Conference Record of 1988 Fortieth Annual Conference of Electrical Engineering Problems in the Rubber and Plastics Industries* (pp. 36-39).

Eason, G., Noble, B., & Sneddon, I. N. (1955). On certain integrals of Lipschitz-Hankel type involving products of Bessel functions. *Phil. Trans. Roy. Soc.*, A247, 529-551.

Edwards, G., Cootes, T., & Taylor, C. (1998). Face recognition using active appearance models. In *Proc. of European Conference on Computer Vision*, (pp. 581-595).

Ekin, A., Tekalp, A. M., & Mehrotra, R. (2003). Automatic soccer video analysis and summarization. *IEEE Trans. on Image Processing, 12*(7), 796-807. doi: 10.1109/TIP.2003.812758.

Elad, A., & Kimmel, R. (2003). On Bending Invariant Signatures for Surfaces. *IEEE Trans. on Pattern Analysis and Machine Intelligence, 25*(10), 1285-1295.

Emerson F.A.L.,P.D. (May, 2004). An Approach to Modelling and Applying Mobile Agent Design Patterns. *ACM SIGSOFT Software Engineering Notes* (pp. 1-8). New York, USA: ACM Press.

Engbers, E., Boomgaard, R. van den, & Smeulders, A. (2001). Decomposition of separable concave structuring functions. *Journal of Mathematical Imaging and Vision, 15*, 181–195.

Falla, M. (n.d.) Results and Achievements from the DTI/EPSRC R&D Programme in Safety Critical Systems.

Faloutsos, C., Equitz, W., Flickner, M., Niblack, W., Petkovic, D., & Barber, R. (1994). Efficient and effective querying by image content. *Journal of Intelligent Information Retrieval, 3*(3/4), 231–262.

Fan, J., Gao, Y., Luo, H., & Xu, G. (2005). Statistical modeling and conceptualization of natural images. *Pattern Recognition, 38*, 865-885. doi: 10.1016/j.patcog.2004.07.011.

Fan, J.P., Gao, Y.L., & Luo, H.Z. (2004). Multi-level annotation of natural scenes using dominant image components and semantic concepts. In *Proc. ACM International Conference on Multimedia.*

Fan, J.P., Gao, Y.L., Luo, H.Z., & Xu, G.Y. (2004). Automatic image annotation by using concept-sensitive salient objects for image content represent. In *27th Annual International ACM SIGIR Conference.*

Fan, X., Xie, X., Li, Z., Li, M., & Ma, W.-Y. (2005). Photo-to-search: using multimodal queries to search the Web from mobile devices. *ACM SIGMM International Workshop on Multimedia Information Retrieval.*

Fatemi, O., Zhang, S., & Panchanathan, S. (1996). Optical flow based model for scene cut detection, *1*, 470-473.

Feibush, E., Gagvani, N., & Williams, D. (2000). Visualization for situational awareness. *IEEE Computer Graphics and Applications, 20*(5), 38- 45.

Feldman, J., & Singh, M. (2005). Information along contours and object boundaries. *Psychological Review, 112*(1), 243-252.

Fellbaum, C. (Ed.) (1998). *WordNet: an electronic lexical database.* MIT Press, Cambridge, Massachusetts.

Felzenszwalb, P. (2005). Representation and Detection of Deformable Shapes. *IEEE Trans. on Pattern Analysis and Machine Intelligence, 27*(2), 208-220.

Felzenszwalb, P., & Huttenlocher, D. (2005). Pictorial Structures for Object Recognition. *International Journal of Computer Vision, 61*(1), 55-79.

Felzenszwalb, P., & Schwartz, J. (2007). Hierarchical Matching of Deformable Shapes. *IEEE Conference on Computer Vision and Pattern Recognition.*

Feng, H., Shi, R., & Chua, T.-S. (2004). A bootstrapping framework for annotating and retrieving WWW images. In *Proc. ACM Multimedia.*

FENG, J., Kwok-Tung, L., & Mehrpour, H. Scene change detection algorithm for MPEG video sequence.

Feng, S., Manmatha, R., & Lavrenko, V. (2004). Multiple Bernoulli relevance models for image and video annotation. *Proc. IEEE Conf. Computer Vision and Pattern Recognition*, (pp. 1002-1009). doi: 10.1109/CVPR.2004.1315274.

Fergus, R., Li, F.-F., Perona, P., & Zisserman, A. (2005). Learning object categories from Google's image search. *Proc. Int'l Conf. Computer Vision, II*, 1816-1823, 2005. doi: 10.1109/ICCV.2005.142.

Fergus, R., Perona, P., & Zisserman, A. (2003). Object Class Recognition by Unsupervised Scale-Invariant Learning, *IEEE Conference on Computer Vision and Pattern Recognition, II*, 264-271.

Fergus, R., Perona, P., & Zisserman, A. (2003). Object class recognition by unsupervised scale-invariant learning. In *Proceedings of the Ninth International Conference on Computer Vision and Pattern Recognition, 2*, 264–271.

Ferman, A.M., Tekalp, A.M., & Mehrotra, R. (2002). Robust color histogram descriptors for video segment retrieval and identification. *IEEE Trans. on Image Processing, 1*(5), 497-508.

Fisher, R.A. (1936). The Use of Multiple Measures in Taxonomic Problems. *Ann. Eugenics, 7,* 179-188.

Flags (2003). Retrieved January 7, 2003, from http://www.flags.nct

Fletcher, N., & Evans, A. (2005). Texture segmentation using area morphology local granulometries. In *International Symposium on Mathematical Morphology (ISMM)* (p. 367-376).

Flickner, M., et al. (1995). Query by image and video content: The QBIC system. *IEEE Computer, 9,* 23-32.

Florack, L. (2001). Non-linear scale-spaces isomorphic to the linear case with applications to scalar, vector, and multispectral images. *International Journal of Computer Vision, 42*(1/2), 39–53.

Foley, C., Gurrin, C., Jones, G., Lee, H., McGivney, S., O'Connor, N. E., Sav, S., Smeaton, A. F., & Wilkins, P. (2004). Trecvid 2005 experiments in dublin city university. In Proceedings of NIST-TRECVID. Gaitherberg, DC.

Forsyth, D.A., & Ponce, J. (2003). Computer vision: A modern approach. *Prentice Hall.*

Fowlkes, C., Martin, D., & Malik, J. (2003). Learning affinity functions for image segmentation: Combining patch-based and gradient-based approaches. In *Proc. of CVPR.*

Fredembach, C., & Finlayson, G. (2008). The 1.5d sieve algorithm. *Pattern Recognition Letters, 29,* 629–636.

Fredembach, C., Schröder, M., & Süsstrunk, S. (2004). Eigenregions for image classification. *IEEE Transaction on Pattern Analysis Machine Intelligence, 26*(12), 1645-1649. doi: 10.1109/TPAMI.2004.123.

Freund, M., Seung, H.S., Shamir, E., & Tishby, N. (1997). Selective sampling using the query by committee algorithm. *Machine Learning, 28,* 133-168.

Freund, Y., & Schapire, R. (1997). A decision-theoretic generalization of online leaning and an application to boosting. *J. Computer and System Sciences, 55*(1), 119-139.

Freund, Y., Seung, H.S., Shamir, E., & Tishby, N. (1997). Selective sampling using the query by committee algorithm. *Machine Learning, 28*(2-3), 133-168.

Friedman, J., Hastie, T., & Tibshirani, R. (2000). Additive logistic regression: a statistical view of boosting. *Ann. Statist., 28*(2), 337–407.

Fu, Y. (2008). *Unified discriminative subspace learning for multimodality image analysis.* Ph. D thesis, Dept of Electrical & Computer Engineering, University of Illinois at Urbana-Champaign.

Fu, Y. Li, Z., Yuan, J., Wu, Y., & Huang, T.S. (2008). Locality vs. globality: Query-driven localized linear models for facial image computing. *IEEE Transactions on Circuits & System for Video Technology, 18*(12), 1741-1752.

Fu, Y., & Huang, T.S. (2005). Locally linear embedded eigenspace analysis, *IFP Technical Report.* Dept of ECE, UIUC.

Fu, Y., & Huang, T.S. (2008). Image classification using correlation tensor analysis. *IEEE Trans. on Image Processing, 17*(2), 226-234.

Fu, Y., Li, Z., Huang, T.S., & Katsaggelos, A. K. (2008). Locally Adaptive Subspace and Similarity Metric Learning for Visual Clustering and Retrieval. *Computer Vision and Image Understanding* (CVIU), *110*(3), 390-402.

Fu, Y., Yan, S., & Huang, T.S. (2008a). Classification and feature extraction by simplexization. *IEEE Trans. on Information Forensics and Security, 3*(1), 91-100.

Fu, Y., Yan, S., & Huang, T.S., (2008b). Correlation metric for generalized feature extraction. *IEEE Transactions on Pattern Analysis & Machine Intelligence, 30*(12), 2229-2235.

Fung, G., & Mangasarian, O. (1999). Semi-supervised support vector machines for unlabeled data classification. *Technical Report 99-05.* Data Mining Institute, University of Wisconsin Madison.

Furnas, G.W., Landauer, T.K., Gomez, L.M., & Dumais, S. T. (1987). The vocabulary problem in human-system communication. Communication of the ACM, 30, 964–971.

Gabbar, H.A. & Naka, Y. (2003, August). *Computer-Aided Operation Design Environment for Chemical Production Plants.* Paper presented at ICCTA'2003 – IEEE, 12th International Conference on Computer Theory and Applications, Alexandria, Egypt.

Gabbar, H.A. (2005). FDS: Fault Diagnostic System, Technical Notes, Okayama University. Retrieved from, http://syslab2.mech.okayama-u.ac.jp/staff/gabbar/fds.html.

Gabbar, H.A. (2006). *Design of Integrated Fault Diagnosis System (FDS).* Paper presented at International Conference of IEEE SMC, Taiwan.

Gabbar, H.A., Aoyama, A., & Naka, Y. (2004a). Model-Based Computer-Aided Design Environment for Operational Design. *Journal of Computers & Industrial Engineering, 46*(3), 413-430.

Gabbar, H.A., Aoyama, A., & Naka, Y. (2004b). Recipe Formal Definition Language For Operating Procedures Synthesis. *Journal of Computers & Chemical Engineering, 28*(9), 1809-1822.

Gabbar, H.A., Chung, P.W.H., Suzuki, K., & Shimada, Y. (2000). Utilization of unified modeling language (UML) to represent the artifacts of the plant design model. In *Proceedings of "PSE Asia 2000" International Symposium on Design, Operation and Control of Next Generation Chemical Plants, PS5* (pp. 387-392). Kyoto-Japan.

Gabbar, H.A., Shimada, Y. & Suzuki, K. (2002). Computer-Aided Plant Enterprise Modeling Environment (CAPE-ModE) – Design Initiatives. *Computers in Industry, 47*(1), 25-37.

Gabbar, H.A., Yamashita, H., & Suzuki, K. (2006). Integrated Plant Maintenance Management Using Enhanced RCM Mechanism. *International Journal of Performability Engineering, 2*(4), 369-381.

Gadre, V., & Patney, R. (1992). Multiparametric multiscale filtering, multiparametric granulometries and

the associated pattern spectra. In *IEEE International Symposium on Circuits and Systems* (pp. 1513–1516).

Gaede, V., & Günther, O. (1998). Multidimensional Access Methods. *ACM Computing Surveys, 30*(2), 170-231.

Gaede, V., &. Gunther, O. (1998). Multidimensional access methods. *ACM Computing Survey, 30*(2), 170-231.

Gandhi, A. (2002). *Content-based image retrieval: Plant species identification.* MS thesis. Oregon State University.

Gao, X., Li, J., & Shi, Y. (2006). A video shot boundary detection algorithm based on feature tracking. *Lecture Notes in Computer Science, 4062,* 651.

Garcia, C., & Delakis, M. (2004). Convolutional Face Finder: A Neural Architecture for Fast and Robust Face Detection. *IEEE Translations on Pattern Analysis And Machine Intelligence, 26*(11), 1408–1423. doi: 10.1109/TPAMI.2004.97.

Gargi, U., Kasturi, R., & Strayer, S. (2000). Performance characterization of video-shot-change detection methods. *Circuits and Systems for Video Technology, IEEE Transactions on, 10*(1), 1-13.

Ghadiali, M., Poon, J., & Siu, W. (1996, September). Fuzzy pattern spectrum as texture descriptor. *IEE Electronic Letters, 32*(19), 1772–1773.

Ghosh, D., & Wei, D. T. (2006). Material classification using morphological pattern spectrum for extracting textural features from material micrographs. In *Asian Conference on Computer Vision (ACCV)* (Vol. 3852, pp. 623–632). Springer-Verlag.

Ghosh, P., & Chanda, B. (1998, October). Bi-variate pattern spectrum. In *International symposium on computer graphics, image processing and vision* (pp. 476–483). Rio de Janeiro.

Ghosh, P., Chanda, B., & Mali, P. (2000). Fast algorithm for sequential machine to compute pattern spectrum via city-block distance transform. *Information Sciences, 124,* 193–217.

Ghoshal, A., Ircing, P., & Khudanpur, S. (2005). Hidden Markov models for automatic annotation and content-based retrieval of images and video. In *28th Annual International ACM SIGIR Conference.*

Ghoshal, A., Ircing, P., & Khudanpur, S. (2005). Hidden Markov models for automatic annotation and content-based retrieval of images and video. In *Proc. 28th Ann. Int'l ACM SIGIR Conf.*, (pp. 544-551). doi: 10.1145/1076034.1076127.

Gimenez, D., & Evans, A. (2008). An evaluation of area morphology scale-space for colour images. *Computer Vision and Image Understanding, 110*, 32–42.

Gionis, A., Indyk, P., & Motwani, R. (1999). Similarity Search in High Dimensions via Hashing. In *Proceedings of 25th International Conference on Very Large Databases* (VLDB).

Goh, K. –S., Chang, E. Y., & Lai, W. –C. (2004). Multimodal concept-dependent active learning for image retrieval. In *Proceedings of International Conference on Machine Learning*, (pp. 564-571).

Goh, K.-S., Chang, E.Y., & Li, B.T. (2005). Using one-class and two-class SVMs for multiclass image annotation. *IEEE Transactions on Knowledge and Data Engineering, 17*(10), 1333-1346. doi: 10.1109/TKDE.2005.170.

Gong, Y., et al. (1994). An Image Database System with Content Capturing and Fast Image Indexing Abilities. *IEEE Computer, 27*(5), 121-130.

Gonzalez, R. & Woods, R. (1992). *Digital image processing.* Reading, MA, USA: Addison Wesley.

Gonzalez, R.C., & Woods, R. (2002). *Digital Image Processing.* Reading, Massachusetts: Addison-Wesley.

Google image. (2008). *http://images.google.com.*

Gorelick, L., Galun, M., Sharon, A., Basri, R., & Brandt, A. (2004). Shape Representation and Classification Using the Poisson Equation. *IEEE Conference on Computer Vision and Pattern Recognition*, (pp. 61-67).

Gosselin, P.H., & Cord, M. (2004). A comparison of active classification methods for content-based image retrieval. In *Proceedings of International Workshop on Computer Vision Meets Databases*, (pp. 51-58).

Goutsias, J., & Heijmans, H. (2000, November). Nonlinear multiresolution signal decomposition schemes. Part I: Morphological pyramids. *IEEE Transactions on Image Processing, 9*(11), 1862–1876.

Grasshopper Mobile Agent Platform. (n.d.). Retrieved 2007, from http://cordis.europa.eu/infowin/acts/analysis/products/thematic/agents/ch4/ch4.htm

Grauman, K. & Darrell, T. (2005). The Pyramid Match Kernel: Discriminative Classification with Sets of Image Features, *Proceedings of the IEEE International Conference on Computer Vision* (ICCV), Beijing, China.

Grauman, K. & Darrell, T. (2005). Pyramid match kernels: Discriminative classification with sets of images features. In *Proc. Int'l Conf. Computer Vision, 2*, 1458-1465. doi: 10.1109/ICCV.2005.239.

Grauman, K., & Darrell, T. (2006). Unsupervised learning of categories from sets of partially matching image features. In *Proceedings of IEEE Conf. on Computer Vision and Pattern Recognition.*

Gray, G.C.R.S. (n.d.). *D'Agents: Applications and Performance of a Mobile-Agent System, 35*(6), 543-573.

Grenander, U., Srivastava, A., & Saini, S. (2007). A Pattern-Theoretic Characterization of Biological Growth. *IEEE Transactions on Medical Imaging, 26*(5), 648-659.

Griffin, G., Holub, A., & Perona, P. (2006). The caltech-256 (Technical Report). Caltech.

Grimson, W.E.L. (1990). *Object Recognition by Computer: The Role of Geometric Constraints.* Cambridge, MA: MIT Press.

Gu, Z., Mei, T., Tang, J., Wu, X., & Hua, X.–S. (2008). MILC²: a multi-layer multi-instance learning approach for video concept detection. In *Proceedings of International Multimedia Modeling Conference*, (pp. 24-34).

Gunturk, B.K., Batur, A.U., Altunbasak, Y., Kayes, M.H., & Mersereau, R.M. (2003). Eigenface-domain super-resolution for face recognition. *IEEE Trans. On Image Proc., 12*(5), 597-606.

Guttman, A. (1984). R-trees: A Dynamic Index Structure for Spatial Searching. In *Proceedings of the 1984 ACM SIGMOD International Conference on Management of Data* (pp. 47-57), Boston, Massachusetts.

Guttman, A. (1984). R-trees: A dynamic index structure for spatial searching. In *Proc. ACM SIGMOD*, (pp.47-57). Boston.

Hadjidemetriou, E., Grossberg, M., & Nayar, S. (2004, July). Multiresolution histograms and their use in recognition. *IEEE Transactions on Pattern Analysis and Machine Intelligence, 26*(7), 831–847.

Haering, N., Qian, R.J., & Sezan, M.I. (2000). A semantic event detection approach and its application to detecting hunts in wildlife video. *IEEE Trans. on Circuits and Systems for Video Technology, 10*(6), 857–868. doi: 10.1109/76.867923.

Halaschek-Wiener, C., Golbeck, J., Schain, A., Grove, M., Parsia, B., & Hendler, J. (2005). Photostuff - an image annotation tool for the semantic web. In Proceedings of the 4th international semantic web conference.

Hall, S.K., Cockerham, K.J., & Rhodes, D.J. (2001). Applying human factors in graphical operator interfaces. In *2001 Conference Record of Pulp and Paper Industry Technical Conference* (pp. 241-246).

Ham, J., Lee, D. D., Mika S., & Schölkopf, B., (2004). A kernel view of the dimensionality reduction of manifolds. In *Proc of Int'l Conf. on Machine learning.*

Hamza, A. B., & Krim, H. (2003). Geodesic Object Representation and Recognition. In I. Nystrom et al. (Eds.), *Discrete Geometry for Computer Imagery, LNCS, 2886*, 378-387.

Hanjalic, A., Lagendijk, R., & Biemond, J. (1999). Automated high-level movie segmentation for advanced video retrieval systems. *IEEE Transactions on Circuits and Systems for Video Technology, 9*(4), 580–588. doi: 10.1109/76.767124.

Hansen, K. (2003). *Lecture 11.* Retrieved 2007, from P2P Lectures: http://www.daimi.au.dk/~marius/p2p-course/lectures/11/talk.html

Haralick, R., Katz, P., & Dougherty, E. (1995, January). Model-based morphology: the opening spectrum. *Computer Vision, Graphics and Image Processing: Graphical Models and Image Processing, 57*(1), 1–12.

Haralick, R.M., et al. (1973). Texture features for image classification. *IEEE Transactions on System, Man and Cybernetics, 3*, 610-620.

Harris, C., & Stephens, M. A. (1988). A combined corner and edge detector. *In Alvey Vision Conference,* (pp. 147–151).

Hashimoto, R., & Barrera, J. (2003). A greedy algorithm for decomposing convex structuring elements. *Journal of Mathematical Imaging and Vision, 18*, 269–289.

Hauptmann, A., & Witbrock, M. (1996). Informedia news on demand: Multimedia information acquisition and retrieval. In Intelligent multimedia information retrieval. Menlo Park, CA.

Hauptmann, A.G. (2005). Lessons for the Future from a Decade of Informedia Video Analysis Research. In *Proceedings of ACM International Conference on Image and Video Retrieval,* (pp. 1-10).

Hauptmann, A.G., Lin, W.-H., Yan, R., Yang, J., & Chen, M.-Y. (2006). Extreme video retrieval: joint maximization of human and computer performance. In Proceedings of the 14th ACM international conference on Multimedia (pp. 385–394). New York, NY, USA.

He, J. R., Li, M., Zhang, H –J., Tong, H., & Zhang, C. (2004b). Mean version space: a new active learning method for content-based image retrieval. In *Proceedings of ACM Workshop on Multimedia Information Retrieval,* (pp. 15-22).

He, J. R., Li, M., Zhang, H.–J., Tong, H., & Zhang, C. (2004a). Manifold-ranking based image retrieval. In *Proceedings of ACM Multimedia,* (pp. 9-16).

He, J., Li, M., Zhang, H.-J., Tong, H., & Zhang, C. (2004). Manifold-ranking based image retrieval. *Proc. ACM Multimedia.*

He, J., Li, M., Zhang, H.-J., Tong, H., & Zhang, C. (2006). Generalized manifold-ranking based image retrieval. *IEEE Transaction on Image Processing, 15*(10).

He, J., Zhang, C., Zhao, N., & Tong, H. (2005). Boosting web image search by co-ranking. In *Proc. International Conference on Acoustics, Speech, and Signal Processing.*

He, X., & Niyogi, P. (2003). Locality Preserving Projections. In *Proc. of NIPS.*

He, X., Cai, D., & Niyogi, P. (2005). Tensor subspace analysis. In *Proc. of Advances in Neural Information Processing,* (p. 18).

Heijmans, H., & Boomgaard, R. van den. (2002). Algebraic framework for linear and morphological scale-spaces. *Journal of Visual Communication and Image Representation, 13*, 269–301.

Helmets (2003). Retrieved January 7, 2003, from http://inside99.net/Helmet_Project/index.htm.

Hempel, C.G. (1937). A Purely Topological Form of Non-Aristotelian Logic. *Journ. Symb. Logic, 2*(3).

Hendriks, C. L., Kempen, G. van, & Vliet, L. van. (2007). Improving the accuracy of isotropic granulometries. *Pattern Recognition Letters*, *28*, 865–872.

Hiary, H., & Ng, K. (2007). A system for segmenting and extracting paper-based watermark designs. *International Journal of Document Libraries*, *6*, 351–361.

Hjaltason, G.R., & Samat, H. (1999). Distance Browsing in Spatial Databases. *ACM Transactions on Database Systems*, *24*(2), 71-79.

Hoffman, D. D., & Richards, W. A. (1985). Parts of recognition. *Cognition*, *18*, 65-96.

Hofmann, T. (2001). Unsupervised learning by probabilistic latent semantic analysis. *Machine Learning*, *42*, 177-196. doi: 10.1023/A:1007617005950.

Hoi, S. C.H., Jin, R., Zhu, J., & Lyu, M.R. (2006). Batch mode active learning and its application to medical image classification. In *Proceedings of International Conference on Machine Learning*, (pp. 417-424).

Hoi, S.C.H., & Lyu, M.R. (2005). A semi-supervised active learning framework for image retrieval. In *Proc. IEEE Conference on Computer Vision and Pattern Recognition*.

Hoi, S.C.H., & Lyu, M.R. (2005). A semi-supervised active learning framework for image retrieval. In *Proceedings of International Conference on Computer Vision and Pattern Recognition*, (pp. 302-309).

Hong, P., Tian, Q., & Huang, T.S. (2000). Incorporate support vector machines to content-based image retrieval with relevance feedback. In *Proceedings of IEEE International Conference on Image Processing* (pp. 750-753).

Hsu, R., & Jain, A. (2002). *Semantic face matching.* In *Proc. of IEEE International Conference on Multimedia and Expo*, (pp. 145-148).

Hsu, R., & Jain, A. (2003). Generating discriminating Carton faces using interacting snakes. *IEEE Trans. on Patter. Recogn. And Machine Intell.*, *25*(11), 1388-1398.

Hsu, W., & Chang, S.F. (2003). A statistical framework for fusing mid-level perceptual features in news story segmentation. *IEEE International Conference on Multimedia and Expo*, (pp. 413-416).

Hsu, W.H., Kennedy, L. S., & Chang, S.-F. (2007). Video search reranking through random walk over document-level context graph. In *Proc. ACM Multimedia.*

Hu, J., & Bagga, A. (2004). Categorizing images in Web documents. *IEEE Multimedia*, *11*(1), 22-30. doi: 10.1109/MMUL.2004.1261103.

Hu, M.K. (1962). Visual pattern recognition by moment invariants. *IRE Transactions on Information Theory*, *8*, 28-32.

Hua, X.S., & Zhang H.J. (2004). An attention-based decision fusion scheme for multimedia information retrieval. *Proceedings of Pacific-Rim conference on Multimedia.*

Huang, C., & Chen, C. (1992). Human facial feature extraction for face interpretation and recognition. *Pattern Recognition*, *25*(12), 1435-1444.

Huang, H.M.. (1996). Operator interface and situation perception in hierarchical intelligent control: a case study. In *Proceedings of the 1996 IEEE International Symposium on Intelligent Control* (pp. 68-73).

Huang, J., et al. (1997). Image indexing using color correlograms. In *Proceedings of Conference on Computer Vision and Pattern Recognition* (pp. 762-768), Puerto Rico.

Huang, J., Kumar, S.R., Mitra, M., Zhu, W.-J., & Zabih, R. (1997). Image indexing using color correlograms. *IEEE Conf. on Computer Vision and Pattern Recognition*, San Juan, Puerto Rico.

Huang, J., Kumar, S.R., Mitra, M., Zhu, W-J., & Zabih, R. (1997). Image indexing using color correlograms. In *IEEE Int. Conference Computer Vision and Pattern Recognition*, (pp. 762–768).

Huang, J., Liu, Z., & Wang, Y. (1998). Integration of audio and visual information for content-based video segmentation. *IEEE International Conference on Image processing*, (pp. 526-530). doi: 10.1109/ICIP.1998.727252.

Huang, T.S., & Zhou, X.S. (2001). Image retrieval with relevance feedback: from heuristic weight adjustment to optimal learning methods. In *Proceedings of International Conference on Image Processing* (pp. 2-5).

Human Factor Analysis and Classification System Presentation Preview. Naval Safety Center. Retrieved from, http://www.safetycenter.navy.mil/PRESENTATIONS/aviation/hfacs.htm

Humpert, B. (1990). Bi-directional associative memory with several patterns. In *Proceedings of International*

Joint Conference on Neural Networks vol. 1 (pp. 741-750), San Diego, California.

Ianeva, T., Vries, A. de, & Rohrig, H. (2003). Detecting cartoons: a case study in automatic video-genre classification. In *IEEE International Conference on Multimedia and Expo (ICME)* (pp. 449–452).

IEC 61508. Proposed framework for addressing human factors in IEC 61508.

Im, C., Nishida, H., & Kunii, T. L. (1998). Recognizing plant species by leaf shapes-a case study of the Acer family. *International Conference on Pattern Recognition, 2*, 1171-1173.

Indyk, P., & Motwani, R. (1998). Approximate Nearest Neighbors: Towards Removing the Curse of Dimensionality. In *Proc of 30th Symposium on Theory of Computing.*

Ionescu, B., Lambert, P., Coquin, D., & Buzuloiu, V. (2007). The cut detection issue in the animation movie domain. *Journal of Multimedia, 2*(4)

Isard, M., & Blake, A. (1998). CONDENSATION—Conditional density propagation for visual tracking. *International Journal of Computer Vision, 29*(1), 5–28.

Itti, L., & Koch, C. (1999). A Comparison of feature combination strategies for saliency-based visual attention systems. *SPIE Human Vision and Electronic Imaging IV (HVEI'99), 3644*, 73-82.

Itti, L., Koch, C., & Niebur, E. (1998). A model of saliency-based visual attention for rapid scene analysis. *IEEE Trans on Pattern Analysis and Machine Intelligence, 20*(11), 1254-1259. doi: 10.1109/34.730558.

Iurgel, U., Meermeier, R., Eickeler, S., & Rigoll, G. (2001). New approaches to audio-visual segmentation of TV news for automatic topic retrieval. *IEEE International Conference on Acoustics, Speech, and Signal Processing.* (pp. 1397-1400). doi: 10.1109/ICASSP.2001.941190.

Jackway, P. (1992). Morphological scale-space. In *IAPR International Conference on Pattern Recognition (ICPR)* (p. C:252-255).

Jackway, P., & Deriche, M. (1996, January). Scale-space properties of the multiscale morphological dilation-erosion. *IEEE Transactions on Pattern Analysis and Machine Intelligence, 18*(1), 38–51.

Jacob, G., Noble, A., & Blake, A. (1998). Robust contour tracking in echocardiographic sequence. In *Proc. Intl. Conf. on Computer Vision*, (pp. 408–413).

Jain, A.K., & Vailaya, A. (1996). Image retrieval using color and shape. *Pattern Recognition, 29*(8), 1233–1244.

Jain, A.K., & Vailaya, A. (1998). Shape-based retrieval: A case study with trademark image databases. *Pattern Recognition, 31*(9), 1369-1390.

Jain, A.K., & Yu, B. (1998). Automatic text location in images and video frames. *Pattern Recognition, 31*, 2055–2076.

Jalba, A., Wilkinson, M., & Roerdink, J. (2004, May). Morphological hat-transform scale spaces and their use in pattern classification. *Pattern Recognition, 37*(5), 901–915.

Jalba, A., Wilkinson, M., & Roerdink, J. (2006). Shape representation and recognition through morphological curvature scale spaces. *IEEE Transactions on Image Processing, 15*(2), 331–341.

Jamieson, G.A. & K.J. Vicente (2005). Designing effective human-automation-plant interfaces: A control-theoretic perspective. *Human Factors, 47*, 12-34.

Jan, S., & Hsueh, Y. (1998). Window-size determination for granulometric structural texture classification. *Pattern Recognition Letters, 19*, 439–446.

Jang, B., & Chin, R. (1998, May). Morphological scale space for 2d shape smoothing. *Computer Vision and Image Understanding, 70*(2), 121–141.

Jeon, J., & Manmatha, R. (2004). Automatic image annotation of news images with large vocabularies and low quality training data. *ACM International Conference on Multimedia.*

Jeon, J., Lavrenko, V., & Manmatha, R. (2003). Automatic image annotation and retrieval using cross-media relevance models. In Proceedings of the 26th annual international ACM SIGIR conference on Research and development in informaion retrieval (pp. 119–126). Toronto, Canada.

Jeon, J., Lavrenko, V., & Manmatha, R. (2003). Automatic image annotation and retrieval using cross-media relevance models. In *Proc. of the Annual Int. ACM SIGIR Conf. on Research and Development in Information Retrieval.*

Jeon, J., Lavrenko, V., & Manmatha, R. (2003). Automatic image annotation and retrieval using cross-media relevance models. In *Proc. ACM SIGIR Conf. on Research and Development in Information Retrieval*, (pp. 119-126). doi: 10.1145/860435.860459.

Jepson, A.D., Fleet, D.J., & El-Maraghi, T.F. (2003). Robust online appearance models for visual tracking. *IEEE Trans. PAMI, 25*, 1296–1311.

Jiang, S.Q., Ye, Q.X., Gao, W., & Huang, T.J. (2004). A new method to segment playfield and its applications in match analysis in sports video, *ACM International Conference on Multimedia*, (pp. 292-295). doi: 10.1145/1027527.1027594.

Jin, Y., Khan, L., Wang, L., & Awad, M. (2005). Image annotations by combining multiple evidence & wordNet. In *Proc. 13th Ann. ACM int'l Conf. Multimedia*, (pp. 706-715). doi: 10.1145/1101149.1101305.

Joachims, T. (1999). Transductive inference for text classification using support vector machines. In *Proc. International Conference on Machine Learning*

Joachims, T. (1999). Transductive inference for text classification using support vector machines. In *Proceedings of the 16th International Conference on Machine Learning* (pp. 200-209).

Johnson, N., & Hogg, D.C. (1996). Learning the distribution of object trajectories for event recognition. *Image and Vision Computing, 14*, 609-615.

Johnsson, C. & Arzen, K.E. (1998). Grafchart for recipe based batch control. *Computers & Chemical Engineering, 22*, 1811-1228

Joliffe, I.T. (1986). *Principal component analysis*. New York: Springer-Verlag.

Jones, D., & Jackway, P. (2000). Granolds: a novel texture representation. *Pattern Recognition, 33*, 1033–1045.

Jones, M., & Viola, P. (2003). Face recognition using boosted local features. In *Proc. of ICCV*.

Jones, R., & Soille, P. (1996). Periodic lines: definitions, cascades, and application to granulometries. *Pattern Recognition Letters, 17*, 1057–1063.

Kalva, P., Enembreck, F., & Koerich, A. (2007). Web image classification based on the fusion of image and text classifiers. In *Proc. 9th Int'l Conf. Document Analysis and Recognition, 1*, 561-568. doi: 10.1109/ICDAR.2007.4378772.

Kang, Y.L.S. (2007). A Landmark-Based Scalable Semantic Resource Discovery Scheme. *E90-D, (6).*

Kashino, K., Kurozumi, T., & Murase, H. (2003). A Quick Search Method for Audio and Video Signals Based on Histogram Pruning. *IEEE Trans. on Multimedia, 5*(3), 348-357.

Katayama N., & Satoh, S. (1997), SR-Tree: An Index Structure for Nearest Neighbor Searching of High-Dimensional Point Data, *Transactions of the Institute of Electronics, Information and Communication Engineers, J80-D-I*, (8), 703-717.

Katsuri, R., & Fain, R. (1991). Dynamic vision. *Computer vision: Advances and applications* (pp. 469-480) IEEE Computer Society Press, Los Alamitos, California.

Ke, Y., & Sukthankar, R. (2004). PCA-SIFT: A more distinctive representation for local image descriptors. In *Proc. Conf. Computer Vision and Pattern Recognition, 2*, 511-517. doi: 10.1109/CVPR.2004.1315206.

Kegan, R,W, (2005). Modelling the simple epidemic with differential equations and random initial conditions. *Mathematical Biosciences , 197*(1).

Kennedy, L.S., Chang, S.-F., & Kozintsev, I.V. (2006). To search or to label? predicting the performance of search-based automatic image classifiers. In *Proceedings of the 8th ACM international workshop on Multimedia information retrieval* (pp. 249–258). New York, NY, USA.

Keogh, E., Wei, L., Xi, X., Lee, S-H., & Vlachos, M. (2006). LB_Keogh Supports Exact Indexing of Shapes under Rotation Invariance with Arbitrary Representations and Distance Measures. *VLDB*.

Khan, F.I., Amyotte, P.R., & DiMattia. D.G. HEPI: A new tool for human error probability calculation for offshore operation. *Safety Science, 44*(4), 313-334.

Kijak, E., Gravier, G., Gros, P., Oisel, L., & Bimbot, F. (2003), HMM based structure of tennis videos using visual and audio cues. *IEEE International Conference on Multimedia and Expo.* doi: 10.1109/ICME.2003.1221310.

Kijak, E., Oisel , L., & Gros, P. (2003). Hierarchical structure analysis of sport video using HMMS. *IEEE International Conference on Image Processing, 2*, II-1025-8.

Kim, C., & Hwang, J.N. (2000). An integrated scheme for object-based video abstraction. *ACM international conference on Multimedia,* (pp. 303 – 311).

Kim, K.I., Jung, K., & Kim, H. (2003). Texture-based approach for text detection in images using support vector machines and continuously adaptive mean shift algorithm. *IEEE Transactions on Pattern Analysis and Machine Intelligence, 25,* 1631–1639. doi: 10.1109/TPAMI.2003.1251157.

Kimia, B. B., Tannenbaum, A. R., & Zucker, S. W. (1995). Shapes, shocks, and deformations, I: The components of shape and the reaction-diffusion space. *International Journal of Computer Vision, 15*(3), 189-224.

Kirkwood, R.L., Locke, M.H., & Douglas, J.M. (1988). A prototype expert system for synthesizing chemical process flowsheets. *Computers & Chemical Engineering, 12*(4), 329-343.

Kohonen, T. (1988). *Self-Organization and Associative Memory.* Berlin: Springer-Verlag.

Koprinska, I., & Carrato, S. (2002). Hybrid rule-Based/Neural approach for segmentation of MPEG compressed video. *Multimedia Tools and Applications, 18*(3), 187-212.

Korn, P., Sidiropoulos, N., Faloutsos, C., Siegel, E., & Protopapas, Z. (1998). Fast and effective retrieval of medical tumor shapes. *IEEE Transactions on Knowledge and Data Engineering, 10*(6), 889–904.

Kosko, B. (1988). Bi-directional associative memories. *IEEE Transactions on Systems, Man and Cybernetics, 18,* 49-60.

Krishnamachari, S., & Abdel-Mottaleb, M. (1999). Image browsing using hierarchical clustering. In *4th IEEE Symposium on Computers and Communications.*

Krishnapuram, R., et al. (2004). Content-based image retrieval based on a fuzzy approach. *IEEE Transactions on Knowledge Engineering, 16*(10), 1185-1199.

Kruskal, J.B., & Wish, M. (1978). *Multidimensional scaling.* Sage Publications.

Kulikowski, J.L. (1986). *Decision Making in a Modified Version of Topological Logic. Proceedings of the Seminar on "Non-conventional Problems of Optimization". Prace IBS PAN, Part I,* 134, Warsaw: IBS PAN, 24-44.

Kulikowski, J.L. (2002). From Pattern Recognition to Image Interpretation. *Biocybernetics and Biomedical Engineering, 22*(2-3), 177-197.

Kulkarni, A.D. (2001). *Computer Vision and Fuzzy-Neural Systems.* Upper Saddle River, New Jersey: Prentice Hall.

Kusek, M.A. (2006). Extending UML Sequence Diagrams to Model Agent Mobility. In *Agent-Oriented Software Engineering, 7th International Workshop* (pp. 51-63). Hakodate, Japan: Springer Berlin/Heidelberg.

Kustanowitz, J., & Shneiderman, B. (2004). Motivating annotation for personal digital photo libraries: Lowering barriers while raising incentives (Technical Report). HCIL, Univ. of Maryland.

Kyriacou, E., Pattichis, M., Pattichis, C., Mavrommatis, A., Christodoulou, C., Kakkos, S., et al. (2008). Classification of atherosclerotic carotid plaques using morphological analysis on ultrasound images. *Applied Intelligence,* online first.

Laaksonen, J., Koskela, M., Laakkso, P., & Oja, E. (2000). PicSOM – content-based image retrieval with self organising maps. *Pattern Recognition Letters,* 21:1197-1207.

Lakshmanan, R. & Stephanopoulos, G. (1990). Synthesis of operating procedures for complete chemical plants – I Hierarchical, structured modelling for nonlinear. *Computers & Chemical Engineering, 14*(3), 301-317.

Lanitis, A., Taylor, C., & Cootes, T. (1997). Automatic interpretation and coding of face images using flexible models. *IEEE Trans. Patter. Analy. And Mach. Intell., 19*(7), 743-756.

Lavrenko, V., Manmatha, R., & Jeon, J. (2003). A model for learning the semantics of pictures. *NIPS.*

Lawrence, S., Ziou, D., Auclair-Fortier, M. F., & Wang, S. (2001). *Motion insensitive detection of cuts and gradual transitions in digital videos* No. 266). Canada: University of Sherbrooke.

Lazebnik, L., Schmid, C., & Ponce, J. (2005). A sparse texture representation using affine-invariant regions. *IEEE Trans. Pattern Anal. Mach. Intell., 27*(8), 1265-1278.

Lazebnik, S., Schmid, C., & Ponce, J. (2006). Beyond bags of features: Spatial pyramid matching for recognizing natural scene categories. In *Proc. IEEE Conf. Computer Vision and Pattern Recognition, II*, 2169-2178. doi: 10.1109/CVPR.2006.68.

Ledda, A., & Philips, W. (2005). Majority ordering and the morphological pattern spectrum. In *International Workshop on Advanced Concepts for Intelligent Vision Systems (ACIVS)* (Vol. 3708, pp. 356–363). Springer-Verlag.

Lee, M. H., Yoo, H. W., & Jang, D. S. (2006). Video scene change detection using neural network: Improved ART2. *Expert Systems with Applications, 31*(1), 13-25.

Lee, M. S., Yang, Y. M., & Lee, S. W. (2001). Automatic video parsing using shot boundary detection and camera operation analysis. *Pattern Recognition, 34*(3), 711-719.

Lefèvre, S. (2007, June). Extending morphological signatures for visual pattern recognition. In *IAPR International Workshop on Pattern Recognition in Information Systems (PRIS)* (pp. 79–88). Madeira, Portugal.

Lefèvre, S., Holler, J., & Vincent, N. (2000). Real time temporal segmentation of compressed and uncompressed dynamic colour image sequences. (pp. 56-62).

Lefèvre, S., Holler, J., & Vincent, N. (2003). A review of real-time segmentation of uncompressed video sequences for content-based search and retrieval. *Real-Time Imaging, 9*(1), 73-98.

Lefèvre, S., Weber, J., & Sheeren, D. (2007, April). Automatic building extraction in VHR images using advanced morphological operators. In *IEEE/ISPRS Joint Workshop on Remote Sensing and Data Fusion over Urban Areas*. Paris, France.

Leibe, B., & Schiele, B. (2003). Analyzing Appearance and Contour Based Methods for Object Categorization. *IEEE Conference on Computer Vision and Pattern Recognition, II*, 409-415.

Leibe, B., Leonardis, A., & Schiele, B. (2004). Combined object categorization and segmentation with an implicit shape model. *ECCV 2004 Workshop on Statistical Learning in Computer Vision*, (pp. 17-32).

Lempel, R., & Soffer, A. (2002). PicASHOW: pictorial authority search by hyperlinks on the web. *ACM Transaction on Information Systems, 20*(1), 1-24. doi: 10.1145/503104.503105.

Lepetit, V., Pilet, J., & Fua, P., (2004). Point matching as a classification problem for fast and robust object pose estimation. In *Proc. of CVPR*.

Li, B.T., Goh, K., & Chang, E. (2003). Confidence-based dynamic ensemble for image annotation and semantics discovery. In *Proc. ACM International Conference on Multimedia*, (pp. 195-206).

Li, F.-F., & Perona, P. (2005). A Bayesian hierarchical model for learning natural scene categories. *Proc. IEEE Int'l Conf. Computer Vision and Pattern Recognition, II*, 524- 531. doi: 10.1109/CVPR.2005.16.

Li, J., & Wang, J. (2003). Automatic linguistic indexing of pictures by a statistical modeling approach. *IEEE Transactions on Pattern Analysis and Machine Intelligence, 25*(9), 1075-1088.

Li, J., & Wang, J. (2006). Real-time computerized annotation of pictures. *ACM International Conference on Multimedia*.

Li, J., & Wang, J. Z. (2006). Real-time computerized annotation of pictures. In Proceedings of the 14th ACM international conference. on Multimedia (pp. 911–920). Santa Barbara, CA, USA.

Li, J., & Wang, J.Z. (2003). Automatic linguistic indexing of pictures by a statistical modeling approach. *IEEE Transactions on Pattern Analysis and Machine Intelligence, 29*(9), 1075-1088. doi: 10.1109/CVPR.2005.16.

Li, J., Wang, G., & Fei-Fei, L. (2007). OPTIMOL: automatic Object Picture collecTion via Incremental MOdel Learning. *IEEE Computer Vision and Pattern Recognition*.

Li, W., & Sun, M. (2006). Semi-supervised learning for image annotation based on conditional random fields. In *Proc. International Conference on Image and Video Retrieval*.

Li, W., Haese-Coat, V., & Ronsin, J. (1997). Residues of morphological filtering by reconstruction for texture classification. *Pattern Recognition, 30*(7), 1081–1093.

Li, X., Wang, X.-J., Wang, C., & Zhang, L. (2007). SBIA: search-based image annotation by leveraging Web-scale images. *ACM International Conference on Multimedia*.

Li, X.R., Chen, L., Zhang, L., Lin, F.Z., & Ma, W.-Y. (2006). Image annotation by large-scale content-based image retrieval. *Proc. Int'l Conf. Multimedia*, (pp. 607-610). doi: 10.1145/1180639.1180764.

Li, Y., Ma, S., & Lu, H. (1998). A multi-scale morphological method for human posture recognition. In *International Conference on Automatic Face and Gesture Recognition (FG)* (pp. 56–61).

Li, Y., Zhang, T., & Tretter, D. (2001). An Overview of Video Abstraction Techniques. *HP Labs Technical Report*, HPL-2001-191, 20010809. Retrieved from http://www.hpl.hp.com/techreports/images/pdf.

Li, Z., Gao, L., & Katsaggelos, A. K. (2006). Locally Embedded Linear Spaces for Efficient Video Shot Indexing and retrieval. In *Proceedings of IEEE Int'l Conference on Multimedia & Expo*, Toronto, Canada.

Li, Z., Katsaggelos, A. K., & Gandhi, B. (2005). Fast video shot retrieval based on trace geometry matching. *IEE Proceedings on Vision, Image and Signal Processing, 152*(3), 367-373.

Li, Z., Liu, W., Lin, D., & Tang, X., (2005). Nonparametric subspace analysis for face recognition. In *Proc of IEEE Conf. on Computer Vision and Pattern Recognition*, (pp. 961-966).

Lieberman, H., Rozenweig, E., & Singh, P. (2001). Aria: An agent for annotating and retrieving images. Computer, 34, 57–62.

Lienhart, R. (1999). Comparison of automatic shot boundary detection algorithms , *3656*, 290–301.

Lienhart, R. (1999). Comparison of automatic shot boundary detection algorithms. In *Proc. IS&T/SPIE Storage and Retrieval for Image and Video Databases VII, 3656*, 290–30.

Lienhart, R., Kuhmünch, C., & Effelsberg, W. (1997). On the detection and recognition of television commercials. In *Proceedings of the International Conference on Multimedia Computing and Systems*, Ottawa, Ontario, Canada, (pp. 509-516).

Lin, C., Tseng, B., & Smith, J. (2003). Video collaborative Annotation forum: establishing ground-truth labels on large multimedia datasets. In *Proceedings of TRECVID Workshop*.

Lin, C., Tseng, B., & Smith, J. (2003). VideoAnnEx: IBM MPEG-7 annotation tool for multimedia indexing

and concept learning. In *Proceedings of International Conference on Multimedia & Expo.*

Lin, T., & Zhang, H. (2001). Video content representation for shot retrieval and scene extraction. *International Journal of Image Graphics, 3*(1), 507–526.

Lin, W.-H., & Hauptmann, A. G. (2006). Which thousand words are worth a picture? experiments on video retrieval using a thousand concepts. In Proceedings of IEEE International Conference On Multimedia and Expo (ICME).

Ling, H., & Jacobs, D. W. (2005). Deformation Invariant Image Matching. *IEEE International Conference on Computer Vision, II*, 1466-1473.

Ling, H., & Jacobs, D. W. (2005). Using the Inner-Distance for Classification of Articulated Shapes. *IEEE Conference on Computer Vision and Pattern Recognition, II*, 719-726.

Ling, H., & Jacobs, D. W. (2007). Shape Classification Using the Inner-Distance. *IEEE Trans on Pattern Anal. and Mach. Intell., 29*(2), 286-299.

Liu, H., Jiang, S., Huang, Q., Xu, C., & Gao, W. (2007). Region-based visual attention analysis with its application in image browsing on small displays. *ACM International Conference on Multimedia*, (pp. 305-308). 10.1145/1291233.1291298.

Liu, J., Lai, W., Hua, X.-S., Huang, Y., & Li, S. (2007). Video search reranking via multi-graph propagation. In *Proc. ACM Multimedia.*

Liu, J., Li, M., Ma, W.-Y., Liu, Q., & Lu, H. (2006). An adaptive graph model for automatic image annotation. In *Proc. ACM International Workshop on Multimedia Information Retrieval.*

Liu, T., & Geiger, D. (1997). Visual Deconstruction: Recognizing Articulated Objects. *Energy Minimization Methods in Computer Vision and Pattern Recognition*, (pp. 295-309).

Liu, W.Y., Dumais, S., Sun, Y., Zhang, H., Czerwinski, M., & Field, B. (2001). Semi-automatic image annotation. In *Proc. Of Interact: Conference on HCI*, (pp. 326-333).

Lotufo, R., & Trettel, E. (1996). Integrating size information into intensity histogram. In *International Symposium on Mathematical Morphology (ISMM)* (pp. 281–288). Atlanta, USA.

Lou, J., Liu, Q., Tan, T., & Hu, W. (2002). Semantic interpretation of object activities in surveillance algorithms in the area of computer vision and machine system. *Pattern Recognition, 3*, 777-780.

Lowe, D. (1999). Object recognition from local scale-invariant feature. *Proc. Int'l Conf. Computer Vision (ICCV 1999)*, (pp. 1150-1157). doi: 10.1109/ICCV.1999.790410.

Lowe, D. (2004). Distinctive image features from scale-invariant key points. *Int'l J. Computer Vision, 2*(60), 91-110. doi: 10.1023/ B:VISI.0000029664.99615.94.

Lucas, B., & Kanade, T. (1981). An iterative image registration technique with an application to stereo vision. In *Proc. DARPA IU Workshop*, (pp. 121–130).

Lundqvist, R., Bengtsson, E., & Thurfjell, L. (2003). A combined intensity and gradient-based similarity criterion for interindividual SPECT brain scan registration. *EURASIP Journal on Applied Signal Processing, 1*, 461 – 469.

Luo, J., Savakis, A.E., & Singhal, A. (2005). A Bayesian network-based framework for semantic image understanding. *Pattern Recognition, 38*, 919-934. doi: 10.1016/j.patcog.2004.11.001.

Ma, Y. F., Lu, L., Zhang, H. J., & Li, M. (2002). A user attention model for video summarization. 533-542.

Ma, Y., Lao, S., Takikawa, E., & Kawade, M. (2007). Discriminant analysis in correlation similarity measure space. In *Proc of Int'l Conf. on Machine Learning, 227*, 577-584.

Ma, Y.F., & Zhang, H.J. (2003). Contrast-based image attention analysis by using fuzzy growing. *ACM international conference on Multimedia*, (pp. 374-381). doi: 10.1145/957013.957094.

Ma, Y.F., Hua, X.S., Lu, L., & Zhang, H.J. (2005). A generic framework of user attention model and its application in video summarization. *IEEE Trans on Multimedia, 7*(5), 907- 919. doi: 10.1109/TMM.2005.854410.

Mandal, M., Idris, F., & Panchanathan, S. (1999). A critical evaluation of image and video indexing techniques in the compressed domain. *Image and Vision Computing, 17*(7), 513-529.

Manjunath, B., Salembier, P., & Sikora, T. (2002). *Introduction to mpeg-7: Multimedia content description interface*. Wiley.

Maragos, P. (1989, July). Pattern spectrum and multiscale shape representation. *IEEE Transactions on Pattern Analysis and Machine Intelligence, 11*(7), 701–716.

Maragos, P. (2003). Algebraic and pde approaches for lattice scale-spaces with global constraints. *International Journal of Computer Vision, 52*(2/3), 121–137.

Martinez, A. (2000). Semantic access of frontal face images: the expression-invariant problem. In *Proc. of IEEE Workshop on Content-based access of images and video libraries.*

Mastroianni, D.T.C. (2005). A Super Peer Model for Building Resource Discovery Services in Grods: Design and Simulation Analysis. In *LNCS: Proceedings European Grid Conference (EGC 2005).*

Matas, J., Chum, O., Urban, M. & Pajdla, T. (2002). Robust wide baseline stereo from maximally stable extremal regions. *British Machine Vision Conference*, (pp. 384-393).

Matheron, G. (1975). *Random sets and integral geometry*. New York: Wiley.

Matsopoulos, G., & Marshall, S. (1992). A new morphological scale space operator. In *IEE Conference on Image Processing and its Applications* (pp. 246–249).

Mauricio, A., & Figucirdo, C. (2000). Texture analysis of grey-tone images by mathematical morphology: a non-destructive tool for the quantitative assessment of stone decay. *Mathematical Geology, 32*(5), 619 642.

McGuinness, N.F. (March 2001). *Ontology Development 101: A Guide to creating Your First Ontology*. Stanford: Stanford Knowledge Systems Laborartory technical report KSL-01-05 and Stanford Medical Informatics Technical Report SMI-2001-0880.

Mehrotra, R., & Gary, J.E. (1995). Similar-shape retrieval in shape data management. *IEEE Computer, 9*, 57-62.

Mehrubeoglu, M., Kehtarnavaz, N., Marquez, G., & Wang, L. (2000). Characterization of skin lesion texture in diffuse reflectance spectroscopic images. In *IEEE Southwest Symposium on Image Analysis and Interpretation* (pp. 146–150).

Meijster, A., & Wilkinson, M. (2002, April). A comparison of algorithms for connected set openings and closings. *IEEE Transactions on Pattern Analysis and Machine Intelligence, 24*(4), 484–494.

Meliopoulos, A.P.S., Cokkinides, G., Beker, B., & Dougal, R. (2000). A new tool for visualization and animation of power component and system operation System Sciences. In *Proceedings of the 33rd Annual Hawaii International Conference on System Sciences* (pp. 4022).

Meng, J., Juan, Y., & Chang, S. F. (1995). Scene change detection in an MPEG compressed video sequence, *2419*.

Mertzios, B., &Tsirikolias, K. (1998). Coordinate logic filters and their applications in image recognition and pattern recognition. *Circuits, Systems and Signal Processing, 17*(4), 517–538.

Metzler, V., Lehmann, T., Bienert, H., Mottahy, K., & Spitzer, K. (2000). Scale-independent shape analysis for quantitative cytology using mathematical morphology. *Computers in Biology and Medicine, 30*, 135–151.

Meyer, F., & Maragos, P. (2000). Nonlinear scale-space representation with morphological levelings. *Journal of Visual Communication and Image Representation, 11*, 245–265.

Miguel Castro, M.C. (2004). *Peer-to-peer overlays: structured, unstructured, or both*? Technical Report MSR-TR-2004-73. Cambridge.

Mikic, I., Krucinski, S., & Thomas, J.D. (1998). Segmentation and tracking in echocardiographic sequences: Active contours guided by optical flow estimates. *IEEE Trans. Medical Imaging, 17*, 274–284.

Mikolajczyk, K., & Schmid, C. (2004). Scale & affine invariant interest point detectors. *Int. J. Computer. Vision, 60*(1), 63-86. doi: 10.1023/ B:VISI.0000027790.02288.f2.

Mikolajczyk, K., & Schmid, C. (2005). A Performance Evaluation of Local Descriptors. *IEEE Trans. Pattern Anal. Mach. Intell., 27*(10), 1615-1630.

Mikolajczyk, K., Choudhury, R., & Schmid, C. (2001). Face detection in a video sequence - a temporal approach. In *Proc. of CVPR*.

Mitchell, T. (1982). Generalization as search. *Artificial Intelligence, 28*, 203-226.

Mitchell, T. (1982). Generalization as search. *Artificial Intelligence*, (pp. 203-226).

Moghaddam, B., & Pentland, A. (1997). Probabilistic Visual Learning for Object Representation. In *IEEE Trans. on Pattern Analysis & Machine Intelligence, 19*(7), 696-710.

Moghaddam, B., Jebara, T., & Pentland, A. (2001). Bayesian face recognition. *Pattern Recognition, 33*, 1771-1782.

Mohan, A., Papageorgiou, C., & Poggio, T. (2001). Example-based object detection in images by components. *IEEE Transactions on Pattern Analysis and Machine Intelligence, 23*(4), 349–361. doi: 10.1109/34.917571.

Mohana-Rao, K., & Dempster, A. (2001). Area-granulometry: an improved estimator of size distribution of image objects. *Electronic Letters, 37*(15), 950–951.

Mojsilovic, A., Gomes, J., & Rogowitz, B. (2002). Isee: Perceptual features for image library navigation. In *Proc. SPIE Human Vision and Electronic Imaging, 4662*, 266-277. doi: 10.1117/12.469523.

Mokhtarian, F., & Abbasi, S. (2004). Matching shapes with self-intersections: application to leaf classification. *IEEE Trans. on Image Processing, 13*(5), 653-661.

Monay, F., & Gatica-Perez, D., (2003). On Image Auto-Annotation with Latent Space Models. In *Proc. ACM Int'l Conf. Multimedia*, 275-278. doi: 10.1145/957013.957070.

Monay, F., & Gatica-Perez, D., (2007). Modeling semantic aspects for cross-media image indexing. *IEEE Transactions on Pattern Analysis and Machine Intelligence, 29*(10), 1802-1917. doi: 10.1109/TPAMI.2007.1097.

Monay, F., & Gatica-Perez, P. (2003). On image auto annotation with latent space models. In *Proc. ACM Int. Conf. on Multimedia*.

Monay, F., & Gatica-Perez, P. (2004). PLSA-based image auto-annotation: constraining the latent space". In *Proc. ACM International Conference on Multimedia*.

Moore, A. (1991). An introductory tutorial on kd-tree, extract from A. Moore's PhD Thesis. *Efficient Memory-based Learning for Robot Control*, University of Cambridge.

Mordacchini, M. (2007). *Grid and Peer-to-Peer Resource Discovery Systems*. Universita Ca Foscari Di Venezia, PhD Thesis.

Mori, G., & Malik, J. (2003). Recognizing Objects in Adversarial Clutter: Breaking a Visual CAPTCHA. *IEEE*

Conference on Computer Vision and Pattern Recognition, 1, 1063-6919.

Mori, Y., Takahashi, H., & Oka, R. (1999). Image-to-word transformation based on dividing and vector quantizing images with words. In *First International Workshop on Multimedia Intelligent Storage and Retrieval Management.*

Mori, Y., Takahashi, H., & Oka, R. (1999). Image-to-word transformation based on dividing and vector quantizing images with words. In *Proc. Int'l Workshop Multimedia Intelligent Storage and Retrieval Management.* From http://citeseer.ist.psu.edu/368129.html.

Muslea, I., Minton, S., & Knoblock, C.A. (2000). Selective sampling with redundant views. In *Proceedings of the 17th National Conference on Artificial Intelligence* (pp. 621-626).

Muslea, I., Minton, S., & Knoblock, C.A. (2002). Active + Semi-supervised learning = Robust multi-view learning. In *Proceedings of International Conference on Machine Learning,* (pp. 435-442).

Muslea, I., Minton, S., & Knoblock, C.A. (2006). Active learning with multiple views. *Journal of Artificial Intelligence Research, 27,* 203-233.

Mylopoulos, M.K. (2001). UML for Agent-Oriented Software Development: The Tropos Proposal. In *Lecture Notes in Computer Science* (pp. 422-441). *Proceedings of UML 2001.*

Nachreiner, F. Nickel, P., & Meyer, I. (2006). Human factors in process control systems: The design of human–machine interfaces. *Safety Science, 44*(1), 5-26.

Nagasaka, A., & Tanaka, Y. (1991). Automatic video indexing and full-video search for object appearance. 113-127.

Nakazato, M., & Huang, T.S. (2001). 3D MARS: Immersive virtual reality for content-based image retrieval. In *IEEE Int. Conference on Multimedia and Expo.*

Nam, J., & Tewfik, A. (2005). Detection of gradual transitions in video sequences using B-spline interpolation. *Multimedia, IEEE Transactions on, 7*(4), 667-679.

Naphade, M., & Smith, J.R. (2004a). Active learning for simultaneous annotation of multiple binary semantic concepts. In *Proceedings of International Conference on Image Processing,* (pp. 77-80).

Naphade, M., & Smith, J.R. (2004b). On the detection of semantic concepts at TRECVID. In *Proceedings of ACM Multimedia,* (pp. 660-667).

Naphade, M., Smith, J. ., Tesic, J., Chang, S.-F., Hsu, W., Kennedy, L., Hauptmann, A., & Curtis, J. (2006). Large-scale concept ontology for multimedia. *IEEE Multimedia Magazine, 13*(3).

Naphade, M., Smith, J. R., Tesic, J., Chang, S.-F., Hsu, W., Kennedy, L., Hauptmann, A., & Curtis, J. (2006). Large-scale concept ontology for multimedia. IEEE MultiMedia, 13, 86–91.

Naphade, M., Smith, J.R., Tesic, J., Chang, S.-F., Hsu, W., Kennedy, L., Hauptmann, A. G., & Curtis, J. (2006). Large-scale concept ontology for multimedia. *IEEE Multimedia, 16*(3).

Naphade, M, Smith, J R, Tesic, J., Chang, S.-F., Hsu, W., Kennedy, L., Hauptmann, A.G., & Curtis, J. (2006). Large-scale concept ontology for multimedia. *IEEE Multimedia Magazine, 13*(3), 86-91.

Napster. (n.d.). Retrieved September 12, 2007, from http://www.napster.com

Naquest, M.V., & Ullman, S. (2003). Object recognition with informative features and linear classification. *Ninth International Conference on Computer Vision, 1,* 281–288. doi: 10.1109/ICCV.2003.1238356.

Navalpakkam, V., & Itti, L. (2006). An integrated model of top-down and bottom-up attention for optimizing detecting speed. *IEEE Conference on Computer Vision and Pattern Recognition, 2,* 2049-2056. doi: 10.1109/CVPR.2006.54.

Nes, N., & d'Ornellas, M. (1999, January). Color image texture indexing. In *International Conference on Visual Information and Information Systems,1614,* 467–474. Springer-Verlag.

Nguyen, H.T., & Smeulders, A. (2004). Active learning using pre-clustering. In *Proceedings of International Conference on Machine Learning,* (pp. 623-630).

Niblack, W., Barber, R., Equitz, E., Flickner, M.D., Glasman, D., Petkovic, D., & Yanker, P. (1993). The QBIC project: Querying images by content using color, texture and shape. In *Conf. on Storage and Retrieval for Image and Video Databases, volume 1908 of Proceedings of SPIE,* (pp. 173–187).

Nigam, K., & Ghani, R. (2000). Analysis the effectiveness and applicability of co-training. In *Proceedings of Information and Knowledge Management,* (pp. 86-93).

Nilsback, M., & Zisserman, A. (2006). A Visual Vocabulary for Flower Classification. *IEEE Conf. on Computer Vision and Pattern Recognition, 2,* 1447-1454.

Nishitani, H., Kawamura, T., & Suzuki, G. (2000). University-industry cooperative study on plant operations. *Computers and Chemical Engineering, 24,* 557-567.

Nishiyama, K. (2005). *Development of human factor analysis system for human errors prevention.* Unpublished Master Thesis, Okayama University, Japan.

Nitta, N., Babaguchi, N., & Kitahashi, T. (2002). Story based representation for broadcasted sports video and automatic story segmentation. *IEEE International Conference on Multimedia and Expo,* 1, pp. 813-816. doi: 10.1109/ICME.2002.1035906.

O'Toole, R.K., & Stark, H. (1980). Comparative study of optical vs. all digital techniques in textural pattern recognition. *Applied Optics, 19,* 2496-2506.

Oh, J.H., Lee, J. K., & Hwang, S. (2005) Video data mining: current status and challenges. In J. Wang (Eds.) *Encyclopedia of Data Warehousing and Mining,* (pp. 104-107). Idea Group Inc. and IRM Press. doi: 10.1002/sam.10003.

Oliva, A., & Torralba, A. (2001). Modeling the shape of the scene: a holistic representation of the spatial envelope. *International Journal of Computer Vision, 42,* 145-175. doi: 10.1023/A:1011139631724.

Omata, M., Hamamoto, T., & Hangai, S. (2001). Lip recognition using morphological pattern spectrum. In *International conference on audio- and video-based biometric person authentication,2091,* 108–114. Springer-Verlag.

Osada, R., Funkhouser, T., Chazelle, B., & Dobkin, D. (2002). Shape Distributions. *ACM Trans. on Graphics, 21*(4), 807-832.

Oshima, D.L. (1998). *Programming and Deploying Java Mobile Agents with Aglets.* Addison Wesley.

Osuna, E., Freund, R. & Girosi, F. (1997). Training Support Vector Machines: an Application to Face Detection. *International Conference on Computer Vision*

and Pattern Recognition, (pp. 130–136). doi: 10.1109/CVPR.1997.609310.

Otsuji, K. Y., Tonomura, & Ohba, Y. (1991). Video browsing using brightness data. *in Proc. SPIE/IS&T VCIP'91, 1606,* 980–989.

Otto, C. (2004). *Textbook of Clinical Echocardiography.* Saunders.

Over, P., Ianeva, T., Kraaij, W., & Smeaton, A. F. (2005). TRECVID 2005-an overview.

Over, P., Ianeva, T., Kraaij, W., & Smeaton, A.F. (2006). Trecvid 2006 overview. In Proceedings of NIST-TRECVID.

Overbye, T.J., Gross, G., Laufenberg, M.J., & Sauer, P.W. Visualizing power system operations in an open market. Computer Applications in Power, *10*(1), 53-58.

Owens, J., & Hunter, A. (2000). Application of the self-organizing map to trajectory classification. In *Proc. Third IEEE Visual Surveillance Workshop,* (pp. 77-83). doi: 10.1109/VS.2000.856860.

Paek, S., & Chang, S.-F. (2000). A knowledge engineering approach for image classification based on probabilistic reasoning systems. In *Proc. IEEE Int'l Conf. Multimedia and Expo, II,* 1133-1136. doi: 10.1109/ICME.2000.871560.

Pan, J. Y., Yang, H.-J., Duygulu, P., & Faloutsos, C. (2004). Automatic image captioning. *Proc. 2004 IEEE Int'l Conf. Multimedia and Expo (ICME'04), III,* 1987-1990. doi: 10.1109/ICME.2004.1394652.

Pan, J., & Faloutsos, C. (2002). GeoPlot: Spatial data mining on video libraries. *Int'l Conf. Information and Knowledge Management,* (pp. 405-412).

Pan, J.-Y., Yang, H.-J., Faloutsos, C., & Duygulu, P. (2004). Automatic multimedia cross-modal correlation discovery. In *Proceedings of the 10th ACM SIGKDD Conference.*

Pan, J.-Y., Yang, H.-J., Faloutsos, C., & Duygulu, P. (2004). GCap: graph-based automatic image captioning. *International Workshop on Multimedia Data and Document Engineering.*

Panda, N., Goh, K., & Chang, E.Y. (2006). Active learning in very large image databases. *Journal of Multimedia Tools and Applications Special issue on Computer Vision Meets Databases, 31*(3), 249-267.

Paolo Trunfio, D.T. (June 2007). *Peer-to-Peer Models for Resource Discovery on Grids*. Italy: Core Grid - Institute on System Architecture.

Papageorgiou, C., Oren, M., & Poggio, T. (1998). A general framework for object detection. In *Proc. of ICCV*.

Pappas, T. N., Chen, J.Q., & Depalov, D. (2007). Perceptually based techniques for image segmentation and semantic classification. *IEEE Communications Magazine*, 45(1), 44-51. doi: 10.1109/MCOM.2007.284537.

Park, H., & Chin, R. (1995, January). Decomposition of arbitrarily shaped morphological structuring elements. *IEEE Transactions on Pattern Analysis and Machine Intelligence*, 17(1), 2–15.

Park, K., & Lee, C. (1996, November). Scale-space using mathematical morphology. *IEEE Transactions on Pattern Analysis and Machine Intelligence*, 19(11), 1121 1126.

Parzen, E. (1962). On the estimation of a probability density function and the mode. *Annals of Mathematical Statistics, 33(3), 1065-1076*.

Pass, G., & Zabih, R. (1996). Histogram refinement for content-based image retrieval. *IEEE Workshop on Applications of Computer Vision*, (pp. 96-102). doi: 10.1109/ACV.1996.572008.

Pass, G., & Zabih, R. (1996). Histogram refinement for content-based image retrieval. In *3rd IEEE Workshop on Applications of Computer Vision*, (pp. 96–102).

Pass, G., Zabih, R., & Miller, J. (1996). Comparing Images Using Color Coherence Vectors. In *Proceedings of the 4th ACM International Conference on Multimedia* (pp. 65-73), Boston, Massachusetts.

Pbmplus (2003). Retrieved January 7, 2003, from http://www.acme.com/software/pbmplus/

Pentland, A., Moghaddam, B., & Starner, T. (1994). View-based and modular eigenspaces for face recognition. In Proc. Of the IEEE Conf. on Comput. Vis. and Patter. Recog., (pp. 84-91).

Perona, P., & Malik, J. (1990). Scale-space and edge detection using anisotropic diffusion. *IEEE Transaction on Pattern Analysis and Machine Intelligence*, 12(7).

Perronin, F. (2007). Universal and adapted vocabularies for generic visual categorization. *IEEE Transaction on Pattern Analysis and Machine Intelligence*, 30(7), 1243-1256. doi: 10.1109/TPAMI.2007.70755.

Pesaresi, M., & Benediktsson, J. (2001, February). A new approach for the morphological segmentation of high-resolution satellite imagery. *IEEE Transactions on Geoscience and Remote Sensing*, 39(2), 309–320.

Pesaresi, M., & Pagot, E. (2007). Post-conflict reconstruction assessment using image morphological profile and fuzzy multicriteria approach on 1-m-resolution satellite data. In *IEEE/ISPRS Joint Workshop on Remote Sensing and Data Fusion over Urban Areas*.

Peters, RJ., & Itti, L. (2007). Beyond bottom-up: Incorporating task-dependent influences into a computational model of spatial attention. *IEEE Conference on Computer Vision and Pattern Recognition*, (pp. 1-6). doi: 10.1109/CVPR.2007.383337.

Petrakis, E.G.M., Diplaros, A., & Milios, E. (2002). Matching and Retrieval of Distorted and Occluded Shapes Using Dynamic Programming. *IEEE Trans. on Pattern Analysis and Machine Intelligence*, 24(11), 1501-1516.

Picard, R.W. (1994). Content access for image/video coding: The fourth criterion. *Technical Report 195*, MIT Media Lab.

Picard, R.W., Minka, T.P., & Szummer, M. (1996). Modeling user subjectivity in image libraries. In *Proceedings of International Conference on Image Processing*, (pp. 777-780).

Plaza, A., Martinez, P., Perez, R., & Plaza, J. (2004). A new approach to mixed pixel classification of hyperspectral imagery based on extended morphological profiles. *Pattern Recognition*, 37, 1097–1116.

Plaza, A., Plaza, J., & Valencia, D. (2007). Impact of platform heterogeneity on the design of parallel algorithms for morphological processing of high-dimensional image data. *The Journal of Supercomputing*, 40(1), 81–107.

Porter, S., Mirmehdi, M., & Thomas, B. (2000). Video cut detection using frequency domain correlation. (pp. 413-416).

Qi, G., Hua, X.-S., Rui, Y., Tang, J., Mei, T., & Zhang, H.-J. (2007). Correlative multi-label video annotation. In *Proceedings of ACM Multimedia*, (pp. 17-26).

Qi, G., Song, Y., Hua, X.-S., Zhang, H.-J., & Dai, L.-R. (2006). Video annotation by active learning and cluster tuning. In *Proceedings of Computer Vision and Pattern Recognition Workshop*.

Qiu, G. (2003). Colour image indexing using BTC. *IEEE Trans. Image Processing, 12*(1), 93–101.

Quelhas, P., Monay, F., Odobez, J.-M., Gatica-Perez, D., Tuytelaars, T. & Gool, L.V. (2005). Modeling scenes with local descriptors and latent aspects. In *Proc. IEEE Int'l Conf. Computer Vision, 1,* 883-890. doi: 10.1109/ICCV.2005.152.

Racky, J., & Pandit, M. (1999). Automatic generation of morphological opening-closing sequences for texture segmentation. In *IEEE International Conference on Image Processing (ICIP)* (pp. 217–221).

Rahmani, R., & Goldman, S. (2006). Multiple-instance semi-supervised learning. In *Proc. International Conference on Machine Learning.*

Ramos, V., & Pina, P. (2005). Exploiting and evolving rn mathematical morphology feature spaces. In *International Symposium on Mathematical Morphology (ISMM)* (pp. 465–474). Paris, France.

Rao, K.R. & Yip, P. (1990). *Discrete cosine transform: algorithms, advantages, applications.* New York: Academic.

Rao, M., Sun, X, & Feng, J. (2000). Intelligent system architecture for process operation support. *Expert Systems with Applications, 19,* 279-288.

Rasheed, Z., & Shah, M. (2005). Detection and representation of scenes in videos. *Multimedia, IEEE Transactions on, 7*(6), 1097-1105.

Rasiowa, H., & Sikorski, R. (1968). *The Mathematics of Metamathematics.* Warsaw: PWN.

Ratnasamy, P.F.S. (2001). A Scalable Content-Addressable Network. In *Proceedings of the 2001 conference on applications, technologies, architectures, and protocols for computer communications.*

Redner, R., & Walker, H. (1984). Mixture densities, maximum likelihood and the EM algorithm. SIAM review, 26(2), 195-239.

Ren, W., Sharma, M., & Singh, S. (2001). Automated video segmentation.

Rivas-Araiza, E., Mendiola-Santibanez, J., & Herrera-Ruiz, G. (2008). Morphological multiscale fingerprints from connected transformations. *Signal Processing, 88,* 1125–1133.

Rivest, J. (2006). Granulometries and pattern spectra for radar signals. *Signal Processing, 86,* 1094–1103.

Robinson, J. (1981). The k-d-b-tree: A search structure for large multidimensional dynamic indexes. In *Proc. Of ACM SIGMOD,* (pp. 10-18).

Rocchio Jr., J.J. (1971). Relevance feedback in information retrieval. In G. Salton (Eds.), *The SMART Retrieval System: Experiments in Automatic Document Processing,* (pp. 313-323). New Jersey: Prentice-Hall.

Rodden, K., Basalaj, D., Sinclair, D., & Wood, K. (1999). Evaluating a visualization of image similarity as a tool for image browsing. In *IEEE Symposium on Information Visualization,* pages 36-43.

Romdhani, S., Gong, S., & Psarrou, A. (1999). A multi-view nonlinear active shape model using kernel PCA. In *Proc. of 10th British Machine Vision Conference,* (pp. 483-492).

Ronse, C. (1990, October). Why mathematical morphology needs complete lattices. *Signal Processing, 21*(2), 129–154.

Ronse, C. (2005). Special issue on mathematical morphology after 40 years. *Journal of Mathematical Imaging and Vision, 22*(2-3).

Ronse, C., Najman, L., & Decencière, E. (2007). Special issue on ISMM 2005. *Image and Vision Computing, 25*(4).

Rosenfeld, A., & Kak, A. (1982). *Digital Image Processing,* Volumes I and II. Orlando, Florida: Academic Press.

Ross, N., Pritchard, C., Rubin, D., & Duse, A. (2006, May). Automated image processing method for the diagnosis and classification of malaria on thin blood smears. *Medical and Biological Engineering and Computing, 44*(5), 427–436.

Roth, S., & Black, M.J. (2005). On the spatial statistics of optical flow. In *Proc. of ICCV.*

Roussopoulos, N., Kelley, S., & Vincent, F. (1995). Nearest neighbor queries. In *Proc of ACM SIGMOD Int'l Conference on Management of Data,* (pp. 71-79).

Roussopoulos, N., Kelley, S., & Vincent, F. (1995). Nearest-Neighbor Queries. In *Proceedings of the 1995 ACM SIGMOD International Conference on Management of Data* (pp. 71-79).

Roweis, S. T., & Saul, L. K. (2000). Nonlinear Dimensionality Reduction by Locally Linear Embedding. *Science, 290*(5500), 2323-2326.

Roweis, S., & Saul, L. (2000). Nonlinear dimensionality reduction by locally linear embeddings. *Science, 290,* 2323-2326.

Roy, N., & McCallum, A. (2001). Toward optimal active learning through Monte Carlo estimation of error reduction. In *Proceedings of International Conference on Machine Learning.*

Ruberto, C. D., Dempster, A., Khan, S., & Jarra, B. (2002). Analysis of infected blood cells images using morphological operators. *Image and Vision Computing, 20,* 133–146.

Rubner, J., Guibas, L., & Tomasi, C. (1997). The earth mover's distance, multi-dimensional scaling, and color based image retrieval. In *Image Understanding Workshop*, pages 661–668.

Rubner, Y., Tomasi, C., & Guibas, L. (2000). The Earth Mover's Distance as a Metric for Image Retrieval. *International Journal of Computer Vision, 40*, (2), 99-121.

Rui, X., Yuan, P., & Yu, N. (2006). Image annotations based on semi-supervised clustering with semantic soft constraints. In *Proc. Pacific-Rim Conference on Multimedia.*

Rui, Y., et al. (1998). Relevance feedback: A power tool for interactive content-based image retrieval. *IEEE Transactions on Circuits and Systems for Video Technology, 8*(3), 644-655.

Rui, Y., Huang, T. S., & Chang, S. F. (1999). Image retrieval: current techniques, promising directions and open issues. *Journal of Visual Communication and Image Representation, 10*(1), 39-62.

Rui, Y., Huang, T., & Mehrotra, S. (1997). Content-Based image retrieval with relevance feedback in MARS. In Proceedings of IEEE International Conference on Image Processing (pp. 815–818).

Rui, Y., Huang, T.S., & Chang, S.-F. (1999). Image retrieval: current techniques, promising directions, and open issues. *Jounal of Visual Communication and Image Representation, 10*(1), 39-62.

Rui, Y., Huang, T.S., & Chang, S.F. (1999). Image Retrieval: Current techniques, promising directions, and open issues. *Journal of Visual Communication and Image Representation, 10*, 39-62.

Rui, Y., Huang, T.S., & Mehrotra, S. (1999) Constructing Table-of-Content for videos, *ACM Multimedia System, 7*(5), 359–368. doi: 10.1007/s005300050138.

Rui, Y., Huang, T.S., Ortega, M., & Mehrotra, S. (1998). Relevance feedback: a power tool in interactive content-based image retrieval. *IEEE Transactions on Circuits and Systems for Video Technology, 8*(5), 664-655.

Ruszala, S.D., & Schaefer, G. (2004). Visualisation models for image databases: A comparison of six approaches. In *Irish Machine Vision and Image Processing Conference*, pages 186–191.

Sabourin, R., Genest, G., & Prêteux, F. (1997, September). Off-line signature verification by local granulometric size distributions. *IEEE Transactions on Pattern Analysis and Machine Intelligence, 19*(9), 976–988.

Saitoh, T., & Kaneko, T. (2000). Automatic Recognition of Wild Flowers. *International Conference on Pattern Recognition, 2,* 2507-2510.

Salembier, P., Oliveras, A., & Garrido, L. (1998, April). Antiextensive connected operators for image and sequence processing. *IEEE Transactions on Image Processing, 7*(4), 555–570.

Sand, F., & Dougherty, E. (1999). Robustness of granulometric moments. *Pattern Recognition, 32,* 1657–1665.

Sangwine, J., & Horne, R.E.N. (1998). *The Colour Image Processing Handbook.* Chapman & Hall.

Santini, S., & Jain, R. (1999). Similarity measures. *IEEE Trans. PAMI, 21*(9), 871–883.

Santini, S., & Jain, R. (1999). Similarity Measures. *IEEE Transactions on Pattern Analysis and Machine Intelligence, 21*(9), 871-883.

Sapiro, G. (2001). *Geometric partial differential equation and image analysis.* Cambridge University Press.

Sasou, K. Human factor analysis on criticality accident, Human Factors Research Center, CRIEPI, Japan.

Saul, L.K., & Roweis, S.T. (2003). Think Globally, Fit Locally: Unsupervised Learning of Low Dimensional Manifolds, *J. Machine Learning Research, 4,* 119-155.

Schaefer, G. (2008). Does compression affect image retrieval performance? *Int. Journal of Imaging Systems and Technology, 18*(2-3), 101-112.

Schaefer, G., & Lieutaud, S. (2004a). CVPIC compressed domain image retrieval by colour and shape. *Springer Lecture Notes in Computer Science, LNCS Vol. 3211,* (pp. 778-786).

Schaefer, G., & Lieutaud, S. (2004b). CVPIC based uniform/non-uniform colour histograms for compressed domain image retrieval. In *7th Int. Conference on VISual Information Systems,* (pp. 344-348).

Schaefer, G., & Qiu, G. (2000). Midstream content access based on colour visual pattern coding. In *Storage and Retrieval for Image and Video Databases VIII, volume 3972 of Proceedings of SPIE,* (pp. 284–292).

Schaefer, G., & Ruszala, S. (2005). Image database navigation: A globe-al approach. In Int. Symposium on Visual *Computing,* volume 3804 *of Springer Lecture Notes on Computer Science,* pages 279-286.

Schaefer, G., & Stich, M. (2004). UCID - An Uncompressed Colour Image Database. In *Storage and Retrieval Methods and Applications for Multimedia 2004,* volume 5307 of Proceedings of SPIE, pages 472–480.

Schaefer, G., & Stich, M. (2004). UCID - An Uncompressed Colour Image Database. In *Storage and Retrieval Methods and Applications for Multimedia 2004, volume 5307 of Proceedings of SPIE,* (pp. 472–480).

Schaefer, G., Lieutaud, S., & Qiu, G. (2004). CVPIC image retrieval based on block colour co-occurance matrix and pattern histogram. In *IEEE Int. Conference on Image Processing,* pages 413-416.

Schaefer, G., Qiu, G. & Luo, M.R. (1999). Visual pattern based colour image compression. In *Visual Communication and Image Processing 1999,* volume 3653 *of Proceedings of SPIE,* (pp. 989–997).

Schneiderman, H., & Kanade, T. (2000). A Statistical Method for 3D Object Detection Applied to Faces and Cars. *IEEE Conference on Computer Vision and Pattern Recognition, 1,* 746-751. doi: 10.1109/CVPR.2000.855895.

Schneiderman, H., & Kanade, T. (2004). Object Detection Using the Statistics of Parts. *International Journal of Computer Vision, 56*(3), 151-177.

Schoeman, M.a. (2003). Architectural Components for the Efficient Design of the Mobile Agent Systems. *ACM International Conference Proceedings Series; Vol. 47* (pp. 48-58). South Africa: South African Institute for Computer Scientists and Information Technologies.

Schohn, G., & Cohn, D. (2000). Less is more: active learning with support vector machines. *Proceedings of the 7th International Conference on Machine Learning* (pp. 839-846).

Sclaroff, S., & Liu, L. (2001). Deformable shape detection and description via model-based region grouping, *IEEE Trans. on Pattern Analysis and Machine Intelligence, 23*(5), 475-489.

Sebastian, T.B., Klein, P.N., & Kimia, B.B. (2004). Recognition of Shapes by Editing Their Shock Graphs. *IEEE Trans. on Pattern Analysis and Machine Intelligence, 26*(5), 550-571.

Seeger, M. (2001). Learning with labeled and unlabeled data. *Technical Report.* University of Edinburgh.

Serra, J. (1982). *Image analysis and mathematical morphology.* Academic Press.

Serrano, N., Savakis, A., & Luo, J. (2004). Improved scene classification using efficient low-level features and semantic cues. *Pattern Recognition, 37,* 1773-1784. doi: 10.1016/j.patcog.2004.03.003.

Seung, H.S., Opper, M., & Sompolinsky, H. (1992). Query by committee. In *Proceedings of Annual Workshop on Computational Theory,* (pp. 287-294).

Shackelford, A., Davis, C., & Wang, X. (2004). Automated 2-d building footprint extraction from high resolution satellite multispectral imagery. In *IEEE International Geosciences and Remote Sensing Symposium (IGARSS)* (pp. 1996–1999).

Shahraray, B. (1995). Scene change detection and content-based sampling of video sequences. *In Proc. IS&T/SPIE, 2419,* 2–13.

Shahraray, B. (1995). Scene change detection and content-based sampling of video sequences, *2419,* 2-13.

Shakhnarovich, G., Darrell, T., & Indyk, P. (2007). *Nearest-Neighbor Methods in Learning and Vision: Theory and Practice,.* MIT Press.

Shen, J., Shepherd, J., & Ngu, A.H.H. (2005). Semantic-sensitive classification for large image libraries. In

Proc. Int'l Multimedia Modeling Conf., (pp. 340-345). doi: 10.1109/MMMC.2005.66.

Shevade, B., & Sundaram, H. (2006). Incentive based image annotation. *Technical Report, Arizona State University.* AME-TR-2004-02.

Shi, J., & Malik, J. (2000). Normalized cuts and image segmentation. *IEEE Transactions on Pattern Analysis and Machine Intelligence, 22*(8), 888-905. doi: 10.1109/34.868688.

Shi, J., & Tomasi, C. (1994). Good features to track. In *Proc. of CVPR,* (pp. 593–600).

Shih, F., &Wu, Y. (2005). Decomposition of binary morphological structuring elements based on genetic algorithms. *Computer Vision and Image Understanding, 99,* 291–302.

Siddiqi, K, Shokoufandeh, A., Dickinson, S.J., & Zucker, S.W. (1999). Shock Graphs and Shape Matching. *International Journal of Computer Vision, 35*(1), 13-32.

Siderean Software. (2003, January). *From Site Search to the Semantic Web.* Los Angeles, CA, USA.

Signs (2005). Retrieved September 7, 2005, from *http://www.geocities.com/jusjih/roadsigns.html#d*

Singh, H.Z.M. (2006). *Infrastructure for Resource Discovery using Mobile Agents.* London.

Sivakumar, K., Patel, M., Kehtarnavaz, N., Balagurunathan, Y., & Dougherty, E. (2000). A constant-time algorithm for erosions/dilations with applications to morphological texture feature computation. *Journal of Real-Time Imaging, 6,* 223–239.

Sivic, J., & Zisserman, A. (2008). Efficient Visual Search for Objects in Videos. *Proceedings of the IEEE, 96*(4), 548-566.

Sivic, J., Russell, B.C., Efros, A.A., Zisserman, A., & Freeman, W. T. (2005). Discovering objects and their locations in images. In *Proc. Int'l Conf. Computer Vision,* (pp. 370-377). doi: 10.1109/ICCV.2005.77.

Smeaton, A., Gilvarry, J., Gormley, G., Tobin, B., Marlow, S., & Murphy, M. (1999). An evaluation of alternative techniques for automatic detection of shot boundaries in digital video. (pp. 45-60).

Smeulders, A. W., et al. (2000). Content-based image retrieval at the end of the early years. *IEEE Transactions on Pattern Recognition and Machine Learning, 22*(12), 1349-1380.

Smeulders, A. W.M., Worring, M., Santini, S., Gupta, A., & Jain, R. (2000). Content-based image retrieval at the end of the early years. *IEEE Transactions on Pattern Analysis and Machine Intelligence, 22*(12), 1349-1380. doi: 10.1109/34.895972.

Smeulders, A.W.M., Worring, M., Santini, S., Gupta, A., & Jain, R. (2000). Content-based image retrieval at the end of the early years. *IEEE Transactions on Pattern Analysis and Machine Intelligence, 22*(12), 1349-1380.

Smeulders, A.W.M., Worring, M., Santini, S., Gupta, A., & Jain, R. (2000). Content-based image retrieval at the end of the early years. *IEEE Trans. Pattern Analysis and Machine Intelligence,* 22(12):1249–1380.

Smeulders, A W M , Worring, M , Santini, S,, Gupta, A., & Jain, R. (2000). Content-based image retrieval at the end of the early years. *IEEE Trans. Pattern Analysis and Machine Intelligence, 22*(12), 1249–1380.

Smith, J., Lin, C., Naphade, M., Natsev, A., & Tseng, B. (2003). Multimedia semantic indexing using model vectors. In *Proc. IEEE Int'l Conf. Multimedia and Expo, II,* 445-448. doi: 10.1109/ICME.2003.1221649.

Smith, J.R., & Chang, S. (1997). VisualSEEK: A Fully Automated Content-Based Image Query System. In *Proceedings of the 4th ACM International Conference on Multimedia* (87-98), Boston, Massachusetts.

Smith, J.R., & Chang, S. F. (1995). Tools and techniques for color image retrieval. In *Proc. SPIE: Storage and Retrieval for Image and Video Database, 2670,* 426-437.

Smith, J.R., & Chang, S.F. (1996). Automated binary texture feature sets for image retrieval. *In Proc IEEE Int Conf Acoust, Speech and Signal Proc,* May, (pp. 2239-2242). doi: 10.1109/ICASSP.1996.545867.

Smith, J.R., & Schirling, P. (2006). Metadata standards roundup. *IEEE Multimedia, 13*(2).

Snoek, C., Worring, M., Geusebroek, J., Koelma, D., & Seinstra, F. (2004). The MediaMill TRECVID 2004 semantic viedo search engine. In Proceedings of NIST-TRECVID.

Snoek, C.G.M., Worring, M., & Smeulders, A.W.M. (2005). Early versus late fusion in semantic video analysis. In *Proceedings of ACM Multimedia,* (pp. 399-402).

Snoek, C.G.M., Worring, M., Gemert, J.C.V., Geusebroek, J.-M., & Smeulders, A.W.M. (2006). The challenge problem for automated detection of 101 semantic concepts in multimedia. In *Proc. ACM Multimedia*.

Soderkvist, O. (2001). *Computer Vision Classification of Leaves from Swedish Trees*. Master Thesis. Linkoping University.

Soille, P. (2002). Morphological texture analysis: an introduction. In *Morphology of condensed matter, 600*, 215–237. Springer-Verlag.

Soille, P. (2003). *Morphological image analysis : Principles and applications*. Berlin: Springer-Verlag.

Soille, P., & Talbot, H. (2001, November). Directional morphological filtering. *IEEE Transactions on Pattern Analysis and Machine Intelligence, 23*(11), 1313–1329.

Solso, R.L., Maclin, M.K. & Maclin, O.H. (2003). Cognitive psychology. *Perception and Attention*, (pp. 70-103). Pearson Education.

Song, Y. Q., Wang, W., & Zhang, A. D. (2003). Automatic annotation and retrieval of images. *World Wide Web, 6*, 209-231. doi: 10.1023/A:1023674722438.

Song, Y., Hua, X.-S., Dai, L., & Wang, M. (2005). Semi-automatic video annotation based on active learning with multiple complementary predictors. In *Proc. ACM International Workshop on Multimedia Information Retrieval*.

Song, Y., Hua, X.-S., Dai, L.-R., & Wang, M. (2005). Semi-Automatic Video annotation based on active learning with multiple complementary predictors. In *Proceedings of ACM Workshop on Multimedia Information Retrieval*, (pp. 94-104).

Song, Y., Hua, X.-S., Qi, G.-J., Dai, L., Wang, M., & Zhang, H.-J. (2006). Efficient semantic annotation method for indexing large personal video database. In *Proc. ACM International Workshop on Multimedia Information Retrieval*.

Southam, P., & Harvey, R. (2005). Texture granularities. In *IAPR International Conference on Image Analysis and Processing (ICIAP), 3617*, 304–311. Springer-Verlag.

SRC (2006). Search result clustering toolbar in Microsoft Research Asia. *http://rwsm.directtaps.net/*.

Stehling, R.O., Nascimento, M.A., & Falcao, A.X. (2002). A compact and efficient image retrieval approach based on border/interior pixel classification. In *11ᵗʰ Int. Conf. on Information and Knowledge Management*, (pp. 102–109).

Stoer, M., & Wagner, F. (1994). A simple min cut algorithm. *Algorithms--ESA '94, LNCS 855*, 141-147.

Stoica, R.M. (2001). Chord: A Scalable Peer-to-Peer Lookup Service for Internet Applications. In *Proceedings of the 2001 ACM SIGCOMM Conference*, San Diego.

Stonebraker, M., Sellis, T., & Hanson, E. (1986). An analysis of rule indexing implementations in data base systems. *Proc. Intl. Conf. on Expert Database Systems*.

Stricker, M., & Orengo, M. (1995). Similarity of color images. In *Conf. on Storage and Retrieval for Image and Video Databases III*, volume 2420 of Proceedings of SPIE, pages 381–392.

Stricker, M., & Orengo, M. (1995). Similarity of color images. In *Proceedings of SPIE 2420, Storage and Retrieval for Image and Video Databases*, (pp. 381-392).

Stricker, M.A., & Orengo, M. (1995). Similarity of color images. In *Proc. SPIE: Storage and Retrieval for Image and Video Database, 2420*, 381-392.

Su, H., Crookes, D., & Bouridane, A. (2007). Shoeprint image retrieval by topological and pattern spectra. In *International Machine Vision and Image Processing Conference* (pp. 15–22).

Sudo, K., Yamato, J., & Tomono, A. (1996). Determining gender of walking people using multiple sensors. In *International Conference on Multisensor Fusion and Integration for Intelligent Systems* (pp. 641–646).

Summers, R., Agcaoili, C., McAuliffe, M., Dalal, S., Yim, P., Choyke, P., et al. (2001). Helical CT of von Hippel-Lindau: semi-automated segmentation of renal lesions. In *IEEE International Conference on Image Processing (ICIP)* (pp. 293–296).

Sumpter, N., & Bulpitt, A.J. (2000). Learning spatio-temporal patterns for predicting object behavior. *Image and Vision Computing, 18*(9), 697-704.

Sundaram, H., & Chang, S.F. (2000). Video scene segmentation using video and audio features. *IEEE International Conference on Multimedia and Expo, 2*, (pp. 1145-1148). doi: 10.1109/ICME.2000.871563.

Swain, M.J., & Ballard, D.H. (1991). Color indexing. *International Journal of Computer Vision, 7*(1), 11-32.

Swain, M.J., & Ballard, D.H. (2001). Color indexing. *Int. Journal Computer Vision, 7*(11), 11–32.

Sychay, G., Chang, E.Y., & Goh, K. (2002). Effective image annotation via active learning. In *Proceedings of International Conference on Image Processing*, (pp. 209-212).

Szummer, M.,& Picard, R. W. (1998). Indoor-outdoor image classification. In *Proc. ICCV Workshop on Content-based Access of Image and Video Databases*, 42-50. doi: 10.1109/CAIVD.1998.646032.

Tang, J., Hua, X.-S., Mei, T., Qi, G.-J., & Wu, X. (2007). Video annotation based on temporally consistent Gaussian random field. *Electronics Letters, 43*(8).

Tang, J., Hua, X.–S., Qi, G., Gu, Z., & Wu, X. (2007). Beyond accuracy: typicality ranking for video annotation. In *Proceedings of International Conference on Multimedia & Expo*, (pp. 647-650).

Tang, J., Hua, X.-S., Qi, G.-J., & Wu, X. (2007). Typicality ranking via semi-supervised multiple instance learning. In *Proc. ACM Multimedia*.

Tang, J., Hua, X.-S., Qi, G.-J., Mei, T., & Wu, X. (2007). Anisotropic manifold ranking for video annotation. In *Proc. IEEE International Conference on Multimedia & Expo*.

Tang, J., Hua, X.-S., Qi, G.-J., Song, Y., & Wu, X. (2008). Video annotation based on kernel linear neighborhood propagation. *IEEE Transactions on Multimedia, 10*(4).

Tang, J., Hua, X.-S., Qi, G.-J., Wang, M., Mei, T., & Wu, X. (2007). Structure-sensitive manifold ranking for video concept detection. In *Proc. ACM Multimedia*.

Tang, X. (1998). Multiple competitive learning network fusion for object classification. *IEEE Transactions on Systems, Man, and Cybernetics, 28*(4), 532–543.

Tang, X., Gao, X.B., Liu, J., & Zhang, H. (2002). Spatial-temporal approach for video caption detection and recognition. *IEEE Transactions on Neural Networks, 13*, 961–971. doi: 10.1109/TNN.2002.1021896.

Taniguchi, Y., Akutsu, A., & Tonomura, Y. (1997). PanoramaExcerpts: Extracting and packing panoramas for video browsing. 427-436.

Tao, D., Li, X., Wu, X., & Maybank, S.J. (2007). General tensor discriminant analysis and Gabor features for gait recognition, IEEE Trans. on Pattern Analysis & Machine Intelligence, *29*(10), 1700-1715.

Taskiran, C., Chen, J. Y., Albiol, A., Torres, L., Bouman, C., & Delp, E. (2004). ViBE: A compressed video database structured for active browsing and search. *Multimedia, IEEE Transactions on, 6*(1), 103-118.

Tavanapong, W., & Zhou, J. (2004). Shot clustering techniques for story browsing, *IEEE Transaction on Multimedia, 6*(4), 517-527. doi: 10.1109/TMM.2004.830810.

Tenebaum, B., Silva, V., & Langford, J. (2000). A global geometric framework for nonlinear dimensionality. *Science, 290*, 23190-2323.

Tenenbaum, J.B., Silva, V., & Langford, J.C. (2000). A Global Geometric Framework for Nonlinear Dimensionality Reduction. *Science, 290*, 2319-2323.

Thayananthan, A., Stenger, B., Torr, P., & Cipolla, R. (2003) Shape context and chamfer matching in cluttered scenes. *International Conference on Computer Vision and Pattern Recognition, 1*, 127-133. doi: 10.1109/CVPR.2003.1211346.

Thayananthan, A., Stenger, B., Torr, P.H.S., & Cipolla, R. (2003). Shape Context and Chamfer Matching in Cluttered Scenes. *IEEE Conference on Computer Vision and Pattern Recognition, 1*, 127-133.

The TRECVID conference website. (2008). Retrieved June 6, 2008, from http://www-nlpir.nist.gov/projects/trecvid/.

Theera-Umpon, N., & Dhompongsa, S. (2007, May). Morphological granulometric features of nucleus in automatic bone marrow white blood cell classification. *IEEE Transactions on Information Technology in Biomedicine, 11*(3), 353–359.

Thompson, D.W. (1992) *On Growth and Form*. (republished), Dover Publication.

Tian, Q., & Zhang, H. J. (1999). Video shot detection and analysis: Content-based approaches. In C. Chen, & Y. Zhang (Eds.), *Visual information representation, communication, and image processing* () Marcel Dekker, Inc.

Tian, Y.H., Huang, T.J., & Gao, W. (2005). Exploiting multi-context analysis in semantic image classification.

Journal of Zhejiang University SCIENCE, 6A(11), 1268-1283. doi: 10.1631/jzus.2005.A1268.

Tieu, K., & Viola, P. (2000). Boosting image retrieval. In *Proceedings of IEEE Conference on Computer Vision and Pattern Recognition* (pp. 228-235).

Tjahyadi, R., Liu, W., An, S., & Venkatesh, S. (2007). Face recognition via the overlapping energy histogram. In *Proc. of International Conf. on Arti. Intell.,* (pp. 2891-2896).

Toda, H. & Kataoka, R. (2005). A search result clustering method using informatively named entities. *7th ACM Workshops on Web Information and Data Management* .

Tong, H., He, J., Li, M., Zhang, C., & Ma, W.-Y. (2005). Graph based multi-modality learning. In *Proc. ACM Multimedia.*

Tong, S., & Chang, E. (2001). Support vector machine active learning for image retrieval. In *Proceedings of the 9th ACM International Conference on Multimedia,* (pp. 107-118).

Tong, S., & Chang, E. (2001). Support vector machine active learning for image retrieval. In Proceedings of the 9th ACM Intl. Conf. on Multimedia (pp. 107–118).

Tong, S., & Chang, E. Y. (2001). Support vector machine active learning for image retrieval. In *Proceedings of ACM Multimedia,* (pp. 107-118).

Tong, S., & Koller, D. (2000). Support vector machine active learning with applications to text classification. In *Proceedings of the 7th International Conference on Machine Learning,* (pp. 999-1006).

Tong, S., & Koller, D. (2000). Support Vector Machine Active Learning with Applications to Text Classification. In *Proceedings of International Conference on Machine Learning,* (pp. 999-1006).

Trec-10 proceedings appendix on common evaluation measures. http://trec.nist.gov/pubs/trec10/appendices/measures.pdf

TRECVID: TREC Video Retrieval Evaluation. http://www-nlpir.nist.gov/projects/trecvid.

TRECVID: TREC Video Retrieval Evaluation. http://www-nlpir.nist.gov/projects/trecvid. In *TREC-10 Proceedings appendix on common evaluation measures.*

From http://trec.nist.gov/pubs/trec10/appendices/measures.pdf.

Tu, Z., & Yuille, A.L. (2004). Shape Matching and Recognition-Using Generative Models and Informative Features. *European Conference on Computer Vision, 3,* 195-209.

Turk, M., & Pentland, A. (1991). Eigenfaces for recognition. *Journal of Cognitive Neuroscience, 3*(1), 71-86.

Turk, M., & Pentland, A.P. (1991). Face Recognition Using Eigenfaces. In *Proc of IEEE Conf. Computer Vision and Pattern Recognition.*

Tushabe, F., & Wilkinson, M. (2007). Content-based image retrieval using shape-size pattern spectra. In *Cross Language Evaluation Forum 2007 Workshop, Imageclef Track.* Budapest, Hungary.

Tzafestas, C., & Maragos, P. (2002). Shape connectivity: multiscale analysis and application to generalized granulometries. *Journal of Mathematical Imaging and Vision, 17,* 109–129.

Uchihashi, S., Foote, J., Girgensohn, A., & Boreczky, J. (1999). Video manga: Generating semantically meaningful video summaries. *ACM international conference on Multimedia,* (pp. 383–392).

Udea, H., Miyatake, T., & Yoshizawa, S. (1991). IMPACT—An integrated natural-motion-picture dedicated multimedia authoring system. *New York. ACM Press,* (pp. 343-250).

Urbach, E., & Wilkinson, M. (2008, January). Efficient 2-d grayscale morphological transformations with arbitrary flat structuring elements. *IEEE Transactions on Image Processing, 17*(1), 1–8.

Urbach, E., Roerdink, J., & Wilkinson, M. (2007, February). Connected shape-size pattern spectra for rotation and scale-invariant classification of gray-scale images. *IEEE Transactions on Pattern Analysis and Machine Intelligence, 29*(2), 272–285.

Vadivel, A., Mohan, M., Sural, S., & Majumdar, A. (2005). Object level frame comparison for video shot detection., *2*

Vailaya, A., Figueiredo, A., Jain, A., & Zhang, H. (2001). Image classification for content-based indexing. *IEEE Transactions on Image Processing, 10,* 117-129. doi: 10.1109/83.892448.

Vanrell, M., & Vitria, J. (1997). Optimal 3 x 3 decomposable disks for morphological transformations. *Image and Vision Computing, 15*, 845–854.

Vapnik, V. (1998). *Statistical learning theory.* Springer.

Vapnik, V. (1998). *Statistical learning theory.* New York: Wiley.

Vapnik, V.N. (1995). *The nature of statistical learning theory.* New York: Springer Verlag.

Vasconcelos, N., & Lippman, A. (2000). Bayesian relevance feedback for content-based access of image and video libraries. In *Proceedings of IEEE Workshop on Content-based Access of Image and Video Libraries* (pp. 63-67).

Vasilescu, M., & Terzopoulos, D. (2003). Multilinear subspace analysis for image ensembles. In *Proc. Of Intl. Conf. On Compt. Vis. and Patter. Recog.,* (pp. 93-99).

Velloso, M., Carneiro, T., & Souza, F. D. (2007). Pattern sepctra for texture segmentation of gray-scale images. In *International Conference on Intelligent Systems Design and Applications* (pp. 347 352).

Veltkamp, R.C., & Hagedoorn, M. (1999). State of the Art in Shape Matching, *Technical Report* UU-CS-1999-27, Utrecht.

Vendrig, J., den Hartog, J., Leeuwen, D., Patras, I., Raaijmakers, S., Rest, J. van, Snoek, C., & Worring, M. (2002). TREC feature extraction by active learning. In *Proceeding of Text Retrieval Conference (TREC).*

Vessel, Ch.A. (1970). On the Topological Logic (in Russian). *Non-Classical Logic.* Moscow: Nauka.

Vetterli, J.K.M. (1995). *Wavelets and subband coding.* Prentice Hall.

Vieira, S. (2001). *Foundation of Intelligent Agents - Agent Communication Language.* FIPA.

Vincent, L. (1993). Grayscale area openings and closings: their applications and efficient implementation. In *EURASIP Workshop on Mathematical Morphology and its Applications to Signal Processing* (pp. 22–27). Barcelona, Spain.

Vincent, L. (2000, January). Granulometries and opening trees. *Fundamenta Informaticae, 41*(1-2), 57–90.

Viola, P., & Jones, M. (2001). Rapid object detection using a boosted cascade of simple features. *IEEE Conference on Computer Vision and Pattern Recognition, 1*, 511-518. doi: 10.1109/CVPR.2001.990517.

Viola, P., & Jones, M., (2001). Rapid object detection using a boosted cascade of simple features. In *Proc. of CVPR.*

Viola, P., & Welles, W.M. (1997). Alignment by maximization of mutual information. *Int. J. Comp. Vision, 24*(2), 137–154.

Viola, P., Jones, M. (2001). Robust Real Time Object Detection. *IEEE ICCV Workshop on Statistical and Computational Theories of Vision, 2*, II- 465-8. doi: 10.1109/ICME.2003.1221654.

Viola, P., Jones, M., & Snow, D. (2003). Detecting pedestrians using patterns of motion and appearance. In *Proc. of ICCV,* (pp. 734– 741).

Vivisimo (2007). *http://www.vivisimo.com.*

Vogel, J. (2004). Semantic scene modeling and retrieval. *No. 33 in Selected Readings in Vision and Graphics,* Houghton Hartung-Gorre Verlag Konstanz, from http://www.vision.ethz.ch/vogel/documents/diss_final_neu.pdf.

Vogel, J., & Schiele, B. (2004). Natural scene retrieval based on a semantic modeling step. *Proc. Int'l Conf. Image and Video Retrieval, LNCS, 3115*, 207-215. doi: 10.1007/b98923.

Vogel, J., & Schiele, B. (2007). Semantic modeling of natural scenes for content-based image retrieval. *International Journal of Computer Vision, 72*(2), 133-157. doi: 10.1007/s11263-006-8614-1.

Volkmer, T., Smith, J., Natsev, A., Campbell, M., & Naphade, M. (2005). A web-based system for collaborative annotation of large image and video collections. In *Proc. ACM International Conference on Multimedia M.*

Volkmer, T., Smith, J.R., & Natsev, A. (2005). A web-based system for collaborative annotation of large image and video collections: an evaluation and user study. In Proceedings of the 13th ACM international conference on Multimedia. Hilton, Singapore.

Volkmer, T., Smith, J.R., & Natsev, A. (2005). A web-based system for collaborative annotation of large image and video collections. In *Proceedings of ACM Multimedia,* (pp. 829-901).

Volkmer, T., Tahaghoghi, S., & Williams, H. (2004). Gradual transition detection using average frame similarity. (pp. 139-139).

von Ahn, L., & Dabbish, L. (2004). Labeling images with a computer game. In Proceedings of the SIGCHI conference on Human Factors in computing systems. Vienna, Austria.

Voyager. (n.d.). Retrieved 2007, from http://www.recursionsw.com

VRML Consortium. (1997). *The Virtual Reality Modeling Language*. ISO/IEC IS 14772-1.

Wada, S., Yoshizaki, S., Kondoh, H., & Furutani-Seiki, M. (2003). Efficient neural network classifier of medaka embryo using morphological pattern spectrum. In *International Conference on Neural Networks and Signal Processing* (pp. 220–223).

Wan, X., & Kuo, C.C.J. (1998). A new approach to image retrieval with hierarchical color clustering. *IEEE Transactions on Circuits and Systems for Video Technology, 8*(3), 628-643.

Wang, B., Li, Z.W., Li, M.J., & Ma, W.-Y. (2006). Large-scale duplicate detection for Web image search. *IEEE International Conference on Multimedia & Expo*.

Wang, C., Jing, F., Zhang, L., & Zhang, H. J. (2006). Image annotation refinement using random walk with restarts. In *Proc. 14th Ann' ACM int'l Conf. Multimedia*, (pp. 647-652). doi: 10.1145/1180639.1180774.

Wang, C., Jing, F., Zhang, L., & Zhang, H. J. (2007). Content-based image annotation refinement. In *Proc. IEEE Computer Vision and Pattern Recognition*, (pp. 1-8). doi: 10.1109/CVPR.2007.383221.

Wang, C., Jing, F., Zhang, L., & Zhang, H.-J. (2006). Image annotation refinement using random walk with restarts. In *Proc. ACM Multimedia*.

Wang, F., & Zhang, C. (2006). Label propagation through linear neighborhoods. In *Proc. 23th International Conference on Machine Learning*.

Wang, F., Zhang, C., Shen, H. C., & Wang, J. (2006). Semi-supervised classification using linear neighborhood propagation. In *Proc. IEEE Conference on Computer Vision and Pattern Recognition*.

Wang, G., Zhang, Y., & Li, F.-F. (2006). Using dependent regions for object categorization in a generative framework. In *Proc. IEEE Conf. Computer Vision and Pattern Recognition*, (pp. 1597-1604). doi: 10.1109/CVPR.2006.324.

Wang, H., Divakaran, A., Vetro, A., Chang, S. F., & Sun, H. (2003). Survey of compressed-domain features used in audio-visual indexing and analysis. *Journal of Visual Communication and Image Representation, 14*(2), 150-183.

Wang, J.Z., & Li, J. (2002). Learning-based linguistic indexing of pictures with 2-D MHMMs. In *Proc. ACM Multimedia*, (pp. 436-445). doi: 10.1145/641007.641104.

Wang, J.Z., Li, J., & Wiederhold, G. (2001). SIMPLIcity: Semantics-sensitive Integrated Matching for Picture Libraries. *IEEE Transactions on Pattern Analysis and Machine Intelligence, 23*(9), 947-963. doi: 10.1109/34.955109.

Wang, L., Chan, K.L., & Zhang, Z. (2003). Bootstrapping SVM active learning by incorporating unlabelled images for image retrieval. In *Proceedings of IEEE Computer Vision and Pattern Recognition*, (pp. 629-634).

Wang, M., Hua, X.-S., Song, Y., Lai, W., Dai, L., & Wang, R. (2007). An efficient automatic video shot size annotation scheme. In *Proc. International Multimedia Modeling Conference*.

Wang, M., Hua, X.-S., Song, Y., Yuan, X., Li, S., & Zhang, H.-J. (2006). Automatic video annotation by semi-supervised learning with kernel density estimation. In *Proc. ACM Multimedia*.

Wang, M., Hua, X.-S., Tang, J., Song, Y., & Dai, L.-R. (2007). Multi-concept multi-modality active learning for interactive video annotation. In *Proceedings of International Conference on Semantic Computing*, (pp. 321-328).

Wang, M., Hua, X.-S., Yuan, X., Song, Y., & Dai, L. (2007). Optimizing multi-graph learning: towards a unified video annotation acheme. In *Proc. ACM Multimedia*.

Wang, P., Liu, Z., & Yang, S. (2005). A probabilistic template-based approach to discovering repetitive patterns in broadcast videos. *ACM international conference on Multimedia*, (pp. 407-410). doi: 10.1145/1101149.1101238.

Wang, T., et al. (2003). Adaptive three similarity learning for image retrieval. *Multimedia Systems, 9*, 131-143.

Wang, T., Li, J., Diao, Q., Hu, W., Zhang, Y., & Duolong, C. (2006). Semantic event detection using conditional random fields. *Computer Vision and Pattern Recognition Workshops*, (pp. 109-109). doi: 10.1109/CVPRW.2006.190.

Wang, X., Li, Y., & Shang, Y. (2006). Measurement of microcapsules using morphological operators. In *IEEE International Conference on Signal Processing*.

Wang, X.-J., Ma, W.-Y., Xue, G.-R., & Li, X. (2004). Multi-model similarity propagation and its application for Web image retrieval. *ACM International Conference on Multimedia*, (pp. 944-951).

Wang, X.J., Ma, W.Y., Xue, G.R., & Li, X. (2004). Multi-model similarity propagation and its application for Web image retrieval. In *Proc. 12th ACM Int'l Conf. Multimedia*, (pp. 944-951). doi: 10.1145/1027527.1027746.

Wang, Z., Chi, Z., & Feng, D. (2003). Shape based leaf image retrieval. *IEEI proc. Vision, Image and Signal Processing*, *150*(1), 34-43.

Weijer, J., Schmid, C., & Verbeek, J. (2006). Learning color names from real-world images. *IEEE Computer Vision and Pattern Recognition*.

Weinberger, K. Q., & Saul, L. K. (2004). Unsupervised Learning of Image Manifolds by Semidefinite Programming. *IEEE Conf. on Computer Vision & Pattern Recognition*, *2*, 988-995.

Weiss, I., & Ray, M. (2005). Recognizing Articulated Objects Using a Region-Based Invariant Transform. *IEEE Trans. on Pattern Analysis and Machine Intelligence*, *27*(10), 1660-1665.

Welk, M. (2003). Families of generalised morphological scale spaces. In *Scale Space Methods in Computer Vision*,*2695*, pp. 770–784. Springer-Verlag.

Wenyin, L., Dumais, S., Sun, Y., Zhang, H., Czerwinski, M., & Field, B. (2001). Semi-automatic image annotation. In Proceedings of Interact: Conference on HCI.

Werman, M., & Peleg, S. (1985, November). Min-max operators in texture analysis. *IEEE Transactions on Pattern Analysis and Machine Intelligence*, *7*(6), 730–733.

White, D. & Jain, R. (1996). Similarity indexing with the SS-tree, *Proc of 12th Intl. Conf. on Data Egnineering*, New Orleans.

Wilhelm, A., Takhteyev, Y., Sarvas, R., House, N.V., & Davis, M. (2004). Photo annotation on a camera phone. CHI '04 extended abstracts on Human factors in computing systems (pp. 1403–1406). Vienna, Austria.

Wilkinson, M. (2007). Attribute-space connectivity and connected filters. *Image and Vision Computing*, *25*, 426–435.

Wilkinson, M. H. F. (2002, August). Generalized pattern spectra sensitive to spatial information. In *IAPR International Conference on Pattern Recognition (ICPR)*, *1*, 21–24. Quebec City, Canada.

Williams, O., Blake, A., & Cipolla, R., (2003). A sparse probabilistic learning algorithm for real-time tracking. In *Proc. of ICCV*, 2003, 353–360.

Witkin, A. (1983). Scale-space filtering. In *International Joint Conference on Artificial Intelligence* (pp. 1019–1022). Karlsruhe, Germany.

Wolf, W. (1996). Key Frame Selection by motion analysis. *IEEE International Conference on Acoustics, Speech, and Signal Processing, (ICASSP'96)*, *2*, 1228-1231. doi: 10.1109/ICASSP.1996.543588.

Wong, G.H.J. (2001). SMART Mobile Agent Facility. *Journal of Systems and Software*, (pp. 9-22).

Wooldridge, M. (2002). *An Introduction of Multi Agent Systems*. John Wiley & Sons, Inc.

Wu, M., & Jing, R. (2006). A graph-based framework for relation propagation and its application to multi-label learning. In *Proc. ACM Conference on Research & Development on Information Retrieval*.

Wu, M., & Scholkopf, B. (2007). Transductive classification via local learning regularization. In *Proc. 11th International Conference on Artificial Intelligence and Statistics*, (pp. 624-631).

Wu, V., Manmatha, R., & Riseman, E.M. (1999). Text-finder: an automatic system to detect and recognize text in images, *IEEE Transactions on Pattern Analysis and Machine Intelligence*, 20, pp. 1224–1229. doi: 10.1109/34.809116.

Wu, Y., Chang, E.Y., Chang, K.C.-C., & Smith, J.R. (2004). Optimal multimodal fusion for multimedia data analysis. In *Proceedings of ACM Multimedia*, (pp. 572-579).

Wu, Y., Kozintsev, I., Bouguet, J.-Y., & Dulong, C. (2006). Sampling strategies for active learning in personal photo retrieval. In *Proceedings of International Conference on Multimedia & Expo*, (pp. 529-532).

Xiaoqi, Z., & Baozong, Y. (1995). Shape description and recognition using the high order morphological pattern spectrum. *Pattern Recognition, 28*(9), 1333-1340.

Xie, L., Chang, S.F., Divakaran, A., & Sun, H. (2003). Unsupervised mining of statistical temporal structures in video. In A. Rosenfeld, D. Doremann, & D. Dementhon (Eds.), *Video Mining*. Kluwer Academic Publishers.

Xie, Z. X., Shyu, M.L., & Chen, S.C. (2007). Video event detection with combined distance-based and rule-based data mining techniques. *IEEE International Conference on Multimedia and Expo*, (pp. 2026-2029). doi:10.1109/ICME.2007.4285078.

Xu, D., & Chang, S.F. (2007). Visual Event Recognition in News Video using Kernel Methods with Multi-Level Temporal Alignment. *IEEE Int. Conf. on Computer Vision and Pattern Recognition*.

Xu, D., Cham, T.J., Yan, S., & Chang, S.F. (2008). Near Duplicate Image Identification with Spatially Aligned Pyramid Matching. *IEEE Int. Conf. on Computer Vision and Pattern Recognition*.

Xu, X., Li. B. (2002). Head tracking using particle filter with intensity gradient and color histogram. *Journal of Computer Science and Technology, 17*(6), 859-864.

Yahiaoui, I., Herve, N., & Boujemaa, N. (2005). *Shape-based image retrieval in botanical collections*.

Yahoo News Search. (2006). *http://news.search.yahoo.com/news*.

Yan, R., & Hauptmann, A.G. (2004). Multi-class active learning for video semantic feature extraction. In Proceedings of IEEE International Conference on Multimedia and Expo (ICME) (pp. 69–72).

Yan, R., & Hauptmann, A.G. (2007). A review of text and image retrieval approaches for broadcast news video. Information Retrieval, 10, 445–484.

Yan, R., & Naphade, M. (2005). Semi-supervised cross feature learning for semantic concept detection in videos. In *Proc. IEEE Conference on Computer Vision and Pattern Recognition*.

Yan, R., Natsev, A., & Campbell, M. (2007). An efficient manual image annotation approach based on tagging and browsing. In *Proceedings of ACM Multimedia Workshop on The Many Faces of Multimedia Semantics*, (pp. 13-20).

Yan, S. C., Xu, D., Zhang, B., Zhang, H., Yang, Q., & Lin, S. (2007). Graph Embedding and Extension: A General Framework for Dimensionality Reduction. *IEEE Trans. on Pattern Analysis & Machine Intelligence, 29*(1), 40-51.

Yanagawa, A., Chang, S.-F., Kennedy, L., & Hsu, W. (2007). Columbia University's baseline detectors for 374 LSCOM semantic visual concepts. *Columbia University ADVENT Technical Report #222-2006-8*.

Yang, H., & Lee, S. (2005, April). Decomposition of morphological structuring elements with integer linear programming. *IEE Proceedings on Vision, Image and Signal Processing, 152*(2), 148–154.

Yang, J., Zhang, D., Frangi, A.F., & Yang, J. (2004). Two-dimensional PCA: a new approach to appearance-based face representation and recognition. *IEEE Trans. on Patt. Analy. And Mach. Intellig., 26*(1), 131-137.

Yang, M.-H. (2002). Kernel eigenfaces vs. kernel fisherfaces: Face recognition using kernel methods. *International Conf. on Auto. Face and Gest. Recog.*, (pp. 215-220).

Yang, S., Kim, S.-K., & Ro, Y.M. (2007). Semantic home photo categorization. *IEEE Transactions on Circuits System and Video Technology, 17*(3), 324-335. doi: 10.1109/TCSVT.2007.890829 .

Yang, S., Wang, C., & Wang, X. (2007). Smoothing algorithm based on multi-scale morphological reconstruction for footprint image. In *International Conference on Innovative Computing, Information and Control*.

Yang, S.Z. (April, 2006). u *11*(2), 201-210.

Yang, Y., & Pedersen, J.O. (1997). A comparative study on feature selection in text categorization. In Proceedings of the 14th International Conference on Machine Learning (pp. 412–420).

Yarowsky, D. (1995). Unsupervised word sense disambiguation rivaling supervised methods. In *Proceedings of the 33rd Annual Meeting of the Association for Computational Linguistics*.

Ye, Q.X., Huang, Q.M., Gao, W., & Jiang, S.Q.(2005). Exciting event detection in broadcast soccer video with mid-level description and incremental learning. *ACM International Conference on Multimedia,* (pp. 455-458). doi: 10.1145/1101149.1101250.

Ye, Q.X., Huang, Q.M., Gao, W., & Zhao D.B. (2005). Fast and robust text detection in images and video frames. *Image and Vision Computing, 23,* (6), 565-576. doi: 10.1016/j.imavis.2005.01.004.

Yeh, T., Tollmar, K., Darrell, T. (2004). Searching the Web with mobile images for location recognition. *IEEE Computer Society Conference on Computer Vision and Pattern Recognition,* (2), 76-81.

Yeo, B. L., & Liu, B. (1995). Unified approach to temporal segmentation of motion JPEG and MPEG video. (pp. 2-13).

Yi, H., Rajan, D., & Chia, L. T. (2006). A motion-based scene tree for browsing and retrieval of compressed videos. *Information Systems, 31*(7), 638-658.

Yi, Z., Gangyi, J., & Yong, C. (1996). Research of oriented pattern spectrum. In *IEEE International Conference on Signal Processing.*

Yilmaz, A. Javed, O., & Shah, M. (2006). Object Tracking: A Survey. *ACM Computing Surveys, 38*(4), doi:10.1145/1177352.1177355.

Yoo, H. W., Ryoo, H. J., & Jang, D. S. (2006). Gradual shot boundary detection using localized edge blocks. *Multimedia Tools and Applications, 28*(3), 283-300.

Yoshitaka, A., & Ichikawa, T. (1999). A Survey on Content-Based Retrieval for Multimedia Databases. *IEEE Transactions on Knowledge and Data Engineering, 11*(1), 81-93.

You, Y., & Yu, H. (2004). A separating algorithm based on granulometry for overlapping circular cell images. In *International Conference on Intelligent Mechatronics and Automation* (pp. 244–248).

Yu, J., Amores, J., Sebe, N., & Tian, Q. (2006). Toward robust distance metric analysis for similarity estimation. In *Proc. of CVPR.*

Yu, J., Tian, B., & Tang, Y. (2007). Video segmentation based on shot boundary coefficient. (pp. 630-635).

Yuan, J., &Wu, Y. (2007). Spatial Random Partition for Common Visual Pattern Discovery. In *Proc. of IEEE Intl. Conference on Computer Vision* (ICCV).

Yuan, J., Duan, L., Tian, Q., & Xu, C. (2004). Fast and Robust Short Video Clip Search Using an Index Structure. In *Proc. of ACM Intl. Workshop on Multimedia Information Retrieval* (MIR).

Yuan, J., Li, Z., Fu, Y., Wu, Y., & Huang, T.S. (2007). Common Spatial Pattern Discovery by Efficient Candidate Pruning. In *Proc. of IEEE Intl. Conference on Image Processing* (ICIP).

Yuan, J., Wu, Y., & Yang, M. (2007a). From Frequent Itemsets to Semantically Meaningful Visual Patterns. In *Proc. of ACM. Knowledge Discover and Data Mining* (KDD).

Yuan, J., Wu, Y., & Yang, M. (2007b). Discovery of Collocation Patterns: from Visual Words to Visual Phrases. *IEEE Int. Conf. on Computer Vision and Pattern Recognition* (CVPR).

Yuan, J., Zhou, X., Zhang, J., Wang, M., Zhang, Q., Wang, W., & Shi, B. (2007). Positive sample enhanced angle-diversity active learning for SVM based image retrieval. In *Proceedings of International Conference on Multimedia & Expo,* (pp. 2202-2205).

Yuan, X., Hua, X.-S., Wang, M., & Wu, X. (2006). Manifold-ranking based video concept detection on large database and feature pool. In *Proc. ACM Multimedia.*

Yuan, X., Hua, X.–S., Wang, M., & Wu, X. (2006). Manifold-ranking based video concept detection on large database and feature pool. In *Proceedings of ACM Multimedia,* (pp. 623-626).

Yunpeng, L., Fangcheng, L., & Yanqing, L. (2005). Pattern recognition of partial discharge based on its pattern spectrum. In *International Symposium on Electrical Insulating Materials* (pp. 763–766).

Zabih, R., Miller, J., & Mai, K. (1995). A feature-based algorithm for detecting and classifying scene breaks. *ACM international conference on Multimedia,* (pp. 189-200). doi: 10.1145/217279.215266.

Zabih, R., Miller, J., & Mai, K. (1999). A feature-based algorithm for detecting and classifying production effects. *Multimedia Systems, 7*(2), 119-128.

Zapater, V., Martinez-Costa, L., Ayala, G., & Domingo, J. (2002). Classifying human endothelial cells based on individual granulometric size distributions. *Image and Vision Computing, 20*, 783–791.

Zeng, H.J., He, Q.C., Chen, Z., & Ma, W.-Y. (2004). Learning to cluster Web search results. In *Proc. of the 27th Annual International Conference on Research and Development in Information Retrieval*, (pp. 210-217).

Zhai, Y., & Shah, M. (2006). Visual attention detection in video sequences using spatio-temporal cues. *ACM international conference on Multimedia*, (pp. 815-824). doi: 10.1145/1180639.1180824

Zhang, C., & Chen, T. (2003). Annotating retrieval database with active learning. In *Proceedings of International Conference on Image Processing*, (pp. 595-598).

Zhang, H. J., Kankanhalli, A., & Smoliar, S. (1993). Automatic partitioning of full-motion video. *Multimedia Systems, 1*, 10-28.

Zhang, H. J., Wu, J., Zhong, D., & Smoliar, S. W. (1997). An integrated system for content based video retrieval and browsing. *Pattern Recognition, 30*(4), 643-658.

Zhang, H., Berg, A.C., Maire, M., & Malik, J. (2006). Svm-knn: Discriminative nearest neighbor classification for visual category recognition. In *Proc. IEEE Conf. Computer Vision and Pattern Recognition*, 2126-2136. doi: 10.1109/CVPR.2006.301.

Zhang, H., Kankanhalli, A., & Smoliar, S. W. (1993). Automatic partitioning of full-motion video. *Multimedia System, 1* 10–28. doi: 10.1007 /BF01210504.

Zhang, H., Low, C. Y., & Smoliar, S. W. (1995). Video parsing and browsing using compressed data. *Multimedia Tools and Applications, 1*(1), 89-111.

Zhang, R.F., Zhang, Z.F., Li, M.J., Ma, W.-Y., & Zhang, H.J. (2005). A probabilistic semantic model for image annotation and multi-modal image retrieval. In *Proc. of the IEEE International Conference on Computer Vision*.

Zhang, T., & Oles, F. (2000). A probability analysis on the value of unlabeled data for classification problems. In *Proceedings of the 17th International Conference on Machine Learning*, (pp. 1191-1198).

Zhang, W., Lin, J., Chen, X., Huang, Q., & Liu, Y. (2006). Video shot detection using hidden markov models with complementary features. (pp. 593-596).

Zhang, X.Y., Cheng, J., Lu, H.Q., & Ma, S.D. (2007). Weighted Co-SVM for image retrieval with MVB strategy. In *Proceedings of IEEE International Conference on Image Processing*, (pp. 517-520).

Zhang, X.Y., Cheng, J., Lu, H.Q., & Ma, S.D. (2008). Selective sampling based on dynamic certainty propagation for image retrieval. In *Proceedings of the 14th International Multimedia Modeling Conference*, (pp. 425-435).

Zhang, Y. J., & Beijing, C. (2006). In Zhang Y. J., Beijing C. (Eds.), *Advances in image and video segmentation* IRM Press.

Zhao, L., & Davis, L. S. (2005). Segmentation and Appearance Model Building from an Image Sequence. *IEEE International Conference on Image Processing, 1*, 321-324.

Zhao, L., & Yang, Y.H. (1999). Theoretical analysis of illumination in PCA-based vision systems. *Pattern Recogn., 32*(4), 547-564.

Zhao, W., et al. (2003). Face Recognition: A Literature Survey. *ACM Computing Surveys, 35*(4), 399-458.

Zhao, Z., & Cai, A. (2006). Shot boundary detection algorithm in compressed domain based on adaboost and fuzzy theory. *LECTURE NOTES IN COMPUTER SCIENCE, 4222*, 617.

Zhong, J.L.Y.Z. (2003). *The Mobile Agent Technology*. ISBN 7-89494-143-3.

Zhou, D., Bousquet, O., Lal, T.N., Weston, J., & Scholkopf, B. (2003). Learning with local and global consistency. *Advances in Neural Information Processing Systems, 15*. MIT Press.

Zhou, D., Bousquet, O., Lal, T.N., Weston, J., & Schölkopf, B. (2004). Learning with local and global consistency. In *Proceedings of Advances in Neural Information Processing Systems*, (pp. 321-328).

Zhou, D., Huang, J., & Scholkopf, B. (2005). Learning from labeled and unlabeled data on a directed graph. In *Proc. 22nd International Conference on Machine Learning*.

Zhou, D., Scholkopf, B., & Hofmann, T. (2005). Semi-supervised learning on directed graphs. *Advances in Neural Information Processing Systems, 17*. MIT Press.

Zhou, H., Yuan, Y., & Sadka, A.H. (2008). Application of semantic features in face recognition. *Pattern Recognition, 41*, 3251-3256.

Zhou, S., Chellappa, R., & Moghaddam, B. (2004). Visual tracking and recognition using appearance-adaptive models in particle filters. *IEEE Trans. Image Processing, 11*, 1434-1456.

Zhou, S., Shao, J., Georgescu, & Comaniciu, D. (2006). Boostmotion: Boosting a discriminative similarity function for motion estimation. *Proc. of CVPR, 2*, 1761–1768.

Zhou, X.S., & Huang, T.S. (2001). Comparing discriminating transformations and SVM for learning during multimedia retrieval. In Proceedings of the 9th ACM international conference on Multimedia (pp. 137–146). Ottawa, Canada.

Zhou, X.S., & Huang, T.S. (2003). Relevance feedback in image retrieval: A comprehensive review. *Multimedia Systems, 8*(6), 536-544.

Zhou, X.S., Comaniciu, D., & Gupta, A. (2005). An information fusion framework for robust shape tracking. *IEEE Trans. PAMI, 27*(1), 115–129.

Zhou, Z.-H. (2004). *Multi-instance learning: a survey.* Technical Report, Department of Computer Science & Technology, Nanjing University, China.

Zhou, Z.H., & Li, M. (2005). Semi-supervised regression with Co-training. In *Proceedings of the International Joint Conference on Artificial Intelligence* (pp. 908-913).

Zhou, Z.-H., Chen, K.-J., & Dai, H.-B. (2006). Enhancing relevance feedback in image retrieval using unlabeled data. *ACM Transactions on Information Systems, 24*(2), 219–244.

Zhu, L., Zhang, A., Rao, A., & Srihari, R. (2000). Keyblock: an approach for content-based image retrieval. In *Proceedings of ACM Multimedia.*

Zhu, X. (2005). *Semi-supervised learning with graphs.* PhD Thesis, CMULTI-05-192.

Zhu, X. (2006). *Semi-supervised learning literature survey.* Wisconsin University, http://pages.cs.wisc.edu/~jerryzhu/pub.

Zhu, X. (2007). *Semi-supervised learning literature survey.* Technical Report (1530), University of Wisconsin-Madison, www.cs.wisc.edu/~jerryzhu/pub/ssl_survey.pdf.

Zhu, X., Ghahramani, Z., & Lafferty, J. (2003). Semi-supervised learning using Gaussian fields and harmonic function. *Proc. International Conference on Machine Learning.*

Zhu, X., Wu, L., Xue, X., Lu, X., & Fan, J. (2001). Automatic scene detection in news program by integrating visual feature and rules. *The second IEEE Pacific-Rim conference on multimedia, 2195*, 837–842.

Zhuang, X., & Haralick, R. (1986). Morphological structuring element decomposition. *Computer Vision, Graphics and Image Processing, 35*, 370–382.

Zingman, I., Meir, R., & El-Yaniv, R. (2007). Size-density spectra and their application to image classification. *Pattern Recognition, 40*, 3336–3348.

About the Contributors

Dacheng Tao received the B.Eng. degree from the University of Science and Technology of China (USTC), the MPhil degree from the Chinese University of Hong Kong (CUHK), and the PhD degree from the University of London (Lon). Currently, he holds a Nanyang titled acadmic post with the School of Computer Engineering in the Nanyang Technological University and a visiting post in Lon. He is a Visiting Professor in Xi Dian University and a Guest Professor in Wu Han University. His research is mainly on applying statistics and mathematics for data analysis problems in computer vision, data mining, machine learning, multimedia, and video surveillance. He has published around 100 scientific papers including IEEE TPAMI, TKDE, TIP, CVPR, ECCV, ICDM; ACM TKDD, Multimedia, KDD etc., with best paper runner up awards and finalists. Previously he gained several Meritorious Awards from the International Interdisciplinary Contest in Modeling, which is the highest level mathematical modeling contest in the world, organized by COMAP. He is an associate editor of IEEE Transactions on Knowledge and Data Engineering, Neurocomputing (Elsevier) and the Official Journal of the International Association for Statistical Computing -- Computational Statistics & Data Analysis (Elsevier). He has authored/edited six books and eight special issues, including CVIU, PR, PRL, SP, and Neurocomputing. He has (co-)chaired for special sessions, invited sessions, workshops, and conferences. He has served with more than 50 major international conferences including CVPR, ICCV, ECCV, ICDM, KDD, and Multimedia, and more than 15 top international journals including TPAMI, TKDE, TOIS, TIP, TCSVT, TMM, TIFS, TSMC-B, Computer Vision and Image Understanding (CVIU), and Information Science.

Dong Xu is currently an assistant professor at Nanyang Technological University at Singapore. He received the B.Eng. and PhD degrees from the Electronic Engineering and Information Science Department, University of Science and Technology of China, in 2001 and 2005, respectively. During his PhD study, he worked at Microsoft Research Asia and The Chinese University of Hong Kong for more than two years. He also worked at Columbia University for one year as a postdoctoral research scientist. His research interests include computer vision, pattern recognition, statistical learning and multimedia content analysis. He has published more than 20 papers in top venues including T-PAMI, T-IP, T-CSVT, T-SMC-B and CVPR. He is an associate editor of Neurocomputing (Elsevier). He is the guest editors of three special issues on video and event analysis in IEEE Transactions on Circuits Systems for Video Technology (T-CSVT), Computer Vision and Image Understanding (CVIU) and Pattern Recognition Letters (PRL), and a coauthor of a forthcoming book entitled "Semantic Mining Technologies for Multimedia Databases". He was awarded a Microsoft Fellowship in 2004

Xuelong Li is the Reader in Cognitive Computing at Birkbeck College, University of London, a Visiting Professor at the Tianjin University, and a Guest Professor at the University of Science and Technology of China.

* * *

Amr Ahmed (BEng'93, MSc'98, PhD'04, MBCS'05) is a Senior Lecturer (equivalent to Assistant Professor in the American system), and the Leader of the DCAPI (Digital Contents Analysis, Production, and Interaction: dcapi.lincoln.ac.uk) research group at the Department of Computing and Informatics, University of Lincoln, UK. His research focuses on the analysis, production, and interaction with digital contents. His research interests include video processing, segmentation, scene understanding, and the integration between computer vision and graphics. Amr worked in the industry for several years, including Sharp Labs of Europe, Oxford, as a Research Scientist. He was working as a Research Fellow at the University of Surrey before joining the University of Lincoln in 2005. Dr. Ahmed is a Member of the British Computer Society (MBCS). He received his Bachelor's degree in electrical engineering from Ain Shams Univerity, Egypt, in 1993, his M.Sc. degree, by research, in Computer and Systems Engineering from Ain Shams Univerity, Egypt, in 1998, and his Ph.D. degree in Computer Graphics and Animation from the University of Surrey, U.K., in 2004. **E-mail address:** Amr.Ahmed@BCS.org. **Web site:** webpages.lincoln.ac.uk/AAhmed.

Leonard Brown is an Assistant Professor in the Computer Science Department at The University of Texas at Tyler. He received his M.S. and Ph.D. degrees in Computer Science from The University of Oklahoma in 1997 and 2003, respectively. Prior to that, he was a Member of Technical Staff-I at AT&T in Oklahoma City. His current research interests include multimedia database management systems and image retrieval. He has published over a dozen refereed technical articles in journals and conference proceedings, and he was awarded a NASA Summer Faculty Fellowship in 2004 at the Jet Propulsion Laboratory. He is a member of ACM and IEEE.

Jian Cheng, associate professor of Institute of Automation, Chinese Academy of Sciences. He received the B.S. and M.S. degrees in Mathematics from Wuhan University in 1998 and in 2001, respectively. In 2004, he got his Ph.D degree in pattern recognition and intelligent systems from Institute of Automation, Chinese Academy of Sciences. From 2004 to 2006, he has been working as postdoctoral in Nokia Research Center. Then he joined National Laboratory of Pattern Recognition, Institute of Automation. His current research interests include image and video retrieval, machine learning, etc.

Xiaochun Cheng Dr Xiaochun Cheng had his BEng on Computer Software in 1992 and his PhD on Artificial Intelligence in 1996. He has been a senior member of IEEE since 2004. He is the secretary for IEEE SMC UK&RI. He is a member of following technical committee of IEEE SMC: Technical Committee on Systems Safety and Security, Technical Committee on Computational Intelligence.

Yun Fu received the B.Eng. in information and communication engineering and M. Eng. in pattern recognition and intelligence systems from Xian Jiao Tong University (XJTU) in 2001 and 2004, the M.S. degree in statistics and the Ph.D degree in Electrical and Computer Engineering (ECE) from University of Illinois at Urbana-Champaign (UIUC) in 2007 and 2008, respectively. From 2001 to 2004, he was a research assistant at the AI&R at XJTU. From 2004 to now, he is a graduate fellow and research assistant at the Beckman Institute for Advanced Science and Technology, ECE department and Coordinated Science Laboratory at UIUC. He was a research intern with Mitsubishi Electric Research Laboratories, Cambridge, MA, in summer 2005; with Multimedia Research Lab of Motorola Labs, Schaumburg, IL, in summer 2006. He jointed BBN Technologies, Cambridge, MA, as a Scientist in 2008.

Hossam A. Gabbar is an Associate Professor in the Faculty of Energy Systems and Nuclear Science, UOIT, Canada. Dr. Gabbar obtained his Ph.D. in Process Systems Engineering from Okayama University (Japan). He joined Tokyo Institute of Technology and Japan Chemical Innovative Institute (JCII) between 2001-2004. In 2004, he joined Okayama University as an associate professor in the division of Industrial Innovation Sciences. From 2007 till 2008, he was a visiting scholar in University of Toronto, in the Mechanical and Industrial Engineering Department. He has contributed significantly to the areas of intelligent green production systems and process systems engineering. He published in reputable international journals, books, book chapters, patent, and industrial technical reports. He is regularly invited to conferences, tutorial, industrial and scientific events as keynote a speaker. He is the Editor-in-Chief of Int. J of Process Systems Engineering (PSE), editorial board member of the international journal of Resources, Energy and Development (READ), senior member of IEEE, chair of technical committee on Intelligent Green Production Systems, and board member of a numerous conferences and scientific committees. His solutions are widely implemented in industry in the areas of energy systems, safety instrumented systems, and process safety management.

Wen Gao (M'92-SM'05) received the BSc and MSc degrees in computer science from the Harbin University of Science and Technology and the Harbin Institute of Technology, China, in 1982 and 1985, respectively, and the PhD degree in electronics engineering from the University of Tokyo, Japan, in 1991. He is currently a professor in the School of Electronics Engineering and Computer Science, Peking University, China. He is the editor-in-chief of the *Journal of Computer* (in Chinese), associate editor of the *IEEE Transactions on Circuit System for Video Technology* and *IEEE Transaction on Multimedia*, and editor of the *Journal of Visual Communication and Image Representation*. He published four books and more than 300 technical articles in refereed journals and proceedings in the areas of multimedia, video compression, face recognition, sign language recognition and synthesis, image retrieval, multimodal interface, and bioinformatics. He is a senior member of the IEEE.

Xin He Mr Xin He received his BSc in Computer Science with First Class Honours from Beijing Union University, P.R. China and BSc in Computer Technology with Second Class (Upper Division) Honours from The University of East London, UK in 2003. He received his MSc in Network Centred Computing with Merit from the University of Reading in 2004. He is currently continuing his study as a PhD student in School of Systems Engineering at the University of Reading. His study is supported by the Research Endowment Trust Fund (RETF). His research includes artificial intelligence, multi-agent system and software engineering.

Xian-Sheng Hua received the B.S. and Ph.D. degrees from Peking University, Beijing, China, in 1996 and 2001, respectively, both in applied mathematics. Since 2001, he has been with Microsoft Research Asia, Beijing, where he is currently a Lead Researcher with the internet media group. His current research interests include video content analysis, multimedia search, management, authoring, sharing and advertising. He has authored more than 130 publications in these areas and has more than 30 filed patents or pending applications. HUA is a member of the Association for Computing Machinery and IEEE. He is an adjunct professor of University of Science and Technology of China, and serves as an Associate Editor of IEEE Transactions on Multimedia and Editorial Board Member of Multimedia Tools and Applications. Hua won the Best Paper Award and Best Demonstration Award in ACM Multimedia 2007.

Qingming Huang (M'04-SM'08) He was born on Dec 23, 1965 in Harbin, China. He obtained his B.S. in computer science in 1988 and Ph.D. in computer engineering in 1994, both from Harbin Institute of Technology, China. He was a postdotoral fellow in the National University of Singapore from 1995 to 1996, and a member of research staff in Institute for Infocomm Research, Singapore from 1996 to 2002. He joined the Chinese Academy of Sciences (CAS) in 2003 under the Science100 Plan, and is now a professor in the Graduate Universwity of CAS. His research interests include multimedia computing, digital video analysis, video coding, image processing, pattern recognition and computer vision. He has published over 100 academic papers in various journals and conference proceedings, and holds/files more than 10 patents in US, Singapore and China

Thomas S. Huang received his Sc.D. from MIT in 1963. He is William L. Everitt Distinguished Professor in the University of Illinois Department of Electrical and Computer Engineering and the Co-ordinated Science Lab (CSL); and a full-time faculty member in the Beckman Institute Image Formation and Processing and Artificial Intelligence groups. His professional interests are computer vision, image compression and enhancement, pattern recognition, and multimodal signal processing. He is a Member of the National Academy of Engineering, a Foreign Member of the Chinese Academies of Engineering and Sciences, and a Fellow of IAPR and OSA, and has received a Guggenheim Fellowship, an A.V. Humboldt Foundation Senior U.S. Scientist Award, and a Fellowship from the Japan Association for the Promotion of Science. He received the IEEE Signal Processing Society's Technical Achievement Award in 1987 and the Society Award in 1991. He was awarded the IEEE Third Millennium Medal in 2000.

Tiejun Huang (M'01) received the BSc and MSc degrees from the Department of Automation, Wuhan University of Technology in 1992, and the PhD degree from the School of Information Technology & Engineering, Huazhong University of Science and Technology, China, in 1999. He was a postdoctorial researcher from 1999 to 2001 and a research faculty member at the Institute of Computing Technology, Chinese Academy of Sciences. He was also the associated director (from 2001 to 2003) and the director (from 2003 to 2006) of the Research Center for Digital Media in Graduate School at the Chinese Academy of Sciences. He is currently an associate professor in the School of Electronics Engineering and Computer Science, Peking University. His research interests include digital media technology, digital library, and digital rights management. He is a member of the IEEE.

David W. Jacobs received the B.A. degree from Yale University in 1982. From 1982 to 1985 he worked for Control Data Corporation on the development of data base management systems, and attended graduate school in computer science at New York University. From 1985 to 1992 he attended M.I.T., where he received M.S. and Ph.D. degrees in computer science. From 1992 to 2002 he was a Research Scientist and then a Senior Research Scientist at the NEC Research Institute in Princeton, New Jersey. In 1998 he spent a sabbatical at the Royal Institute of Technology (KTH) in Stockholm. Since 2002, he has been an Associate Professor of computer science at the University of Maryland, College Park.

Shuqiang Jiang (M'07) received the MSc degree from College of Information Science and Engineering, Shandong University of Science and Technology in 2000, and the PhD degree from the Institute of Computing Technology, Chinese Academy of Sciences in 2005. He is currently a faculty member at Digital Media Research Center, Institute of Computing Technology, Chinese Academy of Sciences. His research interests include multimedia processing and semantic understanding, pattern recognition, and computer vision. He has published over 50 technical papers in the area of multimedia.

Aggelos K. Katsaggelos received the Diploma degree in electrical and mechanical engineering from the Aristotelian University of Thessaloniki, Greece, in 1979 and the M.S. and Ph.D. degrees both in electrical engineering from the Georgia Institute of Technology, in 1981 and 1985, respectively. He is currently Professor of EECS at Northwestern University, and the director of the Motorola Center for Seamless Communications. He is the editor of Digital Image Restoration (Springer-Verlag 1991), co-author of Rate-Distortion Based Video Compression (Kluwer 1997), co-editor of Recovery Techniques for Image and Video Compression and Transmission, (Kluwer 1998), co-author of the books Super-Resolution of Images and Video and Joint Source-Channel Video Transmission (both Morgan & Claypool Publishers 2007). He is a Fellow of the IEEE (1998), and the recipient of the IEEE Third Millennium Medal (2000), the IEEE Signal Processing Society Meritorious Service Award (2001), an IEEE Signal Processing Society Best Paper Award (2001), and an IEEE ICME Best Poster Paper Award (2006).

Arun Kulkarni, Professor of Computer Science, has been with The University of Texas at Tyler since 1986. His areas of interest include soft computing, database systems, data mining, artificial intelligence, computer vision, image processing, and pattern recognition. He has more than sixty refereed papers to his credit, and he has authored two books. His awards include the 2005-2006 President's Scholarly Achievement Award, 2001-2002 Chancellor's Council Outstanding Teaching award, 1999-2000 Alpha Chi Outstanding Faculty Member, 1997 NASA/ASEE Summer Faculty Fellowship award, 1997 Piper award nominee for The University of Texas at Tyler, and the 1984 Fulbright Fellowship award. He has been listed in who's who in America. He has been a software developer for twenty years, and has developed a variety of software packages. He has successfully completed eight research grants during the past ten years. Dr. Kulkarni obtained his Ph.D. from the Indian Institute of Technology, Bombay, and was a post-doctoral fellow at Virginia Tech.

Juliusz L. Kulikowski received MSc degree in electronic engineering from the Warsaw Technical University in 1955, CandSc degree from the Moscow Higher School of Technology in 1959, DSc degree from the Warsaw Technical University in 1966. Since 1966 he was a scientific worker in several Institutes of the Polish Academy of Sciences, since 1981 – in the Institute of Biocybernetics and Biomedical Engineering PAS in Warsaw. Nominated professor in 1973. He published more than 200 papers in information sciences, signals detection in noise, image processing methods, artificial intelligence, application of computers in medicine and 8 books and monographs in these domains. He is the Editor in Chief of a scientific quarterly "Computer Graphics & Vision", a member of IFIP TC13 on "Human-Computer Interaction", of IFAC TC on "Stochastic Systems", a Chairman of Polish National Committee for cooperation with the Committee of Data for Science and Technology CODATA.

Sébastien Lefevre received in 1999 the M.Sc. and Eng. degrees in Computer Engineering from the University of Technology of Compiègne, France, and in 2002 the Ph.D. degree in Computer Science from the University of Tours, France. He is currently an Assistant Professor in the Department of Computer Science and the Image Sciences, Computer Sciences and Remote Sensing Laboratory - LSIIT, University Louis Pasteur, Strasbourg, France. From 1999 to 2002 he was with AtosOrigin as a Research and Development Engineer. In 2003, he was with the Polytechnical School of the University of Tours as an Assistant Professor. His research interests are related to mathematical morphology and its applications to content-based image and video indexing, color image and video analysis, multispectral and multitemporal image processing.

Xirong Li received his B.S. and M.S. both in Computer Science from Tsinghua University, in 2005 and 2007. He was an intern in Microsoft Research Asia from Oct. 2005 to Jun. 2007. He is currently a PhD. student in the Intelligent Systems Lab Amsterdam (ISLA) at University of Amsterdam.

Zhu Li received the PhD degree in Electrical & Computer Engineering from Northwestern University, Evanston, USA, in 2004. He is an Assistant Professor with the Dept of Computing, Hong Kong Polytechnic University since 2008. He was with the Multimedia Research Lab (MRL), Motorola Labs, 2000~2008, where he was a Principal Staff Engineer. He is an IEEE Senior Member, and the elected Vice Chair (2008-2010) of the IEEE Multimedia Communication Technical Committee (MMTC). His research interests include subspace modeling and machine learning in biometrics, multimedia analysis and search, video coding and adaptation, optimization and distributed computing in multimedia networks and systems. He has 12 issued or pending US patents, 30+ publications in these areas. He received the Best Poster Paper Award at IEEE Int'l Conf on Multimedia & Expo, 2006, and the DoCoMo Labs Innovative Paper Award (Best Paper) at IEEE Int'l Conf on Image Processing, 2007

Haibin Ling received the B.S. degree in mathematics and the MS degree in computer science from Peking University, China, in 1997 and 2000, respectively, and the PhD degree from the University of Maryland, College Park, in computer science in 2006. From 2000 to 2001, he was an assistant researcher in the Multi-Model User Interface Group at Microsoft Research Asia. From 2006 to 2007, he worked as a postdoctoral scientist at the University of California Los Angeles. After that, he joined Siemens Corporate Research as a research scientist. Since fall 2008, he has been an Assistant Professor at Temple University. Dr. Ling's research interests include computer vision, medical image analysis, human computer interaction, and machine learning. He received the Best Student Paper Award at the ACM Symposium on User Interface Software and Technology (UIST) in 2003.

Hanqing Lu, professor of Institute of Automation, Chinese Academy of Sciences. He got his B.S. and M.S. from department of computer science and department of electric engineering in Harbin institute of technology in 1982 and 1985. He received his Ph.D. from department of electronic and information science in Huazhong University of sciences and technology. His current research interests include Image similarity measure, Video Analysis, Multimedia Technology and System and so on. He has published over peer-reviewed 200 papers in related journals and conferences. He was award by Second Award of National Nature Sciences, Second Award of CAS Nature Sciences and Third Award of Cultural Department of China.

Wei-Ying Ma received the B.S. degree from the National Tsinghua University in Taiwan in 1990, and the M.S. and Ph.D. degrees from the University of California at Santa Barbara in 1994 and 1997, respectively. He is a senior researcher and research manager in Microsoft Research Asia, where he has been leading a research group to conduct research in the areas of information retrieval, web search, data mining, mobile browsing, and multimedia management. He has published 5 book chapters and over 100 international journal and conference papers.

Guo-Jun Qi received the B.S. degree from University of Science and Technology of China in Automation, Hefei, Anhui, China, in 2005. His research interests include computer vision, multimedia, and machine learning, especially content-based image/video retrieval, analysis, management and sharing. He has been the winner of the best paper award in the 15th ACM International Conference on Multimedia, Augsburg, Germany, 2007. He is now working in Internet Media Group at Microsoft Research Asia as a research intern. Mr. Qi is the student member of Association for Computing Machinery.

Simon Ruszala was awarded a Distinction in MSc Industrial Computing from the Nottingham Trent University in 2005, after gaining a BSC (Hons) 1st in Computing Visualisation from the same university. A career change to telecommunications after graduation has led to him managing a team of engineers aiding the build of Vodafone UK's new core network. Interests in image retrieval and colour image analysis have led to a number of publications during and after university.

Gerald Schaefer gained his PhD in Computer Vision from the University of East Anglia. He worked at the Colour & Imaging Institute, University of Derby as a Research Associate (1997-1999), as Senior Research Fellow at the School of Information Systems, University of East Anglia (2000-2001), and as Senior Lecturer in Computing at the School of Computing and Informaticcs at Nottingham Trent University (2001-2006). In 2006 he joined the School of Engineering and Applied Science at Aston University. His research interests include colour image analysis, physics-based vision, image retrieval, and image coding. He has published more than 150 papers in these areas.

Chunmei Shi is currently working as a dentist in the People's Hospital of Guangxi, Nanning, China.

Manuraj Singh Mr Manuraj Singh received his BEng in Engineering with First Class Distinction from Bangalore University, India in 1999. He is currently working as a System Analyst and Lecturer. He is also pursuing his study as MPhil student in School of Computer Science at Middlesex University. He is member of British Computer Society since 2004. His research includes mobile agents systems, data mining and semantic web.

Yonghong Tian (S'02-M'05) received the MSc degree from the School of Computer Science, University of Electronic Science & Technology of China in 2000, and the PhD degree from the Institute of Computing Technology, Chinese Academy of Sciences in 2005. He is currently an associate professor in the School of Electronics Engineering and Computer Science, Peking University, China. His research interests include machine learning, data mining, semantic-based multimedia analysis, and retrieval. He has published over 40 technical papers in the area of multimedia and machine learning. He is a member of the IEEE.

Jinhui Tang is currently a postdoctoral research fellow in School of Computing, National University of Singapore. He received his B.E. and PhD degrees in July 2003 and July 2008 respectively, both from the University of Science and Technology of China . From Jun. 2006 to Feb. 2007, he worked as a research intern in Internet Media group at Microsoft Research Asia. And from Feb. 2008 to May 2008, he worked as a research intern in School of Computing at National University of Singapore. His current research interests include content-based image retrieval, video content analysis and pattern recognition. Dr. Tang is a member of ACM and a student member of IEEE.

Kongqiao Wang received his Ph.D. in 1999 in signal and information processing from University of Science and Technology of China (USTC). Currently, he is the Visual Systems team leader at Nokia Research Center Beijing and a part-time professor at USTC. Kongqiao has received over 40 granted/pending patents, published four book chapters, and authored or co-authored more than 40 conference and journal papers. His research interests include visual computing technologies, data mining and machine learning.

Meng Wang is currently an Associate Researcher in Microsoft Research Asia. He received the B.E. degree in the Special Class for the Gifted Young and Ph.D. degree in the Department of Electronic Engineering and Information Science from the University of Science and Technology of China (USTC), Hefei, China, in 2003 and 2008, respectively. His current research interests include multimedia content analysis, computer vision and pattern recognition. Dr. Wang is a member of ACM.

Xin-Jing Wang received her PhD degree from Tsinghua University in 2005. She is now an associate researcher in Microsoft Research Asia. Her primary research interests include image retrieval, image understanding, and pattern recognition.

Ying Wu received the B.S. from Huazhong University of Science and Technology, Wuhan, China, in 1994, the M.S. from Tsinghua University, Beijing, China, in 1997, and the Ph.D. in electrical and computer engineering from the University f Illinois at Urbana-Champaign (UIUC), Urbana, Illinois, in 2001. In 2001, he joined the Department of ECE at Northwestern University, Evanston, Illinois, as an assistant professor where he is currently an associate professor of Electrical Engineering and Computer Science. His research interests include computer vision, image and video analysis, pattern recognition, machine learning, multimedia data mining, and human-computer interaction. He is an associate editor of SPIE Journal of Electronic Imaging and an associate editor of IAPR Journal of Machine Vision and Applications. He received the Robert T. Chien Award at UIUC in 2001, and the NSF CAREER award in 2003. He is a senior member of the IEEE.

Rong Yan, **Apostol Natsev**, and **Murray Campbell** are with IBM Research.

Junsong Yuan is currently a Ph.D candidate in Electrical Engineering and Computer Science department of the Northwestern University. His research interests include computer vision, multimedia data mining, and machine learning. During the summer of 2008, 2007 and 2006, he was a research intern with the Communication and Collaboration Systems group, Microsoft Research, Redmond, WA, Kodak Research Labs, Rochester, NY, and Motorola Labs, Schaumburg, IL, respectively. He received his M.Eng. from the National University of Singapore in 2005. From 2003 to 2004, he was a research assistant in the Institute for Infocomm Research (I2R) in Singapore. He was enrolled in the Special Program for the Gifted Young of Huazhong University of Science and Technology and received his B.S. in Communication Engineering in 2002. He was awarded the national outstanding student and the Hu-Chunan fellowship in 2001, by the Ministry of Education in P.R.China.

Yuan Yuan is currently a Lecturer at the Aston University, United Kingdom. She received her BEng degree from the University of Science and Technology of China and PhD degree from the University of Bath, United Kingdom. She published more than forty papers in journals and conferences on visual information processing, compression, retrieval etc. She is an associate editor of the International Journal of Image and Graphics (World Scientific). She was on program committees of several IEEE/ACM conferences. She is a reviewer for several IEEE transactions, other international journals and conferences. She is a member of the IEEE.

Lei Zhang received his PhD degree from Tsinghua University in 2001. He is a researcher and a project lead in Microsoft Research Asia. His current research interests include search relevance ranking, web-scale image retrieval, social search, and photo management and sharing. He is a member of IEEE and a member of ACM.

Huiyu Zhou received his BEng degree in radio technology from Huangzhong University of Science and Technology, P. R. China. He was awarded an MSc degree in biomedical engineering from the University of Dundee and recently the PhD degree in computer vision from Heriot-Watt University, Edinburgh, Scotland. Currently, he is a research fellow in Brunel University, UK. His research interests include computer vision, human motion analysis, intelligent systems and human-computer interface. Since 2002 he has more than 50 papers published in international and national journals and conferences.

Shaohua Kevin Zhou received his Ph.D. degree in Electrical Engineering from University of Maryland at College Park in 2004. He then joined Siemens Corporate Research, Princeton, New Jersey, as a research scientist and currently he is a project manager. He has general research interests in signal/image/video processing, computer vision, pattern recognition, machine learning, and statistical inference and computing, with applications to biomedical image analysis (especially biomedical image context learning), biometrics and surveillance (especially face and gait recognition), etc. He has written two monographes: the lead author of the book entitled Unconstrained Face Recognition and a coauthor of the book entitled Recognition of Humans and Their Activities Using Video, edited a book on Analysis and Modeling of Faces and Gestures, published over 60 book chapters and peer-reviewed journal and conference papers, and possessed over 30 provisional and issued patents. He was identified as Siemens Junior Top Talent in 2006.

Index

W